THE ARTHUR OF THE ITALIANS

ARTHURIAN LITERATURE IN THE MIDDLE AGES

VII

THE ARTHUR OF
THE ITALIANS

THE ARTHURIAN LEGEND IN MEDIEVAL ITALIAN
LITERATURE AND CULTURE

edited by

Gloria Allaire and F. Regina Psaki

CARDIFF
UNIVERSITY OF WALES PRESS

www.uwp.co.uk

British Library Cataloguing-in-Publication Data.
A catalogue record for this book is available from the British Library.

ISBN 978-1-78683-071-5
e-ISBN 978-1-78316-051-8

Typeset by Mark Heslington Ltd, Scarborough, North Yorkshire
Printed by CPI Antony Rowe, Chippenham, Wiltshire

ARTHURIAN LITERATURE IN THE MIDDLE AGES

Series Editor

Ad Putter

CONTENTS

Part Three
Arthur beyond Romance

Part Four
Arthur beyond Literature

PREFACE

This book forms part of the ongoing series Arthurian Literature in the Middle Ages. The purpose of the series is to provide a comprehensive and reliable survey of Arthurian writings in all their cultural and generic variety. For many years, the single-volume *Arthur in the Middle Ages: A Collaborative History* (ed. R. S. Loomis, Oxford, 1959) served the needs of students and scholars of Arthurian literature admirably, but it has now been overtaken by advances in scholarship and by changes in critical perspectives and methodologies. The Vinaver Trust recognized the need for a fresh and up-to-date survey, and decided that several volumes were required to do justice to the distinctive contributions made to Arthurian literature by the various cultures of medieval Europe.

The series is mainly aimed at undergraduate and postgraduate students and at scholars working in the fields covered by each of the volumes. The series has, however, also been designed to be accessible to general readers and to students and scholars from different fields who want to learn what forms Arthurian narratives took in languages and literatures that they may not know, and how those narratives influenced the cultures that they do know. Within these parameters the editors have had control over the shape and content of their individual volumes.

Ad Putter, University of Bristol
(General Editor)

THE CONTRIBUTORS

Gloria Allaire is Senior Lecturer in Italian at the University of Kentucky. She is the author of numerous articles and contributions on Italian manuscripts, chivalric epic and romance. Her edited books include *Il Tristano panciatichiano* (2002), *The Italian Novella* (2003) and *Il Tristano corsiniano* (2015).

Daniela Delcorno Branca is full professor at the University of Bologna. She specialises in medieval and Renaissance Italian literature, in particular courtly literature (the Tristan romances, the *cantari*, Boiardo and Ariosto) and Poliziano. Her scholarship includes both editions and literary-historical criticism.

Keith Busby is Douglas Kelly Professor Emeritus of Medieval French at the University of Wisconsin-Madison. He has published widely in several areas of Old French literature, including Arthurian romance. His current work deals with the manuscript culture of medieval Francophonia, from Ireland to the Levant.

Roberta Capelli teaches Romance languages and literatures at the University of Trent. She focuses on medieval literature and medievalism in contemporary culture, from Guittone d'Arezzo's *Del carnale amore* (2007) to the troubadours of Ezra Pound in *Carte provenzali* (2013).

Franco Cardini is Professor Emeritus at the University of Florence, a research director in Paris and a fellow of Harvard University. His enormous research output has concentrated on pilgrimages to the Holy Land, relations between Europe and the Muslim world and the history of chivalry.

Fabrizio Cigni teaches Romance philology at the University of Pisa. He has specialised in the textual tradition of Arthurian texts in Old French and Italian, particularly around the Arthurian Compilation of Rustichello da Pisa. He is currently studying and documenting the manuscripts produced in the prisons of Genoa–Pisa in the late thirteenth century.

Marie-José Heijkant specialises in Italian Arthurian literature at the University of Leiden. She has published extensively on the reception of the Tristan legend in Italy, including *La tradizione del* Tristan en prose *e proposte di studio sul* Tristano Riccardiano (1989). She has published editions of the *Tristano Riccardiano* (1991) and the *Tavola Ritonda* (1997).

Christopher Kleinhenz is Professor Emeritus of Italian at the University of Wisconsin-Madison. He has published widely on medieval Italian literature, manuscript studies and the interrelationship of art and literature. Books include *The Early Italian Sonnet* (1986), *Courtly Arts and the Art of Courtliness* (2006) and a translation of The Fiore *and the* Detto d'Amore (2000).

Stefano Mula is Associate Professor of Italian at Middlebury College, Vermont. His research focuses on medieval narrative structures and strategies, with particular attention to the Tristan legend and Cistercian *exempla*. He has published various articles in both fields.

Maria Bendinelli Predelli is Professor Emerita at McGill University. Her research focuses on medieval narrative, particularly the relationships between French and Italian literature, and popular genres. Her work on the *cantari* includes *I cantari: Struttura e tradizione* (1984), co-edited with Michelangelo Picone, and *Alle origini del Bel Gherardino* (1990).

F. Regina Psaki is the Giustina Family Professor of Italian Language and Literature at the University of Oregon. She has translated three medieval romances: *Tristano Riccardiano* (2006), the *Roman de la Rose ou de Guillaume de Dole* (1995) and the *Roman de Silence* (1991). She also works on Dante, Boccaccio and medieval misogyny.

Eleonora Stoppino is Associate Professor of Italian, Comparative Literature and Medieval Studies at the University of Illinois. She publishes on Dante, medieval conduct literature, Italian Arthuriana, Tasso and Ariosto, the subject of her *Genealogies of Fiction: Women Warriors and the Medieval Imagination in the* Orlando furioso (2012).

ABBREVIATIONS

BAV	Biblioteca Apostolica Vaticana
BBIAS	*Bibliographical Bulletin of the International Arthurian Society*
BnF	Bibliothèque Nationale, France
BNCF	Biblioteca Nazionale Centrale, Florence
Cigni edn	*Il romanzo arturiano di Rustichello da Pisa*, ed. F. Cigni (Pisa, 1994)
CN	*Cultura Neolatina*
GSLI	*Giornale Storico della Letteratura Italiana*
LI	*Lettere Italiane*
Lös.	Löseth, Eilert. *Le Roman en Prose de Tristan, le Roman de Palamède et la Compilation de Rusticien de Pise: Analyse critique* (1890; rpt 1970)
MR	*Medioevo Romanzo*
PAL 556	*Tavola Ritonda*: *Manoscritto Palatino 556, Firenze Biblioteca Nazionale Centrale*, ed. Roberto Cardini (Rome, 2009)
Panc.	*Tristano Panciatichiano*
Parola	*La parola del testo*
PMLA	*Publications of the Modern Language Association of America*
Ricc.	*Tristano Riccardiano*
StM	*Studi Medievali*
SMV	*Studi Mediolatini e Volgari*
Tav. Rit.	*La Tavola Ritonda*
TLI	D. Delcorno Branca, *Tristano e Lancillotto in Italia: Studi di letteratura arturiana* (Ravenna, 1998)
Tris. Ven.	*Tristano Veneto*

INTRODUCTION: THE ARTHUR OF THE ITALIANS

F. Regina Psaki

The Arthurian material produced in the Italian peninsula has long been something of an object of benign neglect for Anglophone specialists of both continental romance and Italian literature. Certainly broad panoramic works such as Roger Sherman Loomis's *Arthurian Literature in the Middle Ages: A Collaborative History* and Norris J. Lacy's *The New Arthurian Encyclopedia* have included Italian material, and Arthurianists such as Christopher Kleinhenz and Donald Hoffman have given sustained attention to the Italian repertoire.[1] Yet measured against the great romances in French verse and prose on the one hand, and against the great monuments of Dante, Petrarch and Boccaccio on the other, Italian Arthuriana has found itself between a rock and a hard place. Even as scholarship is flourishing on other intertextual connections between England and Italy, the single comprehensive monograph in English on Italian Arthurian literature is over eighty years old – a situation barely conceivable for Dante, Petrarch or Boccaccio studies. This observation is neither plaintive nor indignant. There are concrete reasons why Italian Arthuriana in general has been less visible, and I will survey them in presenting *The Arthur of the Italians*.

Although Anglophone criticism on Italian Arthuriana has been attenuated, Italian-language scholarship on it is abundant, dynamic, meticulous and sophisticated. It is driven and enlivened by many of the contributors to this volume, whose work translated here will give some sense of that body of scholarship represented in Gloria Allaire's Bibliography of Studies. One of our goals for this volume is to make a sampling of Italophone published research on Italian Arthurian literature accessible to the Anglophone scholarly community working on other branches of the Arthurian tradition. Not only is the Italian corpus worth cultivating as an end in itself, but it is also necessary for understanding the Arthurian literature of the rest of Europe.

Italian Arthuriana has been less visible in part because it developed – as did Italian literature in general – later than that of continental Europe and the British Isles. When Chrétien and Marie and Hartmann were writing full-length verse narratives in Old French and Middle High German, there was no parallel extended vernacular production on any topic in medieval Italy. Saint Francis's exalted *Canticle of the Creatures* is one of the earliest vernacular texts, and it dates to 1224. The relative lag in Italian vernacular writing has been explained variously over the years and indeed has recently come to be challenged as a paradigm. A central factor is that the peninsula was strongly multilingual, as much so as medieval Britain or Iberia; with a long presence in Italian territories of populations speaking Greek, Hebrew and Arabic – not to mention French – Latin probably remained a default lingua franca for longer. In fact, some of the earliest evidence for the circulation of the Arthur material in Italy is not in an Italian dialect at all, but in one of the many languages present and flourishing on the peninsula: Latin, of course, but also Hebrew and Greek.

The only surviving Hebrew romance is *Mēlek Arṭûś* (King Arthur), a fragmentary translation from the *Mort Artu* and the *Estoire de Merlin* done in the Umbria/Tuscany area in 1279 – very early for Italy.[2] This text contains two episodes: the deception of 'Izerna' and the conception of Arthur; and the adultery of 'Zinevra' and Lancelot. It is preceded by an intriguing defense of its secular project: 'it is possible to learn wisdom and ethics from these fables concerning a man's conduct towards himself and his fellow man. Therefore they are neither idle nor profane talk.'[3] The only surviving Greek translation of an Arthurian text, 'Ο Πρέσβυς 'Ιππότης (The Old Knight) may date from nearly as early, or perhaps as late as the date of its only surviving manuscript.[4] The Greek text translates part of the first episode of Rustichello da Pisa's Compilation: the Old Knight comes to Arthur's court and, giving no name, defeats every knight there, including the king. The translation may have been done in Cyprus, in Byzantium, or in Italy. Both the Hebrew and the Greek fragments are short, and both are intercultural translations, carefully adapting their matter to and through the authoritative texts and narrative technique normative for their audiences – the Old Testament and the *Iliad*, respectively. We cannot determine whether these translations were unique and anomalous events, or whether there were others in Hebrew and Greek that have not come down to us. Either way, they speak to the multilingual nature of the peninsula, and to the portable, *passe-partout* and polyglot nature of the Arthurian narratives themselves. The corpus we have from Italy is shared among different languages, and of course, some of the most abundant and informative documentation is in French.

For that reason Part One of this volume, 'France and Italy,' is dedicated to the interface between the French and Italian lands in the spread of the Arthurian matter. Keith Busby's chapter, 'Arthuriana in the Italian Regions of Medieval Francophonia', discusses the 'cultural colonisation' willingly courted by Italians in the Angevin court in Naples, in the courts and city-states of Veneto and Lombardy, and of course in Florence. Busby surveys in particular the traces that Chrétien de Troyes's verse narratives left in peninsular writing, finding ample signs that Italian authors knew Chrétien's Arthurian poems and expected their readers to do so as well. In other words, it is not only the influential thirteenth-century French prose texts that were known and active in Italy.

Across the peninsula French texts were not only copied, but composed. Fabrizio Cigni's 'French Redactions in Italy: Rustichello da Pisa' discusses the enormous importance of the Arthurian Compilation written in French (after 1270–4). The Compilation focuses on the generation before that of Arthur, opening with the episode of the Old Knight that was later translated into Greek. Cigni's chapter explores the narrative content of the Compilation, its episodic poetics and its relationship to the *Guiron le Courtois*. These texts exemplify the position of Italian Arthuriana 'between the chairs', as they used to say, of French and Italian studies. In *The Arthur of the French*, Richard Trachsler notes that *Guiron*, 'one of the last Arthurian texts to remain unedited', is 'one of the least well known, such that an overall interpretation may still seem premature'.[5] Because it survives in so many manuscripts and 'sometimes strongly diverging versions', Trachsler says, 'the quest to define the romance of *Guiron le Courtois* … tends to become a mirage, the best example of medieval textual *mouvance*.'[6] In addition to Rustichello's Compilation, therefore, Cigni's chapter also captures some of the developments in progress in the edition and study of *Guiron le Courtois*, one of the two or three most dynamic areas for current research in Italian Arthuriana.

But the most influential Arthurian material in the Italian peninsula is undoubtedly the Tristan story. In 'From France to Italy: The Tristan Texts', Marie-José Heijkant surveys the Tristan versions, both French and Italian, copied and composed there. She surveys the manuscripts which vehicled the various incarnations of the Tristan story circulating on the peninsula and examines the relationships among them, tracking their content using the episodes identified in Löseth's *Analyse*.[7] Heijkant concludes by delineating the '*R* redaction' of the Tristan romance best represented in Italian territory. Daniela Delcorno Branca's chapter focuses on *La Tavola Ritonda*, not only the most artful and individual example of Italian romance, but in her words, 'the only real Arthurian romance of the Italian Middle Ages' (p. 69). This superlative text was 'a holistic attempt to assemble into a single romance the entire Arthurian cycle, from Uther Pendragon to the *Mort Artu*, with Tristan as its focus' (p. 69). The *Tavola Ritonda* exemplifies a specifically Italian focus, reflecting how anonymous authors adapted their sources to the varied political realities and societal tendencies of the peninsula. Delcorno Branca brings a career's worth of experience to bear on this romance, which she notes requires still further study if we are to understand its pedigree and appreciate its literary and ethical value for its varied audiences of fourteenth-century Italy.

The Arthur of the Italians is far from uniformly an Arthur *in* Italian, nor does he appear at all in the guise of long verse romances. There is, nonetheless, a wide array of Arthurian prose romances, *cantari* (short narratives in eight-line stanzas meant for public performance) and Renaissance reprises to explore, as well as an ample presence of Arthurian protagonists, episodes and themes in medieval Italian literature and culture outside of that corpus. Part Two of the volume, 'Arthurian Material in Italian Narrative Forms', treats Arthurian production in Italian vernaculars. Stefano Mula's chapter, 'Narrative Structure in Medieval Italian Arthurian Romance', addresses the techniques by which the Italian romancers laid out the branching tales both to interact with the Arthurian intertext in their audience's reception, and to adapt it to their own aesthetic and ethical framework. The Italian prose romances, even the *Tavola Ritonda*, met early incomprehension and resistance from Arthurian scholars, who tended to compare them unfavourably to their sources rather than exploring them in the light of their own peninsular context. Using the *Tavola Ritonda*, the *Tristano Riccardiano* and the *Tristano Panciatichiano*, Mula discusses how interlace, repetition and compilation work in the Italian romances to create works richer and more subtle than was initially recognised. The mostly anonymous verse narratives known as *cantari*, composed to be sung, were also often dismissed even by their expositors as unsophisticated productions purged of narrative complexity for the capacities of a simpler audience.[8] Maria Bendinelli Predelli's chapter 'Arthurian Material in Italian *Cantari*' presents these stand-alone, non-cyclical narratives, most from the second half of the fourteenth century. Many of them are not adapted directly from French sources: three *cantari* based on the Knight with Enchanted Arms motif, unknown in French romance; Antonio Pucci's *Gismirante*, based on diverse sources, including Germanic; Pucci's *Bruto di Bretagna*, based on Andreas Capellanus' *De amore*; the *Ponzela Gaia*, apparently based on northern Italian rather than French sources; the *cantare* on the vengeance taken for the death of Tristan; the duel of Tristan and Lancelot at Merlin's Stone. Others are more closely rooted in French originals: *Carduino*, based on *Le Bel Inconnu*; *Li Cantari di Lancellotto*; *Febus-el-Forte* (from the *Roman de Palamedes*); and a *cantare* on Tristan's last feats and death.

The Matter of Britain continued to inspire Italian authors and audiences throughout the decades where the late Middle Ages blur into the early and high Renaissance. Eleonora Stoppino's chapter, 'Arthur as Renaissance Epic,' focuses on geographical centres of diffusion, textual circulation, the coexistence of the Arthurian and Carolingian matters, specific tales and characters that were especially successful, and finally, the role of this cycle in the great epic productions of Boiardo and Ariosto. She begins with the *Livre du Chevalier Errant* composed in Paris (1394–6) by Tommaso III, Marchese di Saluzzo. It is written in French in a magnificent verse-prose hybrid form, an imagined chivalric autobiography which blends allegorical and Arthurian conventions and matter. BnF, MS fr. 12559, one of only two manuscripts to preserve this text, is a gorgeous *de luxe* fifteenth-century manuscript with stunning illuminations by the Master of the *Cité des Dames*.[9] Because its Arthurian matter is decidedly subordinated to its allegorical journey, *Le Chevalier Errant* too falls between disciplines, neither covered in *The Arthur of the French* nor thoroughly canvassed in *The Arthur of the Italians*.

The fact is, however, that we have not even finished unearthing the primary corpus of Italian Arthuriana. A flowering of new research and new discoveries makes a definitive study of the Italian Arthurian material very much a moving target. After centuries in which no Lancelot romance was thought to survive in an Italian dialect, Luca Cadioli has discovered a substantial portion of a mid- to late fourteenth-century Tuscan *volgarizzamento* of the prose *Lancelot*.[10] The fifty-six folios that survive contain two scribal hands, and space has been left for miniatures that were never inserted.[11] That the codex did contain the entire romance is clear from the numeration on the remaining folios. The manuscript's owners have donated it to the Fondazione Ezio Franceschini in Florence, where a public presentation on the *Lancellotto* was held on 31 May 2013. This important new discovery will enable – and require – a great deal of study and reconsideration of the Arthurian panorama in Italian vernacular literature.

Outside the circle of Arthurian romances are a variety of Italian texts featuring Arthurian cameos or romance insertions that do a specific kind of cultural work. Part Three, 'Arthur beyond Romance', examines Italian texts that look at the Arthurian corpus from the outside. Roberta Capelli's chapter, 'The Arthurian Presence in Early Italian Lyric', gives a concise overview of how Italian lyric poets from the thirteenth to the fifteenth centuries incorporated Arthurian allusions, showing that their use was both systematic and metatextual: 'Along with biblical and classical figures, the Arthurian *exempla* thus become symbols of absolute autoreferentiality and collective cultural and moral values' (p. 134). She surveys references to the figures of Merlin, Iseut, Morgana, Tristan and Lancelot to show how 'the exemplary comparison adapts itself through metaphorical formulae to the exigencies of narrative synthesis conditioned by prosodic and metrical structures' (p. 134). My chapter, 'Arthur in Medieval Italian Short Narrative', examines thirteenth- and fourteenth-century Italian verse and prose narratives in which Arthurian romance is invoked neither solely for comparison's sake nor as the central focus of the entire narrative. Whether in overtly didactic and allegorical material, or in imaginative fictions which may also bear a didactic charge, the Arthurian material, even at the earliest stages, is borrowed in to carry ethical and aesthetic freight that at this remove we cannot always identify with confidence. Christopher Kleinhenz's chapter, 'The Arthurian Tradition in the Three Crowns', explores the aesthetic and ethical charge of the Arthurian material in the three greatest Italian writers of the fourteenth century (or, it could be claimed, of any century). Although neither Dante nor Petrarch nor Boccaccio actually composed any Arthurian literature, the corpus was strongly present on their cultural horizon: 'Their reception … ranges from an ambivalent appraisal of their moral virtues (Dante) and an almost casual dismissal of their worthiness (Petrarch) to a generally warm embrace of them and their fabulous stories (Boccaccio)' (p. 158). The 'beautiful meanderings of King Arthur' are thus written broadly across Italy's literary patrimony, whatever the language, genre or social context of the tales.

Finally, many vestiges of the circulation of the Arthur material in Italy are not literary at all, but hagiographical, architectural, archaeological, bibliographical and visual. Part Four, 'Arthur beyond Literature', begins with historian Franco Cardini's 'Arthur in Hagiography: The Legend of San Galgano'. Cardini looks at the legend of St Galganus, both in the records of his canonisation hearings and in the Montesiepi sanctuary which features nothing less than a sword embedded in stone: perhaps *the* sword in the stone. Cardini's chapter tracks the hagiography backwards and forwards across centuries, miles and textual forms, to link the chivalric, the anthropological and the archetypal. Gloria Allaire's chapter, 'Owners and Readers of Arthurian Books in Italy', surveys the evidence in and the documentation about manuscripts and early printed books. Archival and codicological research illuminates more than the content and genealogies of texts; it allows us to understand who was reading and producing Arthurian literature in Italy, where and when they were doing so, and how these books traveled and influenced each other. The last chapter in the volume is a survey by Gloria Allaire of the Arthurian-themed artworks made in Italy or by Italians to decorate ecclesiastical and domestic spaces. 'Arthurian Art in Italy' maps the study of frescoes, sculptures, mosaics, ceiling panels and decorative objects, allowing Arthurian scholars to track and find the art historical research published on these artworks. In addition, Allaire has assembled the most complete reference list in print, to facilitate access to not only the analyses but also to the published reproductions of the art.[12]

Daniela Delcorno Branca's 1998 book *Tristano e Lancillotto in Italia: Studi di letteratura arturiana* will recur in these pages so often as to receive its own designated abbreviation. It opens with her generous recognition of the merits of Edmund G. Gardner's 1930 monograph, *The Arthurian Legend in Italian Literature*.[13] Delcorno Branca also noted his limits: a focus limited to literal content, a periodisation at times wobbly, and a complete absence of philological/textual perspective on the relations between texts in French and texts in Italian.[14] Her own life's work in Italian Arthuriana has remedied these and other shortcomings in the secondary literature, and her colleagues and students in this endeavour are dramatically changing and invigorating the field – by the day, as we have seen. There is no way to do justice to Delcorno Branca's importance in Italian Arthurian studies, let alone to overstate it. With full knowledge that it is quite anomalous – indeed, not *done* – to dedicate a volume to a scholar who has contributed a chapter to it, Gloria Allaire and I do dedicate this collaborative history to Daniela Delcorno Branca. We do so impartially, having long admired from afar the erudition, energy, intellectual refinement and generosity of her published work. We hope that any embarrassment this dedication may cause a famously modest colleague may be outweighed eighty years from now, when another team of Anglophones will be taking a snapshot of Italian Arthurian studies. That *futura gente*, tracking and mapping her scholarship and its influence, will see clearly that it is because of Delcorno Branca that Gardner's *The Arthurian Legend in Italian Literature* has at last a successor, though not a substitute, in English.

The last word is given to the many debts we as volume editors have accumulated along the way. For help in obtaining materials, Gloria gives special thanks to Dr. Lezlie S. Knox as well as to the collections and interlibrary loan departments of the Strozier Library at The Florida State University; OhioLink and the Alden Library at

Ohio University; the Purdue University libraries; and the Hesburgh Libraries at the University of Notre Dame. At the University of Kentucky, the William T. Young Library and the Lucille Caudill Little Fine Arts Library and Learning Center have provided invaluable assistance. She also thanks her colleagues, Linda K. Worley and Joseph O'Neil, for help with German references.

For my part, I would like to thank some of the teachers and colleagues who motivated me to look more closely at Italian Arthuriana: Arthur B. Groos; Thelma Fenster; Bonnie Krueger; and Christopher Kleinhenz. I would also like to acknowledge the work of Alison Bron and Stephen P. McCormick in translating the essays of Marie-José Heijkant and Daniela Delcorno Branca, respectively; of Julia Sherman, Ekongkar Khalsa and Erin Kaufman in acquiring secondary materials; and of Laura Berryhill and Bo Adan in formatting and editing many of the volume's essays. The lavish support of the Giustina family of Eugene, Oregon, enabled the collaboration of these translators, research assistants and editors.

Both Gloria Allaire and I wish to acknowledge the generosity of the Vinaver Trust in sponsoring the series Arthurian Literature in the Middle Ages. We also appreciate the apparently boundless patience of Ad Putter, the series editor, and the equally boundless efficiency and good cheer of the professional staff at the University of Wales Press: Commissioning Editor Sarah Lewis, Production Manager Siân Chapman, the Editor Dafydd Jones, and our copy-editor Henry Maas. The Press's external reader made invaluable improvements to the volume that were as learned as they were timely. Our special thanks go to the volume's contributors: for accepting our invitation to contribute to this collaborative history; for reviewing edits and translations that were always pressing; and for remaining focused on a project that proceeded in unpredictable bursts of inexplicable urgency.

Aspro-Coccore, August, 2013

Notes

[1] R. S. Loomis (ed.), *Arthurian Literature in the Middle Ages: A Collaborative History* (Oxford, 1959); N. J. Lacy (ed.), *The New Arthurian Encyclopedia* (New York and London, 1996). The many Arthurian publications of Donald Hoffman and Christopher Kleinhenz appear in Gloria Allaire's Bibliography of Studies (pp. 254–80).

[2] C. Leviant, *King Artus: A Hebrew Arthurian Romance of 1279* (New York, 1969; rpt Syracuse, NY, 2003) contains a Hebrew edition and an English translation; T. Drukker, 'A Thirteenth-Century Arthurian Tale in Hebrew: A Unique Literary Exchange', in *Medieval Encounters*, 15 (2009), 114–29, offers an English translation and analysis. G. Lacerenza discusses the judaising of the Arthurian themes, in '*Mēlek Arṭûś. I temi arturiani ebraizzati nel Sēfer ha-šēmāḏ*', in G. Carbonaro et al. (eds), *Medioevo Romanzo e Orientale. Macrotesti fra Oriente e Occidente* (Soveria Mannelli, 2003), pp. 101–18.

[3] Leviant, *King Artus*, p. 11.

[4] Two new English translations of *The Old Knight* have been published: that of F. Skordili and M. Scordilis Brownlee appears as an appendix to Brownlee, 'The Politics of an Arthurian Prequel: Rustichello, Palamades, and Byzantium', in J. M. Hidalgo (ed.), *La pluma es lengua del alma: Ensayos en Honor de E. Michael Gerli* (Newark, DE, 2011), pp. 53–77; see also A. J. Goldwyn, 'Arthur in the East: Cross-Cultural Translations of Arthurian Romances in Greek and Hebrew, Including a New Translation of '*Ο Πρέσβυς Ἱππότης* (The Old Knight)', *Journal of Literary Artifacts in Theory, Culture, and History*, 5 (2012), 75–105. Goldwyn discusses the uncertain dating; no consensus has emerged, leaving a window of *c.*1300–1450 (pp. 76–7).

[5] F. Bogdanow and R. Trachsler, 'Rewriting Prose Romance: The Post-Vulgate *Roman du Graal* and Related Texts', in *The Arthur of the French: The Arthurian Legend in Medieval French and Occitan Literature* (Cardiff, 2006), pp. 342–92, on p. 364.

[6] Bogdanow and Trachsler, 'Rewriting Prose Romance', p. 365.

[7] E. Löseth, *Le Roman en prose de Tristan, le Roman de Palamède et la Compilation de Rusticien de Pise: Analyse critique d'après les manuscrits de Paris* (Paris, 1890).

[8] M. Picone, 'La "matière de Bretagne"', in Picone and M. Bendinelli Predelli, *I cantari: Struttura e tradizione* (Florence, 1984), pp. 87–102, esp. p. 91.

[9] Tommaso III di Saluzzo, *Il Libro del Cavaliere Errante (BnF ms. fr. 12559)*, ed. M. Piccat et al. (Boves, 2008), p. 23.

[10] L. Cadioli, 'Scoperta di un inedito: il volgarizzamento toscano del *Lancelot en prose*', *MR*, 37 (2013), 177–92. We thank Professors Daniela Delcorno Branca, Fabrizio Cigni and Lino Leonardi for sending us information and bibliography about this important discovery.

[11] L. Leonardi, 'Bella scoperta: Riappare il cavalier Lancillotto', *Il Sole 24 Ore*, 142 (26 May 2013), 41.

[12] Allaire's 'Arthurian Art References' list includes information on manuscript illuminations (pp. 244–6).

[13] Delcorno Branca, *Tristano e Lancillotto in Italia: Studi di letteratura arturiana* (Ravenna, 1998), hereafter *TLI*; E. G. Gardner, *The Arthurian Legend in Italian Literature* (London and New York, 1930).

[14] *TLI*, p. 7.

Part One

France and Italy

1

ARTHURIANA IN THE ITALIAN REGIONS OF MEDIEVAL FRANCOPHONIA

Keith Busby

Medieval Francophonia is a term I use to denote the various regions of Europe where the *langue d'oïl* was in use as a language of social, administrative, legal and literary discourse, beginning in the aftermath of the landing of William I of Normandy at Pevensey Bay in 1066 and continuing to the end of the fifteenth century. The word 'Francophonia', of course, is replete with implications in academic circles, as modern 'Francophone literature' has become a fashionable area within French departments and its growth has gone hand in hand with the rise of colonial and postcolonial studies.[1] Here is not the place for an extended exposé of the parallels between the medieval and modern notions, but they are, *mutatis mutandis*, many and enlightening. The clash, coexistence and assimilation of cultures, languages and religions; tensions between political systems, between coloniser and colonised; problems of the governance of a distant diaspora; perception and awareness of ethnic identity – all feature prominently in the study of both medieval and modern Francophonia. Medieval Francophonia, which stretches geographically from Ireland in the west to the crusader kingdoms of the Levant in the east, did not develop uniformly or predictably. Indeed, it can be argued that the differences between its various regions are sometimes greater than the similarities, but the *langue d'oïl* indisputably provides a common denominator, furnishing not only the means of common discourse but also the prestige of an overachieving vernacular.[2]

If the 'normannisation' of most of the big island was in many ways a classic case of colonisation and largely successful, Ireland, where the Cambro-Normans arrived in 1169, proved more difficult. Even though those parts of Ireland which acceded to Norman rule became thoroughly Norman, much of the smaller island resisted the invaders and remained stubbornly Irish, culturally and politically. The phrase 'Hiberniores Hibernis ipsis', the origin of which is obscure, points to the paradox of Norman success being dependent on Norman assimilation of Irish culture. The provenance of Hiberno-Norman authors and scribes in England, Wales and the continent makes it difficult to identify more than a handful of texts and manuscripts composed and copied in Ireland, but there must have been more than are currently known.[3] The position of French in post-Conquest England is known in its broad outlines, although much work remains to be done rescuing Anglo-Norman (or Anglo-French or the French of England or Insular French) from the contemptuous attitudes of earlier generations.

A much more complex situation obtained on the continent than manuals of literary history suggest. Despite the underlying and enabling *langue d'oïl*, literary and linguistic regionalism is very much the norm, reflecting political situations and the relationship between the monarchy and the aristocracy.[4] In the south, the literary dominance of the *langue d'oc* and the existence of bilingualism and border dialects require us to adjust the map. The courts of Flanders, Brabant and Hainaut in the north sometimes shifted between French and Dutch as a result of the cultural politics of intermarriage, and there is evidence of French literacy as far north as Utrecht.[5]

Francophony in crusader culture of the Levant, centred around Acre but with a legacy that extends to fifteenth-century Cyprus and the great families of Ibelin and Lusignan, is only just beginning to be explored by Cyril Aslanov and Laura Minervini.[6] It resulted, obviously, from a faith-based initiative, although many elements of a typical postcolonial culture are discernible in the wider context. Its cultural heyday was the century between the recapture of Acre by Richard I and Philippe-Auguste (1191) and the taking of the city by the Mamelukes (1291). Several workshops produced illuminated manuscripts of French texts composed there and in France.[7] Aslanov and Minervini have even been able to discern distinctive dialectal features of crusader French.

Italian Francophonia has two principal centres, the Angevin court of Naples and the courts and city-states of the Veneto and Lombardy, with Florence providing a bridge between the two.[8] Savoy is a geographical and cultural link between Francophone communities on both sides of the Alps. Whereas the milieux of the *regno* and Savoy were primarily aristocratic, with French being a language of both administration and culture, in the north the context is both courtly and non-courtly, but in any case basically literary. The merchant classes of the northern city-states and the great aristocratic families such as the Visconti, the Sforza, the Este and the Gonzaga mixed freely and intermarried with French aristocracy and royalty, creating a culture in which French literature became fashionable over a much wider social spectrum than usual. In Angevin Naples, French-language literary activity seems to have been limited, its best-known figure being Adam de la Halle, who composed *Le jeu de Robin et de Marion* there and began the *Chanson du roi de Sicile* for Charles I. Some Latin texts – historical, biblical and classical – were translated into French from the second half of the thirteenth century to the fourteenth, and a small number of manuscripts of existing French texts were copied there.[9]

Within the north, the main region of Italian Francophonia, original works were composed in French and Franco-Veneto, and manuscripts copied in large numbers – of some texts on an almost industrial scale. The French texts copied were in both verse and prose, representing many different genres: *romans antiques* and Alexander romances, *chansons de geste*, some didactic works in verse and prose, (pseudo-)chronicles such as the *Histoire ancienne jusqu'à César*, *Li fait des romains*, the French version of William of Tyre's *Chronique d'Outremer*, and numerous Arthurian prose romances examined in detail by others in this volume. The list is not exhaustive. I have argued elsewhere that most of these texts were popular in Italy because they appealed to a sense of 'national' pride.[10] Those who read or listened to them were proud of Italy's role in the history of the ancient world, as the inheritor of Greek culture and a link in the chain of *translatio studii et imperii*; Italy – Aspramonte in particular – and the general Mediterranean region was the *locus* of action of many *chansons de geste*. These readers and listeners were the same people who commissioned, bought and owned manuscripts. Yet no such arguments can be made to explain the popularity of the Arthurian prose romances, which enjoyed wide dissemination among the aristocracy and merchant classes.

Italian Francophonia is distinct from most of the other regions in that it is not a result of any form of invasion or aggression. This is not to say that political motives and actions never played a part in the spread and acceptance of the French language and literature south and east of the Alps (they clearly did), but outside the Angevin realms in the south, we are not dealing with conquest and colonisation in the usual sense. It may be possible to think of French literature conquering Italy as a form of cultural colonisation, but if so, it is one in which the foreign language and its texts were both welcome and invited by the host.

The reception history of French Arthurian romance in medieval Italy is dominated, as other contributions in this volume amply demonstrate, by the copying, dissemination, ownership and adaptation of prose texts, most notably the *Lancelot-Graal*, the prose *Tristan* and *Guiron le Courtois*. Some of these texts are discussed in this volume by Fabrizio Cigni, Marie-José Heijkant and Daniela Delcorno Branca, while other work by the same scholars, listed in the bibliography, provides a more or less complete and up-to-date overview. Gloria Allaire sums up what is known about ownership of manuscripts.[11] However, it would be false to conclude that earlier and other French Arthurian traditions had no impact in Italy, and more appropriate to argue that the traces they have left are more subtle and less visible.

If the importance of prose romance as the dominant form of Arthuriana in Italy and its popularity among the great Italian families such as the Este and the Visconti-Sforza must be acknowledged, it was equally widespread amidst those of lower social status who sought to enjoy the same French-language culture. This popularity is reflected in large-scale, almost industrial, production of manuscripts. More or less contemporaneous with the rise of Arthurian prose in the last decades of the thirteenth century and the first half of the fourteenth, however, a more discreet influence of the tradition of Chrétien de Troyes can be discerned, and it is that part of the legacy of the great Old French romancers which forms the object of the rest of this chapter. Chrétien may have been caught up in the general prestige of French in the aristocratic Italian courts and their satellites, but his verse clearly came to be seen in Italy as a less appropriate or less accessible medium for Arthurian romance.

The first possible traces of French Arthuriana in Italy are indeed visible and visual ones, namely the Modena archivolt and the Otranto mosaic.[12] The dating of the sculpture on the Porta della Pescheria of Modena cathedral has not been firmly established, although it was most likely executed before 1140.[13] The extensive mosaic covering the entire floor of Otranto cathedral was commissioned in 1163. If the general subject of the former is clear (the abduction, imprisonment and liberation of Guinevere), its precise source is not. Its complexity and numerous figures stand in contrast to the mute and enigmatic simplicity of the Arthurian scene in the latter (a figure captioned REX ARTURUS, holding a club of some kind, sits astride a goat and confronts a large cat-like creature). One French connection of the mosaic at least is known, namely the use of Norman craftsmen by Brother Pantaleone, himself working at the command of Archishop Gionato of Otranto.[14] Neither of these images represents anything from Geoffrey of Monmouth and both predate Chrétien de Troyes. It therefore seems reasonable to conjecture that the sources of both the Modena and Otranto images may have been oral tales, brought over the Alps by itinerant storytellers and/or Norman craftsmen.

The Arthurian history of the written French word in Italy does not begin with prose romance. If the best-known testimony to knowledge of Chrétien in Italy is the excerpt from *Cligés* copied on the second folio of an added *bifolium* (fols 71–72) of Florence, Bibl. Riccardiana, MS Ricc. 2756, it is neither the only one nor the earliest. It is, however, the only textual witness and proof positive of the circulation of at least one manuscript of the romance in Italy sometime after 1300.[15] The bulk of evidence for knowledge of Chrétien is in the form of allusions and quotations in non-Arthurian poetry in Occitan and Italian, the two other principal competing literary vernaculars in Italian Francophonia.

The Venetian troubadour Bertolomé Zorzi, who flourished in the third quarter of the thirteenth century, makes a clear reference to Chrétien. In *En tal dezirs mos cors intra*, a poem marked by the model of Arnaut Daniel, Bertolomé alludes to Perceval's confession to his hermit uncle:

'Don convenra que l'arma l'enfern intra,
Qu'el si gaudet, pois amors i mes l'ongla
Com Percevaus tro qu'anet a son oncle'. (11. 16–8)[16]

(So it's fitting that the soul will enter hell,
for it rejoices once love has put its fingernail in,
like Perceval before he went to his uncle.)

Guittone d'Arezzo, in *Amor tanto altamente*, a poem that may have been written before 1265, compares Perceval's silence at the Grail Castle to his own muteness before his lady:

Fallenza era demando
far lei senza ragione;
poi veggio che, sí stando,

> m'ha sovrameritato el meo servire.
> Però 'n tacer m'asservo,
> perché già guiderdone
> non dea cheder bon servo;
> bisogna i' n'ho, che 'l chere 'l suo servire,
> se no atendendo m'allasso;
> poi m'avvenisse, lasso!
> che mi trovasse in fallo
> sì come Prezevallo – a non cherere.
> Verrei a presente morto!
> Ma non tal penser porto,
> né sí mala credenza,
> ché sola conoscenza – halla in podere. (21, ll. 65–80)[17]

(It was a fault to ask it of her without reason; for I see that as things stand my service has outstripped me. Thus in silence I subject myself, because no good servant must ever ask for a reward; all I need is to ask to serve her, or else, waiting, I bind myself; then I, alas, would find myself at fault just like Perceval – for not asking. Then I would be dead! But I don't think such a thing, or hold such a wrong belief, for only knowledge – has that power.)

Beyond the significance of these allusions in the immediate context of the poems, we should note that they are both to key moments in the narrative of Chrétien's last romance, suggesting that both Zorzi and Guittone had detailed knowledge and good understanding of the text (and expected their audiences to have the same).

In the undated Letter 21 addressed to Orlando da Chiusi, Guittone also includes a partial translation of a couplet from *Cligés*, even mentioning Chrétien by name:

> Unde Cristiano là ove Allessandro Novello dice:
>   'Reposo e loda
>   non concordano bene insieme'.[18]

> (Thus Chrétien, where the new Alexander says, 'Rest and fame do not go well together.')

I take 'Allessandro Novello' to mean that Chrétien's character is a new Alexander the Great. The verbal detail here suggests intimate knowledge of *Cligés*, either from a copy to hand or from a retentive memory. This letter is replete with allusions to, and quotations from, Latin, Old French and Occitan texts: Aristotle, Cicero, Galen, Macrobius, Seneca, Socrates, Augustine, Bernard, Jerome, Gregory, Benoît de Sainte-Maure, Chrétien, Peire Rogier and Peire Vidal. It may well have been written after Guittone's conversion, and cannot be earlier than 1261, the date marking the start of Orlando's conflict with Guglielmino degli Ubertini, bishop of Arezzo.[19] There is a clear difference in the use to which Chrétien has been put in these two contexts, first, as part of a traditional amorous meditation, and second, as the source of a moral *exemplum*. The couplet translated from *Cligés* is essentially a paremiological dictum.

Cligés appears to have left fewer traces in the Middle Ages than Chrétien's other romances – for example, by way of adaptations in other languages.[20] Modern scholars have also tended to pay less attention to it. In Italy, however, it seems to have been relatively well known. In an Italian scribe's attempt to write an Occitan *salut d'amor* on the blank f. 60v of Florence, Bibl. Mediceo-Laurenziana, MS Plut. XLIV, 44 of *Le Roman d'Eneas* (late twelfth century), the two pairs of lovers from Chrétien's text are mentioned along with Floire and Blancheflor:

> Per vos, donna vallenz,
> ch'eu non aus dir
> ni non pos dir
> a vos ma desiranza . . .
> En am plus vos
> de bon cor lialmenz
> che Cliges non ama
> Fenices verament
> ne Floire Blancaflor
> ne Alixandre Soredamors.[21]

(For you, worthy lady, I do not dare nor can I tell you my desire . . . I love you with a true heart more loyally than Cligès loved Fenice, or Floire Blanchefleur, or Alexandre Soredamor.)

L'Intelligenza, an anonymous late thirteenth-century poem in 309 stanzas of *nona rima*, was probably written in Florence. In the first principal section, the poet describes the sixty gems in the crown of his lady in the manner of a lapidary, and in the second, he describes at length her palace. The ceiling is adorned with a series of paintings: Fortune, the God of Love with a procession of famous lovers from different traditions, the story of Cæsar's Civil War, the life of Alexander the Great, the destruction of Troy, and more lovers of romance (stanzas 70–288). The allusion to Guinevere and Lancelot in stanza 73: 'Èvi la bella Ginevra regina, / ed evv' apresso messer Lancialotto', ll. 1–2; ('There is beautiful Guinevere the Queen, and next to her is Sir Lancelot') may either be to Chrétien's *Charrette* or the prose *Lancelot*, but stanzas 74 and 75 undoubtedly refer to three of Chrétien's romances:

> 74
> Èv' Allessandro e Ros[s]enna d'Amore,
> Messere Erecco, ed Enidia davante,
> ed èvi Trasia e 'l prenze Antigonore,
> e d'Apollonio la lira sonante,
> e Archistrate regina di valore,
> Cui sorprese esto Amore al gaio sembiante;
> èvi Bersenda e 'l buono Diomedes[se],
> èvi Penelopè ed Ulizesse,
> ed Eneasse e Lavina davante.

> 75
> E non fallio chi·ffu lo 'ntagliadore
> la bella Analidà e 'l buonn-Ivano;
> èvi intagliato Fiore e Blanzifiore
> e la bell' Isaotta Blanzesmano.
> Si com' ella morio per fin amore,
> cotanto amò Lancialotto sovrano,

> èvi la nobile Donna del Lago;
> quella di Maloalto col cuor vago,
> e Palamidès cavalier pagano.[22]

74: There are Alexander and Roxana of Love, Sir Erec, and Enide before him, and there is Tarsia and Prince Antigonore, and Apollonius playing the lyre, and Archistrata queen of worth, whom this Love with the laughing face surprised; there is Criseida and good Diomedes, and Penelope with Ulysses, and Eneas and Lavinia before him.

75: And he did not err, whoever depicted fair Analidà and good Yvain; depicted there are Floire and Blanchefleur, and beautiful Iseut of the White Hands. Just as she died of noble love for loving the lofty Lancelot so much, the noble Lady of the Lake is there; she of Malehaut, with the loving heart, and Palamedes, the pagan knight.)

The first line of stanza 74 clearly refers to Alexandre and Soredamors from Chrétien's *Cligès*. The form 'Rossenna d'Amore' may be a contamination under the influence of Roxana, wife of Alexander the Great; 'Rossenna' may also derive from the notion that gold ('*sor*' = blonde) has a reddish tinge. In any case, there is clearly an etymological wordplay on '*sora*' and '*rossa*'.[23] The mention of Erec and Enide in the following line confirms the allusion to *Cligés*. And what should be made of the phrasing 'Messere Erecco, ed Enidia davante'? The use of '*davante*' in the last line of stanza 74 probably points to the position of the couples in the fresco, i.e. Eneas and Lavinia in the front of the line. Berisso's punctuation of l. 2, however, suggests that he believes that Enide is in front of Erec, calling to mind how she preceded him on their '*avanture*'.[24]

The second line of stanza 75 completes the three pairs of lovers from Chrétien with Yvain and his lady, although the form of the latter's name is also problematic. The name, usually cited by scholars as 'Laudine', occurs in that form in only two of the ten manuscripts, as 'Laudune' in another and as '*la dame*' in the rest.[25] The name 'Analida' is also noteworthy, occurring to my knowledge only in Chaucer's *Anelida and Arcite*; Chaucer scholars often give its source as *L'Intelligenza*. Since the name Arcite is taken from Boccaccio's *Teseida*, this may indicate that Chaucer encountered the name Anelida in an Italian text; whether or not this was *L'Intelligenza* remains uncertain. In a note to these lines, Berisso points out another reference to *Yvain* in an earlier poem by Bonagiunta Orbicciani da Lucca: 'And Sir Yvain and sweet Tristan were both my inferiors in suffering'.[26]

It seems clear enough in light of the above that Italian poets knew Chrétien and expected their audiences and readers to do so as well. If in France a clear but not absolute distinction was made between the verse tradition of Chrétien and the later rise of the great prose romances, in Italy to some degree the protagonists of early verse romance are not differentiated from those of the prose cycles. For example, stanza 75 of *L'Intelligenza* has Chrétien's characters, Floris, Blanchefleur and Iseut White Hands (probably alluding to verse texts) followed by a reference to the Prose *Lancelot* (the Lady of Malehaut) and the prose *Tristan* (Palamedes).

The regions of Piedmont and Savoy together constituted one of the most important geographical and cultural links between France and Italy. Tommaso III di Saluzzo composed the long *Le Chevalier Errant* in verse and prose during his imprisonment in Turin by Amedeo III of Savoy in the years 1394–6.[27] Tommaso was a serious francophile, and I have tried to demonstrate elsewhere that his reading in French was typical of the French-oriented northern Italian aristocracy, not so much of his own generation, but of a somewhat earlier one.[28] He may have used books from the Savoy library, as well as his own, during his incarceration as the sources for this work. *Le Chevalier Errant* is a nostalgic anachronism already at the end of the fourteenth century, although its encyclopaedic aesthetic is typical of the period. Alongside the Arthurian prose romances used by Tommaso, one verse romance has left its mark; not surprisingly, perhaps, this is Chrétien's *Perceval* along with the First *Continuation*. The Caradoc episode from the *Continuation* is rewritten in prose and there are extensive verse quotations from Chrétien's episode of the Damsel in the Tent. Tommaso encapsulates rather belatedly many aspects of the general situation of Arthuriana in Italy: prose, verse, direct access to French manuscripts, and creative rewriting, among others.

The major development of French Arthurian romance which has left no traces in Italy, as far as one can tell, is that of the so-called epigonal verse romances written in the wake of Chrétien de Troyes, in the period c.1200–75. It is hard to know precisely how to interpret this absence. If Beate Schmolke-Hasselmann is correct that the audience of Arthurian verse romance was a limited one of *cognoscenti*, this may be at least a partial explanation.[29] One would then have to conclude that the appeal of Chrétien's own romances was wider than that of his epigones, an argument which seems to be supported by numbers of surviving manuscripts and adaptations into other vernaculars (of the epigonal romances, only *La vengeance Raguidel* and *Fergus* were adapted into Middle Dutch, and *Le Bel Inconnu* into Middle English). Dissemination of these romances therefore seems to have been north and west; no surviving manuscripts were copied in Italy.

One Arthurian verse romance which was copied in Italy, however, is the sole surviving example of the genre in Occitan, *Jaufre*.[30] This 10,974-line romance is in some ways a crystallisation of diverse features of the post-Chrétien verse romance tradition, although its own intertextual links are primarily to Chrétien and his early aftermath (the First *Continuation* of *Perceval* and *Le Bel Inconnu*, both dating from c.1200). Of the seven manuscripts and fragments of *Jaufre*, three were produced in Italy: Paris, BnF, MS fr. 12571 (probably Bologna, late thirteenth or early fourteenth century); BAV, MS Vat. Lat. 3206 (Occcitan chansonnier *L*, northern Italy, late fourteenth century); and New York, Pierpont Morgan Library, MS M.819 (Occitan chansonnier *N*, Italy, fourteenth century).[31] Despite the general absence of the epigonal tradition in Italy, it would seem that Italian readers and listeners were acquainted with at least one romance in which Arthur, standard Arthurian figures, themes and motifs, were presented in an ironic and humorous manner.

The history of Arthuriana in Italy is part of the literary history of medieval Francophonia. Although the direct textual evidence in the form of surviving manuscripts is predominantly that of the prose tradition, the Modena archivolt and the Otranto mosaic strongly suggest the presence of oral transmission as early as the first half of the twelfth century. The Florence *Cligés* excerpt, the work of Tommaso di Saluzzo, allusions in various poetic forms and the manuscript transmission of *Jaufre*, all confirm considerable knowledge and dissemination in Italy of the verse tradition of Chrétien de Troyes and his successors alongside the more visible presence of prose romance.

Notes

[1] Good introductions to modern Francophonia are P. Corcoran, *The Cambridge Introduction to Francophone Literature* (Cambridge, 2007) and J.-M. Moura, *Littératures francophones et théorie postcoloniale* (Paris, 1999).

[2] K. Busby and A. Putter, 'Introduction: Medieval Francophonia', in K. Busby and C. Kleinhenz (eds), *Medieval Multilingualism: The Francophone World and its Neighbours* (Turnhout, 2010), pp. 1–13.

[3] For French in Ireland, see Busby, 'Livres courtois en mouvement: dans les marges codicologiques de la francophonie médiévale', in I. Arseneau and F. Gingras (eds), *Cultures courtoises en mouvement* (Montreal, 2011), pp. 227–48.

[4] For reflections of this regionalism in patterns of manuscript production, see K. Busby, 'The Geography of the Codex', in *Codex and Context: Reading Old French Verse Narrative in Manuscript*, 2 vols (Amsterdam, 2002), II, pp. 766–97. S. Lusignan sees both persistent regionalism and a movement towards uniformisation, the latter particularly on the administrative level: *La langue des rois au Moyen Âge: le français en France et en Angleterre* (Paris, 2004).

[5] Interesting work has been done on the coexistence of French and Dutch in Brabant and Holland by R. Sleiderink, *De stem van de meester. De hertogen van Brabant en hun rol in het literaire leven (1106–1430)* (Ph.D. diss. Universiteit Leiden, 2003; published Amsterdam, 2003), and J. van der Meulen, 'Au cœur de l'Europe. Littérature à la cour de Hainaut-Hollande (1250–1350)' (Ph.D. diss. Universiteit Leiden, 2010).

[6] By C. Aslanov; see 'Languages in Contact in the Latin East: Acre and Cyprus', *Crusades*, 1 (2002), 155–81; idem, *Evidence of Francophony in Mediaeval Levant: Decipherment and Interpretation (MS Paris BnF copte 43)* (Jerusalem, 2006); and *Le français au Levant, jadis et naguère: à la recherche d'une langue perdue* (Paris, 2006). See also L. Minervini, 'Le français dans l'Orient latin (XIIIe–XIVe siècles). Éléments pour la caractérisation d'une *scripta* du Levant', *Revue de Linguistique Romane*, 74 (2010), 119–98.

[7] For an overview, see Busby, 'Livres courtois'; for manuscript production, see J. Folda, *Crusader Art in the Holy Land, from the Third Crusade to the Fall of Acre, 1187–1291* (Cambridge, 2005).

[8] A useful resource on the French of Italy is L. Morreale and S. Barsella, *French of Italy*, retrieved from *http://www.fordham.edu/academics/programs_at_fordham_/medieval_studies/french_of_italy/index.asp*.

[9] On French in Angevin Naples, see especially L. Formisano and C. Lee, 'Il "Francese di Napoli"', in P. Trovato (ed), *Lingue e Culture dell'Italia meridionale (1200–1600)* (Rome, 1993), pp. 133–62.

[10] Busby, *Codex and Context*, II, pp. 596–634.

[11] See also ibid., pp. 766–97.

[12] Early studies on both can be found in R. S. Loomis and L. H. Loomis, *Arthurian Legends in Medieval Art* (New York, 1938), pp. 32–6, and figs. 4–8, 9–9a. Chapter 13 in this volume discusses these images and provides current bibliography.

[13] In *Arthurian Legends*, the Loomises had argued for an early date for the Modena archivolt, but J. Stiennon and R. Lejeune placed it between 1120 and 1140 ('La légende arthurienne dans la sculpture de la cathédrale de Modène', *Cahiers de civilisation médiévale*, 6 [1963], 281–96).

[14] For a detailed study of the mosaic, see G. Gianfreda, *Il mosaico pavimentale della Basilica Cattedrale di Otranto*, 2nd edn (Frosinone, 1965).

[15] For an edition of this excerpt, see K. Busby, 'Chrétien in Italy', in F. Alfie and A. Dini (eds), *'Accessus ad auctores': Studies in Honor of Christopher Kleinhenz* (Tempe, AZ, 2011), pp. 25–38. See also G. Giannini, 'Il romanzo francese in versi dei secoli XII e XIII in Italia: il "Cligès" Riccardiano', in *Modi e forme della fruizione della 'materia arturiana' nell'Italia dei sec. XIII–XV* (Milan, 2006), pp. 119–58, also with an edition.

[16] E. Levy (ed.), in *Der Troubadour Bertolome Zorzi* (Halle, 1883). The poem is preserved in the Italian *chansonniers I* and *K*. See Gianfranco Folena, *Culture e lingue nel Veneto medievale* (Padua, 1990), pp. 131–2. A quasi-exhaustive list of references to Arthurian tales in all troubadours can be found in F. Pirot, *Recherches sur les connaissances littéraires des troubadours occitans et catalans des XIIe et XIIIe siècles. Les 'sirventes-ensenhamens' de Guerau de Cabrera, Guiraut de Calanson et Bertrand de Paris* (Barcelona, 1972).

[17] F. Egidi (ed.), Guittone d'Arezzo, *Le Rime* (Bari, 1940), pp. 47–9.

[18] C. Margueron (ed.), *Lettere* (Bologna, 1990), pp. 225–40, §16. Cf. *Cligés*: 'Ne s'accordent pas bien ansanble / Repos et los, si con moi sanble' (ll. 157–8). S. Gregory and C. Luttrell (eds), Chrétien de Troyes, *Cligés* (Cambridge, 1993).

[19] Margueron compares the letter with Guittone's poem XVIII (*Lettere*, pp. 225–6).

[20] It survives in a fifteenth-century Burgundian adaptation; the most recent edition is M. Colombo Timelli (ed.), *Le Livre d'Alixandre, empereur de Constentinoble et de Cligés son filz: roman en prose du XVe siècle* (Geneva, 2004).

[21] Thanks to Gabriele Giannini for pointing out that these lines were published in the *Roman d'Eneas* as edited by J. J. Salverda de Grave (Halle, 1891), p. iii.

[22] M. Berisso (ed.), *L'Intelligenza: poemetto anonimo del secolo XIII*, Biblioteca di scrittori italiani (Milan and Parma, 2000), stanzas 74–5.

[23] Berisso (ed.), *L'Intelligenza*, pp. 263–4.

[24] In Chrétien de Troyes, *Erec und Enide*, ed. W. Foerster (Halle, 1890), 'Devant s'est mise' (2777); 'Et Erec, qui aprés venoit' (2934).

[25] Chrétien de Troyes, *Le Chevalier au lion*, ed. and trans. D. Hult (Paris, 1994), pp. 11–12.

[26] Berisso (ed.), *L'Intelligenza*, p. 265. Dante meets Bonagiunta in *Purgatorio* 24.

[27] The text has finally been the object of two critical editions: M. Piccat and L. Ramello (eds), E. Martinengo (trans.), Tommaso III di Saluzzo, *Il Libro del Cavaliere Errante (BnF ms. fr. 12559)* (Boves, 2008); and R. Fajen (ed.), Tommaso III. von Saluzzo, *Le Livre du Chevalier Errant. Kritische Edition* (Wiesbaden, forthcoming 2014).

[28] Busby, 'La bibliothèque de Tommaso di Saluzzo', in C. Galderisi and J. Maurice (eds), *'Qui tant savoit d'engin et d'art': Mélanges de philologie médiévale offerts à Gabriel Bianciotto* (Poitiers, 2006), pp. 31–9.

[29] B. Schmolke-Hasselmann, *The Evolution of Arthurian Romance: The Verse Tradition from Chrétien to Froissart*, trans. M. Middleton and R. Middleton (Cambridge, 1998).

[30] The most useful edition in the present context is C. Lee (ed. and trans.), *Jaufre* (Rome, 2006), with translation into Italian. It also contains an excellent introductory study and critical commentary on the romance.

[31] The manuscripts are described briefly in Lee (ed.), *Jaufre*, pp. 43–5.

2

FRENCH REDACTIONS IN ITALY: RUSTICHELLO DA PISA

Fabrizio Cigni

The name of Rustichello da Pisa (Rusticiaus or Rusticien de Pise, in French manuscripts) is connected to the passage of the Arthurian prose material between France and Italy in the last decades of the thirteenth century. Rustichello evokes certain centres of reception that are particularly important in the Romance literary system, such as the eastern Mediterranean, Pisa and Genoa – in fact, the Mediterranean in general. It is no accident that in 1298 his name is linked with that of the Venetian Marco Polo and the geographical work called *Le Devisement dou Monde*.[1]

I begin this chapter with the historical context Rustichello's introduction invokes: the crusade of Prince Edward of England. I then discuss certain historical-cultural interrelations which are much more complex than Eilert Löseth – who relegated Rustichello's Compilation to an appendix of the prose *Tristan* material – suggested in his critical breakdown.[2] These interrelations are not easy to reconstruct in full, but without them we cannot understand the linguistic and literary value of these new narrative forms – for such were the compilations, anthologies and reassemblages within the same manuscripts. They featured a hybrid linguistic surface and a summary reuse of narrative clichés, simplified and crystallised compared to the French prose works, as we can also see in the Franco-Italian redaction of the *Devisement dou Monde*. In this context I will highlight, first, the direct manuscript tradition of Rustichello's romance, whose outlines, particularly at the end, are not easy to establish, flanked as it is by *Tristan* and *Guiron le Courtois*, the same works from which he takes his matter. I will then also focus on the value of single manuscripts or groups of manuscripts. These are all valuable of course as copies of works, such as *Tristan*, *Guiron* and Rustichello's Compilation; but they are equally valuable as evidence of fundamental editorial/linguistic stages on the one hand, and on the other of representational stages, of the process of acclimatisation of the Breton material to the Italian municipal context. That very process would lead to the prose Tristan romances in Italian, to the *Tavola Ritonda* and to the *cantari*.

Rustichello's Compilation essentially contains, first, a Prologue that serves as an introduction to the first adventure (of the Old Knight Branor li Brun), and then a *florilegium* of favourite Tristan and Grail episodes, such as the combat at Merlin's Stone and Galehaut's submission to Arthur. The Compilation enjoyed a notable French manuscript tradition, one whose language, at least superficially, no longer features the irregularities of the copies made in Italy. That same French manuscript tradition also includes an epilogue as well as episodes either foreign to the Franco-Italian tradition, or related to it in ways that are variously problematic; it has been the subject of vibrant new studies since my 1994 edition of BnF, MS fr. 1463.[3] These studies unveil important new findings on *Guiron le Courtois* and other manuscripts copied in Italy, which contain rewritings and episodes that can in many respects be assimilated to the model of Rustichello.

The second part of this chapter aims to illustrate the narrative content of Rustichello's Arthurian Compilation. Its contours are sometimes elusive, and its novelty vis-à-vis its sources lies precisely in its particular technique of montage, which was probably not subject to a predetermined narrative conclusion. Analysing it anew also requires continual consultation both of the latest research around the earliest matrix of its diffusion, the Pisa–Genoa axis at the end of the thirteenth century, and of the later ramifications, embodied in the French manuscripts. Only a close and reciprocal comparison of the two stages, identified through codicological and linguistic research, can clarify what remained murky for Löseth, Gardner and Rajna.[4]

Rustichello's Compilation: Historical Background

The Compilation, based on materials presumably circulating *c.*1270–4, emerges from the diaspora of Arthurian romance outside France and from the adoption of literary French by certain authors of Italian origin in the second half of the thirteenth century.[5] Rustichello's text is also known as *Meliadus*, the name of Tristan's father, according to the epilogue (perhaps apocryphal) contained in BnF, MSS fr. 340 and 355, and in the sixteenth-century printed editions of *Guiron le Courtois*. The nucleus of Rustichello's adaptation, which we can extrapolate from a complete study of the manuscript tradition, actually bears no title. Only the word *livre* (book) appears several times; based on this *livre*, the unknown Pisan author putatively '*conpilé*' (compiled) some of the Arthurian adventures of the time of Tristan and Lancelot (§§1.3 and 5).[6] The verb *conpiler* yielded the more appropriate descriptor 'compilation' for this prose work of uncertain boundaries. It is the term that Löseth used when he made the first systematic analysis of the text as an appendix to the *Tristan en prose* and the *Guiron* (or *Roman de Palamède*) of BnF, MSS fr. 340 and 355.

The Compilation opens with an introductory paragraph that is both highly recognisable and compact in the manuscript tradition, and very similar in its structure to the prologue of Marco Polo's *Devisement dou Monde*.[7] Rustichello came to be associated primarily with the extraordinary success of that book, on which he collaborated.[8] Nonetheless, because of the network of intertextual relations with its source models, this first literary effort constitutes a necessary stage for understanding the evolution of the Arthurian material in its delicate passage between French and the other medieval languages.[9] The Compilation is particularly important as a link between the most prominent romances, such as the *Tristan en prose* (the redaction circulating most widely in Italy) and the *Guiron* cycle on the one hand,[10] and on the other, the anonymous Italian reworkings in verse and prose.[11]

At this point I must survey the specific textual configuration and organisation of the Compilation within the primarily Italian manuscript tradition. I focus particularly on BnF, MS fr. 1463, one of a large group of romance manuscripts copied in Italy. Although precisely where in Italy they were copied is disputed, this group seems to be most closely connected to the Pisa–Genoa axis.[12] No less important for understanding the Compilation is the historical context from which it emerged: first and foremost, the likely contacts between a 'Pisan' Rustichello and the Mediterranean backdrop of the last crusades. Rustichello calls this a book 'translated' (*treslaités*) from one belonging to, or received from, King Edward during his journey to the Holy Land ('a celui tenz qu'il passé houtre la mer en servise nostre Sire Damedeu pour conquister le saint Sepoucre'; §1.2). This accounts for the earliest circulation of his text in the north-western Italy of the maritime republics, especially Pisa and Genoa, following the battle of Meloria in August 1284, when many Pisans imprisoned in Genoa were involved in literary activities such as copying and translation.[13]

Before proceeding with my analysis, a word about the compiler's name is in order. 'Rustichello da Pisa' is one of the most likely forms to identify with *maistre Rusticiaus de Pise* in BnF, MS fr. 1463, written variously as *Rusticiens de Pise* (BnF, MSS fr. 340 and 355); *messire Rustaciaus* (BnF, MS fr. 1116); and *Rustico da Pisa* (*Tris. Ven.*).[14] Despite his marked authorial profile and this strong codicological evidence, we cannot identify him definitively with any one of the Pisan Rustichellos, primarily notaries, who appear in archival documents of the time.[15] Nonetheless, the manuscript tradition of the Compilation itself, geographically anchored between northern Italy and France, seems to offer more solid and plausible evidence for Rustichello's identity than we can glean for other Arthurian authors such as Walter Map, Luce del Gat or Hélie de Boron. For example, the prologue specifies the broadest imaginable lay audience: an invitation to 'emperors and kings, princes, dukes and counts, lords and knights, vavassours and burghers' (§1.1) to read or hear the book establishes that already the romance no longer has a 'courtly' orientation.[16] This opening, reprised almost verbatim in the *Devisement dou Monde*, tells us that both audiences have been broadened to include everyone who aspires to a literary culture of entertainment. But what gives a sense of concreteness to the circumstances of the composition is the name of Edward I of England, from whom Rustichello claims he received a book of adventures when the future sovereign was sailing to take part in the crusade between 1270 and 1274.[17] The event evoked in the prologue, while comprising a conventional 'source-book' topos, deserves a historical note.

Prince Edward began his Mediterranean crossing at Aigues Mortes, as did King Louis IX of France (who died of malaria in Tunis, in 1270). Edward visited three islands: Sardinia, Sicily (then under the rule of Charles I of Anjou, brother of Louis

IX) and Cyprus; on any of these, he could easily have come into contact with a Pisan writer. For that matter Acre, where Edward landed in May 1271, was an intensely active commercial centre for Pisans, Genoese and Venetians.[18] In Acre the Italian jurist Accursius joined Edward's entourage. The papal legate Tebaldo Visconti, the future Pope Gregory X, was there as well, and had the final say regarding the succession of the English kingdom (news had reached there that King Henry III was gravely ill). Edward's time in the Holy Land was marked by continual clashes with the local sultan, and his stay was forcibly concluded in September 1272. On his return journey Edward again stayed with Charles I of Anjou in Sicily, where he learned of his father's death. He then crossed Italy (overland this time, although not via Pisa) and the French lands, staying in Savoy (in the castle of Saint-Georges d'Espéranche, in the Isère), Paris and Gascony, returning to England for good in August 1274.[19] Even with a clear idea of Edward's movements in these years, however, we still cannot associate a precise date with the verb *conpiler* in the prologue.

It is worth noting that Edward travelled with his young wife Eleanor of Castile (d. 1299), herself the dedicatee of the Anglo-Norman translation of Vegetius' *De re militari*, done in Acre by one Master Richard. The enormous verse romance *Escanor* by Girart d'Amiens, broadly inspired by Arthurian material and probably composed during the couple's homeward journey, was dedicated to her as well. Both Girart and Rustichello address her as 'Queen Eleanor', suggesting that both works were completed after Edward's coronation. In any case we know that by Plantagenet tradition Eleanor had the task of attending to literary relations, as well as of preserving chivalric books, and that she had in her retinue clerks, scribes and miniaturists.[20]

Rustichello's prologue also recalls Edward's well-known interests in King Arthur and in politics. Edward often expressed his political agenda through explicit references to romances in his letters; in frequent political councils inspired by the Round Table; and by participation in tournaments in which nobles adopted blazons and names drawn from Arthurian romance, following contemporary European fashion. Given Rustichello's predilection for duels and combat, it has even been suggested that the Compilation was initially conceived as a kind of military manual, a handbook of basic military encounters, which can be explained as much by the crusading climate of the Latin East as by the English scene immediately following Edward's coronation.[21]

Whatever his identity, Rustichello da Pisa is a literary figure in whom we may detect a *scriptor* of notarial training, which could also account for the qualifier *maistre* in his works.[22] He may have been in occasional contact with the English court (also itinerant); he had a good command of French; and after 1284 he was confined in prison in Genoa, where he was surely in close contact with Dominican scholastic-conventual culture. His *livre* aims to be both concise and pleasurable, selecting or creating adventures that are especially dynamic but above all are adapted to an actualising reading – a reading that is highly responsive to the context in which the book was commissioned. That context seems to have dictated a selection of adventures, more or less well known, which contain at least one of these foundational motifs: a heroic confrontation between old and new generations of knights; help and succour for the weak and defenceless; Christian devotion; and feudal conflicts, vendettas and reconciliations.[23]

The content of the Compilation prologue remains more or less stable in all the redactional phases of the manuscript tradition.[24] Rustichello declares that what is most important to him are the rivalries and enmities of Tristan and Lancelot; this means, among other things, that his principal and initial 'source' remains the *Tristan en prose* and not, as is often claimed, the *Guiron*.[25] Rustichello reads the *Tristan*, moreover, from the canny optic of its intertextual relationship with the Vulgate cycle, whose salient features are the opposition between the two heroes Lancelot and Tristan; the two loves of the respective couples, Lancelot–Guinevere and Tristan–Iseut; and the two worlds of Mark's kingdom and that of Arthur.[26] Nevertheless the militaristic dictates of Rustichello's milieu – whether we consider that milieu to be Edward's crusader entourage or the warring Italian municipalities – reduce all this complexity to a series of duels, recognitions and reconciliations between the two heroes. This series, unlike its models, displays a certain superficiality and formulaic repetitiveness.[27] Rustichello does seem to have invented the adventures of the Old Knight Branor, which immediately follows the prologue of the Compilation. This episode certainly deploys the theme of the comparison between the ancient knights and the 'new' knights (Arthur's contemporaries) already implicit in *Guiron*, a romance organised around the genealogical line of the 'fathers'. The episode also represents a concise and efficient compendium of the major Arthurian *topoi*, from the incognito challenge to the book of adventures compiled at court, which becomes the source of the narration itself. The resulting compendium is perfectly cast in the novellistic taste of municipal Italy of the late thirteenth century, and the theme of the ancient knights' superiority will certainly appear in the *Novellino* and the *Tavola Ritonda*.

The curious image in the prologue, referred to in the phrase 'li quelz est imagines desovre', ('which is pictured above'), is telling for the Italian reception of the romances. Although the phrase is preserved in later manuscript witnesses, only in BnF, MS fr. 1463 does it refer to a crowned figure next to the initial letter S of the same column in which the phrase appears (fol. 1). The male figure is seated on a throne, wearing a red mantle and hood and holding a long sceptre in his hand, like Arthur or Alexander the Great. His pose would suggest that in executing it the illustrator was motivated more by the mention of Edward nearby in the text than by the mention of *Maistre Rusticiaus* on the same page, although the position of the left hand, indicating the beginning of the text, belongs to the iconographic tradition of the medieval *maistre*.[28]

The verb 'to compile' (*conpiler*), which Rustichello uses to refer to the material he 'found' (*treuvé*) in the book, was a technical term that underwent an evolution over the course of the Middle Ages (§1.3). In classical Latin until the early Christian centuries it had a negative valence, that of pillage. In the historical compilations of the twelfth and thirteenth centuries – that is, in the encyclopaedic and scholastic climate of

European literary culture, both courtly and urban – it meant instead 'to make extracts and compose something new'.[29] While the role of the *compilator* could not be considered equivalent to that of a true author, the practice was nonetheless defended with pride and conviction, especially for its twin virtues of brevity and ease of reading. Not surprisingly, compilation found particular favour in the Dominican order: Vincent of Beauvais's *Speculum Historiale* is called a *volumen manuale* (handbook), and Jacopo da Voragine's massive hagiographical collection *Legenda Aurea* is described, between Bologna and Genoa, at the end of the thirteenth century, as *legende conpilate* (compiled legends).[30]

Rustichello da Pisa belongs then to the tradition of those Arthurian authors and pseudo-authors whose names figure above all in liminal spaces such as prologues, epilogues and formulas of transition.[31] Prior Arthurian authors had attempted to produce a complete *summa*;[32] in keeping with the cultural trend of his age, Rustichello redirects their ambition towards selection and *florilegium* instead. Rustichello thus creates a kind of compact compilation, the last of the French series, which would be the model less for the late French redactions of the same romances, than for the Italian translations and reworkings soon to come. The Compilation's importance was always evident to scholars, who consulted this eccentric work in part because of the extraordinary popularity of many of its episodes in late medieval literature. In fact, it would soon lend itself to three new audiences beyond its original one. The first was the Italian municipal middle class at the turn of the thirteenth to the fourteenth century. The second was the more popular and mercantile audience of the *cantari*, which flourished around the middle of the fourteenth century.[33] Not surprisingly, given the Compilation's strongly aristocratic message, its third new audience was the courts of northern Italy, already imbued with late Gothic nostalgia, as demonstrated by the rich libraries which would inspire Boiardo and Ariosto.

Manuscripts

The manuscript tradition of the Compilation, both in French and Italian, is solidly linked to and entwined with the major works from which Rustichello drew his own inspiration. All the manuscript witnesses, in French and other vernaculars, can be described as ambivalent for various texts, bearing in mind the risk of spurious and dubious episodes. In general, the French witnesses range chronologically from the end of the thirteenth century to the beginning of the sixteenth (the print editions of *Tristan*, *Meliadus* and *Guiron*), and geographically from northern Italy to France. A survey of these gives some idea of their complex, often obscure, relations.[34]

The principal manuscripts are:

BnF, MS fr. 1463. Parchment. Late thirteenth century, 305 x 205 mm, 106 fols, Gothic script in two columns, illustrated with ink drawings filled in with a few colours.

(Facsimile and transcription in Cigni edn). One of about thirty manuscripts containing courtly prose texts in French and Italian, previously identified with a Neapolitan scriptorium, but more recently identified as Genoese.[35] Contents: Rustichello's Compilation (§§1–196) and the last adventures and death of Tristan (§§197–236).

BnF, MS fr. 340. Parchment. Early fifteenth century, 420 x 300 mm, 207 fols, three columns. Contents: Rustichello's Compilation (§§1–196); compiled episodes inspired by *Guiron*; a long section of *Meliadus*;[36] a section of *Tristan en prose* (Lös. §§252–344); a section from the Post-Vulgate *Mort Artu*.[37]

BnF, MS fr. 355. Parchment. Fifteenth century, 405 x 285 mm, 413 fols, three columns of 60 lines each. Contents: Rustichello's Compilation (§§1–196) alternates with *Guiron* and *Tristan* similar to MS fr. 340, above, although with more extensive amplifications in the last section.

Berlin, Staatsbibliothek Preussischer Kulturbesitz, MS Hamilton 581. Parchment. Fifteenth century, 400 x 350 mm, 70 fols, two cols, Gothic script. Content: the same as the above manuscripts, up to §195.[38]

Other isolated passages are preserved in the following manuscripts, which primarily contain the prose *Tristan* and *Guiron*:

BnF, MS fr. 99. Fifteenth century. Fols 663d–679a contain §§131a–141 and 2–13.9.

BnF, MS fr. 103. Fifteenth century. Fols 339–372b contain §76.4–15, §§77–157.

Chantilly, Bibliothèque du Château, MSS 645–646–647. Fifteenth century. Contents: resembles BnF, MS fr. 99; fols 138–143 contain; §§131a–141; 2–16.9; 17–19.8; 38–9.

Geneva, Bibliotheca Bodmeriana, MS 96. Fifteenth century. Fols 263a–286b of vol. II contain §§1–39.

New York, Pierpont Morgan Library, MS M.916. Fifteenth century. Fols 82c–136b contain §§163–94; 40–67; 111–17 (condensed into a few lines); 118.5–41; 148–57.

Turin, Biblioteca Nazionale, MS R.1622. Fifteenth century. Badly damaged in 1904 fire. Vol. I.19 (II) contains §§2–39, on reassembled fols 350b, 360, 352, 361, 348, 343, 342, 359, 357, 353, 358, 346, 336.

Viterbo, Archivio di Stato, parchment holdings, box 13, n. 131. End of the thirteenth century, beginning of the fourteenth. To judge by the illustrations at the bottom as well as the text, this two-folio fragment belongs to the same Pisa–Genoa group as BnF, MS fr. 1463. As far as can still be read, it seems to transmit the same text of Rustichello §§131.21–132.22.

The oldest and most authoritative stage of the textual tradition is represented by MS fr. 1463 and by the Viterbo fragment, also because it is represented by few

Franco-Italian witnesses. The texts of two versions composed later in northern Italy (*Tris. Ven.* in Venice, and the BNCF, MS Palatino 556 version of *Tav. Rit.*, in the area around Cremona) are very faithful to the same redaction.[39] Furthermore, only MS fr. 1463 presents characteristics that are not yet adapted to fourteenth-century French, but are instead linguistically closer to BnF, MS fr. 1116 (the Franco-Italian *Devisement dou Monde*) and to the French found in many manuscripts copied in north-western Italy (such as BnF, MS fr. 12599). In particular, the language of MS fr. 1463 presents a series of graphic and phonemic features that can be attributed either to the author's Franco-Italian or to the copyist's western Tuscan origin.[40] In terms of redaction, MS fr. 1463 tends to link the Rustichello text to the *Tristan en prose*.

The first major scholarly contribution to the study of Rustichello's Compilation was Löseth's 1904 *Analyse*, the critical analysis of the redactions of the *Tristan en prose* and the *Roman de Palamède*, in which later criticism would discern a part of the *Guiron le Courtois*. The text Löseth used for Rustichello was the one preserved by BnF, MSS fr. 340 and 355; he took MS fr. 1463 into account only for occasional comparisons, and often interpreted it incorrectly. Yet elsewhere in his work Löseth rightly noted the overall importance of MS fr. 1463, particularly as regards the conjoined tradition of the Compilation and the *Tristan en prose*. Shortly afterwards, scholars such as Luigi Foscolo Benedetto and Giulio Bertoni highlighted, although differently, the authoritative nature and textual specificities of MS fr. 1463, especially its verbal surface and its relation to the Franco-Italian redaction of the *Devisement dou Monde* (BnF, MS fr. 1116).

Comparing the content of MS fr. 1463 to the other codices allowed Löseth to hypothesise a 'first part' of Rustichello's text (Lös. §§620–9). This material, which extends from the prologue to Palamedes' pursuit of the Questing Beast, corresponds to §§1–195. After this episode, the texts of MSS fr. 340 and 355, as well as that of the Berlin manuscript, take advantage of the character Segurades to insert a long transitional series of episodes: a 'Guironian Compilation'. This insertion would be the vestiges of a 'second' compilation, after which the text moves to the interpolated text of the actual *Guiron*. MS fr. 1463, on the other hand, ends the Segurades episode by attaching to it the final section of the *Tristan en prose*, along with its epilogue (§197 Cigni edn; Lös. §§534ff.). In the passage that precedes the actual *Guiron*, the three later manuscripts reproduce the text of a model that had a Guironian Compilation, which the MS fr. 1463 copyist set aside in favour of the Tristan material. The key facts are that some of these episodes are shared by certain manuscripts from the Pisa–Genoa workshop and that a redaction of the text from which the compiler might have taken these episodes is contained in BnF, MS fr. 3325, of Italian origin.[41]

An actual 'second part' of the Compilation, which it is more difficult to attribute to Rustichello, could instead consist of what in MSS fr. 340 and 355 follows the interpolation of the *Guiron le Courtois* text. For the most part, this interpolation is also transmitted by BnF, MSS fr. 357(2) and 3478(2), as well as by Paris, Archives

Nationales, MS AB. XIX 1733. Löseth did not know this last manuscript, identified by Fanni Bogdanow.[42] These episodes, corresponding to Lös. §§639–43, also constitute literal reprises of episodes of the *Tristan en prose*, in particular the correspondence between Iseut and Guinevere, and the *Pays du Servage*, which can be traced to Lös. §§46–8, according to a text which presents points of contact with that transmitted in two manuscripts of Italian origin: BnF, MSS fr. 12599 and 750. Löseth considered their insertion to be at least in part the work of a later adapter responsible for the entire outline of the codices that contain them. This same uncertainty affects the epilogue, transmitted only in MSS fr. 340 and 355. In this epilogue *maistre Rusticien*, reprising the prologue, again invokes the authority of the king of England, identifying him even more explicitly as the patron. Rustichello apologises for chronological incongruities in the organisation of the adventures, such as speaking first of Tristan and then of his father Meliadus, who is given exceptional prominence in the episodes that follow the interpolation of the *Guiron*. Only in the epilogue does he name his book: *Meliadus*. Thus what suggests the work of a continuator is not so much the regularised linguistic and syntactic profile of these codices, as their overall content.[43]

One fundamental reason for privileging MS fr. 1463 lies, as mentioned above, in its distinctive textual-linguistic surface, considered in relation to the French of the Arthurian manuscripts copied in Italy and to the Franco-Italian redaction of the *Devisement dou Monde*. In 1953 L. F. Benedetto recognised the need for better understanding of MS fr. 1463, which Bertoni later judged to be more 'correct' than MS fr. 1116 itself.[44] A linguistic comparison of MSS fr. 1463 and fr. 1116 is fruitless owing to at least three factors concerning MS fr. 1116: the diversity of its topic and genre; the collaboration of two authors, one of whom is Venetian; and its different geographical origin.

The Compiled Material through the Existing Manuscript Tradition

The large section common to all the manuscripts comprises at least eight narrative segments, summarised here on the basis of MS fr. 1463: the Prologue and the Old Knight (§§ 1–39); Merlin's Stone (§§40–75); the Knight of the Vermilion Shield (§§76–141); Perceval, part 1 (§§142–7); the war between the kings of Ireland and Norgales (§§148–57); Perceval, part 2 (§§158–62); the submission of Galehaut; and adventures of Abés, Lamorat and Palamedes (§§163–96). The network of Rustichello's relations to his models is complex and often elusive, given the absence of concrete parallels. The following summary of MS fr. 1463 will sketch that network and trace the narratorial interpolations intended to guide his original reader from one episode to the next, and from one section to the next, of his romance. Again, paragraph numbers throughout refer to my 1994 edition.

In his prologue, Rustichello says that, because he intends to adhere to what he has found written in the book belonging to Edward of England, he will linger longest on the deeds of those who were undoubtedly the best knights (*li meillors chevaliers*) of their time: Lancelot du Lac and Tristan of Leonois (§1). However, he immediately shifts his focus to a tale which seems to him a more worthy beginning, because it contains so many marvellous elements. This episode – the Old Knight Branor at King Arthur's court (§§2–39) – has in a sense become representative of the entire work. Rustichello explains that he decided to place this adventure first because he found it thus in his *livre* (source-book; §16.18–19). He apologises for upsetting the internal chronology of the episodes; although Tristan is already at Arthur's court when Branor arrives, his introduction there will in fact be discussed later.

For Rustichello, Branor, a survivor of Uther Pendragon's Table and last representative of the line of the Bruns, is a personification of a *virtus* which is now lost, or at least greatly diminished, among the knights of the current Round Table. Having come to King Arthur's court at Pentecost to challenge all the kings and knights assembled there, Branor promises to give the beautiful lady he has brought with him to any knight who succeeds in defeating him. No one, not even Arthur himself, can match the strength of this giant knight who easily resists all adversaries, to the astonishment and consternation of the court. He leaves, promising soon to reveal his name. The Old Knight becomes the protagonist of other succinctly narrated valiant exploits that showcase his strength, magnanimity, sense of justice and devotion to higher values. After these noble deeds he finally sends a messenger to Arthur's court to reveal his identity, as promised. The king orders a cleric to add the brave knight's name to the adventures of the day on which he had unhorsed so many kings, barons and knights (§39.7). Only now is his true name revealed. Branor's feats end with his death in the very same year he undertakes the exploits just related – the year in which he took up arms again, sometimes against his will, since he had long avoided doing so (§39.10).

After this initial episode, it becomes clear that Rustichello's compilational technique rests on three strategies: first, the re-elaboration of episodes from the *Tristan en prose*, maintained as a thematic master thread; second, the insertion of minor episodes taken from the Grail Cycle; and third, the rewriting of the part of the *Livre Galehaut* which relates how Galehaut became Arthur's vassal. The following survey of the Compilation will note these impulses and focal points as they emerge in the arc of the plot.

After the Branor episode Rustichello moves to the *Tristan en prose* material, specifically the rivalry and the battles between Lancelot and Tristan, which the prologue had promised would be the favoured theme (§39.12). Along this thematic thread, in fact, will unfold all the adventures that refer to the episode at Merlin's Stone (§§40–52), prominent later in Boiardo and Ariosto. That episode is based on a central passage of the *Tristan en prose* in which the protagonist, through his encounter with the knights of Logres, is introduced at Arthur's court by Lancelot, who takes Tristan there to occupy the seat of the Morholt, whom Tristan slew in his youth. In rewriting this episode, Rustichello eliminated the back story of his model, instead beginning directly with Palamedes' nocturnal love lament (§§40–3).

Intent above all on highlighting the new comradeship of Tristan and Lancelot, Rustichello omits many details regarding Tristan's inclusion among the knights of the Round Table (§51.34–6). When Tristan leaves Arthur's court to seek adventure (§52), we enter the most intricate part of the romance, dense with minor characters and contiguous short adventures. Faced with the possibility of inserting an infinite number of these, Rustichello undertakes a virtuoso work of interlace. The *Tristan en prose* served as source for the Perilous Forest episode where the hero meets Morgan le Fay's thirty-six knights, who have captured two Round Table knights, Dinadan and Dodinel (§53.1–2). Tristan, still little known to the men of Logres, undertakes a heroic rescue yet still manages to conceal his identity. His arrival in that realm causes dismay and anger among the enemies of the Round Table: Morgan le Fay and her knights, whom Tristan must fight (§55). His feats are promptly related at court, where they are recorded at Arthur's command (§56.23). Tristan is then imprisoned and condemned to death by a vavassour, the father of one of the knights he has killed. Tristan's implacable enemy Palamedes, by chance a guest in the same manor, ends up saving his life to avoid the dishonour of letting one of the best knights in the world die (§§57–60).[45]

Thus far, Rustichello has been rewriting episodes from the *Tristan en prose* (§§39–60). At this point, he begins to insert minor episodes from the Grail Cycle. He presents another turning-point in the romance, announcing that he will momentarily suspend the story of Tristan and Palamedes to talk about 'something completely different': the adventures of Lancelot's son Galahad (§60.16–17), the protagonist of substantial episodes of the *Queste del Saint Graal*. Galahad's feat in challenging the son of the generous Dalides (§§61–2) is taken from the Post-Vulgate *Queste*.[46] Rustichello has Galahad meet Tristan and Palamedes (§§63–7), whom (as he mentions) he had earlier left resting at the manor of an old knight, but who now are again on the move. Various astonishing battles with that valorous youth occur, until the inevitable recognition prevents the worst: Galahad suddenly suspects that one of his adversaries may belong to his father's lineage. Galahad hears Tristan narrate his adventure with Lancelot at Merlin's Stone (§67.20–5), and a first segment of adventures thus concludes.

Thanks to the unexpected intervention of Banis, a descendant of King Ban of Benwick, the trio is drawn into a new adventure, and Rustichello returns to the *Tristan en prose* material. Banis is in search of reinforcements to help him free Lamorak and Blioberis from Elis the Red (§§68–71); with the knights' help, he succeeds. Leaving Galahad, Tristan and Palamedes, Rustichello then turns to a new trio, Banis and his two freed companions, who come upon Erec without recognising him, and try to take his wife Enide (§§72–5). This brief adventure ends with the sudden departure of Blioberis, Lamorak, Banis and Erec to free yet another prisoner, Lionel, from Marganor, who also wishes to avenge himself on a member of Ban's lineage

(§75.16–31). This tale breaks off abruptly; although Rustichello promises to pick it up again later, he never does (§75.32).

Rustichello takes up the adventures of the Knight of the Vermilion Shield, whom Tristan follows in hopes of meeting one of the best men in the world. This character is revealed to be Brunor the Black, the Page of the Slashed Surcoat, and Rustichello seems to emphasise primarily his arms: a silver lion rampant on a red shield.[47] The narration of these adventures turns on the clashes that occur in the vicinity of the so-called *Tour du Pin Rond*. Knights seeking to prove themselves strike the shield that hangs there (§§76–141.47); this is another episode imported and shortened from the *Tristan en prose*. With this insertion into the romance, as with Merlin's Stone, Rustichello presages yet another meeting and contest between Tristan and Lancelot. During the battle of Haudebourc – undertaken against Lancelot for a just cause by the Knight of the Vermilion Shield, to whom Tristan has lent his arms – Lancelot mistakenly believes he is fighting his own friend. Along with his brothers and cousins, Lancelot decides to avenge himself on Tristan once and for all. Tristan, meanwhile, has taken refuge at Joyous Guard, along with Iseut, Palamedes, Brunor and Dinadan (§132). The misunderstanding resolved, Lancelot and his relatives stay there for a month as Tristan's guests (§140.20). The group is enlivened not only by the presence of Iseut but also by the conversation of Dinadan, commentator on the Arthurian *gesta*, who will relate to Arthur the latest skirmish between the two 'greatest knights' of their time (§141.11–23).

Once the heroes have returned to court, Rustichello moves on to a new hero, Perceval, who will defend a lady from the evil Argondres (§§142–7). Rustichello will draw on new romance material: this episode's characters and situations are in fact inspired by the *Prose Lancelot*, although we cannot identify any single source passage for it. Perceval is the protagonist of a second episode, in which he fights Sephar (§§158–62); these two episodes frame the war between the kings of Ireland and Norgales over who owns a castle on the border between their two realms (§§148–57). The war results in yet another conflict between Tristan and Lancelot, who was reported to have spoken slightingly of the battle at Joyous Guard (§148.11). This episode, which ends with the reconciliation of Lancelot and Tristan, will be used as well (along with the battle of Haudebourc) in the *Tavola Ritonda* and is present in the cyclical version of the *Tristan en prose*. One element suggesting that we should attribute this revised episode to Rustichello is its allusion to the previous battles of Merlin's Stone and Joyous Guard, present only in the codices which transmit the Compilation (§151.19).

At this point Rustichello turns to his third major strategy, the rewriting of the *Livre Galehaut* section of the *Lancelot*. He announces another adventure, different from the previous ones, and worthy of concluding his book because it is exceptional (§162.13). This is the submission of the mighty Galehaut, Lord of the Distant Isles, to King Arthur, after his failure to conquer the thirtieth kingdom. This episode comes from the famous passage in the *Lancelot*, where it precedes the love story of Lancelot and Guinevere. Rustichello's rewriting gives great emphasis to Lancelot's intercession, using a 'rash boon', on behalf of the king, whom the ambitious prince Galehaut is forced to accept as his liege lord; the narration is then reconfigured in a way that is entirely independent of the *Lancelot*. Rustichello's choices seem the result of a 'political' interpretation of the episode, focused on the relationship between the king and his rebellious vassals; again, this theme must have been a particular favourite of his patron. The love between the queen and Lancelot is mentioned only briefly, and Rustichello safeguards the honour of both by leaving no trace of their meetings (§193.22). Indeed, the text emphasises that Guinevere is so anxious at seeing her husband and all his people in such great danger that she twice urges Lancelot into battle (§181). The psychological profile of the episode's protagonist Galehaut is also strongly modified in order to show that justice and moderation triumph over arrogant overreaching. Galehaut, who had aspired to be Arthur's liege lord, is instead obliged to become Arthur's vassal to keep the promise he made to Lancelot, whom he takes for the most valiant knight in the world.

Peace returns to Camelot and a new character comes to court, a dwarf who asks for Arthur's help on behalf of Abés the Renowned. Abés is imprisoned by a knight who was pursuing the Questing Beast and who turns out to be Palamedes (§194). It will fall to Yvain to intercede peaceably, but Lamorat – mindful of his old jealousy on Iseut's account – decides to pre-empt Yvain in the search, and manages to fight Palamedes. Yvain's intervention will nonetheless succeed in calming the opponents. The prisoner is freed, and returns with the others to thank the king; only Palamedes, still furious, prefers to return to the wilds in pursuit of the Beast (§195).

After this episode the manuscript tradition diverges. The *conte* followed by the redactor of MS fr. 1463 tells of Palamedes who frees his friend Segurades from five unknown knights (§196) and then announces 'how King Mark besieged Camelot' (§196.27). In MS fr. 1463 the abrupt formula of transition to the siege, when King Mark arrives in Logres to take Iseut back, introduces the long and famous passage of the *Tristan* that leads straight to the hero's death. This passage belongs to the French romance, according to the redaction transmitted by other manuscripts that – like MS fr. 1463 – were copied in Italy, but it has absolutely nothing to do with Rustichello's style. The Tristan passage is disconcerting in other ways as well, because it is followed – mechanically, and without any real continuity – by the epilogue. Here the so-called author of the second part of the *Tristan en prose*, Hélie de Boron, continuator of the work of Luce del Gat, promises to continue to write the stories that are still missing from his book, at the request of his protector King Henry of England (none other than the father of Edward, Rustichello's future patron, §236).

In the three complete manuscripts – MS fr. 340, MS fr. 355 and Berlin – two series of episodes compiled from the *Suite Guiron* (the third branch of *Guiron le Courtois*) are added to what is related in §195.[18] After the Guironian Compilation, the Berlin manuscript ends, while MSS fr. 340 and 355 insert the *Guiron le Courtois* proper. After the *Guiron*, MSS fr. 340 and 355 present episodes corresponding to Lös. §§ 639–43, which narrate the liberation from the *Pays du Servage* and the killing of Nabon, another episode taken from the *Tristan en prose*. At that point, MSS fr. 340 and 355 insert an epilogue:

> Here ends Master Rusticien of Pisa, praising and thanking the Father, the Son and the Holy Spirit, one God alone, son of the blessed Virgin Mary, because he has given me world enough and time, strength and wit to bring to a close such a high and noble subject as this one which I have treated in my book, and the deeds and feats of valour of so many noble gentlemen related and recalled in my book. And if anyone were to ask me why in my book I have talked about Tristan before talking about his father King Meliadus, I will answer that my matter required it, for I could not have put all my words in order on account of the intervals which fell between two deeds, and because this book is not properly about one person – it is not only about Lancelot du Lac, nor is it all about Tristan, nor all about King Meliadus. Rather, it is from many histories and many chronicles that I have extracted and compiled them at the request of King Edward of England, as stated at the beginning of my book. And this book is called *Meliadus*, because King Meliadus did more noble deeds in that time than any of the other knights about whom we have spoken.[49]

After the epilogue, both MSS fr. 340 and 355 insert a series of original adventures (which in the explicit are 'signed' by the self-styled Rustichello) that seem to intend to conclude what has already been said: the principal knights who were left in prison at the end of the *Roman de Guiron* (but according to this continuation, all assembled at the castle of Nabon) are freed, after which Meliadus and his companions are received at the court of Camelot. Finally, only MS fr. 340 adds a last section from the *Tristan en prose* (Lös. §§ 252–344).

The content of BnF, MSS fr. 99 and 103, previously analysed by Löseth, deserves separate discussion. These two manuscripts of the *Tristan en prose* show points of contact with Rustichello's text that are much more occasional and fragmentary.[50] Löseth did not know Chantilly, Musée Condé, MSS 645–646–647, nor did Lathuillère mention them.[51] The Chantilly text adds nothing new to BnF, MS fr. 99, where two passages (that of the battle before Joyous Guard and that of the Old Knight) appear in reverse order compared to all the other complete codices, and are considerably shortened as well. However, it corresponds to the passage containing the adventures of the Knight of the Vermilion Shield, thus deriving in some way from the *Tristan en prose*. Now that a thorough comparison with Rustichello's source text is possible, through the edition directed by Philippe Ménard, MSS fr. 99 and 103 can be seen to belong to the same branch as MS fr. 1463 and the *Tris. Ven.*[52]

Conclusion

Rustichello's Compilation reflects a change in taste that came about in the last decades of the thirteenth century. The historical and cultural climate prevailing in Italy, France and perhaps the Middle East must have valued the celebration of illustrious ancestors and justice triumphing over abuses. Adventures that, according to the prologue, should have remained centred on the clashes between Tristan and Lancelot are assimilated more and more into these idealised models (the Knight of the Vermilion Shield, the war of the kings of Ireland and Norgales), until the textual reprise (the death of Tristan and Iseut, the *Guiron* cycle). The technique of juxtaposition, while it favours the detachment of independent narrative nuclei, nonetheless does not diminish the internal coherence of Rustichello's work. His shrewd use of transitional formulas and the consistent presence of internal allusions to episodes – allusions discernible only by careful reading – reveal that the reservations of earlier critics about his foray into Arthurian romance were excessive, or at least premature. Such negative judgements can only stand if we deny the very typology of the work, as well as the modalities of circulation and transmission of Arthurian and Tristanian prose texts during the second half of the thirteenth century.

J. F. Levy's dissertation represents the first modern attempt to return to the tradition of Rustichello's Compilation in the 'correct' French already analysed by Löseth. It utilises only one manuscript, BnF, MS fr. 340, transcribing it in full only as far as the epilogue of 'Rusticien de Pise' (fol. 121e).[53] But it is on the topic of *Guiron le Courtois* that the most promising recent contributions have come, for the text of Rustichello as well. *Guiron* – unfortunately still unedited – had a circulation in Italy that was substantial in both quality and quantity.[54] New research on the complete tradition of the *Guiron* has resulted in the establishment of a cycle, organised into the *Roman de Meliadus*, the *Roman de Guiron* and the connective *Suite*; it has considerably diminished the value of BnF, MS fr. 350, the manuscript which Lathuillère had taken as the basis for his critical analysis but which is now seen to be factitious and contaminated.[55] Among the connections between the *Guiron* and Rustichello, particular prominence belongs to certain materials that can be described as a 'Guironian Compilation',[56] and which conform to portions of the text of the *Guiron* in a manner entirely analogous to the *Tristan* episodes as reworked by Rustichello. From this particular compilation, whose content in its broad outlines was already represented in Lathuillère's analysis, come the materials that fill in the space between Rustichello da Pisa and the *Guiron* of BnF, MSS fr. 340 and 355 and Pierpont Morgan, MS M.916. However, they are present mostly in the form of redactions that are re-elaborated and assembled independently within other Italian manuscripts from the same workshop that produced BnF, MS fr. 1463.

Rustichello's Pisan origins and the period during which he composed his work turn out to be of capital importance in the larger picture of the diffusion of the *Tristan* in Italy (unlike the text of the Guironian compilation, which found greater favour in French manuscripts). Through this channel, in fact, the most representative episodes of the Compilation – the prologue, the Old Knight Branor, Tristan and Lancelot at Merlin's Stone, and the adventures that precede that encounter – reappear in the *Tristano Veneto* and the *Tristano Palatino* (BNCF, MS Palatino 556; and from these in the Greek and Serbo-Russian versions), as well as in the Iberian branch of the prose *Tristan*. Other texts contained in manuscripts that are connected either linguistically or codicologically to BnF, MS fr. 1463 and to the Pisa–Genoa matrix (BnF, MS fr. 12599, for example, or Aberystwyth, National Library of Wales, MS 446E), when they are not directly copying the French romances, feature many 'original' passages in which an anonymous compiler has palpably intervened. Formulating his work on French chivalric models and style, that anonymous compiler has assembled new adventures that respond to the same moralistic dictates as the Compilation.[57] Rustichello's Compilation, far from being the mere appendix to the *Tristan en prose* as eighteenth- and nineteenth-century scholarship tended to view it, represents a fundamental phase in the passage of the Arthurian texts between France and Italy. Only in the last few decades has this essential role been established and clarified in its elemental aspects – and there may yet be new surprises in store.

(Translated by F. Regina Psaki)

Notes

[1] *Le Devisement dou Monde* is the title of the Franco-Italian and French versions of the work; the title of the Italian vernacularisation is *Il Milione*.

[2] E. Löseth, *Le Roman en prose de Tristan, le Roman de Palamède et la Compilation de Rusticien de Pise: Analyse critique* (Paris, 1890; New York, 1970).

[3] N. Morato, *Il ciclo di* Guiron le Courtois: *Strutture e testi nella tradizione manoscritta* (Florence, 2010); C. Lagomarsini, 'Dalla *Suite Guiron* alla *Compilazione guironiana:* Questioni preliminari e strategie d'analisi', *SMV*, 57 (2011), 242–6; and Lagomarsini, 'Tradizioni a contatto: il "Guiron le Courtois" e la "Compilation arthurienne" di Rustichello da Pisa. Studio e edizione critica della "Compilazione guironiana"' (Ph.D. dissertation, University of Siena, 2012).

[4] Löseth, *Analyse*; E. G. Gardner, *The Arthurian Legend in Italian Literature* (London and New York, 1930; rpt 1971); P. Rajna, *Le fonti dell'*Orlando Furioso (Florence, 1876, 1900; rev. edn 1975).

[5] By E. Löseth, see: *Analyse*; *Le* Tristan *et le* Palamède *des manuscrits français du British Museum*, Videnskapsselkapets Skrifter, II (Hist. Fil. Klasse, 4) (Kristiania, 1905), pp. 1–38; and *Le* Tristan *et le* Palamède *des manuscrits français de Rome et de Florence*, Videnskapsselkapets Skrifter, II (Hist. Fil. Klasse, 3) (Kristiania, 1924). See also R. Lathuillère, 'La Compilation de Rusticien de Pise', in *Grundriss der romanischen Literaturen des Mittelalters*, IV/1: *Le Roman jusqu'à la fin du XIIIe siècle* (Heidelberg, 1978), pp. 623–5.

[6] Parenthetical paragraph references are to F. Cigni (ed.), *Il romanzo arturiano di Rustichello da Pisa* (Pisa, 1994), unless otherwise indicated.

[7] V. Bertolucci Pizzorusso, *Scritture di viaggio. Relazioni di viaggiatori e altre testimonianze letterarie e documentarie* (Rome, 2011). New hypotheses have been proposed with regard to the reconsideration of Rustichello's fictitious status as an Arthurian author; see J. F. Levy, '*Livre de Meliadus*: An edition of the Arthurian Compilation of B.N.F. f. fr. 340 attributed to Rusticien de Pise' (Ph.D. dissertation, University of California, Berkeley, 2000); R. Trachsler, 'Rustichello, Rusticien e Rusta pisa. Chi ha scritto il romanzo arturiano?', in G. Brunetti and G. Giannini (eds), *'La traduzione è una forma': trasmissione e sopravvivenza dei testi romanzi medievali*, special issue of *Quaderni di Filologia Romanza*, 19 (2007), 107–23; and N. Morato, *Il ciclo di* Guiron.

[8] His collaboration is clear not only from the short introductory chapter, but especially from the chivalric style displayed by BnF, MS fr. 1116, the Franco-Italian *Devisement dou Monde*, from the fourteenth century.

[9] Not only Romance languages, if we consider the fifteenth-century (?) poem *O presbus ippotes* (The Old Knight), preserved in BAV, MS Gr. 1822, the sole example in medieval Greek of Arthurian material. The poem has always been considered an eastern manifestation of the Compilation, as in Gardner. A more recent hypothesis, consistent with the Franco-Italian manuscript tradition, is that it was composed in one of the many Greek communities in northern Italy; see F. Rizzo Nervo (ed. and trans.), *Il vecchio cavaliere* (Soveria Mannelli, 2000).

[10] R. Lathuillère, Guiron le Courtois, *Étude de la tradition manuscrite et analyse critique* (Geneva, 1966); Morato, *Il ciclo di* Guiron.

[11] Rajna, *Le fonti*; and D. Delcorno Branca, *Tristano e Lancillotto in Italia: Studi di letteratura arturiana* (Ravenna, 1998).

[12] F. Avril, M.-T. Gousset and C. Rabel, *Manuscrits enluminés d'origine italienne* (Paris, 1984), II (*XIIIe siècle*); Benedetti, '"Qua fa' un santo e un cavaliere": Aspetti codicologici e note per il miniatore', in G. D'Aronco et al. (eds), *La grant Queste del Saint Graal. Versione inedita della fine del XIII secolo del ms. Udine, Biblioteca Arcivescovile, 177* (Tricesimo [Udine], 1990), pp. 31–47; Cigni, 'Manoscritti di prose cortesi compilati in Italia (secc. XIII–XIV): stato della questione e prospettive di ricerca', in S. Guida and F. Latella (eds), *La filologia romanza e i codici* (Messina, 1993), II, pp. 419–41; F. Fabbri, 'Romanzi cortesi e prosa didattica a Genova alla fine del Duecento fra interscambi, coesistenze e nuove prospettive', *Studi di Storia dell'Arte*, 23 (2012), 9–32.

[13] Cigni, 'Copisti prigionieri (Genova, fine sec. XIII)', in P. G. Beltrami et al. (eds), *Studi di Filologia romanza offerti a Valeria Bertolucci Pizzorusso* (Pisa, 2006), I, pp. 425–39; and 'Manuscrits en français, italien, et latin entre la Toscane et la Ligurie à la fin du XIIIe siècle: implications codicologiques, linguistiques, et évolution des genres narratifs', in C. Kleinhenz and K. Busby, *Medieval Multilingualism: The Francophone World and Its Neighbours* (Turnhout, 2010), pp. 187–217.

[14] L. F. Benedetto, 'Non "Rusticiano" ma "Rustichello"', in *Uomini e tempi: pagine varie di critica e storia* (Milan, 1953), pp. 71–85; M. G. Capusso, *La lingua del 'Divisament dou Monde' di Marco Polo*, I: *Morfologia verbale* (Pisa, 1980) and 'La produzione franco-italiana dei secoli XIII e XIV: convergenze letterarie e linguistiche', in R. Oniga and S. Vatteroni (eds), *Plurilinguismo letterario* (Soveria Mannelli, 2007), pp. 159–204; Cigni, 'Prima del *Devisement dou monde*. Osservazioni sulla lingua della compilazione arturiana di Rustichello da Pisa', in S. Conte (ed.), *I viaggi del* Milione. *Itinerari testuali, vettori di trasmissione e metamorfosi del* Devisement du monde *di Marco Polo e Rustichello da Pisa nella pluralità delle attestazioni* (Rome, 2008), pp. 219–31, and 'Manuscrits en français'.

[15] G. Del Guerra, *Rustichello da Pisa* (Pisa, 1955).

[16] 'Seingneur enperaor et rois, et princes et dux, et quenz et baronz, civalier et vauvasor et borgiois, et tous le preudome de ce monde que avés talenz de delitier voz en romainz . . .' (§1.1).

[17] M. Prestwich, *Edward I* (London, 1988, 1990), and Cigni edn.

[18] On Pisan citizens and trade on the Mediterranean scene in this period, see C. Otten-Froux, 'Les Pisans en Égypte et à Acre dans la seconde moitié du XIIIe siècle. Documents nouveaux', *Bollettino Storico Pisano*, 52 (1983), pp. 163–90.

[19] Prestwich, *Edward I*, pp. 72–85.

[20] Ibid., p. 123.

[21] This however is speculation, as is the intriguing identification of Rustichello with one Rustike, probably Tuscan and well versed in French, who apparently worked in Henry VII's retinue in northern Italy; see André Joris, 'Autour du *Devisement du monde*. Rusticien de Pise et l'empereur Henri VII de Luxembourg (1310–1313)', *Le Moyen Âge*, 100 (1994), 353–68.

[22] Many notaries were present in Genoa in the years following the battle of Meloria, and many of these left clear documentation of their activity in literature and translation; see R. Mazzanti (ed.), *1284: l'anno della Meloria* (Pisa, 1984).

[23] Lathuillère, *Guiron le Courtois*; Cigni edn; and Cigni, 'Manuscrits en français'.

[24] Such stability does not characterize the *Devisement* prologue, in which over time the very promi-nent figure of Marco as protagonist and co-author came to overshadow his nominal collaborator, to the point of eventually erasing Rustichello entirely; see Bertolucci Pizzorusso, *Scritture di viaggio*, chs 2, 3 and 6.

[25] R. Lathuillère, 'La Compilation de Rusticien', pp. 623–4. Lathuillère puts great emphasis on the *Guiron* as a source for Rustichello, but his interpretation is dependent on how Löseth's *Analyse* presents the narrative material.

[26] Among the many studies dedicated to the Tristan–Lancelot pair, E. Baumgartner, *Le* Tristan en prose*: Essai d'interprétation d'un roman médiéval* (Geneva, 1975) is still useful. It must be comple-mented by *TLI* for the Italian circulation of the romances, especially for the reception of individual characters.

[27] C. Lagomarsini, 'La tradizione compilativa della *Suite Guiron* tra Francia ed Italia: analisi dei duelli singolari', *MR*, 36/1 (2012), 98–127, has also pursued this line of inquiry, comparing the narrative modalities and the processes of *abbreviatio* and *amplificatio* between the *Suite Guiron* and the Guironian compilation; more on this below.

[28] R. Trachsler ('Rustichello, Rusticien'), by contrast, considers that the text refers iconographically to a certain notoriety gained by the author through earlier literary experiments, thus opting for a later date for the Compilation than for the *Devisement dou Monde*.

[29] Cigni, 'Prima del *Devisement*'; M. B. Parkes, 'The Influence of the Concepts of "Ordinatio" and "Compilatio" on the Development of the Book', in J. J. Alexander and M. T. Gibson (eds), *Medieval Learning and Literature. Essays Presented to R. W. Hunt* (Oxford, 1976), pp. 115–40; and A. J. Minnis, 'Late-Medieval Discussions of "Compilatio" and the Role of the "Compilator"', in *Beiträge zur Geschichte der deutschen Sprache und Literatur*, 101 (1979), 385–421.

[30] Genoa produced some hagiographical manuscripts containing both Jacopo's work and anonymous legendaries; see F. Cigni, 'Copisti prigionieri' and 'Manuscrits en français'.

[31] See E. Kennedy, 'The Scribe as Editor', in *Mélanges de langue et de littérature du Moyen Âge et de la Renaissance offerts à Jean Frappier*, 2 vols (Geneva, 1970), I, pp. 523–31.

[32] An example of that aspiration towards completion is contained in the epilogue of the *Tristan* contained in the same BnF, MS fr. 1463: 'Je firai un livre entier, ou je conpilerai, se Diex plaist, tot ce que m.s. Luce del Gaut . . . et maistre Gautier Map . . . et m. Robert de Boron, et je meismes . . . Helyes de Boron, tot ce que nos l'avons menés a ffin' (§236.5).

[33] Cigni, 'Un nuovo testimone del cantare *Ultime imprese e morte di Tristano*', *SMV*, 43 (1997), 131–91.

[34] On all these manuscripts, as well as on French printed books and Italian *volgarizzamenti* (vernacu-larisations), see Cigni edn; and Cigni, 'La ricezione medievale della letteratura francese nella Toscana nord-occidentale', in E. Werner and S. Schwarze (eds), *Fra toscanità e italianità. Lingua e letteratura dagli inizi al Novecento* (Tübingen and Basel, 2000), pp. 71–108.

[35] Avril, Gousset and Rabel, *Manuscrits enluminés*; M.-T. Gousset, 'Etude de la décoration filigranée et reconsitution des ateliers: le cas de Gênes à la fin du XIIIe siècle', *Arte Medievale*, 2 (1988), 121–52; Fabbri, 'Romanzi cortesi'.

[36] Lathuillère §§43n1–49n1.

[37] F. Bogdanow (ed.), *La version Post-Vulgate de la* Queste del Saint Graal *et de la* Mort Artu: *troisième partie du* Roman du Graal, 4 vols in 5 parts (Paris, 1991, 2000, 2001), §§697–9, 701–6.

[38] Bogdanow, 'A Hitherto Unnoticed Manuscript of the Compilation of Rusticien de Pise', *French Studies Bulletin*, 38 (1991), 15–19.

[39] For details, see Cigni edn; and Cigni, 'Pour l'édition de la *Compilation* de Rustichello da Pisa: la version du Ms Paris, B. N., Fr. 1463', *Neophilologus*, 36 (1992), 519–34. On BNCF, MS Pal. 556 and the Compilation, see Cigni, '*Roman de Tristan* in prosa e *Compilazione* di Rustichello da Pisa in area veneta. A proposito di una recente edizione', *LI*, 47 (1995), 598–622.

[40] These features include ç for voiced s; frequent intervocalic voicing; the alternation of liquid consonants l and r; the insertion of h after c with a velar effect; the root conit- of the verb conter (close to Ligurian conitar); the plural perfect forms soufrin, ferin, perhaps influenced by north-western Italian perfect forms –ino; the singular future fi for sera, probably a Pisanism. For a more detailed analysis see Cigni edn; and Cigni, 'Prima del Devisement', as well as V. Bertolucci Pizzorusso, 'Nuovi studi su Marco Polo e Rustichello da Pisa', in L. Morini (ed.), La cultura dell'Italia padana e la presenza francese nei secoli XIII–XV (Alessandria, 2001), pp. 95–110. For further linguistic traits and problems of Franco-Italian pertinent to Rustichello and to the 'Guironian Compilation', through lexicon, see Lagomarsini, 'Tradizioni a contatto', esp. chapter 4.

[41] For the text, a detailed analysis of it, and a discussion of the problems of attribution and the matrix of production, see Lagomarsini, 'Tradizioni a contatto', chapters 1.3 and 5.

[42] F. Bogdanow, 'A New Manuscript of the Enfances Guiron and Rusticien de Pise's Roman du roi Arthur', Romania, 88 (1967), 323–49.

[43] Lagomarsini, 'Dalla Suite Guiron'.

[44] This question is updated in Cigni, 'Prima del Devisement'; Capusso, 'La produzione franco-italiana'; and ead., 'La mescidanza linguistica del Milione franco-italiano', in S. Conte (ed.), I viaggi del Milione (Rome, 2008), pp. 263–83.

[45] These scenes are illustrated in the frescoes of St Floret; see Chapter 13 in this volume.

[46] The French redaction of these episodes is apparently lost, and can be imagined only through the Portuguese and Castilian reworkings.

[47] Brunor's arms are very similar to those of the Montforts, an English family involved during these years in turbulent and bloody political matters; the prose romance genre could be referring to them both through rewritings of the Tristan and via Rustichello. See C. Girbea, 'Flatteries héraldiques, propagande politique et armoiries symboliques dans quelques romans arthuriens (XIIe–XIIIe siècles)', in D. Turrel et al. (eds), Signes et couleurs des identités politiques du Moyen Âge à nos jours (Rennes, 2008), pp. 365–80.

[48] The episodes that follow §195 are taken from the third branch of the Guiron. The Berlin manuscript finishes at that point, whereas MSS. fr. 340 and 355 insert, respectively, the final part of the Roman de Meliadus (Lathuillère §43 n. 1–49 n. 1) and the two principal branches (Meliadus, Guiron). In this description I follow the recent classification by Morato, Il ciclo di Guiron. Part of the Suite Guiron is preserved in Paris, Arsenal, MS 3325. From a similar text, a pseudo-Rustichello perhaps compiled – changing the order of episodes and narrative modalities – a compilation, now comprising four textual sequences (S1, S2, S2*, S3). This 'Guironian Compilation' is preserved only in discontinuous fashion. For details, see Lagomarsini, 'La tradizione compilativa', 'Tradizioni a contatto' and 'Rustichello da Pisa ed il Tristan en prose: un esercizio di stemmatica arturiana', SMV, 58 (2012), 49–77.

[49] In MS fr. 355 the epilogue concludes differently: after the words 'que ma matiere' ('that my matter'), it concludes, 'was not known. For I cannot know it all, nor place all my words in order. And thus my tale ends. Amen. Explicit the romance of Meliadus.'

[50] The survival of scattered Rustichello episodes in later but complete manuscripts of the Tristan en prose poses a knotty problem which will require future study.

[51] Again, the references are to Löseth's Analyse and Lathuillère's 'Compilation'.

[52] Lagomarsini, 'Rustichello da Pisa'. The Cigni edn proposed a stemma which added, to the two groups a and b proposed by Löseth, a third, independent group c which would include MSS fr. 99 and 103. That 1994 stemma may well be modified further in light of new terms of comparison and methodological approaches, specifically since it can be demonstrated that the c group, despite the limited scope of its Rustichello episodes, can be included in the same a group as MS fr. 1463.

[53] J. Pourquery de Boisserin also focuses on BnF, MS fr. 340, examining the relationship between text and image. See 'L'énergie chevaleresque: Étude de la matière textuelle et iconographique du manuscrit BnF fr. 340 (Compilation de Rusticien de Pise et Guiron le Courtois)', Université Rennes 2, Haute-Bretagne, 2009–10. Content viewable at tel.archives-ouvertes.fr/tel-00458206/en/.

⁵⁴ See Cigni, 'Per la storia del *Guiron le Courtois* in Italia', *Critica del testo*, 7/1 (2004), 295–316; and 'Mappa redazionale del *Guiron le Courtois* diffuso in Italia', in *Modi e forme della fruizione della 'materia arturiana' in Italia dei sec. XIII–XIV: Milano, 4–5 febbraio 2005* (Milan, 2006), pp. 85–117.

⁵⁵ Morato, *Il ciclo di* Guiron.

⁵⁶ Again, see Lagomarsini, 'Dalla *Suite Guiron*' and 'Tradizioni a contatto'.

⁵⁷ See Cigni edn, and C. Lagomarsini, 'Dalla *Suite Guiron*'.

3

FROM FRANCE TO ITALY: THE TRISTAN TEXTS

Marie-José Heijkant

The Reception of the *Tristan en prose* in Italy

Among the Arthurian romances written from the mid-twelfth century on, Italians pre-ferred that of Tristan, who quickly became the exemplary knight *par excellence*. Indeed the Tristan story was 'the only one to assimilate, taking on not only the Italian language, but a truly Italian narrative vitality as well'.[1] That the metrical versions by Thomas and Béroul circulated in Italy early on is clear both from proper names in his-torical archives and from references in the earliest lyric poetry. Re Giovanni mentions the love potion, and Giacomo da Lentini mentions the *Salle aux images* and Tristan's disguise as a pilgrim (see Chapter 8). The famous tryst, where King Mark spies on Tristan and Iseut in the garden, was reprised by the anonymous Tuscan *Novellino* author (see Chapter 9). Episodes and motifs from the metrical versions also appear in the early Italian translations of the *Tristan en prose*, especially in the *Tavola Ritonda*.[2]

The new prose *Roman de Tristan*, a triumph in France in the period around 1230, promoted a purely secular and worldly chivalric ideal.[3] The author, identified in his prologue as 'Luce, knight and lord of the Castle of Gat', set out to write the biography of Tristan on the model of the prose *Lancelot*, setting the Tristan tale in the Arthurian and Grail context.[4] The rapid success of the *Tristan en prose*, spreading beyond France and Italy across Iberian, English, Germanic and even Slavic regions, is probably due to the prose author's attempt to mitigate those aspects of the original myth that were politically transgressive for feudal-courtly environments: passionate love in conflict with society on the one hand, and on the other the betrayal of Mark, Iseut's husband and Tristan's uncle and king. Love for Iseut spurs Tristan to become one of the most illustrious knights of the Round Table; jealousy turns King Mark into an ignoble traitor who kills his nephew with a poisoned lance. The prose *Tristan* also exemplifies the tendency of prose romance to form vast story cycles with a centrifugal structure, which attempted to combine the Aristotelian principle of cohesion with the need for multiplicity. In the epilogue of some manuscripts, one Hélie de Boron, who was interested in completing the romance *summa*, calls himself a continuator of Luce. Interlace narrative structure favoured the interpolation of passages from other Arthurian tales, such as the Vulgate and Post-Vulgate *Questes*, and the insertion of originally independent stories about single characters such as the Vallet à la Cotte Maltaillée ('Page with the Slashed Surcoat'). One feature of the *Tristan en prose* derivations is the insertion of lyric passages – *lais*, soliloquies, love laments, letters – into the prose narrative.

The French Model

Within the complex textual tradition of the *Tristan en prose* there are two principal versions, starting from Lös. §184: V.I, shorter and slightly earlier; and V.II, the Vulgate.[5] Emmanuèle Baumgartner concluded that both versions were re-elaborations written after 1240, given that interpolations attributed to Robert de Boron from the Post-Vulgate *Queste* can be found in both V.I (in a shorter form) and V.II (in more developed form).[6] V.I, less commonly found in France, is actually the main version found in Italy, especially in texts written in Italian; the most complete witness of V.I, BnF, MSS fr. 756–757, was copied in Naples around the second half of the fourteenth century. This does not seem to be a version destined strictly for readers abroad, as Blanchard had suggested;[7] a fragment of V.I preserved on the verso of the final folio of Florence, Bibl. Riccardiana, MS Ricc. 866 was clearly of French origin. This fragment, datable to the last decades of the fourteenth century, contains the tournament at *Roche Dure* (Lös. §192), previously known in only one V.I source: MS fr. 757.[8] Traces of the now-lost *Estoire de Monseigneur Tristan* can be deduced in the first part of the romance, which contains the oldest episodes of the legend. Renée Curtis, in the introduction to her critical edition, presents a five-branched *stemma* in which the *a* family is considered to represent the original romance.[9] Besides the exemplary 'best manuscript' of Carpentras, this early and authoritative branch consists mainly of codices produced in Italy.[10]

From the second half of the thirteenth century on, the *Tristan en prose* spread through various cultural centres of the Italian peninsula; these included the aristocratic and francophile circles of Angevin Naples, the feudal courts of the Po Valley and the communal-mercantile environments of Tuscany and the Veneto. Thanks to the foundational work of Edmund G. Gardner and the seminal studies of Daniela Delcorno Branca, we know which specific texts circulated on the peninsula and how this romance was received by a highly diverse audience.[11] The enormous and continued success of the *Tristan en prose* in Italy is attested by entries in the inventories of princely libraries, by the French manuscripts copied in Italy and by many translations into Italian vernaculars. *Tristan* was the Arthurian romance most assiduously translated into and redacted in Italian.[12] In the rivalry between Lancelot and Tristan set in motion by Luce del Gat, Tristan is the clear winner in the Italian texts.[13] While the Orphic dimension of Tristan – a musician and poet as well as a valiant knight[14] – may explain the success of this character in Italy, other features of the legend may also have seduced Italian readers: the synthesis of *sapientia* and *fortitudo* in a single hero; the tragic fate of Tristan and Iseut, united in love and death; and the love potion, which allowed sympathetic readers to morally absolve the adulterous lovers.

The *Tristan* Manuscripts Copied and Owned in Italy

Italian production of various Old French versions of the *Tristan en prose* was lively and fertile from the mid-thirteenth century on. Fully a quarter of the one hundred surviving manuscripts were copied in Italy. Thanks to methodical work by Longobardi, Benedetti, Cingolani and Scalon to identify and catalogue fragments, new scraps of parchment codices are constantly surfacing, which from the seventeenth century on had been recycled as book bindings and document covers.[15] The most current census of *Tristan en prose* manuscripts produced in Italy is by Delcorno Branca.[16] To date twenty-six manuscripts and fragments in Old French have been identified as Italian in origin, shown below.[17]

W: Aberystwyth, National Library of Wales, MS 446 E. Late thirteenth century, now attributed Pisa–Genoa. 128 fols, Lös. §§18–60, 71a–74a, 538–49.

W¹: Aberystwyth, National Library of Wales, MS 5667 E. Fols 1–85, fifteenth century, Italian origin, Lös. §§171–247. Fols 89–523, early fourteenth century, French, Lös. §§252a–282a, 338b–571.

Bo¹: Bologna, Archivio di Stato, Tribunale di Rota, volume *Debitorum anni 1613–1614* of the notary Sassi. Late thirteenth century, *bifolium*, Lös. §§504, 510.

Bo²: Bologna, Bibl. dell'Archiginnasio, MSS Casini, Folder 18. Thirteenth–fourteenth century, *bifolium*, Lös. §§73a–74a.

Brescia, Bibl. Queriniana. Fourteenth century, central Italy. One fol., Lös. §368.[18]

L: Florence, Bibl. Medicea Laurenziana, MS Ashburnham 123. Late thirteenth century, Pisa–Genoa. Miscellany, 132 fols, Lös. §§1–21.[19]

G: Geneva, Bodmer Collection, MS 164. Dated 1316. 655 fols, Lös. §§10–570.[20]

Inn: Innsbruck, Universitätsbibliothek, MS Fragment B4. Thirteenth or fourteenth century, northern Italy. Two fols, Lös. §§376, 379.

Add: London, British Library, MS Additional 23929. Late fourteenth century, north-eastern Italy (possibly Padua). 86 fols, Lös. §§1–44.

H: London, British Library, MS Harley 4389. Late thirteenth century, Pisa–Genoa. 61 fols, Lös. §§18–41.

Mb: Milan, Bibl. Nazionale Braidense, MS AC. X. 10. Fourteenth century, northern Italy. Miscellany, eight fols, Iseut's *lai* 'Folie n'est pas vasselage' (fols 6v–7r), Lös. §100.

M: Modena, Bibl. Estense, MS α F. 3. 15 (E 40). Fourteenth century, northern Italy. 79 fols, Lös. §§331–7, 338b–84.

M¹: Modena, Bibl. Estense, MS α T. 3. 11 (E 59). Late thirteenth century, Pisa–Genoa. 102 fols, Lös. §§18–60, 71a–75a, 534–70.

Ox: Oxford, Bodleian Library, MS Douce 189. Late thirteenth century, northern Italy. Miscellany, 78 fols, Lös. §§534–70.

Oxford, Bodleian Library, MS Douce 379. Fourteenth century. Fols 117–18, fragment of *Queste*, version V.II.[21]

Paris, BnF, MS fr. 755. Fourteenth century (*c.*1320–30), Lombardy. 160 fols, Lös. §§338b–99.

Paris, BnF, MSS fr. 756–757. Fourteenth century, Naples. 265 and 268 fols, Lös. §§1–570.

Paris, BnF, MS fr. 760. Late thirteenth century, Pisa–Genoa. 127 fols, Lös. §§338b–84, 534–70.

Paris, BnF, MS fr. 1463. Late thirteenth century, Pisa–Genoa. 106 fols, Rustichello's Compilation and *Tristan,* Lös. §§449d–92, 534–70.

Paris, BnF, MS fr. 12599. Late thirteenth century, northern Italy (possibly western Tuscany). Miscellany, 511 fols, Lös. §§59–71 (fragments 74; 57; 418; 85); 202–282a, 291–299a, 338b–417, 538–69).

Ud: Udine, Archivio di Stato, Fondo Notarile Antico, envelope 5221. Mid-fourteenth century, north-eastern Italy (possibly Friuli). Two fols, Lös. §§41, 43.[22]

Vb: Vatican City, BAV, MS Barb. lat. 3536. Fourteenth century, northern Italy (Veneto). 160 fols, Lös. §§18–41, 338b–383.[23]

Vb[1]: Vatican City, BAV, MS Barb. lat. 3953. *c.*1325–35, Veneto. Niccolò de' Rossi, *Canzoniere*; Iseut's letter to Tristan on fol. 25r, Lös. §71a.

Vb[2]: Vatican City, BAV, MS Vat. lat. 14740. Fourteenth century, north-central Italy, *bifolium*, Lös. §§538, 547–8.[24]

Ve: Venice, Biblioteca Nazionale Marciana, MS fr. XXIII (234). Late thirteenth century, Pisa–Genoa. 64 fols, Lös. §§26–41, 546–70.

Vt: Viterbo, Archivio di Stato, Parchment, file 13, no. 131. Late thirteenth century, Pisa–Genoa. One fol., Lös. §§479, 488–9.

The *Tristan* manuscripts copied in Italy appear to date from between *c.*1275 and *c.*1350, though some were completed and restored at the end of the fourteenth century (**M**) and in the fifteenth (**W[1]**, first section). Book production seems to have been target-specific; we have *de luxe*, finely illustrated manuscripts aimed at the aristocratic market, as well as rapidly produced manuscripts in cursive script using humbler materials, for use by the rising mercantile class.[25] Eight *Tristan* codices have been indicated as coming from the same Pisa–Genoa workshop (**W, L, H, M[1]**, BnF, MSS fr. 760 and fr. 1463, **Ve, Vt**). These belong to a vast corpus of manuscripts which share the same codicological features and iconography, and which transmit French texts, primarily chivalric-Arthurian romances. This unified subset of codices, with generic illustrations at the bottom or in the middle of each folio, has been variously assigned to Lombardy, Angevin Naples and more recently, Genoa. Roberto Benedetti linked the activity of the Ligurian scriptorium, which mass-produced copies of didactic-courtly prose works, to the many Pisans imprisoned in Genoa from 1284 to 1299, following the battle of Meloria.[26] This theory is supported by the many works that were signed by incarcerated scribes.[27] For more prestigious commissioned work, Fabrizio Cigni posits a strong link to Dominican *studia* at Genoa and perhaps even Pisa. BnF, MS fr. 12599, connected to the Pisa area, is a late thirteenth-century bilingual collection which includes not only large sections deriving from the Old French Arthurian tales (*Guiron le Courtois*, *Tristan en prose*, Post-Vulgate *Queste* and the *Suite du Merlin*), but also a fragment of *Guiron* in Pisan dialect.[28] Pisa, the city of Rustichello, was a centre for the diffusion of Arthurian literature and chivalric ideas, and a military company named for the Round Table was active there as early as 1238.[29] Cigni's scholarship demonstrates Pisa's cultural vitality, highlighting the trade, pilgrimage and crusade routes travelled by Pisans and their direct contact with Genoa, with the Hohenstaufens in southern Italy and with the crusader kingdoms of the Latin East.[30]

In the fourteenth century, Lombardy too was a busy centre, known especially for its manuscript miniatures. The well-known *Tristan* (BnF, MS fr. 755) is richly ornamented with 320 sumptuous illustrations.[31] London, British Library, MS Add. 23929 was probably produced in Padua, to judge by its illustrations.[32] Evidence that the lords in the Po Valley were collectors and keen readers of the French romances includes fifteenth-century inventories of princely libraries, registers of loans and payments, and letters and notes written in the codices themselves.[33] Exact inventory entries that state title, *incipit, explicit* and length have allowed scholars to identify several codices owned by the Visconti and the Gonzaga families. BnF, MS fr. 755 is listed in the 1426 inventory of the Visconti library in Pavia. **W**[1] belonged to the Dukes of Milan, and was finished by an Italian scribe during the fifteenth century. The 1407 inventory of the Gonzaga library mentions **Add** (or its direct antigraph), a twin of MS fr. 755, and the Pisa–Genoa-based **Ve**. The inventories of the Estense libraries are much less complete, but they included four copies of *Tristan* which have not yet been identified.

In southern Italy, the Angevin dynasty in Naples prompted a greater interest in the transalpine imaginative fictions. The richly illustrated exemplar BnF, MSS fr. 756–757 is the only survivor of the *Tristan* codices circulating in Naples, but it is well documented that noble Neapolitan families were still reading *Tristan* in the fifteenth century. Evidence for the circulation of the *Tristan* includes the Tristan books documented in household library inventories in Florence, Pavia, Mantua, Padua and the Friuli region.[34] Filipone Bonacolsi's 1325 will attests to the migration of Tristan texts from Tuscany to the Veneto; it mentions six codices in pawn to a Florentine banker, among them a copy of *Tristan*. Three years later the volumes passed into the hands of the Gonzaga family.[35]

Although these early inventories give few details about the content of the manuscripts themselves, from the librarians' notes we can surmise that some contained Tristan material. The *Liber nativitatis Tristani et mortis suae* mentioned in the 1488 Estense inventory seems to juxtapose Tristan's youth and his death.[36] Extant Italian manuscripts of French *Tristan* texts sketch more clearly the contours of the Italian *Tristan* tradition.[37] The *Tristan* that reached Italy is strongly linked to the Carpentras version for the first part of the story. Curtis's *a* family includes five thirteenth-century manuscripts produced in western Tuscany (**W, L, H, M¹, Ve**); three produced a few decades later in the northern Italian/Veneto areas (**Add, Vb, Ud**); and one, MS fr. 756, that is Neapolitan.[38] Within the *a* family, **W** and **M¹** bear remarkable similarities; both are the base text for the most faithful Italian translation, the *Tristano Veneto*. These manuscripts contain the earliest phase of the *Tristan en prose*,[39] but they lack many prominent episodes (Lös. §§57–74). The narratives of **W** and **M¹** proceed directly to Tristan's adventures in Darnantes, consistent with the chronology of the tale (Lös. §§71a–75a).

One collateral version is represented by BnF, MSS fr. 750 and fr. 12599, which constitute the separate family *f*.[40] In place of the Darnantes episode, these codices continue with a series of adventures of Brunor, the Vallet à la Cotte Maltaillée (Lös. §§71–4), forming a kind of romance within the romance.[41] BnF, MS fr. 750, the oldest witness of the *Tristan en prose*, was copied by a French scribe in 1278, probably in Acre or Antioch.[42] The thirteenth-century bilingual compilation BnF, MS fr. 12599 was produced in central Italy. Cigni has examined the hands, illustrative programs, *mise en page*, material structure and content of the miscellany, using and correcting descriptions by Bogdanow and Baumgartner.[43] The scribe (possibly Pisan) who signs himself Oddo, is responsible for the first *Tristan* fragment, which contains a *florilegium* of letters and part of the Brunor material (Lös. §§59–71). Tristan's adventures in the *Pays du Servage* and Brunor's adventures are also found in the *Tristano Panciatichiano*, produced in western Tuscany.[44] Thus a unique redaction of the *Tristan en prose* may be localised between Pisa and the Latin East, with which Pisa had direct contact until the fall of the colonial empire in 1291.[45] The *florilegium* of letters and passages on lyrico-erotic *topoi* in MS fr. 12599 is one of the early witnesses to the rhetorical and formal assimilation of the *Tristan en prose* in the Italian tradition.

In the second part of *Tristan*, we can observe a singular consistency in the Franco-Italian codices, as compared to BnF, MS fr. 757, in the specific assembling of episodes of the tournament at Louvezerp (Lös. §338b, §§352–80), found only in **M**, MSS fr. 755 and 760 (V.I, *yxc* group), **W¹** and MS fr. 12599. A similar consistency can be seen at the end, in that **W, M¹, Ox**, MSS fr. 1463 and 12599, **Ve** and **Vb²** all give a single version. Only a bare minimum of content derives from the *Queste* (Lös. §§534–51 and 568–70); the same is found in early witnesses MSS fr. 104 and fr. 1628.[46] For Delcorno Branca, the most notable feature of the Italian texts is their modular structure, often but not always conditioned by the material that was locally available for this sprawling tale.[47] In Italy, the copies in circulation were either partial texts, texts with missing episodes, or abbreviated versions resulting from the juxtaposition of non-contiguous episodes. We have exemplars in which two large sections are linked by connective tissue which was clearly inserted by the copyist (**W, M¹, Ve** and MS fr. 760). Others reveal a montage of extracts from widely different sources, either expressly connected (MS fr. 12599) or knitted together to make one unified text (**W, M¹, Vb**). There is also a complete witness bound in two codices (MSS fr. 756–757).

Delcorno Branca develops the hypothesis of Gioia Paradisi and Arianna Punzi that the manuscripts copied in Italy represent a very specific narrative selection which preserves all the key events of the Tristan story: his youth, the Louvezerp tournament, and his death.[48] Tristan's birth to his marriage and adventures in Darnantes (Lös. §§ 19–74a) is transmitted in MS fr. 756 and G (the most complete), in H, Ve, MS fr. 12599 (partial), and in W and M¹ (complete). The segment from the Joyous Guard to the Louvezerp tournament (Lös. §§ 338b–384) is preserved in MS fr. 757 and G (also the most complete for this segment), as well as by W¹, M, MSS fr. 755, fr. 760 and fr. 12599, and Vb (an essentially free-standing piece). The final segment – Tristan's last chivalric adventures and last musical performance, the death of the lovers and Arthur's court in mourning (Lös. §§ 534–51, 568–70) – can be found in MS fr. 757, G and W¹ (the most complete); MS fr. 1463, Ox and Vb² (in a separate section); in W, M¹ and Ve (juxtaposed with his *enfances*); in MSS fr. 760 and fr. 12599 (juxtaposed with Louvezerp). This cutting and pasting was facilitated by the interlace technique, which divides the story into narrative units marked by fixed formulae of introduction and transition. This compilation method is well illustrated by the *Tristan* texts translated into Italian, which maintain more or less the same divisions of the romance. All these redactions, whether abbreviated or elliptical, met the demand for more linear narratives with a quicker pace, and reveal new interpretative strategies.[49]

Italian Translations and Adaptations of *Tristan*

The prose translations and adaptations that date from the mid-thirteenth century to the late fourteenth comprise the most interesting phase of the reception of the Tristan material in Italy. These texts were initially produced in Tuscany, where aristocratic chivalric customs had been adapted to a distinctively urban and mercantile context.[50] Pisa, even more than Florence, seems to have been the early centre for disseminating the *Tristan* in Italy. The Pistoia fragments (second half of the thirteenth century) contain the oldest extant *Tristano*, which demonstrates marked Pisan traits.[51] Gaddo de' Lanfranchi, also from Pisa, owned an authoritative Tristan exemplar repeatedly invoked by the Tuscan author of the *Tavola Ritonda*.[52]

Prose Narratives
R: *Tristano Riccardiano*, Florence, Bibl. Riccardiana, MS Ricc. 2543. Late thirteenth century, north-western Tuscany. 180 fols (damaged at the end), Lös. §§19–57, 71a–74a.
P: *Tristano Panciatichiano*, BNCF, MS Panc. 33. Early fourteenth century, Pisa–Lucca. 284 fols, Lös. §§19–101, 338b, 352–81, 539–51, 568–80.
Pistoia fragments: Pistoia, Bibl. Forteguerriana, Documenti Antichi. Thirteenth century, Pisa–Genoa (?). Lös. §§28 and 56.

Todi fragments: Todi, Archivio di Stato. Mid-fourteenth century, Pisa–Lucca. Fols
    32–4, 38–9 and 64–7, Lös. §§367–8 and 374–5.
F: Florence, Bibl. Riccardiana, MS Ricc. 1729. First half fifteenth century,
    Veneto–Emilia. 193 fols, Lös. §§20–49, 544–51, 568–70.
Tristano Veneto: Vienna, Österreichische Nationalbibliothek, MS 3325. Dated
    1487, Veneto. 166 fols, Lös. §§18–59, 70–74a, 623–7, 449d, 458–72, 488–92,
    620–2, 537–51, 568–70 and Rustichello's Compilation.
Zibaldone da Canal: New Haven, Beinecke Library, MS 327. Dated 1312, Venice.
    On fols 44r–45r, Lös. §§20 and 22–3.
Tristano Corsiniano: Rome, Bibl. Corsiniana MS 55.K.5. Last quarter fourteenth
    century (?), Veneto. 114 fols (acephalous and damaged), Lös. §§361–81.
Tavola Ritonda: 8 manuscripts; Lös. §§19–74a, 623–6. See Chapter 4.
Conto di antichi cavalieri, 'Conto de Brunor e de Galeocto suo fillio'; Lös. §41.
Reggimento e costumi di donna, Bellicies's suicide; Lös. §§26–7.

Cantari
BNCF, MS Magl. VIII, 1272. Fourteenth century. *Le Ultime imprese e morte di
    Tristano*; *Vendetta per la morte di Tristano* (partial); *Cantare di Lasancis*
    (partial).
Milan, Bibl. Ambrosiana, MS N. 95 Sup. Dated 1430. *Morte di Tristano*; *Vendetta
    per la morte di Tristano*.
Florence, Bibl. Riccardiana, MS Ricc. 2971. Second half fifteenth century. *Le
    Ultime imprese e morte di Tristano*, Lös. §§516, 518, 524, 533–51, 568–70.
Florence, Bibl. Riccardiana, MS Ricc. 2873. Dated 1432. *Tristano e Lancillotto al
    Petrone di Merlino*; Rustichello's Compilation with Lös. §623.
Florence, Bibl. Medicea Laurenziana, MS Tempi 2. Antonio Pucci's *Zibaldone*;
    fifteen stanzas of Tristan jousting.

Tristano Riccardiano

The most authoritative translation, for both linguistic and editorial importance, is preserved in Florence, Bibl. Riccardiana, MS Ricc. 2543. This parchment codex of 180
folios, mutilated at the end, is from the end of the thirteenth century. Its first editor E.
G. Parodi dubbed it the *Tristano Riccardiano*.[53] Parodi's philological, linguistic and
comparative introduction pays particular attention to the distinct outline of *Ricc.*, a
version concise in its expression yet still complete in its narration.[54] It is impossible to
determine *Ricc.*'s exact audience. On the basis of external data, Parodi posited that the
text had originally been translated in north-eastern France by an Italian writing for a
colony of fellow Italian merchants. Gianfranco Folena and then Antonio Scolari contested this hypothesis; to them it seems much more likely that the text was composed

in Italy, imitating French models.[55] In any case, palaeographical and linguistic details place the text in a mercantile Tuscan context: its domestic, cursive appearance, typical of 'saddle-bag' books, suggests a non-aristocratic audience.

The text of *Ricc.* exhibits traits from various dialects, but the copyist's Florentine dominates. Antonio Scolari showed that the linguistic colouring of south-eastern Tuscany, which Parodi had attributed to areas near Cortona and Umbria, is overlaid on an older stratum from Pisa–Lucca.[56] Within this mix, many Gallicisms add a certain 'exotic flavour' to the text.[57] The semi-gothic script – with obvious features of mercantile writing – varies in colour and letter in a great number of narrative formulae which break the tale down into short narrative units. This material feature scans the text to guide a collective or intimate reading, one perhaps mediated by aural reception, keeping the sequence of events very clear. The frequent explicative formula 'and if someone were to ask me . . . I would tell them . . .' reinforces the complicity between storyteller and audience in typical *jongleur* fashion.[58] *Ricc.* has too often been studied for its linguistic interest alone, being considered clumsy in terms of its narrative.[59] Recently, however, the text has aroused new interest: Parodi's edition has been reprinted, and a new edition has recently been published with an English translation.[60]

Ricc. begins abruptly with the death of Felix, Tristan's grandfather, following the coronation of his successors Meliadus (king of Leonis) and Mark (king of Cornwall): 'Lo re che Filicie iera chiamato' ('The king whose name was Filicie'). The same opening can be found in **Vb**, an Old French manuscript produced in the Veneto: '[Li roi]s que feliz estoit apele'.[61] The redactor has presented the oldest portions of Tristan's biography (Lös. §§19–57) in a style that is both concise and singularly effective in narrative terms. These episodes include: Tristan's birth in the woods, persecution by his stepmother and service at King Faramond's court; Bellicies's tragic love for Tristan; Tristan's fight with Morholt and healing by Iseut; the tournament in Ireland and rivalry with Palamedes; the rivalry between Tristan and Mark for the Lady of Acqua della Spina; Tristan's embassy to win Iseut for Mark; the fateful love potion; the Isle of the Giants; Iseut's marriage to Mark and her abduction by Palamedes; the plots and death sentence against the lovers; their escape to and exile in the forest; the war in Brittany, Tristan's marriage to Iseut White Hands and the announcement to Iseut the Blonde of Tristan's marriage. Returning to Cornwall after receiving her letter, Tristan arrives in the forest of Darnantes (in *Ricc.*, 'Nerlantes'), where he meets famous knights of the Round Table and frees Arthur from a damsel's spell (Lös. §§71a–74a). The text breaks off shortly before the Darnantes episode ends, leaving the story unresolved with a second duel between Tristan and Perceval which does not appear in the French version.

Features specific to *Ricc.* point to a municipal and middle-class reception of this version. The anonymous *Ricc.* author likes to linger over the joys of the lovers, whether on board ship or hiding in the forest. The Wise Damsel's palace, surrounded by gardens and welcoming meadows, can be likened to the villas of the *Decameron* frame-story, which expresses a similar ideal of courtly life. The epic-chivalric episode in Brittany, far more detailed than in the original French version, is interpreted in a political and civic key. The feudal conflict between the father of Iseut White Hands and his nephew, the count of Agippi, is seen as a fight between municipalities; the episode features Tristan in the unusual role of peacemaker, endowed with all the virtues required in a balanced leader as outlined in contemporary mirrors for princes.[62] The wrenching scene in which Iseut White Hands climbs a tower to watch Tristan's ship set sail reveals a sensitivity to the abandoned woman's tragic destiny. Unusual in versions of the prose *Tristan*, it will influence Boccaccio's *Elegy of Lady Fiammetta*.[63] Other Italian redactions show Tristan's wife driven mad by her love for him (*Tris. Ven.*) or dying of grief (*Tav. Rit.*). The letters written by Bellicies and Iseut the Blonde are clearly influenced by the rules for epistolary prose laid out in contemporary *artes dictaminis* by rhetoricians such as Boncompagno da Signa, Guido Faba and Brunetto Latini.[64]

A vivid example of parody is the comic-realistic portrayal of Palamedes sitting before Iseut's locked tower door, first mocked by the besieged queen and later awoken from an erotic dream by Governal tugging at his helmet.[65] In terms of structure, the seemingly episodic narrative sequences[66] actually follow an order ideal for creating a climax. *Ricc.* relates Tristan's maturation through trials which contrast his behaviour to the ignoble court of Cornwall, until he reaches the courtly ambience of Camelot. Hence the importance of the Darnantes episode, which confirms that the new knight has a right to a place in Arthur's world despite coming from a land despised by the Round Table elite.[67] Such an exemplary reading of his *enfances* seems a particularly apt metaphor for the new ruling classes of the Italian communes, who aspired to the dignity of knighthood.[68]

A one-folio parchment fragment (BNCF, MS Nuovi Acquisti 1329, *maculatura* 44) used to cover a sixteenth-century manuscript owned by the banker Filippo Strozzi, was discovered by Donatella Limongi and transcribed by Gloria Allaire.[69] This fragment, from the fourteenth or fifteenth century, is from the area around Florence, but linguistic traits from Pisa–Lucca can also be detected, as well as many Gallicisms. It contains the scenes of Bellicies in love and Morholt arriving in Gaul (Lös. §§24–5), in a redaction somewhere between *Ricc.* and *Tav. Rit.* Allaire indicates many correspondences between the fragment and *Ricc.* which are absent from *Tav. Rit.*; to these we must add King Faramond's proclamation, his daughter's rash boon and the transitional formula which marks the return to the Bellicies episode.

Tristano Panciatichiano

Also of Tuscan origin is the *Tristano Panciatichiano* (BNCF, MS Panc. 33), a translation of the prose *Tristan* into the vernacular of Pisa–Lucca.[70] The text, from the beginning of the fourteenth century, is an anthology of five substantial Arthurian fragments copied in a single hand. These are juxtaposed in a series of compact blocks, linked by standard transitional formulae:

1. the first part of the *Queste del Saint Graal*: from the Grail Pentecost to the repentant Lancelot's confession;[71]
2. the first part of the prose *Tristan*: from his birth to his madness (Lös. §§19–101);
3. the first part of the *Mort Artu*: from the Winchester tournament to the liberation of Guinevere falsely accused of murder (probably followed by the lovers' escape to the Joyous Guard, on three missing pages);
4. two sections of the prose *Tristan*: Tristan and Iseut at the Joyous Guard, and the tournament of Louvezerp (Lös. §338b; 352–81);
5. the final adventures culminating in the death of Tristan (Lös. §§ 539–51; 568–70).

The first narrative segment of *Panc.* is a translation of the *Sangradale* which used the same antigraph as the *Queste* in Udine, Biblioteca Arcivescovile MS 177, part of the Pisa–Genoa corpus.[72] The juxtaposition of the *Mort Artu* with the Tristan story is already visible in the **Ox** manuscript,[73] which exhibits some ties to the Pisa–Genoa scriptorium.[74] The most notable feature of the partial translation of the *Mort Artu* (akin to BnF, MS fr. 342) is the abandonment of interlace technique in favour of a serial construction, a popular feature of Italian texts, which tend towards simpler structures.[75] The compilation only appears to lack coherence; in fact, a close reading reveals a sophisticated play of echoes based on the repetition of motifs and the selection of episodes with parallel themes.[76] The montage aims to recount the life of Tristan, having him reach the peak of his fame with his triumph at Louvezerp, the tournament proclaimed to establish the hierarchy of the knights. Tristan's feats are set alongside those of Lancelot, creating a diptych which shows the new hero and the model he must equal or surpass, against a backdrop of similar experiences of forbidden love.

Tristan's story contained in *Panc.* echoes the *Ricc. incipit*, mentioned above: 'the king who was called Felix'. The first *Tristan* section narrates, concisely and linearly, the episodes from birth up until his marriage (Lös. §§19–56, *R* redaction), followed by the adventures of Tristan and Iseut of the White Hands in the *Pays du Servage*; the exchange of letters between Tristan and Lancelot (Lös. §§62–3, 74–5, *f* family); the puddle that reveals that Tristan's wife is still a virgin (from the metrical version);[77] the letter from Iseut the Blonde (Lös. §71a); the correspondence between Ghedino (Kahedin) and Iseut; Tristan's madness; the false news of his death; Iseut's *lai mortel* and attempted suicide; Palamedes's leave-taking (Lös. §§ 76, 80, 84, 86, 91, 101, 83; redaction similar to BnF, MS fr. 750); and finally, after two folios left blank, the adventures of Brunor, imprisoned by Breus and freed by Lancelot (Lös. §§71–2, *f* family). The prose anthology of Breton cycle material, which is similar to MS fr.

12599, contains various stylistically elaborate passages: the two generic love letters; the specifically Tristanian letters; and the *lai* 'Le solex luist et clers et beaux'. *Panc.* independently develops the episode of Tristan's madness, which corresponds in part to BnF, MS fr. 750[78] and to *Tav. Rit.*[79] This episode contains many didactic and exemplary features found only here: Tristan's animalesque metamorphosis, covered in hair and eating grass; his fight with a bear; the companionship of a grateful dog who licks his wounds; Tristan's intervention as a peacemaker both in a family feud and in the fight between Lamorat and Gawain.[80]

The second major Tristan section in *Panc.* is more prolix and follows the original French version very closely.[81] It begins with the lovers' arrival in Logres (Lös. §338b), as in Pisa–Genoa manuscripts **M**, **Vb**, and BnF, MSS fr. 755, 760 and 12599.[82] The *locus amoenus* of Joyous Guard, 'an enclave of the *Lancelot* in the *Tristan*',[83] reveals the courtly dimension of the passion of the Cornish lovers, perfectly integrated into the Arthurian world. The long description of the tournament at Louvezerp shows the Tuscan merchant class's fascination with tales of knightly games; this can be seen in the visual arts as well, such as a late thirteenth-century fresco painted in the San Gimignano town hall.[84] Starting from Lös. §378, the *Panc.* redactor begins to condense, excising various episodes of Dinadan, Palamedes and Lancelot.

Owing to the loss of some folios, the final section (Lös. §§539–70) starts *in medias res* with the combat of Tristan and Astore De Mare against the knights of Norgales; this section is very close to the Pisa–Genoa group, as well as to the *Tris. Ven.* The *Panc.* is the only non-French text which places the epilogue of Hélie de Boron immediately after the mourning at Arthur's court, as do all the French manuscripts copied in Italy (**M¹**, **Ox**, **Ve**, and BnF, MSS fr. 760, 757 and 1463).[85] A notable divergence from the Vulgate lies in the fact that it is Iseut rather than Tristan who sings the *lai* and accompanies herself on the harp during their last fatal meeting. This unusual inversion of gender roles occurs only in manuscripts (including illustrations) copied and translated in Italy: **W**, **M¹**, **Ox**, MSS fr. 760 and 1463, *Panc.*, *Tris. Ven.*, *Tav. Rit.*[86] Another exemplar of *R*, MS Ricc. 1729, should also be added to this list.[87]

Other Italian Prose Witnesses

Very close to *Panc.* are the two thirteenth-century parchment fragments written in Pisan (Pistoia, Bibl. Forteguerriana, Documenti Antichi 1). They contain the arrival of Morholt in Cornwall (Lös. §28) and the abduction of Iseut from the Wise Damsel's Palace (Lös. §56). The drawing in the lower margin of the first fragment resembles the figurative style of the Pisa–Genoa workshop.[88] Also similar to *Panc.*, in both language and redaction on the one hand and codicology on the other, are the Todi fragments (Archivio di Stato, fols 32–4, 38–9, 64–7) identified and published by Paradisi and Punzi.[89] These parchment pages (Lös. §§367–8 and 374–5) are from a mid-fourteenth-century codex which its editors claim also contained the entire Louvezerp section.

A key manuscript witness for the transmission of the Tristan material from Tuscany to the Veneto is the unedited Florence, Bibl. Riccardiana, MS Ricc. 1729 (first half of the fifteenth century).[90] Despite features of Veneto–Emilian dialect, this manuscript also contains distinct traces of a Pisa–Lucca antecedent.[91] The first ninety folios of MS Ricc. 1729 contain a *Fiore di Virtù* and various moral treatises; they are followed by two non-contiguous episodes from the prose *Tristan*, juxtaposed and introduced by a rubric that emphasises the protagonist's misfortunes. The first section, closely akin to the *R* redaction, begins with Meliadus's abduction by an enchantress and Tristan's birth in the woods; it ends with a series of traps set for the lovers (Lös. §§20–49). The ellipsis occurs when the banished Tristan receives Mark's letter inviting him to return. The redaction then skips to the last part of the romance, told in the same concise style typical of *R*: Tristan's return to Cornwall, the death of the lovers and the mourning at Arthur's court (Lös. §§544–51 and 568–70).

Northern Italian Texts: The *Tristano Veneto*

The most important northern Italian Tristan text is the early fourteenth-century translation into Venetian (Vienna, Österreichische Nationalbibliothek, MS 3325, dated 1487). The *Tristano Veneto* contains two sections from *Tristan* (Lös. §§18–74a and 537–51; 568–70), which are interspersed with long passages from Rustichello's Compilation. The linguistic surface shows that it was strongly influenced by the texts copied in French in the north-west of Tuscany.[92] The use of Latin note forms and the addition of religious expressions suggest the Venetian redactor may have been a churchman. He displays his eloquence in the stylistically elaborate letter from Iseut the Blonde to her faithless lover and in the extended description of the beauty of Iseut White Hands.[93]

The narrative begins with the last part of the tragic events in the lives of Tristan's ancestors: Apollo, the first king of Leonis, is killed by the son of Clodvis, the first king of Cornwall. The beginning coincides with that of Pisa–Genoa **W** and **M¹** (*a* family), which are followed faithfully until the Darnantes episode (Lös. §§18–56 and 71a–74a). There are also some connections with the Udine fragment.[94] After Arthur's liberation, the Venetian redactor changes his source; he skips to the duel between Tristan and Lancelot at Merlin's Stone, following MS fr. 1463, the most authoritative manuscript of Rustichello's Compilation (also Pisa–Genoa).[95] The two different sources are linked by one of the rare transitional formulae in this text, and Rustichello's narrative sequence is inverted for greater continuity. Rustichello's sequence of the Old Knight Branor is moved to the end, while two episodes – the two incognito champions who fight each other, and Tristan joining the Round Table – are moved earlier, as if to crown his feats in Darnantes.[96]

With this change of model, ethical and political themes are added to the *Tris. Ven.*'s love story. The knights errant are portrayed as an invincible military elite characterised primarily by 'vengefulness, a caste spirit and the defence of "family" interests'.[97] In addition to the various duels between Tristan and Lancelot, and Palamedes and Galehaut, other episodes narrate the feats of many other Arthurian knights. The love theme returns in the last Tristan section, which is signalled by a transitional formula and the rubric *Morte de miser Tristan* (Death of Sir Tristan). The narration of the final part accords with that of the Pisa–Genoa manuscripts and with *Panc.*[98] The Veneto text coincides above all with **W**, using the same transitional formula and starting from the very same point: the arrival of the maiden with the harp at Breus's castle.[99] At her request Tristan sings and plays the *lai D'amor vient mon chant et mon plor*, transcribed in French along with a faulty translation.[100] Italian texts reveal a singular interest in this episode, which appears again in *Tav. Rit.* and in *cantari*.[101] The Veneto version coincides with other Italian versions in that Tristan – a guest in disguise – is recognised by the lady not because of his good looks (as in MS fr. 757), but because of his excellent musical performance. Back in Cornwall, Tristan is wounded by Mark as he listens to Iseut playing the *lai* which he – not she – had composed. In this detail, *Tris. Ven.* corresponds to the reading of MS fr. 1463 (Rustichello's Compilation) rather than to the other Italian versions.

The feud mentality, predominant in the part taken from Rustichello, reappears in the vengeance taken for Tristan's death: eight hundred Arthurian knights led by Lancelot invade Cornwall, defeat Mark's army, kill the king and destroy Tintagel. The source of this exceptional insertion is unknown, since in the prose *Tristan* the Cornish people's expectation of an avenger is not fulfilled. Given that the episode is told in a quick, lively, almost folkloric narrative style, this addition shows debts to the *cantare* tradition. An identical sequence of events occurs in the fourteenth-century *cantare Vendetta per la morte di Tristano* ('Revenge for the death of Tristan'), unlike in *Tav. Rit.*, where the revenge expedition is very different and led by Dinadan.[102] The Italian versions of the epilogue have no direct parallels with the primary *Tristan* tradition.[103] Moreover, these versions are a long way both from the few traces of Lancelot's revenge present in BnF, MSS fr. 99 and 112, and from Dinadan's vengeful expedition related in the late redaction in MS fr. 24400 in which Mark escapes (Lös. §409). In a fifteenth-century Castilian version, Lancelot instigates the revenge, as he does in *Tris. Ven.* and *Vendetta per la morte di Tristano*. In the Castilian, too, Mark survives, repents and cedes his kingdom to Arthur, but Aldret dies at the stake.[104]

Another witness from Venice is the short Tristan fragment in the *Zibaldone da Canal*, a fourteenth-century mercantile manuscript (Yale University, Beinecke Library, MS 327, fols 44r–45r). It gives a strongly condensed version of Tristan's childhood, closely connected to the *R* redaction and featuring Meliadus's abduction by the enchantress; Tristan's birth, Eliabel's death, Meliadus's second marriage and the plots of Tristan's stepmother; the murder of Meliadus and Tristan's revenge (Lös.

§§20 and 22–3). This is an exceptional fragment, given the commercial nature and focus of the *Zibaldone*.[105]

The *Tristano Corsiniano*, produced in the Veneto, dates from the last quarter of the fourteenth century.[106] It is preserved only in Rome, Bibl. Corsiniana, MS Cors. 55.K.5 (paper, 114 folios, acephalous and damaged). This is another economical witness to the autonomous tradition of the tournament at Louvezerp, which starts with the adventures of Tristan and Dinadan at Joyous Guard (Lös. §§361–81). The manuscript is embellished with 188 pen drawings with coloured ink wash. The *Corsiniano* was long neglected by critics, who considered it a servile translation of an unknown French antigraph, but it has recently garnered more interest. A modern critical edition and new studies have been published (re-examining the dialectal, codicological and iconographic data of this version, probably produced in a notarial or mercantile milieu), and the first English translation is forthcoming.[107]

The latest editor, Roberto Tagliani, disputes the earlier views of Galasso and Allaire that the *Corsiniano* derives directly from a French version or that it can be traced back to an intermediate Tuscan version based on MS fr. 757.[108] Highlighting dialectal elements typical of the western Veneto, overlaid by other typically Venetian linguistic features, Tagliani posits the existence of a lost Veronese antigraph from the beginning of the fourteenth century. Based on the linguistic traces of Venetian, as well as on the illustrations drawn by three different hands, Tagliani believes the codex was produced in a workshop in or around Venice. The illustrations – stylized and schematic, yet functional and expressive – are perhaps inspired by the iconographic *clichés* found in manuscripts generated in the Pisa–Genoa workshop. He suggests further study of the claim that scenes in the manuscript closely resemble images in recently discovered tempera panels used to decorate ceilings in Udine and Pordenone.[109] The illustrative program, tightly linked to the plot, confirms that the *Corsiniano* was aimed at an audience of middle rank. Both the narration and the drawings emphasize the epic themes of battle and chivalry – feats of arms, duels, and tournaments – far more than the love scenes and courtly passages. Tagliani connects this choice to the political and cultural climate of late fourteenth-century Venice, which needed 'new' knights for its hegemonic ambitions over the mainland. This rereading of the Tristan romance in an epic register would have offered the emerging class a new behavioural model which exalted the military prowess of a wise and valiant knight.

Tavola Ritonda

The most innovative and complex Italian Arthurian text is the *Tavola Ritonda*, composed by an anonymous Tuscan author in the first third of the fourteenth century. Since Daniela Delcorno Branca analyses it in this volume, I will add only that although its content owes much to the prose *Tristan*, it also drew on the *Lancelot-Grail*, the *Mort Artu*, *Guiron le Courtois* and Rustichello. It begins with Tristan's direct ancestors

(Lös. §18), as do **W**, **H**, **M¹**, **Vb** and *Tris. Ven.*, and follows the *R* redaction until the liberation of Arthur from the Palace of Desire (Lös. §§19–74a). At this point the anonymous Tuscan inserts a series of episodes borrowed from Thomas, and then continues with Tristan episodes taken mainly from V.I.[110] Many elements from the early tradition are preserved in the Po Valley redaction of *Tav. Rit.* preserved in BNCF, MS Palatino 556, dated 1446. In the first part of the romance (Lös. §§20–75a) MS Pal. 556 shows close ties to the *R* redaction, especially to MS Ricc. 1729.[111] In the second part, Pal. 556 differs from the Tuscan version of *Tav. Rit.* in its abrupt insertion of the duel at Merlin's Stone taken from Rustichello (Lös. §§623–6), following a model close to *Tris. Ven.*[112]

Roberto Benedetti has identified and transcribed two fragments of a *Tav. Rit.* in a Veneto dialect, which come from a single volume written in the mid-fourteenth century: one in Padua (Biblioteca Universitaria, MS 609) and the other in Udine (Archivio Arcivescovile, MS 86).[113] These contain the Grail liturgy in Corbenic (*Queste*) and King Mark's invasion of Logres to retake Iseut (Lös. §516). The last Tristan section from *Tav. Rit.* – Tristan's death and the revenge taken for it – circulated independently in the area around Verona; this is proven by BAV, MS Vat. Lat. 6789, which also contains Guido delle Colonne's *Historia destructionis Troie*. This Tristan exemplar was copied in 1422 by Ventura de' Cerutis, Castellan of Montebello, and published by Giovanni Cassini in Paris in 1854.[114]

Shorter Narrative Forms in Prose and Verse

During the mid-thirteenth century other shorter versions of the Tristan tale began to circulate in Italy. The episodic structure and linear narrative of the Italian prose *Tristan* tradition made it easy to extract isolated episodes or sequences, turning them into short stories with didactic messages.[115] The 'Conto de Brunor e de Galeocto suo fillio' is an exemplary biography of Galehaut inserted into the *Conti di antichi cavalieri*.[116] It juxtaposes two episodes, one from *Lancelot* (the battle between Galehaut and Arthur) and one from *Tristan* (Tristan at the Isle of the Giants, Lös. §41). Delcorno Branca highlights the 'politico-civic' portrayal of the protagonist as a wise and just prince.[117] Bellicies's unhappy love and suicide (Lös. §§26–7) becomes an *exemplum* in Francesco da Barberino's *Reggimento e costumi di donna* (1318–20).[118] The episode follows the order of the *R* redaction (unrequited love, suicide, letter) which removes the surprise created by the prose *Tristan*'s analeptic structure; in that version, only while reading her letter in its diegetic insertion do we learn that Bellicies has killed herself with Tristan's sword.[119]

In *Novellino* 65, the meeting of the lovers spied on by Mark (Lös. §282) derives from the metrical versions rather than from the prose romance. This can be seen from certain details also found in *Tav. Rit.*: the identification of the tree as a pine; the king revealed by his shadow, not a reflection; and Iseut's quick reaction.[120] In *Novellino* 45,

Lancelot's single combat at a fountain is in all likelihood modelled on the combat between Tristan and Helye of Saxony (Lös. §399).[121] Tristan's madness as found in *Panc*. makes an appearance as Novella 99 of the Borghiniana edition (1572).[122]

The Tristan material became a popular subject for *cantari*, *ottava rima* settings of episodes both emotional and epic, which were sung in town squares for a mixed and semi-learned audience.[123] In the *Cantare de' Cantari* (*c*.1380–1420), the Tuscan *cantastorie* or tale-singer boasts of his repertoire, listing a whole series of *cantari* on Tristan at octave 44. Only a few of these compositions survive, most in BNCF, MS Magl. VIII, 1272, whose Tristan-themed *cantari* are: *Le Ultime imprese e morte di Tristano* ('The last feats and death of Tristan'); two fragments of the *Vendetta per la morte di Tristano* ('Revenge for the death of Tristan'); and the beginning of the *Cantare di Lasancis*. Milan, Bibl. Ambrosiana, MS N. 95 Sup., written in 1430 by Milanese Giovanni de' Cignardi, preserves a Lombard version of the *Morte di Tristano* as well as the *Vendetta*. Cigni published a third, Florentine redaction of *Le Ultime imprese* (Florence, Bibl. Riccardiana, MS Ricc. 2971, second half of the fifteenth century).[124]

The *ottava rima* poems are faithful adaptations of the French models. The *Ultime imprese*, for example, opens with Mark's brutal abduction of Iseut from Joyous Guard while Tristan is away (Lös. §516). This is a narrative turning-point in the prose *Tristan*; Mark's invasion of Logres prompts the final break between the tale of the Arthurian knights and that of Tristan, who abandons the Quest after hearing this news.[125] The war between Mark and Arthur (Lös. §518), Galehaut's intervention (Lös. §524) and Mark's return to Cornwall (Lös. §533) are followed by Tristan's last feats and death (Lös. §§534–51 and 568–70). The events related in *Vendetta* have much in common with *Tris. Ven.*: Lancelot takes the initiative and kills Mark during a fierce fight.[126]

Another *cantare* based on the Matter of Britain is the *Tristano e Lancillotto al Petrone di Merlino* (42 stanzas, in Florence, Bibl. Riccardiana, MS Ricc. 2873, dated 1432). The account follows Rustichello's Compilation, with a few variants from the prose *Tristan* (Lös. §623). Its author seems particularly interested in the misunderstanding which causes the two knights to fight fiercely at Merlin's Stone.

The *Cantare di Lasancis* contains the beginning of a fabulous adventure from *Tav. Rit.* which has no parallel in the prose *Tristan*. The Old Knight with a magical lance, sent him by an evil enchantress to destroy the Round Table, defeats all Arthur's strongest knights, but is eventually defeated by Tristan's cunning. This episode, an example of the 'knight with the enchanted weapons' *topos*, is often found in other *cantari*, but also recalls the episode of the Old Knight Branor le Brun, created by Rustichello.[127] Lasancis is mentioned in the boasting catalogue of the *Cantare dei Cantari* (stanza 44), and reappears in the figure of King Samsiž in the Serbo-Russian *Tristan*, which draws on various texts that circulated in the Veneto.[128]

Finally, a Tristan fragment in Antonio Pucci's *Zibaldone* (Florence, Bibl. Medicea Laurenziana, MS Tempi 2) is too generic to allow us to identify its source. Its fifteen stanzas recount a series of standardized duels between Tristan and the familiar Arthurian knights Gawain, Dodinel, Palamedes and Breus.[129]

Non-textual Evidence[130]

Sicilian artists embroidered magnificent scenes from the Tristan story onto a wall hanging, of which one part is preserved in the Victoria and Albert Museum, the other in the Bargello. The scenes represent Tristan's departure from King Faramond – the scene of Bellicies's suicide has been lost – and his duel with Morholt (Lös. §§26–8). The embroidered captions follow *R*. This work was probably created for the 1395 wedding joining the Guicciardini and the Acciaioli, two important Florentine banking families influential in southern Italy. Tristan's shield shows the Guicciardini arms – three hunting horns – which the hero also carried in *Ricc.*[131] A second, similar textile belongs to the Marchesi Pianetti of Florence, in which Tristan and Iseut are part of a group of allegorical figures.

Between 1377 and 1380, scenes from some version of the Tristan romance were also painted on the wooden ceiling of Palazzo Chiaramonte, or *Lo Steri*, in Palermo, seat of the most powerful feudal family of the time. Palazzo Ricchieri in Pordenone contains frescoes which date roughly to the second half of the fourteenth century. They depict the combat with Palamedes at the tournament in Ireland; the love potion on the ship; the Isle of the Giants. The Ricchieri were urban nobles who owed their social rise to trade in textiles and fabrics.

Attestations and Outline of the *R* Redaction

In the light of this complete list of Tristan texts in Italian vernaculars, and summary overview of Tristan references in material culture, we can specify the textual physiognomy of the biographical slant of the *R* redaction, the most widespread and popular in Italy. It is a short but not a shortened redaction, in which the deeds narrated follow a logical and linear sequence of events.

The Tristan texts in Italian, most often incomplete or fragmentary versions of long French models, privilege four key episodes:

1. Tristan's *enfances* (*Ricc.*; *Panc.*; *Tris. Ven.*; *Tav. Rit.*; Pistoia and Florence fragments; *Zibaldone da Canal*; *Reggimento*; Sicilian wall hanging);
2. the duel at Merlin's Stone (*Tris. Ven.*; *Tav. Rit.*; the eponymous *cantare*);
3. the Louvezerp tournament (*Panc.*; *Tav. Rit.*; *Corsiniano*; Todi fragments);
4. Tristan's death (*Panc.*; MS Ricc. 1729; *Tris. Ven.*; *Tav. Rit.*; *cantari*).

The first section (birth–marriage–Darnantes, Lös. §§19–75a) was not only widespread but also diverse in the various redactions: the *a* family, the *f* family and the *R* redaction. With the Tristanocentric *R* redaction, Italy is able to document a very early stage of elaboration of the prose *Tristan*, possibly close to that of Luce's *Estoire*, which spread through two other collateral areas, the Iberian and the Slavic.[132] Many Italian versions belong to *R*: Ricc. MS 2543 (= **R**); MS. Ricc. 1729 (= **F**); *Panc.* (= **P**); *Tav. Rit.* (= **S**); Pal. 556 (= **L**); the Pistoia and Florence fragments, the *Zibaldone da Canal*, the *Reggimento* and the Sicilian wall hanging.[133] The *Tris. Ven.*, a faithful translation of **W** and **M**[1], cannot be said to belong to *R*, even if these versions – more prolix overall – lack most of the details of Tristan's ancestors' story, as well as lacking an identical series of secondary adventures (Lös. §§57–74). Ultimately their divergence from *R* is too marked, at the level of both macrostructure and microstructure.

The main Iberian witnesses of *R* are the Castilian-Aragonese redaction of the *Cuento de Tristán de Leonís* (BAV, MS Vat. lat. 6428, late fourteenth century = **V**), and the Castilian redaction of *Tristán de Leonís* (*editio princeps*, Valladolid, 1501 = **TL**).[134] In addition, fifteenth-century fragments that have emerged in Galician-Portuguese, Catalan and Aragonese, and fifty-nine in Castilian, are also crucial witnesses to the romance's circulation in Iberia before the age of print.[135] **V**, acephalous and truncated, juxtaposes Tristan's youth (Lös. §§19–75a) and Louvezerp (Lös. §§343–80). Similarly, **TL** juxtaposes Tristan's youth (Lös. §§24–75a) and Louvezerp (Lös. §§343–78), Rustichello's Compilation (Lös. §§620–6) and the death of the lovers (Lös. §§545–50). The Louvezerp passage has many *sui generis* elements,[136] but the **TL** text seems to be close to MS fr. 760.[137] The Castilian *Don Tristán de Leonís* effects a combination of *Tristan* and Rustichello, as do MS fr. 1434, *Tris. Ven.* and MS Pal. 556, which must have been typical of the northern Italian tradition. The final section of *Don Tristán*, which is influenced by the *novela sentimental*, reproduces some details of the Italian vernacular texts, such as Iseut's song at the moment of the ambush, Tristan's Christian death and Iseut's death from a broken heart.[138] The Castilian *Tristan* probably ended with Lancelot's revenge, as did the *Tris. Ven.* and the *cantare Vendetta per la morte di Tristano*.[139]

The Serbo-Russian *Tristan* (Raczyński, Public Library, MS 94, sixteenth century) also belongs to the *R* redaction, since this text, through an as yet unidentified Serbo-Croatian intermediary, has as its source an unknown Veneto text abbreviated like the fragment from the *Zibaldone da Canal*.[140] Like *Tris. Ven.*, the text begins with Lös. §18. After Iseut has been freed from Palamedes's siege (Lös. §44), the Slavic text skips to the lovers' flight to Domolot (Lös. §322), continuing with a completely original plot which seems to have some parallels with the Italian narrative and *cantare* traditions.[141] Finally, elements from the *R* redaction are found even in areas where there was absolutely no direct contact, such as Malory's *Tristram*.[142]

The *R* redaction is marked by several distinctive features.[143] At the level of macrostructure, it notably lacks both collateral episodes and later insertions such as the myth of Tristan's ancestors (Lös. §§1–18); the knight who rescues Iseut abducted by Palamedes (Lös. §43); the exchange of letters; the *Pays du Servage* and the Brunor episodes (Lös. §§57–74); and Gawain and Lamorat's encounter in Darnantes (Lös. §72a), which introduces the hatred between the sons of Lot and Pellinor, interpolated from the Post-Vulgate *Suite du Merlin*.[144] Also missing are the synoptic references to events in the *Lancelot* and the *Suite du Merlin* regarding Galehaut, Lancelot and Merlin, in keeping with the goal of *'accomplir'*.[145] Various scenes have been added: Tristan's stepmother's third attempt to poison him; Bellicies's suicide; Joseph of Arimathea's martyrdom on the Isle of the Giants; Tristan's premonitory dream; and Camelot rejoicing at Arthur's liberation. The attacks by Tristan's stepmother are given in inverted order (Lös. §22),[146] and the order of the traps set for the lovers is also very different (Lös. §§45–9). Other significant details which prove the cohesion of the Italo-Hispanic group include the name Ghedin (rather than Andret) for Tristan's cousin and rival; the inversion of the characters Lambegues and Sigris (Segurades); Perceval's association with the Questing Beast; the periphrastic name of the Lady of Acqua della Spina,[147] with Blanor as her kidnapper; the Island Without Adventure as the place where Tristan and Morholt fight; and the poisoned arrow with which Morholt then wounds Tristan. There are also notable similarities between *Panc.* and the Spanish translations alone, such as the sword as one of Bellicies's gifts to Tristan.

The clear relation between the Italian and Iberian versions of the Tristan texts was recognised long ago by Northup in his edition of the *Cuento de Tristán de Leonis*. Northup hypothesised that the Iberian texts had all stemmed from one original Italian source, on the grounds that the *Ricc.* is much older than the two Castilian texts; that they are much further from the French than the Italian versions are; and that both **V** and **TL** contain many Italianisms. The existence of *R* has not been refuted, but its antecedent is still subject to debate: it has been hypothesised to be an archaic and 'anomalous' version of *Tristan* preserved in the south of France;[148] a condensed yet complete 'southern version', similar to the **M¹** family;[149] a 'peripheral' French *Tristan* which was shortened and contaminated with Rustichello's Compilation.[150] After examining all the Iberian texts in detail, and presenting the debate on antecedents of *R*, Enrique Andrés Ros Domingo proposed a new, bipartite *stemma* that foregrounds the role of Catalonia in the diffusion of the Tristan material over the Iberian peninsula.[151] In his opinion the Italian adaptations derived directly from the non-orthodox French **Y**, while the Spanish translations descend from a Gallo-Romance sub-archetype **Y'**, to which the Catalan fragments are closer. The Catalan model **Y″** is the intermediary text of **V**, which also drew directly on **Y'**, and of **TL**, which was also influenced by Rustichello.

Sebastian Iragui maintained that only the Iberian texts have preserved the second part of the Southern version; Parodi and Northup, however, were not convinced that there had ever existed any further material beyond the ending of the *R* version of Tristan.[152] The narration of *Ricc.*, the main representative of *R*, stops at the end of the

Darnantes episode owing to loss of folios. At this critical point of the tradition, all other witnesses to *R* either stop (even before Lös. §74a), draw on other sources (Thomas or Rustichello) or link up again with V.I and the *a* family (**W**, **M¹**, **Ve**). According to Delcorno Branca, the change of the name of Tristan's cousin could indicate a change of source: while in the first part, Tristan's antagonist is called Ghedin in **TR**, **P**, **F**, **L**, **V** and **TL**, in the final section he is called Andret in **P**, **L** and **TL**, but Dorin in **F**, which is the only text to give a concise narration of the final part of the tale as well.[153]

Identifying behind the Italian and Iberian texts of the *Tristan* a common redaction, *R*, containing its own characteristics, shows that the Italian Tristan material had a more various and multiform life than the French versions alone would lead us to suppose. Its afterlife in early print editions is addressed in Chapter 7 of this volume.

Conclusion

The *Tristan*, rewritten in prose by a French redactor, served as the model for the Italian versions of the romance. Manuscripts in French of Italian origin, and the many adaptations in the vernaculars of Tuscany and the Veneto, attest to the clamorous success of the *Tristan en prose* in diverse social and cultural environments. The texts produced in Italy, based on various redactions (V.I, V.II, the *a* and *f* families, *R*) relate the most important stages of Tristan's knightly itinerary: the conquest of his heroic and courtly identity; his absolute triumph in the Arthurian world as both knight and lover; and his tragic death. In the vernacular versions, the protagonist becomes the exemplary representative of the Round Table. Tristan emerges as an ideal mirror for that new middle class which, having adopted the universal aristocratic ideal, could recognise in the Cornish hero's quest its own aspirations of social advancement.

(Translated by Alison Bron)

Notes

[1] D. [Delcorno] Branca, *I romanzi italiani di Tristano e la Tavola Ritonda* (Florence, 1968), p. 18.

[2] See Delcorno Branca, *Tristano e Lancillotto in Italia. Studi di letteratura arturiana* (Ravenna, 1998), pp. 117–42, henceforth *TLI*; and *ead.*, 'Diffusione della materia arturiana in Italia: per un riesame delle "tradizioni sommerse"', in F. Benozzo et al. (eds), *Culture, livelli di cultura e ambienti nel Medioevo occidentale* (Rome, 2012), pp. 321–40.

[3] E. Baumgartner, 'The Prose *Tristan*', in G. S. Burgess and K. Pratt (eds), *The Arthur of the French: The Arthurian Legend in Medieval French and Occitan Literature* (Cardiff, 2006), pp. 325–92.

[4] For the *Roman de Tristan en prose* (= prose *Tristan*), scholars typically refer to three editions which supplement each other in terms of both content and redaction. For content, Löseth's 1891 summary divides the complex plot into 619 paragraphs (indicated throughout as Lös. §§). R. L. Curtis's edition (*Le*

Roman de Tristan en prose, 3 vols [Munich, 1963; Leiden, 1976; Cambridge, 1985]), based on Carpentras, Bibliothèque Municipale, MS 404, contains Lös. §§1–92. The edition directed by P. Ménard (*Le Roman de Tristan en prose* [Geneva, 1987–97]), based on Vienna, Österreichische Nationalbibliothek, MS 2542, contains Lös. §§93–517. Finally, *Le Roman de Tristan en prose (version du manuscrit fr. 757 de la Bibliothèque nationale de Paris)* (Paris, 1997–2007), which begins with Lös. §184, was published by a team of scholars also directed by Ménard.

⁵ The V.I and V.II theory has been much debated and continues to be so; basic bibliography on it must include R. Curtis, 'Les deux versions du *Tristan* en prose: examen de la théorie de Löseth', *Romania*, 84 (1963), 390–8; E. Baumgartner, Le Tristan en prose. *Essai d'interprétation d'un roman médiéval* (Paris, 1975) and 'Histoire d'Helain le Blanc: du *Lancelot* au *Tristan* en prose', in J. C. Aubailly (ed.), *'Et c'est la fin pour quoy sommes ensemble'. Hommage à Jean Dufournet*, 3 vols (Paris, 1993), I, pp. 139–48; E. Polley, 'La retransmission de la *Queste* Vulgate par le *Tristan en prose*', *Questes*, 11 (2007), 17–25; Baumgartner, 'The Prose *Tristan*', pp. 329–30; P. Ménard, '"Monseigneur Robert de Boron" dans le *Tristan* en prose', in L. Harf-Lancner et al. (eds), *Des 'Tristan' en vers au 'Tristan' en prose* (Paris, 2009), pp. 359–70; and F. Cigni, 'Per un riesame della tradizione del *Tristan* in prosa, con nuove osservazioni sul ms. Paris, BnF, fr. 756–757', in Benozzo et al. (eds), *Culture, livelli di cultura*, pp. 247–78.

⁶ Baumgartner, *Tristan en prose*. See F. Bogdanow and R. Trachsler, 'Rewriting Prose Romance: The Post-Vulgate *Roman du Graal* and Related Texts', in Burgess and Pratt (eds), *Arthur of the French*, pp. 342–92. It is possible that long passages of this compilation, reconstructed by F. Bogdanow in *The Romance of the Grail: A Study of the Structure and Genesis of a Thirteenth-century Arthurian Prose Romance* (Manchester and New York, 1966), were the work of an Italian compiler (Bogdanow, 'La tradition manuscrite de la *Queste del Saint Graal*: Versions *Vulgate* et *Post-Vulgate* en Italie', in D. Buschinger and W. Spiewok [eds], *Die kulturellen Beziehungen zwischen Italien und den anderen Ländern Europas im Mittelalter* [Greifswald, 1993], pp. 25–45, on pp. 40–1).

⁷ J. Blanchard (ed.), *Le Roman de Tristan en prose: Les deux captivités de Tristan* (Paris, 1976), p. 31 n. 9; and T. Delcourt, 'Un fragment inédit du cycle de la Post-Vulgate', *Romania*, 109 (1988), 247–79, on 253.

⁸ L. Leonardi, 'Un nuovo frammento del *Roman de Tristan* in prosa', in D. De Robertis and F. Gavazzeni (eds), *Operosa parva per Gianni Antonini* (Verona, 1996), pp. 9–24, and 'Il torneo della Roche Dure nel *Tristan* in prosa: versioni a confronto (con l'edizione dal ms. B.N., fr. 757)', *CN*, 57 (1997), pp. 209–51.

⁹ Curtis (ed.), *Roman de Tristan* ([1963], pp. 18–23; [1976], pp. 26–32; [1985], pp. xxxiii–v).

¹⁰ D. Delcorno Branca, 'Per la storia del *Roman de Tristan* in Italia', *CN*, 40 (1980), 211–29, on 218–19.

¹¹ E. G. Gardner, *The Arthurian Legend in Italian Literature* (London and New York, 1930; rpt 1971), and the many works by Delcorno Branca cited in the present chapter.

¹² On the dissemination of Tristan material in the peninsula, see Kleinhenz, 'Tristan in Italy: The Death or Rebirth of a Legend', *Studies in Medieval Culture*, 5 (1975), 145–58; H. Krauss, 'Der Artus-Roman in Italien', in H. R. Jauss and E. Köhler (eds), *Grundriss der romanischen Literaturen des Mittelalters, IV: Le roman jusqu'à la fin du XIIIe siècle* (Heidelberg, 1978), I, pp. 667–75; M.-J. Heijkant, *La tradizione del 'Tristan' in prosa in Italia e proposte di studio sul 'Tristano Riccardiano'* (Nijmegen, 1989); F. Cigni, 'Tristano e Isotta nelle letterature francese e italiana', in M. Dallapiazza (ed.), *Tristano e Isotta. La fortuna di un mito europeo* (Trieste, 2003), pp. 29–129; and A. Punzi, *Tristano. Storia di un mito* (Rome, 2005), pp. 121–63. A focused research tool is Cigni's *Bibliografia degli studi italiani di materia arturiana (1940–1990)* (Fasano, 1992), supplemented in 'Bibliografia degli studi italiani di materia arturiana: Supplemento 1991–2005', in *Modi e forme della fruizione della 'materia arturiana' nell'Italia dei sec. XIII–XIV* (Milan, 2006), pp. 183–226.

¹³ *TLI*, pp. 177–99.

¹⁴ Baumgartner, *La harpe et l'épée: Tradition et renouvellement dans le* Tristan *en prose*, Moyen Age (Paris, 1990), and V. Bertolucci Pizzorusso, 'L'arpa d'Isotta: Variazioni testuali e figurative', in J. C.

Faucon et al. (eds), *Miscellanea Mediaevalia: Mélanges offerts à Philippe Ménard*, 2 vols (Paris and Geneva, 1998), I, pp. 101–19.

[15] An extensive list of these publications is available in the general bibliography of the present volume.

[16] *TLI*, pp. 51–7, and 'Lecteurs et interprètes des romans arthuriens en Italie: un examen à partir des études récentes', in C. Kleinhenz and K. Busby (eds), *Medieval Multilingualism: The Francophone World and Its Neighbours* (Turnhout, 2010), pp. 155–86.

[17] I use Delcorno Branca's *sigla* in *TLI*, pp. 51–7. To her list of manuscripts we must add the Brescia fragment; see P. M. Galimberti, 'Censimento dei frammenti manoscritti della Biblioteca Queriniana di Brescia', *Aevum*, 76 (2002), 471–515, on 478 [INC.A.VI.7]. M.-L. Chênerie ('Étude et édition des fragments du *Tristan en prose* de Toulouse', *BBIAS*, 50 [1998], 231–64, on 241) has noted northern Italian linguistic features in the late thirteenth-century Toulouse *Tristan* fragment (Lös. §§116 and 138, close to BnF, MS fr. 750). For the classification of the manuscripts, see Baumgartner, *Tristan en prose*; and Cigni, 'Per un riesame'.

[18] This fragment is transcribed by R. Benedetti in 'Frammenti arturiani. Percorsi e nuove individuazioni. *L'Estoire del Saint Graal*', in Paradisi and Punzi (eds), *Storia, geografia, tradizioni manoscritte*, special issue of *Critica del testo*, 7/1 (2004), 257–93, on 274–5.

[19] L is described extensively in F. Cigni, 'Manuscrits en français, italien, et latin entre la Toscane et la Ligurie à la fin du XIIIe siècle: implications codicologiques, linguistiques, et évolution des genres narratifs', in Kleinhenz and Busby (eds), *Medieval Multilingualism*, pp. 187–217, on pp. 197–203.

[20] On the Italian scribe, see F. Bogdanow (ed.), *La Version Post-Vulgate de la* Queste del Saint Graal *et de la* Mort Artu, 4 vols in 5 parts (Paris, 1991, 2000, 2001); I, pp. 166–71, on p. 167.

[21] Perhaps a fragment of the Post-Vulgate *Queste*, according to Bogdanow; 'La tradition manuscrite', pp. 26 and 29.

[22] For the announcement and transcription of this fragment, see R. Benedetti, '"Qua fa' un santo e un cavaliere . . .": Aspetti codicologici e note per il miniatore', in G. D'Aronco et al. (eds), *La grant Queste del Saint Graal* (Udine, 1990), pp. 31–47; and Benedetti, 'Un frammento del *Roman de Tristan en prose* fra tradizione toscana e tradizione veneta (Udine, Archivio di Stato, fr. 110)', *SMV*, 49 (2003), 47–69.

[23] See Benedetti, 'Un frammento'; and R. Zanni, 'Il Barberiniano latino 3536 e la tradizione del *Tristan en prose*', *Parola*, 12 (2008), 35–67.

[24] The fragment is edited by A. Radaelli in 'Il testo del frammento Vb² del *Roman de Tristan en prose* (Bibl. Apostolica Vaticana, Vat. lat. 14740)', *SMV*, 50 (2004), 185–223. She thinks the quire began with the *Lai du plor* and ended with the lovers' death and the mourning in Camelot. The text shows affinities with the Pisa–Genoa branch, as well as with BnF, MS fr. 12599.

[25] Cigni, 'Manoscritti di prose cortesi compilati in Italia (secc. XIII–XIV): stato della questione e prospettive di ricerca', in S. Guida and F. Latella (eds), *La filologia romanza e i codici*, 2 vols (Messina, 1993), II, pp. 419–41.

[26] R. Benedetti, '"Qua fa' un santo"'. For details on the Pisa–Genoa attributions, see F. Cigni, 'La ricezione medievale della letteratura francese nella Toscana nord-occidentale', in E. Werner and S. Schwarze (eds), *Fra toscanità e italianità. Lingua e letteratura dagli inizi al Novecento* (Tübingen and Basel, 2000), pp. 71–108, on pp. 81–9. See also V. Bertolucci Pizzorusso, 'Testi e immagini in codici attribuibili all'area pisano-genovese alla fine del Duecento', in M. Tangheroni (ed.), *Pisa e il Mediterraneo. Uomini, merci, idee dagli Etruschi ai Medici* (Milan, 2003), pp. 196–201. See also F. Cigni, 'I testi della prosa letteraria e i contatti col francese e col latino. Considerazioni sui modelli', in L. Battaglia Ricci and R. Cella (eds), *Pisa crocevia di uomini, lingue e culture. L'età medievale. Atti del Convegno, Pisa, 25–27 ottobre 2007* (Rome, 2009), pp. 157–81, on pp. 159–61 and 172–7; and 'Manuscrits en français'.

[27] F. Cigni, 'Copisti prigionieri (Genova, fine sec. XIII)', in P. Beltrami et al. (eds), *Studi di Filologia romanza offerti a Valeria Bertolucci Pizzorusso*, 2 vols (Pisa, 2006), I, pp. 425–39.

[28] F. Cigni, 'Guiron, Tristan, e altri testi arturiani. Nuove osservazioni sulla composizione materiale del Ms. Parigi, BNF, fr. 12599', *SMV*, 45 (2000), 31–69; and 'Per la storia del *Guiron le Courtois* in

64 MARIE-JOSÉ HEIJKANT

Italia', in G. Paradisi and A. Punzi (eds), *Storia, geografia*, pp. 295–316. The *Guiron* fragment was edited by A. Limentani, *Dal Roman de Palamedés ai Cantari di Febus-el-Forte* (Bologna, 1962); see also Cigni, 'Manuscrits en français', pp. 190–1.

[29] Delcorno Branca, *Romanzi italiani*, pp. 174–5.

[30] See Cigni, 'Copisti prigionieri', 'I testi della prosa', and 'Manuscrits en français'.

[31] F. Avril and M.-T. Gousset, *Manuscrits enluminés d'origine italienne*, III: *XIVe siècle, I. Lombardie-Ligurie* (Paris, 2005), pp. 16–26.

[32] Delcorno Branca cites the findings of B. Degenhart and A. Schmitt (*TLI*, p. 53 n. 11).

[33] *TLI*, pp. 13–48; 'I Tristani dei Gonzaga', in J.-C. Faucon et al. (eds), *Miscellanea Mediaevalia: Mélanges offerts à Philippe Ménard*, 2 vols (Paris and Geneva, 1998), I, pp. 385–93; and 'Lecteurs et interprètes'.

[34] For bibliographical sources, see *TLI*, pp. 29–30 and 33 n. 46.

[35] Delcorno Branca, 'I Tristani dei Gonzaga', p. 386.

[36] *TLI*, p. 40.

[37] *TLI*, pp. 58–76.

[38] Cigni, 'Per un riesame'.

[39] Curtis (ed.), *Roman de Tristan* (1985), III, pp. xiv–xvi, xxi–xxiv.

[40] Curtis (ed.), *Roman de Tristan* (1985), III, pp. xxxix–xliii.

[41] Curtis, 'A Romance within a Romance: The Place of the *Roman du Vallet à la Cote Maltailliée* in the Prose *Tristan*', in *Studies in Medieval French Language and Literature Presented to Brian Woledge in Honour of his 80th Birthday* (Geneva, 1988), pp. 17–35.

[42] Cigni, 'Guiron, Tristan', p. 41 n. 26.

[43] Cigni, 'Guiron, Tristan'; F. Bogdanow, *La Folie Lancelot: a hitherto unidentified portion of the Suite du Merlin contained in MSS B.N. 112 and 12599* (Tübingen, 1965), pp. l–li; Baumgartner, *Tristan en prose*, pp. 63–7.

[44] *TLI*, p. 62.

[45] Cigni, 'Manoscritti di prose cortesi', pp. 439–41. Circulation of the *Pays du Servage* episode in the Veneto has been confirmed by a note erased from **Vb**; *TLI*, pp. 71–2.

[46] Cigni, 'Per un riesame'.

[47] *TLI*, pp. 65–9; D. Delcorno Branca, 'Le storie arturiane in Italia', in P. Boitani et al. (eds), *Lo spazio letterario del Medioevo. II: Il Medioevo volgare. III: La ricezione del testo* (Rome, 2003), pp. 385–403, on 389–92.

[48] *TLI*, pp. 62, 72–3; G. Paradisi and A. Punzi, 'La tradizione del *Tristan en prose* in Italia e una nuova traduzione italiana', in G. Hilty (ed.), *Actes du XXème Congrès International de Linguistique et de Philologie Romanes*, 5 vols (Tübingen and Basel, 1993), V, pp. 323–37; Punzi, *Tristano. Storia di un mito*, pp. 151–63.

[49] Delcorno Branca, 'Le storie arturiane', pp. 390–2.

[50] F. Cardini, 'Concetto di cavalleria e mentalità cavalleresca nei romanzi e nei cantari fiorentini', in D. Rugiadini (ed.), *I ceti dirigenti nella Toscana tardo comunale* (Florence, 1983), pp. 157–92.

[51] G. Savino, 'Ignoti frammenti di un *Tristano* dugentesco', *Studi di Filologia Italiana*, 37 (1979), 5–17.

[52] Delcorno Branca, *Romanzi italiani*, p. 173; S. Guida, 'Sulle "fonti" della *Tavola Ritonda*', in *Umanità e Storia. Scritti in onore di Adelchi Attisani* (Messina, 1971), II, pp. 129–55, on pp. 145–6.

[53] E. G. Parodi, *Il Tristano Riccardiano* (Bologna, 1896).

[54] I discuss below the conservative *R* redaction – Parodi's own term for the four manuscripts he was editing (p. lxv) – free of later interpolations by scribes and adapters, which after developing in Tuscany and the Veneto subsequently appeared in Iberian and Slavic versions.

[55] G. Folena, 'Ernesto Giacomo Parodi', *LI*, 14 (1962), 395–420; A. Scolari, 'Sulla lingua del *Tristano Riccardiano*', *MR*, 13 (1988), 75–89, on 85–7.

[56] Scolari, 'Sulla lingua'; Parodi (ed.), *Ricc.*, pp. cxxix–ccx.

[57] G. Holtus, 'La "matière de Bretagne" en Italie: quelques réflexions sur la transposition du vocabulaire et des structures sociales', in *Actes du 14ème Congrès International Arthurien* (Rennes, 1985), I, pp. 324–45.

[58] Delcorno Branca, *Romanzi italiani*, pp. 120–1; M.-J. Heijkant, 'L'emploi des formules d'introduction et de transition stéréotypées dans le *Tristano Riccardiano*', in K. Busby and E. Kooper (eds), *Courtly Literature: Culture and Context* (Amsterdam and Philadelphia, 1990), pp. 271–82.

[59] M. Dardano, 'Il *Tristano Riccardiano* e la *Tavola Ritonda*', in *Lingua e tecnica narrativa nel Duecento* (Rome, 1969), pp. 222–48. On the various literary evaluations of the text, see F. R. Psaki (trans. and intro.), *Tristano Riccardiano* (Cambridge, 2006), pp. xiii–xvi.

[60] Recent published editions are *Tristano Riccardiano*, rpt Parodi, intro. Heijkant (Parma, 1991) and A. Scolari (ed.), *Il romanzo di Tristano* (Genoa, 1990); the latter was republished in Psaki (trans.), *Tristano Riccardiano*.

[61] *TLI*, p. 70.

[62] M.-J. Heijkant, 'L'assedio della città di Gippi nel *Tristano Riccardiano*', in G. Angeli and L. Formisano (eds), *L'imaginaire courtois et son double* (Naples, 1992), pp. 323–31.

[63] M.-J. Heijkant, 'Iseut aux Blanches Mains dans le *Tristano Riccardiano*. Le motif de l'*homme entre deux femmes* et le motif de la *femme abandonée*', *Tristania*, 16 (1995), 63–76. For the influence of courtly literature on Boccaccio, see Delcorno Branca, *Boccaccio e le storie di re Artù* (Bologna, 1991).

[64] M.-J. Heijkant, '"E' ti saluto con amore". Messaggi amorosi epistolari nella letteratura arturiana in Italia', *MR*, 23 (1999), 277–98.

[65] A, Scolari, 'Volgarizzamenti e intertestualità. Il sogno erotico di Pallamides', in M. Bonafin (ed.), *Intertestualità: Materiali di lavoro del Centro di ricerche in scienza della letteratura* (Genoa, 1986), pp. 89–100.

[66] This is the judgement of R. Morosini, '"Prose di romanzi" . . . or novelle? A Note on Adaptations of "franceschi romanzi." The Case of the *Tristano Riccardiano* and the *Novellino*', *Tristania*, 22 (2003), 23–48.

[67] Heijkant, *La tradizione*, pp. 287–312.

[68] Cardini, 'Concetto di cavalleria'. Such features will be developed further in the *Tavola Ritonda*, in which a new spirit of pragmatism and realism, based on the ideals of *libertas*, *civilitas* and *urbanitas*, reach maturity. On this concept, see Delcorno Branca, *Romanzi italiani*; Krauss, 'Der Artus-Roman in Italien'; and Chapter 4 of the present volume.

[69] D. Limongi, 'Le maculature della Biblioteca Nazionale Centrale di Firenze', *Accademie e Biblioteche*, 59 (1991), 18–61, on 55–7; and G. Allaire, 'Un nuovo frammento del *Tristano* in prosa (Biblioteca Nazionale Centrale di Firenze, ms. Nuovi Acquisti 1329, maculatura 44)', *LI*, 53 (2001), 257–77.

[70] Cigni, 'La ricezione medievale', p. 79; M. Infurna (ed.), *La Inchiesta del San Gradale* (Florence, 1993), pp. 80–3.

[71] This section is followed by two autonomous and anonymous love letters, the first from a lady and the second from her lover, paraphrasing Guittone d'Arezzo's famous letter *Alla Donna Compiuta*, in C. Margueron (ed.), *Guittone d'Arezzo, Lettere* (Bologna, 1990), pp. 87–8.

[72] M. Infurna, 'La *Queste del Saint Graal* in Italia e il manoscritto udinese', in *La grant Queste*, pp. 49–57.

[73] D. Delcorno Branca, 'La tradizione della *Mort Artu* in Italia', *Critica del testo*, 7/1 (2004), 317–39, on 327–8.

[74] Cigni, 'La ricezione medievale', p. 88.

[75] Delcorno Branca, 'La tradizione della *Mort Artu*', 333.

[76] Heijkant, 'La compilation du *Tristano Panciatichiano*', in B. Besamusca et al. (eds), *Cyclification: The Development of Narrative Cycles in the Chansons de Geste and the Arthurian Romances* (Amsterdam, 1994), pp. 122–6.

[77] This episode is from the Turin fragment of Thomas's *Tristan*. The annotations from a thirteenth-century Italian hand reveal that the manuscript has perhaps reached Tuscany by that period; see L. Fontanella and A. Vitale-Brovarone, 'Due frammenti francesi all'Accademia delle Scienze di Torino: L'*Estoire du Graal* e il *Tristano* torinese', in A. Cornagliotti et al. (eds), *Miscellanea di Studi romanzi offerta a Giuliano Gasca Queirazza per il suo 65° compleanno*, 2 vols (Alessandria, 1988), I, pp. 299–314.

[78] P. Michon, 'L'épisode de la folie de Tristan dans le *Tristano Panciatichiano*', *Le Moyen Âge*, 101 (1995), 461–73.

[79] Delcorno Branca, 'Per la storia del *Tristan*', 224.

[80] Heijkant, 'Tristan "pilosus": la folie de l'héros dans le *Tristano Panciatichiano*', in A. Crépin and W. Spiewok (eds), *Tristan-Tristrant: Mélanges en l'honneur de Danielle Buschinger à l'occasion de son 60ème anniversaire* (Greifswald, 1996), pp. 231–42.

[81] Heijkant, review of Allaire (ed. and trans.), *Il Tristano panciatichiano*, in *Romance Philology*, 58 (2004), 136–47, on 142–3.

[82] Other differences from BnF, MS fr. 757 contradict Allaire's hypothesis that MS fr. 757 may have been *Panc.*'s main source (Allaire [ed.], *Il Tristano panciatichiano*, p. 7).

[83] Baumgartner, *La harpe et l'épée*, p. 95.

[84] M. Saksa, 'Cavalleria e iconografia', in F. Cardini and I. Gagliardi (eds), *La civiltà cavalleresca e l'Europa* (Pisa, 2007), pp. 139–58.

[85] Delcorno Branca, 'Per la storia del *Tristan*', p. 226.

[86] Bertolucci Pizzorusso, 'L'arpa d'Isotta', pp. 115–16.

[87] Parodi (ed.), *Ricc.*, p. xi–xix.

[88] Savino, 'Ignoti frammenti'.

[89] G. Paradisi and A. Punzi, 'La tradizione del *Tristan*', and 'Il *Tristano* dell'Archivio Storico di Todi. Edizione', *Critica del testo*, 5 (2002), 541–66.

[90] Gloria Allaire is preparing a transcription and English translation of this exemplar.

[91] M. Corti, 'Emiliano e veneto nella tradizione manoscritta del *Fiore di Virtù*', *Studi di Filologia Italiana*, 18 (1960), 29–68.

[92] A. Donadello (ed.), *Il libro di messer Tristano ('Tristano Veneto')* (Venice, 1994), pp. 44–5.

[93] Donadello (ed.), *Tris. Ven.*, §353, p. 597.

[94] Infurna, 'La *Queste del Saint Graal*', pp. 54–5.

[95] F. Cigni, *Il romanzo arturiano di Rustichello da Pisa* (Pisa, 1994), §§40–52; idem, 'Roman de Tristan in prosa e Compilazione di Rustichello da Pisa in area veneta. A proposito di una recente edizione', *LI*, 47 (1995), 598–622, on 611–2.

[96] *TLI*, pp. 180, 192.

[97] 'La caratteristica di questi cavalieri erranti, autentici pretoriani di Artù, è la vendicatività, lo spirito di casta, la difesa delle ragioni di "famiglia".' (Introduction to Donadello edn of *Tris. Ven.*, p. 23.)

[98] On the Pisa–Genoa manuscripts, see Cigni, 'Una recente edizione', 613; on Panc., see Parodi (ed.), *Ricc.*, pp. cxxiv–v.

[99] *TLI*, pp. 67–8.

[100] Donadello (ed.), *Tris. Ven.*, §§560–1; R. Brusegan, 'Les insertions lyriques dans les *Tristan* italiens. Le lai en Italie au Moyen Âge', in Harf-Lancner et al. (eds), *Des Tristan en vers au Tristan en prose*, pp. 63–83. On Iseut's *lai mortel*, see T. Fotitch, *Les lais du roman de Tristan en prose d'après le manuscrit de Vienne 2545. Edition critique* (Munich, 1974), pp. 120–2, and G. Bertoni, 'I *lais* del romanzo in prosa di Tristano', *StM*, 2 (1929), 140–51, on 145.

[101] Delcorno Branca, *Boccaccio e le storie*, p. 23.

[102] D. Delcorno Branca, 'I cantari di Tristano', *LI*, 23 (1971), 289–305, on 297–300.

[103] R. Trachsler, 'Il tema della *Mort le roi Marc* nella letteratura romanza', *MR*, 19 (1994), 253–75.

[104] C. Alvar and J. M. Lucía Megías, 'Hacia el códice del *Tristán de Leonís* (cincuenta y nueve nuevos fragmentos manuscritos en la Biblioteca Nacional de Madrid)', *Revista de Literatura Medieval*, 11

(1999), 9–135, on 133–5; L. Soriano Robles, '"E qui vol saver questa ystoria, leçia lo libro de miser Lanciloto": a vueltas con el final original del *Tristan en prosa* castellano', *SMV*, 49 (2003), 203–17; M. L. Cuesta Torre, 'La venganza por la muerte de Tristán: la reconstrucción de un episodio del *Tristán* castellano medieval del ms. de Madrid a la luz de sus paralelos con versiones francesas e italianas y con el *Tristán el Joven* de 1534', in A. Chas Aguión and C. Tato García (eds), *'Siempre soy quien ser solía'. Estudios de literatura española medieval en homenaje a Carmen Parilla* (A Coruña, 2009), pp. 83–106.

[105] This fragment has been edited by A. Stussi, *Zibaldone da Canal: Manoscritto mercantile del sec. XIV* (Venice, 1967), pp. 73–5; and translated by J. E. Dotson (ed. and trans.), *Merchant Culture in Fourteenth-Century Venice: The Zibaldone da Canal* (Binghamton, NY, 1994), pp. 125–7.

[106] R. Tagliani (ed.), *Il Tristano Corsiniano. Edizione critica* (Rome, 2011) gives this dating.

[107] R. Tagliani, 'Una prospettiva veneziana per il *Tristano Corsiniano*, *MR*, 32 (2008), 303–32, and 'La lingua del *Tristano Corsiniano*', *Rendiconti dell'Istituto Lombardo, Accademia di Scienze e Lettere*, 142 (2008), 157–296. Allaire's edition with English translation is forthcoming (Boydell).

[108] M. Galasso (ed.), *Il Tristano Corsiniano* (Cassino, 1937), p. 21; G. Allaire, 'An Overlooked Italian Manuscript: The *Tristano Corsiniano*', *Tristania*, 24 (2006), 37–50, on 39–40.

[109] E. Cozzi, 'Per la diffusione dei temi cavallereschi e profani nella pittura tardogotica. Breve viaggio nelle Venezie, tra scoperte e restauri recenti', in E. Castelnuovo (ed.), *Le Stanze di Artù. Gli affreschi di Frugarolo e l'immaginario cavalleresco nell'autunno del Medioevo* (Milan, 1999), pp. 116–27, on pp. 123–4; L. Battaglia Ricci, 'Frammenti di storie dipinte', in G. Ganzer (ed.), *Le favolose historie di Palazzo Ricchieri. Testimonianze tardogotiche nei soffitti lignei di Pordenone* (Pordenone, 2008), pp. 51–65 and 93–115.

[110] Delcorno Branca, 'Per la storia del *Tristan*', 220–2.

[111] *TLI*, pp. 102–3.

[112] Cigni, 'Una recente edizione', 614–20.

[113] Benedetti, '"Qua fa' un santo"', pp. 44–5.

[114] Delcorno Branca, *Romanzi italiani*, pp. 36–7; 'Cantari di Tristano', 294 n. 14.

[115] D. Delcorno Branca, 'Dal romanzo alla novella e viceversa. Il caso dei testi arturiani', in G. Albanese et al. (eds), *Favole–Parabole–Istorie. Le forme della scrittura novellistica dal Medioevo al Rinascimento* (Rome, 2000), pp. 133–50.

[116] A. Del Monte (ed.), *Conti di antichi cavalieri* (Milan, 1972), pp. 149–55.

[117] *TLI*, pp. 228–32.

[118] G. E. Sansone (ed.), Francesco da Barberino, *Reggimento e costumi di donna* (Turin, 1957), pp. 355–8.

[119] Delcorno Branca, 'Dal romanzo alla novella', pp. 140–2.

[120] *TLI*, pp. 119–26.

[121] *TLI*, pp. 131–5.

[122] Allaire (ed.), *Il Tristano panciatichiano*, p. 8.

[123] See also Delcorno Branca, 'Cantari di Tristano'; and Cigni, 'Tristano e Isotta', pp. 113–15. On all the Arthurian *cantari* and related criticism, see Chapter 6 in this volume.

[124] F. Cigni, 'Un nuovo testimone del cantare *Ultime imprese e morte di Tristano*', *SMV*, 43 (1997), 131–91.

[125] R. Trachsler, *Clôtures du cycle arthurien. Etude et textes* (Geneva, 1996), p. 173.

[126] Delcorno Branca, 'Cantari di Tristano', 298–9.

[127] D. Delcorno Branca, 'Il cavaliere dalle armi incantate: circolazione di un modello narrativo arturiano', *GSLI*, 159 (1982), 353–82; and *TLI*, pp. 201–23.

[128] E. Sgambati (ed.), *Il Tristano Biancorusso* (Florence, 1983), pp. 51–2.

[129] Delcorno Branca, 'Cantari di Tristano', 301–5.

[130] On these visual artifacts and the history of their study, see Chapter 13 in this volume.

[131] Heijkant, *La tradizione*, p. 123. On the coats of arms mentioned in chivalric romances, see Cardini, 'Concetto di cavalleria', pp. 165–6.

[132] M.-J. Heijkant, 'Le *Tristano Riccardiano*, une version particulière du *Tristan en prose*', in C. Foulon et al. (eds), *Actes du 14ème Congrès International Arthurien*, 2 vols (Rennes, 1985), I, pp. 314–23; and *La tradizione*.

[133] My *sigla* follow Parodi edn, *Ricc.*

[134] G. Northup (ed.), *El Cuento de Tristán de Leonís, edited from the unique manuscript Vatican 6428* (Chicago, 1928); M. L. Cuesta Torre (ed.), *Tristán de Leonís (Valladolid, Juan der Burgos, 1501)* (Alcalá de Henares, 1999).

[135] The Iberian evidence has been examined by E. Ros Domingo, *Arthurische Literatur der Romania: Die iberoromanischen Fassungen des Tristanromans und ihre Beziehungen zu den französischen und italienischen Versionen* (Bern, 2001). For the edited Castilian fragments, see Alvar and Lucía Megías, 'Hacia el códice'.

[136] Ros Domingo, *Arthurische Literatur*, pp. 476–83.

[137] S. Iragui, 'The Southern Versions of the Prose *Tristan*: The Italo-Iberian Translations and their French Source', *Tristania*, 17 (1996), 39–54, on 48.

[138] Heijkant, review of Ros Domingo, *Arthurische Literatur*, in *Estudis Romànics*, 26 (2004), 384–9, on 389.

[139] Soriano Robles, '"E qui vol saver"'; Cuesta Torre, 'La venganza'.

[140] M. Sgambati, 'Note sul *Tristano Bielorusso*', *Ricerche Slavistiche*, 24–6 (1977–9), 33–53; and B. Lomagistro, 'Tristano e Isotta nelle letterature slave', in M. Dallapiazza (ed.), *Tristano e Isotta*, pp. 175–88.

[141] Heijkant, *La tradizione*, p. 57.

[142] H. L. Sharrer, 'Malory and the Spanish and Italian Tristan Texts: The Search for the Missing Link', *Tristania*, 4 (1979), 36–41

[143] Heijkant, *La tradizione*, pp. 125–32.

[144] Baumgartner and Roussineau presume instead that the hatred between the two families was created by Luce del Gat. See Baumgartner, *Tristan en prose*, p. 42; Bogdanow, *Romance of the Grail*, pp. 20–1; G. Roussineau, 'Remarques sur les relations entre la *Suite du Roman de Merlin* et sa continuation et le *Tristan en prose*', in J. C. Faucon et al. (eds), *Miscellanea Mediaevalia*, II, pp. 1149–62.

[145] *TLI*, pp. 181–4.

[146] This is an element typical of *R*, present in the Italian texts and not only the Spanish translations as Soriano Robles had maintained ('"E que le daria"', p. 324). The stepmother's third attempt is found not only in *Ricc.* but also in MS Ricc. 1729 and *Panc.*

[147] Cigni pointed out that, in the thirteenth century, a district of Pisa was called '*La Spina*' (review of Heijkant, *La tradizione*, *SMV*, 36 [1990], 267–78, on 274).

[148] Cuesta Torre, *Aventuras amorosas y caballerescas en las novellas de Tristán* (León, 1994).

[149] Iragui, 'The Southern Versions'.

[150] C. Alvar, '*Tristanes* italianos y *Tristanes* castellanos', in F. Cigni and M. P. Betti (eds), *Testi, generi e tradizioni nella Romània medievale*, special issue of *SMV*, 47 (2001), 57–75.

[151] Ros Domingo, *Arthurische Literatur*, and his 'Gallica, Italica, Hispanica. Anmerkungen zu einer umstrittenen Dreiecksbeziehung. Zur Theorie des italienischen Ursprungs der spanischen Fassungen des Tristanromans', in P. Wunderli et al. (eds), *Italica – Raetica – Gallica. Studia linguarum litterarum in honorem Ricarda Liver* (Tübingen and Basel, 2001), pp. 655–77.

[152] Parodi (ed.), *Ricc.*, p. lxxxvii; G. Northup, 'The Italian Origin of the Spanish Prose Tristram Versions', *Romanic Review*, 3 (1912), 194–222, on 197.

[153] *TLI*, p. 103.

4

THE ITALIAN CONTRIBUTION: *LA TAVOLA RITONDA*

Daniela Delcorno Branca

The *Tavola Ritonda* (Round Table) has an incontestable claim to be the only real Arthurian romance of the Italian Middle Ages. Italian offers many translations and reworkings of the great French prose romances, but in my view they are of mainly linguistic or philological interest, useful for determining which texts and versions were circulating alongside the many codices in North French copied by Italian scribes.[1] In general they do not boast a narrative outline that is original with respect to their models; even the better attempts, such as the *Tristano Riccardiano* and the *Tristano Corsiniano*, are limited to a subset of the episodes of the *Roman de Tristan*. The *Tav. Rit.*, by contrast, represents a holistic attempt to assemble into a single romance the entire Arthurian cycle, from Uther Pendragon to the *Mort Artu*, with Tristan as its focus. The *Tav. Rit.* proposes its own interpretation of the chivalric world, one inflected by religious and civic ideals and able to respond to the tastes and expectations of both urban audiences and of the *signorie* of the Po Valley, as the complex history of its diffusion and its adaptations shows.

The *Tavola Ritonda*: Witnesses and Editions

The conventional title *Tavola Ritonda* refers to a Tuscan prose romance most likely composed in the first half of the fourteenth century. Doubtless owing to its exceptional narrative and stylistic merits, it enjoyed a wide circulation as well as a lasting success from the fourteenth to the seventeenth centuries.[2] Other Arthurian versions composed in Italian – whether preserved in single manuscripts (*Ricc.*, *Panc.*, *Tris. Ven.*, *Tristano Corsiniano*) or in fragments (*Zibaldone da Canal* and others) – were not similarly successful.

The *Tav. Rit.* survives in ten manuscripts, one incomplete and another fragmentary, as follows:[3]

Florence, Bibl. Medicea Laurenziana:
MS Plut. XLIII, 10 (=**L¹**). Dated 1447. Florentine, copied by Antonio di Taddeo Mancini.
MS Plut. XLIV, 27 (=**L**). Second half of fourteenth century. Florentine.
Florence, Bibl. Nazionale Centrale:
MS II.II.68 (=**M**). Dated 1391. Florentine.

MS Palatino latino 556 (=**P¹**). Dated 1446. Lombard area (Cremona–Mantua), copied by Zuliano de Anzoli of Cremona.

MS Palatino latino 564 (=**P²**). Fifteenth century. Umbrian area (Perugia).

Florence, Bibl. Riccardiana:

MS Ricc. 2283 (=**R**). Sixteenth century. Florentine.

Padua, Bibl. Universitaria:

MS 609 (fragment). Second half of fourteenth century. Northern Italy. A fragment preserved in Udine, Bibl. Arcivescovile, MS 86 originates from this same codex.[4]

Siena, Bibl. Comunale:

MS I.VII.13 (=**S**). Dated 1478. Siena area, copied by Daniello di Gheri Bolgarini.

Vatican City, Bibl. Apostolica Vaticana:

MS Vat. lat. 6789. Dated 1422. Verona area, copied by Ventura de Cerutis. Partial: fols 57v–59v recount the episode of the return to Cornwall and the deaths of Tristan and Iseut.[5]

MS Urbinate lat. 953 (=**U**). Early seventeenth century. Florentine.

Of the ten manuscript witnesses, three date from the second half of the fourteenth century (**L**, **M**, Padua/Udine); five from the fifteenth century (**L¹**, **P¹**, **P²**, **S**, Vat. lat. 6789); one from the sixteenth century (**R**); and one from the seventeenth (**U**). The two latest codices (**U** is copied from **M**) reflect the particular interests of the sixteenth- and seventeenth-century scholars of the Italian language associated with the *Vocabolario della Crusca*; these early philologists had identified the *Tav. Rit.* as an invaluable source for examples of medieval Tuscan.[6] The geographical spread of these textual witnesses, as we shall see, entails not only a variety of redactions but also a spectrum of linguistic coloration. The manuscripts come from Florence (**L**, **L¹**, **M**, **R**, **U**); Siena (**S**); the region between Cremona and Mantua (**P¹**); the Veneto (MS Vat. lat. 6789 and the Padua and Udine fragments); and Umbria (**P²**). The title *Tavola Ritonda* reflects the undoubtedly cyclical narrative ambitions of the prologue, which opens thus:

> Let it be clear to you, lords and good people, that this book briefly recounts and treats and relates great battles and fine acts of chivalry and noble tournaments which took place at the time of King Uther Pendragon and of the great lords of the Old Table, three hundred years and more after the passion of our Lord Jesus Christ, son of God the Father, the true and living and eternal spirit. And this book also treats and relates the great adventures and noble tournaments that occurred at the time of King Arthur, son of King Uther Pendragon, and of the valorous knights of the New Table, especially Sir Tristan and Sir Lancelot and Sir Palamedes and Sir Galahad and indeed all the other knights errant who belonged to the company of the Round Table, and also all the other knights of distant lands, who were testing themselves in deeds of arms at that time. And this book also tells me of the high Quest of the Holy Grail, and how by that undertaking the aforementioned Table was destroyed, and how it failed because of the sin and the fault of certain knights.[7]

In fact, however, the text narrates the story of Tristan according to the version of the French prose romance which circulated throughout Italy; this Tristan story is framed by episodes relating to the Old Table of Uther Pendragon (from *Guiron*), Lancelot's youth (*Lancelot*) and the tragic epilogue of the *Mort Artu*. Tristan of Cornwall was by far the favourite hero in the Italian tradition, and the success of the *Tristan en prose* had eclipsed the other versions of his tale in Italy. This gave rise to a proliferation of copies in French, as well as of translations and adaptations in Italian, both of which circulated in Italy.[8] The *Tav. Rit.* also incorporates sections from other major Arthurian prose romances as a complement to a clearly 'Tristanocentric' narration, as if to guarantee a dimension of cyclical completeness desired and expected by its Italian audience.

The spike of sixteenth- and seventeenth-century interest in the text for the purposes of linguistic investigation is attested by the gleanings of Leonardo Salviati and by the citations in the *Vocabolario della Crusca*.[9] After that time, the *Tav. Rit.* would have to wait until the mid-nineteenth century for a critical edition, published by Filippo-Luigi Polidori in 1864.[10] Although the text presented in that edition forms the basis of most studies and analyses to the present day, it is philologically flawed: it blithely uses a later codex, **S**, alongside **M** and **L**, while ignoring **L**[1] and failing to check against other witnesses. Beyond its philological defects, however, the Polidori edition is especially problematic in that it presents a peculiar version, which contains additions and modifications; because of Polidori's edition, that reading is still identified today as representative of the romance itself. The period of intense scholarship that followed Parodi's 1896 edition of the *Tristano Riccardiano* has established with increasing clarity the richness and complexity of the Italian tradition of the *Tristan en prose*. Scholars have focused especially on the transmission history and the attested traditions, also using the *Tav. Rit.* for this purpose.[11] It has become clear that the *Tav. Rit.* has come down to us through various redactions subsequent to the hypothetical original (which I call *Tav. Rit. X*), all corresponding to different geographical areas.[12] Based on extant manuscripts, we can confidently identify a fourteenth-century Tuscan redaction which was produced in Florence and Siena (*Tav. Polidori*); a Po Valley–Veneto version (**P**[1]); and an Umbrian version (**P**[2]).[13] The Po–Veneto and the Umbrian versions are preserved in two fifteenth-century manuscripts, BNCF, MSS Pal. 556 and Pal. 564, respectively. An edition of **P**[1] appeared in 2009,[14] while the characteristics of **P**[2] have only been illustrated in a sampling of published excerpts.[15] Each of these textual witnesses presents its own additions and modifications and, at the same time, preserves older passages that have been suppressed in the other redactions.

At this point we must ask what the primary features of *Tav. Rit. X* (the original text) were, and whether it is possible to outline its characteristics. These are problems well known to scholars of the great French prose Arthurian romances and of their layers of adaptations. The task is delicate and exacting, but it is precisely this comparison between the surviving versions and the other Tristan versions that circulated in Italy that reveals a strong authorial personality capable of structuring and reformulating the polymorphous Arthurian material in an original fashion, consonant with its Italian context.[16] Far from being a deformation of the tradition, the successive redactions ultimately confirm the narrative vitality of that tradition. In the next two sections of this chapter, I will examine the content and characteristics of the *Tav. Rit.* based on those elements that can be determined to belong to the hypothetical original (again, *Tav. Rit. X*). In the final section, I will discuss the characteristics of individual redactions.[17]

Content and Sources

After the ambitious promises of his prologue, the *Tav. Rit.* author attempts to suture the adventures of the knights of the Old Table – that is, of the generation of Uther Pendragon – to those of the knights of King Arthur's time, in a kind of synoptic plot. The opening revisits Uther's tournament and the adventure of Guiron the Courtly, who was deceived by the wicked maiden, and summarizes the adventure of the Old Knight, the same episode that opens the Arthurian Compilation of Rustichello da Pisa (I–II).[18] The scenes that follow include Tristan's genealogy (incomplete and abbreviated); the deeds of King Mark and Meliadus, who has here become an ally of Galehaut in the war against Arthur; Lancelot's youthful exploits and his love for Guinevere; the war and ensuing peace between Arthur and Galehaut, sealed by Meliadus's marriage to a maiden of the lineage of King Ban (III–IX). From ch. XII on, after using narrative material from *Guiron* and *Lancelot*, *Tav. Rit.* shifts decisively to narrating the story of Tristan. As has been clearly shown,[19] *Tav. Rit.* draws on the specific redaction of the *Tristan en prose* which circulated in Italy (and which is also attested in the Spanish versions).[20] This redaction, identified as *R*, is represented above all by the *Ricc.* (preserved in Florence, Bibl. Riccardiana, MS Ricc. 2543), and partially by other versions.[21] The *Ricc.* contains the Tristan material only from his birth up until the episode of Darnantes (Lös. §74a); it was most likely limited to the hero's youth, his first successful exploits, his love for Iseut, his conflict with King Mark, his marriage to Iseut of the White Hands, and finally his liberation of Arthur in Darnantes, when his valour becomes officially known to the Arthurian court. All of this material is found in *Tav. Rit.* XII–LXIII[1], with some recourse to the *Tristan en prose*.

Perhaps because the *R* model breaks off, the second part of the *Tav. Rit.* is considerably more free and composite. This section draws again – before the obligatory episode of the lovers' death (CXXVI[2]–CXXXIII) – on the central section of the *Tristan en prose*, in particular from version V.I.[22] It relates the madness of Tristan; his adventures once he has been banished from Cornwall; his encounter with Lamorat at the Chastel Cruel; the counterfeit shield and the tournament of Roche Dure (LXVIII–LXXXII). It then narrates Tristan and Iseut's journey to Joyous Guard; the tournament of Louvezerp; and the related sections devoted to the lively presence of Dinadan (LXXXVIII–XCIX). This section, which precedes the introduction of the

Queste del Saint Graal material, is considerably altered, especially by the insertion of episodes that are found in other parts of the *Tristan*: the giant Lucanor (LXXIV); Hervis li Aspres (LXXVI); the victory of Tristan over Caradoc (LXXXIII–LXXXVI); the enmity between Lancelot and Tristan provoked by the Vallet à la Cotte Maltailliée and later by Gauvain (C–CV). In this same, structurally open, section, we find the conspicuous presence of newly invented episodes introducing fabulous characters known to an Italian audience, such as the Gaia Donzella (Cheerful Damsel), daughter of Morgan le Fay (LXXX),[23] and the treacherous sorceress who sends the knight with the enchanted armour (LXXXVII).[24] Other innovations include novellistic comic variations on the character of Dinadan (LXXV, LXXXIX, XCIII[1]), or the enchantments of the Lady of the Lake (CV–CVII). These innovative elements, as we will see, prompted later compilers to modify the narrative material further.

Chapters CVIII–CXXI are dedicated to the Grail Quest, in which Tristan takes part, as he had in the *Tristan en prose*. The story is recounted succinctly: Galahad's arrival at court; the appearance of the Grail; the adventures of the chosen three, Bors, Perceval and Galahad; the sacred rite at Corbenic; the conclusion of the Quest. We cannot exclude the use of the Post-Vulgate *Queste*, known to our author and well disseminated throughout Italy;[25] however, the *Tav. Rit.* seems here to follow closely the text of the *Queste* rather than the version inserted in the *Tristan*.[26] The portion of the *Tav. Rit.* that is dedicated to the Quest is also marked by the prominent insertion of new episodes, in particular the adventure of the Cavaliere Fellone (Wicked Knight). The aim of these episodes is principally to illustrate the problem of the chivalric supremacy disputed among Galahad, Tristan and Lancelot (CXI–CXII and CXIII[2]–CXV). It is no accident that the emblematic duel between Tristan and Lancelot at Merlin's Stone (CXIII[1]) is placed in this section, specifically to promote the comparison of the two major heroes.[27]

With the return of Tristan to Cornwall, the trap set for the two lovers and their death, the final portion of the romance (CXXII–CXXXIII) for the most part follows the *Tristan en prose*, although the author includes two amplifications centred on the treacherous Breus and on the damsel imprisoned by a terrible snake. The author also presents his own original version of the two lovers' death, as we shall see below.

As the prologue had promised, the next episode recounts the vengeance taken for Tristan's death by Arthur and Lancelot (CXXXIV–CXXXVII). This episode, attested only later and in a different form in the French texts, is characteristic rather of the Italian and Spanish traditions.[28] Aside from the *cantare* and the epilogue – probably added – of *Tris. Ven.*,[29] which concur, the material returns in varied form in the *Tav. Rit.*, in the Castilian fragments, and in the later variations of the *Innamoramento de Tristano* by Niccolò degli Agostini (published 1515 and 1520; see Chapter 7 in this volume).

The epilogue recounts the destruction of the Round Table according to *La Mort Artu* or, as seems more likely, to the Post-Vulgate *Queste*.[30] Only a few salient episodes are recalled: the ambush of Lancelot by Gawain and his brothers; Guinevere's abduction and her return; Arthur's war against Lancelot; his duel with Gawain and the latter's death; the treachery of Mordred; Arthur's wounding and healing by Morgan le Fay; Lancelot's vengeance on Mordred; Guinevere's death (not in a convent, and in Lancelot's presence); Lancelot's retreat to the hermitage and his death (CXXXVIII–CXLV).

Narrative Features and the Historical-Cultural Context

By comparing the various witnesses of *Tav. Rit.*, first as a group and then with the *Tristan en prose* and the Italian versions, we can identify as accurately as possible the characteristics of this text.[31] The *Tav. Rit.* author, unlike those of *Tris. Ven.* and *Panc.*, is anything but a passive translator.[32] More like the redactor of his problematic model (*Ricc.*), he tends to renew and reinterpret the Tristan story according to the expectations and mindset of his audience, certainly urban and mercantile. This audience had an appetite for alternative paradigms of the chivalric ideal, and for escape into the marvellous and the fantastic. This same audience, however, was also concretely interested in the 'historical', pragmatic and behavioural aspects of the Arthurian world.[33]

As my summary has shown, the author has a good mastery of the Arthurian texts: he draws not only on the *R* version but also on the French prose romance (reintroducing for example part of the protagonist's genealogy) as well as on *Guiron*, *Lancelot*, the *Queste* and *La Mort Artu* (these last two most likely in the Post-Vulgate version). His most striking quality, however, is his ability to arrange and combine episodes and traditional elements with material either newly invented or drawn from secondary traditions. In this way Ferragunze, tutor to Tristan's mother Eliabel, is introduced early on (X–XI) as a counterpart to the later role of Governal, tutor to Tristan himself. Ferragunze is an example of wisdom and *mesure*, based on both experience and on the biblical Proverbs: his boasts (that he is noble, does not fear his enemies, is not jealous of his wife, never allows himself to get drunk) are all carefully demonstrated. This is a reprise – with novellistic and fabliau-like variations – of the tradition of *gabs* or vaunts common in the chivalric tradition (*Le Pelèrinage Charlemagne*, for example), in a form particularly close to *Les Voeux de Baudoin*.[34] Arthur's war against Galehaut is reworked according to the demands of the Tristan plot, so that Meliadus becomes an ally of Galehaut (thus creating a generational gap between Tristan and Lancelot). The peace between the two opponents is solemnly sealed by Tristan's father's marriage to Eliabel, who is Lancelot's cousin. Only in passing does the author mention the consummation of Lancelot and Guinevere's love (XI[2]), while the mediating role of Galehaut goes unmentioned.[35] Conversely, adding the amusing storyline of Ferragunze not only varies the slightly repetitive nature of the previous conflicts, but seems almost to compensate for the abbreviated genealogy of Tristan, providing him with a background of 'common' exemplarity (though one, we must note, with a patent of nobility) worthy of Ferragunze and his wife Verseria, who instruct his mother. Placing this model of wisdom in the opening section seems to suggest the work's utility for contemporary readers who belong to the Tuscan communal context rather than to a courtly one.

The most notable additions are the episodes of a more fabulous kind, which are nonetheless always introduced using deft connective tissue and for a specific purpose. Although the narrative technique of *entrelacement* is substantially simplified in *Tav. Rit.*, as in Arthurian texts in Italy in general,[36] it has still informed the way in which our author inserts these new elements.

The traditional motif of the enemy knight armed with magical or demonic weapons is introduced as a consequence of one of Tristan's most noted adventures: his liberation of Arthur from the enchantress of Darnantes. This enemy knight places the Arthurian court in extreme danger by defeating all its best champions, until he himself is defeated by Tristan, the hero *par excellence*.[37] The malevolent sorceress who sends the dreaded knight Lasancis, armed with a magic lance, is in fact identified as the mother of the slain enchantress, who is seeking revenge (LXXXVII). The traditional adventure is however completely transformed so as to exalt the protagonist Tristan, a goal which comprises the most pronounced focus of *Tav. Rit.* Here it is the shrewd Tristan who succeeds in defeating the treacherous Lasancis; in the older tradition, Galahad, forewarned by an angel, had triumphed over his adversary's demons by making the sign of the cross.[38] We can understand the addition of the Cavaliere Fellone (Wicked Knight) episode as an attempt to assimilate Tristan in some way to the three knights chosen for the Grail Quest. Here, as in many other instances, the protagonist not only proves superior to Lancelot, but is also instructed by a hermit and subjected to powerful carnal temptation; this he overcomes with the sign of the cross, analogous to what happens to Perceval in the same context (CXIII²–CXV).[39]

Characters like Morgan and the Lady of the Lake naturally evoke references to, and variations on, fabulous elements. When Tristan is a guest of Morgan, the author makes sure to mention her beautiful daughter the Gaia Donzella (LXXX¹), unknown in the French tradition but a favourite figure in folk tales in Tuscany and the Veneto. As will be recalled later at the encounter of Tristan and Breus, the daughter has been taken from her treacherous mother by her lover Gawain (CXXIV).[40] The Lady of the Lake, unlike her wicked sister Morgan, treats lovers kindly: she gladly rescues the two pairs of lovers (Tristan and Iseut, Lancelot and Guinevere) by the trick of the apparent corpses, so that the lovers can secretly enjoy the delights of love and courtly life within her palace (CV–CVII). This episode, greatly expanded, is the culmination of the famous declaration attributed to Galehaut on the Island of the Giants,[41] and recounted in the *Conti di antichi cavalieri*: "'Whoever had the Queens Iseut and Guinevere and the knights Tristan and Lancelot together, could say that he had all the beauty and goodness of the entire world.'"[42]

Tav. Rit.'s comic dimension also reflects the influence of the original text. Greater attention is given to the quirky character of Dinadan and his role as an anti-chivalric and anti-amorous counterweight. His discourse on Love occurs twice, in two separate passages of the romance: once shortly before Dinadan briefly falls in love with Losanna della Torre Antica (LXXVII; Autine in the prose *Tristan*); and again (as in *Tristan*) immediately before Iseut extends hospitality to the Savio Disamorato (the Wise Man Disabused of Love, an epithet for Dinadan), whom she pretends to want as a champion for her defence (XCIII). But at the first occurrence, which Iseut will later teasingly recall, *Tav. Rit.* introduces an original episode of playful provocation towards Dinadan (LXXV): a beautiful maiden pretends to be in love with him; impersonating her, Tristan concocts a nocturnal surprise, provoking Dinadan's resentful protest. These are lively pages of brisk dialogue, decidedly more akin to the *fabliau* or the *beffa* than to the courtly romance.[43]

The *Tav. Rit.* author, however, does more than merely demonstrate a sound knowledge of the Arthurian narrative material and structures as found in the great French prose romances. Rather, a closer stylistic familiarity seems to emerge from the strategic insertion of epistles and lyric passages on the model of the *lais*,[44] with the purpose of commenting on the characters' emotions or narrative developments, as well as of establishing Tristan's traditional attributes of musician and poet and lover, not to mention those of his beloved pupil Iseut. Similarly, we find a controlled and functional use of transition formulae ('Now the story stops telling of ...') and of deferred explanation ('But if someone were to ask me ...').[45]

Tav. Rit. achieves a version of the Tristan story which has been renewed in terms of style and narrative construction: more brisk and action-oriented,[46] it is tailored to the tastes of a new audience. Furthermore, it presents an original interpretation of the tale of the Cornish hero and of his Arthurian world. Setting aside for the moment the additional textual modifications due to later redactions, it is clear that from its conception, *Tav. Rit.* sought to identify Tristan as the paradigm of the perfect knight. This interpretation of Tristan discards the hesitations and reservations of its model, the *Tristan en prose*, which tends to present Tristan as either equal in prowess to Lancelot, or in a three-way tie with Lancelot and either Galehaut or Galahad.[47] *Tav. Rit.* makes Lancelot a contemporary of Meliadus rather than of Tristan, a distinct generational shift; moreover, the entire Italian romance is sprinkled with minute and regular reminders – especially during tournaments, duels and battles – that Tristan's valour is greater than Lancelot's. This innovative tendency reaches its peak in the final section, when the author intervenes explicitly to affirm that the death of the two lovers occurs 'not because of the embrace, or any other outside force, but from weakness and for very sorrow' (CXXIX). The author thus sets aside the mortal embrace in the *Tristan en prose* (recalled also by Boccaccio)[48] in favour of the death purely for love, already found in Thomas. The mortal embrace could then be read as a contrast to the clearly Christian and virtuous overtones that the Italian author had given to the entire episode

(CXXVII–CXXIX). Tristan pardons King Mark, who had treacherously struck him, and then asks forgiveness in his turn. What follows is Tristan's confession, his prayer to God, and his humble and loving words to his friends and to Iseut. To eliminate any scruple in the reader's mind regarding the adulterous couple, the author reports the indulgence given by not one but two popes to all those who would pray for the lovers' souls, 'sappiendo che loro peccare era stato per opera d'incantamento e no' per altra malvagia volontà' ('knowing that their sin had been caused by enchantment and not by any evil will' [CXXXIII]).

Thus Tristan is pre-eminent not only in valour but also in moral virtue. It is his death, as our author explicitly affirms, that brings about the downfall of the Round Table narrated in the epilogue of the romance (CXXVII). This interpretation of Tristan's knightly perfection corresponds naturally to a civic version of chivalry placed at the service of the community, an interpretation of the Arthurian world that was typical of Italian communal society.[49] In the early thirteenth century, Boncompagno da Signa refers to the widespread phenomenon of urban associations which adopt chivalric customs and names, such as 'de Tabula Rotunda'. This practice was particularly common in Tuscany, where such groups have been documented in several cities, especially Pisa. In various texts, from Armannino Giudice's *Fiorita* to Boccaccio's *De casibus virorum illustrium*, the Arthurian court appears as the ideal model of a civil society.[50] In *Tav. Rit.*, this civic dimension is seen when Tristan offers to challenge Morholt to end a tyrannical tribute and a ceremony of knighthood is described (XVII^2–XVIII^1), and again when both Tristan and Lancelot confront fierce giants in wild and dangerous places in order to restore justice and to free those lands (CX–CXII).

The pragmatic chivalry of this interpretation of the Tristan story is sustained explicitly throughout *Tav. Rit.* by the invocation of an authoritative book defined as 'la fontana di tutti libri e romanzi che si leggano' ('the wellspring of all the books and romances that are read' [CXXVIII]), and the 'Libro della Fontana' ['Book of the Fountain'], *PAL 556*, p. 323). The author invokes this ostensibly written authority whenever he needs to clarify the problematic meaning of inscriptions (XIII^1), images (XXIX^1) or dreams (XXXII and CXXVI), but especially to explain or discuss why the reader is to consider Tristan the best knight (XXXIII, CIX and CXXVIII). Such passages and discussions are entirely without precise parallels in the French texts. We cannot dismiss this putative source text as fictitious, since the author specifies in detail the authoritative sequence of the volume's owners: a certain Viero di Guascogna, followed by Pietro, Count of Savoy, and 'al presente' (presently) Sir Gaddo de' Lanfranchi of Pisa. The French origin of the volume is strongly emphasised; it is described variously as a book 'ritratto dal primo reame di Francia ('drawn from the first kingdom of France', *PAL 556*, p. 105); a book 'trato da prima da quelo dillo re di Franza' ('originally derived from the one owned by the king of France', *PAL 556*, p. 180); a 'bono e grande libro francescho' ('great and good French book', *PAL 556*, p.

323). What it says about at least two of these individuals, Pietro Count of Savoy and Gaddo de' Lanfranchi, corresponds exactly to historical reality.[51] That the author, who writes in the first half of the fourteenth century, consults a French text 'presently' belonging to a member of a noble Pisan family, underscores the extraordinary role this city played in the diffusion of French and especially Arthurian texts during the thirteenth and fourteenth centuries.[52] The fact that the 'libro di Gaddo' is cited in all redactions of *Tav. Rit.* proves that this source was an integral element of the text from the very beginning (*Tav. Rit. X*). Indeed, it is this very 'documentary' characteristic that may have contributed to the success and diffusion of the romance.[53]

Most likely, as Guida has demonstrated,[54] *Tav. Rit.* was a treatise in which questions concerning the characters and situations of chivalric literature were discussed from a moral and theological point of view: it was a kind of *Glossa Ordinaria* that helped to resolve doubts and interpret romance narratives.[55] We may consider a typical example in the passage that discusses the *quattro openioni* (four opinions) concerning who was the best knight:

> . . . because the decision of kings, counts, and barons was that Tristan was certainly the best knight in the world. If you searched among the best, the finest, the most approved, Tristan was first.
>
> However, there were and are four opinions, for those of you who are interested to hear them, and those four opinions are in the wellspring of all the books and romances that are read. This book belonged first to Sir Pietro, Count of Savoy, and was copied from one belonging to the king of France. Now it belongs to Sir Gaddo de' Lanfranchi of Pisa. The book has this to say about the four opinions held: some say the knights of the Old Table were the boldest in the world, and some say Sir Lancelot, and some say Sir Galahad, while others affirm that it was Sir Tristan. The book does not choose among these opinions, but says this: 'It is written that Tristan fought with knights of the Old Table in the Valle Bruna and the Valle Franca, and suffered no dishonor. By force of arms he put to death Sir Brunor the Brown who was the flower of the Old Table, and he killed many giants who were of that same era.'
>
> The second opinion was that Sir Lancelot was the best knight in the world and equal to Sir Tristan, but in our book we do not find a single joust in which Lancelot has the advantage over Tristan, but rather Tristan always has it over Lancelot. Nor, whenever they fought with swords, was it Tristan who asked for respite, no matter how long the encounter might last.
>
> The third opinion is that Sir Galahad was the best knight in the world, and our book affirms this, saying about him, 'He was the best by far in grace, virtue, and the prowess which proceeds from the Holy Spirit. I do not say in secular prowess, which comes from boldness of heart.'
>
> For know that Galahad had in himself a grace more than that of any other knight, and it was through grace that he was called the best knight in the world, and through grace that he conquered in battle. Therefore he is not counted among the knights who fought for the love of ladies and maidens . . .
>
> Therefore our book does set down the decision that Sir Tristan was the best worldly knight and the boldest that nature ever formed, and this is the fourth opinion. (*Tav. Rit.* CXXVIII)

By distinguishing thus between the 'heavenly' chivalry of Galahad (whose prowess is due to divine grace) and the 'worldly' chivalry of knights such as Tristan (who fight for the love of ladies and maidens), the *Tav. Rit.* author can assign to Tristan that undisputed primacy in the chivalric world which he has carefully constructed throughout the romance. That primacy holds not only in duels and tournaments, but in acts of clemency and courtesy going all the way up to Tristan's death, characterised by words and gestures of Christian piety.[56]

Redactions and Circulation

Thus far I have deliberately concentrated on the elements that unquestionably belonged to the original text. Beyond permitting at least a partial reconstruction of the text's original character, the redactions I have identified also document later elaborations and the expansion of readership. I will survey them here, recapitulating the principal conclusions I laid out in *Tristano e Lancillotto in Italia*.[57]

The Tuscan Redaction (*Tavola Polidori*)

The Tuscan redaction (*Tav. Polidori*), datable to the second half of the fourteenth century, is the most widely attested (**L, L¹, M, S, R, U**), and until recently was considered to be the most authoritative text of the romance. It circulated in Florence and Siena among artisans and readers of modest culture. In 1391 the copyist of **M** borrowed the copy 'of Fede the shoemaker and his sons'; Antonio di Taddeo Mancini, the copyist of **L¹** in 1447, also transcribed Dati's *La Sfera*, the *cantare Geta e Birria*, and the vernacular translation of the *Distruzione di Troia*;[58] and in 1478 the Sienese Daniello di Gheri Bolgarini, castellan of Montecchiello and formerly of Rocca di Cetona, copied **S**.[59] The Tuscan redaction fully reflects the spirit and interests of the communal and mercantile class. Only in this text does the character Ferragunze affirm, "'If I boast and say that I am noble, this is not a bad thing; any person who has good manners and habits may be noble, and gentle speech confers nobility.'"[60]

The *Tav. Polidori* contains a series of additions taken from the Thomas and Béroul tradition, even if they are probably not by its elaborator (LXIII–LXVII). These sections include famous episodes: the secret garden meeting where Mark spies upon the lovers; the test of the red-hot iron; the trap of the flour on the bedroom floor. These were already known to the reading audience from other sources. This material is inserted between the end of the Darnantes episode and Kahedin's falling in love with Iseut, that is, at the moment that the *R* redaction breaks off. The clear goal of narrating the story in its entirety is achieved by using other sources. There is also an echo of the *Folies Tristan* and an allusion to the story of Iseut's statue (LIV).[61] In the first part of the romance, the Tuscan redactor presents of his own initiative a series of parallel adventures of Lancelot and Tristan. These additions, occurring before Tristan's journey to Brittany, anticipate the first meeting of the two champions at Merlin's Stone (XLVIII–L), a scene which is duplicated in the romance. The reference to Morgan's daughter, the Gaia Donzella, leads to a discussion about her between Morgan and Tristan (LXXX). This scene also gives rise to the introduction of an entirely new episode (LXXXI) which follows the traditional theme of the 'pucele esforciée'; here, after Lancelot had taken to task the unpleasant and ignoble knight who had tried to rape the Gaia Donzella, Tristan definitively punishes him.[62]

Again, what particularly distinguishes the *Tav. Polidori* is the emphatically communal and civic orientation of Arthurian chivalry. The material taken from the 'good' book of Gaddo de' Lanfranchi is devoted to problems of an essentially theoretical and intellectual nature: who is to be identified as the best knight? Should Galahad's chivalry be distinguished from that of Tristan? What is the meaning of the lovers' dreams the night before their death? The *Tav. Polidori* compiler, by contrast, takes on more practical and timely questions: what was the function of the knight in society? How did knights arrange their wanderings through deserted lands? What was the Round Table actually like, and what were its rules? Some of the most representative and revealing pages of the *Tav. Polidori* include the mini-lesson that Tristan gives to Kahedin on the status and function of the knight, as they wander through Darnantes unable to find anything to eat (LVII); the detailed description of the system of 'fine lodgings' established for knights errant (LVII); and the description of the hall which held the Round Table, and of the categories of those allowed to participate in it (LXII).

The Po Valley Redaction (MS Pal. 556)

P^1, the text preserved in BNCF, MS Pal. 556, was long considered to be either entirely distinct from *Tav. Rit.* or, at best, a late reworking that had conflated *Ricc.* and *Tav. Rit.* A more careful analysis, however, reveals that this text is an invaluable witness not derived from the *Tav. Polidori*, but rather a parallel tradition that also stems, like the *Tav. Polidori*, from the *Tav. Rit. X*. In fact, P^1 allows us on the one hand to identify certain characteristics of this original source, and on the other to understand precisely how several passages from the *Tav. Polidori* have been interpolated.[63] P^1 is certainly not without interventions and manipulations of its own, in particular an extended passage from the Compilation of Rustichello da Pisa.[64] Copied in 1446 in the Po Valley between Cremona and Mantua,[65] the manuscript offers an extraordinary iconographical support in the form of 289 pen drawings.[66] The iconography conforms completely to the codex's textual content, and specialists have linked it to the Cremonese artistic circle of the Bonifacio Bembo workshop.[67] This manuscript is an exceptional witness to the migration of *Tav. Rit.* north of the Apennines, and from the Tuscan communal context to that of the *signorie* of northern Italy.[68] One of the copyists of MS Pal. 556 (P^1) signs his name: Zuliano de Anzoli of Cremona, who owned a copy of Boccaccio's *Filostrato* and a French *Lancelot* produced in Italy.[69] Although Zuliano cannot be identified as the (or an) illustrator, his intervention as an expert in Arthurian books in the design of this special volume cannot be denied. This volume does not have the characteristics of a true *de luxe* codex, being prepared on parchment, but not large format; written in calligraphic script with drawings, not miniatures; and incomplete in its decorative programme in the last pages. Nonetheless, the volume was most likely prepared for a distinguished buyer. The text is divided into chapters of unequal length (some very brief), introduced by summary rubrics, and chapter *incipits* show a marked use of traditional formulae ('Now the tale tells . . .'; 'The story shows . . .'; 'The story relates . . .').

One of the most pronounced characteristics of MS Pal. 556 is the textual and iconographical space dedicated to Grail Quest passages: in particular, to the adventure of the Wicked Knight and to the Grail liturgy.[70] This redaction contains details lacking in the parallel texts and gives increased importance to the relics of the Passion and the blood of Christ. Throughout the text the redactor uses only the pseudo-etymological form *Sangue Gradale* for *Sangradale*. This linguistic emphasis, combined with the presence of Gonzaga family emblems diegetically associated with Bors, and a certain resemblance between the manuscript's illustrations and the Pisanello frescoes completed a few years earlier in the Gonzaga palace in Mantua and dedicated to the origins of Bors, point strongly to the possibility that this manuscript was created for that circle.[71] The Gonzaga family tended to present itself as the heirs of the chosen Grail knight, and thus as the authorised keepers of the Holy Blood and of the spear of Longinus.[72]

Another characteristic of this unique Po Valley redaction is a revalorisation of the role of Lancelot alongside that of Tristan.[73] The text opens with Lancelot's *enfances*, under the title '*Dito di lo principio di Lanceloto*' ('Tale of Lancelot's Youth'), and features a highly distorted attempt at a versification in octaves in the first two folios. It is not known whether the limited skill evident in these poetically unrefined octaves belongs to the copyist or to the author. In other places, the text juxtaposes the orphaned and difficult childhoods of Lancelot and Tristan (*PAL 556*, pp. 150 and 287), and presents Lancelot as a penitent outside Corbenic (p. 312), narrated in more detail than the cursory description found in the *Tav. Polidori* (CXV). This text also prevents Lancelot from lapsing back into adultery after the Grail Quest ends (*PAL 556*, pp. 330–1). It is also significant that the romance ends with two drawings dedicated to Lancelot. The first of these depicts Guinevere dying in his arms; although this scene is not narrated in the text, the illustration establishes a kind of parallel with the death of Iseut alongside Tristan. The second image shows the surviving hero received into a hermitage by Bors.[74]

The Umbrian Redaction (MS Pal. 564)

The Umbrian redaction, preserved in the fifteenth-century BNCF, MS Pal. 564 (**P²**), is difficult to characterise, both because it contains many lacunae and because it has not yet been systematically compared with the other two. The Umbrian redaction generally abbreviates the story, although the absence of certain passages may be attributed to the fact that this manuscript was copied from a text predating the *Tav. Polidori* that must have resembled the *Tav. Rit. X*, rather than to intentional omissions, as Guida had suggested.[75] This is the case with the attempted rape of the Gaia Donzella, which is missing in the Umbrian version and is one of the additions of the *Tav. Polidori*. **P²** shows textual independence from the *Tav. Polidori* witnesses,[76] as well as sporadic convergences with **P¹** which could be considered traces of the original *Tav. Rit. X*.[77]

The presence – in *Tav. Polidori*, but known in **P¹** – of a section of episodes deriving from the Thomas and Béroul tradition suggests that the Umbrian redaction represents an earlier stage of the *Tav. Rit.* tradition than the Tuscan reworking. **P²** would then be deriving from a text that already contained these additions, unlike the one known in northern Italy (**P¹**). The episode of the Iseut statue, another element derived from the Thomas tradition, is extensively and creatively developed in the Umbrian redaction; the inclusion of this scene is especially noteworthy in a text that is so succinct in nature. This episode, which tells how Tristan had the statue made and how Kahedin mistook it for the queen herself (**P²**, fol. 30v),[78] is mentioned only briefly in *Tav. Polidori* (LIV) and is entirely absent in **P¹**, either not in the model or deliberately omitted.

Beyond its tendency toward compendium, the Umbrian version stands out for its distinctly sententious quality: it is quick to introduce proverbs, learned allusions and doctrinaire reflections. Linguistically associated with the area around Perugia, the text also tends to insert Latinate and French locutions, as well as a number of Gallicisms.[79]

Conclusion

Scholarly work done in the last few decades on the textual tradition of the French *Tristan* and its diffusion in Italy has undoubtedly removed *Tav. Rit.* from a certain critical isolation, by illuminating the historical, cultural and linguistic matrix out of which this original narrative grew.[80] At the same time, more detailed comparison with the versions of the *Tristan* actually present in Italy, and with translations and adaptations recently available in modern editions, has allowed us to recognise more clearly the singularity and the merits of *Tav. Rit.*[81] The author remains unknown, but he undoubtedly belonged to the Trecento Tuscan communal environment. In addition, he was probably connected to Pisa, which from the end of the thirteenth century on was the most active centre for the diffusion of Arthurian texts. Another feature of *Tav. Rit.* is its adaptability to diverse social contexts, from the urban mercantile class to the courts of northern Italy. As I have shown, this romance – in keeping with the 'open' structure typical of Arthurian narrative – has come down to us in versions enriched by additions and manipulations, and its original outline can be reconstructed only approximately, though with reasonable confidence. But its intricate textual stratification, which demands further investigation, is proof of the vitality of *Tav. Rit.*, a romance which was able to interpret the expectations, curiosities, nostalgias and ideals of the Italian audience vis-à-vis the Arthurian chivalric world.

(Translated by Stephen P. McCormick)

Notes

[1] D. Delcorno Branca, 'Lecteurs et interprètes de romans arthuriens en Italie: un examen à partir des études récentes', in C. Kleinhenz and K. Busby (eds), *Medieval Multilingualism: The Francophone World and Its Neighbours* (Turnhout, 2010), pp. 155–86.

[2] D. [Delcorno] Branca, *I romanzi italiani di Tristano e la Tavola Ritonda* (Florence, 1968); M.-J. Heijkant, *La tradizione del* Tristan *in prosa in Italia e proposte di studio sul* Tristano Riccardiano (Nijmegen, 1989); F. Cigni, 'Tristano e Isotta nelle letterature francese e italiana', in M. Dallapiazza (ed.), *Tristano e Isotta. La fortuna di un mito europeo* (Trieste, 2003), pp. 29–129, on pp. 102–15.

[3] I use the *sigla* adopted in my *I romanzi italiani*, pp. 32–6; the two partial witnesses have no *sigla*. A complete list is found in A. Punzi, 'Per una nuova edizione della *Tavola Ritonda*', in G. Ruffino (ed.), *Atti del XXI Congresso Internazionale di Linguistica e Filologia Romanza (Palermo 18–24 settembre 1995)* (Tübingen, 1998), VI/7, pp. 727–39, on pp. 727–8. A modern copy of **S** is BNCF, Nuovi Acquisti 575.

[4] On the two fragments, see R. Benedetti, '"Qua fa' un santo e un cavaliere . . .": Aspetti codicologici e note per il miniatore', in G. D'Aronco et al. (eds), *La grant Queste del Saint Graal. Versione inedita della fine della XIII secolo del ms. Udine, Biblioteca Arcivescovile, 177* (Tricesimo [Udine], 1990), pp. 31–47, on pp. 44–5.

[5] Delcorno Branca, 'I cantari di Tristano', *LI*, 23 (1971), 289–305, on 294.

[6] A. Punzi, 'Per la fortuna dei romanzi cavallereschi nel Cinquecento. Il caso della *Tavola Ritonda*', *Anticomoderno*, 3 (1997), 131–54.

[7] Translation McCormick. All other translated textual excerpts from Polidori are by Shaver, with minor corrections. Here, I quote the prologue from **M** (Punzi, 'Nuova edizione', p. 732), not from *Tav. Polidori*, which uses **S**. 'Manifesto sia a voi signori e buona giente ch'esto libro brievemente conta e tratta e divisa di gran battaglie e di belle cavallerie e di nobili torniamenti che fatti furono al tempo dello re Uter Pandragon e di grandi baroni della Tavola Vecchia, nel treciento anni e più dopo la passione del nostro Signiore Giesù Cristo, figliuolo di Dio padre vivo e vero e spirito eternale. E anche questo libro tratta e divisa di grandi avventure e nobili torniamenti che fatti furono al tempo dello re Artù figliuolo dello re Uter Pandragon e degli pro' cavalieri della Tavola Nuova, e spetialmente messer Tristano e di messer Lancielotto e di messer Palamides e di messer Galasso e gieneralmente degli altri cavalieri erranti iscritti nel collegio della Tavola Ritonda, e anche di tutti gli altri cavalieri di lontano paese, li quali a quell tempo provarono loro persone in fatti d'arme. E anche questo libro mi narra dell'alta inchiesta del Sangradale e sì come per tale impresa fu distrutta la detta Tavola, e con che venne meno per lo peccato e per lo difetto d'alcuno cavaliere.'

[8] F. Cigni, 'Manoscritti di prose cortesi compilati in Italia (secc. XIII–XIV). Stato della questione e prospettive di ricerca', in S. Guida and F. Latella (eds), *La filologia romanza e i codici* (Messina, 1993), II, pp. 419–41; D. Delcorno Branca, 'Per la storia del *Roman de Tristan* in Italia', *CN*, 40 (1980), 211–29, and *TLI*, pp. 49–76.

[9] Punzi, 'Fortuna dei romanzi'.

[10] *La Tavola Ritonda o l'Istoria di Tristano*, ed. Filippo-Luigi Polidori (Bologna, 1864–6). Heijkant reprinted this critical edition as *La Tavola Ritonda* (Milan and Trent, 1991).

[11] [Delcorno] Branca, *Romanzi italiani*; Delcorno Branca, 'Per la storia', *TLI* and 'Lecteurs et interprètes'; Heijkant, *La tradizione*; Cigni, 'Manoscritti di prose' and 'Tristano e Isotta'.

[12] For the sake of clarity I use the following abbreviations: *Tav. Rit. X* indicates specifically the original version of the romance, as it can be reconstructed through subsequent redactions; *Tav. Polidori* is the Tuscan redaction edited by Polidori in 1864; **P¹** and **P²** indicate the textual readings preserved in Pal. 556 and Pal. 564 respectively.

[13] Delcorno Branca, *TLI*, pp. 99–113, and '"Le carte piene di sogni"', Introduction to *Tavola Ritonda: Manoscritto Palatino 556, Firenze Biblioteca Nazionale Centrale*, ed. R. Cardini, 2 vols (Rome, 2009), pp. 3–18.

84 DANIELA DELCORNO BRANCA

14 Cardini (ed.), *Tavola Ritonda: Manoscritto Palatino* 556. I will cite this facsimile edition parenthetically as *PAL 556*.

15 M. Eusebi, 'Reliquie del *Tristano* di Thomas nella *Tavola Ritonda*', *CN*, 39 (1979), 39–62; S. Guida, 'Per il testo della *Tavola Ritonda*. Una redazione umbra', *Siculorum Gymnasium*, n.s. 32 (1979), 637–67; Punzi, 'Nuova edizione'.

16 See Heijkant, *La tradizione*, and her Chapter 3 in this volume; Cigni, 'Tristano e Isotta'.

17 For a detailed analysis of the diversity of the content, see *TLI*, pp. 99–113, and Guida, 'Per il testo'.

18 On Rustichello, see Chapter 2 in this volume, and Cigni's '*Roman de Tristan* in prosa e Compilazione di Rustichello da Pisa in area veneta. A proposito di una recente edizione', *LI*, 47 (1995), 598–622. For convenience I cite the Polidori edn by chapter number, indicated by capitalized roman numerals. Superscript 1 and 2 indicate the first or the second parts of a chapter. A summary of the *Tav. Rit.* with the parallels to the French *Tristan* and other texts is found in [Delcorno] Branca, *Romanzi italiani*, pp. 49–61. For the section *Tav. Rit.* shares with *Ricc.*, see Heijkant, *La tradizione*, pp. 136–237. However, these summaries do not reflect fully the diversity of the various redactions.

19 [Delcorno] Branca, *Romanzi italiani*; Delcorno Branca, 'Per la storia'; Heijkant, *La tradizione*.

20 C. Alvar and J. M. Lucía Megías, 'Hacia el códice del *Tristán de Leonis* (cincuenta y nueve nuevos fragmentos manuscritos en la Biblioteca Nacional de Madrid)', *Revista de Literatura Medieval*, 11 (1999), 9–135; C. Alvar, '*Tristanes* italianos y *Tristanes* castellanos', in F. Cigni and M. P. Betti (eds), *Testi, generi, e tradizioni nella Romània medievale: Atti del VI Convegno della Società Italiana di Filologia Romanza, Pisa, 28–30 settembre 2000*, special issue of *SMV*, 47 (2001), 57–75.

21 Chapter 3 in this volume profiles the *R* redaction.

22 Delcorno Branca, 'Per la storia', and *TLI*, pp. 49–76.

23 [Delcorno] Branca *Romanzi italiani*, pp. 78–9; and B. Barbiellini Amidei (ed.), *Ponzela Gaia* (Milan and Trent, 2000).

24 *TLI*, pp. 201–23.

25 See the works by F. Bogdanow: *The Romance of the Grail: A Study of the Structure and Genesis of a Thirteenth-Century Arthurian Prose Romance* (Manchester and New York, 1966); 'La tradition manuscrite de la *Queste del Saint Graal*, versions *Vulgate* et *Post-Vulgate*, en Italie', in D. Buschinger and W. Spiewok (eds), *Die kulturellen Beziehungen zwischen Italien und den anderen Ländern Europas im Mittelalter: 4ème Congrès annuel de la Société Reineke (Florenz, 28.–31. Mai 1993)*, Jahrbücher der Reineke-Gesellschaft, series 4; Wodan, 28 (Greifswald, 1993), pp. 25–45; *La Version Post-Vulgate*.

26 [Delcorno] Branca, *Romanzi italiani*, pp. 91–4.

27 Ibid., pp. 79–80; F. Benozzo, 'Per la storia di un *topos* del ciclo bretone. Il combattimento in incognito di Tristano e Lancillotto (i testi del gruppo cornico)', *Francofonia*, 16/31 (1996), 21–46; *TLI*, pp. 177–99.

28 R. Trachsler, 'Il tema della *Mort le roi Marc* nella letteratura romanza', *MR*, 19 (1994), 253–75; L. Soriano Robles, '"E qui vol saver questa ystoria, leçia lo libro de miser Lanciloto". A vueltas con el final original de *Tristan en prosa* castellano', *SMV*, 49 (2003), 203–17; Delcorno Branca, 'Lecteurs et interprètes', pp. 181–2.

29 Delcorno Branca 'Cantari di Tristano', 297–300; A. Donadello (ed.), *Il libro di messer Tristano ('Tristano Veneto')* (Venice, 1994), pp. 557–8.

30 [Delcorno] Branca, *Romanzi italiani*, p. 91; Delcorno Branca, 'La tradizione della *Mort Artu* in Italia', *Critica del testo*, 7/1 (2004), 317–39; on pp. 330–1.

31 *TLI*, pp. 99–113.

32 On *Tris. Ven.*, see Heijkant, *La tradizione*; Donadello (ed.), *Il libro di messer Tristano*; and Cigni, '*Roman de Tristan* in prosa'. On *Panc.*, see M.-J. Heijkant, 'La compilation du *Tristano Panciatichiano*', in B. Besamusca et al. (eds), *Cyclification: The Development of Narrative Cycles in the Chansons de Geste and the Arthurian Romances* (Amsterdam, 1994), pp. 122–6, and G. Allaire (ed. and trans.), *Il Tristano panciatichiano* (Cambridge, 2002). Both Heijkant and Allaire attribute a degree of initiative to the compiler rather than to the translator.

[33] F. Cardini, 'Concetto di cavalleria e mentalità cavalleresca nei romanzi e nei cantari fiorentini', in D. Rugiadini (ed.), *I ceti dirigenti nella Toscana tardo comunale. Atti del III Convegno, Firenze, 5–7 dicembre 1980* (Florence, 1983), pp. 157–92.

[34] Heijkant, 'The Custom of Boasting in the *Tavola Ritonda*', in L. E. Whalen and C. M. Jones (eds), *'Li premerains vers': Essays in Honor of Keith Busby* (Amsterdam, 2011), pp. 143–56.

[35] *TLI*, pp. 143–54 and 225–38.

[36] Delcorno Branca, 'Le storie arturiane in Italia', in P. Boitani et al. (eds), *Lo spazio letterario del Medioevo*, II: *Il Medioevo volgare*, III: *La ricezione del testo* (Rome, 2003), II, pp. 385–403.

[37] This plot is familiar in popular Italian literature; see my *Cantari fiabeschi arturiani* (Milan and Trent, 1999).

[38] *TLI*, pp. 201–23.

[39] Heijkant, 'Tristan im Kampf mit dem treulosen Ritter. Abenteuer, Gralssuche und Liebe in dem italienischen *Tristano Palatino*', in X. von Ertzdorff and R. Schulz (eds), *Tristan und Isolt im Spätmittelalter* (Amsterdam and Atlanta, 1999), pp. 453–72.

[40] [Delcorno] Branca, *Romanzi italiani*, pp. 78–9; *Ponzela Gaia*, ed. Barbiellini Amidei.

[41] *Roman de Tristan*, ed. Curtis, §482, ll. 5–10.

[42] A. Del Monte (ed.), *Conti di antichi cavalieri* (Milan, 1972): 'Chi avesse la reina Isolda, la reina Genevria, Tristano et Lancelocto insieme, porria dire che la beltà e la bontà tucta avesse del mondo' (p. 154). See [Delcorno] Branca, *Romanzi italiani*, pp. 76–7; and M.-J. Heijkant, 'Die seltsame Gefangenschaft von Tristan und Lancelot bei der Dama del Lago in der *Tavola Ritonda*', in T. Ehlert (ed.), *Chevaliers errants, demoiselles et l'Autre: höfische und nachhöfische Literatur im europäischen Mittelalter, Festschrift für Xenja von Ertzdorff zum 65. Geburtstag* (Göppingen, 1998), pp. 245–56; *TLI*, p. 233.

[43] [Delcorno] Branca, *Romanzi italiani*, pp. 81–3; F. Zambon, 'Dinadan en Italie', in K. Busby and R. Dalrymple (eds), *Comedy in Arthurian Literature* (Cambridge, 2003), pp. 153–64.

[44] That the lyric passages were already present in *Tav. Rit. X* is proven by the fact that a majority of them occur in **P¹**: see *TLI*, p. 109 n. 26. On the formal-rhetorical aspects of Arthurian texts in Italy, see M.-J. Heijkant, '"E' ti saluto con amore": Messaggi amorosi epistolari nella letteratura arturiana in Italia', *MR*, 23 (1999), 277–98; Cigni, '*Guiron, Tristan* e altri testi arturiani. Nuove osservazioni sulla composizione materiale del Ms. Parigi, BNF, fr. 12599', *SMV*, 45 (1999), 31–69, on 42–7 and 58–9; Delcorno Branca, 'Le storie arturiane', p. 392.

[45] [Delcorno] Branca, *Romanzi italiani*, pp. 122–5. Several summary echoes of Dante's *Commedia* have been identified in the *Tav. Rit.*; see for example, E. G. Gardner, *The Arthurian Legend in Italian Literature* (London and New York, 1930), p. 153; and S. Guida, 'Sulle "fonti" della *Tavola Ritonda*', in *Umanità e Storia: Scritti in onore di Adelchi Attisani* (Messina, 1971), II, pp. 129–55, on p. 137 n. 12. In *I romanzi italiani*, I judged these echoes to be incidental or of little consequence (p. 98 n. 73), and I find them to be all the more so now that they appear to belong rather to the *Tav. Polidori* (the passage of chapter CXIX cited in *I romanzi italiani*, belongs only to this redaction).

[46] The source text's extended '*parlements*' (councils) are systematically deleted or abbreviated.

[47] *TLI*, pp. 177–99.

[48] G. Boccaccio, *Elegia di madonna Fiammetta*, ed. Carlo Delcorno (Milan, 1994), VIII.7.1–4: see Delcorno Branca, *Boccaccio e le storie di re Artù* (Bologna, 1991), pp. 15–49, esp. 25–30.

[49] [Delcorno] Branca, *Romanzi italiani*, pp. 173–97; Cardini, 'Concetto di cavalleria'; Delcorno Branca, 'Le storie arturiane', pp. 396–8.

[50] Delcorno Branca, *Boccaccio e le storie*, pp. 69–112, esp. pp. 78–9; *TLI*, pp. 89–97.

[51] Guida, 'Sulle "fonti"', pp. 145–55.

[52] Cigni, 'Manoscritti di prose'; 'La ricezione medievale della letteratura francese nella Toscana nord-occidentale', in E. Werner and S. Schwarze (eds), *Fra toscanità e italianità: Lingua e letteratura dagli inizi al Novecento* (Tübingen and Basel, 2000), pp. 71–108; 'I testi della prosa letteraria e i contatti col francese e col latino. Considerazioni sui modelli', in L. Battaglia Ricci and R. Cella (eds), *Pisa*

crocevia di uomini, lingue, e culture. L'età medievale (Rome, 2009), pp. 157–81; and 'Manuscrits en français, italien, et latin entre la Toscane e la Ligurie à la fin du XIIIe siècle. Implications codicologiques, linguistiques, et évolution des genres narratifs', in Kleinhenz and Busby (eds), *Medieval Multilingualism*, pp. 187–217. See also V. Bertolucci Pizzorusso, 'Testi e immagini in codici attribuibili all'area pisano-genovese alla fine del Duecento', in M. Tangheroni (ed.), *Pisa e il Mediterraneo. Uomini, merci, idee dagli Etruschi ai Medici* (Milan, 2003), pp. 196–201.

⁵³ Of the seven 'explanations' taken from the book of Gaddo de' Lanfranchi in the *Tav. Polidori*, only two are missing in **P¹**. The remaining five do appear, three of which make explicit reference to the book of messer Gaddo. In my opinion, this tends to support the idea that these citations were present in the original stage of the romance. See also [Delcorno] Branca, *Romanzi italiani*, p. 173 n. 3.

⁵⁴ Guida, 'Sulle "fonti"', pp. 146–55.

⁵⁵ *TLI*, pp. 196–8.

⁵⁶ [Delcorno] Branca, *Romanzi italiani*, pp. 212–19.

⁵⁷ For a detailed analysis of the differences between the *Tav. Rit. X*, the *Tav. Polidori* and the MS Pal. 556 versions, see *TLI*, pp. 99–113.

⁵⁸ See L. Bertolini, 'Censimento dei manoscritti della *Sfera* del Dati: I manoscritti della Biblioteca Nazionale Centrale e dell'Archivio di Stato di Firenze', *Annali della Scuola Normale Superiore di Pisa*, ser. III, 18/2 (1988), 417–588, on 456–7.

⁵⁹ See Polidori edn, p. lvi (however, the date he gives for **S** is inaccurate).

⁶⁰ *Tav. Polidori*, ch. XI: 'perché io mi vanti e dica che io sia gentile, questo non è male; chè gentile può éssare [*sic*] ogni persona che à belli atti e costumi; et dolce parlare fa gentilezza.'

⁶¹ *TLI*, pp. 109–10.

⁶² M.-J. Heijkant, 'La mésaventure érotique de Burletta della Diserta et le motif de la pucelle esfor-ciée dans la *Tavola Ritonda*', *Zeitschrift für romanische Philologie*, 118/2 (2002), 182–94.

⁶³ *TLI*, pp. 99–113, and 'Le carte piene di sogni'.

⁶⁴ Cigni, '*Roman de Tristan* in prosa'.

⁶⁵ L. Bertolini, 'La lingua del Palatino 556', in *PAL 556*, pp. 19–58.

⁶⁶ High-resolution images of the entire manuscript may now be seen on line at *http://www.bncf.firenze.sbn.it/Bib_digitale/Manoscritti/Pal_556/main.htm*.

⁶⁷ For early studies on MS Pal. 556, see the section on Manuscript Illumination in the 'Arthurian Art References' of the present volume.

⁶⁸ Note too the other attestations of the *Tav. Rit.* in northern manuscripts from the Veneto: MS Vat. lat. 6789 and the Padua and Udine fragments. A. Tissoni Benvenuti announced that she has discovered a reference to a manuscript of the **P¹** version in the early fifteenth-century inventories of the Visconti library. Other traces of **P¹** appear in chivalric poems of the Po Valley printed in the fifteenth and sixteenth centuries, such as the anonymous *Libro de l'Ancroia* or Niccolò degli Agostini's *Innamoramento di Lancillotto* (both 1521). Already in 1896, Parodi (pp. lxi–lxv) had discerned notable points of contact between **P¹** and the *Tristano* conserved in Riccardiano MS 1729 (**F**). The latter is a partial vernacular rendition copied in the Veneto, but with a linguistic substrate from the Pisa–Lucca area. See M. Corti, 'Emiliano e veneto nella tradizione manoscritta del *Fiore di Virtù*', *Studi di filologia italiana*, 18 (1960), 29–68; and *TLI*, pp. 103–112.

⁶⁹ *TLI*, pp. 99–100.

⁷⁰ On the Wicked Knight, see Heijkant, 'Tristan im Kampf'. On the Grail liturgy, see P. Breillat, 'Le manuscrit Florence Palatin 556: la *Tavola Ritonda* et la liturgie du Graal', *Mélanges d'Archéologie et d'Histoire de l'École Française de Rome*, 55 (1938), 341–73; and A. Hoffmann, 'Il rapporto testo-immagine: un caso particolare', in *PAL 556*, pp. 83–102.

⁷¹ V. Bertolucci, 'I cavalieri di Pisanello', *SMV*, 20 (1972), 37–48; Delcorno Branca, 'I *Tristani* dei Gonzaga', in J.-C. Faucon et al. (eds), *Miscellanea Mediaevalia: Mélanges offerts à Philippe Ménard* (Paris and Geneva, 1998), I, pp. 385–93; and ead., 'Le carte piene di sogni', pp. 6–7.

[72] Although S. A. Luyster and A. Di Domenico offer divergent explanations for the codex's commissioning, both propose the noble class of the Po Valley. See Luyster, 'Playing with Animals: The Visual Context of an Arthurian Manuscript (Florence, Palatino 556) and the Uses of Ambiguity', *Word and Image*, 20 (2004), 1–21; and Di Domenico, 'Un cavaliere sotto l'insegna del leone rampante. Una nuova ipotesi di committenza', in *PAL 556*, pp. 113–22. For additional sources concerning the Grail cult at Mantua, see the 'Arthurian Art References' in this volume.

[73] Delcorno Branca, 'Le carte piene di sogni', p. 14.

[74] Delcorno Branca, 'La tradizione della *Mort Artu*', 337–9.

[75] Guida, 'Per il testo', p. 641.

[76] M. Eusebi, 'Reliquie del *Tristano*', and Guida, 'Per il testo'.

[77] Guida, 'Per il testo', pp. 652–3 and 658–9.

[78] Ibid., pp. 660–2

[79] Ibid., pp. 647–50.

[80] See the authoritative editions of the *Roman de Tristan en prose*: R. L. Curtis (ed.), *Le Roman de Tristan en prose* (Munich, 1963; rpt Cambridge, 1985); P. Ménard (gen. ed.), *Le Roman de Tristan en prose* (Geneva, 1987–97); Ménard (gen. ed.), *Le Roman de Tristan en prose (version du manuscrit fr. 757 de la Bibliothèque nationale de Paris* (Paris, 1997–2007). See also Delcorno Branca, 'Per la storia' and 'Lecteurs et interprètes'. Finally, see the studies by Cigni cited above: 'Manoscritti di prose'; 'La ricezione medievale'; 'I testi della prosa'; and 'Manuscrits en français'.

[81] Recent editions include Donadello's edition of *Tris. Ven.*, Allaire's edition of *Il Tristano panciatichiano*, and R. Tagliani (ed.), *Il Tristano Corsiniano* (Rome, 2011).

Part Two

Arthurian Material in Italian Narrative Forms

5

NARRATIVE STRUCTURE IN MEDIEVAL ITALIAN ARTHURIAN ROMANCE

Stefano Mula

I do not know whether, as the proverb says, things that are repeated are pleasing, but I believe that they are least significant. (Roland Barthes, *Mythologies*)[1]

The Arthurian legends have, in Michel Stanesco's words, a 'European destiny'.[2] The legends and the texts spread quickly throughout Europe, carrying with them themes, characters and narrative structures. In Italy as elsewhere in Europe, authors modified the original renditions with the tools at their disposal – rhetorical and narrative tools they shared with the authors of the stories they were retelling. To talk about narrative structures in Italian prose texts thus requires that we refer to the more abundant research conducted, in particular, on the French prose tradition of the Arthurian legends. When Arthurian romances first arrived on the Italian peninsula they wore their French garb, but soon donned different dress. Early diffusion of the legends may predate extant written versions, but Italian renditions of the French prose romances start appearing towards the end of the thirteenth century, at the confluence of different traditions. Narrative structures of *Il Tristano Riccardiano* (*Ricc.*) or *La Tavola Ritonda* (*Tav. Rit.*) reflect not only the French prose cycles, but also contemporary Italian prose traditions.

Arthurian works were popular in Italy not only as entire cycles, but also as single episodes circulating independently, or in early collections such as the *Novellino* and the *Conti di antichi cavalieri*.[3] Diffusion in the form of self-contained short narratives is not, paradoxically, a sign of the weakness of the unity of the Arthurian material, but on the contrary proves its vitality and strength. Single episodes and shorter works in Italian could be read and understood not in isolation, but only against the backdrop of the whole tradition transmitted by familiar longer works. The retelling of single episodes was influenced by the tendency to brevity typical of contemporary collections of short narratives (e.g., *novelle* and *exempla*). The originality of the Italian tradition lies also in the fruitful encounter between the French prose tradition and the new Italian interest in the short *novella*. The study of narrative structure is connected to the question of how Arthurian works were construed and, consequently, how they were read when they were first composed. Although there is no book-length study on narrative structure in medieval Italian Arthurian romance, the topic is raised in many articles and introductions to editions. This chapter proposes an overview and some paths for future research. I will describe three major narrative devices used in Italian

Arthurian prose narrative: interlace, repetition and compilation. To highlight the specific characteristics of the Italian texts, these devices will be considered in the broader perspective of the French and English traditions, and illustrated primarily with examples from *Tav. Rit.*, *Ricc.* and *Il Tristano Panciatichiano* (*Panc.*).

The earliest modern critical reactions to medieval Italian Arthurian works mainly privileged their linguistic value, in large part because they were seen as artless modifications of original French texts, considered as their models.[4] Only with Gardner's 1930 monograph did the Italian Arthurian tradition receive a full-length study, though one not always admiring;[5] more recently, scholars such as Daniela Delcorno Branca have shown how productive this tradition was for writers such as Boccaccio.[6] In a salutary corrective to older studies, Giorgio Agamben neatly articulates a methodological principle that should guide our understanding of medieval works: 'our ignorance of an author's motivations does not authorise us to posit that they were incoherent or deficient.'[7] Although Agamben was referring to Dante, his comments apply also to our anonymous Arthurianists. We should not assume that what we see today as incoherence or pointless repetition evidences a lack of literary skill. Authors of medieval prose texts exploited narrative structures that today have lost much of their meaning and effect. Consequently, readers and scholars have sometimes lost the ability to derive pleasure and significance from structures that, while still common in film and popular literature, have lost their effectiveness in 'art' fiction. Hans Robert Jauss described the medieval aesthetic of repetition:

> The reader's pleasure can spring today, as it already did with the medieval listener, from an attitude which does not presuppose a self-submersion in the unique world of a single work, but which rather presupposes an expectation which can only be fulfilled by the step from text to text, for here the pleasure is provided by the perception of difference, of an ever-different variation on a basic pattern.[8]

This aesthetic explains the medieval use of narrative devices such as interlace and repetition, and in particular helps us to appreciate the many incomplete or isolated Arthurian texts in the Italian tradition.

Interlace

The long prose works of the Middle Ages were held together by various narrative strategies, of which three are interconnected and particularly useful for understanding the Italian Arthurian prose romances. Before offering examples of how each one works I will briefly introduce all three, from the better-studied interlace to repetition and compilation, which support and interact with it.

One of the defining features of the long French prose cycles is *entrelacement,* or interlace. Ferdinand Lot was the first to develop the concept of interlace as one of the structural principles behind the organisation of the French prose *Lancelot*.[9] The complexity of this work led to the idea of a single mind behind the creation of the cycle: the Architect, responsible for carefully weaving the many threads of the Arthurian knights' adventures.[10] No single adventure was ever told from start to finish; instead, each was interrupted by other stories in a complex, interconnected web. Expanding on Lot, Eugène Vinaver highlighted the role of analogy in the construction of interlace: the adventures intersected not randomly, but on the basis of similar content. Narrators linked the various adventures 'by means of significant parallels' that could guide readers in their search for meaning.[11] The great expansion of the prose romances was obtained by inserting adventures that were never completely new, but modelled on previous ones, each a different strand that would resurface and intersect over and over, making the reader lose 'every sense of limitation in time or space'.[12]

Vinaver's analysis of Malory's *Morte Darthur* led him to identify the reduction or elimination of the interlace structure as a principal element of Malory's originality. Already in some later versions of the French prose cycles, authors were reducing their reliance on interlace, but in Vinaver's view, Malory brought this stylistic tendency to its extreme consequence. Malory divided the longer originals into seven distinct tales which, as his style evolved, grew more and more independent from each other and from the whole cycle of Arthurian adventures. The simplification of the structure in order to achieve a stronger coherence in each volume was for Vinaver the defining feature of Malory's Arthuriad.[13] The poetics of interlace, however, did not come to an end with Malory, nor was this narrative structure always used as it was in the prose *Lancelot*. Vinaver notes that signs of the changing nature of interlace were already present as early as the French prose *Tristan*, and innovations such as that later found in Malory were already visible in Italian works of the fourteenth century.[14] However, if we adopt the *Lancelot en prose* as the model to which all other Arthurian prose works should conform, and accept *entrelacement* as the only glue capable of keeping the long narratives together, we risk overlooking other important narrative structures that were present at the same time in the long prose works of the period.[15] In the *Morte Darthur,* the disintegration of the tightly knit pattern of the prose *Tristan* is due to Malory's conscious choice to exploit a different strategy. It is thus not the decay of a perfectly built cathedral, but a case of reuse: Malory was interested in building a different monument by exploiting older construction materials, and in cementing it by repetition.

Repetition

To describe the device of repetition I could use the particular case of analogy, in which episodes are linked by having almost exactly the same plot. When the story happens to the same character, we can talk about duplication of episodes; when the same adventure happens to two different knights we have parallelism, where the analogy between the episodes invites comparison and reflection. Repetition is not only fundamental for the long prose romances;[16] it is also used to organise the miniatures that often accompany Arthurian manuscripts.[17] In one of her last articles, Elspeth Kennedy discussed the French prose *Lancelot*, noting in the miniatures the common device of repetition, which she calls 'pairing':

> Another important factor in the thematic and narrative structure of the romance in this part of the tale of Lancelot is that of pairing, a common structural device in medieval literature. There are two kings, brothers, who both die, two queens, sisters, who are both separated from their children, both take the veil and are nuns in the same abbey. Lancelot, who has lost land and father, has two cousins, Lyonel and Bohort, who have lost land and father and who, eventually, join Lancelot in the Lake.[18]

What happens in the miniatures closely resembles what happens in the texts, as noted by Emmanuèle Baumgartner, who stresses the important role of repetition in the French prose *Tristan*:

> The true originality of the *Tristan*, however, lies in the doubles the authors have created around Tristan, knights who are direct rivals in both love and chivalric prowess, such as Kaherdin and especially Palamedes, or who are made more or less in Tristan's image, like Lamorat, the lover of the queen of Orcanie, or even Alixandre l'Orphelin. This technique is not only useful for prolonging the narrative; it also has an ethical purpose.[19]

Although Kennedy called this technique 'pairing', in fact medieval authors often did not stop at a pair. The reason for duplicating and multiplying similar characters and episodes can be summarised briefly, and illustrated by detailed examples. In short, the simple pairing of characters or of episodes can serve as a balancing strategy, one that supports the interlace structure by providing sturdier threads. Moreover, multiple instances of such repetition show the growth of a character and deepen the audience's understanding of the character's development and psychology. The structure is used specifically to give a fuller, more rounded view of the main characters; as we will see, the Italian authors in particular exploit it to reinforce Tristan's personality at the expense both of his fellow companions of the Round Table and of his enemies.

Repetition in the Italian Prose Tradition

In the Italian tradition, the use of interlace is diminished in favour of more frequent repetition and, as I will discuss in the next section, compilation. The fresh attention to the Arthurian legend in Italy has alerted scholars and readers to many texts which until recently were available only in older editions or in manuscript.[20] By comparing different rewritings of the same text, we can discern and analyse the changing narrative structures in the prose versions of the Italian Tristan legend.

In Italy, treatment of the Arthurian texts as independent works rather than as mere translations from the French is a relatively recent development, and one due in large part to the innovative work of Daniela Delcorno Branca. Already in 1968, her study of *Tav. Rit.* helped focus attention on Italian versions as works in their own right.[21] Defining what distinguishes a translation from an adaptation is not always easy. *Il Tristano Veneto (Tris. Ven.)*, for instance, certainly can be considered a relatively faithful translation of the *Tristan en prose*; but even there the adapter/translator made important choices, such as eliminating long sequences and inserting episodes taken from Rustichello's Compilation.[22] All choices – of which passages to translate, where to abbreviate, where to summarise and how to connect passages between originally separated episodes – are indications of a conscious effort on the part of a translator/ redactor to adapt the original text to a different taste.[23] Taste is subject to change, however, and as Maurizio Dardano noted in studying *Ricc.*, some of the author's narrative choices can generate boredom in a modern reader. In *Ricc.*, interlace is greatly reduced; the hero's adventures are repeated, multiplied and juxtaposed; and we do not find the same degree of psychological introspection present in earlier versions of the Tristan story, such as that of Thomas.[24] And yet the repetitions and the juxtaposition of similar episodes are precisely what show the different authorial attitudes towards the main characters. Through the same devices, the hero acquires a psychological depth, which, if easily overlooked today, was understood and appreciated by the original audience.[25] The alterity of the repetition device in *Ricc.* is not, however, an insurmountable obstacle for our understanding, even if modern readers bring a different appreciation to the story.[26] Multiple instances of same words and formulae, and the repetition of episodes and characters, are prominent features that characterise and unify works such as *Ricc.* and *Tav. Rit.* In what follows I will show how repetition works in a few specific examples.

Marie-José Heijkant's analysis of narrative repetitions in *Ricc.* stresses how analogy works to provide an intertextual coherence for each single Arthurian work. She remarks that references to Lancillotto are meant to provide a comparative background, rather than a chronological framework, for Tristano's adventures.[27] Even more than a comparative model, parallels and repetitions serve to show the evolution of a character, especially but not only Tristano. To see how repetition in the form of parallelism works at a macro level in *Ricc.*, we can follow Tristano's rise from being Lancillotto's equal to being indisputably the best knight, recognised as such even by Lancillotto himself. Their equality is first stated by Galeotto in his letter to Arthur and Guinevere:

> 'Wherefore know, my lord King Arthur and my lady Queen Guinevere and all other knights of your realm, that in the world there are only two knights and two ladies, and in these two knights there is all the goodness and all the valor in the world, and in the two ladies there is all the nobility and all the beauty in the world; I see no prowess in other knights, or beauty in other ladies, than these two.'[28]

By the end of *Ricc.* Lancillotto openly acknowledges Tristano's superiority: 'I am truly delighted that Sir Tristan has rescued King Arthur, for I want you to know that he is the best knight you ever heard of.'[29] Queen Guinevere follows suit indirectly, telling her husband: 'We can truly say that Sir Tristan has done you greater honour than any other knight.'[30] The text of the damaged manuscript ends a few paragraphs later, but Tristano has already achieved the summit of his chivalric career.

Sometimes repetition adds an additional layer to an already rich, intertextual tradition. Dante knew well the *Arturi regis ambages pulcerrime*, and he exploited Lancelot and Guinevere's story in the famous fifth canto of the *Inferno*.[31] Soon after, *Tav. Rit.* referred to that same canto when commenting on Bellicies's infatuation for Tristan, but the use of repetition proposes to the readers a stronger commentary. Donald L. Hoffman shows convincingly how the intertextual relationship with Dante's *Inferno* 5 brings love back to the centre of *Tav. Rit.*,[32] and Joan Tasker Grimbert has argued vigorously that *Tav. Rit.* makes 'a number of radical changes and additions clearly designed to refocus attention on a love portrayed as both overpowering and exemplary'.[33] To this interpretation we could incorporate the psychological depth that these repetitions add to the traditional elements of the love story. The strength of the love potion, for example, is highlighted by the original creation of parallels with Governale and Brandina (whose loyalty to the lovers is enhanced by the smell of the potion) and with Isotta's pet dog Idonia falling so deeply in love with them both that it dies three days after they do.[34] Other elements were already present in the French prose *Tristan*, such as Bellicies's love for Tristano, but they are reshaped in a fresh way. Thanks to the backdrop of *Inferno* 5, the *Tav. Rit.* narrator distinguishes more clearly why Bellicies's love is not to be reciprocated: 'No love is perfect, if the other party is not in agreement. And since Tristano's will was not in agreement with Bellicies's, she suffered greatly from it.'[35] This discussion of love is clearly in intertextual dialogue with Francesca's powerful speech in the *Inferno*, but the episode derives even more poignancy from the intratextual repetition of Tristano's love affairs: his tryst with the Donzella dell'Aigua della Spina and, later, his fateful encounter with Isotta. In particular, the tryst shows yet a different kind of love from the one we would expect from such a famous lover: there is no stability, no eternity in this love. This time, the dwarf is the one who makes the case, and in his words we may perhaps see another reference to *Inferno* 5: 'And you should know, that love does not look at equality of beauty or of riches, but enters wherever pleasure leads him.'[36]

A representative case of parallelism is the opposition between the Old and New Round Tables (*Tavola Vecchia* and *Tavola Nuova*) typical of Italian versions, and here inserted into the larger context of Tristano's life.[37] *Tav. Rit.* begins with Gurone, a knight of the *Tavola Vecchia*, who wins a lady in a duel, only to be humiliated through deception and lies. The lady pretends to accept Gurone, planning to slander him at the court of King Meliadus, where she accuses him of cowardice for refusing to defend his own damsel. At first sight the episode is not immediately connected to the rest of the Tristan narrative; it does, however, provide the necessary background for all subsequent actions. While Gurone's old world is presented as full of courage, wisdom and truthfulness, the new world and the new *tavola* is a place where deception can bring shame to worthy knights. But this basic parallelism is not the only one that matters: the same basic pattern of taking a lady from another knight, a common *topos* of Arthurian stories, foreshadows the adventures of Tristano and offers a key to the interpretation of his actions and behaviour.

At this point, a more detailed example will illustrate how repetition by duplication works in *Tav. Rit.* In the early Tristan poems, as evidenced in Gottfried's *Tristan*, the Irish Baron Gandin asks King Mark for a gift in exchange for playing the harp.[38] To Mark's great displeasure, after Gandin performs he asks to be given Isolde. The king now realises that he had agreed to the bargain too quickly; nevertheless, bound by his word, he must allow the queen to leave. Joseph Bédier, reconstructing this episode in his edition of Thomas's *Tristan*, christened it 'La Harpe et la Rote' for the two instruments played by Gandin and later by Tristan, who played the same trick on Gandin to recover Iseut.[39] The episode does not appear in this form in any of the later Tristan works, but its main theme – the kidnapping of a lady loved by Tristan and Mark – is exploited first in the French romances (Lös. §34) and later by the anonymous *Tav. Rit.* author.

The author of the French prose *Tristan* anticipates Mark and Tristan's competition for the love of a woman by creating a new character, the wife of the otherwise unremarkable knight Segurades. The story goes that a foreign knight named Blioberis arrives one day at Mark's court, and promptly asks the king for a gift. Mark, not much wiser in this version than in Gottfried's, happily consents, only to be surprised by the request: Blioberis wants Segurades's wife (Lös. §375). The most relevant difference from the removal of Isolde in Gottfried's text is Tristan's attitude. In the prose *Tristan*, worried about having his love affair discovered by his uncle, Tristan decides to stay put and not go at once to rescue his beloved: 'If it were not for his uncle, Tristan would have followed them; but he was afraid of his uncle, since he already and certainly knew that he loved the lady, and that he hated him for that same one. That is why he gave it up.'[40] At the same time her rightful husband, Segurades, ignoring his wife's well-known adulterous behaviour, fights Blioberis and is unhorsed. A damsel then scolds Tristan, calling him a coward and the worst knight ever to carry arms in the kingdom of Cornwall (and we recall that Cornish knights were not known for their courage). Tristan does not understand why she reproaches him, realising only later that it is because he was reluctant to rescue the woman he supposedly loved. The entire episode closely follows the basic pattern of the Harp and the Rote, the sole exception being Tristan's immediate reaction. His behaviour shows everyone – readers, fictional characters and himself – that he is not a perfect lover and, consequently, not a perfect knight. Later, Tristan finally confronts Blioberis, and after a long battle they decide to leave the choice to the woman: whom does she prefer, Blioberis or Tristan? To Tristan's chagrin the woman chooses Blioberis and chastises Tristan for his cowardice (Lös. §393). The French prose *Tristan* thus highlights Tristan's uncourtly behaviour and his lack of will to fight for his beloved.

With just a few additions and modifications to the story of Segurades's wife from the French prose *Tristan*, the *Tav. Rit.* author will offer the reader yet a different view of Tristano's personality and role in the story – a role much more in keeping with the ideals of the emerging Italian merchant class, as Delcorno Branca has argued.[41] The changes in the *Tav. Rit.* rendition of the episode show how the Italian author exploits the duplication device to stress not Tristano's flaw, but only his youth and inexperience. Unlike in the *Tristan en prose*, no mention is made of any fear of Mark that would prevent the hero from rescuing the lady, but it is Mark who immediately and courteously asks Tristan to act in order to protect the honour of the court: 'And King Mark, seeing Tristano, told him: "Dear nephew, don't you see how much dishonour that knight with that lady has brought to us? I pray you to go and rescue her."'[42]

Comparing the kidnapping of Segurades's wife in the prose *Tristan* and its version in *Tav. Rit.* sharply focuses their differences and similarities. In the French prose *Tristan* the hero is afraid of King Mark, while in *Tav. Rit.* he seems simply somewhat absent-minded. The Donzella dell'Aigua della Spina, as the woman is called here, is taken from before his very eyes, yet he waits to attempt her rescue until Mark encourages him. The other addition is to the woman's character. In *Tav. Rit.* her unnamed husband, in fact, leaves the court and unhorses Brunoro, yet the lady decides to stay with Brunoro. That is indeed a remarkable if brief episode: against all chivalric rules, after a successful duel the husband does not win back his wife, who instead chooses Brunoro. Against this backdrop of a strong-willed woman, we are invited to read what follows: Tristano's arrival and his duel with Brunoro.

The fight clearly goes in Tristano's favor, but before it ends Brunoro suggests that it is for the woman to choose with whom she will stay. When the duel between Tristano and Brunoro is suspended pending her decision, her attitude and her words are even more striking. In the same situation, we remember, the wife in the *Tristan en prose* was so appalled by Tristan's behaviour that she chose her kidnapper, to Tristan's surprise and shame: 'Tristan, I did love you greatly, but since I saw that you were so vile and cowardly as to allow me to be taken from your uncle's court by one knight, I will never love you again.'[43] In *Tav. Rit.* the lady chastises Tristano and calls him a traitor, but nevertheless decides to stay with him: 'And the lady said: "Even if Tristano is a traitor, since he should never have allowed me to be taken away form the court, I still prefer him."'[44] The Italian author not only shows Tristano to be the best choice, but he even portrays him as a defender of the institution of marriage: 'Tristano and the lady go back to court, and he gives her back to her husband.'[45] We are left wondering what will happen to the lady who rejected her husband for a kidnapper, chose Tristano and finds herself with her husband again; but she immediately leaves the narrative and does not return. The Italian author focuses only on Tristano, and the episode allows the author to compare him to three different knights: to Mark, who cannot act; to the kidnapper Brunoro, clever but not a strong fighter; and to the rightful, unnamed husband who fights for his lady but, although rewarded at the end, does not have the qualities that his wife desires. Tristano, on the other hand, has one major flaw: inexperience. He has not yet learned how to love, and his feelings for the lady are not true. This is why he does not act immediately to rescue her, thus earning her rebuke. Everything else he does correctly, even defending the institution of marriage by reuniting the wife and her rightful husband. We soon find out, in an episode that duplicates this same plot, whether he has learned anything from his adventure.

The occasion arises, in the French prose *Tristan*, as a consequence of Iseut's attempt to kill Brangaine. Palamedes, whose love for Iseut is not returned, saves Brangaine and, exploiting the rash boon, leaves the court with Iseut (Lös. §43). The situation is the same, only this time Tristan's behaviour changes dramatically. As soon as he hears the news, Tristan openly shows his grief before Mark and swears never to come back without Iseut. Now there is no fear or doubt: the hero has learned how to love, and he is amply rewarded. This time the queen is not asked to choose between the knights, but she does intervene of her own will. Iseut too has matured as a character, and from the comparison with the maiden of the earlier episode, we appreciate her strength and her wisdom. Recognising that Palamedes truly loves her, she does not want him to die, but only to carry her message to Guinevere. Her thoughtful words prevent the death of a valorous knight, and she returns with Tristan to Mark's court. As in the first episode, Tristan returns the wife to the husband, but in *Tav. Rit.* the story does not end there. Where the French Tristan stresses the honour of the king and of the kingdom, the Italian Tristano makes a point of comparing courtly gestures to practical results: 'Once at the palace Tristano takes Isotta by the hand and brings her before King Mark, saying, "Dear Sir, take your wife, and next time don't be as courteous, because it takes more to get something back than to give it away."'[46] The episode gains all its significance from being compared with its earlier analogue. By this duplication in the plot, listeners and readers are encouraged to see the differences in behaviour of all the characters involved. Certainly, Tristano is the one who has grown the most; he is now a fearless, true lover. However, we also learn much about the other characters, such as Mark (who again falls for the same trick) and Isotta (whose comparison with the *donzella* is all in her favour). The *Tav. Rit.* narrator also adds a personal touch, turning Tristano into a spokesperson of contemporary values. By his effective understanding and use of the repetition device, the *Tav. Rit.* author manages to create an original work while modifying only slightly the French version of the same story.

Compilation

The third major structural device, compilation, I would define as the creation of new meaning and a new work from the juxtaposition within a codex of different, pre-existing texts or excerpts. Compilation is a development of the undoing of inter-lace, and of the poetics of repetition. Interlace allows the reader to move from one

story to another with the briefest of transitions; duplication provides a model for juxtaposing two stories from the same text; and compilation is a further step in the same
direction. Unravelling the many threads they found in the long French prose romances,
later authors added cohesion to their works by duplicating plots and episodes. At the
same time, thinking in terms of parallelisms between adventures contained in a single
work may have encouraged them to bring together elements that were originally disparate, to create new coherence and new meaning by juxtaposing excerpts from
separate works in the same codex.

     Formal parallels are structurally present in early collections of *novelle*, such as the
Conti di antichi cavalieri and the more famous *Novellino*, where thematic and formal
symmetries are the structural glue of the whole work.[47] Roberta Morosini has
highlighted the influence of this peculiar aspect of the recent novella tradition on the
longer Arthurian compilations: *Ricc.* 'looks more [like] a book of *novelle* like the
contemporary *Novellino*, than a "simple" version of the Prose Tristan.'[48] Morosini
concludes her analysis with an explicit reference to the use of interlace as a narrative
device that is still fully functional, though more freely used.[49]

     Together with full adaptations such as the *Tav. Rit.*, and translations/adaptations
such as *Tris. Ven.*, we also find single episodes of the Arthurian tradition treated
independently. Some are transmitted in the form of the *novella*, as in the *Novellino* or
the *Conti di antichi cavalieri*; but a more curious and intriguing example of
compilation is offered in BNCF, MS Panciatichiano 33. *Panc.* is a unique collection of
six texts – five of Arthurian origin – dating from the beginning of the fourteenth
century, juxtaposed without any effort to connect the disparate parts. We find a version
of the *Queste* coming from the *Lancelot en prose*; two love letters; the beginning of
Tristano's story until the false news of his death (roughly corresponding to Lös. §§19–
101); the death of King Arthur; the story of Tristano at the Tournament of Louvezerp
(Lös. §§352–81); and finally the last adventures and death of Tristano and Isotta (Lös.
§§539–51 and 568–70).[50] Until very recently, this last section was the only Tristan
portion of the manuscript in print. At first glance the manuscript seems to be a
collection of independent, though related, texts, but Heijkant has convincingly
suggested that *Panc.* preserves a set of texts organised around one main theme: the life
of Tristano. Its different sections are not smoothly sutured together, but only copied
contiguously. Their meaning, however, also lies in the logic of the composition:
Tristano's life, deeds and death are all there, his love for Isotta and his competition
with Lancelot as the best knight of the Arthurian world linked logically and
thematically but not by explicit, textual connective tissue.[51]

     The form of *Panc.*, the presence of a number of fragmentary manuscripts, and the
emergence of collections of *novelle* excerpted from larger works, all seem to indicate
the existence of what we might call a poetics of compilation. With the authors probably
influenced by contemporary *exempla* collections, and the audience influenced by the
use of *exempla* in preachers' sermons, the fourteenth-century Italian audience's taste

moved away from the long compilations so popular in France, and towards the short story. On the other hand, this move was accompanied by the preservation in different degrees of many of the same narrative devices and structures, such as interlace, repetition and compilation. Delcorno Branca stresses that the limited availability of complete texts should not be seen as the only reason behind the creation of anthology manuscripts, although it might have encouraged the new formations.[52] Lack of complete copies would then lead to works where the junctures are not always perfect, but where the interpretation of the texts leads to new, original narrative voices such as that of *Tav. Rit.*[53]

The presence of Arthurian matter in the *Novellino* is well known,[54] but many other works such as the *cantari* also attest to the success and influence of the Arthurian tradition as a whole in the Italian peninsula.[55] Individual Arthurian stories present in the popular *cantari* in *ottava rima* were not necessarily based on the most famous episodes of the legends, but relied on their audiences' broad knowledge of the tradition for their better understanding. Direct and indirect influences show the creative power of the legend in the form of the individual episode, and hint at how each single short text was always considered and perceived as part of a larger unit: the Arthurian world.

The author of the early and unique Hebrew version of the Arthurian tradition in Italy, *Mēlek Arṭûś* (*King Artus*, 1279), was probably influenced by the same poetics of compilation.[56] In his introduction, the medieval author claims that he will translate the whole *Mort Artu*; unfortunately, the manuscript ends after only a few folios that contain an abridged version of Arthur's conception, followed immediately by the end of the *Queste* and the beginning of the *Mort Artu*. The text comes to an abrupt end in the middle of a sentence. Given the context of the Italian Arthurian tradition, the author of *Mēlek Arṭûś* could have relied on a complete Italian text as its model, though he may have had a compilation instead. That source, certainly longer than the Hebrew translation we have, may well be an early example of the narrative tendency to reduce the long French Arthurian prose romances, which were structured using interlace, to texts whose coherence lies in their intra- and extra-diegetic references and parallels.

Conclusion

Intrigued by the Arthurian stories coming from France, Italian authors adapted the long and convoluted French prose romances to the taste of their audience. They did not try to create something completely new, but instead built on the strength of their sources to transform the adventures of knights and ladies in ways that fit a different audience. The interlacing threads were kept, though reduced in size and number. At the same time, fewer separate narrative lines helped highlight parallels between stories, leading authors to exploit repetition as a primary device to show their characters' psychological evolution, or in some cases their lack of it. Finally, perhaps encouraged in some cases by difficulty in finding complete copies, and certainly helped by their habit of looking for connections between works, various authors employed the compilation as a unifying tool for their work. As Heijkant states, 'Analogy also gives intertextual coherence, presenting the individual text as part of the Arthurian reality existing outside the romance.'[57] Manuscripts with different sections not explicitly linked together, then, should not necessarily be seen as collections of independent works, but rather as single works knowingly assembled by the process of compilation. They were in this sense very open works, where the readers were invited to interpret and find connections for their continued enjoyment. The parallels, repetitions and analogies readers and listeners find in the Italian Arthurian texts help us see each of the single, only apparently dispersed fragments of the legend as the many bricks of that immense construction that is the Arthurian world.

Notes

[1] 'Je ne sais si, comme dit le proverbe, les choses répétées plaisent, mais je crois que du moins elles signifient.' Roland Barthes, *Mythologies* (Paris, 1957), p. 10. Unless otherwise indicated, translations are mine.

[2] M. Stanesco, 'Le destin européen de la littérature arthurienne', in *Modi e forme della fruizione della 'materia arturiana' nell'Italia dei sec. XIII–XIV* (Milan, 2006), pp. 7–28.

[3] A. Conte (ed.), *Il Novellino* (Rome, 2001) and A. Del Monte (ed.), *Conti di antichi cavalieri* (Milan, 1972).

[4] F. R. Psaki (trans.), 'Introduction', *Tristano Riccardiano*, rpt of the critical edition by A. Scolari (Cambridge, 2006), pp. xiii–xvi.

[5] E. G. Gardner, *The Arthurian Legend in Italian Literature* (New York, 1930; rpt 1971).

[6] D. Delcorno Branca, *Boccaccio e le storie di re Artù* (Bologna, 1991).

[7] '[L]a nostra ignoranza delle motivazioni di un autore non può autorizzare alcuna illazione quanto alla loro incoerenza o manchevolezza' ('Comedìa', in G. Agamben, *Categorie italiane. Studi di poetica e di letteratura* (Rome and Bari, 2010), pp. 3–26, on p. 5).

[8] H. R. Jauss, 'The Alterity and Modernity of Medieval Literature', *New Literary History*, 10/2 (1979), 181–229, on 189.

[9] F. Lot, *Étude sur le* Lancelot en prose (Paris, 1954), esp. pp. 17–28.

[10] J. Frappier, 'Plaidoyer pour l'"architecte", contre une opinion d'Albert Pauphilet sur le *Lancelot en prose*', *Romance Philology*, 8 (1954), 27–33.

[11] E. Vinaver, *The Rise of Romance* (Oxford, 1971), p. 110.

[12] Ibid., p. 76.

[13] Vinaver (ed.), *The Works of Sir Thomas Malory*, rev. P. J. C. Field, 3 vols (Oxford, 1990), esp. I, pp. xlvi and lvii–xcix.

[14] For the Italian tradition, see D. [Delcorno] Branca, *I romanzi italiani di Tristano e la Tavola Ritonda* (Florence, 1968), pp. 67–72.

[15] '[T]he prose *Tristan* enables us to see what happens when the disintegration takes place. Loose threads are scattered everywhere: quests are undertaken and abandoned, interpolations occur that have no bearing on any of the earlier or later episodes, and the work as a whole tends to become a vast *roman à tiroirs*' (Vinaver, 'The Prose *Tristan*', in R. S. Loomis [ed.], *Arthurian Literature in the Middle Ages: A Collaborative History* [Oxford, 1959], pp. 339–74, on p. 345).

[16] E. Baumgartner, *Le* Tristan en prose. *Essai d'interprétation d'un roman médiéval* (Geneva, 1975), pp. 279–81.

[17] E. Ruhe, 'Repetition und Integration. Strukturprobleme des *Roman de Tristan en prose*', in E. Ruhe and R. Schwaderer, *Der altfranzösische Prosaroman. Function, Functionswandel und Ideologie am Beispiel des* Roman de Tristan en prose (Munich, 1979), pp. 131–59.

[18] E. Kennedy, 'The Placing of Miniatures in Relation to the Pattern of Interlace in Two Manuscripts of the Prose *Lancelot*', in K. Busby and C. M. Jones (eds), *'Por la soie amisté': Essays in Honor of Norris J. Lacy* (Atlanta, 2000), pp. 269–82, on p. 271.

[19] E. Baumgartner, 'The Prose *Tristan*', in G. S. Burgess and K. Pratt (eds), *The Arthur of the French: The Arthurian Legend in Medieval French and Occitan Literature* (Cardiff, 2006), pp. 325–41, on p. 335.

[20] See Chapter 3 in this volume.

[21] [Delcorno] Branca, *Romanzi italiani*.

[22] Ibid., pp. 26–7, and A. Donadello (ed.), 'Introduzione', *Il libro di messer Tristano ('Tristano Veneto')* (Venice, 1994).

[23] J. Tasker Grimbert, 'Introduction', *Tristan and Isolde: A Casebook* (New York and London, 1995; rpt 2002), pp. xiii–ci. 'Four of these [Italian prose romances] are fragments, of which the earliest (late thirteenth century) and longest, *Tristano Riccardiano*, strays the farthest from its source, actually exaggerating the preference for chivalric adventures over love' (p. xl).

[24] M. Dardano, 'Il *Tristano Riccardiano* e la *Tavola Ritonda*', in *Lingua e tecnica narrativa nel Duecento* (Rome, 1969), pp. 222–48, on p. 224.

[25] E. Stoppino, '"Lo più disamorato cavaliere del mondo": Dinadano fra *Tristan en prose* e *Tavola Ritonda*', *Italica*, 86/2 (2009), 173–88; S. Mula, 'Dinadan Abroad: Tradition and Innovation for a Counter-Hero', in K. Busby, B. Besamusca and F. Brandsma (eds), *The European Dimension of Arthurian Literature*, Arthurian Literature, 24 (Cambridge, 2007), pp. 50–64.

[26] Dardano, 'Il *Tristano Riccardiano*', p. 227.

[27] M.-J. Heijkant, 'Introduzione', *Tristano Riccardiano*, rpt of the critical edition by E. G. Parodi (Parma, 1991), pp. 31–2.

[28] '"Onde sappiate, messer lo ree Arture e madonna la reina Ginevra e·ttutti igl'altri cavalieri del vostro reame, ke nel mondo non sono se·nnoe due cavalieri e·ddue donne: e in questi due cavalieri si àe tutta la bontade e·ttutta la prodezza del mondo, e ne le due donne si è·ttutta gentilezza e·ttutta la bellezza del mondo; né inn-altri cavalieri io non veggio prodezza, ned inn-altre donne non veggio bellezza, se·nnoe in·lloro.'" Psaki (trans.), Scolari edn, §64.

[29] Psaki (trans.), Scolari edn, §208. '"[C]erto io sono molto allegro che monsignor Tristano àe diliverato lo ree Arturi, impercioe ch'io voglio che voi sappiate ch'egli èe lo migliore cavaliere che voi unquanche udiste parlare."'

[30] Psaki (trans.), Scolari edn, §212. "Certo noi po[ssia]mo dire che monsignor Tristano v'àe fatto piue d'onore che nullo altro cavaliere".

[31] S. Botterill (ed. and trans.), Dante Alighieri, *De Vulgari eloquentia* (New York and Cambridge, 1996), 1.10.2 (p. 23).

[32] D. L. Hoffman, 'Radix Amoris: The *Tavola Ritonda* and Its Response to Dante's Paolo and Francesca', in J. T. Grimbert (ed.), *Tristan and Isolde*, pp. 207–22.

[33] Grimbert, 'Translating Tristan-Love from the Prose *Tristan* to the *Tavola Ritonda*', *Romance Languages Annual*, 6 (1994), 92–7, on 93.

[34] For *Tav. Rit.* I cite M.-J. Heijkant (ed. and intro.), *La Tavola ritonda*, rpt of the critical edition by F.-L. Polidori (Milan and Trent, 1997), §34.

[35] '[N]ullo perfetto amore non è, se l'altra parte non è in concordia. E perché Tristano non era in concordia sua volontà con quella di Bellices, di ciò ella molto si doleva' (*Tav. Rit.* §16).

[36] '"Chè dovete sapere, amore non guarda paraggio di bellezza, nè di ricchezza, ma entra secondo piacere lo porta"' (*Tav. Rit.* §25).

[37] 'The distinction, and the opposition, between the two "Tables" is a characteristic trait of the Italian tradition until the end of the Quattrocento' (F. Cigni, 'Mappa redazionale di *Guiron le Courtois* diffuso in Italia', in *Modi e forme*, pp. 85–117, on pp. 89–90).

³⁸ This episode is missing from Thomas's text, but it was clearly part of the French tradition, and this is the link with the Italian texts. A single episode in the verse tradition gave rise to two episodes in the French *Tristan en prose*, and to further repetition and elaboration of the strategy in the Italian works. Gottfried's *Tristan* offers the earliest extant example of the basic plot.

³⁹ Thomas, *Le Roman de Tristan*, ed. J. Bédier (Paris, 1902–5), pp. 763–76.

⁴⁰ 'Se messire Tristanz nel lessast por son oncle, il alast aprés; mes il dotoit son oncle, car il avoit ja tant apris qu'il savoit vraiement qu'il amoit la dame, et qu'il le haoit por cele dame meïsmes. Ce fu la chose por quoi il le lessoit' (R. L. Curtis [ed.], *Le Roman de Tristan en prose* [Cambridge, 1985], I, §377).

⁴¹ Recently Delcorno Branca has again stressed that in *Tav. Rit.* Tristano has become a model and the embodiment of all virtues. See 'Diffusione della materia arturiana in Italia: per un riesame delle "tradizioni sommerse"', in F. Benozzo et al. (eds), *Culture, livelli di cultura e ambienti nel Medioevo occidentale* (Rome, 2012), pp. 321–40.

⁴² '[. . .] e lo re Marco, vedendo Tristano, sìe gli disse: "Dolce nipote, or non vedi tu quanto disinore ci à fatto quello cavaliere per quella dama? Priégoti che tue la vadi a riscuoterla"' (*Tav. Rit.* §25).

⁴³ 'Lors parole la dame et dit a Tristan: "Tristanz, mout vos ai amé. Mes quant je ai veü que vos si mauvés et si coarz fustes que de la cort vostre oncle m'en lessastes mener a un chevalier sol, sachiez que jamés ne vos amerai"' (Curtis edn, *Tristan en prose*, I, §393).

⁴⁴ 'E la donzella disse: "Avvegna che messer Tristano sia traditore, chè mai per nulla cagione non mi dovea lasciare menar via di corte; ma non di meno, io voglio pur più tosto lui"' (*Tav. Rit.* §25).

⁴⁵ '[E] Tristano e la donzella si ritornano a corte; e rendèlla al suo marito' (*Tav. Rit.* §25).

⁴⁶ 'Essendo al palagio, e Tristano piglia Isotta per la mano, e sì la rappresenta allo re Marco, e dice: "Bel sire, prendete vostra dama, e non siate altra fiata tanto cortese; però ch'egli è maggior briga lo racquistare che non è lo donare"' (*Tav. Rit.* §42).

⁴⁷ M. Dardano, 'Il *Novellino*', in *Lingua e tecnica narrativa*, pp. 148–221, on pp. 164–7. The author of the *Novellino* also seems to have built his collection around the same symmetries.

⁴⁸ '"Prose di romanzi" . . . or novelle? A Note on Adaptations of "franceschi romanzi". The Case of the *Tristano Riccardiano* and the *Novellino*', *Tristania*, 22 (2003), 23–48.

⁴⁹ '[T]he possibility that the fragmentation and the "strange" use of formulae, even in transitions where they are unnecessary (since both passages involve the same hero and the same action), can be attributed to a free use of *entrelacement*. It is clear that the author is trying both to respect his sources and to resize them for the modern taste. His continuous jump-cutting shares the tendency of a contemporary text, the *Novellino*, in favor of *narratio brevis* and the rising genre, the *novella*, and points toward the art of storytelling that Boccaccio celebrates' (Morosini, 'Prose di romanzi', 47–8).

⁵⁰ Heijkant's Chapter 3 in this volume offers a more detailed description of the content; see also G. Allaire (ed. and trans.), *Il Tristano panciatichiano* (Cambridge, 2002).

⁵¹ 'La compilation du *Tristano Panciatichiano*', in B. Besamusca et al. (eds), *Cyclification: The Development of Narrative Cycles in the* Chansons de Geste *and the Arthurian Romance* (Amsterdam/Oxford/New York/Tokyo, 1994), pp. 122–6, on p. 126.

⁵² D. Delcorno Branca, 'Le storie arturiane in Italia', in P. Boitani, M. Mancini and A. Vàrvaro (eds), *Lo spazio letterario del Medioevo*, II: *Il Medioevo volgare*, III: *La ricezione del testo* (Rome, 2003), pp. 385–403, on p. 390.

⁵³ Delcorno Branca, 'Le storie arturiane', p. 391.

⁵⁴ Gardner, *Arthurian Legend*, pp. 85–113; *TLI*, pp. 117–42.

⁵⁵ D. Delcorno Branca (ed.), *Cantari fiabeschi arturiani* (Milan and Trent, 1999). See Chapter 6 in this volume.

⁵⁶ Curt Leviant (ed. and trans.), *King Artus. A Hebrew Arthurian Romance of 1279* (New York, 1969; rpt Syracuse, 2003).

⁵⁷ Heijkant re-ed. of *Tristano Riccardiano*, 'Introduzione', p. 31.

6

ARTHURIAN MATERIAL IN ITALIAN *CANTARI*

Maria Bendinelli Predelli

Cantari are short narrative poems, from 400 to several thousand lines, that emerged as a genre in late medieval Italy.[1] Although some *cantari* represent religious or classical episodes, most have epic or romance subjects. In the hands of semi-learned authors, the genre furnished a matrix in which the Matter of France and the Matter of Britain became conflated. *Cantari* are characterised by eight-line stanzas (*ottava rima*), with alternating rhymes in the first six lines, and a rhyming couplet (*rima baciata*) for the final two – ABABABCC – but a few *cantari* have stanzas of only six lines, ABABCC. The genre was destined for oral presentation, being 'sung' in public by a *canterino*, a latter-day descendant of the *jongleur*. The verb *cantare* (to sing), here used as a noun, can refer to the poem itself or to the internal divisions which occur in the longer examples. While the *cantare* is usually considered a popular genre, the form and rhyme scheme were also used by Boccaccio in his lengthy poems *Teseida* and *Ninfale fiesolano* to impressive effect, and would later attain literary greatness in the hands of Pulci, Boiardo and Ariosto.

The majority of *cantari* that employ Arthurian material seem to date to the second half of the fourteenth century. It is difficult to discuss exact dates or relative order of composition since so few extant manuscripts are dated. A noteworthy exception is BNCF, MS Magl. VIII, 1272 (former MS Gaddi 520), which contains *Il Bel Gherardino*, *Le Ultime imprese e morte di Tristano* and fragments of other *cantari*, and has dates ranging from 1369 to 1373 written in various places throughout. Another useful date is 1388, the year of Florentine composer Antonio Pucci's death. Although Pucci's name survives, most *cantari* are anonymous: many exemplars of the genre are found in fifteenth-century manuscripts, but the poems themselves were often composed earlier than the witnesses that preserve them.

The group of *cantari* that feature Arthurian characters or episodes testify to the popularity of the Matter of Britain in Italy. The lengthy French romances had already been translated or reworked into vernacular Italian prose texts; these *volgarizzamenti* (vernacularisations) would have facilitated transmission of the stories among readers who did not know French, while serving as the putative sources for the shorter versifications. However, the identification of sources presents many problems. Sometimes it is clear that two works tell the same story, but their exact relationship is difficult to establish, one work being an early French courtly poem and the other a late Italian popular *cantare*. At times it is possible to recognise only bits and pieces of motifs found in other works, as the singer picks and chooses from the extensive material of the genre. Every composer followed his own inspiration in order to present innovative tales and please his public. A *cantare* may be an economical version of a lengthy *roman* and the redactor may allude to omissions, indicating that he knew the content of the longer version, or it may be built around a single episode of a long story. Several *cantari* may elaborate on the same motif with completely different results.

Typically, there is an impoverishment of language and meaning as the material moves from courtly romance to the less learned, simplified *cantare*. In the *cantare* the intrusion of elements from the epic cycle with its emphasis on battles and duels brings more visceral excitement to the high-flown rhetoric of romance, as does the insertion of magical elements – the 'marvellous'. Both of these innovations began with the humble, anonymous *canterini* long before the advent of Boiardo's Renaissance masterpiece, the *Inamoramento de Orlando*. The addition of theatrical, dramatic elements (fight scenes, magic) would have been useful in capturing the attention of listeners when these poems were performed in public. Such deviations from the models created variety and novelty; yet despite the stylistic differences among the *canterini*, their awareness of Arthurian narrative is a common denominator.

With a few exceptions, the *cantari* of Arthurian subject matter appear to have been composed as 'stand-alone' poems, without attempting to form a saga or cycle; in this they differ from the *cantari* of Carolingian subject matter, which often provided a basis for lengthy poems such as *La Spagna*, *L'Aspramonte* and *Rinaldo da Monte Albano*. There are surprisingly few appearances of the major Arthurian characters, even though the protagonists belong to Arthur's court. Lancelot has a major role only in the *ottava rima* version of *La Mort le roi Artu*; Gawain appears as protagonist only in the *Ponzela Gaia*; and Lancelot's son Galahad, already a hermit, overcomes adversaries with demonic connotations in the *Cantare del Falso Scudo*. On the other hand, Tristan is the hero of a handful of *cantari* which are centred on the episode of his death at the hand of King Mark. This is entirely in keeping with the popularity that Tristan enjoyed in Italy. Remarkably, the rest of the *cantari* have as their protagonists minor figures, some of whose names are not even directly traceable to the best-known French sources.

The Knight with Enchanted Arms Motif

Three *cantari* are constructed around a narrative motif that is unknown in the French romances: a knight who, with enchanted arms, brings harm and havoc to Arthur's court before being defeated *in extremis* by an extraordinary defender of Arthur's cause.[2] The first – and probably the oldest, to judge by manuscript evidence – is the *Cantare di Lasancis*. Although only ten octaves of this poem survive, it is very likely that the *cantare* told an episode that appears – with a protagonist of the same name – in the prose *Tavola Ritonda*.[3] According to this analogous text, Lasancis's sister gives him a magical lance that will unhorse anyone it touches. By this means, he defeats and imprisons the best knights of the Round Table and even King Arthur himself. Lasancis intends to put them to death in order to avenge the death of certain of his relatives (in the *Tav. Rit.*) or of his brother whom Lancelot had killed (in the *cantare*). According to the *Tav. Rit.,* Queen Guinevere seeks out Tristan in King Mark's kingdom; then, with the advice of a hermit, Tristan brings the duel with Lasancis to a happy conclusion, thereby freeing the prisoners. It is not certain that the *Cantare di Lasancis* had the same ending as the *Tav. Rit.*; the author of the latter may have modified the story in order to exalt the favourite hero of the book, Tristan.[4] In the two other *cantari* that elaborate the same motif the rescuer is Galahad, Lancelot's son, and not Tristan.

In the *Cantare del Falso Scudo* the enchanted weapon is a shield, called 'false' because it is magical and because it is used for a treacherous purpose. Here, the heroic liberator is Galahad. This *cantare* is preserved in a later manuscript than that of *Lasancis*, but may actually preserve an older version of the motif.[5] The Knight of the False Shield is said to be the son of a noble-born fairy who had a magical castle in a lake (*Falso Scudo* I 11.1–5). This description brings to mind Mabuz, son of the Lady of the Lake in *Lanzelet*, an early thirteenth-century German poem which may have had as its model a lost Anglo-Norman poem. The Knight's declared motive – to reveal Lancelot and Guinevere's adulterous relationship – is an archaic one, and recalls Morgana's attempts in the romances to alert Arthur to the adultery, and the *Lai du Cor* (1170–80), in which an enchanted horn will spill its contents on any adulterous woman who tries to drink from it.[6]

Notwithstanding the presence of a very old narrative motif, the *Cantare del Falso Scudo* is probably a late reworking, as is deducible from the heavy contamination with hagiography and Carolingian cycle epic. The magical element is explicitly associated with the diabolical: the shield has three demons in it (I 13.5), and Galahad is a hermit to whom God sends an angelic message.

In the *Cantare di Astore e Morgana*, the setting is more consonant with the Breton cycle. Here, Morgana gives a new suit of armour to Astore (Hestor de Mares in the French), and the knight is transported to Britain on a magical ship. Galahad is again the liberating hero, but a lacunose manuscript prevents us from knowing further plot details. Again, the magical element – always hostile to Arthur's court – is presented in a demonic key.

The three 'knight with enchanted arms' *cantari* appear to elaborate the same motif independently of each other; it is therefore reasonable to assume that there once existed in Italy a source known to all three authors. This now lost source must have drawn its inspiration from French texts, as echoes and analogues of the motif appear in Arthurian tales. For example, *Astore e Morgana* (32.3–8) shares with Rustichello da Pisa's Arthurian Compilation the episode in which Guinevere desperately attempts to dissuade King Arthur from jousting against a powerful knight who is deemed to have enchanted arms because he has defeated all of Arthur's best champions.[7] One may also recall the 'scudo contraffatto' (counterfeit shield) that Tristan puts on at the Tournament of Rocca Dura (Roche Dure) in Tav. Rit.[8] As in the other texts, this enchanted shield presents a threat to the Round Table because it, too, would reveal the adultery between Lancelot and Guinevere.

Antonio Pucci's *Gismirante*

The preceding three examples are relatively restrained in their use of source material, adapting a single episode that focuses on an enemy of Arthur's court who is endowed with enchanted arms. In contrast, *Gismirante* by Antonio Pucci juxtaposes narrative sequences apparently drawn from diverse sources. Its traditional narrative structure is bipartite, similar to that of the courtly poems of Chrétien de Troyes. In the first 'act', the young hero Gismirante solves the vexing problem of Arthur's court – that one cannot be seated at the table until news of some adventure arrives – by bringing a blonde hair that has undoubtedly come from the head of an exceptionally comely lady. In the second 'act', Gismirante travels to a far-off land, finds the lady and wins her. On the return trip, his adventure takes a new twist when the princess is carried off by a Wild Man, causing the quest to be reopened. The figure of the Wild Man enjoys a long tradition in the Breton cycle, appearing in Geoffrey of Monmouth's *Vita Merlini*, Chrétien's *Yvain*, *Partonopeu(s) de Blois* and *Claris et Laris*, although in these texts he never figures as an abductor of women.

   Gismirante's diverse narrative elements include the folkloristic, but it is noteworthy for its numerous links to Arthurian romance. In addition to the motifs already mentioned, Pucci employs the dying father who sends his son to Arthur's court, as in *Cligés*, and the hero who encounters seductive fairies during his quest. Gismirante reacts to the news of a demanded tribute payment much as Tristan, in the *Tristan en prose*, reacts to the announcement of a tribute due to Morholt. In addition, the *cantare* preserves archaic Breton material such as the search for a wife on the basis of a golden hair, which is mentioned in Gottfried of Strassburg's *Tristan*, and the fantastic 'Porco Troncascino' which finds parallels in the 'Porcus Troit' of the *Historia Brittonum* and the Twrch Trwyth of *Kulhwch and Olwen*.[9]

Ponzela Gaia

As Pucci does in *Gismirante*, the anonymous author of *Ponzela Gaia* derives his motifs from disparate sources, but this time they mostly have French origins (as opposed to Celtic), which lends greater coherence to the *cantare*. The well-known hero Gawain is the protagonist, but the adventure in which he participates belongs to a secondary branch of the Arthurian narrative tradition. Gawain is involved in a bet on who will bring back the best wild game to court. While hunting in the forest, Gawain battles with a serpent. As the combat draws to an end, the serpent discovers the knight's identity. The creature is, in fact, Gaia, daughter of Morgana, who loves Gawain. Here, the *canterino* draws on Marie de France's *Lanval* for the motif of the jealous queen who secures the hero's condemnation unless he reveals his lover. In the *cantare*, however, the episode ends on a cruel note: when Morgana discovers her daughter's love for Gawain, she imprisons her in a cell that is partly submerged in water. To the *Lanval* material, the *canterino* now links the typical quest theme: the hero must find and liberate his beloved, and punish her oppressor.

When we examine the motifs of this *cantare* and compare them to others, it seems possible that the *Ponzela Gaia* was composed on the basis of contemporary narratives circulating in northern Italy rather than employing earlier French sources. The motifs woven through the story are reminiscent of corresponding motifs in French sources, but have no crisp parallels in them. The only exception is the imitation of Marie's *Lanval*, a work that was presumably well known in Italy. The wager motif is found in *Madonna Elena*, a widely known *cantare* with Carolingian cycle epic overtones.[10] The transformation of a serpent into a damsel appears in the *Roman de Belris*, a fragmentary Franco-Venetian poem, and is central to the *Cantare di Carduino* (below). Other narrative traits find parallels in *Aymeri de Narbonne*, a *chanson de geste* belonging to the William of Orange cycle, well known in northern Italy. One wonders if the depiction of *Ponzela Gaia*'s prison, where the prisoner is partly submerged in water, echoes the historical reality of the Venetian prisons called *pozzi* (wells), rather than referring to an otherwise unknown literary motif. The *pozzi* were, in fact, situated in the basement of Venice's Palazzo Ducale under sea level, and flooded with two feet of seawater.[11]

The language of *Ponzela Gaia* is a strange mixture of Venetian and Tuscan dialects.[12] Many end rhymes conserve typical features of the northern pronunciation and morphology. Thus the *cantare* has served to strengthen the thesis that most 'Italian' (i.e. Tuscan) renderings of French works, both Arthurian and Carolingian, derive from Franco-Italian intermediate sources rather than from French models directly.

Carduino

The *Cantare* of *Carduino* is clearly related to the short French poem *Le Bel Inconnu* by Renaut de Beaujeu (variously spelled 'de Bâgé') and to the analogous Middle English lay *Lybeaus Desconus*. However, no intermediary source or witness exists to prove transmission into Italy. The story results from a combination of motifs which flourished in French romance tradition at the end of the twelfth and the beginning of the thirteenth centuries. These motifs include the arrival at court of a '*nïce*' (i.e., an

uncouth youth) who is at first mocked but later develops into one of the best champions; a series of combats in which the opponents are increasingly formidable; the
encounter and eventual defeat of a seductive sorceress; a serpent's kiss which frees a
princess from a spell; and revenge upon a father's enemies.

The motif of the 'nice' defines such young heroes as Perceval in the *Conte du
Graal*, Tyolet of the eponymous *lai*, and the protagonist of the German *Lanzelet*.
There are noteworthy similarities between the *enfances* of Carduino and those of
Perceval, and both share the motivation that takes them to Arthur's court. Beyond that
point, however, *Carduino* begins to follow the plot of *Bel Inconnu*. The occasion of
Carduino's departure from court; to some extent, the progression of his quest; the
difficult test of kissing a monstrous serpent; and the resulting marriage with the
enchanted princess whom he has freed, all follow the content of *Bel Inconnu*. The
same type of quest, albeit with variations, is also found in the second part of *Ipomedon*
by Hue de Ruotelande (*c*.1180) and in Chrétien's *Erec*. For the encounter with a
sorceress, however, *Carduino* departs from the French poem; certain aspects of the
episode recall a parallel one in Chrétien's *Lancelot* (ll. 1184–7), but it is not a precise
source for the passage in *Carduino*. Indeed, the types of divergence between *Carduino*
and *Bel Inconnu* raise the possibility that the *cantare* does not derive directly from the
French poem, but from a parallel narrative source, perhaps contemporary if not much
older. The linguistic similarity of the name Carduino with Kaherdin (Kaheddin) in
Thomas's verse *Tristan* may even indicate that the story has Celtic roots.

La Struzione della Tavola Ritonda (Cantari di Lancellotto)

One of the most noteworthy Italian reworkings into verse from an identifiable French
source is the *cantare* published as *Li chantari di Lancellotto* (the title appears in the
copyist's *explicits* at the end of each internal division of the poem). It is, however, the
composer's given title – *La Struzione della Tavola Ritonda* ('The Destruction of the
Round Table'), which appears in the text of the first octave and in the copyist's last
explicit – that more accurately reflects the subject of the poem. The *cantare* is clearly
based on the French prose romance *La Mort le roi Artu* (*c*.1230). The existence of a
definite model allows us to examine the reworking process, which, in turn serves to
illustrate characteristics of the *cantare* genre. Probably the author had before him not
the French *roman*, but an intermediate 'Italian' version that had already undergone a
transformation from the original. We know that reworkings into Italian vernacular of
La Mort Artu circulated in Italy: a lengthy portion survives in the Arthurian compilation BNCF, MS Panciatichiano 33, and there is an extant Hebrew version based on an
Italian original.[13]

We have seen how *cantari* were based on or inspired by Arthurian romance material,
but what is remarkable about *La Struzione* is the way in which the *canterino* renders a

large 'block' of the *Lancelot-Grail* cycle into a compact, autonomous narrative. The French *Mort Artu* is the concluding romance of a huge cycle and, as such, conserves in its opening allusions links to the events that preceded it. The opening of *La Struzione* alludes naturally to Arthur's court as its setting, but presents Lancelot as though he were an unknown character:

> Regnando i·re Artù in Camellotto,
> aveva in suo corte un cavaliere,
> chiamato era per nome Lancelotto;
> consorti avea con seco e buona gente,
> che sempre intorno a·llui facíen ridotto,
> quand'egli stava in corte risedente.
> Costui de·re la donna si teneva
> e con carnale amor co·llei giaceva.[14]

(While reigning in Camelot, King Arthur had at his court a knight called Lancelot; he had with him companions – good people – who were always near him when he was residing at court; that fellow kept the king's lady for himself and lay with her carnally.)

Not only is Lancelot presented as though he were a new character, but the famous adultery between him and Guinevere is here reinterpreted and emphasised. From the first octave, their carnal relationship will serve as a unifying thread that runs throughout the entire poem. In reinterpreting the *Mort Artu* narrative, the *canterino*'s intent is clear: he wishes to refashion the story as a moral *exemplum*. From the beginning, the reader/listener is guided to see the parallels between the fall of ancient Troy and the destruction of the Round Table, including even Arthur's death and the death of his barons. The admittedly misogynistic root cause of both is an adulterous queen.

> Com'è notorio a ttutto quanto il mondo
> i ma' che già per femina so\<n\> stati,
> e come Troia ne fu messa in fondo,
> e terre e genti a morte consumati,
> così simile i·re Artù giocondo
> con tutti i suo baron' d'onor pregiati,
> per la suo donna Ginevra reina
> tutti morinno con crudel rovina.[15]

(As the whole world knows the evils that have already been caused by women, and how Troy was brought low, and lands and people consumed by death: so the same [befell] happy King Arthur with all his barons – so worthy of honour – because of his lady Queen Guinevere: all died with cruel ruin.)

As critics have noted, this theme is also found in *La Mort Artu* and in many ways, serves as an implicit rationale for the whole *Lancelot-Grail* cycle.[16] However, in the French romance, the notion that adulterous love is responsible for destroying Arthur's court is perceived rather than explicitly stated. Beneath the plethora of other themes and motifs, it remains hidden, overwhelmed by the rest of the narrative. In these much shorter *Cantari*, the central theme of adultery remains exposed and visible throughout the entire account, being referred to explicitly and implicitly in various sections.[17] The end of the poem presents a sternly worded *exemplum* that warns against stealing another man's woman, and advises men to guard their 'pretty and comely' ladies – winter and summer – so that they do not play any tricks, as Guinevere did on Arthur.[18]

Despite the economical retelling of the French romance, *La Struzione* actually amplifies passages within the Guinevere–Lancelot love story. For although adultery is morally denounced as the cause for the Table's destruction, these added passages highlight the affection that Lancelot and the queen feel for each other. *La Struzione* stresses the sorrow the lovers feel when forced by papal order to separate.[19] When Lancelot returns to Great Britain and learns that Guinevere has become a penitent – even saintly – abbess, he offers up a moving prayer for the salvation of her soul.[20] The *canterino*'s condemnation of adultery notwithstanding, he cannot entirely resist describing the more pleasant aspects of an amorous relationship.

Compared to the French *roman*, *La Struzione* presents a compact story in which episodes succeed one another at a breathless pace. Naturally, the *canterino* was forced to make deep cuts in his source material, but even where omissions were made, allusions to omitted events prove his knowledge of the more complete source. Despite the need for brevity, he has a predilection for duels and battle scenes: these he narrates with rare vivacity, avoiding the triteness and clichés which too often accompany such action. To tighten the story and keep the focus on the main theme of adultery, the *canterino* changes Arthur's rationale for announcing the tournament at Vincestri (Winchester). In *La Mort Artu* it is held to recruit and test his mounted forces; in *La Struzione*, it is to test the relationship of Lancelot and the queen. Elsewhere, there is drastic simplification of passages that express courtly ideals and sentiments; instead of an idealising romance ethos, the versification presents characters and events as well grounded in realistic contemporary social mores. In the final portion of the story, *La Struzione* preserves Gawain's concern for avenging his brothers but contains no trace of the interior conflicts and psychological complications of the romance's characters.

Cantari di Febus-el-Forte

We can notice a similar reworking process in the *Cantari di Febus-el-Forte*, which utilises a portion of the *Roman de Palamède*. The author probably worked from an intermediary Italian prose version.[21] As in the case of *La Struzione della Tavola Ritonda*, he creates an autonomous narrative, drastically reducing its length and stripping away everything not related to the main argument. In particular, he omits psychological descriptions and moments of internal reflection, which are at most restated as quick remarks made in external dialogue. Even more than changes in style and pacing, one is struck by the deliberate shift in central theme. In the *Roman de Palamède*, the *ubi sunt* theme runs throughout as the narrator exalts the 'good old days' of Arthur's father Uther Pendragon; the past generation is shown as stronger and more courtly than the current one in order to exalt the moral value of knighthood in general. In the best tradition of courtly love, the *Palamède* links a knight's prowess and courage to his love for the beautiful lady who inspires him. By contrast, the *Cantari* focus on the hero's physical prowess and the feats of arms he accomplishes through his own extraordinary strength. The fact that Febus feels love for a damsel is seen as a tragic weakness: "'One weakness only divided my heart: that was Love, because of which I dedicated myself to serving a damsel who made me die.'"[22]

The love theme never completely disappears, but the *canterino* is clearly uncomfortable with the language and tropes of courtly love. In the scenes with female characters, the courtly atmosphere and decorum so evident in the *Palamède* are lost amid a more mechanical and pedestrian presentation of events. As with other *cantari*, due to the influence of Carolingian cycle epics, scenes of combat have been expanded to create a larger-than-life hero. It is impossible to say whether these changes are the work of *Febus*'s redactor or whether they had already appeared in an intermediary text.

Despite the undeniable impoverishment of language with respect to the *Roman*, the Italian reworking displays an admirable narrative efficacy. Everything is described in a lively fashion, riveting the listener/reader's attention with a sense of wonder. Certain episodes are skilfully juxtaposed in a way that creates surprise and delight. The superhuman feats performed by the hero represent an aspect of the marvellous that is shared by many *cantari* and has even been called the defining characteristic of the genre.[23]

Ultime imprese e morte di Tristano; Vendetta di Tristano

An even more drastic reduction of sources at the hands of *canterini* occurs with respect to the French *Roman de Tristan*. Tristan was more popular in Italy than other Arthurian heroes.[24] Consequently, the *cantare* that deals with his last adventures and death has been handed down in more than one manuscript. Italian authors even composed a *Cantare della Vendetta di Tristano* ('Revenge for the Death of Tristan') for which no French source has survived. The final adventures of Tristan do occur in the French Vulgate version, but the *Ultime imprese* contains omissions and discrepancies which can either be attributed to specific narrative choices on the part of the author or suggest the possibility of lost intermediary sources. For instance, the episode with the giant Lucanor is omitted; the traitor who summons King Mark is called Alibruno; the lance Mark uses to mortally wound Tristan is the same lance Tristan himself left at the doorway to Iseut's chamber, and so on.[25]

Given the lack of clear sources, it is not possible definitively to ascribe such changes in content to a single author. More profitable in a discussion of this *cantare* is the poet's skilful use of *ottava rima*, that purely Italian metre. When one thinks of the continuous flow of the lengthy French prose account, one could hardly expect a compact eight-line stanza in verse to achieve a similarly smooth advancement of the plot. Yet after the first six octaves, which introduce and summarise the foregoing story, the account is divided into short scenes, each with its own organic conclusion. Often the octaves begin with a secondary clause that sets up the main sentence, displacing the focus of the utterance to the central verses of the octave, while the final couplet either sums up the short narrative unit or, more often, provides a 'hook' to the content of the following stanza, thereby ensuring the continuity of the narration.

The formal arrangement of the octave is used for another purpose: to lend balance to the poem by equally distributing dialogue. Very often a character's remark is situated entirely within one octave, whether in direct discourse with another interlocutor or when indirectly expressing his or her thoughts or feelings; the next speaker's reply is assigned to the following stanza. The appearance of direct discourse creates a more vivid characterisation and lends theatricality to the story. A brief comparison to an extant Italian prose romance, the *Tristano Panciatichiano*, illustrates this quality. The prose romance is bald and repetitive: 'When Sir Tristan feels himself wounded, he knew at once that he was mortally wounded.'[26] The *cantare*, by contrast, amplifies the pace and emotion of the moment:

> Quando Tristano si sentì ferito
> alla reina cominciò a ddire:
> 'Gentil madonna, i' sono a tal partito,
> da vvoi per forza mi convien partire . . .'[27]

(When Tristan felt himself wounded / he began to say to the queen / 'Noble lady, I have come to such a pass / that I am forced to leave you . . .')

In conjunction with the octave's inherent rhythm and the concise presentation of material demanded by the eight-line form, the addition of direct discourse enlivens the tale, imparting a greater emotional immediacy to capture and hold the public's attention more effectively.

The *Duello al Petrone di Merlino*

The duel between Lancelot and Tristan at Merlin's Stone (*Perron Merlin*) is a crucial episode in the *Roman de Tristan*: this is where Lancelot tries to convince Tristan to come with him to Arthur's court. In the larger literary tradition, it is a vital 'suture' that fuses the Tristan cycle with the Lancelot material.[28] The episode was re-elaborated in Rustichello da Pisa's Arthurian Compilation, written in French (after 1272/4), a fragment of which was already included in an anthology of Tristan material written in Italy by the late Duecento (BnF, MS fr. 12599).[29] The *cantare* appears to follow the version of the duel given by Rustichello's Compilation rather than that of the *Roman de Tristan*.[30]

Despite the fact that the *Duello* contains allusions to other Arthurian characters and their adventures, the *cantare* appears to be a self-contained composition and not a fragment of a now lost longer poem. The *canterino* was obviously writing for an Italian public well aware of the Arthurian tradition: the *cantare* opens with a typical courtly springtime scene, and major characters are introduced by first name with no epithet or special expository remarks. When compared, however, to Rustichello's Compilation, the closest extant source, one notes certain plot differences. For instance, the *Duello* concludes happily with Tristan and Lancelot embracing, and includes a brief reference to making peace with Palamedes, a notion not found in the Compilation. Minor discrepancies may be attributed to the *canterino*'s embellishments for the purpose of winning over his audience, a typical feature of the reworking process. In the *Duello*, the helmeted knights – who do not recognise each other – always exchange a few pointed remarks before engaging in combat, and the description of their sword blows constantly alternates with additional threats and imprecations. The revelation of their respective names is prolonged for suspense, and the moment in which each finally discovers the other's identity is presented to good dramatic effect. Even ambiguous references to 'the queen' deliberately create a misunderstanding regarding the knight's beloved. Only when Tristan finally names Iseut aloud does Lancelot realise the identity of his opponent and withdraw in surprise. The emotions of the combatants are exaggerated and presented in a rather blunt, even plebeian manner. After requesting a truce, Lancelot removes his helmet and Tristan finally learns his identity. This sort of blatant theatricality would have been useful to the street performer; such a device conforms to oral transmission and can be identified as another characteristic of the *cantare* genre.

Bruto di Bretagna

This short *cantare* in forty-six octaves is one of the few for which an author is known – the Florentine herald Antonio Pucci (*c.*1310–88), who also composed the *Gismirante*. It is also one of the few that has an extant, identifiable source. However, instead of deriving Arthurian characters and content from a French romance, in this case the poet had in front of him Andreas Capellanus' well-known Latin treatise *De amore*. Andreas himself employed Arthurian tropes in the second book of his *Art of Love*: the topic for discussion – the Rules of Love – is introduced by the adventure that brings an unnamed knight to Arthur's court. The knight's quest is to assemble all the rules for loving and then deliver them to all the ladies and knights engaging in 'courtly love'.

In the *cantare*, the knightly protagonist is given a name: Bruto di Bretagna (Brutus of Brittany). This is probably a misreading of the adjective 'Brito' (Breton) assigned to the hero in the Latin text.[31] As with other derivative literary works in medieval Italy, one cannot be sure whether Antonio Pucci knew the Latin original or was relying on an Italian *volgarizzamento*; either Pucci or an earlier translator may have assigned the name 'Brutus' to the character.

Both Andreas and Pucci appreciated the Matter of Britain and recognised its popularity, although they adapted it for different purposes. The erudition and rhetoric of Andreas' treatise gives way to the demands of oral performance in Pucci's *cantare*. Whereas in *De amore* the purpose of the knight's search for King Arthur is revealed gradually, in the *cantare* his mission is explicit from the outset. The allegories and symbols of *De amore* – the sparrowhawk, which represents difficulty in amorous conquest; dogs who guard the virtue of Love; the apparition of the *chartula amoris* (rules of love) – are transformed in the *cantare* into actual creatures and objects, albeit with magical significance, as one would find in folk tales.[32]

We have seen the importance of clear exposition, quick pacing and the inclusion of the marvellous in other *cantari*. Pucci retains mythical elements and courtly references for their entertainment value, but transposes them into a key more consonant with the sensibilities of his non-courtly milieu: the merchants and citizens of late medieval Florence.

Conclusion

From this brief overview of Arthurian *cantari*, one can recognise certain common traits in the versification of the courtly romance tradition: adaptation of the narrative into a form accessible to the general public; displacement of symbols and allusions into purely magical elements; a gradual shift in tone, structure and content towards the folk or fairy tale. The *cantare* strips away from the original narrative all those elements that reflect the values of a particular social class at a particular historical moment. As the traditional romance vicissitudes are distilled into their most elementary components – a warrior's prowess, diffidence at an unavoidable affair of the heart – they become atemporal and, as such, are transmissible to a different audience in a different place. Concurrently developing in Italy was the art of narrating quickly and succinctly in a compact form, with episodes closely following one after the other. The shift in focus combined with the tighter structure aided the material's penetration and guaranteed its success among new strata of the population (one thinks of the contemporary development of the Italian *novella* as another response to lengthy narratives in prose). The metrical and stylistic solutions afforded by the octave constitute a rich soil from which would flower the great chivalric epic poems of the Renaissance.

(Translated by Gloria Allaire)

Appendix
Finding List of Manuscript Exemplars and Modern Editions

Astore e Morgana

MS: Florence, Bibl. Riccardiana, MS Ricc. 2971. Second half of fifteenth century. Acephalous. 40-octave fragment with lacuna between octaves 35 and 36.

Edition: *Cantari fiabeschi arturiani*, ed. D. Delcorno Branca (Milan and Trent, 1999). Text: pp. 85–94; Notes: pp. 165–71.

Bruto di Bretagna

MS: BNCF, MS Nuovi Acquisti 333 ('Kirkup codex'). Datable to 1370–90. Tuscan, with some traces of a northern dialect. Acephalous. Contains only *cantari* by Antonio Pucci: the last four octaves of *Madonna Leonessa*; *Reina d'Oriente*; *Bruto di Bretagna*; *Apollonio di Tiro; Guerra di Pisa*.

Editions: E. Benucci (ed.), in *Cantari novellistici dal Tre al Cinquecento,* ed. E. Benucci et al., Intro. by D. De Robertis. 2 vols (Rome, 2002). Text: I, pp. 109–27; Notes: II, p. 888; Apparatus: II, pp. 937–8; N. Sapegno (ed.), *Poeti minori del Trecento* (Milan and Naples, 1962), pp. 869–81.

Carduino

MS: Florence, Bibl. Riccardiana, MS Ricc. 2873. Dated 1432.

Editions: P. Rajna (ed.), *I Cantari di Carduino, giuntovi quello di Tristano e Lanciellotto quando combattettero al Petrone di Merlino*, Scelta di curiosità letterarie inedite o rare, 135 (Bologna, 1873; 1968); D. Delcorno Branca (ed.), *Cantari fiabeschi arturiani*. Text: pp. 39–64; Notes: pp. 135–51.

Duello al Petrone di Merlino (Cantare quando Tristano e Lancelotto combattettero al petrone di Merlino)

MS: Florence, Bibl. Riccardiana, MS Ricc. 2873. Dated 1432. A collection of texts, including moral and religious ones in *ottava rima*, alongside other *cantari*: *Gismirante, Carduino, Madonna Leonessa*. Southern and western Tuscan traits.

Edition: Rajna (ed.), *I Cantari di Carduino*.

Cantari del Falso Scudo

MS: BNCF, MS Magl. VII, 1066. Copied first half fifteenth century .

Edition: Delcorno Branca (ed.), *Cantari fiabeschi arturiani*. Text: pp. 65–84; Notes: pp. 152–64.

Cantari di Febus-el-Forte

MS: BNCF, MS Banco Rari 45 (former Magl. II.II.33; former CI. VII. P.2, cod. 19). Second half fourteenth century or early fifteenth. Sienese linguistic traits. Also referred to as 'Febusso e Breusso' or 'Il Febusso'.

Editions: A. Limentani (ed.), *Dal Roman de Palamedés ai Cantari di Febus-el-Forte* (Bologna, 1962). Text: pp. 189–285.

Galasso dalla Scura Valle
MS: Archivio di Stato di Venezia, Miscellanea di Atti diversi, manoscritti, busta 137, lettera a. Fifteenth century. Paper. 10–fol. fragment. Veneto dialect.
Edition: Delcorno Branca (ed.), *Cantari fiabeschi arturiani*. Text: pp. 125–34; Notes: pp. 185–92.

Gismirante
MS: Florence, Bibl. Riccardiana, MS Ricc. 2873. Florentine. Dated 1432.
Editions: F. Zabagli (ed.) in *Cantari novellistici dal Tre al Cinquecento*, ed. Benucci et al. Text: I, pp. 131–64; Notes: II, pp. 888–9; Apparatus: II, pp. 938–40; Antonio Pucci, *Gismirante. Madonna Leonessa*, M. Bendinelli Predelli (ed.), with English translations by J. Myerson, A. Glover and A. Saunderson. British Rencesvals Publications, 6 (Edinburgh, 2013).

Cantare di Lasancis
MS: BNCF, MS Magl. VIII, 1272. *c.*1372. Fragment (10 octaves plus one line).
Edition: Delcorno Branca (ed.), *Cantari fiabeschi arturiani*. Text: pp. 110–2; Notes: pp. 180–4.

Cantari di Lancellotto. See *La Struzione della Tavola Ritonda*

Ponzela Gaia
MS: Venice, Bibl. Marciana, MS It. Cl. IX 621 (=10697). Second half of fifteenth century; watermark dates 1467. Veneto dialect with strong Tuscan patina.
Editions: B. Barbiellini Amidei (ed.), *Ponzela Gaia. Galvano e la donna serpente* (Milan, 2000); R. Manetti (ed.), in *Cantari novellistici dal Tre al Cinquecento* (Rome, 2002). Text: I, pp. 407–48; Notes: II, pp. 913–5; Apparatus: II, p. 958.

La Struzione della Tavola Ritonda
MS: Florence, Bibl. Medicea Laurenziana, MS Plut. LXXVIII, 23. Composite MS. One section (of paper folios) contains an anthology of *cantari*: *Cantari di Amadio, Cantare di Piramo e di Tisbe, Cantare del Mercatante, Cantari di Lancellotto*.
Editions: E. T. Griffiths (ed.), *Li chantari di Lancellotto*, with introduction, notes and glossary by (Oxford, 1924); M. Bendinelli Predelli (ed.), '*La Struzione della Tavola Rotonda*', *Letteratura italiana antica*, 13 (2012), 17–111.

Ultime imprese e morte di Tristano

MSS: 1. BNCF, MS Magl. VIII, 1272 (former MS Gaddi 520). *c*.1372. Also contains a complete *Bel Gherardino*, and fragments of *Cantare della Vendetta*, *Cantare di Lasancis*, *Guerra di Troia*.

  2. Milan, Bibl. Ambrosiana, MS N.95 Sup. Dated 1430. Octave 58 to the end, but begins with an original introductory octave not found in the longer BNCF witness.

  3. Florence, Bibl. Riccardiana, MS Ricc. 2971. Datable to second half of fifteenth century.

Editions: G. Bertoni (ed.), *Cantari di Tristano* (Modena, 1937). For corrections to this edition, see D. De Robertis, 'Cantari antichi', *Studi di filologia italiana*, 38 (1970), 67–175. Bertoni arbitrarily split the story into two parts which he titled *Le ultime imprese di Tristano* (56 octaves) and *La morte di Tristano* (35 octaves); A. Balduino, *Cantari del Trecento* (Milan, 1970) restored the *cantare*'s unity according to the BNCF and Riccardiana manuscripts. F. Cigni, 'Un nuovo testimone del cantare *Ultime imprese e morte di Tristano*', *SMV*, 43 (1997), 131–91. 'Morte di Tristano' in *Poeti minori del Trecento*, ed. N. Sapegno (Milan and Naples, 1962), pp. 938–46.

Cantare della Vendetta (La vendeta che fe' meser Lanzelloto de la morte de miser Tristano)

MSS:

  1. Milan, Bibl. Ambrosiana MS N.95 Sup. Dated 1430. Complete witness.

  2. BNCF, MS Magl. VIII. 1272. *c*.1372. Florentine dialect. Fragmentary: 16 octaves and 3 lines.

Edition: Bertoni (ed.), *Cantari di Tristano*.

Notes

[1] For a concise discussion of the genre, see G. Allaire, 'Cantare', in C. Kleinhenz (ed.), *Medieval Italy: An Encyclopedia*, 2 vols (New York, 2004), I, pp. 180–1.

[2] *TLI*, pp. 201–23.

[3] F.-L. Polidori (ed.), *La Tavola Ritonda* (Bologna, 1864–6); reprinted by M.-J. Heijkant (Milan and Trent, 1997), ch. 87.

[4] *TLI*, p. 209.

[5] Ibid., p. 209.

[6] See E. K. Heller, 'The Story of the Magic Horn: A Study in the Development of a Mediaeval Folk Tale', *Speculum*, 9/1 (1934), 38–50.

[7] F. Cigni (ed.), *Il romanzo arturiano di Rustichello da Pisa* (Pisa, 1994), §11.

[8] *Tav. Rit.*, chs 80 and 82; Lös. §§190 and 192.

[9] E. G. Gardner, *The Arthurian Legend in Italian Literature* (London and New York, 1930), note on p. 250. See also C. Kleinhenz, 'The Quest Motif in Medieval Italian Literature', in K. Busby and N. J. Lacy (eds), *Conjunctures: Medieval Studies in Honor of Douglas Kelly* (Amsterdam, 1994), pp. 235–51, on p. 250.

[10] The tendency toward contamination of courtly romance with *chanson de geste* material, already begun in *Cligés* and *Partonopeus*, becomes continually more marked in Italian literature. Between 1377 and 1380, the *Madonna Elena* story was painted on the ceiling of Palazzo Chiaramonte in Palermo, proving its wide transmission. See Chapter 13 in this volume.

[11] G. Casanova, *Histoire de ma fuite des prisons de la République de Venise qu'on appelle les Plombs* (Bordeaux, 1884), p. 126.

[12] B. Barbiellini Amidei (ed.), *Ponzela Gaia. Galvano e la donna serpente* (Milan and Trent, 2000), pp. 12 and 46–50.

[13] G. Allaire (ed. and trans.), *Il Tristano panciatichiano* (Cambridge, 2002); C. Leviant (ed. and trans.), *King Artus: A Hebrew Arthurian Romance of 1279* (Syracuse, NY, 2003).

[14] Bendinelli Predelli (ed.), '*La Struzione della Tavola Rotonda*', *Letteratura italiana antica*, 13, 17–111; see also E. T. Griffiths (ed.), *Li chantari di Lancellotto* (Oxford, 1924), I.3.

[15] Ibid., I.2.

[16] J. Frappier (ed.), *La Mort le roi Artu* (Geneva, 1956), pp. xiii–xiv; N. J. Lacy, 'The Sense of an Ending: *La Mort le roi Artu*', in C. Dover (ed.), *A Companion to the Lancelot-Grail Cycle* (Cambridge, 2003), pp. 115–24, on p. 117.

[17] Bendinelli Prendelli edn, II, 1.6–8; II, 44.4–6; IV, 2.8–3.2; V, 1.4–8.

[18] '[E] chi ha dama bella ed avenente, / guardila sì nel verno e nella state / ch'ella non facci <ma'> malizie alcune, / sì come fé Ginevra a·re Artune' (Bendinelli Predelli edn, VII, 51.5–8).

[19] Bendinelli Predelli edn, IV, 46.1–5; 48.1–5; 49.6–8.

[20] Bendinelli Predelli edn, VII, 8–10.

[21] A. Limentani (ed.), *Dal* Roman de Palamedés *ai* Cantari di Febus-el-Forte. *Testi francesi e italiani del Due e Trecento* (Bologna, 1962), Introduction, p. xviii.

[22] '[U]na sola viltà mi partì el core . . . / ciò fu Amore, per cui mi diei a servire / una pulzella che mi fé morire' (Limentani edn, I, 27.5–8).

[23] V. Branca, 'Nostalgie tardogotiche e gusto del fiabesco nella tradizione narrativa dei cantari', in *Studi di varia umanità in onore di Francesco Flora* (Milan, 1963), pp. 88–108, on pp. 99 and 108.

[24] See Chapter 4 in this volume.

[25] F. Cigni, 'Un nuovo testimone del cantare *Ultime imprese e morte di Tristano*', *SMV*, 43 (1997), 131–91, on 143; G. Bertoni (ed.), *Cantari di Tristano* (Modena, 1937), pp. 250–4.

[26] 'Quando messer Tristano si sente fedito, elli conobbe inmantenente ch'elli era fedito mortalmente' (Allaire edn, *Il Tristano panciatichiano*, §524).

[27] Cigni edn, *Ultime imprese*, 66.1–4.

[28] *TLI*, p. 180.

[29] Cigni edn, *Il romanzo arturiano* (based on BnF, MS fr. 1463), §§ 44–8. Unfortunately, owing to a lacuna, MS fr. 12599 does not preserve the duel.

[30] See Chapters 2, 4 and 7 in this volume.

[31] P. G. Walsh (ed. and trans.), *Andreas Capellanus on Love* (London, 1982), pp. 272–3, §§ 11, 12, 14, 19.

[32] M. Lecco, '*Bruto di Bertagna* e Andrea Cappellano. Analisi delle fonti e considerazioni comparative su un *Cantare* del XIV secolo', *Forum Italicum*, 38/2 (2004), 545–61, on 553.

7

ARTHUR AS RENAISSANCE EPIC

Eleonora Stoppino

Between the fifteenth and the sixteenth centuries, Arthurian cycle texts circulated widely in the Italian peninsula. This circulation varied with respect to audiences, languages, literary forms and media. From the lords of the northern courts to the *cantimpanca* (the popular singers of the *piazze*), from the short *cantari* on Merlin and Tristan to Florentine *zibaldoni* (commonplace books), from the compilations in French to the authoritative reworkings operated by Boiardo and Ariosto, the Arthurian legend represents a conspicuous and lively component of the literary tradition of the Italian Renaissance. The pervasive presence of Arthurian themes in the life of the Renaissance courts finds evocative witnesses in the frescoes scattered throughout northern Italy. The rediscovery in the mid-1960s of a cycle attributed to Pisanello in the Palazzo Ducale of Mantua is only one striking example of the tales narrated on the walls of castles such as Frugarolo, Roncolo and La Manta, near Saluzzo.[1]

This chapter follows the arc of Arthurian literature in the Italian Renaissance, focusing on specific aspects of its production and its later study. It offers an overview of Arthurian texts from the end of the fourteenth century to the mid-sixteenth, from the post-Petrarchan rise of Latin humanism to the monumental change in chivalric epic initiated by the Counter-Reformation (1545–63). Through a discussion of the literature, I will touch on geographical centres of diffusion; textual circulation; coexistence of the Arthurian and Carolingian matters; several specific tales and characters of the Arthurian cycle that were particularly successful in the Italian Renaissance; and finally, the role of this cycle in the chivalric epics by Matteo Maria Boiardo and Ludovico Ariosto. I should note at the outset that, as in medieval and Renaissance chivalric literature in general, most texts are anonymous and circulated without reference to an author.[2]

The history of Arthurian texts in the Italian Renaissance both begins and ends with peripheral and little-read monumental poems, whose originality seems to be connected with their neglect: *Le Chevalier Errant* by Marquis Tommaso III di Saluzzo (written between 1394 and 1396) and Alamanni's *Girone (Gyrone) il cortese* (published for the first time in 1548). *Le Chevalier Errant*, written a century after Rustichello's Arthurian text, turns to French verse with prose insertions to narrate the adventures of a knight – a figure of the author-narrator – in his search for love.[3] The tales of Tristan and Lancelot find ample space in this highly allegorical text, which does not appear to have enjoyed a vast audience. The book is particularly important to mention in the beginning of this review of Arthurian literature in the Italian Renaissance, both because it opens it temporally and also because it provides a spatial connection, an ideal bridge from French-speaking Italy to the region of the peninsula where chivalric epic had its explosion. Tommaso di Saluzzo's dynastic connections provide a suggestive link with the court of Ferrara, one of the most important centres of circulation and production of chivalric epic in the Italian Renaissance.[4] In 1431, Rizarda of Saluzzo, Tommaso's daughter, married none other than Niccolò III Este, lord of Ferrara.

Archival research confirms that the north-eastern courts, and Ferrara in particular, favoured Arthurian texts. In particular, in the inventory of Niccolò III (1436) is a 'Gurone in francexe', and the most important inventories compiled during the reign of Ercole I (1471 and 1495) mention texts of the same subject.[5] Borso d'Este (Duke of Ferrara, 1441–50) was extremely fond of Arthurian narratives: in a letter to Ludovico da Cuneo (a town close to Tommaso's lands), Borso says that he has read all of his own French books, and asks for books 'of the Old Table . . . from which we will receive more pleasure and satisfaction than from the conquest of a city'.[6] If Borso and Ercole I were avid consumers of Arthurian literature, Ercole's daughter Isabella d'Este, Marchioness of Mantua and one of the most important female patrons of the sixteenth century, was so fond of chivalric texts that she asked for them specifically, by title. In a letter written in 1491 to Giorgio Brugnolo, one of her book-finders, she sends a long list that includes a *Merlino*.[7]

As these examples demonstrate, one avenue of research on Arthurian literature in the Renaissance has been the exploration of archival materials to assess the presence of these texts in the age between manuscript and print. A particularly interesting example of this presence takes us from northern Italy to Florence, where in the first half of the sixteenth century the bibliophile Stradino assembles an annotated list of chivalric romances on a guard leaf of a manuscript. Stradino, a book collector whose real name was Giovanni Mazzuoli, conveys a passion for the Arthurian stories, reconstructing the genealogy of characters 'from Breus and Febus, knights errant of the old and new table, with the Graal in the times of King Uther Pendragon, to King Arthur of Camelot, with the battles waged by Lancelot of the Lake and Tristan of Leonis and the other errants'.[8] The same passion for the same heroes had emerged almost a century earlier in the Tuscan *Cantare dei cantari*, which lists – in octaves – the materials available to a popular singer in order to entertain his public in the *piazza*.[9]

Recent research on the material production and circulation of these texts has greatly expanded our knowledge of the impact they had on all strata of society and on different readers, from lords to commoners. It has also highlighted the presence of Arthurian texts in various areas of the peninsula. The area of highest French influence – modern-day Piedmont – was a vital centre of circulation and production of Arthurian texts, embodied by *Le Chevalier Errant* by Tommaso III; the northern courts, Ferrara and Mantua in particular, had these texts as prized possessions in their libraries;

Florence and Tuscany continued the medieval tradition of Arthurian tales so dear to the readers of Rustichello; and the region around Venice continued to be a focal point of production and diffusion, also by virtue of the advent of print.

Another aspect of the research on the *matière de Bretagne* is the study of specific traditions within the Arthurian corpus, such as the exploration of the vital legend of Merlin, reworked in Italy through the centuries. The Merlin tradition is embodied in the Renaissance by the *Historia di Merlino* or *Vita di Merlino* (*editio princeps*, Venice, 1480), which was known, for instance, to Ludovico Ariosto. The *Historia di Merlino* is probably the last great compilation of Arthurian material in prose, and its success is witnessed by its vitality in print in the sixteenth century.[10]

Like the *Historia di Merlino*, in the fourteenth and the fifteenth centuries other Arthurian texts also bridge the illusory boundary between the Middle Ages and the Renaissance. Circulating predominantly in Tuscany and copied in the Quattrocento, but most likely composed in the preceding century, these texts are popular *cantari*, short poems written in octaves.[11] Daniela Delcorno Branca has subdivided these texts into three thematic categories.[12] *Cantari* such as *Bel Gherardino*, *Liombruno*, *Ponzela Gaia* narrate a knight's encounter with a fairy and their love; after the love is revealed, the knight loses his beloved and finally recovers her.[13] The second theme, that of the *Bildungsroman* of a young knight, is modelled on Chrétien's *Perceval* and Renaut de Beaujeu's *Le Bel Inconnu*, and is present in the *Cantare di Carduino*: a boy, raised in the forest by his mother, enters Arthur's court and conquers a bride by overcoming a series of enchantments. Finally, in *cantari* such as the *Falso scudo* and the fragmentary *Astore e Morgana*, a knight sent by an evil sorceress threatens Arthur's court, but is ultimately defeated by a hermit knight.

In the Italian Renaissance, as in the preceding period, the Arthurian tradition coexists, or rather mixes and intersects, with Carolingian epic, the other pole of medieval French literature on the axis of epic and romance. A double phenomenon exists, apparently contradictory. On the one hand, the Arthurian texts seem to have been the vast majority;[14] the great chivalric production of the sixteenth century, on the other hand, takes as its protagonists the heroes of the Carolingian cycle. This apparent contradiction is best explored through the work of Matteo Maria Boiardo, the Renaissance author who revitalized the Arthurian tradition, raising it to a learned, authorial context.

Recent studies have complicated the traditional view that Boiardo, in his *Inamoramento de Orlando* [*Roland in Love*], coupled the Carolingian and Arthurian cycles.[15] From a structural point of view, Boiardo realized a profound combination of the two traditions, applying to the Carolingian narratives the technique of *entrelacement*, typical of the Arthurian texts.[16] From the point of view of content, Boiardo presents the Carolingian heroes as affected by the 'Arthurian' force of love, as the title itself demonstrates. Orlando, the hero of the Frankish army, falls in love with the beautiful pagan princess Angelica and is drawn to the adventures (*venture* or *aventure*) typical of the Arthurian tradition. This mixture, however, was already a specific trait of the tradition of the *cantari* and *poemi cavallereschi*, a popular epic genre widespread in northern Italy during the century preceding Boiardo's poem. Carolingian poems such as the *Ancroia* and the *Inamoramento de Carlo Magno* already provided models for the successful integration of the themes of romance with the epic matter of war.

What is innovative in Boiardo's treatment of the Arthurian cycle, however, is the explicit poetic reflection on the history of the two cycles in the Italian context of the early Renaissance:

Fo glorïosa Bretagna la grande	Britain the great was glorious
Una stagion, per l'arme e per l'amore.	once, in arms and love
(Onde ancor hoggi il nome suo si spande	(and still today her name resounds
Sì ch'al re Artuse fa portar honore),	and brings honour to King Arthur),
Quando e bon cavalieri a quele bande	when the good knights in that region
Mostrarno in più batalie il suo valore,	showed their valour in battle,
Andando con lor dame in aventura	setting out on adventures with their ladies,
Et hor sua fama al nostro tempo dura.	and their fame still lasts in our times.
Re Carlo in Franza poi tenne gran corte,	King Charles then held court in France,
Ma a quela prima non fo somiliante,	but his court did not resemble that first one,
Ben che assai fosse ancor robusto e forte	even though he was valiant and strong
Et avesse Renaldo e 'l sir d'Anglante:	and had Rinaldo and Orlando on his side:
E sol se dete ale bataglie sante,	he devoted himself only to holy battles,
Non fo di quel valor o quela estima	his court had not the same valour and esteem
Qual fo quel'altra ch'io contava in prima.[17]	as the other I mentioned before.

In these two octaves, Boiardo seems to demonstrate awareness not only of the poetic distinction between the two cycles, which in his day was certainly common knowledge, but also of the passage from one to the other in the favour of his audience. Boiardo's choice is unwavering: his faithfulness to the Arthurian matter and his predilection for its themes and narrations are apparent throughout the *Inamoramento*. The Arthurian court is a transparent double for the Ferrarese court Boiardo addresses with his poem, and Tristan and Lancelot are models for the behaviour of anyone who aspires to love and honour:

E qual fia quel che odendo de Tristano	And who could, hearing the story
E de sua dama ciò che se ne dice,	of Tristan and his lady,
Che non mova ad amarli il cor humano	not be moved to love by his human heart,
Reputando il suo fin dolcie e felice?	thinking their end happy and sweet?
Ché viso a viso essendo, e man a mano	As face to face and hand in hand
E cor con cor più streti ala radice,	and heart to heart, tied at the root,
Nele braza l'un l'altro, a tal conforto	in each other's arms, to such comfort
Ciascun di lor rimase a un ponto morto.	each of them died in the same instant.
E Lanciloto e sua Regina bela	And Lancelot and his fair Queen
Mostrarno l'un per l'altro un tal valore	showed such valour, each for each,
Che dove de soi giesti si favela	that where their deeds are told

Par che d'intorno el ciel arda d'amore.	it seems that the skies around burn with love.
Tragasse avanti adonque ogni dongiella,	Come forward then, every damsel
Ogni baron chi vòl portar honore,	and every lord who seeks honor,
Et oda nel mio canto quel ch'io dico	and listen to what I say in my song
De dame e cavalier del tempo antiquo.[18]	of ladies and of knights of old.

If the reminiscence of Dante's Francesca and Paolo, damned forever by the irresistible power of the Arthurian tale, is strongly present in these lines, the courtly settings of the tale and of its audience have now made them the mirror images of each other.[19]

After Boiardo (d. 1494) left his poem unfinished, the coexistence of Arthurian and Carolingian literature continued, but there were also texts predominantly focused only on the characters of the Old Table. One of the poets who sought to complete Boiardo's unfinished poem, Niccolò degli Agostini, began publishing his continuations of the *Inamoramento de Orlando* in 1505–6. Niccolò, a Venetian poet and soldier, also wrote an *Inamoramento di messer Tristano e madonna Isotta* in three books (1515–20), and an *Innamoramento di messer Lancillotto e madonna Ginevra* (1521) in two books. By 1520, according to his own request for permission to publish submitted to the Venetian Senate, he had already completed all his work on the Arthurian poems. Niccolò's poems on the Old Table have no direct relation to the tradition of the *Tavola Ritonda*, and they are conceived for consumption and blockbuster success. The author mixed themes, characters and episodes; his writing shares much with the simpler, popular style of the *cantari*. A peculiar trait of Niccolò's work is the insertion of Ovidian episodes within the fabric of the Arthurian legend, a feature certainly connected to his work in translating the *Metamorphoses*.[20]

The three books of Niccolò's *Tristano* treat, respectively, Tristan's childhood and adventurous youth; his love for Iseut and the couple's death; and the revenge Tristan's friends take on King Mark. While in the framework of the Breton legend, the narrative makes space in the third book for characters from Boiardo's plot. The tone of the narration, moreover, inclines more towards the comic.

Comic tones are also present in the three books Niccolò devoted to Lancelot, published in Venice by Zoppino. The first two books (fifteen cantos) appeared in 1521 as *Lo inamoramento di messer Lancilotto e di madonna Genevra, nel quale si trattano le horribili prodezze e le strane venture de tutti li cavalieri erranti nella Tavola rotunda* ('The Falling in Love of Sir Lancelot and Lady Guinevere, in which are treated the Horrible Feats and Incredible Adventures of All the Knights Errant of the Round Table'). In 1526, probably the year of Niccolò's death, Zoppino published the third and last book with a final addition by Marco Guazzo (*Il libro terzo e ultimo del inamoramento di Lancillotto de Zenevra... agiuntovi el fine de tuti li libri de Lancilotto del strenuo milite Marco Guazzo*). In this work, Niccolò treated the Arthurian matter with even more freedom than in the *Tristano*: Guinevere is not truly a protagonist, whereas the loves of Lancelot for other characters take centre stage. In particular, the 'polzella Gaggia', the lady-snake of the traditional *cantari*, gains a more central role along with Bellisandra, Ersilla and other figures from the popular tradition. To give an example of Niccolò's reworking of the Arthurian tradition, the 'polzella Gaggia', out of jealousy, starves Bellisandra, wife of the protagonist, to death. After her death, she embalms Bellisandra's corpse and adorns it with inscriptions about modesty. Galehaut remains a warrior who fights against King Arthur, and it is a serving-maid who performs the role of intermediary between the lovers.

Evangelista Fossa, a friar from Cremona born in the third quarter of the fifteenth century to an ancient and noble family, received a humanistic education and was the prior of the Convent of Saint Mary of the Fountain in Casalmaggiore in 1497–8. He belonged to the Venetian cultural milieu (as proven by the dedication of his poem to a 'ser Lorenzo Loredano, Venetian patrician') and translated Virgil and Seneca into Italian. His chivalric poem in thirteen cantos, *Libro novo de lo innamoramento di Galvano* ('New Book of the Falling in Love of Gawain'), was printed in Milan before 1497, possibly in 1494.

Re-utilising tales like those sung in the above-mentioned *Cantare di Astore e Morgana* and the *Ponzela Gaia*, the *Innamoramento di Galvano* focuses on the figure of Gawain and his unlucky adventures and love for Gaia, as well as on the evil deeds of Morgana, Gaia's mother, through her minion Estorre. In all likelihood, Fossa had envisaged a sequel to his poem: in the course of the thirteen cantos he frequently refers to events that will follow, but these do not appear in the book. This first book ends with the preparations that precede the confrontation of Arthur and Morgana's opposing armies. As a peculiar trait, the text demonstrates a marked interest in necromancy and revives the magical tradition of Arthurian discourse.[21]

Boiardo's most famous continuator, Ludovico Ariosto, who published the first edition of his *Orlando furioso* in 1516, had a profound knowledge of Arthurian literature.[22] Just a few threads of the Arthurian tapestry within the *Orlando furioso* will serve to explore the conscious combination of different intertexts on Ariosto's part, and will link once more the tales of Lancelot and Tristan to the Este court of Ferrara.

Ariosto connects the Arthurian element with dynastic prophecy, one of the central themes of his poem. In canto 3, when the woman warrior Bradamante, founding mother of the Estense dynasty, receives the first prophetic communication from the sorceress Melissa and sees the spirits incarnating her future descendants, the episode takes place in Merlin's tomb. The *Historia di Merlino* had provided a succinct account of how the magician, madly in love with the Lady of the Lake, was entombed alive by her. His body decomposed, but his prophetic spirit remained alive and continued prophesying the future. Ariosto reprises this textual element and makes Merlin a silent presence in the canto, leaving to Melissa the task of the prophetic conjuring of spirits. The setting and its ominous memories, however, remain in the text as a memory of the potentially dangerous side of the magical gift. Finally, Merlin reappears again as pure simulacrum in Canto 26, when Ruggiero sees the sculptures of the '*Fonte di Merlino*' illustrating the allegorical fight of European princes against avarice.

The connection between the dynastic theme and the Arthurian discourse is explicit in the *Rocca di Tristano* episode in Cantos 32 and 33, an addition to the 1532 edition of the poem. The *Rocca*, so named because it is at the centre of one of Tristan's *aventures*, can accommodate for the night only the most beautiful lady and the most valiant knight. Bradamante enters it with the lady Ullania, whose companions she has just defeated, disguised as a knight. But as soon as the lord of the castle understands that she is a woman, he wants to banish Ullania, because she is less beautiful than Bradamante. Only Bradamante's negotiating ability and her threats will convince the lord to change his custom. On the frescoed walls of the *Rocca*, the two ladies see other prophetic scenes that further educate the woman warrior on her destiny as a founder.

The *Rocca* episode in the *Furioso* provides insight into another element evoked by the use of Arthurian material together with the theme of prophecy. This is the idea of the inflexible custom or *coutume*, the fixed law that prevents humans from fully realizing themselves. The Arthurian tradition had established *coutume* as one of its defining features: one could claim that the quintessential obstacle of many Arthurian narratives is the result of an arbitrary law (such as, for instance, the *coutume de Logres*, which prescribes that a lady whose companion is defeated be at the mercy of the knight who defeated him). Social inflexibility is at the centre of another Arthurian episode in the *Orlando furioso*, the tale of the damned Lidia in Canto 34. This time the episode derives from the *Palamedes* tradition, which acquired great popularity in the Italian peninsula during the Middle Ages.[23] The anonymous daughter of the King of Norbelanda in the *Cantari di Febus-el-Forte* lends her story to the cruel Lidia, whom Astolfo meets in Hell because she refused a lover and made him die of heartbreak. A few chronological adjustments in the plot and the combination with the Ovidian tale of Atalanta, however, turn this tale into a bitter reflection on the inflexibility of the dynastic logic, which forces women into pre-defined positions and denies any real possibility to choose.[24]

As new texts are discovered and unexpected relations between texts unearthed, the Arthurian tradition in the Italian Renaissance seems far from the creative dead end that these legends would reach a few decades into the seventeenth century.[25] Ariosto's revitalization of a reflection on the law, for instance, seemed to promise further developments for these narrations: the potential for a reflection on choice, both political and moral, seems called into question by Ariosto's treatment of an Arthurian thread. The ideological framework of the final text of our survey, Luigi Alamanni's *Girone (Gyrone) il Cortese*, leads instead in a radically different direction.

Luigi Alamanni (1495–1556), a Florentine, studied with famous humanists of his time and was an active participant in the circle of the Orti Oricellari, one of the most important cultural centres of sixteenth-century Florence. In 1522, he participated in a conspiracy to overturn the Medici rule and, after its failure, spent most of his life in the service of the French kings. The poem *Girone il Cortese* was commissioned by

King Francis I of France in 1546 and published for the first time in Paris in 1548, with a dedication to King Henry II. It consists of 3,590 stanzas, divided into 24 books.[26]

The *Girone il Cortese* is a rendition of the prose *Guiron le Courtois*, from the Compilation written in French by Rustichello da Pisa in the last quarter of the thirteenth century.[27] In keeping with its model, Alamanni's poem has at its centre the friendship between Girone and Danain, threatened by the possible love between Girone and Danain's wife, the lady of Maloalto (Malehaut). The narrative is based only loosely on the Arthurian matter that had produced it. Among the heroes who surround Girone are Meliadusse and Bruno, already familiar to the audiences of the Italian peninsula throughout the Middle Ages.

The *Girone* blends the Arthurian theme of the *Guiron le Courtois* with the dynastic theme and with a changed model of *courtoisie* and chivalry. As Stefano Jossa has observed, 'the *Girone* constitutes . . . a move from the chivalric world based on courtly love to the modern world, where courtliness is a military and political value.'[28] On a poetic level, this corresponds to the adoption of a single hero, as opposed to the variety and multiplicity of heroes and actions of the tradition after Chrétien. Such unity foreshadows the strict Aristotelian poetics of Tasso, and it is certainly remarkable to find it connected with the Arthurian legend, by definition wandering and multifarious. The knight errant has become a courtier,[29] and the parable that began with the nostalgic knight of Tommaso di Saluzzo has reached its end.

Notes

[1] Dates for these images are hotly contested; see Chapter 13 in this volume.

[2] A great number of texts on epic and chivalric heroes circulated in manuscripts and early printed books between the late fourteenth and the sixteenth centuries, which have not been re-edited or studied in detail; see the appendices in M. Beer, *Romanzi di cavalleria: il* Furioso *e il romanzo italiano del primo Cinquecento* (Rome, 1987).

[3] The text of *Le Chevalier Errant* preserved in BnF, MS fr. 12559 has recently been published by M. Piccat, with a critical edition by L. Ramello and a translation into modern Italian by E. Martinengo (Boves, 2008).

[4] On Tommaso di Saluzzo's literary culture, see K. Busby, 'La bibliothèque de Tommaso di Saluzzo', in C. Galderisi and J. Maurice (eds), *'Qui tant savoit d'engin et d'art'. Mélanges de philologie médiévale offerts à Gabriel Bianciotto* (Poitiers, 2006), pp. 31–9.

[5] See Chapter 12 in this volume, and A. Tissoni Benvenuti, 'Il mondo cavalleresco e la corte estense', in *I libri di* Orlando Innamorato (Modena, 1987), pp. 13–33. On the Estense library, see also G. Bertoni, *La Biblioteca Estense e la coltura ferrarese ai tempi del duca Ercole I (1471–1505)* (Turin, 1903). On the importance of Arthurian texts between the Middle Ages and the Renaissance, see *TLI*, pp. 13–48, as well as the list of Arthurian manuscripts compiled by G. Allaire (ed. and trans.), *Il Tristano panciatichiano* (Cambridge, 2002), pp. 13–25.

[6] The letter is quoted by Tissoni Benvenuti in 'Il mondo cavalleresco', p. 23. Unless otherwise noted, translations are my own.

[7] Ibid., p. 24. On Isabella's literary tastes, which tend towards Carolingian epic rather than Arthurian romance, see A. Luzio and R. Renier, *La coltura e le relazioni letterarie di Isabella d'Este Gonzaga*, originally published in *GSLI* between 1899 and 1903, and since reprinted by S. Albonico (Milan, 2005).

[8] Beer, *Romanzi di cavalleria*, pp. 221–3.

[9] M. Villoresi, *La letteratura cavalleresca. Dai cicli medievali all'Ariosto* (Rome, 2000), p. 42.

[10] 'The Census of Italian Sixteenth-Century Editions' (EDIT 16) for Italian printed books (*http:// edit16.iccu.sbn.it/web_iccu/eimain.htm*) reports two *cinquecentine*: Venice, 1539 (Venturino di Roffinello) and Venice, 1554 (Bartolomeo Imperatore). On the Merlin tradition in Italy, see O. Visani, 'I testi italiani dell'*Historia di Merlino*: prime osservazioni sulla tradizione', *Schede umanistiche*, n.s. 1 (1994), 17–61; D. Delcorno Branca, 'Appunti su Merlino', in *TLI*, pp. 77–97.

[11] See Chapter 6 in this volume. On the form of the *cantare*, see M. Picone and M. Bendinelli Predelli (eds), *I cantari. Struttura e tradizione* (Florence, 1984); M. C. Cabani, *Le forme del cantare epico-cavalleresco* (Lucca, 1988); and Picone and L. Rubini Messerli (eds), *Il cantare italiano fra folklore e letteratura* (Florence, 2007).

[12] D. Delcorno Branca (ed.), *Cantari fiabeschi arturiani* (Milan and Trent, 1999), pp. 12–15.

[13] See also B. Barbiellini Amidei (ed. and intro.), *La Ponzela Gaia* (Milan and Trent, 2000).

[14] See Tissoni Benvenuti, 'I testi cavallereschi di riferimento dell'*Inamoramento de Orlando*', in Picone (ed.), *La letteratura cavalleresca dalle chansons de geste alla Gerusalemme liberata* (Pisa, 2008), pp. 239–55.

[15] Boiardo's *Inamoramento*, also known as *Orlando innamorato*, was first published in 1482–3 (books 1 and 2) and 1495 (book 3, posthumous). This view – that the poem is a successful and influential blend of the two great epic cycles, Carolingian and Arthurian – was canonised by P. Rajna in *Le fonti dell'Orlando furioso* (Florence, 1876).

[16] See M. Praloran, *'Maraviglioso artificio'. Tecniche narrative e rappresentative nell'Orlando innamorato* (Lucca, 1990); R. Donnarumma, *Storia dell'Orlando innamorato. Poetiche e modelli letterari in Boiardo* (Lucca, 1996), p. 27; and T. Matarrese, 'Il racconto cavalleresco dal cantare ai canti. L'inamoramento de Orlando di M. M. Boiardo', in Picone (ed.), *Letteratura cavalleresca*, pp. 225–38, on p. 225.

[17] I quote the text from Tissoni Benvenuti and C. Montagnani (eds), M. M. Boiardo. *Opere. L'inamoramento de Orlando* (Milan and Naples, 1999), II xviii, 1–2.

[18] Tissoni Benvenuti and Montagnani edn, *Inamoramento de Orlando*, II xxvi, 2–3.

[19] On Boiardo's 'neo-Breton' ideology, see R. Bruscagli, 'Matteo Maria Boiardo', in E. Malato (ed.), *Storia della letteratura italiana. Il Quattrocento* (Rome, 1996), pp. 635–708; and R. Bruscagli, *Studi cavallereschi* (Florence, 2003), pp. 3–36.

[20] *Tutti li libri de Ovidio Metamorphoseos tradutti dal litteral in verso vulgar con le sue Allegorie in prosa* ('All the Books of Ovid's Metamorphoses Literally Translated into Vernacular Verse with Prose Allegories'), also published in Venice by Zoppino, in 1522.

[21] On Evangelista Fossa, see Villoresi, 'Niccolò degli Agostini, Evangelista Fossa, Francesco Cieco da Ferrara. Il romanzo cavalleresco fra innovazione e conservazione', in his *La fabbrica dei cavalieri: cantari, poemi, romanzi in prosa fra Medioevo e Rinascimento* (Rome, 2005), pp. 345–83. An excerpt of the *Innamoramento di Galvano* may be found in the appendix to Delcorno Branca, *Cantari fiabeschi arturiani*, pp. 95–109 with Notes on pp. 172–9.

[22] Rajna traced endless points of contact between Ariosto's poem and the *Tristan* and *Lancelot* cycles. C. Dionisotti cautioned against Rajna's concentration on the Old French sources, however, favouring instead the fifteenth-century Italian popular tradition: 'Appunti sui "cinque canti" e sugli studi ariosteschi', in his *Studi e problemi di critica testuale* (Bologna, 1961), pp. 369–82.

[23] A. Limentani (ed.), *Dal Roman de Palamedés ai cantari di Febus-el-Forte* (Bologna, 1962), pp. xvii–xix.

[24] E. Stoppino, 'Il destino della storia. Genealogie e gerarchie di modelli nel canto XXXIV dell'*Orlando furioso*', *Schifanoia. Rivista dell'Istituto di Studi Rinascimentali di Ferrara*, 26 (2004), 211–22.

[25] With post-Renaissance readers the Arthurian material still found favour, but it did not inspire writers to generate the same volume of new imaginative fictions.

[26] For printing history, see F. Montorsi, 'L'autore rinascimentale e i manoscritti medievali: sulle fonti del *Gyrone il cortese* di Luigi Alamanni', *Romania*, 127 (2009), 190–211.

[27] See Chapter 2 in this volume.

[28] S. Jossa, *La fondazione di un genere. Il poema eroico tra Ariosto e Tasso* (Rome, 2002), p. 163.

[29] On the moralistic turn of Arthurian literature in *Girone*, see also Z. Rozsnyói, *Dopo Ariosto: Tecniche narrative e discorsive nei poemi postariosteschi* (Ravenna, 2000), pp. 37–40.

Part Three

Arthur beyond Romance

8

THE ARTHURIAN PRESENCE IN EARLY ITALIAN LYRIC

Roberta Capelli

The Arthurian Tradition in Medieval Italy

From the twelfth century on, signs of the popularity of the heroes of the Round Table appeared in various forms in Italy, revealing a remarkably consolidated presence. Arthurian naming patterns are found in archival documents, particularly in northern and north-eastern Italy. The Modena archivolt and the Otranto mosaic (discussed in Chapter 13) represent Arthur and Arthurian characters. Authors writing in Latin such as Henricus of Settimello and Godfrey of Viterbo allude to Arthurian figures and stories. Between the last quarter of the thirteenth century and the first half of the fourteenth, the Italian *scriptoria* are at the height of their manuscript production of Arthurian legends in Old French, a trend that only begins to decline during the fifteenth century, when the Arthurian tradition consists mostly of vernacularisations.[1] Old French and Old Provençal works were usually read in their original languages in the aristocratic courts of northern Italy; in the *comuni* (municipalities) of central Italy, however, and especially in Tuscany, the cultural needs of the rising merchant class gave a strong impulse to the vernacularisation process.

In thirteenth- and fourteenth-century Italian poetry, we find significant and pervasive signs of the assimilation of the Arthurian repertory. Dante is escorted to Paradise by a Beatrice who is compared periphrastically to the Lady of Malehaut (*Par.* 16.14–15). The early fourteenth-century poet Folgore da San Gimignano is accompanied to table by an 'entourage' of friends 'more courtly than Lancelot, / since if need be, with lances in hand / they would engage in tournaments at Camelot'.[2] Franciscan friars answer the call as 'soldiers of the Round Table, who battle in remote and deserted places'.[3] In his essay 'Arthurian Influences on Italian Literature from 1200 to 1500', Antonio Viscardi observes that 'as the verses of the troubadours were placed on an equal plane with academic Latin poetry by the cultivated classes of Italy, so also the Matter of Britain was adopted into the historical manuals along with the narratives of the Bible and of pagan antiquity.'[4] The immense success of King Arthur's adventures produced socio-literary icons whose stylised and highly evocative nature turned them into symbolic examples of human, cultural and rhetorical values, absorbed by the Italian artistic and ideological framework and adapted to its needs and directions.[5]

Early Italian lyric poets most often mention Arthurian characters, as they do the prominent Christian and classical ones, as emblems of unattainable qualities, celebrated for their physical or moral perfection. Both aulic (courtly) forms and most popular genres refer to the Matter of Britain, demonstrating the broad success of chivalric literature among aristocratic as well as merchant classes. In a wide range of lyrics preserved in miscellaneous songbooks, the Arthurian insertions occupy definite and recurring positions in the verse and the strophe; these associations and resonances on the horizontal and vertical axes of a poem aim at accentuating the visual significance and symbolic effectiveness of the Arthurian names. This chapter's survey ranges from the early thirteenth century to the end of the fifteenth; it excludes the production of Dante, Petrarch and Boccaccio, the extent and complexity of which require separate study (see Chapter 10 in this volume).

The Arthurian *Exempla*

The active assimilation in Italy of the chivalric literature written in Old French reveals specific tendencies in the reception and re-adaptation of Arthurian quotations. The allusions in thirteenth- and fourteenth-century Italian poetry to deeds and heroes of the Old French romances demonstrate a convergence in the creation of typologies of the Arthurian 'loans' absorbed in the form of the *exemplum vel figura* ('example or symbol'), a paradigmatic comparison which links the legendary past with the contemporary world in order to illustrate a point,[6] supported by the moralising nature of hagiographic and didactic literature. Along with biblical and classical figures, the Arthurian *exempla* thus become symbols of absolute autoreferentiality and collective cultural and moral values.

The exemplary comparison adapts itself through metaphorical *formulae* to the exigencies of narrative synthesis conditioned by prosodic and metrical structures. This new kind of telegraphic comparison accentuates the visual-evocative weight of the *exemplum* through morpho-syntactic formulations at key junctures in poetic verse, such as the *incipit*, rhyme words, mid-verse rhyme and so on. My evidence suggests that in moving from prose to poetry, what I would call the *exemplum*-function remains a constant rhetorical intersection among diverse genres and registers. On a synchronic level, the Arthurian *exemplum* allows us to determine the coexistence and consistency of a narrative and thematic repertory within multiple literary contexts. Diachronically, the same *exemplum* potentially reveals geographically specific tendencies of reception and re-adaptation.

Merlin

We can observe an informative dissimilarity in the vertical development of two poetic trajectories: the courtly tradition from the troubadours to the Stilnovists, and the long tradition of burlesque and parodic verse from the Goliards to the comic poets of the fourteenth century. Both trajectories may be found in a single author who composes in two styles in separate contexts: Monte Andrea da Firenze writes, in his *canzone Donna, di voi si rancura*, that 'Troy was overthrown, and Merlin and Solomon were conquered by love' (ll. 81–2), while in his sonnet in debate with Schiatta, *Chi di me conoscente è, a rasgione*, the author considers himself wiser than two legendary wise men, Aristotle and Solomon (ll. 1–4).[7] These two examples rely on diverse narrative antecedents and pursue opposite artistic objectives. The *canzone* enlists Arthurian *exempla* to define the poet's sentimental and poetic submission to love, based on the collective symbolic weight of illustrious lovers from the past; among these is Merlin, imprisoned by Vivian through the magical arts that he himself has revealed to her. In contrast, in the poetic debate with Schiatta, the self-irony of the *gap* (boast) brings to the poetic scene Merlin and a host of eloquent characters whose proverbial knowledge and wisdom offer Monte an implicit and mockingly provocative contrast to the presumed merits of his poetic correspondent, Schiatta.

A dense network of information folded into the simple name-reference reveals and attests to the sedimentation of the collective image-hoard contained in the reservoir of socio-literary materials, which poetry attains only when these names and facts have become communicative codes that are immediately recognised. The sonnet's triad of Aristotle, Merlin and Solomon finds numerous antecedents and echoes: first in Schiatta's response, *Eo non sono Aristotol né Platone* – 'I am neither Aristotle nor Plato, and I am not so clever as Merlin; and I am not even as intelligent as Solomon' (ll. 1–3) – and elsewhere in the many translations and poems of a didactic, scientific and moral nature.

In those citations and allusions associated with the figure of Merlin, we note that the satirical-comic poetry of the thirteenth and fourteenth centuries gives almost exclusive attention to the *topos* of the soothsayer-prophet. This emphasis is probably influenced by that quasi-political, quasi-religious literature in Italy which produces, from the end of the twelfth century on, texts such as *Versus Merlini, futura praesagia Lombardiae, Thusciae, Romagnuolae . . . per Merlinum recitata* and the *Expositio Sibyllae et Merlini*, erroneously attributed to Joachim of Fiore. That tradition continues right up to the *Prophecies de Merlin*, written between 1276 and 1279 by Maistre Richart d'Irlande,[8] identifiable with a Venetian Grey Friar. Merlin, the paragon of wisdom and yet of vainglorious claims as well, appears as a central figure in some of the principal voices of burlesque poetry: Rustico Filippi, *Quando egli apre la bocca de la tomba*; Monte Andrea, *S'e' ci avesse alcun segnor più 'n campo*; Pacino Angiulieri, *Lo mio risposo invio a lo camino*; Cecco Angiolieri, *Ogne mie 'ntendimento mi ricide*; Meo de' Tolomei, *Si·sse' condott'al verde, Ciampolino*. Either as a simple name or as a deeply evocative image, Merlin is the metaphorical and syntactic fulcrum of the composition; his name is often in rhyme position and establishes a complex network

of phonic and visual correspondences within the poems. The most striking example is
Rustico's visual poetics:

> Quando egli apre la bocca de la tomba
> per dir parole, messer Casentino,
> sì nel gozzo la boce gli rimbomba
> che diserta le donne e guasta 'l vino.
> E Baldanza si dorme, quando tromba,
> ed hal per gica messere Ugolino:
> ma quest'è il gran fastido, che colomba
> si crede che ver' sé fosse Merlino. (ll. 1–8)

(When Sir Casentino opens his mouth to speak, a dreadful voice resounds in his throat, and his
putrid breath makes women run away and spoils the taste of wine. Boldness is asleep each time he
lets his voice resound like a trumpet; nevertheless, Sir Ugolino listens to that as if it were a sweet
melody: what bothers me is the fact that Sir Casentino regards Merlin as a fool in comparison with
himself.)

In this poem, the three names Casentino, Ugolino and Merlino are associated with
vino (wine) in a play of derisive implications in the diminutive suffix *-ino*, and then
collide with profound comic resonance with the bombastic series of rhymes in *-omba*.

If we can say, then, that burlesque poetry recontextualises Merlin the sage-prophet
in a humorous vein, we must distinguish the tendency of courtly love lyric to utilise
Merlin in the more tragic guise of the 'fool in love'. Merlin's perdition in love,
mentioned above in Monte's *canzone Donna, di voi si rancura*, appears also in
Lunardo del Guallacca's misogynous *sirventes Si come 'l pescio al lasso*, in reply to
Galletto Pisano's courtly *canzone Credeam' essere, lasso*, in which all the *topoi* in the
troubadour manner and the *descriptio puellae* theorised by rhetorical manuals unfold
in their most basic and illuminating forms. Lunardo's sardonic Arthurian counterpoint
– Merlin was betrayed by a woman just as Samson, Paris and Adam were, 'per
femmina treccera / sì·ffo Merlin derizo' (ll. 14–5) – becomes an implicit attack on the
overload of qualities extolled in the canonical female beauties (such as Vivian,
Delilah, Helen and Eve). Galletto installs his own lady among them, through a slavish
description of his beloved that follows the rules of the *ars versificatoria* (golden hair,
perfect skin, heavenly smile, etc.).[9] The object of Galletto's praise and Lunardo's
attack, a woman crystallised in a network of rhetorical virtues that transcend time and
author, is traceable to the classical citation of celebrated beauties to exalt the poet's
beloved. This technique, widely utilised by the troubadours, is taken up by the
Sicilians and the poets of the *Stilnovo* with specific cultural, formal and thematic
elaborations.

Iseut the Blonde and Morgan le Fay

While the process of mythologisation of female beauty is perhaps readily understand-able in the case of Iseut the Blonde, especially in light of her love story with Tristan, it would seem less automatic in the case of a character like Morgan, now stripped of her ambiguous negative traits in the literary tradition. Let us consider the anonymous son-net addressed to the *Compiuta Donzella* ('Accomplished Maiden') of Florence, a 'gentle damsel high and learned, worthier of honour than Morgan the Fay and the Lady of the Lake' (ll. 1–5). The beauty and wisdom of the *Compiuta Donzella* reach the apex of perfection, to the point that she deserves to be praised more than Vivian/Lady of the Lake and Morgan (two female figures gifted with supernatural powers), or Constance of Sicily, empress and regent of Frederick II. In this enumerative sequence, the proper name *Morgana* is coupled with the epithet *la fata* (Morgan le Fay), creating a fixed and repeatable morpho-syntactic unit used by other authors in similar contexts, with the same rhetorical function. The fascination with the fay of royal lineage, sister of Arthur and with familial links to the Sicily–Avalon line of Norman conquerors, could actually be partially based on the phonic features of her name, which – thanks to a certain musicality – presents itself as perfect in rhyme, where it is often found cou-pled with courtly adjectives like *sovrana* (supreme) and *diana* (gorgeously bright).[10]

Curiously, Morgan and Iseut monopolise the repertory of female figures, second only to Thisbe, in the prolific thirteenth-century poet Chiaro Davanzati. All three women always appear within an enumerative comparison syntactically coordinated by disjunctives – i.e., *né . . . né* (neither . . . nor), or *o . . . o* (either . . . or) – reminiscent of the formulaic compactness and rhythmic repeatability of Latin and Romance epics: the lady loved by the poet is 'more charming' or 'more praiseworthy and cultivated' or 'more full of joy' than Thisbe and Iseut, or than Helen and Morgan the Fay.[11] The combination of Iseut, Morgan and Thisbe implicitly confirms the success in Italy of the *matière de Bretagne*, which was clearly able to compete in the construction of meta-literary heroes with the more ancient and articulated diffusion of the tale of the tragic love of Pyramus and Thisbe, a legend whose uninterrupted vitality links Ovid's *Metamorphoses* and the poem *Piramus et Tisbé* through numerous medieval Latin and Gallo-Romance versions.

In addition to the evocative power of the names Iseut and Thisbe, we should consider the emblematic value of their respective literary and legendary *gestes*. According to the ideological needs of the poetic discourse, this associative background supplied by simple names potentially shifts the axis of the simile from the individual exemplarity of a single character to the exemplary nature of the episode in which the character serves as protagonist: the subject is *like* or even *better than* the Breton heroes/heroines. The best example of this particular kind of shift is the forbidden love of Iseut and Tristan in the Sicilian, early Tuscan and Bolognese traditions: Giacomo da Lentini 'loves more intensely than Tristan and Iseut' (*Dal core mi vene*, ll. 39–40);

Filippo of Messina 'can bear for love more pain than did Tristan for Iseut' (*Ai, Siri deo, con forte fu lo punto*, ll. 10–1); Bonagiunta da Lucca is 'in love with his lady far more than Tristan with Iseut' (*Donna, vostre belleze*, ll. 31–4); and the anonymous author of the poem in the Memoriali Bolognesi (n. 119, 1309) 'suffers more intensely' than the two Breton lovers (*Placente vixo, adorno, angelicato*, ll. 5–6). In all four cases, the two lovers are invoked squarely in the category of the didactic *exemplum*, even though its unique dynamic resides in the implicit narrativity of pre-existing and well-known Arthurian plots that poetry can take for granted. In such a case the simile does not amplify the quality of a characteristic, but rather the intensity of an action.

It is worth emphasising that the similes I have just examined are usually gender-consistent: men are compared with famous male characters, and women are compared with famous female characters. Moreover, multiple enumerative sequences consisting of two or more characters aim at uniformity, listing exclusively male or female examples according to the gender of the subject referred to. Of course, some exceptions are allowed, as shown in Stoppa de' Bostichi's ballad *Se la Fortuna gira o 'l mondo*, and these have particular relevance: 'Dov'è la gran fortezza / ch'ebber le dure braccia di Sansone? / Dov'è la gran bellezza / di Ginevra, d'Isotta e d'Ansalone?' (ll. 77–80) ('Where is the great strength of Samson's arms? And where is the great beauty of Guinevere, Iseut and Absalom?'). Here Stoppa directs his moralistic anathema against those who waste their lives pursuing worldly pleasures and goods: the fact that Absalom, the third son of King David, could be associated with Guinevere and Iseut depends not only on the generic moral category the three of them represent (beauty), but also – and principally – on the demands posed by rhyme (*Sansone : Ansalone*), a choice that confirms the metrical value of these emblematic insertions.

Tristan

Just as Merlin attains a dual referential nature, Tristan's double exemplarity as lover and knight assures him a double role in the spheres of the amorous and the comic. Tristan, the paladin of *fin'amor*, belongs to a cultural and literary tradition that is not solely Arthurian but generically courtly, and his presence reverberates between the-matic and formal intertextuality in two *canzoni*, by Inghilfredi (*Del meo voler*) and Pallamidesse di Bellindote (*Amore, grande pecato*). Inghilfredi openly cites Arnaut Daniel's sestina, *Lo ferm voler qu'el cor m'intra*, accentuating the sensual double meanings of the flesh-and-nail metaphor[12] that reaches its apex not in the seemingly limitless and usually fruitless devotion of so many troubadours but in Tristan, whose erotic passion becomes a kind of symbol – the 'model my faith strives to emulate' (l. 60) – for tangible reward and physical fulfilment.

The absorption of models, in this case the simultaneous penetration of a troubadour and Arthurian substratum, produces examples of multireferentiality that emphasise the symbolic value of a simple proper name. In the coda of Pallamidesse's *canzone*, the episode of the Joyous Guard is reformulated on the basis of a Tristan-*senhal* pseudonym (used by Bernart de Ventadorn in his *canso*, *Can vei la lauzeta mover*), para-etymologically explained by the adjective *dolorosa*.

> A la Guardia Gioiosa
> te·n va al mio Tristano,
> mia chanzone dolorosa,
> e dì che Speranvano
> a lei tosto verrà. (ll. 61–5)

(Go, my sorrowful song, to the Joyous Guard, to my Tristan; and say that Hope-in-Vain will soon come to her.)

Pallamidesse, hidden behind the *senhal Speranvano*, sends his poem to his beloved Lady, hidden behind the *senhal Tristano*, who is staying in a distant place represented by the Joyous Guard to announce to her his forthcoming visit.[13] The Arthurian quotation expresses and describes the action of the poet, condensing the key segments of the plot into heavily freighted words interconnected with one another both ideally and visually. Following the trajectory drawn by the rhyme scheme, we obtain the antithetical coupling *Gioiosa ~ dolorosa* and the analogical, para-etymological coupling *Tristano* (the unhappy one)[14] ~ *Speranvano* (Hope-in-Vain);[15] by combining adjacent terms, we encounter an emblematic opposition between the positive pole represented by the Lady (*Gioiosa ~ Tristano*) and the negative pole represented by the poet (*dolorosa ~ Speranvano*).

Our resulting theoretical formula might then be: Tristan the lover is to courtly lyric as Tristan the knight is to comic-burlesque poetry. Through the comic poets' anti-romanticism and overturning of courtly values, Tristan's proverbial valour becomes a model for boastfulness and irony. Tristan's original courtly value turns comical in the anti-heroic and provocative tones of Cecco Angiolieri:

> In una che' danar' mi dànno meno,
> anco che pochi me n'entrano 'n mano,
> son come vin, ch'è du' part'aqua, leno
> e son più vil che non fu pro' Tristano.
> Enfra le genti vo col capo 'n seno,
> più vergognoso ch'un can foretano,
> e per averne dì e notte peno,
> ciò è in modo che non sia villano. (ll. 1–8)

(Then I run out of money, though little money comes into my hands, I am like diluted wine that is two parts water, and I am more gutless than Tristan was brave. I wander with downcast eyes; I feel more diffident than a stray dog, and I strive night and day to get some money without being base.)

Comic poets[16] repeat the anti-courtly *topoi* common to all medieval romance, the expression of a much older tradition of *vituperium* and *iniuria*, revived in goliardic songs and laced with moralistic anathema. Stylistically, the visual significance of the Arthurian insertions is also enhanced by rhyme schemes. The series of rhymes *mano* :

Tristano : *foretano* : *villano* in Angiolieri's sonnet creates what we might call 'combining strings', associative strings of rhymes 'spendable' in different poetic contexts. These associative rhyme-strings formulated on the basis of *Tristano* utilise a technique typical of *affabulatio*, relying on the mnemonic codification of repeatable syntactic units which become conventional rhyme combinations in popular poetry and current speech – we still say: *gioco di mano, gioco di villano*, i.e., 'never use your fists' – and which are already widely attested at the chronological height of this survey.[17] Other combinations, like *Galeotto* : *otto* (eight; in Francesco di Vannozzo, *Dé, buona zente, poneteli mente*, ll. 78 and 79) and *Lancillotto* : *vintiotto* (twenty-eight; in Giuntino Lanfredi, *Morte dogliosa, ché non vien' di botto*, ll. 5 and 8), illustrate the popular nature of this category of occurrence.

Lancelot

Strangely enough, this analysis of the figure of Tristan does not carry over to Lancelot, whose poetic 'consecration' is relatively late and very much tied to the production of short prose genres and *cantari*. In fact, in the lyrical corpus taken for analysis, the pairing Tristan ~ Lancelot has only one attestation, in the fourteenth-century author Franco Sacchetti's *Firenze bella, confortar ti dèi* (ll. 12–14). While references to Lancelot occur in Italian lyrics, these appearances do not suggest widespread trends in the re-utilisation of the Arthurian character and his episodic lore. Rather, they seem to suggest a developmental phase in the penetration of the Lancelot model into Italian lyric. Regarding the overall diffusion of tales from the Breton cycle in Italy, Delcorno Branca notes that among the Arthurian romances, Tristan enjoyed a far longer period of integration and reuse in Italian literature, while translations of Lancelot seem to have been relatively scarce.[18] Thus, in marked contrast to the large number of preceding cycles devoted to Merlin, Tristan and Iseut, my analysis of the citational formula based on the character of Lancelot in early Italian lyric will be limited to two examples from the second half of the thirteenth century: a sonnet by Guittone d'Arezzo, *Ben aggia ormai la fede*, and a *canzone* by Lapuccio Belfradelli, *Donna senza pietanza*.

   In Guittone's sonnet – where it is said that 'even a knight as valiant as Lancelot is lost in wonder when he meets a lady as tough as the one the poet loves' (ll. 9–11) – Lancelot enjoys two noteworthy functions. Taken together with the other Arthurian allusions found in Guittone's production, this occurrence of Lancelot expresses the poet's own erudition.[19] In addition, viewed in the context of this specific sonnet, the poet's self-comparison to Lancelot clarifies the ideological function of the Lancelot reference. Analysing the significance of Guittone's comparison to Lancelot inevitably leads us to Dante. The Arthurian character Lancelot – the exemplar of *prodezza* (valour) – assumes in Guittone's post-conversion sonnet the metonymic value of a symbol of the courtly love ethic that Guittone seeks to deny and condemn in the name of religious purification. It is not by chance that this is the same moralistic attitude that Dante advances in *Inferno* 5 in the face of Paolo and Francesca's sin of lust.

The attestation of Lancelot in Lapuccio Belfradelli's *Donna senza pietanza* confirms the presence of the *Lancelot-Graal* as one of the primary sources for the diffusion of Lancelot in early Italian culture:

> Pemsate a Galeotto
> di ciò c'a Lancalotto
> promise im sua volglienza,
> che no volle mentire;
> poi ch'ebe dato il botto
> ad Artù re, d'u·motto
> li si diede im servanza. (ll. 54–60)

(Think of Galehaut, of what he promised Lancelot spontaneously, for he did not want to argue with him: after he had defeated King Arthur, at a word he committed himself to him.)

In Lappuccio's *canzone*, Lancelot is the symbol of chivalry and loyalty not independently but together with Galehaut, and solely in the context of the episode of Galehaut's submission to Arthur. This exemplarity of this famous episode has already been established in Rustichello's Compilation and in the *Conti di antichi cavalieri* (see Chapters 2 and 9 of this volume). Lappuccio does not simply allude to it; he synthetically summarises it in seven verses.

This typology of Arthurian narrative digression comes down to us in a series of texts of diverse origin, metrical construction and content. Despite this diversity they can all be classified as lyric even though they eschew courtly registers and the noble form of the *canzone*. These texts are Re Giovanni's *descort Donna, audite como*; Ruggieri Apugliese's *sirventes Tant'aggio ardire e conoscenza*; and the three anonymous semi-narrative poems known as *Il Mare amoroso, Il Detto del Gatto lupesco* and *L'Intelligenza* (see Chapter 9). Though they operate in separate ways and with distinct socio-literary goals, collectively these texts give us an idea of the liveliness and extent of the independent circulation of Arthurian tales and legends beyond the standardised literary codes more strictly connected to the romances themselves. These texts also reveal the vitality of extraordinarily diverse narrative influences in the creation of local traditions and cultural tastes and preferences. In the free-wheeling combination and cross-fertilisation of stories somewhere between literary creation and tradition, between recitational technique and standard themes, my examination of the resulting versions of legends and tales constantly negotiates the active and passive reception of materials that supply us alternately with general tendencies and isolated details. In fact, testimonials of the literary authoritativeness of the *matière de Bretagne* can also be found in the manuscript tradition of early Italian poetry. This range of information is especially important in our editing of medieval texts, for which the indispensable selection of variant readings cannot overlook the cultural significance of every level of the manuscript tradition.

Textual Evidence of Arthurian Lore

To suggest the editorial implications of the citational adaptation of Arthurian characters in Italian verse, I will focus on two significant examples. In Petrocchi's critical edition of Dante's *Divine Comedy, Inferno* 4.141 reads: 'Tullio e Lino e Seneca morale' ('Tully, Linus, and Seneca the moralist'); the fifteenth-century manuscript Oxford, Bodleian Library, MS Canon. Ital. 97, reads instead 'Tullio e Merlino e Seneca morale'.[20] In ecdotic terms the variant *Merlino* is poor, but this reading tells us that 'wise Merlin' was more familiar to the copyist than *Lino,* a Theban lyre-player poet, son of Apollo and Calliope, sometimes confused on different levels of the *stemma codicum* with Alano, sometimes with Pliny, sometimes with Livy. In the eyes of the compiler – and probably to readers of the time as well – Merlin appeared worthy of figuring alongside *auctoritates* of the calibre of Cicero and Seneca, as he was endowed with autonomous and acclaimed exemplarity.

A similar example comes from one of Cecco Angiolieri's sonnets, *I' sum sì magro che quasi trallucho.* The main tradition of this text reads: 'Ma non ci ha forza, ch'i' so' 'nnamorato; / ché, s'i' avesse più òr che non è sale, / per me saria 'n poco tempo assommato' (ll. 9–11; 'It does not matter if I am poor, because I am in love; even if I owned more gold than salt, I would soon run through it all').[21] In the early fourteenth-century Escorial, MS e.III.23, copied by a scribe from the Veneto, an Arthurian variant demonstrates the textual *mouvance* that has to be considered in determining the 'fixity' of these highly open texts:

> Ma laxia andar, ch'i' sum ben avïato:
> se io avesse tra man' lo san grahale,
> en pocho tenpo l'avrey consumato. (fol. 86v)

(Let it go, I am done already: / if I could hold the Holy Grail in my hands, / I would waste it in a second.)

From what we could deem a general trivialisation of the text found in MS Escorial e.III.23, emerges the unique variant in line 10: 'se io avesse tra man' lo san grahale' in lieu of – and notably in rhyme position, rather than within the line – 'più òr che non è sale'. This variant is probably of northern Italian origin, given the disappearance of intervocalic fricative stops (non-continuants) graphically indicated by the 'h' (*grahale*) and in light of the manuscript's general linguistic patina; in the larger picture of Cecco's poetry it is probably of no more than minor interest, relegated to the apparatus of the critical edition. But in the context of the Escorial codex, this variant reading tells us that at a given moment in the transmission of Cecco's texts, and in the Veneto, the proverbial and thus popular comparison of salt and gold is replaced in rhyme by the equally popular and telegraphic image of the Holy Grail. It should come as no surprise that in the same region in which we find the courts of the Da Romano family, the land of the *Prophecies de Merlin* and the birthplace of the *Entrée d'Espagne*, we find an emblematic reference to Arthurian lore applied to everyday life.

Conclusion

We have seen that features and functions of exemplary Arthurian episodes are subject to recurrent formal and theoretical conditions: within a single stanza, chivalric and courtly models can coexist with characters and stories taken from the Bible and from the classical world, so that the opposition between *Christian* and *pagan*, *religion* and *myth* is neutralised by the shared purpose of offering a symbolically and morally persuasive *exemplum*. Verses appear to be built on identifiable morpho-syntactic nuclei that are highly predetermined in their structures, consisting of binary or ternary sequences of names, usually formalised as epithetic junctures and often placed in rhyme position. The blend between deeds of war and matters of the heart confirms that the reception of the material in Arthurian fictions tends to emphasise chivalrous-courtly bipartition (that is, between pairs of paladins or couples of lovers). Moreover, the significance and variety of Arthurian allusions confirm the breadth of knowledge of the *matière de Bretagne*, the favour in which it is held and its subjects' earned authoritativeness by the middle of the fourteenth century, suggesting that the literary repertoire employed by medieval authors and copyists fulfilled the demands of a large audience.

Notes

[1] D. Delcorno Branca, *TLI*, pp. 27–8; E. G. Gardner, *The Arthurian Legend in Italian Literature* (London and New York, 1930; rpt 1971), Chapter 1.

[2] Folgore da San Gimignano, *Alla brigata nobile e cortese*, ll. 12–14. I give *incipits* in Italian, but translate into English the lines I am examining; all translations are mine unless otherwise noted. Where no other source is specified, I cite the data and reference editions from *Tesoro della Lingua Italiana delle Origini*, consulted at *www.ovi.cnr.it*, 'Opera del Vocabolario Italiano'.

[3] '[M]ilites Tabulae Rotundae, qui latitant in remotis et desertis locis', in *Leggenda antica di san Francesco*, trans. V. Gamboso, in *Fonti francescane. Scritti e biografie di san Francesco d'Assisi* (Padua, 1983), p. 1237.

[4] In R. S. Loomis (ed.), *Arthurian Literature in the Middle Ages: A Collaborative History* (Oxford, 1959), pp. 419–29, on p. 421.

[5] My argumentation proceeds by *specimina*; see also my two-part analysis 'Presenze arturiane nella lirica italiana delle origini', *Quaderni di lingue e letterature*, 31 (2006), 43–56, and 32 (2007), 17–27, as well as 'Caratteri e funzioni dell'elemento cavalleresco-cortese nella lirica italiana del Due e Trecento', in M. Picone (ed.), *La letteratura cavalleresca dalle* chansons de geste *alla* Gerusalemme liberata (Pisa, 2008), pp. 91–122.

[6] See J. Le Goff, 'L'*exemplum* et la rhétorique de la prédication aux XIIIe et XIVe siècles', in C. Leonardi and E. Menestò (eds), *Retorica e poetica tra i secoli XII e XIV. Atti del secondo Convegno internazionale di studi dell'Associazione per il Medioevo e l'Umanesimo latini (AMUL), Trento e Rovereto 3–5 ottobre 1985* (Perugia, 1988), pp. 3–29, esp. p. 4; See also P. von Moos, 'Sulla retorica dell'*exemplum* nel Medioevo', in the same volume, pp. 53–77, esp. p. 59.

[7] F. F. Minetti (ed.), *Monte Andrea da Fiorenza. Le rime* (Florence, 1979), ll. 81–2 and 1–4, respectively.

[8] *TLI*, p. 77. See also P. Zumthor, *Merlin le prophète. Un thème de la littérature polémique de l'historiographie et des romans* (Lausanne, 1943; rpt Geneva, 2000).

⁹ See for example Matthew of Vendôme's thirteenth-century reference book *Ars versificatoria* III.38–118; F. Munari (ed.), *Mathei Vindocinensis: Opera*, 3 vols (Rome, 1977–88). See also Brunetto Latini's *Livres dou Tresor*, III.13.11, when Tristan describes the beauty of Queen Iseut; P. G. Beltrami et al. (eds), *Tresor* (Turin, 2007).

¹⁰ See the anonymous Sicilian *canzonetta*, *Quando la primavera*, ll. 14–18; Guido delle Colonne, *La mia gran pena e lo gravoso affanno*, ll. 34–6; Giacomo da Lentini, *Madonna mia, a voi mando*, ll. 45–8; Dante da Maiano, *Rosa e giglio e flore aloroso*, ll. 13–14; and the anonymous poem from BAV, MS Vat. lat. 3793, *Lo grande valore di voi, donna sovrana*, ll. 5–8.

¹¹ See, respectively, *Lo disïoso core*, ll. 7–8; *Madonna, lungiamente aggio portato*, ll. 7–8; *Ringrazzo amore de l'aventurosa*, ll. 3–4.

¹² Arnaut's sestina uses the image of flesh and nail: 'de lieis serai ainsi cum carn e ongla' (l. 17; 'I will be to her as flesh is to nail'), and the verb *enongla* (en-nails) in 'Aissi s'empren e s'enongla / mos cors en lieis cum l'escors'en la verja' (l. 31; 'my body is fixed and clings to her / like the bark to the rod'). Inghilfredi deploys both in the first stanza of *Del meo voler*: 'Amor m'inunglia' (l. 4; 'Love has become incarnate in me') and 'esendo due semo un, con' carne ed unglia' (l. 7; 'though we are two, we are one, like flesh and nail'). M. Eusebi (ed.), *Arnaut Daniel: Il sirventese e le canzoni* (Milan, 1984).

¹³ Picone suggests a different interpretation of the *senhal*, in 'Temi tristaniani nella lirica dei siciliani', in R. Castagnola and G. Fioroni (eds), *Le forme del narrare poetico* (Florence, 2007), pp. 21–33, on p. 31.

¹⁴ See, for instance, Arrigo da Settimello's early twelfth-century *Elegia de diversitate fortunae et philosophiae*: 'Quis ille / Tristanus qui me tristia plura tulit?' and the early fourteenth-century vernacularisation: 'E quale è quello Tristano ch'à più tristizia di me?' In C. Fossati (ed.), *Arrigo da Settimello: Elegia* (Florence, 2011); and E. Bonaventura (ed.), 'Lo libro d'Arrighetto fiorentino disposto di grammatica in volgare,' *StM*, 4 (1912–13), 110–92.

¹⁵ The idea of 'waiting and hoping in vain' expressed by the *senhal* 'Speranvano' could be ideally connected with the feeling of useless hope expressed by the image of *esperansa bretona* (Breton hope) in Bernart de Ventadorn's *La dousa votz ai ausida*, l. 38. Bernart compares the troubadour's love for his unattainable lady with the unshakeable belief of the Bretons that King Arthur did not die and would return. See P. Cherchi, 'Gli *adynata* dei trovatori', in his *Andrea, i trovatori e altri temi romanzi* (Rome, 1979), pp. 19–51; and D'A. Silvio Avalle, *Le maschere di Guglielmino. Struttura e motivi etnici nella cultura medievale* (Milan and Naples, 1989), pp. 8–10.

¹⁶ Tristan serves as an anti-model also in Cecco Nuccoli's sonnet *El mi rincresce sì lo star di fuore*, in poetic debate with Giraldello's *Ben me rincrebbe perch'io foi lontano*.

¹⁷ Of the many extant examples, I will quote only three: the *Cantilena* of a Tuscan *jongleur* (second half of the twelfth century) uses the rhyme words *san Germano* : *sovrano* : *cristiano* : *(lor) mano* : *delitiano* : *villano* (ll. 13–18); in the *Detto dei villani* of Matazone da Caligano, the rhyme words are *vilan* : *man* (ll. 21–2); in the *lauda Omo, de te me lamento* in the Florence *laudario*, we read *villano* : *mano* (ll. 12 and 14).

¹⁸ See *TLI*, pp. 17 and 50; this relative rarity remains true despite the prose *Lancellotto* newly discovered by L. Cadioli (see the Introduction to this volume).

¹⁹ For examples of Guittone's familiarity with Arthurian sources, see Chapter 1 in this volume.

²⁰ Dante Alighieri, *La Commedia secondo l'antica vulgata*, ed. G. Petrocchi (Milan, 1967); E. Moore, *Contributions to the Textual Criticism of the* Divina Commedia, *including the complete collation throughout the* Inferno *of all the mss. at Oxford and Cambridge* (Cambridge, 1889), pp. 282–3.

²¹ On the Escorial manuscript, see Capelli, *Sull'Escorialense (lat. e.III.23). Problemi e proposte di edizione* (Verona, 2006); on the manuscript tradition of Cecco, see G. Contini, 'Postilla angiolieresca', in G. Breschi (ed.), *Frammenti di filologia romanza. Scritti di ecdotica e linguistica (1932–1989)* (Florence, 2007), pp. 495–500.

9

ARTHUR IN MEDIEVAL ITALIAN SHORT NARRATIVE

F. Regina Psaki

In a broad but lapidary summation, Christopher Kleinhenz describes two poles for the spectrum of Italian Arthurian literature:

> In Italian literature, the principal players in the Arthurian drama assumed a new, double life: a 'symbolic' existence as emblematic figures in superficial allusions, and a 'real' literary life as principal characters in a sustained narrative or sequence of episodes. On the one hand, lyric poets used these figures as standards of comparison against which they measured elements of their own experience: beauty, prowess, wisdom, and the like. On the other hand, other authors mined the rich (mainly French) Arthurian treasure trove and composed a number of prose romances, *novelle*, and *cantari*, thus creating a large and distinct body of Italian Arthurian literature.[1]

On the whole, this characterisation is accurate. Between these two poles however we find short narratives whose use of the Arthurian material consists neither of superficial allusions nor of sustained narratives, and these will be the focus of this chapter.

In Chapter 8 in this volume, Roberta Capelli surveys the many references to Arthurian figures, places, motifs, episodes and tropes to be found in medieval Italian lyric production.[2] Because of their familiarity, such references – often desultory and generic – could be lifted wholesale from lyric models in Old French or Old Provençal without indicating precise knowledge of specific Arthurian texts.[3] In Chapter 10 of this volume, Kleinhenz examines how Dante, Petrarch and Boccaccio deploy the content and ethos of the Arthurian material. In the Three Crowns even the briefest of allusions carries a significant ethical charge and indicates a substantial engagement with the imaginative world of Arthurian and courtly fictions.

Daniela Delcorno Branca provides an analysis both minute and wide-ranging that indicates the presence of a range of Arthurian sources in Italy, well beyond the prose romances that have been the most visible and substantial conduits of the Arthurian matter.[4] She probes the specific sources of allusions to Arthurian episodes mostly in the Italian narrative corpus. The greater detail and scope of these allusions, found in texts composed in Italian territory rather than texts translated or adapted there from continental models or originals, can give more nuanced clues to the Arthurian texts and traditions actually known in the Italian peninsula. Delcorno Branca establishes the clear availability to Italian authors of French verse romances, particularly versions by Thomas, Béroul and Chrétien de Troyes. She pinpoints as well the availability of sources from German lands, such as Eilhart von Oberg; this is hardly surprising, given the visual evidence surveyed in Chapter 13 of this volume, as well as the political link between the Holy Roman Empire and the peninsula.

The present chapter presents Italian short narratives from the thirteenth and fourteenth centuries that make pointed references to Arthurian matter. Some short narratives make only a perfunctory nod to it: Brunetto Latini's *Tesoretto* mentions 'Lancialotto e Tristano' (1. 40) to quickly praise his 'valente segnore' (valiant lord) (1. 1) as their equal.[5] But in other cases specific episodes, narrative arcs, psychological profiles and entire landscapes can be imported in summary form, yet carry the full weight of their allusive freight. To bridge the gap between research *foci* of Italian and of continental Arthurianists, I will discuss the narratives in this category that have received the most attention from Arthurianists writing in Italian. The first four are verse narratives that invoke the Arthurian material in a matrix that is primarily amorous, allegorical, didactic, or some combination of these: *Il Detto del Gatto lupesco*; *Il Mare amoroso*; *L'Intelligenza*; and *Il Dittamondo*. The last two are collections of short prose fictions, though a didactic or moralising aim is not excluded: *Il Novellino* and the *Conti di antichi cavalieri*.

Amorous/Didactic Material in Verse

The short *Detto del Gatto lupesco* survives, untitled and unattributed, only on the fly-leaf of BNCF, MS Magl. II.IV.111, a codex containing various treatises of moral topics. The *Detto* was copied onto the flyleaf just after 1274, according to Petrucci, or perhaps in the early Trecento.[6] It is a first-person narration of 77 eight- and nine-syllable rhyming couplets. The text's verse form, its length (consistent with that of a *dit*), and its many French locutions, indicate French influence. The speaking voice begins by describing his own peregrinations through the world and his encounter with two Breton knights who had sought their lost King Arthur in Mongibello, i.e., Mount Etna (ll. 1–40).[7] Asked his identity, the narrator calls himself a 'wolf-like cat' (*gatto lupesco*) (l. 15). After they part, the narrator lodges with a hermit who sets him on the right way to the East (ll. 41–105). In the last part of the poem (ll. 106–44) the narrator encounters a variety of animals, some familiar and some fantastic, after which he says he completed his journey through the many eastern lands he had listed earlier (ll. 56–65), and then returned home. This 144-line text thus points in shorthand to an enormous sweep in terms of place, frame of reference, and even time, to end in a truncated rush.

This deft text is so enigmatic that its various expositors locate it at different points on a spectrum ranging from religious allegory to humorous parody.[8] Because the *Detto* nods at a variety of genres and invokes a variety of referents as well as of registers, it seems to invite a metanarrative focus. It may be a humorous play on the *Tesoretto* or a precursor of the *Divine Comedy*. It may be linked to the beast fable genre. The wolf-like cat may be a lynx; since in the bestiaries both wolves and cats were credited with night vision, the poem may aim to 'unmask the visionary pretensions of allegorical-didactic journeys'.[9] Luciana Borghi-Cedrini considers the poem a game playing on the schemata of the journey-vision and of travel accounts fictitious and factual.[10]

Just as the whole text is interpretatively enigmatic, so is its prominent Arthurian import. The narrator opens with a thumbnail sketch of the human journey, which he qualifies by saying that he walks along 'thinking of a love of [his]' (l. 6) with his 'head bent' (l. 7).[11] However we interpret this brief invocation of a quest or a pilgrimage, the Arthurian reference in the beginning does not appear determinative for the seeking protagonist, who seems both tangential and indifferent to the knights' suspended search. The Arthurian intertext is inconclusive, a false start:

> 'Cavalieri siamo di Bretagna,
> ke vegnamo de la montagna
> ke·ll'omo apella Mongibello.
> Assai vi semo stati ad ostello
> per apparare ed invenire
> la veritade di nostro sire
> lo re Artù, k' avemo perduto
> e non sapemo ke·ssia venuto.
> Or ne torniamo in nostra terra,
> ne lo reame d' Inghilterra.' (ll. 25–34)

> ('We are knights of Britain,
> coming from the mountain
> that men call Mongibello.
> Long did we stay there
> to learn and find out
> the truth about our lord,
> King Arthur, whom we have lost,
> and know not what has become of him.
> Now we are returning to our land,
> in the kingdom of England.')

After the narrator parts from the knights, neither they nor Arthur recur in the poem. The narrator's lodging in the wilds with the hermit recalibrates both the encounter and the quest from the profane to the sacred, but this is standard in chivalric quest narrative from *Li Contes del Graal* on, especially in the post-1230 material. The *Gatto lupesco* seems to harness an array of genres – love lyric, allegorical romance, Arthurian romance, visionary journey and travel narrative – and to thematise lexically truth (ll. 17, 30, 52, 55, 86–7) and falsehood (or loss, or ignorance; ll. 32, 54, 89ff.) in order to interrogate the kinds of truth that different narrative modes can tell. It is a little too jokey to be an earnest religious allegory, and a little too earnest to be a joke.

The *Mare amoroso* (1270–80), of 334 lines, also a *unicum*, is preserved in Florence, Biblioteca Riccardiana, MS Ricc. 2908 (fols 42r–50r), a manuscript that also contains the *Tesoretto*. Its speaking voice addresses a beloved who is, if not unalterably indifferent, at least disappointingly uneven in her receptiveness to the narrator's attentions and desires. The entire poem constitutes a request for her love, but a request so overloaded with elaborate learned comparisons that they wag the dog. Like Richard de Fournival's *Bestiaire d'Amour*, the *Mare amoroso* narrator compares himself and his beloved lady to all the creatures that erudition has endowed with meaning in the bestiary tradition, among others. The comparisons are mostly to animals, but also to the zodiac, to the planets, and to characters biblical, mythological and Arthurian. So refined is the erudition that the poem in the form we now have it appears to have absorbed its own commentary. What were probably once marginal glosses on a hendecasyllabic text have migrated into the body of the poem, resulting in a mix of eleven-syllable lines and hypermetric lines, unrhymed.[12]

Within the diegesis, the purpose of all these refined comparisons is to show the high worth of the beloved and the narrator's exemplary love and suffering. Outside the diegesis, of course, they reveal the author's recondite knowledge and his dexterity at thematising and parodying a literary register. The poem seems a pretext for playfully fanning out, like a peacock's tail, all the book-learning a posturing author or a suffering lover can muster. At first glance the central conceit has the effect of draining the exalted love of its immediacy and individuality, or parodying it by aligning it – even in superlative relation – with all the parallels and analogues that a learned tradition can offer. But the poem can still read as a sincere homage to love poetry,[13] and once the reader has accepted that central conceit of learned comparison, it is played out quite gracefully indeed.

The Arthurian references in this poem include the *Val sans retour* from the *Lancelot en prose* (ll. 31–3); the Loathly Maiden, from the continuation of *Perceval* by Wauchier de Denain (ll. 209–11); Merlin's enchanted vessel, from the *Prophecies de Merlin* (ll. 212–6); the love potion drunk by Tristan and Iseut (ll. 217–21); and 'Nadriano' [?] and 'Caedino' (Kahedin), who died of unrequited love (ll. 332–3). Like the lyric poets, this poet invokes the Arthurian world with approbation, drawing on it as a shorthand term of comparison for his own experience; unlike them he does so systematically, variously and repeatedly throughout his text. Delcorno Branca gives strong evidence that in addition to the new and popular prose romances, the *Mare amoroso* is referring to the verse romance *Tristan*, specifically to the version of Thomas.[14] She points out that 'the Italian circulation of Thomas's version of Tristan is precisely one of those "hidden traditions" that we need to re-examine'.[15]

A third Tuscan verse narrative that refers to a broad sampling of the Matter of Britain is the allegorical poem *L'Intelligenza*, composed around 1300 by an unidentified author. Preserved in two manuscripts, the poem is composed of 309 nine-line stanzas of eleven-syllable lines, an unusual stanza length. This work too has an elegant conceit: the speaking voice has been forced by *fin'amor* to love a beautiful lady whom he reveals at the end to be an allegory for intelligence itself, both human and divine. The poet begins with an exemplary springtime opening rich in thematic and lexical echoes from courtly lyric and romance, and describes his hyberbolically lovely lady (stanzas 1–15). The first 'encyclopaedic digression'[16] describes the sixty gems in her crown with their assigned virtues (stanzas 16–58). Some 200 stanzas then describe the lady's elaborately painted palace, offering an extended *ekphrasis* of the founding stories of classical antiquity, as well as a few Arthurian characters and episodes.[17] The amorous pretext of the poem is dwarfed by the classical material: the Civil War between Caesar and Pompey (stanzas 77–215); the life of Alexander the Great (stanzas 216–39); the destruction of Troy (stanzas 240–86). After a short reprise of the Arthurian material (stanzas 287–8), the poem returns to describing the lady and her court (stanzas 289–98) and ends by unveiling her allegorical significance and that of her palace (stanzas 299–309). The last stanza seems a rapid palinode of the whole: 'Amor, che mia vertute signoreggia, / m'ha fatto vaneggiare in questo dire' ('Love, which dominates my strength, / has made me rave in this poem') (309.1–2). The limited scope of the Arthurian references (ten stanzas out of 309) and their generality have seemed to its most recent editor to indicate only a vague or indirect knowledge of the Arthurian corpus. Keith Busby and Delcorno Branca argue instead that the allusions bespeak a substantial familiarity with that corpus, especially with the works of Chrétien.[18]

These three anonymous poems, all Florentine from the last twenty years of the thirteenth century, are contemporary with the earliest Arthurian narratives we have from the Italian peninsula. All are secular in theme, and their references to the Arthurian material are positive rather than dismissive or ambivalent. All have some kind of echo in Dante, whether in content or in phrasing, suggesting that they were known and influential in Florence despite leaving few manuscript witnesses. More overtly parallel to the *Divine Comedy* – indeed, deeply influenced by it – is the *Dittamondo* by the Pisan poet Fazio degli Uberti, composed from *c.*1350 on, but left unfinished in Book Six when he died in 1368.[19] This fascinating text uses Dante's *terza rima* form in a putative journey ranging over the known world, guided by the mid-third-century geographer Solinus. As in *L'Intelligenza*, the Arthurian invocations are a small proportion of the historical and geographical whole, but they are wide-ranging and strongly approving.[20] In Book Two the narrator sets the Arthurian legends solidly in the fifth and sixth centuries, saying that they were known in the time of Theodoric:

> In questo tempo giá parlar s'udia
> di Uter Pendragon e di Merlino
> e del lavor che, fondato, sparia.
>
> . . .
>
> Artú benigno, largo e franco in guerra,
> con l'alta compagnia Francia conquise,
> Fiandra, Norvegia e ciò che quel mar serra. (Book 2.15.31–3 and 46–8)
>
> (In this time talk was already heard
> of Uther Pendragon and of Merlin
> and of the work which, once founded, vanished.

. . .

Arthur, benign, generous, and brave in war,
with his high company conquered France,
Flanders, Norway, and what that sea encloses.)

In Book Four the narrator and his guide visit Brittany (4.22) and Great Britain (4.23, 4.24, 4.26) and survey the sites and events of the Arthurian tales. Delcorno Branca extrapolates from the unusual details of the tombs of Tristan and Iseut, the specific source Fazio drew on to compose the following passage:

Poi vidi l'isoletta dove uccise
Tristano l'Amoroldo e dove ancora
Elias di Sansogna a morte mise.
In Tintoil udii contare allora
d'un'ellera, che de l'avello uscia
lá dove 'l corpo di Tristan dimora,
la quale abbarbicata se ne gia
per la volta del coro, ove trovava
quello nel quale Isotta par che sia.
Per le giunture del coperchio entrava
e dentro l'ossa tutte raccogliea
e come viva fosse l'abbracciava:
e ciò di novo trovato parea. (4.22.97–109)

(Then I saw the islet where
Tristan killed Morholt, and where too
he put Helye of Saxony to death.
I then heard tell of an ivy
in Tintagel which came out of the tomb
where Tristan's body lies,
and it went climbing out
over the vault of the choir, where it met
the tomb where it seems Iseut lies.
Through the gaps in the lid it entered,
and gathered up all the bones
and embraced them as though she were alive;
and that seemed recently found.)

The detail of the plant growing from Tristan's tomb and reaching to Iseut's 'is very close to the specific version of the episode given in BnF, MS fr. 103 of the *Tristan en prose*, which relays Thomas's version of the death of the lovers'.[21]

The *Dittamondo*'s description of Britain overall – its resources, qualities and people – is admiring and positive:[22]

Tanto è l'isola grande, ricca e bella,
che vince l'altre che in Europa sono,
come fa il sole ciascun'altra stella.

. . .

[Q]uivi divota a Dio vidi la gente,
forti, costanti e schifi a ciascun fallo.

> Maraviglia non pare, a chi pon mente,
> se prodezza, larghezza e leggiadria
> vi fun, come si dice, anticamente. (4.23.7–9, 44–8)
>
> (The island is so great, rich and fair,
> that it surpasses all of those in Europe
> as the sun surpasses every other star.
> . . .
> I saw the people there faithful to God,
> strong, constant and averse to every error.
> It seems no wonder, to anyone who thinks about it,
> that valour, liberality and grace
> were there, as they say, in the old days.)

Fazio's qualifier *anticamente* (of old) reveals his generation's interpretation of the Matter of Britain, still circulating and valid in Italy some two centuries after its conception, and their positive impression of the British Isles. Indeed, six centuries later, Dante Gabriel Rossetti and the Pre-Raphaelite Brotherhood express a similarly nostalgic conception of courtliness and chivalry. E. G. Gardner identifies Fazio's next lines as 'the true note of Arthurian romance',[23] and Rossetti captures that nostalgic and elegiac tone in his own translation of the passage:

> We went to London, and I saw the Tower
> Where Guenevere her honour did defend,
> With the Thames river which runs close to it.
> I saw the castle which by force was ta'en
> With the three shields by gallant Lancelot,
> The second year that he did deeds of arms.
> I beheld Camelot despoiled and waste;
> And was where one and the other had her birth,
> The maids of Corbonek and Astolat.
> Also I saw the castle where Geraint [Erec]
> Lay with his Enid; likewise Merlin's stone,
> Which for another's love I joyed to see.
> I found the tract where is the pine-tree well,
> And where of old the knight of the black shield
> With weeping and with laughter kept the pass,
> What time the pitiless and bitter dwarf
> Before Sir Gawaine's eyes discourteously
> With many heavy stripes led him away.
> I saw the valley which Sir Tristram won
> When having slain the giant hand to hand
> He set the stranger knights from prison free.
> And last I viewed the field, at Salisbury,
> Of that great martyrdom which left the world
> Empty of honour, valour, and delight.
> So, compassing that Island round and round,
> I saw and hearkened many things and more
> Which might be fair to tell but which I hide.[24]

Fazio degli Uberti's project, resembling Dante's *Comedy* in the superstructure of its allegorical journey in *terza rima*, also shares Dante's project of braiding together the different strands of his legendary, historical and scientific culture – Christian and classical, local and universal. Fazio also shares Dante-pilgrim's admiring and wistful view on the 'ancient ladies and the knights' (*Inferno* 5.71) as a centre of positive value in the world, lost to us now but awaited, like Arthur, as though it were to return ('che dovesse tornare fu aspettato', 4.24.51).

Short Prose Fiction

The earliest collection of Italian short fiction in prose, the *Novellino* (*c*.1280) requires and rewards study both extensive and minute. The complexity of the *Novellino*'s textual tradition entails nuances to which a study of this scope cannot do justice.[25] The prologue's announced programme is to assemble fine utterances of the past which can serve as a model for its day: 'fiori di parlare, di belle cortesie e di belli risposi, e di belle valentie, di belli donari e di belli amori . . . a prode e a piacere di coloro che non sanno e disiderano di sapere' ('flowers of speech, fine courtesies and fine answers, and fine noble gestures, and fine gifts and fine loves . . . for the benefit and pleasure of those who do not know and who wish to know'). Of the approximately one hundred tales, five are specifically derived from the narrative tradition of Arthurian romances; three come from the prophetic Merlin tradition;[26] two contain comparative references only, without relating episodes concerning the characters they invoke; and one attributes to a Lancelot a proverb or moral without any indication that it is indeed the Arthurian Lancelot. The *Novellino*'s importance for this volume lies in the evidence it offers both for the circulation of Arthurian material and for the relative prestige and moral valence of Arthuriana in Italy around 1280.[27]

Three tales concern Lancelot: the tale of the cart (28), a single combat at a fountain (45) and the Lady of Shalott (82). *Novellino* 28 is one of the few moralisations – and the most emphatic – of the collection.[28] It links Lancelot's journey in the cart, wandering aimlessly 'through many places' (*per molte luogora*), to one of his episodes of madness rather than to a conscious sacrifice made in pursuit of a focused goal (the rescue of Guinevere). The narrative focuses on how Lancelot's adoption of the cart reversed the shame and opprobrium previously attached to it, making it instead a 'stylish vehicle for the nobility'.[29] The narrator bursts into a reproach to the ungrateful world and base humankind, willing to reverse a custom to imitate a mere Lancelot (a madman and a foreigner, at that) when Christ Himself could not inspire mankind to abandon its custom of hatred and vengeance in favour of forgiveness.[30]

A more admirable and honourable Lancelot is featured in *Novellino* 45, in which a knight fighting him incognito at a fountain is undaunted until he learns who Lancelot is. 'Your name harms me more than your valour does,' says the suddenly intimidated knight, offering one of the elegant ripostes that the *Novellino* prologue announces as its narrative agenda. The theme of chivalric supremacy is regularly entwined with that of fame and reputation in the Arthurian romances, though it is less typical for Lancelot to announce his name while fighting incognito.[31] While no specific source for this episode emerges from the Lancelot sources, Delcorno Branca proposes a very convincing one – with strong confirmation from the narrative specifics – in an episode from the *Tristan en prose*, with a change of protagonist from Tristan to Lancelot.[32]

Novellino 82 contains the third episode from the Lancelot matrix, in which the Lady of Shalott arranges for her corpse to be dressed sumptuously and placed in a luxurious ship, to be wafted to Camelot with a letter in her bag to be read there:

> E lo nobile re Artú vi venne, e maravigliavasi forte ch'era sanza niuna guida. Il re entrò dentro: vide la damigella e l'arnese. Fe' aprire la borsa. Trovaro quella lettera. Fecela leggere.

> (And the noble King Arthur came there, and wondered greatly that the ship was without a pilot. The king went in: he saw the lady and her panoply. He had the bag opened. They found that letter. He had it read.)

The letter calls Lancelot 'lo migliore cavaliere del mondo e . . . lo più villano' ('the best knight in the world and . . . the most base'). The elaborate staging of the scenario by the lovesick maiden; the hyperbolic luxury of her array; the marvellous unmanned ship: all are from the *La Mort le roi Artu* (§§70–1).[33] What seems to have the most value for the context of the *Novellino* is the paradox of Lancelot's simultaneous greatness and baseness, to which Arthur is, not by chance, the privileged witness.

Novellino 65 relates at unusual length a much-loved episode from Béroul, when Tristan and Iseut meet in the garden and narrowly escape betraying themselves to the suspicious King Mark, hiding in a tree. This encounter is often represented in visual art, especially the so-called decorative arts, as an epitome of courtly love: its secretive delight, its risks of exposure and its hair's-breadth escapes. The lovers' constant vigilance enables both their detection of the trap and their doubled discourse, an exchange which assuages the king's suspicion even as it declares their love for each other. Because Iseut spotted the king, and because of her calculated speech, Tristan 'non fu sorpreso né ingannato per lo savio avedimento ch'ebbero intra lor due' ('was not taken by surprise or deceived because of the wise discernment that there was between them').

Delcorno Branca analyses the specific elements of this version of the episode, tracing the individual details back (and forward) to sources and influences to discover 'a multiple and contaminated use of Tristanian antecedents'.[34] That the tree in question is a pine is a detail found only in Béroul and in all the Italian Tristan romances; that it is the king's shadow in the tree that warns the lovers is unique to Thomas and present in the Italian romances (in Béroul and Eilhart it is his reflection in the water that betrays the king). Details taken from Eilhart include the stream that runs through the palace, Mark's hunt and his departure from it. In the Panciatichiano version of the *Novellino* (as in Eilhart and *Sir Tristrem*), it is Tristan who spots the king and warns

Isotta with coded speech. Delcorno Branca's analysis reveals 'the use of a text close to Eilhart von Oberg and to Béroul . . . with elements of the Thomas redaction, as it is attested by Gottfried of Strassburg, the Norse saga, and *Sir Tristrem*'.[35]

One *Novellino* tale draws on the Old Table material so present and influential in Italy, the generation before Arthur and his knights. *Novellino* 63 relates two vivid examples of magnanimity between King Meliadus and the Knight Without Fear, magnanimity made even more noble by the implacable hostility prevailing between them. As the *Novellino* prologue had promised, the tale portrays natural, effortless *valentie* or courtesies, when two valorous knights defer to each other despite their enmity. Their courtesy is emphasised by the churlish brutality of the servants of the Knight Without Fear who, unaware that he is their lord, abuse him for declaring King Meliadus the greatest knight. Both knights conceal their names in order to appropriately praise the other; the Knight Without Fear will not identify himself even to restrain his servants, and King Meliadus, after rescuing the Knight, instructs him not to look at the saddle-cover of the horse he has given him, until he is far away. Only then does the Knight realise that it is his mortal enemy who has rescued him.[36]

Italian Arthurian authors often depart notably from their source material in order to create an ethical or civic vision more consonant with peninsular political structures (varied as these can be). The character of Galehaut, for example, is imported into the *Conti di antichi cavalieri* (*c*.1270–1300), in the only Arthurian tale of its twenty.[37] This collection has been described as a mirror of princes, and as Delcorno Branca notes, it downplays the original contours of the Galehaut of the *Prose Lancelot* and the *Tristan en prose*:

> [T]he author has removed the connection with the violent, pagan lineage of the giants, the excessive ambition for conquest, the role of intermediary between Lancelot and Guinevere, the wrenching chivalric friendship destined to lead to his death: all the fantastic, obscure, and disquieting features of the character.[38]

The *Conti* author has, moreover, inserted material describing Galehaut's altruistic and egalitarian character even as a child, material for which there are no parallels in the tradition he is appropriating: the boy lets his companions win at games, and shares his food and fine clothing as his father tutors and tests him in these virtues. Coming first, this material conditions the familiar Galehaut narrative differently, so that the two remaining episodes figure as natural outgrowths of his goodness. He conquers twenty-nine kingdoms not out of ambition and violence, but to extirpate the evil customs that abounded then:

> In quello tempo assai re aveano usanze e costumi rei e vilane multo, de li quali grandi mali e descionori seguiano a cavalieri e a donne e a donzelle. Esso se puse in core d'abactere ciascuno malvagio costume.[39]
>
> (In that time many kings had customs and practices that were very wicked and base, and from which great evil and dishonour befell knights and ladies and maidens. He set his heart on defeating every evil custom.)

After he has sworn allegiance to Arthur out of love for Lancelot, Galehaut fights Tristan to avenge his own parents whom, because of the evil custom of *their* land, Tristan had been forced to kill. But because this Galehaut too had loathed that evil custom, he forgives Tristan his unwilling murder and peace is restored. The Galehaut of this short narrative, in other words, is strongly reconfigured, by dint of inserted material, connective tissue and explanatory additions, to reflect an ethos quite different from that of the source texts.

Franco Sacchetti's *Trecentonovelle* (*c*.1385–97) similarly invokes Tristan and Lancelot aslant, in an anecdote about Dante Alighieri.[40] Hearing a blacksmith singing his verses, ruining and mangling them, the great poet hurls the man's tools out in the street. Asked 'Che diavol fate voi? Sète voi impazzato?' ('What the devil are you doing? Are you crazy?'), the poet retorts, 'Tu canti il libro [mio] e non lo di' come io lo feci; io non ho altr'arte, e tu me la guasti' ('You're singing my book, and you're not telling it the way I made it; I have no other art [or craft, or skill], and you're ruining it'). Thereafter, if the chastened smith wanted to sing, 'cantò di Tristano e di Lancelotto e lasciò stare il Dante' ('he sang of Tristan and of Lancelot, and let Dante be'). The clear implication is that Dante's divine *terza rima* should not be entrusted to a tradesman; an *ottava-rima cantare* version of Tristan or Lancelot could more appropriately be sung in the streets.

In a similar way, the episode of Bellicies's suicide for love is imported, strongly reconfigured from its romance version, into Francesco da Barberino's *Reggimento e costumi di donna*, as Marie-José Heijkant notes in Chapter 3. Not surprisingly for a conduct book, the *Reggimento* does not invoke her suicide favourably or recommend Bellicies as a model. It is worth noting that some other thirteenth- and fourteenth-century texts concerned with women's behaviour – proper and improper – do not mention Arthurian fictions at all, unless *as* fictions, as reading matter in which women overindulge (as Christopher Kleinhenz notes in Chapter 10). The *Proverbia super natura feminarum* and Antonio Pucci's *Il Contrasto delle donne* draw their *exempla* of misbehaving females from history, myth and the Bible, but give the Arthurian matter a wide berth. Sacchetti invokes it once or twice, a presence that calls attention to the absence of a corpus he has no use for; the *Proverbia* and the *Contrasto* occlude the Arthurian material completely, an absence that calls attention to the presence of that corpus in the feminine realm they examine.

Conclusion

It is clear that by the 1270s the Arthurian material was fully present and available to Italian authors and audiences, not only in the prose romances that were so very influential, but also in many metrical versions. The Arthurian stories performed a variety of cultural work in the different verse and prose compositions discussed here. Whether serving as centres of positive value or as negative *exempla*, they are imported to carry a specific ethical and aesthetic charge that at this remove we cannot always confidently identify. Only by continuing to scrutinise the entire literary horizon can we speculate on precisely what the Arthurian material meant in these carefully crafted cameos.

Notes

[1] C. Kleinhenz, 'Italian Arthurian literature', in *The New Arthurian Encyclopedia*, ed. N. J. Lacy (New York and London, 1991; rpt 1996), pp. 245–7, on p. 245.

[2] See also R. Capelli, 'Caratteri e funzioni dell'elemento cavalleresco-cortese nella lirica italiana del Due e Trecento', in M. Picone (ed.), *La letteratura cavalleresca dalle* chansons de geste *alla* Gerusalemme liberata (Pisa, 2008), pp. 91–122.

[3] D. Delcorno Branca, 'Diffusione della materia arturiana in Italia. Per un riesame delle "tradizioni sommerse"', in F. Benozzo et al. (eds), *Culture, livelli di cultura e ambienti nel Medioevo occidentale* (Rome, 2012), pp. 321–40, on p. 324.

[4] Delcorno Branca, 'Diffusione della materia'.

[5] Julia Bolton Holloway's edition of Brunetto Latini's *Tesoretto*, from Florence, Bibl. Medicea Laurenziana, MS Strozziano 146, is available at *http://www.florin.ms/Tesorett.html*.

[6] Petrucci is cited in A. Carrega (ed.), Il Gatto lupesco e Il Mare amoroso (Alessandria, 2000), p. 36.

[7] C. Lee notes that this alternative Arthurian matter seems to have remained 'at the margins of the "official" codification of the legend', and that it 'was received and circulated for the most part in works coming from the Mediterranean region, and elaborated first in Italian territory' ('Artú dall'Italia alla Spagna,' in R. Morosini and C. Perissinotto [eds], *Mediterranoesis: Voci dal Medioevo e dal Rinascimento mediterraneo* [Rome, 2007], pp. 43–60, on p. 44).

[8] Carrega surveys the range of interpretative positions in her introduction to the *Detto* (pp. 8–14).

[9] Ibid., p. 20.

[10] Cited in ibid., p. 21.

[11] Translations are mine unless otherwise noted.

[12] On the fusion of text and commentary, and on scholarship on it, see Carrega (pp. 53–4) and J. Bartuschat, '"Il mare amaro dell'amore": Autour du *Mare amoroso*', in C. Cazalé Bérard et al. (eds), *La mer dans la culture italienne* ([Nanterre], 2009), pp. 47–58, on p. 47 n. 2.

[13] Bartuschat, '"Il mare amaro"', p. 48.

[14] Delcorno Branca identifies several data that point to the *Tristan* of Thomas, including the foregrounding of the potion drunk on the ship and of a death for love (though attributed here to Kahedin, Tristan's double), and the funerary inscription on the lover's future tomb, 'a series of insistent paronomasia and verbal play on *amare / marinaio / mare / amaro / amore / morto / amarore / morto* (ll. 327–34)', 'the intensity and concentration of which constitutes the stylistic hallmark typical of the Carlisle fragment of Thomas' ('Diffusione', p. 327). See also Bartuschat, '"Il mare amaro"'.

[15] 'La diffusione italiana della versione tristaniana di Thomas è appunto una di quelle "tradizioni sommerse" che occorre riesaminare' ('Diffusione', p. 329).

[16] M. Berisso (ed.), *L'Intelligenza: poemetto anonimo del secolo XIII* (Parma, 2000), p. xi. Since this poem's Arthurian passages are discussed in Chapter 1 in this volume, I will treat it in shorthand here.

[17] The Arthurian stanzas are 71–6, 207, 287–8 and 294. See Chapter 13 in this volume for discussion of extant frescoes of Arthurian figures.

[18] Busby in Chapter 1 of this volume; Delcorno Branca 'Diffusione', p. 333.

[19] Fazio degli Uberti, *Il Dittamondo e le Rime*, ed. G. Corsi, 2 vols (Bari, 1952).

[20] The *Dittamondo*'s Arthurian allusions (Book Two, 15.31–3 and 43–8; Book Four, 22.91–109, 23.46–75, 24.40–51, 26.4–12) show its debt to the *Historia Regum Britanniae*, to the *Vulgate Lancelot-Graal*, the *Tristan en prose* and *Guiron le Courtois* (Delcorno Branca, 'Diffusione', p. 337).

[21] Delcorno Branca, 'Diffusione', p. 337.

[22] Indeed, an anecdote describes a small island where people are said to be born with tails, mothers are said to refuse to tend their babies and trees are said to bear birds as their fruit; Fazio emphasises that this is hearsay, and that he does not necessarily believe it (*Dittamondo*, 4.23.28–39).

[23] E. G. Gardner, *The Arthurian Legend in Italian Literature* (London and New York, 1930), p. 225.

[24] *Dittamondo* (4.23.52–78), trans. D. G. Rossetti, *The Early Italian Poets*, ed. Sally Purcell (Berkeley, CA, 1981), pp. 110–11.

[25] The *Novellino* should be examined in its two major incarnations: the *editio princeps* of 1525, and the earliest and best manuscript witness, BNCF, MS Panc. 32. Differences between the two are often important and significant. A. Conte's edition *Il Novellino* (Rome, 2001) contains both.

[26] This tradition is discrete, unconnected to the Arthurian narrative world; in it Merlin unveils various secrets through his gift of prophecy.

[27] The major study of the *Novellino*'s Arthurian tales is Delcorno Branca, 'I racconti arturiani del *Novellino*' (*TLI*, pp. 117–42). She surveys various critical hypotheses for the sources used in *Novellino*; I follow the sources she proposes.

[28] *TLI*, p. 135.

[29] *TLI*, p. 136.

[30] *TLI*, p. 136.

[31] *TLI*, p. 132.

[32] *TLI*, pp. 133–5.

[33] C. Segre discusses the complex syncopation of the *novella*'s temporal sequence as a function of its deracination from the romance matrix, in 'Deconstruction and Reconstruction of a Tale: From *La mort le roi Artu* to the *Novellino*', in *Structures and Time: Narration, Poetry, Models*, trans. J. Meddemmen (Chicago, 1979), pp. 58–64.

[34] *TLI*, p. 125.

[35] *TLI*, p. 119.

[36] As Delcorno Branca notes, this exchange of courtesies does not lead to any 'forgiveness' of the enemy, although *Novellino* 28 had deplored the persistence of violent resentment; it is merely 'a habitus, the expression of a mode of being' (*TLI*, p. 129), one which the *Novellino* clearly finds worthy of admiration.

[37] A. Del Monte (ed.), *Conti di antichi cavalieri* (Milan, 1972), ch. 21, 'Conto de Brunor e de Galeocto suo fillio', pp. 149–55.

[38] *TLI*, p. 238.

[39] *Conti di antichi cavalieri*, p. 150.

[40] Sacchetti, *Il Trecentonovelle*, I classici italiani, ed. A. Lanza (Florence, 1984), ch. 114, pp. 231–3.

10

THE ARTHURIAN TRADITION IN THE THREE CROWNS

Christopher Kleinhenz

In the writings of the 'Three Crowns' of Italy – Dante (1265–1321), Petrarch (1304–74) and Boccaccio (1313–75) – allusions to Arthurian literature often appear in lists of famous people from the past, who serve an emblematic or didactic function.[1] For the Three Crowns, Arthurian literature was a rich source of amorous intrigues and courtly adventures, presenting a host of characters with well-known personalities and individual traits that could serve as the basis for appropriate comparisons, descriptions and moralising commentary. This chapter will examine the many and diverse ways in which each author incorporates figures from the Arthurian tradition in his works. These uses reflect a shift in the understanding of the historicity of 'the ladies and the knights of old', from Dante's attitude of general acceptance to Petrarch's serious reservations and Boccaccio's milder ones.[2] Their reception in the writings of the Three Crowns ranges from an ambivalent appraisal of their moral virtues (Dante) and an almost casual dismissal of their worthiness (Petrarch) to a generally warm embrace of them and their fabulous stories (Boccaccio).

Petrarch

Of the three authors, Petrarch appears to be the least interested in and the most critical of Arthurian literature, for his few references to that tradition are generally derogatory. Unlike the earlier lyric tradition in Italy, Petrarch's *Canzoniere* contains no allusions to the intense but tragic passions of Tristan for Iseut or Lancelot for Guinevere; indeed, the only references to the Matter of Britain in his vernacular works occur in the *Trionfi* (Triumphs). In the *Triumphus Cupidinis* (Triumph of Love), Petrarch not unsurprisingly includes several figures from the Arthurian tradition among the myriad lovers who follow in Love's sorrowful train:

> Here are those who fill the pages with dreams – Lancelot, Tristan and the other knights errant, whom the errant masses naturally crave. Behold Guinevere, Isolde and other paramours, and the couple from Rimini who together go uttering sorrowful laments.[3]

The word play on *erranti* is both descriptive (the 'knights errant' who wandered about in search of adventure) and judgemental (the moral aberrancy of those same individuals).[4] The general populace (''*l vulgo errante*') is also criticised for their 'errant' literary tastes, and this is typical of Petrarch's view of the common folk, who are easily swayed by their enthusiasms rather than their intellect. The passage also emphasises

Petrarch's negative view of Arthurian romance, based primarily on the lack of historical foundation for these pleasant but fatuous tales, even though some of the individuals in Love's train were historical figures (e.g. the 'couple from Rimini', Paolo and Francesca).[5]

Similarly, in the *Triumphus Fame* (Triumph of Fame), after listing the great heroes of the past, Petrarch passes to the late classical and medieval world when he notes the earthly glory of King Arthur: 'I compress many great things into a small package: Where is a King Arthur, and three August Caesars [i.e. emperors], one from Africa, one from Spain, one from Lorraine?'[6] Petrarch prefaces this new section with the comment that he will necessarily condense and abbreviate his narration, which suggests that the greatness of these later heroes can be dealt with much more succinctly and is thus of lesser value. He begins with Arthur, whose name is followed by a precise reference to three emperors: Septimius Severus ('one from Africa'), Theodosius I ('one from Spain') and Charlemagne ('one from Lorraine'). Petrarch also downplays Arthur when he uses the indefinite article 'a' (*un*) with his title and name ('un re Arturo'). This suggests that Arthur is not in the triumph on account of his own merit as a king but rather as the representative of a type of hero whose fame rests on legends that cannot be verified historically. By contrast, Petrarch presents the three emperors as genuine by using the definitive phrase 'tre Cesari Augusti' followed by the toponym which indicates their birthplace.

In his Latin works, Petrarch alludes to figures from Arthurian legend only a few times, and always negatively. In one of his letters (*Seniles* 15.3), he addresses the question of fame, noting that rarely can earthly renown be gained through marriage or children:

> How great would Plato's or Aristotle's or Homer's and Virgil's name be today, if they had thought it was to be gotten through matrimony and offspring? These are not the paths to glory, as they are said to be, but sidetracks and roamings; they do not lead to the splendor of fame, but often to dangers, and more often to disgrace, and almost always to disgust; and certainly the examples of dangers and disgrace are countless.[7]

Following these examples of men who achieved fame, Petrarch refers to numerous other classical figures – e.g. Julius Caesar, Domitian, Claudius – whose adulterous wives brought them 'disgrace'. In this context he alludes to the cuckolded kings, Mark and Arthur – 'I pass over King Mark and King Arthur and the tales of Britain' – in reference to the negative influence of their unfaithful wives, Isolde and Guinevere.[8]

In his series of moralising dialogues, *De remediis utriusque Fortune* ('Remedies for Fortune Fair and Foul'), Petrarch draws examples from Arthurian literature on three occasions. In Book Two, Dialogue 6, *Ratio* (Reason) and *Dolor* (Sorrow) debate the question of 'Shameful Origin' (*De obscena origine*). Reason notes that, despite illegitimate or incestuous origins, many individuals have risen to high places:

> Constantine himself was born of a concubine, although a very distinguished one, and was advanced to be emperor in preference to his legitimate brothers. To these I could add King Arthur, were it not

for the fact that this would mean mixing historical evidence with fable and dilute the truth with lies.[9]

Although acknowledging Arthur's dubious legitimacy, Petrarch carefully refrains from using this example because it is not historical.[10] This choice is consistent with his unwillingness to accept evidence that does not come from reliable sources, as well as his general reluctance to attribute value to anything that enjoys popularity among the masses.

In Dialogue 21 of Book Two of *De remediis,* the debate between Sorrow and Reason is concerned with 'An Immoral Wife' (*De impudica uxore*); here, one example of a betrayed husband is Arthur, whose wife Guinevere dallied with Lancelot: 'Think of the kings and rulers of nations you have seen yourself. Then consider those about whom you have read or heard, and you will remember the legend of Arthur and some others.'[11] The explicit contrast between the 'fable' (*fabulam*) of Arthur and the 'histories' (*historias*) of other heroes suggests the lesser value given to Arthurian tales. In *De expectatione filii, vel amici* ('Expecting Family and Friends'), Reason mentions Arthur when tempering the expectations of Hope:

> *Reason*: Who is surprised that living people are expected to return when, it is reported, some expect dead ones to come back. Although no one save a madman believes anything like this, the Britons are said to expect the return of Arthur.[12]

Here too, Petrarch disparages Arthurian material on the grounds that it is a fiction.

Dante Alighieri

Unlike Petrarch, Dante did not appear to doubt the historical validity of Arthur and other characters in the legends. His perspective on the Arthurian tradition does, however, change and mature over time, from a generally positive view in his early works to a distinctly more negative one in the *Comedy*. In his early sonnet, *Guido, i' vorrei che tu e Lapo ed io* ('Guido, my wish would be that you and Lapo and I'), Dante voices his intense wish, couched in the conditional and subjunctive moods, to be caught up in a state of enchantment in a small boat together with two friends – Guido Cavalcanti and Lapo Gianni – and their respective ladies:

> Guido, my wish would be that you and Lapo and I
> might be taken by a magic spell
> and placed on a boat that would be blown
> about the sea as you and I wanted,
>   such that neither storm nor any other foul weather
> could impede our course;
> indeed, by sharing one same desire,
> our wish to be together would be increased.
>   And may the good magician put with us
> Lady Vanna and Lady Lagia with that lady

who rests on number thirty:
   and there we would always speak of love,
and each of our ladies would be happy,
as I think we, too, would be.)[13]

The three friends would share this lovely idyll with their ladies: Cavalcanti's Monna Vanna, Lapo's Monna Lagia and Dante's lady whom he identifies only as the one 'who rests on number thirty'. In this periphrasis, Dante may be alluding to the woman listed thirtieth in his list of the sixty most beautiful women of Florence, provided in a now-lost *sirventese* (the 'pistola sotto forma di serventese') mentioned in the *Vita nova*.[14] Whomever he means, in line 9 Dante expresses his wish that the *buono incantatore* (good magician) might magically convey the ladies to their *vasel* (boat), thus transforming their apparently mundane world into a sort of enchanted paradise or at least into a romantic cruise. Most critics agree that the good magician is Merlin, and that with this reference Dante proves his awareness of the Arthurian legend and its principal figures.[15] Although he does not name Merlin here, elsewhere in his works Dante does make precise allusions to other characters from the chivalric romances – Lancelot, Tristan, Guinevere, Galehaut, Mordret, Arthur and the Lady of Malehaut.

In his treatise on language and poetry, *De Vulgari eloquentia* (1304–7), Dante refers to the 'beautiful tales of King Arthur' ('Arturi regis ambages pulcerrime', 1.x.2) narrated in *lingua oïl* (Old French), a reference that suggests his great appreciation of Arthurian literature:

Thus the language of *oïl* adduces on its own behalf the fact that, because of the greater facility and pleasing quality of its vernacular style, everything that is recounted or invented in vernacular prose belongs to it: such as compilations from the Bible and the histories of Troy and Rome, and the beautiful tales of King Arthur . . . [16]

Here, Dante associates Old French with prose narrative and expository writings of 'history and doctrine' ('ystorie ac doctrine'). Indeed, his knowledge of Arthurian literature seems to have been limited almost exclusively to the prose romances, specifically the prose *Lancelot* and the *Mort Artu*. Moreover, he appears not to harbour any of the reservations that Petrarch would eventually have concerning the lack of historical veracity in the tales of Arthur.

There has been some discussion about the meaning of *ambages* in this passage – either 'digression' or 'ambiguous tale' or 'to go wandering' – but the intent seems clear: Dante is referring to the 'very beautiful rambling tales of Arthur', equating in a way the ambiguity of the term *ambages* itself with the lovely interlaced fables of the king and his knightly companions.[17] It should be noted, however, that while the term *ambages* was employed in a positive way in this treatise, it has undergone a complete transformation in its unique appearance in the *Comedy*. In *Paradiso* Dante contrasts Cacciaguida's 'plain words' and 'clarity of thought' with the enigmatic and ambiguous phrases of pagan prophets – *ambage* – thus placing these errant beliefs in opposition to the true word of God:

> Not with *cloudy sayings*, by which the foolish folk
> were once ensnared, before the Lamb of God,
> who takes away our sins, was slain,
> but in plain words and with clear speech,
> that paternal love replied . . . (*Paradiso* 17.31–5; my emphasis)[18]

By employing the loaded term *ambage*, Dante is able in the *Comedy* not only to correct his earlier view but also to place the entire courtly tradition into a more universal perspective. These lines set the stage for Cacciaguida's foretelling of Dante's exile from Florence for political reasons, a prophecy expressed in simple, direct and unequivocal language. This use of *ambage* in the *Comedy*, coupled with the allusion (discussed below) to the Lady of Malehaut and the first fault of Guinevere in the previous canto (*Par.* 16.13–15), suggests that Dante was consciously thinking of and referring to the Arthurian tradition in this episode.

One example that demonstrates Dante's familiarity with the Old French prose tradition is his portrayal of Lancelot, whom he praises in *Convivio*. Here, Lancelot figures as a prime example of the noble soul who, at the end of his life, abandons the active life and its earthly pleasures and embraces the spiritual, taking refuge in religion:

> Certainly the knight Lancelot did not wish to enter with his sails raised high, nor the most noble of our Italians, Guido of Montefeltro. These noble men did indeed lower the sails of their worldly preoccupations and late in life gave themselves to religious orders, forsaking all worldly delights and affairs.[19]

Dante does not differentiate between the fictional Lancelot and the historical Guido in describing souls who lower their sails to enter a safe port.[20] However, Lancelot's positive act of repentance is not immediately apparent when Dante presents the story of his adulterous relationship with Guinevere as a negative *exemplum*.[21]

In fact, the first reference to Arthurian literature in the *Comedy* occurs in *Inferno* 5, when Virgil includes Tristan among the great lovers of antiquity – Semiramis, Dido, Cleopatra, Helen, Achilles, Paris: '"See Paris, Tristan," and he showed me more / than a thousand shades, naming as he pointed, / whom love had parted from our life' (*Inf.* 5.67–9).[22] The last verse of Virgil's catalogue juxtaposes classical Paris with medieval Tristan and, in this way, prepares for the entrance of the two truly 'modern' lovers – Paolo and Francesca – who complete the movement from antiquity to the present. In response to Virgil's list and brief comments on seven of the great lovers of the past, Dante the Pilgrim shows extreme compassion: 'When I heard my teacher name the ladies / and the knights of old, pity overcame me / and I almost lost my senses' (*Inf.* 5.70–2).[23] Here Tristan, and later in this same canto Lancelot and Guinevere, appear as negative *exempla* of the many sinners who succumbed to lust: 'I understood that to such torment / the carnal sinners are condemned, / they who make reason subject to desire' (*Inf.* 5.37–9).[24]

In an oft-cited passage, Francesca da Rimini relates to Dante the Pilgrim how their first kiss was occasioned by their reading of a courtly romance:

'One day, to pass the time in pleasure,
we read of Lancelot, how love enthralled him.
We were alone, without the least misgiving.
    More than once that reading made our eyes meet
and drained the color from our faces.
Still, it was a single instant overcame us:
    When we read how the longed-for smile
was kissed by so renowned a lover, this man,
who never shall be parted from me,
    all trembling, kissed me on my mouth.
A Galeotto was the book and he who wrote it.
That day we read in it no further.' (*Inf.* 5.127–38)[25]

This well-known story focuses on the literary source that precipitated their amorous liaison: they read in the Old French prose *Lancelot* the circumstances of the first kiss the titular character and Guinevere shared, how their meeting was orchestrated by Galehaut. By imitating that particular action, Francesca and Paolo began their love affair, which would eventually lead to their death at the hand of her jealous husband, Gianciotto. In this context, Dante intends the allusion to Lancelot and Guinevere to impart a moral lesson, one that should warn against engaging in similarly adulterous behaviour. Francesca uses the Italian name of the Old French go-between, Galehaut, in the declaration 'Galeotto fu 'l libro e chi lo scrisse' ('Galeotto was the book and he who wrote it'), as a double indictment of both the book itself and its author as those responsible for the sinful passion that ultimately condemned them to Hell. This episode in the *Inferno* has also been read as a commentary on the act of reading and its dangers, on the purpose and power of literature and on the great responsibility an author assumes in writing. Another instance of multiple interpretations in this episode is Paolo and Francesca's 'mis-reading' of the text of the prose *Lancelot*. The question of who kissed whom is an open one, for there is no consensus in the manuscripts of the *Lancelot*; in some Guinevere takes the initiative and kisses Lancelot, and in others it is the opposite. We do not know the version with which Dante was familiar. Therefore, when the poet has Francesca say that Lancelot kissed Guinevere, is this the variant version of the story that he had read? Or is he having her alter the story, and, if so, why? The mystery continues.

Another allusion to this particular episode in the *Lancelot* is found in *Paradiso* 16:

With that *You* which had its origin in Rome
and which her offspring least preserve by use,
I once again began to speak,
    and Beatrice, who stood somewhat apart,
smiled, like *the lady who discreetly coughed*
at the first fault inscribed of Guinevere. (*Par.* 16.10–15; emphasis added)[26]

Here, having just learned the identity of his great-great-grandfather Cacciaguida, Dante addresses him with the honorific *voi*; this discloses the earthly pride he feels in having so famous an ancestor, an emotion inappropriate for the Heavenly Spheres.

Recognising both Dante's sudden awareness of his noble lineage and his indiscreet pride in that knowledge, Beatrice smiles, and in this she is compared with 'the Lady [of Malehaut] who discreetly coughed / at the first fault written about Guinevere'. This is a complex allusion. In the Old French prose romance, during the meeting between Lancelot and Queen Guinevere orchestrated by Galehaut, the lady of Malehaut, one of Guinevere's ladies-in-waiting, coughs as a sign to Lancelot. She does so for two reasons: (1) because she, too, loves Lancelot and does not want that fact to harm his relationship with the Queen, and (2) to inform Lancelot that she, too, now knows his genealogy, following the Queen's acknowledgement of her awareness of Lancelot's identity and noble lineage. Like the Lady of Malehaut who stands apart and coughs, Beatrice also 'stood somewhat apart' and smiled, providing a gentle warning to Dante, who is the counterpart of Guinevere in the allusion and whose 'first fault' is his obvious pride in his family's nobility.

One final Arthurian allusion in the *Comedy* occurs in *Inferno* 32, where the Pilgrim encounters the souls of the traitors to kin. Among them is Mordret, Arthur's illegitimate and rebellious son who, while giving the king a mortal wound on the battlefield was in turn slain by him. Dante describes Mordret as 'him whose breast and shadow were pierced / by a single blow from Arthur's hand' (*Inf.* 32.61–2; 'quelli a cui fu rotto il petto e l'ombra / con esso un colpo per la man d'Artù'). This description derives directly from the *La Mort le roi Artu*: 'and the king, who came at him with all his might, wounded him so strongly that he broke the chain mail of his hauberk and struck him in the chest with his sword; and the story says that after the sword was removed, a ray of sunlight passed through the wound'.[27] With this vivid description of Mordret and his death, Dante focuses attention on the disastrous consequences of treason and warfare – the rending of the 'body politic', figured in the perforated body of Mordret – and again uses Arthurian legend to make this point.

Boccaccio

Of the Three Crowns, Boccaccio made the most extensive use of Arthurian material in his literary corpus, as Daniela Delcorno Branca demonstrates.[28] In the *Amorosa visione* ('The Amorous Vision', 1343), an allegorical dream vision in *terza rima* divided into fifty cantos, Boccaccio follows the metrical example of Dante's *Comedy* and provides the conceptual model for Petrarch's *Trionfi*. Both Boccaccio and Petrarch saw the 'paradigmatic value of the Greco-Latin world' and presented numerous examples in their works.[29] Boccaccio devotes considerable space to the triumph of earthly Glory ('la Gloria del popol mondano'), painted on the walls in the noble castle ('nobile castello').[30] He begins the eleventh canto with a presentation in fifty-four verses of no fewer than nineteen characters from the Arthurian romances:

Venia dopo costor gente gioconda
ne' loro sembianti, tutti cavalieri
chiamati della Tavola ritonda.
 Il re Artù quivi era de' primeri,
a tutti armato avanti cavalcando
ardito con pensier sublime e altieri.
 Seguielo appresso il splendido e onorando
Pricivalle ed il saggio *Galeotto*
a picciol passo 'nsieme ragionando.
 E dietro ad essi vidi *Lancellotto*,
con vago sguardo ed aspetto grazioso,
a passo celer, via più che di trotto,
 ferendo il caval fiero e valoroso
per appressarsi alla donna piacente,
cui di toccar tutto era disioso.
 Oh quanto adorna quivi e risplendente
allato lui *Ginevra* seguitava,
sovra un bianco corsier orrevolmente!
 Stella micante al tutto somigliava
la luce del suo viso e aver biltate
quanta fu mai; e tutta si mostrava
 sorridendo negli atti, di pietate
piena, parlando in atto assai discreto
con silenti parole e grazie ornate.
 Era con quel che già ne visse lieto
per lunga fiata, lei sanza misura
amando, ben che poi seguisse fleto.
 Non molto dietro ad esso con gran cura
era il fier *Galeotto*, il cui valore
più ch'altri suoi compagni s'affigura;
 ed appo lui 'l vittorioso *Astore*
veniva insieme con *messer Ivano*,
disioso ciascun d'etterno onore.
 L'Amoroldo d'Irlanda ed *Aravano*,
Pallamide seguiva e *Lionello*,
e *Polinor* col strenuo *Calvano*.
 Mordretto poscia e con lui *Dodinello*,
e il valido *Tristan* seguiva appresso
sopra arduo corsier feroce e isnello.
 Isotta bella venia allato ad esso,
la man di lui con la sua giunta e presa
e rimirandol nella faccia spesso.
 Oh quanto si mostrava in viso offesa
dalla forza d'amor, di che parea
ch'avesse l'alma dentro tutta accesa!
 Di che negli atti quasi dir volea:
'Tu sei colui cui solo sol disio',
con soavi sguardi; e poscia soggiognea:
 'In qua, ti priego, volgi il volto pio,
acciò fruisca il mio bel paradiso

per cui sicura in tal camin m'invio'.
   Rietro a costor, sovra un corsiero assiso,
rubesto e ardito 'l fier *Brunor* venia
con altri molti, i quai qui non diviso.[31]

(After these came people joyous / in appearance, all knights / called 'of the Round Table'. / *King Arthur* was among the first, / riding before them in armor, / bold in his sublime, proud thoughts. / After him came the splendid and honorable / *Percival* and wise *Galahad*; they spoke together as they slowly went along. / Behind them I saw *Lancelot*, / with his longing look and charming face, / moving quickly, more than at a trot, / spurring his high-spirited brave horse / in order to draw near the lovely lady, / whom he greatly wished to touch. / Oh how well turned out, how splendid / was *Guinevere* there, following at his side, / in an honorable fashion, upon a white charger! / The light which shone from her face / in every way resembled that from a star; / she seemed more beautiful than anyone ever was. / Smiling, she showed herself full of compassion, / speaking in a most discreet way, / with quiet utterance and charming, graceful manners. / She was with the one who because of her enjoyed / long-lasting happiness, loving her without measure, / even if sorrow was to follow later. / Not far behind him, with solicitous air, / was proud *Gallehault*, whose valor / is accounted greater than that of his companions. / And next to him victorious *Astorre* / came with *Messire Yvain*, / each desirous of eternal honor. / *Amoroldo of Ireland*, *Hargdabrant*, / and then *Palamedes* followed; also *Lyonel* / and *Pellinor*, along with energetic *Gauvain*. / *Mordret* then, and with him *Dodiniel*, / and brave *Tristan* came after, / on an ardent charger, fierce and swift. / *Isolde* the fair came at his side, / her hand joined fast with his, / frequently gazing into his face. / Oh did her expression reveal how greatly she was / wounded by the power of love, by which it seemed / that the soul within her was altogether consumed! / From her gestures it seemed as though she said: / 'You are the one alone whom alone I desire', / with sweet glances, then adding: / 'Turn in my direction, I pray you, your / compassionate face, so that I may enjoy my lovely / paradise; toward it, secure, I follow such a path'. / Behind these, seated on his charger, / fierce and brave, came proud *Brunoro* / with many another whom I do not here set down.)[32]

The many exemplary figures gathered here reflect Boccaccio's familiarity with the French courtly romances (gained in large part during his stay in the Angevin court in Naples),[33] as well as with the Italian versions of these exemplars, including the more popular oral narratives, the *cantari*, sung by *jongleurs* in the town square. The ordering of the Arthurian characters begins with the legend's founding figure, Arthur, just as the subsequent series featuring Carolingian epic heroes begins with Charlemagne. Alongside the Arthurian protagonists (Arthur, Lancelot, Guinevere, Tristan), Boccaccio mentions heroes who participated in the Grail Quest (Percival and Galahad) as well as a number of lesser-known knights (Morholt of Ireland, Hargdabrant, Lionel, Dodinel).

Later in the *Amorosa visione*, at the conclusion of his description of the artistic representation of the Triumph of Love, Boccaccio alludes to the two most famous pairs of lovers from Arthurian legend: 'And next to this pleasing representation / I saw Lancelot figured there / with her in whom so long he gloried. / There, after him, to his right, / was Tristan and the one of whom he was / enamoured more than of any other.'[34] While naming the male partner of each couple (Lancelot and Tristan), Boccaccio elides their ladies' names (Guinevere and Iseut), referring to them simply with the feminine-gendered demonstrative pronoun *quella* (that one). Given their widespread fame, to read or hear the name of one lover would automatically bring to mind the name of the other.

Boccaccio also refers to Tristan and Iseut in the *Elegia di Madonna Fiammetta* ('The Elegy of Lady Fiammetta', 1343–4) where the titular character compares her amorous suffering with that of earlier women, noting in the process a number of famous pairs of lovers (e.g. Hero and Leander, Pyramus and Thisbe).[35] Chapter 8, Section 7 opens with Fiammetta acknowledging her source texts: 'At times I remember reading French romances in which, if they can be trusted, Tristan and Iseult loved one another more than any other lovers did and spent their earliest youth in pleasure mixed with innumerable adversities.'[36] Fiammetta explicitly refers to the French romances that she has read and which provide her with the prime example of a couple beset by 'innumerable adversities': Tristan and Iseut. She alludes to the couple's shared death, when the mortally wounded Tristan holds Iseut in an embrace so strong that she too dies: 'Tristan's death and that of his lady were in his own hands; if it had been painful when he tightened its grip, he would have loosened it, and the pain would have ceased.'[37] Fiammetta concludes by noting that, 'although Tristan and Iseult ended pleasures and pains at once', her sorrow is much greater: 'but the lengthy period of my incomprehensible grief surpasses the pleasures I have had'.[38] As often happens in such narratives, the trials and tribulations of the protagonist are compared with those of a restricted set of literary examples and are found to be much greater.

In his virulently misogynous work, *Il Corbaccio* ('The Old Crow', 1355), Boccaccio tells the story of a rejected lover, who, in a dream vision, is visited by a spirit who cures him of his passion for a widow (who, as it happens, was the Spirit's wife) by painting a grim picture of her earthy and carnal desires. In the course of the narration we observe, as Anthony Cassell has noted, 'vituperation colored with obscenity and clothed with the worst of classical and medieval antifeminist abuse'.[39] As a result, the references to the Arthurian legend here assume a very different tone than in other works by Boccaccio. In discussing the widow's love of male prowess, the Spirit notes that it is valour not on the field of battle that the widow likes, but in the bedroom.

> 'That prowess which she likes . . . is used in the boudoir, in hidden places, beds, and similar loca-
> tions suited to it, where without the coursing of horses, or the sound of brass trumpets, one goes to
> the joust at a slow pace. And she considers him to have the prowess of either Lancelot, Tristram,
> Roland, or Oliver, whose lance does not bend for six, eight, or ten jousts in one night in such a way
> that it is not then raised again . . . Therefore, if the years have not sapped your usual strength, you
> should not, as you did, despair of pleasing her with your prowess, believing that she wished you to
> be, perhaps, Morold of Ireland.'[40]

With thinly veiled sexual innuendo, the Spirit characterises the nature of the widow's insatiable lust for the 'joust'. The heroes of both Arthurian and Carolingian legends become terms of comparison for the bold man who would attempt to satisfy her carnal cravings. The allusions to the sexual prowess of Lancelot, Tristan and Morold of Ireland reflect the coarser but much more realistic view of the Arthurian knights which would have appealed to the fourteenth-century popular imagination.

The Spirit continues his denunciation of the widow by speaking sarcastically of her 'sacred texts':

'But I spoke so confidently because I believed and now know that her prayers and paternosters are French romances and Italian songs in which she reads of Lancelot and Guinevere, Tristram and Isolde, and of their great exploits, their loves, jousts, tournaments, and battles; and when she reads that Lancelot, Tristram, or someone else meets with his lady secretly, and alone, in her bedchamber, she goes all to pieces because she thinks she can see what they are doing and would willingly do as she imagines they do – although she manages to suffer her craving for it only a short time.'[41]

Just as Lady Fiammetta spoke of her reading of French romances, so too does the widow exult in reading the same materials. Indeed, the intimate scenes she encounters in her reading arouse her; ultimately, she finds that she is able to satisfy these libidinal desires much more quickly than the protagonists do in the romances.

In the *Corbaccio*, Boccaccio makes a few other allusions to Arthurian characters. Galehaut and Febus are exemplars of bravery: '"To disapprove of her stories and lies, of which she has a greater store than any other woman, would be the same as wanting to fight with her – this she would do at the drop of a hat, because she thinks she excels Galehaut of the Distant Isles or Febus in bravery."'[42] Similarly, Lancelot's father, King Ban of Benwick, is an example of noble lineage: '"But I want to tell you this: if you had any speck of nobility in your spirit, or had you that which once the lineage of King Ban of Benwick possessed, you would have sullied and spoiled it by loving her."'[43] Boccaccio's almost casual use of these Arthurian figures attests to how familiar they would have been to his readers. Allusions of this sort are, however, not overtly present in his *magnum opus*, the *Decameron*.

Boccaccio was a fervent admirer of Dante and an able supporter of his cult in Florence. By subtitling the *Decameron* 'Prencipe Galeotto', he is clearly borrowing the name of a well-known character in Arthurian romance, which was also used in a pertinent allusion in *Inferno* 5. While his exact meaning in adopting this subtitle is unclear, Boccaccio may have intended to suggest that, as Galeotto's role in the prose *Lancelot* was to serve as a go-between and friend of lovers, so he and his collection of one hundred tales would serve as a sort of friend and go-between, providing some consolation for ladies experiencing distress in amorous matters. Or, if the reference is directed towards the apostrophe in *Inferno* 5 – 'Galeotto fu 'l libro e chi lo scrisse' ('A Galeotto was the book and he who wrote it') – then the subtitle would appear to serve as a warning to readers about the dangers that books and their reading pose to one's moral health. Even though there are many subtle borrowings – lexical, stylistic and thematic – from the Arthurian tradition in the *novelle* of the *Decameron*, Boccaccio includes no direct allusions to specific names or episodes.[44]

Boccaccio's devotion to Dante included copying his works in several manuscripts, writing a highly laudatory life of the poet and presenting public lectures on the *Comedy* in Florence. The lectures became the *Esposizioni sopra la Comedia* (Expositions on Dante's *Comedy*), which Boccaccio wrote at the end of his life. In these, he provides some putatively historical glosses on the Arthurian characters who are mentioned in or who have some connection to *Inferno* 5: Tristan (and Iseut), Galehaut, Lancelot and Guinevere (and Arthur). Glossing Tristan, Boccaccio says:

> Tristan, according to the French romances, was the son of King Meliadus and the nephew of King Mark of Cornwall. In these French romances, he was a handsome and valiant knight. He loved Queen Isolde, the wife of King Mark, somewhat less than respectably, which is why his uncle wounded him with a poisoned arrow. Isolde went to see him and Tristan, realizing he was about to die, embraced her and squeezed her so tightly against his chest that both of their hearts were crushed. They died together and were likewise buried in the same tomb. He lived during the time of King Arthur and the Round Table.[45]

For the story of Lancelot and Guinevere, which Francesca da Rimini cites as the cause of her love affair with Paolo, Boccaccio provides the following gloss:

> *We ... were pleasure reading one day of Lancelot*, of whom the French romances relate many beautiful and praiseworthy things. I believe, however, that these things were composed more for entertainment than as truths. And we were reading of *how love bound him*, since it is written in these romances that Lancelot was quite fervently in love with Queen Guinevere, the wife of King Arthur ... *Gallehault was the book and he who wrote it*. It is written in the aforementioned romances that Prince Gallehault ... (at the urging of Lancelot, whom he most dearly loved) one day took Queen Guinevere with him into a chamber with the pretext of chatting with her. There the go-between summoned Lancelot and to no small effect revealed his love for her ... he [Gallehaut] saw to it that the couple exchanged a kiss. Thus ... that book, which she and Paolo were reading, performed the same task for the two of them that Gallehault fulfilled for Lancelot and Queen Guinevere. She also says that that same man was the one who wrote it. This is because, were it not he who wrote it, what happened would never have taken place.[46]

Boccaccio's reading and exposition of Dante's *Comedy* discloses how much knowledge concerning the Arthurian legends was available to him and how he transmitted it to those in attendance at his lectures in Florence and to his readers, both contemporary and posthumous. Boccaccio's vernacular witness to Arthurian material is complemented by his treatment of this subject in his more scholarly Latin works.

In Book 8 of *De casibus virorum illustrium* ('The Fates of Illustrious Men', 1355–60), Boccaccio devotes a chapter to 'Arthur, King of the Britons' ('De Arturo Britonum rege'), which he prefaces by noting the lack of historical evidence surrounding him:[47]

> But Arthur the King, in misery, came forward and stood in front of me. He has been famed in the celebrated English fables. Although we do not recognize the evidence of his greatness and his fate as worthy of credence, still let us surely relate his story, for subsequently the whole world seems to have given witness to him.[48]

Whereas Petrarch would not have continued the narrative under these circumstances, Boccaccio, recognising a good story when he sees it, pursues it with gusto. Given the moral nature of the treatise, the tale of Arthur and the Knights of the Round Table is a cautionary one: Arthur attains worldly glory only to be betrayed by his natural son Mordret. Having left England to invade Gaul, Arthur trusted Mordret

> to defend the seat of the kingdom during his absence. The youthful Mordret was strong and bold in all his actions, and for a long time had been spurred by a desire for power. He considered the

absence of the king a chance offered to him by Fortune, and began to incite the oppressed to liberty, to capture the minds of all men with gifts, to guard the cities and the castles, and to show that he was going to be a very benign king. He called his friends together, trained men, and united a very large band of mercenaries. Then he denied victuals and help to his father, and did everything that had the appearance of a rebellion. When the time was ripe, he published false letters stating that King Arthur had died in battle and that he, Mordret, was to be king.[49]

According to Boccaccio, Arthur hears of these events and immediately returns to England to fight his rebellious son. In the ensuing battle, most of Arthur's men are slain. In the final combat between Arthur and Mordret, the king impales his son with a lance, making '[a] wound . . . so wide that through it could be seen the rays of the setting sun'.[50] In the process Arthur is wounded by a sword blow to his head, and this leads to his mysterious journey to Avalon: 'The King, . . . knowing that this was his last day, came down from his horse and going to a boat, ordered that he be carried to the island of Avalon, and there death released him from his misery.'[51] Boccaccio then refers to the legend that, given the absence of a tomb prepared for him Arthur did not die, but will eventually return once his wounds have healed. Boccaccio summarises the moral of the tale:

> What can be concluded from this? In a very short time Arthur's huge kingdom was shrunk and his own life lost through the temerity of one evil man. The famous Round Table, enriched by such brave men, was entirely deserted and broken up by Arthur's death, though it lives on in the fabulous tales of ordinary people. The triumphant glory of King Arthur and his brilliant renown gave way to shame and obscurity by this rebellion and destruction. From this example people can learn, if they wish, that in this world only the humble things endure.[52]

In this passage and throughout the treatise Boccaccio is keenly attuned to the sadness arising from the inevitable loss of earthly glory, but is quick to remind – and perhaps also to encourage and reassure – his non-aristocratic readers of the moral 'that in this world only the humble things endure'. The popularity of this work among future generations, evident in the large number of editions and translations, was guaranteed in part by its presentation of familiar figures, and among these King Arthur has a place of prominence.

Conclusion

As we have observed, the Three Crowns often alluded to Arthurian characters and interpreted these tales in varying ways. Their reliance on this tradition for *exempla* is indicative of the many uses that will be made of this rich hoard of tales and legends during the thirteenth and fourteenth centuries in Italy. Arthurian literature was for everyone, from those listening to oral performances of this material by *giullari* (performers) in the piazza to the readers of courtly romances in their palaces. The three major intellectuals of late medieval Italy – Dante, Petrarch and Boccaccio

– counted on the characters' instant name recognition to convey ethical and aesthetic lessons, both positive and negative. By reflecting various interpretations attached to certain Arthurian figures, the works of the Three Crowns attest to the richness of the tradition and contribute to its continuance in Western culture.

Notes

[1] This differs from the earlier practice in the Italian lyric tradition where protagonists from the Arthurian romances generally served as terms of comparison, to express the greatness of a poet's love, the beauty of his beloved lady, or the prowess of the male lover. See Roberta Capelli's Chapter 8 in this volume.

[2] '[L]e donne antiche e ' cavalieri', *Inferno* 5.71. Quotations from the *Divine Comedy* follow Giorgio Petrocchi (ed.), *La Divina Commedia secondo l'antica vulgata* (Florence, 1994), and Robert Hollander and Jean Hollander (eds and trans.), *Inferno* (New York, 2000) and *Paradiso* (New York, 2007).

[3] This and subsequent translations are mine except where otherwise noted. 'Ecco quei che le carte empion di sogni: / Lancilotto, Tristano, e gli altri erranti, / ove conven che 'l vulgo errante agogni. / Vedi Ginevra, Isolda, e l'altre amanti, / e la coppia d'Arimino, che 'nseme / vanno facendo dolorosi pianti' (V. Pacca and L. Paolino [eds], Petrarca, *Trionfi, Rime estravaganti, Codice degli abbozzi* [Milan, 1996; 2000], III.79–84).

[4] Roberta Capelli argues the same point in 'Caratteri e funzioni dell'elemento cavalleresco-cortese nella lirica italiana del Due e Trecento', in M. Picone (ed.), *La letteratura cavalleresca dalle* chansons de geste *alla* Gerusalemme liberata (Pisa, 2008), pp. 91–122.

[5] Petrarch claims never to have read Dante's *Commedia*, but his reference to 'la coppia d'Arimino' would suggest a more than casual acquaintance with the Circle of the Lustful (*Inferno* 5). Moreover, as I discuss below, in that canto Tristan is identified as one of the punished souls, and Francesca describes how she and Paolo fell in love while reading about the first kiss of Lancelot and Guinevere. As Michelangelo Picone argues, the amorous adventures of the Arthurian knights – as well as those of the three famous couples mentioned in this passage – provide a model of sorts for Petrarch's own *innamoramento* with Laura; '"Ecco quei che le carte empion di sogni": Petrarca e la civiltà cavalleresca', in Picone (ed.), *Letteratura cavalleresca*, pp. 139–52.

[6] 'Molte gran cose in picciol fascio stringo: / ov'è un re Arturo, e tre Cesari Augusti / un d'Affrica, un di Spagna, un Lottoringo?' (Pacca and Paolino [eds], Petrarca, *Trionfi*, II.133–5).

[7] A. S. Bernardo, S. Levin and R. A. Bernardo (trans.), *Letters of Old Age: Rerum senilium libri I–XVIII*, 2 vols (Baltimore, 1992), II, p. 565. 'Quantum hodie Platonis, aut Aristotelis, quantum Homeri ac Virgilii nomen esset, si matrimonio illud ac sobole comparandum censuissent. Non sunt hae viae ad gloriam, quae dicuntur, sed devia et errores. Neque hac ad splendorem fame pergitur, sed saepe ad pericula, saepius que ad dedecora et fere semper ad taedia, et certe periculorum atque dedecorum innumerabilia sunt exempla' (Petrarch, *Opera omnia* [Basileae: Per Sebastianum Henricpetri (*sic*), 1581], II, p. 936).

[8] Bernardo et al. (trans.), *Letters*, II, p. 566. 'Omitto Marcum, et Arcturum reges, fabulasque Britannicas' (*Opera omnia* [1581], II, p. 936).

[9] C. H. Rawski (trans.), *Petrarch's Remedies for Fortune Fair and Foul: A Modern English Translation of De remediis utriusque fortune, with a Commentary*, 5 vols (Bloomington, IN, 1991), III, p. 30. 'Constantinus ipse, ex concubina genitus, licet insigni, pre legitimis fratribus ad imperium venit. Adderem his Arturum regem, nisi quod historiis miscere fabulas, nichil est aliud quam mendacio veri fidem imminuere' (Christophe Carraud [ed.], Petrarch, *Les Remèdes aux deux Fortunes. De remediis utriusque Fortunae. 1354–1366*, 2 vols [Grenoble, 2002], I, p. 580).

[10] Another example of this particular view of Arthur and his legendary survival on the island of Sicily may be observed in Petrarch's metrical epistle to Pope Benedict XII (1.5): 'Hinc feror Oceano, qua nobilis insula vivum / Praedicat Arcturum et quicquid sibi fabula mendax / Persuadet. Sylvas, fontes, mirandaque vulgo / Praelia et insanos equitum decantat amores / Gallia quae magnum Carolum, duodena virorum / Praesidia et regnum tot opimis dotibus auctum / Ostentat longaque iacet iam fessa quiete', in D. Rossetti (ed.), *Poesie minori del Petrarca: sul testo latino ora corretto*, 3 vols (Milan, 1829–34), III, pp. 142–4, ll. 72–8, with minor alterations. ('From here I am borne across the Ocean, where a noble island proclaims a living Arthur and whatever else a lying tale persuades itself is true. Gaul reels off woods, fountains, battles amazing to common folk, and the obsessive loves of knights. She holds up to view great Charles, the twelvefold protection of heroes, and a kingdom increased by very many splendid gifts; now weary, she rests in long stillness.') I thank my colleague John Dillon for his elegant translation of these verses.

[11] Rawski (trans.), *Petrarch's Remedies*, III, p. 69. I omit from Rawski's translation the elevating title 'King', as it is pointedly not in Petrarch's text: 'Reges cogita quos vidisti ac terrarum dominos; dehinc scriptis famaque cognitos recordare; respice et Arthuri fabulam et historias reliquorum' (Carraud [ed.], *Les remèdes*, I, p. 662).

[12] Rawski (trans.), *Petrarch's Remedies*, I, p. 309. '*Ratio*: Quis miretur expectari vivos, cum mortui expectentur, ut perhibent, quod nisi inter fatuos veri faciem non habet? Arcturum Britannos expectare fama est' (Carraud [ed.], *Les remèdes*, I, p. 504).

[13] 'Guido, i' vorrei che tu e Lapo ed io / fossimo presi per incantamento, / e messi in un vasel ch'ad ogni vento / per mare andasse al voler vostro e mio, / sì che fortuna od altro tempo rio / non ci potesse dare impedimento, / anzi, vivendo sempre in un talento, / di stare insieme crescesse 'l disio. / E monna Vanna e monna Lagia poi / con quella ch'è sul numer de le trenta / con noi ponesse il buono incantatore: / e quivi ragionar sempre d'amore, / e ciascuna di lor fosse contenta, / sì come i' credo che saremmo noi' (Dante, *Rime*, in *Opere minori*, ed. D. De Robertis and G. Contini, 2 vols in 3 tomes [Milan and Naples, 1995], vol. I, tome 1).

[14] G. Gorni and M. Tavoni (eds), *Vita nova*, in *Opere*, I: *Rime. Vita nova. De vulgari eloquentia* (Milan, 2011), 6.1–2.

[15] The '*vasel*' also has a correlative in the legends of Merlin: the '*nef de joie et de deport*' ('boat of joy and pleasure'). See Contini's note in *Rime*, p. 35.

[16] S. Botterill (trans.), *De Vulgari eloquentia* (Cambridge, 1996), p. 23. 'Allegat ergo pro se *lingua oïl* quod propter sui faciliorem ac delectabiliorem vulgaritatem quicquid redactum est sive inventum ad vulgare prosaycum, suum est: videlicet Biblia cum Troianorum Romanorumque gestibus compilata et Arturi regis ambages pulcerrime . . .' (P. V. Mengaldo [ed.], *De vulgari eloquentia*, in Mengaldo et al. [eds], *Opere minori* [Milan and Naples, 1979], vol. II, tome 2, pp. 82 and 84).

[17] For the debated meaning of this term, see among others A. Duro, 'Ambage', in *Enciclopedia dantesca*, 6 vols (Florence, 1966), I, pp. 199–200; A. Marigo, in his commentary on the second edition of *De vulgari eloquentia*, Opere di Dante (Florence, 1948), VI, pp. 77–8; Mengaldo et al. (eds), *Opere minori*, II, p. 84; Picone, 'Dante e la tradizione arturiana', *Romanische Forschungen*, 94 (1982), 1–18; P. Rajna, '*Arturi regis ambages pulcerrime*', *Studi danteschi*, 1 (1920), 91–9; and K. Stierle, 'Il mondo cavalleresco nella *Commedia*', in Picone (ed.), *La letteratura cavalleresca*, pp. 123–38.

[18] 'Né per *ambage*, in che la gente folle / già s'inviscava pria che fosse anciso / l'Agnel di Dio che li peccata tolle, / ma per chiare parole e con preciso / latin rispuose quello amor paterno . . .'

[19] R. Lansing (trans.), *Dante's Il Convivio (The Banquet)* (New York, 1990), p. 233. 'Certo lo cavaliere Lanzalotto non volse [in porto] intrare colle vele alte, né lo nobilissimo nostro latino Guido montefeltrano. Bene questi nobili calaro le vele delle mondane operazioni, che nella loro lunga etade a religione si rendero, ogni mondano diletto ed opera disponendo' (F. Brambilla Ageno [ed.], *Convivio: Testo* [Florence, 1995], II, 4.28.7–8).

[20] Both examples reappear in the *Comedy* but in two different guises: Lancelot and Guinevere are alluded to in *Inferno* 5 as models for adulterous behaviour, and Guido da Montefeltro is condemned to Hell (*Inferno* 27) for the sin of evil counsel.

[21] Because Lancelot, unlike Tristan, never appears as a character in the *Comedy*, we do not know where Dante would have placed him. It may be that because of his repentance, Dante believes him to be among the saved, but this is unknowable. What we know is that Lancelot's adulterous relationship with Guinevere has disastrous consequences both in the prose *Lancelot* (it ultimately leads to the destruction of Arthur's court) and in Dante's poem (Francesca says the tale led to her adulterous affair with Paolo and their subsequent damnation).

[22] '"Vedi Parìs, Tristano"; e più di mille / ombre mostrommi e nominommi a dito, / ch'amor di nostra vita dipartille.'

[23] 'Poscia ch'io ebbi 'l mio dottore udito / nomar le donne antiche e ' cavalieri, / pietà mi giunse, e fui quasi smarrito.'

[24] 'Intesi ch' a così fatto tormento / enno dannati i peccator carnali, / che la ragion sommettono al talento.'

[25] '"Noi leggiavamo un giorno per diletto / di Lancialotto come amor lo strinse; / soli eravamo e sanza alcun sospetto. / Per più fïate li occhi ci sospinse / quella lettura, e scolorocci il viso; / ma solo un punto fu quel che ci vinse. / Quando leggemmo il disïato riso / esser basciato da cotanto amante, / questi, che mai da me non fia diviso, / la bocca mi basciò tutto tremante. / Galeotto fu 'l libro e chi lo scrisse: / quel giorno più non vi leggemmo avante."'

[26] 'Dal "voi" che prima a Roma s'offerie, / in che la sua famiglia men persevra, / ricominciaron le parole mie; / onde Beatrice, ch'era un poco scevra, / ridendo, *parve quella che tossio* / al primo fallo scritto di Ginevra.'

[27] '[E]t li rois, qui li vient de toute sa force, le fiert si durement qu'il li ront les mailles del hauberc e li met par mi le cors le fer de son glaive; et l'estoire dit que aprés l'estordre del glaive passa par mi la plaie uns rais de soleill' (J. Frappier [ed.], *La Mort le roi Artu* [Geneva, 1964], p. 245).

[28] See D. Delcorno Branca, *Boccaccio e le storie di re Artù* (Bologna, 1991); J. Levarie Smarr, 'Boccaccio, Giovanni', in N. J. Lacy (ed.), *The New Arthurian Encyclopedia* (New York, 1996), pp. 42–3.

[29] Vittore Branca, 'Introduction' to R. Hollander, T. Hampton, and M. Frankel (eds and trans.), *Amorosa Visione* (Hanover, NH, 1986), p. xxii.

[30] Hollander et al., *Amorosa Visione*, 6.75 and 6.59 respectively.

[31] V. Branca (ed.), *Amorosa Visione*, 11.1–54 (emphasis added), in V. Branca (ed.), *Tutte le Opere di Giovanni Boccaccio*, 9 vols (Milan, 1974), III. The Italian text in this edition is the later 'B' version.

[32] Hollander et al., *Amorosa Visione*, 11.1–54 (emphasis added).

[33] Delcorno Branca, *Boccaccio e le storie*, pp. 8–9.

[34] Hollander et al., *Amorosa Visione*, 29.37–45. 'E dopo questa piacevole istoria, / vi vidi Lancelotto effigiato / con quella che sì lunga fu sua gloria. / Lì dopo lui, dal destro suo lato, / era Tristano e quella di cui elli / fu più che d'altra mai inamorato . . .'

[35] The rubric reads, 'Eight. In which Lady Fiammetta, comparing her pains to those of many ancient ladies, demonstrates that hers are greater and then finally concludes her lamentation' (M. Causa-Steindler and T. Mauch [eds and trans.], *The Elegy of Lady Fiammetta* [Chicago, 1990], p. 142).

[36] Causa-Steindler and Mauch (trans.), *Elegy*, p. 145. 'Ricordami alcuna volta avere letti li franceschi romanzi, alli quali se fede alcuna si puote attribuire, Tristano e Isotta oltre ogn'altro amante essersi amati e con diletto mescolato a molte avversità avere la loro età più giovane essercitata' (C. Delcorno [ed.], *Elegia di Madonna Fiammetta*, in V. Branca [gen. ed.], *Tutte le opere* [Milan, 1994], vol. V, tome 2, p. 175).

[37] Causa-Steindler and Mauch (trans.), *Elegy*, p. 146. 'Ne le braccia di Tristano era la morte di sé e della sua donna: se quando strinse li fosse doluto, egli avrebbe aperte le braccia, e saria cessato il dolore' (C. Delcorno edn, p. 175).

[38] Causa-Steindler and Mauch (trans.), *Elegy*, p. 146. '[F]inirono . . . ad una ora li diletti e le doglie . . . [m]a a me molto tempo in doglia incomparabile è sopra li avuti diletti avanzato' (C. Delcorno edn, p. 175).

[39] A. Cassell (trans. and intro.), *The Corbaccio* (Chicago, 1975), p. xxv.

[40] Cassell (trans.), *Corbaccio*, pp. 49–50. 'Quella prodezza addunque, che le piace ... s'usa nelle camere, ne' nascosti luoghi, ne' letti e negli altri simili luoghi acconci a ciò, dove, senza corso di cavallo o suono di tromba di rame, alle giostre si va pian passo; e colui tiene ella che sia o vuogli Lancelotto o vuogli Tristano, Orlando o Ulivieri di prodeza, la cui lancia, per sei o per otto o per dieci aringhi, la notte non si piega in guisa che poi non si dirizi ... Per che, se gli anni non t'hanno tolta l'usata virtù, non ti dovevi per prodeza disperare di piacerle, come facesti, credendo tu ch'ella volesse che tu fossi l'Amaroldo d'Irlanda' (G. Padoan [ed.], *Corbaccio*, in V. Branca [gen. ed.], *Tutte le opere* [Milan, 1974], pp. 264–5).

[41] Cassell (trans.), *Corbaccio*, p. 60. 'Ma io così fidatamente ne favellava, per ciò che saper mi parea, e so, che le sue orazioni e paternostri sono i romanzi franceschi e le canzoni latine, e' quali ella legge di Lancelotto e di Ginevra e di Tristano e d'Isotta e le loro prodeze e i loro amori e le giostre e i torniamenti e le semblee. Ella tutta si stritola quando legge Lancelotto o Tristano o alcuno altro colle loro donne nelle camere, segretamente e soli, raunarsi, sì come colei alla quale pare vedere ciò che fanno e che volentieri, come di loro imagina, così farebbe; avvenga che ella faccia sì che di ciò corta voglia sostiene' (Padoan edn, *Corbaccio*, p. 316).

[42] Cassell (trans.), *Corbaccio*, p. 51. 'E 'l non consentirle le favole e bugie sue, delle quali ella è più ch'altra femmina piena, niuna cosa sarebbe se non un volersi con lei azuffare; la qual cosa ella di leggieri farebbe, sì come colei alla qual pare di gagliardia avanzare Galeotto delle lontane Isole o Febus' (Padoan edn, *Corbaccio*, p. 272).

[43] Cassell (trans.), *Corbaccio*, p. 70. 'Ma così ti vo' dire che, se punto di gentileza nello animo hai, o quella avessi che già ebbe il legnaggio del re Bando di Benvich, tutta l'avresti bruttata e guasta, costei amando' (Padoan edn, *Corbaccio*, p. 372).

[44] See Delcorno Branca, 'Strategie allusive nel *Decameron*', in *Boccaccio e le storie*, pp. 15–49. With regard to specific names, in *Decameron* 10.6 the two daughters of messer Neri degli Uberti are named 'Ginevra la bella' and 'Isotta la bionda', names that, together with the general tone of the *novella*, evoke the world of courtly romance.

[45] M. Papio (trans.), *Boccaccio's Expositions on Dante's* Comedy (Toronto, 2009), p. 277. 'Tristano, secondo i romanzi de' Franceschi, fu figliuolo del re Meliadus, e nepote del re Marco di Cornovaglia, e fu, secondo i detti romanzi, prode uomo della persona e valoroso cavaliere; e d'amore men che onesto amò la reina Isotta, moglie del re Marco, suo zio, per la qual cosa fu fedito dal re Marco d'un dardo avelenato. Laonde vedendosi morire ed essendo la reina andata a visitarlo, l'abracciò e con tanta forza se la strinse al petto che a lei e a lui scoppiò il cuore e così insieme morirono e poi furono similmente sepelliti insieme. Fu costui al tempo del re Artù e della Tavola Ritonda, ed egli ancora fu de' cavalieri di quella Tavola' (G. Padoan [ed.], *Esposizioni sopra la Comedia*, in V. Branca [gen. ed.], *Tutte le opere* [Milan, 1965], VI, canto 5, 1.135–6).

[46] Papio (trans.), *Boccaccio's Expositions*, pp. 285–6. '*Noi ... leggiavamo un giorno per diletto Di Lancialotto*: del quale molte belle e laudevoli cose racontano i romanzi franceschi, cose, per quel ch'io creda, più composte a beneplacito che secondo la verità; e leggiavamo *come amor lo strinse*, per ciò che ne' detti romanzi si scrive Lancialotto esser stato ferventissimamente inamorato della reina Ginevra, moglie del re Artù ... *Galeotto fu 'l libro e chi lo scrisse*. Scrivesi ne' predetti romanzi che un prencipe Galeotto ... ad istanzia di Lancialotto, il quale amava maravigliosamente, tratta un dì in una sala a ragionamento seco la reina Ginevra, e a quello chiamato Lancialotto, ad aprire questo amore con alcuno effetto fu il mezzano: e ... fece che essi si basciarono insieme. E così ... quello libro, il quale leggevano Polo ed ella, quello officio adoperasse tra lor due che adoperò Galeotto tra Lancialotto e la reina Ginevra; e quel medesimo dice essere stato colui che lo scrisse, per ciò che, se scritto non l'avesse, non ne potrebbe esser seguito quello che ne seguì' (Padoan edn, *Esposizioni*, canto 5, 1.180, 183–4).

[47] See Delcorno Branca, 'Storiografia e romanzo: *De Arturo Britonum Rege*', in *Boccaccio e le storie*, pp. 69–112.

[48] L. B. Hall (trans.), Boccaccio, *The Fates of Illustrious Men* (New York, 1965), pp. 214–15: 'Sed obstitit Britonum celebris fabula, Arturus rex veniens gemebundus, cuius magnitudinem atque casum, etsi ex fide digna testimonio non noscamus, pro comperto existimamus postquam universi orbis testari

videtur opinio' (P. G. Ricci and V. Zaccaria [eds], Boccaccio, *De casibus virorum illustrium*, in V. Branca [gen. ed.], *Tutte le opere* [Milan, 1983], IX, 8.18.7).

[49] Hall (trans.), *Fates*, pp. 214–15. 'Dum ergo armis interiora infestaret Gallie, Mordretus eius ex concubina filius – cui sedem regni, se absente, tutandam liquerat – acer iuvenis ad omne facinus audax, iam dudum regnandi cupidine captus, oblatum sibi tempus a Fortuna regis absentia ratus, cepit ad libertatem iugo pressos regio irritare, animos omnium donis allicere, se regem benignissimum futurum ostendere, civitates arcesque regni suis presidiis servare, amicos convocare, vires parare, mercennariorum militum maximam manum conducere, regi patri supplementa et commeatus negare et ad rebellionem spectantia cuncta peragere; et cum iam precogitatum tempus adesset, ficticiis literis regem bello mortuum demonstrare, sese regem dicere . . . et regalia cuncta tractare' (Ricci and Zaccaria edn, 8.xix.6).

[50] Hall (trans.), *Fates*, p. 217. 'Rex vero transvectus equo, dum lanceam ex pectore moribundi retraheret, aiunt adeo ampliatum vulnus ut per illum in partem alteram cadentis iam solis transparerent radii' (Ricci and Zaccaria edn, 8.xix.12). This detail Boccaccio, like Dante, knew from *La Mort le roi Artu*; see my discussion of *Inf.* 32, above.

[51] Hall (trans.), *Fates*, pp. 217–18. 'Rex autem dierum extremum iam sentiens continuo prosiluit ex equo navimque conscendens, iussit se moriturum in insula Avalonis deferri. Ibique ex felicissimo miser moriens' (Ricci and Zaccaria edn, 8.xix.13).

[52] Hall (trans.), *Fates*, p. 218. 'Quo ergo unius nepharii hominis ausu parvissimo temporis tractu ampliatum, Arturi regnum diminutum est illique cum vita subtractum. Tabula Rotunda tot probis splendida viris cesis omnibus deserta fractaque et in vulgi fabulam versa est. Gloria ingens regis et claritas desolatione in ignominiam et obscuritatem deleta est adeo ut possint, si velint, mortales advertere nil in orbe preter humilia posse consistere' (Ricci and Zaccaria edn, 8.xix.15–16).

Part Four

Arthur beyond Literature

11

ARTHUR IN HAGIOGRAPHY:
THE LEGEND OF SAN GALGANO

Franco Cardini

One of Italy's most noted Arthurian sites is located in a magical corner of Tuscany, bounded by Siena, Grosseto and the Metalliferous Hills. On a clear day, the azure Tyrrhenian Sea glitters away to the south-west. Through hills planted with grapes and olives flows the Merse, a small tributary of the river Ombrone. Atop a small hill sits the sanctuary of Montesiepi, usually called *La Rotonda*: a cylindrical red brick building adorned with bands of white travertine. The massive Romanesque structure had been repeatedly modified, but has been restored in the modern period. A few dozen yards downhill, the imposing ruins of the Gothic Cistercian abbey dedicated to St Galganus soar upward. Now in the archdiocese of Siena, Colle di Val d'Elsa and Montalcino, Montesiepi and the abbey of San Galgano have become well known as a tourist destination.

Both monuments are also documents of the historical, not legendary, events surrounding a figure with an intriguing and unsettling name. St Galganus is attested by important written sources, not least of which are the voluminous Acts of his canonisation hearing. Unlike his colleague St George, this 'saint-knight' does not belong to medieval Christian mythology: he was an actual historical figure. A short biographical summary and a survey of his canonisation and cult are thus in order.[1]

We have concrete historical evidence regarding the existence of one Galganus, born around the middle of the twelfth century in the castle of Chiusdino (about eighteen miles south of Siena), at that time in the diocese of Volterra. Galganus' death date is less vague: his biographer, a Cistercian monk who belonged to the abbey of San Galgano, and who wrote during the first half of the thirteenth century, reports it as 30 November 1181, although other sources tend towards 1183.[2] Beyond the *Vita sancti Galgani*, repeatedly revised and only recently published in correct form, we have other, later hagiographies.[3] In addition, the text of the canonisation hearing held 4–7 August 1185, contains invaluable information on the saint's personality and his life.[4]

What definite information can we extract from these sources? The earliest sources mention no surname; the young Galganus would come to be associated with the family name of Guidi or Guidotti (a *consorteria* associated with Siena); otherwise, he was called more simply 'son of Euidotto'. In any case, he must have belonged to 'a family group of that lower military aristocracy bound in vassalage to the bishop of Volterra, lord of Chiusdino'.[5] Very early on he lost his father, who seems to have had a special devotion for the Archangel Michael; although this would be particularly apt for a knight, it is not enough to establish with any certainty that Galganus' father was in fact a *miles*. Certainly, the young Galganus also aspired to the dignity of knighthood.

At the canonisation hearing, Galganus' mother Dionigia testified that the vocation of her son, who later converted to the hermit's life, began with two portentous visions that came to him in dreams. In the first vision, the Archangel Michael asked the widowed Dionigia to give the child to him. When Galganus told his mother of this dream, Dionigia drew from it the happy conclusion that both she and Galganus had the archangel's special protection. In the second vision, Galganus saw himself being led by the archangel along a rough path, reaching a bridge that was long and very difficult to cross. Beneath the bridge raced a churning, perilous river dominated by a mill with its incessantly moving paddles, explained as a symbol of earthly life with its endless and vain daily cares. After this test, Galganus came to a beautiful flowering meadow which undoubtedly symbolised Paradise or, perhaps more properly, the Garden of Eden. Beyond the meadow, the youth entered an underground cave, through which he finally reached a hill apparently easily identifiable with that of Montesiepi, near the town of his birth. Atop the hill, in a splendid circular building suffused with a divine perfume, he met the Apostles, who gave him a book to read. When he declined it on the grounds that he could not read, the Apostles instructed him to look up so that he could admire the 'divinae maiestatis quaedam imago et species'.[6] This seems to indicate that what Galganus saw was a painting or sculpture, rather than a direct vision of God. The Apostles ordered him to build on that very site a circular building resembling the one in his vision, in honour of God, the Blessed Virgin Mary and the Archangel Michael.

Following this vision, Galganus sought the necessary funds to build the 'house' as the Apostles had instructed him, but he received only derision and refusal from his friends and acquaintances. Sometime afterwards, riding from his native Chiusdino to nearby Civitella, he noticed that at a certain point his horse obstinately stopped. Galganus let the reins hang loose on the horse's neck, and it carried him up to the top of the Montesiepi hill. Then and there he chose the hill for his dwelling-place and dismounted. Either not finding or not wanting to seek wood to make himself a cross, he unsheathed his sword – cruciform, as swords were in the twelfth century – and thrust it into the ground. The sword struck deep into the rock and afterwards could not be removed. That stone, topped by the sword-cross, served as an altar and, more significantly, as a symbol of Calvary. Before it, the aspiring knight lived and prayed as a hermit until the end of his life – a short period, as his biographers say that he died in less than a year. Later on, certain miracles were reported, and the cult of Galganus became established. When the Cistercians arrived they built their splendid basilica in the flatland surrounding the hill, leaving intact the round altar on the hill.

Other episodes of the saint's life have been recorded, but three elements of the Galganus legend pertain to Arthur. These are the story of the second dream, with the journey of initiation under the guidance of the Archangel Michael; the discovery of the real place which Galganus had dreamed about; and the symbol of the sword in the stone. This last episode recalls an Arthurian theme quite different, even opposite, in function: Arthur proved that he was destined for the throne by removing the sword held fast in a tree or anvil; Galganus by contrast abandoned the world of sin and signalled his conversion by fixing his sword in the stone and thereby renouncing his arms, to worship the cross whose form the sword suggests.

The saint's vocation revealed to him in a dream is a *topos* capable of infinite variations, but common enough in its essential outlines. However, there is something in Galganus' dream that impresses us with its archetypal depth. At the same time, it demands interpretation in terms of its literary – and perhaps also anthropological – ties to an entire tradition that for the sake of convenience we can call 'chivalric'. Let us trace the main lines of this complex and delicate discourse.

The elements of Galganus' dream are clear: the apparition of the Archangel Michael and his command to follow him; the journey to a river; the difficult river crossing; the mill of earthly cares;[7] the *locus amoenus* beyond the river; the underground cave; the circular structure inhabited by the twelve Apostles; the presentation of a holy book; the divine vision. This is the structure of a journey to the afterlife which we could call Dantean: from the guide figure to the crossing of the river, to the visit to the meadow and the underworld, to the ascent of the mountain and the concluding vision, the journey of initiation contains all these recognisable motifs.

Michael, as the guide figure, fulfils one of his traditional functions. He confers upon Galganus the dignity of knighthood; thus in the first of Galganus' dreams Michael is both flanked by and replaces the mother. The resulting scenario closely recalls the initiatic sequence of Chrétien de Troyes's *Perceval*. It could be said that we are witnessing Galganus' transition from maternal authority and teaching to heavenly authority and teaching. Michael, as *princeps caelestis militiae* (prince of the heavenly host), completes on the level of divine knighthood the instruction and apprenticeship that Galganus' mother had begun on the level of earthly duties.

The journey of initiation that Galganus undertakes under Michael's guidance is a *peregrinatio spiritualis*, a journey to the afterlife which should perhaps be interpreted as a *metanoia* (change of heart): the bridge (conversion) which overcomes the mill (earthly cares, vanities) and the waters (events). Through that journey Galganus attains the state of renewed prelapsarian purity: first in adopting the hermit's life, figured as edenic (the flowering meadow), and then in the passage through death (the journey underground), to eternal life, to Paradise (the circular building), to the vision of God.[8] On the other hand, the act of crossing water is itself a symbol (as in baptism) of death and regeneration, of the return to an unformed state like that which precedes birth, and of the subsequent assumption of a new form. The bridge – like the divine wind which thrust back the waters of the Red Sea before Moses and the Israelites – is the instrument that allows one to cross over water yet remain dry. On the other hand, its very status as place of passage makes the bridge a dangerous object, a dangerous instrument and of course a dangerous path.[9] We think at once of the Sword Bridge in Chrétien's *Chevalier de la Charrette*, to which we will return shortly.

But first let us note that the presence of the guide Michael indubitably characterises the journey as an initiation, with the associated ritual stages of death and resurrection. Whether or not Galganus' journey is to be considered as strictly oneiric – the terms *visio* and *somnium* are not always or entirely interchangeable, nor for that matter always or entirely distinguishable – the journey is an initiation insofar as, symbolically speaking, a journey (and most particularly, a pilgrimage) always is.[10] The sculpted capital in the church of San Lorenzo di Siponto on the Gargano peninsula, where the archangel guides the pilgrim mounted on an ass, holding the animal's reins, could easily serve to illustrate the model of Michael's guidance as Galganus' *Vita* presents it.

An important consideration in this context – and I must emphasise that I am working with textual evidence deriving from late exemplars of the tradition – is that Galganus' journey corresponds to an itinerary common in folklore as well.[11] Since Tuscany was a region in which Lombard culture was well rooted, I will use a Lombard source which claims to report an episode about the historical Frankish hero Gunthram:

> When [King Gunthram] went once upon a time into the woods to hunt, and, as often happens, his companions scattered hither and thither, and he remained with only one, a very faithful friend of his, he was oppressed with heavy slumber and laying his head upon the knees of this same faithful companion, he fell asleep. From [the king's] mouth a little animal in the shape of a reptile came forth and began to bustle about seeking to cross a slender brook which flowed near by. Then he in whose lap [the king] was resting laid his sword, which he had drawn from its scabbard, over this brook and upon it that reptile of which we have spoken passed over to the other side. And when it had entered into a certain hole in the mountain not far off, and having returned after a little time, had crossed the aforesaid brook upon the same sword, it again went into the mouth of Gunthram from which it had come forth. When Gunthram was afterwards awakened from sleep, he said he had seen a wonderful vision. For he related that it had seemed to him in his slumbers that he had passed over a certain river by an iron bridge and had gone in under a certain mountain where he had gazed upon a great mass of gold. The man however, on whose lap he had held his head while he was sleeping, related to him in order what he had seen of it. Why say more? That place was dug up and countless treasures were discovered which had been put there of old.[12]

All these elements – the soul as an animal (and as a reptile in particular), the separation in the dream of the soul from the body and the link between the cavern and treasures – are elements which belong both to a widespread folk patrimony and to oneiric experiences repeatedly addressed in psychoanalysis. It is noteworthy that in Gunthram's dream there is no actual guide figure, but the soul is a reptile; whereas in Galganus' dream Michael is the guide figure: the archangel, as a *sauroctonus*, is thus 'king of the reptiles'. Both cases retain the link between the soul and the reptile.

The analogies between Gunthram's dream and that of Galganus are evident. First, the fact of the dream in itself; then the idea of a journey made by the soul (with the theriomorphisation of Gunthram's soul); the bridge; the river; the cave. While Gunthram finds a treasure in the cave, Galganus discovers nothing less than the gate to Paradise. The symbol of the sword returns as well, as the material instrument of

Gunthram's journey and the fulcrum around which the principal scene of Galganus' conversion takes place.

Medievalist readers, undoubtedly familiar with Gunthram's dream, will quickly connect Galganus' dream to the well-known *exemplum* of the lizard-soul in Paul the Deacon. The following variant of it circulated in the third decade of the fourteenth century, in the context of a Catharism which had already permeated the folklore of the now famous Pyrenean village of Montaillou:

> Once upon a time, said Philippe d'Alayrac of Coustaussa, two believers found themselves close to a river. One of them fell asleep. The other stayed awake, and from the mouth of the sleeper he saw emerge a creature like a lizard. Suddenly the lizard, using a plank (or was it a straw?), which stretched from one bank to the other, crossed over the river. On the other bank there was the flesh-less skull of an ass. And the lizard ran in and out of the openings in the skull. Then it came back over the plank and re-entered the sleeper's mouth. It did that once or twice. Seeing which, the man who was awake thought of a trick: he waited until the lizard was on the other side of the river and approaching the ass's skull. And then he took away the plank! The lizard left the ass's head and returned to the bank. But be could not get across! The plank was gone! Then the body of the sleeper began to thrash about, but it was unable to wake, despite the efforts of the watcher to arouse it from its sleep. Finally the watcher put the plank back across the river. Then the lizard was able to get back and re-enter the body of the sleeper through the mouth. The sleeper immediately awoke; and he told his friend the dream he had just had.
>
> 'I dreamed,' he said, 'that I was crossing a river on a plank; then I went into a great palace with many towers and rooms, and when I wanted to come back to the place from which I had set out, there was no plank! I could not get across: I would have been drowned in the river. That was why I thrashed about (in my sleep). Until the plank was put back again and I could return.'[13]

The alternation of plank and straw – that is, the *topos* of the bridge that expands and shrinks – is particularly prominent in Zoroastrian beliefs: the *Chinvat* bridge expands or shrinks according to whether or not the soul crossing it is just. The theme of the lizard coming and going from the dreamer's mouth could refer to a shamanic journey to the afterlife, a journey which is however actually and not only ritually accomplished by the soul in slumber. Also interesting is the building/equid skull, which refers to the magical and psychagogic role of the horse and its skull or skeleton.[14] Between the sixth and eighth centuries, and indeed later, the Pyrenees were affected by Visigothic culture, relatively close to the Lombard (both were Germano-oriental), and like it deeply influenced by cultures of Ural-Altaic and North Persian origin, which were endowed with strong shamanistic traits.

At this point, the field of inquiry becomes extremely broad: the theriomorphic or lizard-soul; shamanic dreams; the dreams of modern patients placed in a trance or emerging from a cataleptic state.[15] Anthropology and psychoanalysis both afford ample scope for comment on both the episode from Paul the Deacon, and the testimony reported by Le Roy Ladurie. In the medieval Pyrenees, Cathar beliefs – perhaps of Manichaean origin, or perhaps attributable to the local ethno-folkloric matrix – blended with a folkloric production that was to a certain degree autochthonous (but this is hard to establish). I will simply recall that Catharism has deep roots in gnosis and in Manichaean mythology. Lombard culture, in its turn, has close ties to both the Ural-Altaic world on the one hand (the Huns and the Avars) – a world of shamanic culture – and the North Persian world (the Scythians and Sarmatians) on the other. These elements will illuminate other texts that I will examine shortly. For now I must invoke another text, this time a chivalric one, and return to the Cistercian order as the hagiographical/chivalric medium of the elaboration of the Galganus legend.

Chrétien's *Chevalier de la Charrette* is rooted in an ancient myth: the rescue of a woman carried off to the Otherworld and then brought back again. It is the myth of Orpheus and Eurydice, also widespread in Celtic culture. The status of the Celtic underworld in the medieval imaginary is rather different from that of both the Greco-Roman underworlds and the Christian afterlife, although it has links to both, and perhaps influenced the latter. The myth returns – this time in a patently Celtic-Christian acculturation – in the *Vita sancti Gildae*, in the version composed around 1136 by the Welsh cleric Caradoc of Larcavan. Some believe this hagiographic text to have been one of Chrétien's direct sources.[16]

Are there typological links between Galganus and Lancelot? I would be tempted to locate them especially in the almost somnambulistic certainty with which both knights, each in his own context, move toward the test of crossing from one world to the other. Lancelot is plunged deep in thoughts of Guinevere; Galganus is guided by the archangel and is literally asleep. Later, outside the dream, he is entrusted to his horse, on whose neck he has let the reins drop. The content of the test with its fundamental analogies is most remarkable. Let us examine Chrétien's text.

Queen Guinevere is held prisoner by Meleagant, son of King Bademagus of the kingdom of Gorre, which is in essence a kingdom of the dead. If Lancelot wishes to save the Queen, he faces the fate of Orpheus, Theseus and Hercules. He must find the way to the Otherworld, and then cross to it over terrible, rushing waters. There are two ways to cross: the Water Bridge, submerged under water, which Arthur's nephew Gawain chooses; and the Sword Bridge, which Lancelot will take.

> Late in the afternoon, just before dusk, they reached the sword-bridge. At the foot of this treach- erous bridge they dismounted and looked down at the menacing water, black and roaring, dense and swift. Its muddiness and terror made it seem like the devil's river. Anything in the whole world that fell into the perilously deep current would disappear as if it had fallen into the icy sea. The bridge spanning the water was unlike all others: to be honest, there never was, nor would there ever be, such a menacing bridge or footbridge. The bridge across the cold water consisted of only a brightly polished sword, though the sword, the length of two lances, was strong and stiff. Since the sword was fastened to a huge stump on each bank, there was no need to worry about falling off because of the sword's bending or breaking. But to the eye it seemed incapable of sustaining heavy weight.[17]

Regarding the narrow-bridge test and its role in the Grail romances (especially *Perlesvaus*), Pierre Gallais connects them to the world of Zoroastrian beliefs rather than to the Celtic matrix.[18] On the archetypal level the relationship between bridge and sword so clearly exemplified in both Gunthram's dream and the Lancelot episode is easily understood given that *Chinvat* is a test for souls, and the sword is a symbol of justice. Like the scales, the sword is an attribute of the Archangel Michael, who plays the double role of guide and benevolent judge in the Galganus episode.

Galganus' bridge, described as very long and crossable only by great exertion, would seem to be the equivalent of Lancelot's Sword Bridge. Where the chivalric romance presents the dark and furious waters,[19] the more allegorical-moralistic hagiographical text places upon those waters the mill of life with its vain cares and source of sin: in effect, a mill of the vanities. In both cases, the waters beneath the bridge are the currents of sin and death. For Lancelot the agonised crossing of the blade set between the two banks – which could also be interpreted as a penance – marks the passage from the world of the living to that of the dead; for Galganus the crossing of the water which powers the mill of the vanities instead seems to have an ascetic significance.

In truth, the crossing of the Perilous Bridge is an archetypal theme with a long historical and anthropological tradition of which I can sketch only the outline here.[20] We find the theme already fully formed in the *Avesta*. In this text, the test of the *Chinvat-perethu* ('the bridge that joins', but also 'the bridge of the one who chooses') awaits every dead man, who reaches it on the fourth day after death, accompanied by figures who personify his good and evil actions. It is a test of strength and ability, but both are ultimately secondary to – or at any rate predetermined by – the behaviour of the dead man during life. For the just man, the bridge is broad and secure and leads to heaven; for the evil man it is so narrow and unsteady that he cannot help but fall.[21] In the Scythian lands and among the Ossetes, guardians of the Scytho-Sarmatian traditions, the myths of the 'bridge-sword' and of the 'bridge as wide as a sword-blade' were prominent.[22]

The motif of the bridge test may have passed from the Iranian into the Islamic tradition, as some of the most ancient *hadith* attest. But in the Second Epistle to the Corinthians, Paul too speaks of being caught up to the third heaven (12:2–4). The *Visio sancti Pauli*, which would undergo various redactions between the ninth and the twelfth centuries, developed around the nucleus of an apocryphal Greek Apocalypse, datable to the third or fourth century.[23] In any case, it is a text that Paul the Deacon could well have known. The narrow-bridge motif also appears in a text by St Gregory the Great, the narrative of a warrior who returned to life after death, and in the *Vision of Tundal*, a twelfth-century Irish text that circulated throughout Europe, including in Italy.[24] The theme is equally widespread in Italian folk traditions and in popular narratives of various countries. In fact it is a variation on a crucial traditional symbol: the crossing – of bridge or ladder, rope or rainbow, tree or pillar – which allows for passage between separate cosmic spheres, and which can occur after death or even during life, thanks to certain ecstatic practices known in shamanic cultures.

Miguel Asín Palaciós indicated a series of *hadith* – like those collected in the *Kitab al-Ulum al-fahirah fi an-Nazar fi umur al Ahirah* ('The Book of the Splendid Sciences for Observing the Things of the Beyond') of Ibn Mahluf; or those attributed to Ibn Abbas and apparently collected no later than the tenth century; or one collected by Abu Dardah – in which the journey to the Beyond is littered with difficult crossings: now a path or a road (*sirat*), now a bridge or a viaduct (*qantarah*), now a natural bridge or a slippery passage (*jisr*), now a steep slope or incline (*aqabah*).[25] The intermediate *sirat* is interpreted almost like a veritable Christian Purgatory in the *Futuhat* of Ibn Arabi of Murcia who, commenting on words of the Prophet, maintains that the souls who do not go to Hell will be confined on the *sirat* over the mound of Hell; that only by walking across it will they be able to enter Paradise; and that it ends in a meadow which stretches to the outer wall of the celestial Paradise.

Asín Palaciós has shown that the nucleus of Dante's representation of the journey to the afterlife depends on a Muslim text, the *Kitab al-Miraj*. In fact, as this brief overview of the 'Narrow Bridge' mytheme confirms, not only are the Christian and Muslim imaginaries of the fate of souls after death closely connected, but they draw on an imaginative reservoir which, given its earliest and most complete articulation in Zoroastrianism, seems to correspond to an archetypal knowledge hoard common to many traditional civilisations, one which requires further study.[26]

I have emphasised that Galganus' dream could well be a reminiscence of the 'journey to the afterlife' tales that were widespread in the Christian tradition of the time, which had in its turn inherited and elaborated – in multiple forms of acculturation – Greek, Italic, Etruscan, Celtic, Germanic, Illyrian and later also Baltic and Slavic models, without needing to trouble either the Ossetes or the Muslims. But in this case analyses based on assumptions regarding circulation, structure or archetype all seem equally plausible, and probably no one of these three approaches needs invalidate the other two. The theme of certain *visiones* is undoubtedly very close to some of the tales found in chivalric romance. The 'journey to the Otherworld' and the 'fantastic voyage' are themes present in many literary genres and subgenres, and they have produced innumerable cases of encounter and of synthesis/synchresis in allegorical-moral, chivalric, hagiographic and other text-types.[27] In the specific case of chivalric culture, this kind of tale emerges as characteristic of, though not exclusive to, *aventure*.[28] All of this, however, while taking us to depths that are folkloric or even archetypal, gives us no help on an issue that is absolutely central: did Galganus of Chiusdino know anything about Arthurian literature? Was anything known about it in the Tuscany of his time?

The name *Galganus* was fairly widespread in Tuscany in the mid-twelfth century. It was the name of an important member of the Pannocchieschi family, a bishop and lord of Volterra; and it is likely that St Galganus, if he belonged to a family of military rank bound to that household by vassalage or clientele, bore the name in his honour.[29] We must ask whether the form *Galgano* could be a Tuscanism for the French *Gauvain*, name of the renowned Arthurian hero, which was more commonly Italianised as *Galvano*; if so, then we could posit that in those years there was already at least some knowledge, whether direct or indirect, of the Arthurian cycle. The spelling *Galgano* is however more likely to be a version of the name 'Gargano', the result of a typically Tuscan hypercorrection of *r* to *l*. This would send us back to an even older sanctuary in Puglia dedicated to the same Archangel Michael to whom Galganus of Chiusdino and his family seem to have been devoted. The sanctuaries in his honour – Mont-Saint-Michel between Brittany and Normandy, Saint-Michel l'Aguilhe in Le Puy, the Sacra di San Michele in the Valle d'Aosta, the church of San Michele in Lucca and Monte Gargano itself – were well known along the *Via Francigena*, whose route through Val d'Elsa, Siena and Acquapendente passed not far from Volterra.

The Arthurian legends were known in Italy by the early thirteenth century, as Arturo Graf demonstrated in a study that was prompted by the story that the mythical king of the Bretons was imprisoned in the bowels of Mount Etna.[30] Arthur's fame reached Sicily with the Normans, who came from an area close to Britain; this would justify the early connection of the Arthur legend with Etna. The Arthurian-inspired images sculpted in the Modena archivolt in the early twelfth century and depicted in the Otranto Cathedral floor mosaic in the late twelfth century prove at least oral circulation of the themes, if not necessarily of texts to be read or heard.[31] But we cannot make a similar case for Tuscany, where so far as I know no such early traces exist.

By the end of the twelfth century the Matter of Britain would spread to Tuscany, site of a lively romance production. Arrigo da Settimello (a town near Florence) recalls 'Arturus . . . vetus ille Britannus' in his poem *De diversitate fortunae et philosophiae consolatione*, composed not long after 1190; this appears to be the earliest extant written Tuscan evidence for knowledge of Arthur in Italy.[32] The eminent master of rhetoric Boncompagno da Signa, in his *Cedrus* (1190?–1210?), attests that in his time there existed *in multis partibus Ytaliae alcune iuvenum societates* – military companies – which boasted heraldic names such as 'of the hawks', 'of the lions' and 'of the Round Table'.[33] We cannot exclude the possibility of indirect or oral transmission of the Arthurian cycle to Tuscany. This hypothesis could account for the name *Galgano,* if it could be etymologically justified as a version of *Galvano*; until the emergence of the Siculo-Tuscan poetic school, however, we cannot claim for a fact that the Tuscans knew Arthur directly.[34] Ultimately, the name *Galgano/Galvano* and the echo of the 'sword in the stone' – attested since the end of the twelfth century in the written sources, but present as a material and concrete datum further back than we can pinpoint – could actually suggest an idea that was born in the episcopal-seigneurial court of Volterra and in the Cistercian order during the Duecento, when Arthur *was* well known, to popularise the 'sanctuary' of Montesiepi and the adjacent abbey.

(Translated by F. Regina Psaki)

Notes

[1] See E. Susi, *L'eremita cortese: San Galgano fra mito e storia nell'agiografia toscana del XII secolo* (Spoleto, 1993); A. Gianni (ed.), *Santità ed eremitismo nella Toscana medievale* (Siena, 2000); F. Cardini, *San Galgano e la spada nella roccia* (Siena, 2000); A. Papi Benvenuti (ed.), *La spada nella roccia: San Galgano e l'epopea eremitica di Montesiepi* (Florence, 2004).

[2] The anonymous Cistercian *Vita sancti Galgani* is preserved in a manuscript in Veroli (Frosinone), Bibl. Giovardiana, MS 42, fourteenth century, fols 253r–254v; it is published in Susi, *L'eremita cortese*, pp. 177–213.

[3] Susi, *L'eremita cortese*, pp. xxiv–xxvi.

[4] *Inquisitio in partibus*, in F. Schneider (ed.), 'Die Einsiedler Galgan von Chiusdino und die Anfänge von San Galgano', *Quellen und Forschungen aus italienischen Archiven und Bibliotheken*, 17 (1914–24), 71–7.

[5] Susi, *L'eremita cortese*, p. 5.

[6] As cited in Schneider (ed.), 'Die Einsiedler Galgan'.

[7] On the mill, ordinarily a Eucharistic symbol, see the entry for *Müle, mystische* in G. Heinz-Mohr, *Lexikon der Symbole: Bilder und Zeichen der christlichen Kunst* (Düsseldorf and Cologne, 1971), p. 217; see also M. Zink, 'Moulin mystique. A propos d'un chapiteau de Vézelay: figures allégoriques dans la prédication et dans l'iconographie romanes', *Annales*, 31 (1976), 481–8.

[8] The *topoi* which the legend presents are, with very few variations, traditional to the genre which has its model in the Christian context in the apocryphal Greek Apocalypse of Paul (third century CE). The archetypes can be seen in the *Epic of Gilgamesh*, as well as in the *nekya* proposed in the *Odyssey* and in the vision of Er the Chaldean in Plato, which is given the comprehensive title *Visiones Animarum*. See M. Lecco (ed.), Introduction to *La visione di Tungdal* (Alessandria, 1998), pp. 5–27.

[9] See A. Seppilli, *Sacralità dell'acqua e sacrilegio dei ponti* (Palermo, 1990).

[10] On *visio* and its complex relation to *somnium*, see W. H. Stahl (trans.), *Macrobius: Commentary on the Dream of Scipio* ([New York], 1952); P. Dinzelbacher, *Vision und Visionsliteratur im Mittelalter* (Stuttgart, 1981); T. Gregory (ed.), *I sogni nel Medioevo* (Rome, 1985).

[11] Among the abundant sources on this topic, some are essential: H. R. Patch, *The Other World according to Descriptions in Medieval Literature* (Cambridge, MA, 1950); J. Le Goff, *The Birth of Purgatory*, trans. A. Goldhammer (Chicago, 1986); C. Segre, 'L'invenzione dell'altro mondo' and 'Viaggi e visioni d'oltremondo sino alla *Commedia* di Dante', both in Segre, *Fuori del mondo. I modelli nella follia e nelle immagini dell'aldilà* (Turin, 1990), pp. 11–23 and 25–48, respectively; and J. B. Russell, *A History of Heaven: The Singing Silence* (Princeton, 1997).

[12] W. D. Foulke (trans.), Paul the Deacon, *History of the Langobards* (Philadelphia, 1907), pp. 147–8. See C. Ginzburg's commentary on this episode in *Ecstasies: Deciphering the Witches' Sabbath*, trans. R. Rosenthal (New York, 1991), pp. 138, 151–2 n. 109, 281 n. 119 and 296.

[13] E. Le Roy Ladurie, *Montaillou: The Promised Land of Error*, trans. B. Bray (New York, 1978), p. 351.

[14] On the horse as companion on the journey to the afterlife, see Cardini, *Alle radici della cavalleria medievale* (Florence, 1981), pp. 31ff.

[15] See M. Oldoni, '*A fantasia dicitur fantasma*. (Gerberto e la sua storia)', *StM*, 18 (1977), 629–704; 21 (1980), 493–622 (esp. 579ff.); 24 (1983), 167–245.

[16] Susi, *L'eremita cortese*, surveys the relevant literature (pp. 145–6).

[17] Chrétien de Troyes, *The Knight of the Cart*, in D. Staines (trans.), *The Complete Romances of Chrétien de Troyes* (Bloomington, 1990), pp. 207–8.

[18] P. Gallais, *Perceval et l'initiation* (Paris, 1972), pp. 136–9.

[19] See A. Renoir, 'The Terror of the Dark Water: A Note on Virgilian and Beowulfian Techniques', in L. D. Benson (ed.), *The Learned and the Lewed: Studies in Chaucer and Medieval Literature* (Cambridge,

MA, 1974), pp. 147–60; and G. Chandès, 'Recherches sur l'imagerie des eaux dans l'oeuvre de Chrétien de Troyes', *Cahiers de civilisation médiévale*, 19 (1976), 151–64.

[20] In addition to the works on this theme cited above, see Seppilli, *Sacralità dell'acqua* and I. P. Culianu, *Expériences de l'extase: Extase, ascension et récit visionnaire de l'héllenisme au moyen âge* (Paris, 1984).

[21] Seppilli, *Sacralità dell'acqua*, pp. 249–9; J. Duchesne-Guillemin, 'L'Iran antico e Zoroastro', in H.-C. Puech (ed.), *Storia delle religioni*, II: *Da Babilonia a Zoroastro*, 7 vols (Rome and Bari, 1977), p. 137.

[22] See G. Dumézil, *Le livre des héros: légendes sur les Nartes* (Paris, 1965), which tells of the journey of the hero Soslan to the Land of the Dead (pp. 134ff.).

[23] T. Silverstein (ed.), *Visio sancti Pauli: The History of the Apocalypse in Latin Together With Nine Texts* (London, 1935). For a seventh- or eighth-century Anglo-Saxon vision of similar content, see C. S. Lewis, *The Allegory of Love* (Oxford, 1936), pp. 86–7.

[24] See M. Lecco (ed.), *La visione di Tungdal*, which presents a French version and an Anglo-Norman fragment; see also F. Corazzini (ed.), *Visione di Tugdalo* (Bologna, 1872; rpt 1968), for a fourteenth-century Italian version.

[25] M. Asín Palaciós, *Islam and the Divine Comedy*, trans. Harold Sunderland (New York, 1926; rpt London 1968), p. 183.

[26] See C. Kappler et al. (eds), *Apocalypses et voyages dans l'Au-delà* (Paris, 1987).

[27] I refrain from exploring the distinction between the 'imaginary', the 'marvellous' and the 'fantastic'. While the distinction is essential in epistemological, philological, semantic, sociological and literary discussion, and affects Medieval Studies broadly construed, it actually touches my properly historical perspective only up to a certain point.

[28] On the concept of adventure in general, see the seminal work by Erich Köhler, *L'Aventure chevaleresque: idéal et réalité dans le roman courtois, études sur la forme des plus anciens poèmes d'Arthur et du Graal*, trans. Éliane Kaufholz (Paris, 1974); and A. Pioletti, *Forme del racconto arturiano: Peredur, Perceval, Bel inconnu, Carduino* (Naples, 1984). Within Italy, see F. Cardini, 'L'avventura cavalleresca nell'Italia tardomedievale: modelli letterari e forme concrete', in *Mediterraneo medievale. Scritti in onore di Francesco Giunta*, 3 vols (Soveria Mannelli, 1989), I, pp. 243–88.

[29] Susi, *L'eremita cortese*, p. 8.

[30] A. Graf, 'Artù nell'Etna', in *Miti, leggende, e superstizioni del medioevo* (Florence and Rome, 1892), II, pp. 303–59; rpt Milan, 2002, pp. 375–408.

[31] The Modena archivolt bas-reliefs have been variously dated, but consensus has formed around a dating of *c.*1120–40; the Otranto mosaic dates to *c.*1165. See Chapter 13 in this volume.

[32] C. Fossati (ed.), *Arrigo da Settimello: Elegia* (Florence, 2011).

[33] Cited in A. R. Falzon, *Re Artù in Toscana: Inchiesta sul ciclo arturiano in Toscana dal XII secolo a oggi* (Siena, 1996), p. 12.

[34] See Chapter 8 in this volume.

12

OWNERS AND READERS OF
ARTHURIAN BOOKS IN ITALY

Gloria Allaire

The question of who in Italy read the narratives of King Arthur and his court is vast, spanning different centuries, different geographical areas and various languages. Using extant manuscripts and fragments as transmission evidence, Daniela Delcorno Branca has examined the interface between books copied in French and their Italian counterparts, a phenomenon which occurred as early as the thirteenth century.[1] Linguistic evidence allows us to localise book production and readership by country or region, but falls short of revealing the precise identity or status of a given reader; to learn more, we must consider private library inventories and owners' marks that appear on extant manuscripts. Surviving inventories from the northern courts of the Este, Visconti-Sforza and Gonzaga prove that these aristocratic families possessed numerous Arthurian romances – more in French than in Italian vernaculars.[2] Even when using inventories or published library catalogues, it may be difficult, if not impossible, to judge from a title alone whether the book was written in French or Italian: the designation 'in volgare' may refer to either French or Italian vernacular as distinct from Latin. In addition, inventory and catalogue evidence, however valuable, is still only a part of the picture for yet another reason, as Paul Grendler notes:

> Because chivalric romances portrayed a feudal society led by heroes and heroines of noble blood, it might be assumed that members of the upper classes were the primary intended audience . . . It is much more likely that the reading and listening audience transcended class boundaries.[3]

Indeed, new evidence is constantly coming to light that deepens our understanding of the readership of Arthurian material in Italy. By focusing on the colophons and own-ers' notes of extant manuscripts, we can discover the names of actual Italian readers, copyists and book owners, their places of origin and sometimes their professions or trades.[4] We may even glimpse how these books were produced and used: where they were copied and by whom; when they were loaned; later owners who conserved them; and how they travelled from place to place.

Northern Italian Ownership

Although the once extensive collections of northern Italian princes and dukes have been dispersed, surviving inventories indicate the large number of Arthurian manu-scripts that Este of Ferrara, the Visconti of Milan and the Gonzaga of Mantua once owned, read and shared. Precious archival evidence also shows that members of these powerful families borrowed such books from one another. Loaning a book opens up various possibilities for its use: the person requesting it may have read it himself; a borrowed book could have further circulated among other readers at a given court; it may have served as a model text and been copied. As can happen today, books could be returned, borrowed again at a later date or perhaps lost and never returned.

Records for Borso d'Este's library show that Francesco Accolti of Arezzo, the noted legal scholar at the *studium* of Ferrara, borrowed a *San Gradale* (Holy Grail) on 30 January 1458. On 17 June 1458 he borrowed a *Merlino* and a *Meliadux*. The next year, on 2 March, he again borrowed the *San Gradale*.[5] Giacomo (di Folco) Ariosto, great-uncle of the famous Ferrarese poet, was an avid reader of Arthurian texts. From Borso's library Giacomo borrowed a *Meliadux* on 1 February 1455, which he kept for fourteen days; in the same year, he read a *Lanzeloto*. In 1457 he again read a *Meliaduse*, which he returned and then reborrowed.[6] In 1458 he requested a *Lanzeloto*, which he loaned to his *nipote* (nephew or grandson) Nicolò. In 1461 he took home a *Tristano*.[7]

At the recommendation of a favoured courtier Ludovico Casella, Alberto della Sala borrowed a *Tristano* from Borso's library in 1460. In that same year, Anselmo Salimbeni and Bertolazzo dei Pizzolbeccari read *Lanzeloto*, and Galeotto di Campofregoso requested a *Merlino*. In 1461, Count Gian Francesco della Mirandola asked to borrow a '*Lanzaloto* v[u]lgare', perhaps translated into Italian. Miniatto Buregatto, a *sottospendedore* (assistant bursar or treasurer) at Borso's court, borrowed a '*Lanzilotto* in v[u]lgare' in 1461.[8] Count Ludovico di Channo (Cuneo) borrowed a French book called *Galioto le bruns* on 17 December, and the aforementioned Anselmo Salimbeni borrowed his *Lanzeloto* on 23 December.[9] The frequency of December borrowing dates suggests that the colder winter months may have been an opportune time to read these lengthy romances.

Documents indicate book use and transportation outside the Estense library itself. When Borso went to his villa in 1461, he took with him a '*Lanzaloto* in v[u]lgare' (*Lancelot* in vernacular Italian) and another '*Lanzaloto* in franzexe' (*Lancelot* in French), along with a French Bible.[10] Inventories make it clear that the princely northern libraries owned more than one codex of the same title. Books were also sent out to *cartolai* (stationers) for binding: Grigorio di Gasparino bound a *Gurone* for Borso in 1457, a *Merlino* in 1458 and *un libro di brus* (probably, *Bruns*).[11] As late as 1494–5, Duke Ercole I's library contained three copies each of *Meliadus* and *Guiron le Courtois*.

Wealthy lords borrowed books from each other: Sigismondo d'Este borrowed a *Tristano*; from Ludovico Gonzaga, Borso obtained a *Gurone* in 1464 and a *Lancillotto* in 1468.[12] In a letter dated 15 June 1378, Luchino Visconti, lord of Milan, asks Ludovico Gonzaga to loan him 'unum romanzum loquentem de Tristano vel Lanzaloto aut de aliqua alia pulchra et delectabili materia' ('a romance that speaks of Tristan or

Lancelot or some other lovely and delectable material') because he wanted to read a romance to relieve the tedium during his next sea voyage to Cyprus.[13]

The Visconti–Sforza library did not lack its own copies of Arthurian narratives. Inventories from as late as 1488 and 1490 show thirty-three discrete manuscripts that contained the Matter of Britain: *Tabula/taola rotonda*; *Re Artus/Artuxo*; *De morte regis Artus*; *Lancelotus/Lanceloto/Lanzeloto*; *Istoria Tristani*; *Merlinus in profetiis* (Prophecies of Merlin); and one *Istoria Sanregalis* (Holy Grail).[14] Inventories were frequently written by learned compilers, meaning that titles given in Latin may actually refer to a book written in a vernacular. A manuscript book could include more than one romance: various texts copied by different people may have been collected later and bound together as a composite manuscript, or a single copyist-redactor may have created a compilation by selecting complementary texts and copying them end to end. One example of a codex that contains various Arthurian stories is the *Liber Galasii ystoriati* (present-day BnF, fr. MS 343), which contains the *Quest for the Holy Grail*, stories of *Tristan* and the *Death of King Arthur*. Another manuscript that once belonged to the Visconti is preserved in Aberystwyth, National Library of Wales, MS 5667 E. This book, copied on vellum in various hands, contains passages from the *Roman de Tristan* in French; on fol. 89r, we find the Visconti emblem.[15]

In the early fifteenth century, the Gonzaga Library in the ducal palace at Mantua contained sixty-seven French texts of all genres, comprising probably the largest collection anywhere on the Italian peninsula.[16] Among the romances, Delcorno Branca notes that *Tristan* was the most popular: nine manuscripts recount the knight's birth and adventures.[17] In addition, there were copies of *Merlin*, *Lancelot*, *Queste du Saint Graal*, *Guiron le Courtois*, and *La Table Ronde*.[18] The fascination with heroes like Lancelot, Tristan and Meliadus extended to decorative objects and furnishings; in more than one instance, entire rooms were frescoed with chivalric legends.[19] In one of the oldest buildings at the Mantuan court, the 'Saleta Lanzaloti' was decorated with a wall painting of Lancelot's adventures, made in the fourteenth century. An elegantly detailed fresco cycle was created by Pisanello. The surviving underdrawings for his frescoes identified various warriors with Gothic lettering beside their images: lesser knights of the Round Table include *Cabilor as dures mains*, *Arfassart li gros [cuer]*, *Malies de l'Espine* and *Meldons l'envoissiez* (Cabilor with the Hard Hands, Arfassart the Great [Hearted], Melior of the Thorn, Meldons the Joyful). These unusual names of minor characters allow us to pinpoint literary sources such as *Lancelot* and *Guiron le Courtois*, in addition to the well-known *Roman de Tristan*.[20]

Arthurian texts and their readers were scattered across northern Italy. Extant evidence show that these narratives were copied and owned by a troubadour poet, by military commanders, by doctors of law and by notaries who even retained fragments of manuscripts that had been copied in earlier centuries. Romances were sometimes used as collateral on loans and could be passed on to heirs along with other property. Some of the oldest documents reveal a group of otherwise unidentified 'books of romances' that were owned in the area of Genoa or brought there from afar. Bonvassallo de Pallareto gave his brother Lanfranco 'librum unum de romanciis' as surety for a loan in 1226. When Sinibaldo of Poggibonsi, in Tuscany, died in a Genoese hospital in 1247, he left 'libros suos de romanciis' among his belongings. The aptly named troubadour poet Percivale Doria gave five romances, whether bound or individual quires, to the judge Iacopo de Platealonga as collateral for a loan.[21]

Although codicological evidence for the thirteenth and fourteenth centuries is scarce, the Matter of Britain made its way along the Po Valley and to the Veneto well before 1400. Owing to house fires, wars and other calamities, fewer books and household possessions survive than for the fifteenth century onward. A precious early exemplar, *La Mort le roi Artu* (Chantilly, Musée Condé, MS 1111 = 649), was copied by Giovanni Gualandi for his patron, Lord Brisciano de Salis, who served as *capitano del popolo* at Modena *c.*1281: 'Liber domini Brexiani de Salis. Qui scripsit Zo[hannes?] de Gualandis existens cum eo in regimine Mutinensi'.[22] The important pseudo-historical source for many of the Arthur stories, Geoffrey of Monmouth's *Historia regum Britanniae*, was known in Italy by the second half of the thirteenth century, to judge by a four-folio fragment written on parchment in *littera textualis*. The fragment's sixteenth-century owner was Francesco di Andrea Pittiani, a notary in San Daniele, of the Friuli region in north-eastern Italy. A later owner named Ser Francesco wrote various dates (1537, 1538, 1546, 1547) on the folios.[23] Another notary, Decio di Leonardo Deciani in Tolmezzo, preserved among his books a one-folio fragment of a thirteenth-century *romanzo arturiano*, also copied on parchment in *littera textualis*. This fragment, of French or northern Italian production, was not better identified in the inventory of Ser Decio's possessions, which was drawn up in 1598-9.[24] A two-folio fragment of an early *Roman de Tristan en prose* on parchment was owned in 1457-8 by Lorenzo di Domenico Lovaria, notary in Udine.[25] As with the Geoffrey of Monmouth fragment, it was copied in the second half of the fourteenth century, in a *littera textualis* hand, on parchment.

Also in northern Italy, the Library of Savoy included the late fourteenth-century French book *Le Chevalier Errant* by Tommaso III di Saluzzo as well as two volumes of Robert de Boron's *Histoire du Saint Graal*.[26] *Le Chevalier Errant* still appears as item 252 in the 1497-8 inventory that was prepared after the death of Filippo II.[27] The Savoy libraries also included a *Meliadus* (item 130) and a parchment manuscript identified no better than as 'paincte de parsonnaiges à quarreaulx à mode de la table ronde' (item 116).[28]

In northern Italy as elsewhere, one finds *aficionados* who possessed more than one Arthurian romance. An inventory of the possessions of the Paduan Benvenuto de' Lanzarotti, prepared in 1402 after his death, shows that, among the dozen or so books that he owned, four contained Arthurian texts: two parchment volumes of *Tristano*, a *San Gradale* and a *Liber Lanzaroti*.[29] The *Roman de Lancellot* copied on paper (Turin, Biblioteca Nazionale, MS L.V, 30) was badly burned in that library's tragic fire. Its colophon (now destroyed) once read: 'Deo gratias hunc librum expletum et scriptum fuit per me Johannem de Cour de Sonzio in Pergamo mcccciii de mense octobre' ('Thanks be to God. This book was finished and written by me, John of the court of Sonzio in [Bergamo?] in the month of October 1403').[30]

Another romance reader from the Veneto region, Zuliano di Anzoli – his names are spelled variously – finished copying a unique version of *Tristan* followed by the *Tavola Ritonda* material on 20 July 1446. The colophon of a *Filostrato* (1437) that Zuliano also owned identifies him as Cremonese.[31] Given his *ductus* script, he may have been a professional copyist.[32] The lengthy *Tristan* that Zuliano copied – sometimes called the *Tristano Palatino* or *Historia di Lancilotto del Lago* – is conserved in BNCF, MS Palatino 556 (formerly 198²; Pal. E.5.4.47).[33] One of Zuliano's notes (fol. 36) indicates two earlier owners/readers of this important Italian prose compilation: he says that his model for one section was a book that he borrowed from Geno deli Franceschi of Pisa, which had first belonged to Messer Pietro de Savoia.[34] This beautiful parchment codex contains 289 pen-and-ink designs by the artist Bonifacio Bembo, also from Cremona, who was 'the favorite painter of Bianca Visconti Sforza'[35] and court painter for Francesco and Galeazzo Sforza. Bembo executed frescoes in the great hall of the castle in Pavia and in the nearby Carthusian monastery, as well as an altarpiece for the cathedral in Cremona. Zuliano di Anzoli also owned a *Lancelot* in French prose, copied on 383 parchment folios (Venice, Bibl. Marciana, MS fr. Z.XII [255]; former CIX, 8; Recanati XVII). The note of possession in this manuscript reads: 'Libro del cantare de messer Lancelotto el quale è de Ziliano di Anzuli' ('Book of the poem of Sir Lancelot, which belongs to Giuliano di Anzuli').[36]

Although evidence is scarce, Arthurian material was well known in medieval Verona and Venice. Venetian dialect elements were a feature of a now untraceable *Vita di Merlino*, which had been translated from French. The manuscript was dated 20 November 1379 and was owned by 'Magnifico M. Pietro Delfino del fu Magnifico M. Giorgio' ('the magnificent Messer Pietro Delfino, son of the late magnificent Messer Giorgio'). Pier Delfino has been variously identified as a Venetian nobleman or as a general of the Camaldolite order.[37] The fourteenth-century *Tristano Corsiniano,* so named for the library that preserves it (Rome, Accademia dei Lincei, Biblioteca Corsiniana, MS 2593 [formerly Rossi 35; 55.K.5; N.11.19]), is an abbreviated version of the French prose *Tristan* that exhibits strong Veronese linguistic traits.[38] A short fragment of the last part of *Tavola Ritonda*, which treats the death of Tristan and the ensuing vengeance (BAV, MS Vat. lat. 6789, fols 57r–59v), was copied in 1422 by Ventura de Cerutis of Verona, then *castellano* of Montebello. The principal text in the manuscript is the *Historia destructionis Troie* by Guido delle Colonne (fols 1–57r).[39]

Florence and Tuscany

Even though the earliest Tuscan manuscripts have not always survived, it is clear that the Arthurian legends were known to Florentines by the early fourteenth century. As Christopher Kleinhenz notes in Chapter 10 in this volume, Dante Alighieri refers to various characters throughout his *Commedia*: Tristan in *Inferno* 5.67; Lancelot in *Inferno* 5.128; Guinevere in *Paradiso* 16.15; Galehaut in *Inferno* 5.137; and King Arthur's slaying of Mordred in *Inferno* 32.62. A famous passage in *Inferno* 5 describes the adulterous lovers, Paolo and Francesca, as reading the Old French *Lancelot* when they were murdered.

The *Tristano Panciatichiano* (BNCF, MS Panc. 33), a unique compilation of Arthurian legends, was copied in Tuscany in the fourteenth century. Its various sections correspond to *La Queste del Saint Graal*, in abbreviated form; lengthy portions of the prose *Roman de Tristan*, including the well-known Tournament at Louvezerp; *La Mort le roi Artu*; and Tristan's final adventure and death of the lovers, with the epilogue by Hélie de Boron. The site of the codex's original production is not known, but notes and designs contained within it indicate later Florentine ownership: 'Jacopo di Firenze' (fol. 117r), and amateur sketches of the coat of arms of Duke Cosimo I de' Medici and Eleonora da Toledo (fols 119v, 199r).[40] The name 'P[ietr?]o Fantoni' appears twice, on fols 200r and 246r.

A dated codex containing Arthurian texts was produced in Florence, and was later owned and read by different generations of Florentines: BNCF, MS II.II.68 (Magliab. Cl. VI, 158; Strozzi MSS in fol. 883). It was completed 6 December 1391 by a copyist who lived in the *Ghonfalone del Vaio*, in the San Giovanni quarter (fol. 158v). The copyist apparently had as his model a book belonging to a shoemaker named Fede and his sons. The book's 240 folios contain a *Tavola Ritonda* (fols 1–158) and a Post-Vulgate *Queste* fragment (at fol. 182). It was later owned by Pietro del Nero and entered the Strozzi library on 7 July 1786.[41]

Another exemplar of the *Tav. Rit.* in Italian vernacular (Florence, Bibl. Medicea Laurenziana, MS Pluteus XLIV, 27) was owned by messer Piero di Guascogna.[42] A rough sketch on fol. 74r seems to represent the Bracciolini coat of arms, as suggested by Polidori, who used this manuscript as a base text for his edition.[43]

A little-known document (BNCF, MS Nuovi Acquisti 509) lists the titles of a handful of books owned by Giovanni di Carlo Strozzi, among which were individual quires or fragments of Arthurian material. The little inventory appears on the recto of a parchment endpaper at the rear and is written in two different cursive fifteenth-century hands, the first of which gives the date 1424. In 1434, various members of the aristocratic Strozzi family were exiled from Florence for opposing the Medici. Having settled in Ferrara, Giovanni di Carlo Strozzi kept tabs on political developments by corresponding with his relatives who had remained in Florence.[44] Giovanni Strozzi's library was not extensive nor was it particularly valuable, to judge by the pejorative or diminutive descriptions he uses, such as 'due quadernuzzi', 'un libracciuolo di carte piccholissime', 'uno libro piccholo', 'un libro ... guasto' ('two gatherings or notebooks'; 'a little book with very small pages'; 'a little book'; 'a damaged book'). Even though these items apparently lacked resale value or had been damaged, the fact that they were conserved indicates that they still had value as reading material. This group of vernacular books – most in Italian and two in French – was probably representative of an early fifteenth-century Florentine's library. Titles include 'a piece of' the *Donadello*, the ubiquitous grammar text used for learning Latin; the *Lucidario*; the Passion of Christ; saints' lives and didactic *exempla*; prophecies and prognostications by Frate Stoppa and others; and recipes for cures. The unusual title *incoronate di Dante* (nine folios) may indicate a small anthology of Dante's writings, perhaps a selection of sonnets from the *Vita Nuova*.[45] There are four *cantari* – *ottava rima* poems especially popular in Tuscany – and selections from the *Alexander Romance*, *Apollonius of Tyre*, the *Destruction of Troy* and Arthurian romances. Under the rubric of 'legends', Item Four includes 'un pezzo di quello di Trisstano' ('a piece of that [book] about Tristan'). Item Five, a miscellany or composite manuscript written on sixty-nine 'very small' folios, in paper, contained as its last two portions two 'quadernuzzj di Trisstano e di Lanciolocto'. *Quadernuzzi* may indicate quires which were dilapidated or in some other way not very pristine or precious. Item Six, another miscellany or composite manuscript, contained ten 'legends': the sixth was about *messer Galasso*, possibly the Florentine *cantare* that has been edited under the title 'The Knight of the False Shield'.[46] The seventh item – twelve folios long – was about 'Carduino', probably the *Cantare di Carduino*.[47] Item Six also contained two quires about the adventures of 'Banduic[c]he', the Italian name for the character Ban of Benwick in the Vulgate Arthurian cycle. The first of these quires was twenty-two folios in length, and the second totalled twenty folios, as the inventory notes. Given the presence of French romances translated into Italian, it is tempting to suggest that the two untitled French books may have included longer portions of the French originals. The Strozzi inventory describes the first of these as 'uno libro lo quale dice i[n] franciozo di molte belle cose ed è foli 08[6?] e guasto' ('A book which tells many lovely things in French, and it is 86[?] folios in length and damaged').[48] The second was 'uno libro piccholo i[n] francioso il quale è fogli 88 carte dj pechora – folj 88' ('a small-format parchment book in French, written on 88 folios'). The vagueness of these two descriptions with respect to their content, and their lack of titles, indicate that the inventory's compiler may not have been literate in French.

Long after the French originals had been composed, Arthurian material continued to be copied, redacted and read in Florence. In 1433, one of the Alberti family of Florence copied Biblioteca Riccardiana, MS Ricc. 2759, which contains a *Joseph d'Arimathie* (i.e., a *San Graal*) and a *Merlin*: 'Iste liber est Francisci Altoblanchi de Albertis de Florentia posuit hoc manu propria V novembris MCCCCXXXIII' ('This book belongs to Francesco Altoblanchi of the Albertis of Florence written in his own hand 5 November 1433').[49] Armando Petrucci has identified Francesco as a professional scribe; strangely, the codex is a partial palimpsest.[50] Similarly, Florence, Bibl. Laurenziana, MS Plut. XLIII, 10 containing the adventures of Lancelot and Tristan in prose was owned and copied in 1447 by Antonio di Taddeo Mancini, as his colophon states.[51] In 1455 Antonio Mancini copied Guido delle Colonne's *Storia di Troia* in vernacular translation (BNCF, MS II.IV.43).[52] The Mancini were an important ruling family in Florence from 1284 on, and lived in the *Bue* (Ox) district.[53] Andrea di Taddeo Mancini, perhaps the copyist's brother, was a 'prominent and respected statesm[a]n of generally conservative leanings' who was elected to the *Signoria* in 1434 (1433 *stile fiorentino*) to represent the Santa Maria Novella quarter.[54]

Another native of Florence, Francesco di Tommaso Sassetti, worked for the Medici bank in Geneva, where he was promoted to manager in 1447. After returning to Florence, he eventually became general manager of the Medici bank there. His investments prospered, and he was extremely rich by the 1460s. Among the vernacular books he owned in November 1462 was one 'libro di Tristano in francioxo' ('Book of Tristan in French').[55]

The Tuscan soldier-poet Michelangelo di Cristofano di Giovanni da Volterra, a self-described *tronbetto* (trumpeter), composed an unedited *Storia del conte Ugo d'Avernia* ('Story of Count Huon d'Auvergne') in octaves based on the epic romance in prose by Andrea da Barberino. Michelangelo worked on composing this verse redaction from March 1487 to 6 June 1488, according to the dates he jotted in his book (fols 1r, 169r). The unique exemplar survives in Florence, Bibl. Laurenziana, MS Med. Pal. 82, which entered Duke Ferdinando's private library by 1588.[56] Michelangelo was an *aficionado* of *libri di battaglia* ('battle books') that treated the fictional adventures of Charlemagne and his paladins; a list of titles in Michelangelo's hand appears at the end of the codex. Among these epics is a single copy of '*La tavuola Rito[n]da*' (fol. 166r). In the sixteenth century, members of the Florentine Accademia della Crusca were consulting Arthurian romances and other medieval texts to obtain lexical samples for the first dictionary of the Italian language: Piero di Simone del Nero (fl. 1590) studied the witness conserved in BNCF, MS Pal. 564 [formerly 305; E.5,5,4]. This codex was loaned to him by 'Stritolato', the nickname for Messer Pier Francesco Cambi, another member of the noted Academy.[57]

By the sixteenth century, the two Pluteus manuscripts mentioned above had found their way into the Medici Library, where they were chained to reading benches (*plutei*) in the elegant room that Michelangelo Buonarroti designed in 1571. Another Arthurian narrative entered the Medici private library by 1588, when Domenico Mellini prepared its inventory (conserved in BNCF, MS II.II.309): this was the so-called *Storia del re Artù* (BNCF, MS II.I.17), a late prose version of *Girone il Cortese*.[58] MS II.I.17 had previously belonged to Giovanni Mazzuoli, called 'Lo Stradino' after the name of his birthplace, Strada in Chianti.[59] Stradino was a professional soldier who faithfully served Giovanni dalle Bande Nere and, later, Duke Cosimo de' Medici. Given his profession, it is not surprising to find Stradino's *armadiaccio* (cabinet of books) filled with Carolingian cycle 'battle books'. Stradino had also once owned MS Plut. XLIV, 27, mentioned above; he described this book in his 1553 inventory as 'Libro della tauola uechia et nuoua' ('The Book of the Old and New [Round] Table').[60]

For obvious reasons, narratives concerning Arthurian knights and their adventures must have appealed to readers who were military men: we have seen the examples of the Veronese Ventura de Cerutis, Michelangelo di Cristofano from Volterra and the Florentine Stradino. Another *castellano* stationed in Tuscany owned a manuscript of the *Istoria della Tavola Ritonda* (fols 4r–154v), which also contained the *Ninfe fiorentine* ('Florentine Nymphs') by Boccaccio, copied on paper (Siena, Biblioteca Comunale degli Intronati, MS I.vii.13). The detailed colophon (fol. 189v) reads: 'Scritto per me Daniello di Ghery Bolgharini al presente chastellano di Montecchiello questo dì xx di maggio MCCCCLXXVIII' ('Written [i.e. copied] by me, Daniel, son of Gheri Bulgarini, presently serving as *châtelain* of Montecchiello this 20th day of May 1478').[61] Montecchiello is a medieval hill town in Tuscany, about thirty miles south-east of Siena. The Bulgarini were a noble Sienese family that dated back to the early thirteenth century.[62] An apparent ancestor of this copyist was Simone di Gheri Bulgarini, a miniaturist who in 1344 finished illuminating a Lectionary for the Hospital at Siena.[63] A probable brother of the copyist Daniello was 'dominus Bulgarinus Gherii De Bulgarinis senensis' ('Lord Bulgarino, son of Gheri de' Bulgarini of Siena'); Gheri (1441–97) held posts as lecturer in civil law at the university in Pisa in 1483–90 and as *capitano del popolo* in 1491.[64] He also held posts at Ferrara, Bologna and Padua. In the 1490s, Bulgarino de' Bulgarini published three books of legal commentaries with the printer Henricus de Harlem, in Siena.[65] A final example of an Arthurian book that was owned by a Tuscan is the *Libro del Lancilotto*, which belonged to 'Giovanni di Benedetto di Marco Cecchi da Pescia' in 1597.[66] Cecchi is a Florentine name, still today; Pescia is a small Tuscan town, founded in the Middle Ages, to the north-west of Florence.

Naples and Sicily

Older studies by Bernhard Degenhart and Annegrit Schmitt compared numerous man-uscripts of different genres, suggesting that these were produced under the Angevins in Naples. Three exemplars – all with Arthurian texts in French – later made their way northward: to the French court; to the Gonzaga library in Mantua, and thence to Venice; into the hands of a Visconti supporter and, still later, to a Florentine owner. This is not the place to summarise previous studies on Neapolitan production, but three quick examples will be illustrative. The best witness of the shorter version of the French prose *Roman de Tristan* (BnF, MSS fr. 756–757) was owned by the Carafa, a powerful family closely allied to the Angevin court. The manuscript's ornamentation includes an unusual coat of arms and a star of David. In the early sixteenth century, the book was owned by Jérôme de Monteux, medical counsellor to Francis I.[67] The sixty-four folios of Venice, Bibl. Marciana, MS fr. XXIII (234) contain episodes from the first part of the French prose *Roman de Tristan*. This illuminated manuscript was produced in Naples in the first decade of the 1300s. By 1407, this book had made its way to Francesco I Gonzaga's library at Mantua.[68] *Guiron le Courtois* in French was produced at Naples in the second decade of the fourteenth century (Venice, Bibl. Marciana, MS fr. IX [227]). The manuscript bears several amateur sketches of the Visconti coat of arms, indicating that it was owned by a Visconti client or ally, someone who perhaps resided in Visconti territory. Other owners' notes include one by a doctor of law: 'Liber domini Johannis de Zevio juris utriusque doctoris' ('This book belongs to John of Zevio, doctor of civil and canon law') written in a fifteenth-century hand (fol. 73v); and a brief comment in the purest Florentine: 'questo libro è di Taldo' ('This is Taldo's book') (fol. 74).[69]

A portion of the prose *Lancelot* is preserved in Venice, Bibl. Marciana, MS fr. Z.XI (254). The narrative segment this manuscript contains corresponds to *Lancelot*, Book III, 'Agravain'.[70] Written in French on parchment and decorated with pen and ink miniatures, the manuscript has been connected to Neapolitan *scriptoria*. At some point, the book came into the hands of a Tuscan owner, as indicated in a note on fol. 75: 'Rudolfo da Sangimingniano'. A note in a later hand mentions an otherwise unidentified 'Rodolfo di Lese' as owner or reader.[71]

A fourteenth-century French prose *Meliadus*, now London, British Library, MS Add. 12228, has a Neapolitan provenance. It is a heavily decorated vellum book, 'the backgrounds of several of [whose] early miniatures, behind the figures of kings, bear the arms of Louis of Taranto, who married Queen Joanna of Naples in 1347'. Louis (Ludovico) was crowned in 1352 and then founded the first Italian order of knighthood, the *Nodo* (knot), a symbol that appears 'in the first large miniature (at fol. 4). Meliadus, the hero of the romance, is always represented . . . as bearing the arms of Naples'.[72]

Books in French also made their way to fifteenth-century Palermitan libraries, although existing inventories do not always furnish titles. The nobleman 'Fridericus de Symone' possessed a single book 'in lingua francigena' ('in the French language'; 1457); 'Petrus de Speciale', a knight and lord of Alcamo and Calatafimi, who died in 1474, had owned two French books, one of which was copied on large-sized folios: 'Liber in carta bonbicina magnus in lingua francorum' ('a large book on cotton paper in the French language') and 'liber in carta membrana in lingua galica' ('a book on parchment in Gallic language'). On his death in 1484, Jacobus de Chirco, doctor of law, left an extensive collection of over one hundred books, one of which was a book 'in lingua francigena in pergameno' ('in the French language on parchment'). A fragmentary inventory (*c*.1490), now lacking its owner's name, mentions 'certa frustra librorum in lingua francorum' ('certain scraps of a book in the French language').[73]

Three other inventories from Sicily are more helpful, providing clear evidence of Arthurian titles. The inventory of Giovanni de Cruyllas (1423) names 'unu Galeoctu lu bruns in francescu' (a *Galehaut the Brown* in French).[74] *Tristan* was also read in Palermo, Sicily. Documents of a 17 July 1434 sale of property show one book of *Tristayno* redacted by 'Peri Ferreri' ('Librum unum de Tristayno Peri Ferreri'); Henri Bresc suggests this may have been the Catalan translation.[75] At the time of his death in 1482, Petrus de Burgio of Sciacca, Sicily, owned '[u]nu libru di parchiminu cum cuverti di tavuli chamatu Galiotu' ('a parchment book with board covers, called *Galehaut*').[76] This book was copied on parchment and covered with boards, i.e. bound, which suggests a lengthy romance, perhaps even rather luxuriously done.

A final example of an Arthurian text that was once in the hands of an Italian is London, British Library, MS Add. 23929. This *Tristan* in French was copied on eighty-six vellum folios in the late fourteenth century. The book is decorated with illuminated initials. A sixteenth-century owner's memorandum on the last flyleaf reads: 'Memoria di trouar prõns [?] – ad marcantonio di beltramo'.[77]

Conclusion

Surviving codicological evidence indicates that transmission to various regions of the Italian peninsula must have taken place rapidly – indeed, almost simultaneously – during the later thirteenth century. Transmission was due to travel by land or sea for pilgrimages, commerce, diplomatic missions or military assignments. Political, social and familial relationships provided additional occasions for cultural exchange. Manuscripts could be loaned to friends and associates, who sometimes made their own copies. Arthurian narratives, like other books, were copied either on commission by professional scribes or, more economically, by amateur owners for their own use. Romances were sometimes used as collateral on loans and could be passed on to heirs along with other property. Such narratives were owned and read by a troubadour poet, by professional soldiers, by doctors of law and notaries. In the sixteenth century, scholars studied these stories for linguistic purposes, and later bibliophiles retained the lengthy Arthurian manuscripts that had been copied in earlier centuries.

Notes

[1] D. Delcorno Branca, 'Lecteurs et interprètes de romans arthuriens en Italie: un examen à partir des études récentes', in C. Kleinhenz and K. Busby, *Medieval Multilingualism: The Francophone World and its Neighbours* (Turnhout, 2010), pp. 155–86. See also Chapter 4 in the present volume.

[2] See, for example, G. Bertoni, 'Notizie sugli amanuensi degli Estensi nel Quattrocento', *Archivum romanicum*, 2 (1918), 29–57; A. Cappelli, 'La Biblioteca estense nella prima metà del secolo XV', *GSLI*, 14 (1889), 1–30; G. Mazzatinti, 'Inventario dei codici della Biblioteca Visconteo-Sforzesca redatto da

Ser Facino da Fabriano nel 1459 e 1469', *GSLI*, 1 (1883), 33–59; Anna Giulia Cavagna, '"Il libro desquadernato: la carta rosechata da rati". Due nuovi inventari della Libreria Visconteo-Sforzesca', *Bollettino della Società Pavese di Storia Patria*, n.s. 41 (1989), 29–97.

³ P. F. Grendler, 'Chivalric Romances in the Italian Renaissance', in *Studies in Medieval and Renaissance History*, ed. J. A. S. Evans and R. W. Unger (New York, 1988), X, pp. 59–102, on p. 83.

⁴ For a brief survey, see R. Middleton, 'The Manuscripts', in G. S. Burgess and K. Pratt (eds), *The Arthur of the French. The Arthurian Legend in Medieval French and Occitan Literature* (Cardiff, 2006), pp. 8–92, on pp. 81–2. A longer study, which improved upon E. G. Gardner's earlier work, is Delcorno Branca's '"Franceschi romanzi": copisti, lettori, biblioteche', in *TLI*, pp. 13–48. A concise census of Arthurian codices produced or owned by Italians appears in *Il Tristano panciatichiano*, ed. and trans. G. Allaire (Cambridge, 2002), pp. 13–25. I have not personally examined all manuscripts mentioned in that Appendix nor in the present study.

⁵ G. Bertoni, 'Lettori di romanzi francesi nel Quattrocento alla corte estense', in *Studi su vecchie e nuove poesie e prose d'amore e di romanzi* (Modena, 1921), p. 254. I rely on Bertoni's transcription of fifteenth-century librarians' remarks and did not personally examine these archival records; these may contain additional information that Bertoni did not publish.

⁶ Since these private libraries did not yet use a shelfmark system, inventories and archival documents do not always make clear if they are speaking of the same codex. *Meliadux* and *Meliaduse* are spelling variants of the same hero's name. Identification requires detailed research to reconstruct early libraries, subject to the vagaries of extant documents and surviving codices.

⁷ Bertoni, 'Lettori', p. 255; Delcorno Branca, 'Tradizione italiana dei testi arturiani. Note sul *Lancelot*', *MR*, 17/2 (1992), 215–50, on 235: 'Iacomo de Ariosti have uno libro franchois dito Meliadus a dì XIII de novembre. rese a dì XIII dicembre.' The archival source cited is: ASE, *Camera ducale, Guardaroba* 50, *Memoriale* 1457–62, fol. 10r.

⁸ Bertoni, 'Lettori', pp. 257–8.

⁹ Delcorno Branca, 'Note sul *Lancelot*', 235.

¹⁰ Bertoni, 'Lettori', p. 257.

¹¹ Bertoni, 'Lettori', p. 258; Delcorno Branca, 'Note sul *Lancelot*', 235 n. 49.

¹² Bertoni, 'Lettori', p. 257; Delcorno Branca, 'Note sul *Lancelot*', 235.

¹³ Letter published by Osio, cited in C. Santoro, 'La Biblioteca dei Gonzaga e cinque suoi codici nella Trivulziana di Milano', in *Arte, Pensiero e Cultura a Mantova nel Primo Rinascimento in rapporto con la Toscana e con il Veneto* (Florence, 1965), p. 89. The term 'romance' indicated a text written in one of the European vernaculars, as opposed to Latin. Since courtly narratives written in French were such an influential literary genre, 'romance' would come to connote stories of love and adventure.

¹⁴ M. G. Albertini Ottolenghi, 'La Biblioteca dei Visconti e degli Sforza: Gli inventari del 1488 e del 1490', *Studi Petrarcheschi*, n.s. 8 (1991), 1–238.

¹⁵ E. S. Murrell, 'Quelques manuscrits méconnus du *Roman de Tristan* en prose', *Romania*, 56 (1930), 277–81, on 277–8.

¹⁶ C. H. Clough, 'The Library of the Gonzaga of Mantua', *Librarium. Revue de la Société Suisse des Bibliophiles*, 5 (1972), 50–63, on 52.

¹⁷ Delcorno Branca, 'I *Tristani* dei Gonzaga', in J. D. Faucon et al. (eds), *Miscellanea Mediaevalia. Mélanges offerts à Philippe Ménard*, 2 vols (Paris and Geneva, 1998), I, pp. 385–93, on p. 387. On the popularity of Tristan in Italy, see Chapter 4 of this volume.

¹⁸ W. Braghirolli, P. Meyer and G. Paris, 'Inventaire des manuscrits en langue française possédés par Francesco Gonzaga I, capitaine de Mantoue, mort en 1407', *Romania*, 9 (1880), 497–514, on 501.

¹⁹ See Chapter 13 in the present volume.

²⁰ G. Paccagnini, *Pisanello*, trans. J. Carroll (New York, 1973), pp. 46, 56, 72.

²¹ G. Petti Balbi, 'Il libro nella società genovese del sec. XIII', *La Bibliofilía*, 80 (1978), 1–46, on 14, 33, 37, 43.

²² Bénédictins du Bouveret, *Colophons de manuscrits occidentaux des origines au XVIe siècle*, Spicilegii Friburgensis, Subsidia 4, 6 vols (Fribourg, 1973), III, p. 310, no. 9926.

[23] Cesare Scalon, *Libri, scuole e cultura nel Friuli medievale. 'Membra disiecta' dell'Archivio di Stato di Udine* (Padua, 1987), pp. 147–8.

[24] Scalon, *Libri, scuole e cultura*, pp. 176–7, tav. XLI. A partial photo facsimile of the *romanzo* is included among the black and white plates at the end.

[25] Scalon, *Libri, scuole e cultura*, p. 178.

[26] S. Edmunds, 'The Medieval Library of Savoy (III): The Documents', *Scriptorium*, 26 (1972), 274, 278–9, 281–2.

[27] P. Vayra, 'Le Lettere e le arti alla Corte di Savoia nel secolo XV: Inventari dei castelli di Ciamberì, di Torino e di Ponte d'Ain 1497–98 pubblicati sugli originali inediti', *Miscellanea di Storia Italiana (Torino)*, 22 (1884), 6–212, on 73.

[28] Vayra, 'Le Lettere e le arti', 50 and 53.

[29] G. Folena, 'La cultura volgare e l' "umanesimo cavalleresco" nel Veneto', in V. Branca (ed.), *Umanesimo europeo e umanesimo veneziano* (Florence, 1963), pp. 141–58, on p. 153.

[30] Edmunds, 'Medieval Library of Savoy', 289.

[31] D. De Robertis, 'Censimento dei manuscritti delle *Rime* di Dante', *Studi Danteschi*, 38 (1961), 167–276, on 276: 'Magnanimus Iulianus de Ançolis de Cremona frater dilectissimus meus possidet hunc librum' ('My generous and dearly beloved brother Giuliano di Anzoli of Cremona owns this book'). Thanks to J. Francis, Abigail Firey and Calvin Higgs for help with translations from Latin.

[32] Delcorno Branca, 'Note sul *Lancelot*', 243.

[33] *Tavola Ritonda: Manoscritto Palatino 556, Firenze Biblioteca Nazionale Centrale*, ed. R. Cardini, intro. D. Delcorno Branca, 2 vols (Rome, 2009). On this codex, see Chapter 4 in the present volume.

[34] N. Rasmo, 'Il Codice palatino 556 e le sue illustrazioni', *Rivista d'arte*, 21 (1939), 245–81, on 248.

[35] G. Moakley, *The Tarot Cards Painted by Bonifacio Bembo for the Visconti-Sforza family. An Iconographic and Historical Study* (New York, 1966), pp. 19 and 22.

[36] D. Ciàmpoli, *I codici francesi della R. Biblioteca nazionale di S. Marco in Venezia* (Venice, 1897), pp. 33–4; Delcorno Branca, 'Note sul *Lancelot*', 227, 243–4.

[37] Ciàmpoli, *I codici francesi*, pp. 152–3.

[38] I am grateful to Roberta Capelli her help in confirming this. See also R. Tagliani, '*Il Tristano Corsiniano: edizione, studio codicologico, iconografico e linguistico*' (Ph.D. diss. Università di Siena), abstract online: *www.unisi.it/ricerca/dottorationweb/filologia. . ./abstract_tagliani.pdf*.

[39] M.-J. Heijkant, *La tradizione del 'Tristan' in prosa in Italia e proposte di studio sul Tristano Riccardiano* (Nijmegen, 1989), p. 41.

[40] *Il Tristano panciatichiano*, ed. and trans. Allaire, pp. 6–7.

[41] The original copyist's name was obliterated by a later owner. G. Mazzatinti, *Inventari dei manoscritti delle Biblioteche d'Italia*, 116 vols (Forlì, 1898), VIII, pp. 178–9; *La Tavola ritonda o L'Istoria di Tristano. Testo di Lingua*, ed. F.-L. Polidori (Bologna, 1864), pp. lii–liv.

[42] A. M. Bandini, *Catalogus codicum manuscriptorum Bibliothecae Medicae Laurentianae* (Florentiae: Caesareis, 1778), V: *Italicos scriptores exhibens*, pp. 227–8. Bandini gives the date as fourteenth century. For a photo facsimile of one page, see F. Arese (ed.), *Prose di romanzi. Il romanzo cortese in Italia nei secoli XIII e XIV* (Turin, 1962), plate between pp. 320–1.

[43] *Tavola Ritonda*, ed. Polidori, pp. li–lii.

[44] M. M. Bullard, *Filippo Strozzi and the Medici. Favor and Finance in Sixteenth-Century Florence and Rome* (Cambridge, 1980), pp. 46, 52, 76; M. Hollingsworth, *Patronage in Renaissance Italy from 1400 to the Early Sixteenth Century* (Baltimore, 1994), p. 208; D. Kent, *The Rise of the Medici Faction in Florence 1426–1434* (Oxford, 1978), p. 357.

[45] I am indebted to Christopher Kleinhenz and Gino Casagrande for this suggestion.

[46] '*Il Cavaliere del Falso Scudo*. Cantari due di anonimo fiorentino del sec. XV', ed. C. Milanesi, in *Raccolta di scritture varie pubblicata nell'occasione delle nozze Riccomanni-Fineschi* (Turin, 1863), pp. 79–84.

[47] See Chapter 6 in the present volume.

[48] This item is crossed out; the book may have been sold, loaned or perhaps destroyed owing to its damaged condition.

[49] Delcorno Branca, 'Note sul *Lancelot*', 227.

[50] A. Petrucci, 'Storia e geografia delle culture scritte (dal secolo XI al secolo XVIII)', in *Letteratura italiana. Storia e geografia*, II: 'Produzione e consumo' (Turin, 1988), pp. 1195–1241, on p. 1225.

[51] This text is also known as the *Tavola Ritonda,* but was not included in Polidori's edition. 'Questo Libro si è d'Antonio di Taddeo Mancini el quale lo schrisse di sua mano propria, e fu finito a dì 10 di Giugno MCCCCXLVII a ore XV' (Bandini, *Catalogus,* V, p. 209). See also P. Breillat, 'La *Quète du Saint-Graal* en Italie', in *Mélanges d'Archéologie et d'Histoire de l'Ecole française de Rome*, 54 (1937), 262–300, on 284 n. 1.

[52] Mazzatinti, *Inventari* (Forlì, 1900), X, 104–5; Bénédictins, *Colophons* (of series vol. 2), tome I (1965), p. 141, no. 1120 shelfmark as II, IV, 44.

[53] Kent, 'The Florentine *Reggimento* in the Fifteenth Century', *Renaissance Quarterly*, 28 (1975), 575–638, on 629.

[54] Kent, *Rise of the Medici*, p. 317.

[55] A. de la Mare, 'The Library of Francesco Sassetti (1421–1490)', in C. H. Clough (ed.), *Cultural Aspects of the Italian Renaissance. Essays in Honour of Paul Oskar Kristeller* (New York, 1976), pp. 160–201, on 161 and 172–3.

[56] The indication '1626' corresponds to Domenico Mellini's 1588 inventory of the Medici Library.

[57] S. Guida, 'Per il testo della *Tavola Ritonda.* Una redazione umbra', *Siculorum Gymnasium*, n.s. 32 (1979), 637–67, on 639.

[58] *Girone il cortese. Romanzo cavalleresco di Rustico o Rusticiano da Pisa . . .* , ed. F. Tassi (Florence, 1855), p. xvii.

[59] I am grateful to Carla Masaro for sharing her unpublished findings regarding Stradino's library.

[60] B. Maracchi Biagiarelli, 'L'*Armadiaccio* di Padre Stradino', *La Bibliofilía*, 84 (1982), 51–7, on 51, 55, 57.

[61] For the complete manuscript description, see 'CODEX. Inventario dei manoscritti medievali della Toscana' at *http://codex.signum.sns.it/Isis*.

[62] For identification of the Bulgarini as nobles, see V. Spreti, *Enciclopedia storica-nobiliare italiana*, 7 vols (Milan, 1928–35), II, p. 204.

[63] The Lectionary, which has since vanished, was completed by Lippo Vanni in 1344. See G. Milanesi, *Sulla storia dell'arte toscana. Scritti vari* (Siena, 1878; rpt Soest, 1973), p. 73.

[64] A. F. Verde and R. M. Zaccaria, *Lo studio fiorentino 1473–1530. Ricerche e Documenti*, Istituto Nazionale di Studi sul Rinascimento, 6 vols (Florence, 1973–2010), II (1973), pp. 141–3, 331; IV, pt. 2 (1985), pp. 567–8, 725, 885, 896, 901, 981.

[65] Bulgarinus de Bulgarinis, *Quaestiones de bonorum possessione* (15 March 1491); *Interpretatio super Rubrica 'soluto matrimonio quemadmodum dos petatur'* (15 September 1491), and *Disputatio de testamentis. Consilium* (4 April 1493).

[66] C. Bec, *Les livres des Florentins (1413–1608)* (Florence, 1984), p. 286.

[67] *Le Roman de Tristan en prose (version du manuscrit fr. 757 de la Bibliothèque nationale de Paris),* ed. J. Blanchard and M. Quéreuil (Paris, 1997), I, pp. 12–13 nn. 5 and 6.

[68] B. Degenhart and A. Schmitt, *Corpus der Italienischen Zeichnungen* (Berlin, 1980), II, pt. 2, p. 226.

[69] Degenhart and Schmitt, *Corpus*, II, pt. 2, pp. 239–40. A recent reassessment by F. Fabbri argues that MSS fr. IX (227) and fr. XXIII (234) were actually Genoese in origin ('Romanzi cortesi e prosa didattica a Genova alla fine del Duecento fra interscambi, coesistenze e nuove prospettive', *Studi di Storia dell'Arte*, 23 [2012], 9–32, on 11). The lively debate regarding the so-called Neapolitan manuscripts has still not been resolved. It is clear that there were many active centres of manuscript production scattered throughout medieval Italy.

[70] Degenhart and Schmitt, 'Frühe angiovinische Buchkunst in Neapel. Die Illustrierung französischer Unterhaltungsprosa in neapolitanischen Scriptorien zwischen 1290 und 1320', in F. Piel and J. Traeger (eds), *Festschrift Wolfgang Braunfels* (Tübingen, 1977), pp. 71–92, on p. 89 n. 10.

[71] Ciàmpoli, *I codici francesi*, pp. 31–2; Degenhart and Schmitt, *Corpus*, II, pt. 2, p. 237.

[72] H. L. D. Ward, *Catalogue of Romances in the Department of manuscripts in the British Museum* (London, 1883), I, p. 364.

[73] H. Bresc, *Livre et société en Sicile (1299–1499)*, Centro di Studi filologici e linguistici siciliani. Bollettino, Supplementi 3 (Palermo: [Luxograph], 1971), pp. 211, 252, 284–90, 311.

[74] Bresc, *Livre et société*, p. 280 note to inventory 188.

[75] Bresc, *Livre et société*, p. 161 note to inventory 70.

[76] Bresc, *Livre et société*, p. 280.

[77] Ward, *Catalogue of Romances*, I, p. 357.

As this book was in press, the following new study came to my attention: Armando Antonelli, 'La sezione francese della biblioteca degli Este nel XV secolo: sedimentazione, evoluzione e dispersion. Il caso dei romani arturiani', TECA, 3 (2013), 53–82 online at *www.teca.patroneditore.it*.

13

ARTHURIAN ART IN ITALY

Gloria Allaire

As we have seen in Chapters 11 and 12, some of the most copious evidence for the circulation of the Arthurian legend in Italy is not textual at all, but material. By examining visual representations, we can often understand which specific texts circulated in a given area. Unfortunately art historians and literary scholars have not always communicated their discoveries to each other, a problem which this chapter attempts to address. Any survey of artistic representations of the Arthurian legend which survive in Italy or which were produced by Italians must begin with the 1938 *Arthurian Legends in Medieval Art* by Roger Sherman Loomis and Laura Hibbard Loomis.[1] Although great strides have been made in all areas of Medieval Studies since then, this study still has value, not least for the 'shrewd recognition of the necessity of multiple approaches' to this vast topic.[2] The Loomises' book was a remarkable achievement: they identified Arthuriana in lesser-known applied arts – such as ivories, enamels and ceramics – which have yet to be fully examined by modern scholars.

Although the Loomises' cursory – and sometimes judgemental – interpretations have largely been revised, their inventory of Arthurian art in Italy was surpassed only in 1990 by Muriel Whitaker's ambitious and lavishly illustrated *The Legends of King Arthur in Art*.[3] Of the handful of Arthurian art surveys produced recently, the impetus is most often literary, and much research has been done in the area of manuscript studies. Although many texts and codices were unknown to the Loomises (the lengthy *Tristano Veneto* and *Tristano Panciatichiano* still had not been edited), to their credit they cited available published editions and even mentioned *cantari* such as the *Sala di Malagigi* and the *Padiglione di Carlomagno*.[4] While many manuscripts – 'the richest sources of Arthurian art' – have since been identified,[5] Whitaker rightly notes the difficulties of doing a comprehensive analysis of illuminations in any given group of Italian Arthurian manuscripts. One can only hope that some day we shall have a study such as has been produced for those of Chrétien de Troyes[6] or a database of images which could be readily consulted.[7]

Several recent surveys have approached the subject in terms of single characters or authors. Norbert H. Ott's 1975 pan-European 'Katalog' identifies the Tristan story across centuries, genres and national borders; following the Loomises, he provides more detailed information on castle frescoes, the Guicciardini wall hanging, Italian ivories and the maternity tray.[8] Julia Walworth's 2002 update includes the Guicciardini '*coperta*' and a brief review of Italian illuminated manuscript studies from the 1970s and 1980s.[9] Ott's 'Tristano e Isotta nell'iconografia medioevale', centred on Eilhart, is addressed to an Italian audience, but alludes only to Marciana, MS fr. XXIII and the Guicciardini wall hanging.[10] More comprehensive is the chapter 'Arthur in the Arts' in *The Arthurian Handbook*, a global study that includes cinematic and American rewritings of the legend.[11] The Italian references are limited to the well-known cathedrals of Modena and Otranto, castle and palace decorations, and wall hangings, with a nod to manuscripts in Italy.[12] Following this blueprint, Whitaker's 2006 contribution 'Early Arthurian Art' mentions manuscripts, Modena, Otranto, the wall hanging, the wall paintings at Runkelstein, Saint Floret, Mantua and the ceiling of *Lo Steri* in Palermo.[13] Another book which tackles visual representation of the Arthur legends is the 2009 *Companion to Arthurian Literature*; its only references to Italy appear in Jeanne Fox-Friedman's examination of Arthurian imagery in medieval churches.[14] Fox-Friedman provides a valuable analysis of the Modena archivolt (subject of her 1992 dissertation) and also mentions the Otranto floor mosaic, without attempting to unravel its enigmatic significance.[15]

Even though the Matter of Britain was widely transmitted throughout medieval Europe, surveys of the Arthurian legend in art have – with the exception of Ott – been produced by English-speaking scholars. A language barrier may have inhibited access to the numerous studies which exist in Italian. In fact, during the last quarter of the twentieth century, Italianists have produced numerous studies on manuscript illumination and palace decoration. New editions and translations of Italian Arthuriana have appeared. Frescoes have been cleaned, and palaces themselves restored and opened to the public as museums. Once-lost courtly scenes in wall paintings have come to light, following natural or man-made disruptions. The oft-mentioned Guicciardini wall hanging itself has undergone extensive repair, and the noteworthy Otranto cathedral floor has been excavated, rebuilt and cleaned. From the later twentieth century onward, specialists of diverse disciplines have dedicated their talents to preserving the visual remnants of the Arthurian tradition in Italy. The results of their efforts have furnished the material for the scientific, photographic and literary studies collected in an analytical bibliography that accompanies this chapter. It may seem paradoxical to discuss Arthurian-themed art without providing illustrations; however, this chapter and its accompanying bibliography indicate where good-quality reproductions have been published. It is my hope that collating these findings here will inspire future scholars to fill in the critical gaps in order to provide a holistic view of the visual representations of the Matter of Britain . . . in Italy.

Cathedral Decoration

The Modena Archivolt

The earliest extant visual representation of Arthur in Italy, sculpted on the Modena cathedral's Porta della Pescheria (Fishmarket doorway) has been dated to *c.*1120–40.

Here, *Artus de Bretania* and his knights rescue queen Winlogee (Guinevere in the legend's later retellings) from Mardoc's castle. Whitaker briefly analyses the figures and suggests narrative analogues for the abducted queen story.[16] Although no such written account survives, the scene resembles the Dolorous Tower episode in Caradoc's *Vita Gildae* (pre-1129).[17] Using stylistic and literary evidence, Loomis dismantled Olschki's notion that the sculpture postdates 1150 and noted that the names incised above the figures are Welsh with Latin -*us* endings.[18] Loomis also hypothesised the story's arrival in Italy: a Breton duke had wintered in Bari at the time of the First Crusade. Because the Modena archivolt resembles one at San Nicola in Bari, Loomis suggests that workmen and/or storytellers travelled from there to Modena.[19] Stiennon and Lejeune used palaeographic analysis of the inscriptions throughout the Modena cathedral and comparison to contemporary sculptures to date the archivolt to the second quarter of the twelfth century.[20]

A restoration attempt in 1973 and a public exhibition in 1984 dedicated to the cathedral's construction and decoration sparked critical interest: several book-length studies appeared within ten years. The exhibition's lavishly illustrated catalogue was published in 1985; in the same year a conference was held, the proceedings of which were published.[21]

Soon afterwards, the portal itself was restored, occasioning a book-length study, *La Porta della Pescheria nel Duomo di Modena*; Monica Chiellini Nari's essay on the fables, symbols and Arthurian 'cycle' is of special interest.[22] Although the archivolt itself has received the lion's share of critical interest, Chiellini Nari perceptively examines the Arthurian episode within the iconographic context of the entire doorway. Using classical and medieval sources, she deduces that the woods and animals represent largely negative *exempla*. The humans portrayed in the Arthurian scene illustrate the futility of war as denounced by St Bernard, for whom chivalry is reprehensible because killing is a mortal sin; instead of *milizia*, he would call it *malizia*.[23] Chiellini Nari notes that this early Arthur figure is not labelled 'rex', nor does he wear a crown; however, he and two knights have flags on their lances which identify them as valorous war captains. Their armour and attack strategy, including the new way of carrying the lance against the body and beneath the arm, correspond to contemporary arts of war.

Jeanne Fox-Friedman reprises her dissertation in an article which interprets the Modena cathedral in the context of the crusades.[24] She furnishes a critical survey on the architrave, providing additional bibliography. In her analysis, she brilliantly signals the importance of the cathedral's other door: the Porta dei Principi (Door of Princes), where officials entered. Its lintel shows Modena's patron, San Geminiano, rescuing the eastern emperor's daughter who had been captured by the devil. This religious story parallels the secular rescue shown on the other portal, where the populace entered. Countess Matilda, who ruled the region and had founded the cathedral, was an ardent supporter of the papacy and of the crusades. Chronicles of the

First Crusade helped establish it as part of cosmic history. According to this Church-sanctioned view, Jerusalem needed deliverance 'from the evil grasp of the infidel', just as the abducted women portrayed on the two doorways needed rescue.[25]

Finally, Giovanni Lorenzoni and Giovanna Valenzano compare the Modena cathedral to the Basilica of San Zeno in Verona, hypothesising that Lanfranco also worked there. Their evidence suggests that the Modena architectural work was essentially done by the 1130s.[26] Although nothing at San Zeno has been identified as Arthurian, its sculptures include a scene of jousting and a sword battle on foot under scenes of the life of Christ.[27]

The Otranto Mosaic

Under the influence of Normans, the Arthurian legend swept throughout Italy. By 1165, a mounted figure of *Rex Arturus* was included in the iconographic programme of the Otranto cathedral floor in Puglia; the presbyter Pantaleone created this mosaic during William I's reign. Chiara Settis Frugoni's 1968 art-historical study is funda-mental to understanding these images; her subsequent 1970 essay views the mosaic in its broader contexts and demonstrates the penetration of Norman culture even into the Church.[28] In the mosaic, Arthur rides a quadruped which has been variously identified as a ram, a bear or a panther; for Walter Haug, it represents the middle Welsh *Cath Palug*, known to Italians as *il Gatto di Losanna*.[29] Arthur wrestles a similar beast on the bas-relief of the Ghirlandina tower in Modena.[30] The Loomises consider it a goat, the symbol of lechery: indeed, its horns, cloven hooves and short tail are the attributes of a goat rather than of a feline.[31] Although many photographs of the mosaic show Arthur wearing a crown, this was added in an 1818 restoration.[32] Inspired by archaeo-logical findings at a Roman city in Upper Carinthia (Austria), Alice Schulte compares Otranto's ornamental motifs to examples that range across centuries and cultures.[33] Martin Wiershin studied the figures of Arthur and Alexander;[34] however, other royal figures appear as well: Solomon, the queen of Saba and the king of Nineveh.[35] Carl Arnold Willemsen's *L'enigma di Otranto* builds on Frugoni's work and includes excellent pre-restoration photographs and updated bibliography; this book has both Italian and German editions.[36] In 1986, the entire pavement was excavated prior to restoring the mosaic; this process and its noteworthy results are documented in Grazio Gianfreda, *Il mosaico di Otranto: Biblioteca medioevale in immagini*.[37] Gianfreda provides background on the cathedral and its cultural context before proceeding to a reading of the individual images in the nave. The restoration of the mosaic even inspired a historical novel by Giovanni Barba and a fanciful moralistic interpretation by Claudio Saporetti.[38]

Castles and Palaces

Castel Rodengo

An astounding pictorial cycle of Yvain survives in the north-eastern Italian Castel Rodengo, built *c*.1140 near Bressanone (Brixen). Known variously as Schloß Rodenegg or Rodeneck, the castle's name derives from the medieval owner's surname: Federico I di Rodank or Rodanc. These frescoes *a secco* were unknown to the Loomises, having been covered by late sixteenth-century vaulting and flooring to construct a cannon emplacement. Josef Garber mentioned the remnants of chapel frescoes, but proposed a much later date based on when the chapel itself was finished.[39] Only in the 1970s, under the direction of Nicolò Rasmo, were the Yvain frescoes uncovered. In an early publication Rasmo provides early close-up photographs of figures and discusses the discovery and conservation efforts.[40] Later, in *L'età cavalleresca*, he furnishes details on the history and location of the castle, the floor plan and colour plates of the exposed frescoes.[41] His digressive introduction includes a speculative discussion of the diffusion of Breton and other chivalric stories throughout Europe in the thirteenth century. Seizing upon the name Maestro Ugo (Master Hugo), Rasmo tried to establish a single 'court painter' who had produced various frescoes in the area; Heinz Mackowitz and the contributors to *Trentino Alto Adige* concurred.[42] This oft-repeated notion has since been discredited: Maestro Ugo had witnessed a contemporary document pertaining to the bishop of Rodank, but he cannot be identified as a painter. Furthermore, Anne-Marie Bonnet and A. Rainer have argued against the hand of a single painter for works done in different sites.[43]

Because the end of the story is not portrayed, Rasmo believed that the frescoes were executed *c*.1200, before Hartmann had finished his poem. The dating controversy has been variously addressed within the context of comparative art history, notably by Peter and Dorothea Diemer; Birlauf-Bonnet narrowed the date to the 1220s, which is now generally accepted.[44] The precise date notwithstanding, Castel Rodengo's Yvain cycle is an 'extraordinary document without known precedent: the oldest surviving . . . representation in the monumental arts of the High Middle Ages of a profane narrative subject in the context of profane architecture'.[45] Paola Bassetti Carlini summarises the various critical controversies, suggests that the room may have been the family's winter apartment and provides colour photographs of the entire space after the cycle was restored in the 1990s.[46]

Scholars have repeatedly compared the Rodengo images to extant literary versions of *Yvain/Iwein*.[47] Inevitable comparisons of the Rodengo cycle to another, later series of Yvain paintings in Schmalkalden, Germany, offer reception evidence for Arthurian legends.[48] Bonnet's 1986 book *Rodenegg und Schmalkalden* provides useful diagrams of the room and a detailed comparative table of narrative scenes.[49] Ott expands the comparisons, using pictorial evidence from the two Italian castles

Rodengo and Roncolo (discussed below) as well as two German tapestries with chivalric themes.[50]

Given the Tyrolean location of the castle and the dating of the cycle, critics have tended to focus on Hartmann von Aue's German reworking of Chrétien de Troyes's *Yvain*. However, the images themselves 'reread and restage' the texts known to us.[51] Interpretation of the scenes selected and their iconography has been a rich source of scholarly inquiry. The lack of precise visual-literary correspondence perplexed scholars; Bonnet was 'the first critic to recognize the negative emphasis of the Rodenegg narrative'.[52] Over the years, Curschmann and Rushing have complemented each other's work; their subtle arguments are too complex to summarise here adequately.[53] Briefly, the Rodengo Yvain cycle was executed before the painterly arts had developed a profane vocabulary; thus, as Rushing persuasively demonstrates, the iconography borrowed heavily from sacred art.[54] More than as a simple transposition of a written story into visual images, these revolutionary frescoes must be read on a sociotextual level.[55] They belong to an emerging discourse on the didactic properties of the romance genre as expressed by Thomasin of Zirclaria.[56] Thomasin's tract, written 1215/16, is a 'quasi-official authorization . . . of courtly romance as morally defensible, even beneficial': his use of the terms *Aventiure* and *Bild* places romance alongside *exemplum*, and even profane images can be a means whereby 'illiterate laity may gain limited access to the truth.'[57]

Castel Roncolo (Schloß Runkelstein)

In the Tyrolean Alps near Bolzano (Bozen), this imposing castle stands on a rocky crag above the Talverna river. Built in the 1230s by the Vanga brothers, it was acquired between 1385 and 1388 by wealthy financiers Niklaus and Franz Vintler. Eager to enhance their social status, the Vintlers decorated their buildings with scenes from romances that were over a century old: the splendid images which 'glowed with the idealizing patina of time past' would have surrounded the Vintlers and their guests.[58] The so-called Summer House features three separate fresco cycles which are detailed enough to allow identification of their literary sources: (1) Wirnt von Gravenberg's poem *Wigalois* (from French: Guiglain, Gawain's son and the protagonist of *Le Bel Inconnu*); (2) the Tristan story according to Gottfried of Strassburg's poem; and (3) the imitative Arthurian romance, *Garel von dem Blühenden Tal* by Der Pleier (composed 1260/80). Known in Italian as *Garello di Vallefiorita*, the latter borrows the Arthurian character's name – *Garel* from French: *Gaeres, Gaheret* – and generic scenes of war and chivalry from earlier German poems and contemporary re-enactments. In addition, a 'unique expansion of the Nine Worthies topos' was painted on the loggia which connects the Summer House to the palace.[59] Here, a series of 'triads' includes three Round Table knights – Parzival, Gawain and Ywain – and three pairs of lovers, including Tristan and Iseut. Inside the palace are additional frescoes showing a tournament, a bathhouse scene, courtly pastimes, heraldry etc. In addition, the Vintlers' town house in Bolzano, called Casa Schrofenstein, contains a fresco cycle dedicated to Tristan; these poorly preserved frescoes await restoration and, if possible, better identification of pictorial-literary content.[60]

The Roncolo paintings were clearly done by several artists; newer evidence does not support early attempts to attribute them to Hans Stotzinger.[61] After the Vintler brothers died, the property changed owners, eventually coming into the possession of Emperor Maximilian I. The chivalric nostalgia of his society prompted him to restore the paintings: this time, we know names of painters involved, but their additions (such as beards and plumes) are anachronistic.[62] Centuries of neglect caused deterioration until mid-nineteenth-century medievalism awakened interest in the castle and its frescoes. Local theatricals damaged the *Tristan* cycle with 'smeared on' decorations.[63] Simple line drawings of the cycles were made by Ignaz Seelos in 1857; these preserve the narrative content of *Garel* and *Tristan* scenes that were lost when a wall collapsed in 1868.[64] Painted copies displayed in 1877 attracted popular interest, spurred scholarship and led to the eventual restoration of the castle.

Several books in English contain good introductory summaries about the Roncolo frescoes. The Loomises' descriptions, arranged thematically by characters, are still largely valid; these cover many aspects of the frescoes and their relation to literary sources. Margaret Scherer's 1945 art-historical analysis contains astute remarks as well as striking exterior photographs of the site.[65] James Rushing gives a succinct description of the castle's history, the frescoes' content and the history of German criticism; he also provides a specialist's interpretation of the figure of Ywain.[66]

Italian and German scholars have produced an array of articles and books on Castel Roncolo. Giuseppe Gerola studied coats of arms and historical personages in the tournament scene to date the fresco as begun *c*.1395 and finished prior to a siege of 1407.[67] In a concise yet thorough article, Eva Tea traces archival documents, compares the painters' styles to regional artistic production and sensitively describes the frescoes within their architectural context, noting the importance of courtly values in the residence.[68] Antonio Morassi's *Storia della pittura nella Venezia Tridentina*, an early history of the region's medieval painting, indicates courtly frescoes in other castles;[69] many of these have since received their own book-length studies. Morassi's remarks on the Roncolo narrative cycles are rather superficial, but his photographs show the frescoes in the context of their rooms: we are able to view entire walls, including doorways, windows and glimpses of the wooden ceilings. In part II, section V of a multi-part journal article, Marisa Viaggi surveys earlier criticism and assembles an updated bibliography. Although she relies overmuch on hypotheses and was clearly enamoured of the Torre dell'Aquila frescoes of the Castello del Buonconsiglio in Trent, she usefully describes the remnants of damaged hunting scenes, and points out medallions of emperors and allegorical figures of the Liberal Arts which had been ignored. Viaggi also provides a summary of dates and painters' names for the sixteenth-century restoration campaigns and transcribes certain epithets done in red chalk at that time.[70] Her detailed eyewitness descriptions of the frescoes as they appeared in 1950 may prove useful to scholars, in cases where wear and damage has ensued.

Silvia Spada Pintarelli briefly summarises earlier criticism on Castel Roncolo, unfortunately repeating notions which had been debunked long since. Her book's value lies in the full-colour photos, scattered throughout, of the 'recently restored' frescoes.[71] More reliable are books by the indefatigable Nicolò Rasmo, who directed restoration efforts in the early 1970s; his photographs feature details which had escaped earlier scholars.[72] Published post-restoration, his *L'età cavalleresca* (1980) is a precious tome dedicated not only to this castle and its painted narratives, but also to the impact of courtliness on late medieval society in northern Italy. *L'età cavalleresca* includes a good discussion of the unfamiliar *Garello* story and furnishes new evidence about its transmission: in the Alto Adige region, parchment fragments used as register bindings conserve about 5,000 lines of the 21,310-line poem.[73]

Oswald Trapp's summary of Rasmo's work appears in German translation in a volume which documents the castle's changing appearance through paintings, photographs and a floor plan showing different phases of construction or collapse.[74] Complementing Trapp is the guidebook-like *Burg Runkelstein*: focusing on the construction of the castle itself, it contains a list of important dates, geographical map, floor plans and reconstructive drawings.[75] More specialised studies in German are Haug et al., *Runkelstein: Die Wandmalereien* (cited above) and Curschmann's *Vom Wandel im bildlichen Umgang* which includes Castel Roncolo.[76] The most authoritative and comprehensive book to date is André Bechtold's edited volume *Castel Roncolo: Il maniero illustrato*, also available in German.[77] An excellent group of essays explores all aspects of the castle, including the Arthurian cycles, erotic graffiti and photographs of rooms not shown in earlier sources.

Mantua, the Sala di Pisanello

An elegant Arthurian fresco cycle in the Ducal Palace at Mantua was not visible to the Loomises. Its sensational rediscovery in the mid-1960s provided art historians with an important example of Antonio di Puccio Pisano's work, much of which has been lost. The planned frescoes had never been finished, but the extant *sinopie* and partially destroyed condition of the remnants furnish precious examples of Renaissance painting techniques. Letters written in 1480 mention a ceiling collapse in that room; in later centuries, various remodelling campaigns obscured the original walls and ceiling. Although scholars knew of the cycle's existence – the room was referred to as the Sala di Pisanello – they were not sure where in the sprawling complex it had been located or if any of it had survived.[78] Located in the *Corte Vecchia* ('Old Court'), the room had been redone in the late eighteenth century and its ceiling lowered, so that the entire cycle was obscured.[79] As a result of initial restorations directed by Giovanni Paccagnini, the Arthurian frescoes were uncovered.

With the work still in progress, Paccagnini wrote early notices of the find.[80] The book *Pisanello alla corte dei Gonzaga* was a show catalogue to the completed project. It contains a history of the family, photos of the room and plates of other Pisanello designs and works, and discusses the importance of chivalric tropes at court. Although much of the intended programme survives only in *sinopia*, two sections that were partially executed show a chivalric tournament and knights errant in a wilderness setting. French names inscribed in the paintings identify several characters as those of known Arthurian romances.[81] Bernhard Degenhart praised the unique find and related its narrative content to literary ideas and manuscripts that had once circulated at the Gonzaga court: in 1407 their library had contained more French romances than any other.[82]

Joanna Woods-Marsden's 1988 book-length study of the frescoes examines their iconography, their political context and Pisanello's style and method of working, along with a detailed formal analysis. Her book includes a bibliography and a wide range of photos of the frescoes and the room itself, some while still under restoration. Woods-Marsden rightly argues that the term 'battle' used by earlier scholars is inaccurate, due to the presence of female spectators in the scene; in discussing contemporary iconographic conventions, she shows that Pisanello's asymmetrical treatment of the mêlée is revolutionary.[83] Given later discoveries, she perhaps insists too much on Lodovico as patron: he inherited the marquisate in 1447–8, rather late in Pisanello's active career.[84] Archival documents have since come to light that prove that Pisanello remained strictly tied to the Gonzaga court from 1422 to 1442; from October 1442 until well into 1444, the year of Gianfrancesco's death, the painter was exiled from Mantua and Verona. In addition, armour in the frescoes closely resembles that produced *c*.1440, so Pisanello was probably working on them soon before his exile.[85]

Following Valeria Pizzorusso Bertolucci's discussion of the inscription of French knights' names and Roman numerals, Woods-Marsden and later, Syson and Gordon, look to the prose *Lancelot* episode of Bors's visit to King Brangoire's castle as the literary source for Pisanello's tournament scene.[86] Woods-Marsden posits that the frescoes celebrate Bors as the central hero, a notion repeated by certain other scholars. By contrast, Paccagnini, Goodman and Whitaker point to the famous three-day tournament at Louvezerp from the prose *Tristan* (expanded to include the reopening of the Grail quest) as a more likely source.[87]

We have seen how Arthurian stories could be adopted by both Church and state: the Sala di Pisanello frescoes employ the secular and sacred themes from the Arthurian legend in a single room. A smaller, partially executed section alludes to the Grail quest. This story appears as the fourth section of the Vulgate *Lancelot* as well as at the end of the expanded prose *Tristan*. E. L. Goodman notes that 'Pisanello has captured the religious message of his source'; according to local lore, in 36 CE Longinus had buried a vessel containing drops of Christ's blood in Mantua.[88] This legend and local sites associated with it are examined in *Il sangue e la coppa* by Giannino Giovannoni and Giovanni Pasetti.[89] While their comments are at times too conjectural, their photographs (three drops of blood; a flaming heart; a round, dish-like 'grail' in S. Maria del Gradaro; chalices on Renaissance coins) offer convincing evidence of the importance of the Grail cult at Mantua. Aldo Cicinelli's examination of overlooked motives in the Pisanello frescoes reveals among the religious themes a pelican piercing its breast and a crown of thorns with a second, similar pelican inside it.[90] Although he does not attempt an interpretation, these surely allude to the Blood of Christ relic so revered at Mantua: in medieval moralised bestiaries, the pelican symbolised Christ. Giovanni Pasetti suggests the turtle dove device as a link to the Grail knights.[91]

During the restoration project done in the 1990s,[92] Cicinelli was able to examine the frescoes, their characters and emblems up close. A fully armed knight with a long lance who emerges triumphant from the mêlée is covered with Gonzaga symbols: the baton of the *Capitano del Popolo* at Mantua decorates his helmet; the family's calendula floral motif decorates his arms and his horse; the horse's head has the belt-with-buckle emblem repeated throughout the ornamental *fregio* (frieze) across the top of the wall. Between the metal bosses on the horse is repeated a Gothic inscription written with abbreviations which Cicinelli expands as *Iohannes Franciscvs*.[93] Cicinelli also discerns an eagle on the knight's pennant: Gianfrancesco was prince of the Holy Roman Empire, and in 1433 or 1434 Emperor Sigismondo had renewed his concession to bear the imperial eagle. Given that Gianfrancesco died in 1444, Cicinelli proposes that the frescoes are datable to this period; new data support an earlier dating of *c*.1436.[94]

Leandro Ventura also supports Gianfrancesco rather than Ludovico as patron, but does not believe that the inscription or the mounted knight represent the former: the name is too heavily abbreviated and the figure is a 'giovane scudiere' ('young squire') loaded down with his lord's weapons.[95] Ventura's 'Noterelle pisanelliane' marshals archival documents and stylistic and technical evidence to show that Gianfrancesco was the likely patron, and that the commission and painting date to 1436–42. Inscriptions match those of a contemporary Gonzaga register done by a professional scribe; preparatory sketches for the frescoes and for medallions of Gianfrancesco feature an identical profile; the imaginary architecture in the frescoes is like that of Sant'Anastasia in Verona, done in 1438. Most convincing is the fact that the Arthurian frescoes at Mantua are filled with emblems and colours favoured by Gianfrancesco; singularly absent is the sun symbol that Ludovico used in his commissions.[96]

Finally, *Pisanello: Painter to the Renaissance Court* was produced for an exhibition at the National Gallery in London in 2001–2; its useful chapter 'The Culture of Chivalry in Italy' summarises earlier criticism and compares iconographical features of the Mantua frescoes to medallions designed by Pisanello and contemporary manuscript illuminations.

Saint Floret

The largest surviving Arthurian mural cycle in France was rediscovered in 1861: of forty original scenes, only thirteen or fourteen remain. Despite its full restoration in the late 1990s, the cycle has attracted surprisingly little critical attention.[97] The Saint Floret wall paintings are a case in point of the need for collaboration between art historians and literary specialists: lack of knowledge in either sphere can lead to faulty interpretations. The story of this castle's *aula magna* illustrates the importance of rediscovering and facilitating the accessibility of surviving evidence – whether cleaning and preserving visual images or editing manuscripts – for the larger study of Arthuriana.

The castle, located near Issoire, in the *département* of Puy-de-Dôme in the Auvergne region of France, is linked to Italy by virtue of the paintings' literary source. Despite the all too frequent critical insistence on the better-known prose *Tristan*, the narrative scenes and characters portrayed are found at the beginning of *Meliadus* by Rustichello da Pisa (see Chapter 2 in this volume). Anatole Dauvergne, the first to examine the murals, employed Italian restorers to clean them, took tracings of the figures and published an eyewitness account of a walk through the castle. Dauvergne also transcribed the 'metres' of painted textual citations which border the scenes, but his work is error-ridden. Although Dauvergne's full-sized copies were burned in a fire in 1870, lithographs of certain scenes were made later by Racinet for a history of costume; these, in turn, were traced by Gélis-Didot. In 1902 and 1909 Yperman made watercolour copies of the surviving scenes. In *Arthurian Legends in Medieval Art* (1938), Loomis and Loomis included many black-and-white close-up photographs which are still useful: for the rest of the century, their account stood as the most complete and accurate. The Loomises corrected Dauvergne's transcription errors and carefully compared the scenes to Rustichello's romance. According to the Loomises, Tristan is 'somewhat effeminately painted', which seems inappropriate to an 'oft wounded hero of a hundred desperate encounters'.[98] Yet rather than this being an artistic liberty, such representation accurately reflects Rustichello's text, which repeatedly refers to Tristan's physical beauty.[99]

Brief references to the cycle occur in histories of French painting: inaccuracies often arise from the unrestored condition of the paintings or a lack of literary knowledge. For example, one tracing of Tristan sleeping near his horse reveals details which have since been lost, but is wrongly captioned 'Chevalier blessé'.[100] Michèle Beaulieu's observations on details of costume, hair and armour allow broad dating to 1340/80, and more precisely to 1364/70.[101]

Muriel Whitaker points to 'the artist's skill in adapting his design to the architectural structure'.[102] In an extremely perceptive study, Amanda Luyster analyses the 'unusual complexity' of the images within their architectural spaces. This provides an interesting corollary to the Yvain cycle at Rodengo done over a century earlier where, lacking models for his profane subject, the painter adopted sacred iconography.

According to Luyster, sacred art had began using larger narrative cycles in imitation of profane art c.1300; later, the Saint Floret cycle follows the by-then established norms of contemporary religious wall paintings. Although Luyster insists overmuch on the prose *Tristan* as source, on artistic matters she is on a firmer footing. She praises the Saint Floret images for their amazing plasticity: not being confined to a flat surface, the designer employs the segmented spaces of the room to great advantage. The choice of narrative scene as framed within a given space provides unity to the composition. The result is a remarkably complex and sophisticated production in which space, time, wide bands of actual text and image overlap to varying degrees. This makes the narration economical, but also propels it forward. The scenes are set up almost theatrically in the huge room to represent various geographical spaces: Camelot, Mark's castle, the wilderness etc. Just as written texts are read from left to right, the entire cycle moves from left to right, as do the movement of major characters within individual scenes.[103] Luyster furnishes a schematic drawing of the room which demonstrates this admirably.

Although the Saint Floret cycle is based largely on *Meliadus*, it incorporates the famous tryst under a pine tree next to a fountain. Several critical studies refer to this scene and include photographs of it without mentioning Béroul's *Tristan*.[104] The Loomises do allude to Béroul, while pointing out that no known text 'contains any such dialog as that recorded in the . . . inscription'.[105] Here, Iseut refers to a fish which she has not seen for a very long time, and Tristan replies that he has seen it before. According to Whitaker, the fish as a warning device shows up in Dirk Potter (1411/12).[106] In addition, in the late Middle Ages, the word 'fish' colloquially alluded to the penis.[107] This metaphoric reading opens up erotic allusions which are entirely appropriate to the adulterous situation.

Views of the castle's exterior and the great room itself may now be found on various websites; Luyster's study includes excellent photos. Taken together, these recent sources indicate the scale, technical quality and lustrous colours of this phenomenal painted cycle.

Frugarolo

Another extensive Arthurian fresco cycle was found in a fortified dwelling in Frugarolo, near Alessandria, in Piedmont. Fifteen skilfully done segments illustrate the prose *Lancelot*; textual excerpts are included which identify the images. The so-called *torre*, a squat rectangular structure, and the surrounding agricultural lands had once belonged to the Knights of Malta. In 1391, the property passed to Andreino Trotti for services rendered to Spain in helping to stave off a French invasion. Trotti was an ardent supporter and confidant of Gian Galeazzo Visconti. In 1393, Visconti approved his request to reinforce the building for defensive purposes. Presumably, Trotti commissioned the wall decorations at this time; the anonymous painter is therefore known as 'The Master of Andreino Trotti'.

When the frescoes were rediscovered in 1971, their upper-floor location had been used as a dovecot since 1611. Nearly 2 metres high, the frescoes were detached for preservation, but nearly thirty years would pass before they were properly cleaned and restored. In that interval, the cycle received very little critical attention. Ten years later Franco Mazzini announced the find, but the frescoes were still unrestored and not yet well studied, so his remarks were rather superficial.[108] Alessandro Vitale Brovarone indicated the literary source of the images; Elena Rossetti Brezzi summarised hypotheses and findings to date.[109] The frescoes were displayed at a 1999 exhibition; for this occasion, the comprehensive and heavily illustrated *Le Stanze di Artù: Gli affreschi di Frugarolo* was prepared under the direction of Enrico Castelnuovo. This catalogue contains a collection of essays on the geographical location, the building's architecture, Trotti family history and broader discussions of the importance of chivalry in late medieval culture. Maria Luisa Meneghetti's excellent study describes the content of the scenes, transcribes the textual excerpts which were painted in the frescoes, identifies the citations by using the *Lancelot* critical edition and compares this cycle to extant Arthurian wall paintings in other buildings.[110] *Le Stanze di Artù* contains colour plates of all the restored frescoes. Apparently, they had been photographed but not studied *in situ* before their hasty removal; Giorgio Rolando Perino furnishes schematic drawings of how the cycle must have appeared in its original space.[111]

Pordenone, Palazzo Ricchieri

This mid-fourteenth century palace contains another Arthurian fresco cycle that had been covered with plaster and was unknown to the Loomises. Two different cycles – one romance, one epic – located on different floors came to light during the course of restorations undertaken in 1965–9. (The building had been bequeathed to the Comune di Pordenone by the last surviving descendant of the noble Ricchieri family.) The site, which opened to the public in 2005, houses the Civic Museum of Pordenone. Enrica Cozzi notes that, although the discovery created a furore among scholars, early studies were superficial and inaccurate owing to lack of knowledge concerning both medieval art history and literary texts which circulated in Friuli and the Veneto; hypotheses on dating and the content of the frescoes were haphazardly proposed. Cozzi herself was the first to indicate the connections to chivalric subject matter, based on an awareness of manuscripts decorated in the International Gothic style.[112] Restoration efforts and Aulo Donadello's 1994 edition of the *Tristano Veneto* allowed better identification of the frescoes.[113] The manuscript Donadello edited proves by its language that a version of the French prose *Tristan* was known specifically in north-eastern Italy and that it circulated there in written form.

In *Tristano e Isotta in Palazzo Ricchieri a Pordenone*, a slim volume rich with colour plates and information, Cozzi and other contributors briefly describe the family's history, architecture of the building, and details of the restoration process

– and, for the first time, provide an analysis of the images. Located in one room on the *primo piano*, this cycle portrays episodes from the Tristan and Iseut story. We cannot ascertain the original dimensions of the room, but surviving portions suggest that it would have contained numerous scenes from the romance. The two largest remnants show that the cycle was meant to be read from right to left. The fresco painter used space economically, arranging more than one scene within each bordered wall segment. Portions still legible relate to passages from the *Tris. Ven.*, conveniently cited in Cozzi's study.[114] The centre of the longest wall shows a much-damaged scene with pavilions and pennants. Next, Iseut and another woman on a castle watch two rival knights jousting below: Tristan – from 'Leonis' – is recognisable by the lion on his shield, his traditional emblem. After this, we see Tristan and Iseut aboard ship – clearly enamoured of one another – while an elderly man (probably Governal) looks on benignly. In the same section, a sword battle among foot soldiers takes place on the Distant Isles ruled by the giant (plates I–IX). The recovery of a fresco cycle dedicated to Tristan nicely complements the evidence of other medieval wall paintings which show the adventures of Lancelot, Meliadus, Yvain and other knightly heroes. The Palazzo Ricchieri cycle offers additional evidence of the prose *Tristan*'s cultural importance in Italy, as has been discussed elsewhere in this volume.

La Manta

King Arthur himself features in an exquisite fresco cycle in the castle of La Manta, near Saluzzo, in Piedmont. There, a rectangular baronial hall was decorated with an elaborate programme: along one wall, a demographically varied group of 'pilgrims' make their way to the regenerative Fountain of Youth; on the opposite wall is a formally structured series of eighteen exemplary men and women.[115] On an end wall, a massive fireplace bears the family's coat of arms and motto, 'Leit'. In the hands of the same family until 1983, the room had never undergone remodelling nor suffered destruction. In an early listing of national monuments to be preserved, C. F. Biscarra alerted authorities to its uniqueness.[116] Years later, Paolo D'Ancona published the first substantive study; he summarises the plot of Tommaso III, Marquis of Saluzzo's romance *Le Chevalier Errant* (begun 1394), and surveys other artistic representations of the Nine Worthies, including the 'triads' at Castel Roncolo (above).[117] In the Fountain of Youth fresco, D'Ancona points out the second artist's clumsy handling of naked humans and poorly proportioned horses. His appendix includes transcriptions of the French verse epigrams painted beneath the Worthies, as well as textual variants from the two extant manuscripts of Tommaso's romance.

The comparison of the frescoes to actual manuscript books is a recurrent strain of La Manta criticism; Marco Piccat collates the epigrams with the surviving manuscripts and concludes that the artist did not directly consult either of them. Errors (especially in the 'Heroines' series), omissions and simplifications show that the painted legends were copied from a source late in the textual tradition.[118] Anna Maria Finoli studies

Tommaso's literary representation of the heroes in *Le Chevalier Errant*, alluding to the frescoes only briefly; she concludes that although Tommaso was working within the literary norms of the Nine Worthies, he was not concerned with the 'culto degli eroi e neppure di un ideale estetico di vita "bella"' ('cult of heroes, nor even an ideal courtly aesthetic').[119] Instead, Tommaso's portrayal includes a moralistic – even pessimistic – meditation on death and the transitory nature of Fame. Maria Luisa Meneghetti found another manuscript connection to the Manta frescoes: during a Paris sojourn in 1403–5, Tommaso had purchased several books, one of which contained a unique redaction of the *Roman de Fauvel* (BnF, MS fr. 146).[120] In one episode, Fauvel visits the Fountain of Youth.

In a survey of late Gothic art in the region, Noemi Gabrielli provided information about the castle's history; their family tree demonstrates the high political and social position which the Saluzzese dukes enjoyed.[121] Tommaso's grandfather had married a Visconti daughter; his own daughter, Ricciarda, married Niccolò d'Este, Duke of Ferrara. Tommaso's legitimate son, Ludovico, served for long periods of time as lieutenant under the Dukes of Savoy. Gabrielli believed that the frescoed figure of Hector was a portrait of Valerano, Tommaso's natural son: his figure begins the series and stands adjacent to his father, who is shown in the guise of Alexander the Great.[122] The long nose was apparently a physical trait typical of the Saluzzesi. It seems likely that the Penthesilea figure represents Valerano's wife, Clemenzia dei Ricci of Provana: she holds the symbol of the French Order of the Broom-cod, which had been conferred upon Valerano in Paris in 1411. The garments of both Hector and Penthesilea bear the family motto 'Leit'.[123] Continuing the notion that these figures were historical portraits, Theuca is believed to represent Tommaso's widow, Margherita de Roussy (d. 1419). Daniel Arasse considers the dynastic implications of the iconography, noting several singular things about Hector: his placement differs from typical Nine Worthies ordering; he is the only hero who does not touch a weapon; his left hand is placed against a tree, signifying familial ties; and his right hand is raised in a gesture of investiture as he accepts power from his father, adjacent.

Although various attributions have been proposed, the painter's identity remains elusive.[124] Giovanni Romano sensibly opts for calling the painter of the Worthies 'Il Maestro della Manta'.[125] Restoration work revealed differences in techniques and different amounts executed in a single day; these discoveries support D'Ancona's earlier remarks on stylistic differences and lead to the conclusion that the walls were done by different painters.[126] Dating remains conjectural as well: most scholars assume that the Worthies fresco was commissioned by Valerano after he inherited the property upon his father's death in 1416. Riccardo Passoni has studied the fashionable clothing of the heroes and heroines, concluding that those historical styles would not have lasted beyond 1415–20.[127]

Wooden Ceiling Panels

Scattered among the various sources on La Manta are several photographs that show the great hall in its entirety. In addition to the frescoes, another striking element of the well-preserved room is its wooden ceiling.[128] Every available space on such ceilings was decorated: corbels, cross beams and the vast expanses between were covered with small, painted wooden panels. Although many such ceilings have been lost owing to termites, water damage, intentional remodelling or natural and man-made disasters, enough remain – especially across northern Italy – that we can imagine what the late medieval noble residence must have looked like. From extant examples, we know that all three 'Matters' – the Matter of Rome, the Matter of France and the Matter of Britain – furnished visual images in this type of decoration.[129] Although these are often generic chivalric or courtly scenes for which an exact source cannot be pinpointed, many correspond to the story of Tristan. The Pordenone panels are not labelled as neatly as some of the figures discussed above, but a 'T' on the shield of one knight and on a ship's flag surely alludes to Tristan.[130] One panel shows a knight fighting a dragon;[131] without having seen the image in person, I wonder if this is yet another representation of Gottfried's Tristan.

This category of applied arts in medieval Italy has been neglected by art historians, a void which Enrica Cozzi has attempted to fill. Her 1996 essay 'Tavolette da soffitto tardogotiche di soggetto cavalleresco a Pordenone' is a fine introduction to the subject. The small panels – also referred to as *cantinelle* or *pettenelle* – were painted in tempera mostly using three colours: ochre, red and brown.[132] The average size of panels from one Friuli ceiling is 36 x 18 cm. By the second half of the fifteenth century, *tavolette* production had become a sort of industry; we even know the names of certain artisans who specialised in this genre: the Floriano family (fl. 1492–1506), and their son Giovanni, nicknamed 'delle cantinelle' (1486–1540).[133]

Cozzi has studied the ceilings that survive from three different residences in Friuli: the Palazzo Ricchieri at Pordenone; a second, private dwelling nearby, whose panels were detached and reassembled unsystematically into a large *tableau*; and a third, in the former Casa Vanni degli Onesti, in Udine.[134] These ceilings came to the notice of scholars after 1971, so they were unknown to the Loomises. Depending on the artist and, no doubt, on the size of the commission, the style of these images ranges from crude, quickly produced 'industrial grade' to detailed, high-quality ones. Although simpler in design and execution, the scalloped style of plate armour and the massive crest on a knight's helmet in the Udine example resemble those found in Pisanello's frescoes at Mantua, datable to the mid-fifteenth century.[135] Cozzi underscores the need for more editions and facsimiles of manuscripts to enable art historians to better identify unlabelled figures and stories, a persistent problem which predates the Loomises.[136]

Palermo, Palazzo Chiaramonte 'Lo Steri'

Painted wooden ceilings were not unique to northern Italy. An Arabic-style ceiling was commissioned by Manfredi III of the Chiaramonte (or Chiaromonte) family in 1377 and completed on 1 July 1380, as an inscription shows precisely. The three artists' names also appear in Sicilian dialect spellings, shown here in their Tuscanised forms: Simone da Corleone, Cecco di Naro and Maestro Pellegrino d'Arena of Palermo.[137] Again, in this ceiling the colours are 'predominantly red, ochre, brown and black'.[138] In 1438 carpenters repaired a damaged section, and the Spanish miniaturist Juan de Valladolid was hired to do the necessary touch-ups; additional repairs were done 1495–1509, under the influence of humanism.[139]

When Manfredi III commissioned the decoration, his family was at the height of its fortunes; defeated in a power struggle with the Aragonese, his successor, Andrea, was beheaded in front of the palace in 1392. The palace and the space in front of it would long be connected with law enforcement, imprisonment and execution. It became the seat of the Spanish viceroys, was the official seat of the Bourbon kings and from 1601–1782 housed the tribunal of the Inquisition. After that, the palace was variously used as a refuge for the poor, or as offices for the lottery, the court of appeals, and customs.

Although the medieval subject matter of the images was no longer appreciated, Agostino Inveges (1651) and others after him mined the baronial *stemmi* – a veritable heraldic map of Sicily – for proof of noble ancestry. In the 1750s, Francesco Maria Emanuele, Marquis of Villabianca, studied the various painted captions that identify the stories. With ninteenth-century Romanticism, the applied arts movement and a new appreciation of Arabic culture among British, French and German scholars, the ceiling attracted foreigners to study it. Jules Gailhabaud examined Lo Steri in 1869–70 and did black-and-white drawings *in situ*. By then the room had been crudely divided by a brick wall across the middle, and the ceiling gravely damaged by rain and bad repairs. At some point, a false ceiling had been installed to hide the original wooden beams. Not until 1898–9 did Lo Steri come under the restorative care of Giuseppe Patricolo, regional director for the conservation of monuments. Giuseppe Alfano published a series of watercolour reproductions of the ceiling's details in a Milanese decorative arts review; he brought to light the names of two of the original painters.[140] Gioacchino Di Marzo (1899) praised the artistic and historical value of the ceiling. Although some of his assertions have since been disproven, three of his conclusions are still valid: the ceiling's importance for art history; the presence of the 'Islamic matrix' in Palermo for 250 years; and the cycle's iconographical richness.[141]

The 1932 study by art historian Ettore Gabrici and Romance philologist Ezio Levi remains the most thorough and, despite some errors, was still unsurpassed in the 1970s.[142] Gabrici consulted the preceding published studies, and used archival documentation and the titles in the ceiling itself along with the architecture of the building to ground his interpretation. Levi brought a new awareness of the content, adjudging it rightly according to various aspects of medieval culture and discarding the misleading notions of the preceding century. He offered proof of the literary culture of Manfredi III's day, a line of thinking supported by Toesca and Henri Bresc. Toesca related the format of the ceiling to medieval manuscript illumination, and Bresc's work on Sicilian book ownership, as evidenced by inventories, demonstrated the penetration of Arthurian romances into Sicily.[143]

Among the images are courtly scenes which have been proposed as *Lancillotto e Ginevra*.[144] Unlike many of the stories represented, these are not identified with captions. More convincing is the evidence for Tristan and Iseut panels. Gabrici and Levi analyse these with detailed reference to various known literary sources: Arthurian elements in the designs correspond variously to episodes from Thomas, Béroul, the French prose *Tristan*, the *Folies Tristan* and the *Tristano Riccardiano*. Although the segments are not always adjacent or even in the correct order (probably due to repairs), the recurrent figures of Iseut, Tristan, his squire Perinis, the faithful dog Husdent and even the horses are painted with the same armour, hairstyles, clothing or colours, so the panels can be linked to the same general story.[145] A device used on a ship's banner in one Palermitan ceiling panel matches Tristan's arms in the London portion of the Guicciardini '*coperta*' (see below), which was also produced in Sicily; this indicates that a particular redaction of a Tristan text circulated on the island.[146]

Decorative Objects

Textiles

A famous embroidered example of the Tristan and Iseut story exists in two pieces: one in the Bargello Museum in Florence and the other in London. The Guicciardini wall hanging was first studied in the nineteenth century by Pio Rajna, the noted philologist and scholar of chivalric literature. Rajna incorrectly thought that the separated panels were bed coverings – '*coperte*', a term which has been repeated *ad infinitum*.[147] We now know more about medieval domestic life, and art historians have properly identified them as part of a single wall hanging that was produced for a Guicciardini wedding in 1395. Since the captions within the panels are in Sicilian dialect, they were probably manufactured in Sicily or by Sicilian artisans. In 1922, Morelli studied and photographed the portion which is now in the Bargello while it was still in a Guicciardini villa near Prato.[148] The '*coperta*' did not escape the notice of the Loomises: they included helpful summaries of each segment, relating the contents to the only two published Italian Tristan texts then available in critical editions: the *Tristano Riccardiano* and the *Tavola Ritonda*.

We find brief, though sometimes inaccurate, references to this wall hanging in histories of embroidery or textiles.[149] Averil Colby provides transcriptions with translation of the inscriptions and furnishes unique sketches that show the stitch patterns.[150] Norbert Ott includes the 'coperta' in his iconographic surveys on the Tristan legend; Arthurian art surveys by Whitaker and Walworth also refer to it.[151] The most comprehensive book on this topic was produced as a result of the restoration project of the Bargello portion; scientific in approach, with essays in Italian and extensive colour photographs, La 'coperta' Guicciardini: Il restauro delle imprese di Tristano (2010) is the definitive study to date. Photographs show the reverse of the hanging; a chart indicates different thread colours used; and individual panels are shown in close-up, under different types of lighting, radiographic analysis and even microscopically to distinguish linen threads from cotton.

Ivory Objects

Ivory carvings were produced all over Europe for centuries, and production centres have been identified in Milan, Venice, central Italy, Salerno and the Amalfi coast. North African ivory was imported into Italy through its ports.[152] Intricately decorated luxury objects included small chests (cofanetti), mirror covers, combs, game boards and saddles. By the thirteenth and fourteenth centuries, the iconography of many courtly subjects was becoming standardised. Koechlin catalogued some 1,300 ivory objects from the Gothic period. He and other scholars nationalistically tended to privilege the flourishing industry of fourteenth-century Paris and inaccurately ascribed objects of lesser quality to countries outside France.[153] Later studies identified competing workshops which existed in Venice after 1350 and on into the sixteenth century.[154] Foremost among these was the Embriachi (or Ubriachi), who had connections by marriage to a branch of the Davanzati from Florence. Inventories reveal that such pieces belonged not only to princely owners, but to wealthy entrepreneurs.[155]

Among profane subjects, one finds scenes derived from Arthurian romances. Richard H. Randall, Jr's fine overview 'Popular Romances Carved in Ivory' includes a few Italian examples.[156] Other courtly motifs are more generic: a rendezvous in a garden or by a fountain; a young lover handing his heart to his lady; a lover wearing a garland of flowers, or a garland alone; couples meeting, riding, hunting with falcons, playing chess or taking leave of one another. Zastrow's Museo d'arti applicate: gli avori includes various northern Italian examples, but does not attempt to identify the sources for their subjects. The literary and iconographic content of some of these demands more study: for example, a couple facing each other with a pine tree in between surely suggests the famous scene from Béroul.[157] Several ivories feature attractive ladies and couples accompanied by sexual symbols: a rabbit, a pair of affectionate oxen and a pair of rabbits (?) copulating.[158]

Ivory carvings present challenges for the scholar: it is difficult to determine precisely dates, workshops or even areas of production.[159] The often anonymous craftsmen travelled and were influenced by other regional styles.[160] Models could be imitated for decades. To judge by the penetration of French language, courtly literature, manuscript illumination, clothing and customs into Italy, it seems likely that wealthy Italians of the fourteenth and fifteenth centuries would have sought to acquire ivory objects. *Cofanetti* made of ivory or bone occur in medieval inventories from Friuli.[161] Charlotte of Savoy and Valentina (Sforza) of Milan owned ivory pieces;[162] Claudia de' Medici owned a *cofanetto* made by the Embriachi;[163] the Este and Gonzaga employed their own carvers.[164]

Although much about decorative objects is ephemeral, a few tantalising facts suggest that at least some of the objects owned by Italians represented Arthurian scenes. A Treviso inventory dated 1335 of possessions owned by a rich businessman, Oliviero Forzetta, refers to an ivory chess board acquired in Venice with – apparently – a King Arthur piece.[165] The enamelled foot of a golden chandelier once owned by the Savoy also showed the famous episode from Béroul: Tristan and Iseut by the fountain, with King Mark hiding in a tree above.[166] Two other pieces in the Vatican and in Turin – the latter probably from the Savoy – portray the same scene.[167] A mirror cover preserved in Bologna shows Gauvain on the Perilous Bed, from Chrétien's *Perceval*.[168] Romance scenes on a small composite chest in the Trivulziano at Milan include Lancelot on the Sword Bridge and possibly the story of Galahad.[169] Koechlin's 1924 catalogue lists several other ivory pieces with courtly motifs which were extant in Italian collections in Naples, Florence's 'Musée National' (now the Bargello), Perugia, Venice, Bologna, the Vatican and the former Stroganoff collection in Rome.[170] A remarkable ivory scene of a tournament is still in Ravenna.[171]

Other Decorative Objects

Despite the ubiquitous ceramic production throughout Italy, one seeks in vain anything resembling the narrative cycle of the paving tiles found at Chertsey.[172] Among fragments and extant majolica, Italian-made pieces are less narrative in nature: earlier designs tended to be floral, geometric or armorial. A noteworthy exception is a Tuscan plate of *c.*1480 which shows a lady on horseback holding a falcon.[173] The rise of Latin humanism in the mid-fifteenth century was accompanied by an iconographic shift away from French romances and towards classical antiquity.[174] One observes the same stylistic shift in *cassoni* (wedding chests) and in the ivory objects from the Embriachi workshop: now Paris and Helen appear alongside Tristan and Iseut among pairs of lovers.[175] Niccolò degli Agostino's paraphrases of Ovid's *Metamorphoses* (1498), woodcuts, engravings and even Michelangelo's Sistine Chapel figures served as models for Urbino's ceramics painters. During the Counter-Reformation, biblical subjects become more common than chivalric and secular ones.[176]

Conclusion

The rich record of Arthurian art in Italy includes a substantial corpus of manuscript illustrations to which I cannot do justice here: that would be a book in itself. I do, however, offer a select bibliography that pertains to images in Italian manuscripts. The field of Italian Arthurian study needs an interlinguistic as well as international approach, with scholars collaborating across disciplinary and linguistic boundaries. By mapping the various areas of Italian Arthurian-themed art, as well as the major scholarship on it, I hope to promote just such collaborative projects in the future.

Notes

[1] R. S. Loomis, *Arthurian Legends in Medieval Art* (London, 1938). Part II was done in collaboration with L. H. Loomis.

[2] A. Stones, in W. Van Hoecke et al. (eds), *Arturus Rex: Acta Conventus Lovaniensis 1987*, 2 vols (1991), II, pp. 21–54, on p. 22.

[3] M. Whitaker, *The Legends of King Arthur in Art* (Cambridge, 1990).

[4] Loomis and Loomis, *Arthurian Legends*, pp. 22 and 23, respectively.

[5] M. Whitaker, 'Early Arthurian Art', in N. J. Lacy (ed.), *A History of Arthurian Scholarship* (Cambridge, 2006), p. 202. See 'Arthurian Cycle Manuscripts Copied, Decorated or Owned by Italians' in *Il Tristano panciatichiano*, ed. and trans. G. Allaire (Cambridge, 2002), pp. 13–25. To this, I must add Florence, BNCF, Fondo nazionale II.I.17 (former Magl. Cl. VI, no. 11), a *Tavola Ritonda* that once belonged to the Medici Library; and New York, Columbia University, Rare Book and Manuscript Library, Western MS 24, a fourteenth-century *La Mort le roi Artu* copied in Italy, which was a bequest of Dr Loomis himself. As this volume was in preparation, an unedited fourteenth-century manuscript, referred to as *Lancellotto del Lago* (an Italian version of the prose *Lancelot*) was announced by Luca Cadioli and Lino Leonardi: MS. 1 of the Biblioteca della Fondazione Ezio Franceschini in Florence. Blank spaces were left for intended illuminations which were never executed. See the Introduction to this volume.

[6] K. Busby et al. (eds), *Les Manuscrits de Chrétien de Troyes*, 2 vols (Amsterdam, 1993).

[7] For example, the lavishly illuminated BNCF, Pal. MS 556 is now accessible online: *www.bncf.firenze.sbn.it/Bib_digitale/Manoscritti/Pal_556*.

[8] N. H. Ott, 'Katalog der Tristan-Bildzeugnisse: Zusammengestellt', in H. Frühmorgen-Voss (ed.), *Text und Illustration im Mittelalter: Aufsätze zu den Wechselbeziehungen zwischen Literatur und bildender Kunst* (Munich, 1975).

[9] J. Walworth, 'Tristan in Medieval Art', in J. Tasker Grimbert (ed.), *Tristan and Iseut: A Casebook* (New York, 1995; 2002), pp. 274–5, 292, and 294, and plates 7, 8, 17.

[10] Ott, 'Tristano e Isotta nell'iconografia medievale', in M. Dallapiazza (ed.), *Tristano e Isotta. La fortuna di un mito europeo* (Trieste, 2003), pp. 208–24, on pp. 215 and 218, respectively.

[11] N. J. Lacy and G. Ashe (eds), *The Arthurian Handbook*, with D. N. Mancoff, 2nd edn (New York, 1997), pp. 197–270.

[12] Lacy and Ashe (eds), *Arthurian Handbook*, pp. 199, 201, 205–6, 210–11, 213–14.

[13] Whitaker, 'Early Arthurian Art', pp. 202, 205–10.

[14] J. Fox-Friedman, 'King Arthur in Art', in H. Fulton (ed.), *Companion to Arthurian Literature* (Chichester and Malden, MA, 2009), pp. 381–99.

[15] Fox-Friedman, 'King Arthur in Art', pp. 383–4.

[16] Whitaker, *Legends*, pp. 86–8.

[17] Loomis and Loomis, *Arthurian Legends*, p. 34.

[18] R. S. Loomis, 'The Modena Sculpture and Arthurian Romance', *StM*, n.s. 9 (1926), 1–17, on 11.

[19] Loomis, 'The Modena Sculpture', 12; see also Loomis and Loomis, *Arthurian Legends*, p. 34.

[20] J. Stiennon and R. Lejeune, 'La légende arthurienne dans la sculpture de la cathédrale de Modène', *Cahiers de Civilisation Médiévale*, 6 (1963), 281–96, on 286.

226   GLORIA ALLAIRE

²¹ M. Armandi Barbolini (ed.), *Lanfranco e Wiligelmo: Il Duomo di Modena* (Modena, 1985); for Arthur, see pp. 390–3, 454, 499, 500. Concerning the Arthurian figures on the archivolt, see S. Piconi, 'Restauri nel Duomo di Modena: la Porta della Pescheria e il bassorilievo di Agostino di Duccio', in Enrico Castelnuovo (ed.), *Wiligelmo e Lanfranco nell'Europa romanica: Atti del Convegno . . . 24–27 ottobre 1985* (Modena, 1989), pp. 189–96. Lanfranco was the architect and Wiligelmo the craftsman who sculpted the figures.

²² M. Chiellini Nari, 'Le favole, i simboli, il "ciclo di Artù": il fronte istoriato nella "Porta della Pescheria"', in C. Settis Frugoni et al. (eds), *La Porta della Pescheria nel Duomo di Modena* (Modena, 1991), pp. 32–59.

²³ Chiellini Nari, 'Le favole', p. 47.

²⁴ Fox-Friedman, 'Messianic Visions: Modena Cathedral and the Crusades', *Res: Anthropology and Aesthetics*, 25 (1994), 77–95.

²⁵ Fox-Friedman, 'Messianic Visions', pp. 81, 84, 95.

²⁶ G. Lorenzoni and G. Valenzano, *Il duomo di Modena e la basilica di San Zeno* (Verona, 2000), p. 88.

²⁷ Lorenzoni and Valenzano, *Il duomo di Modena*, p. 152, plate 156.

²⁸ Settis Frugoni, 'Per una lettura del mosaico pavimentale della cattedrale di Otranto', *Bullettino dell'Istituto storico italiano per il Medio Evo e Archivio muratoriano*, 80 (1968), 213–56, and 'Il mosaico di Otranto: modelli culturali e scelte iconografiche', *Bullettino dell'Istituto storico italiano per il Medio Evo e Archivio muratoriano*, 82 (1970), 243–70. The Church's struggle against the influence of romance produced different responses. On this interaction in France, see F. Gingras, 'Le bon usage du roman: cohabitation de récits profanes et de textes sacrés dans trois recueils vernaculaires de la fin du XIIIe siècle', in D. Kullmann (ed.), *The Church and Vernacular Literature* (Toronto, 2009), pp. 137–56.

²⁹ C. A. Willemsen surveys the hypotheses in *L'enigma di Otranto: Il mosaico pavimentale del pres-bitero Pantaleone nella Cattedrale*, Italian trans. Raffaele Disanto (Galatina, 1980), p. 164. W. Haug, *Das Mosaik von Otranto: Darstellung, Deutung und Bilddokumentation* (Wiesbaden, 1977), pp. 31–9.

³⁰ Stiennon and Lejeune, 'La légende arthurienne', 291, plate 23; Settis Frugoni, 'Per una lettura', 238–9.

³¹ Loomis and Loomis, *Arthurian Legends*, p. 36.

³² Settis Frugoni, 'Per una lettura', fig. 12; Willemsen, *L'enigma di Otranto*, p. 53, fig. 33, plate XXVIII.

³³ A. Schulte, 'Mosaik von Otranto und ein Vergleich mit dem Mosaik von Teurnia', in G. A. Küppers-Sonnenberg et al. (eds), *Flecht- und Knotenornamentik: Mosaiken (Teurnia und Otranto). Beiträge zur Symboldeutung* (Bonn, 1972), pp. 155–227.

³⁴ M. Wierschin, 'Artus und Alexander im Mosaik der Kathedrale von Otranto', *Colloquia Germanica*, 13 (1980), 1–34.

³⁵ Settis Frugoni, 'Per una lettura', pp. 218, 244, 247, and 'Il mosaico di Otranto', p. 257.

³⁶ Willemsen, *Das Rätsel von Otranto: das Fussbodenmosaik in der Kathedrale. Eine Bestands-aufnahme*, trans. Raymund Kottje (Sigmaringen, 1992).

³⁷ G. Gianfreda, *Il mosaico di Otranto: Biblioteca medioevale in immagini* (Lecce, 1998); for Arthur, see pp. 63–5.

³⁸ G. Barba, *L'opera ingenua: una nuova lettura del mosaico pavimentale della cattedrale di Otranto* (Perugia, 2005); and C. Saporetti, *Mosaico: Una storia inventata per un'interpretazione vera del capola-voro pavimentale di Otranto* (Rome, 2006).

³⁹ J. Garber, *Die romanischen Wandgemälde Tirols* (Vienna, 1928), pp. 109–10.

⁴⁰ N. Rasmo, *Pitture murali in Alto Adige* (Bolzano, 1973).

⁴¹ N. Rasmo, *L'età cavalleresca in Val d'Adige* (Milan, 1980), pp. 40–53.

⁴² Rasmo, *L'età cavalleresca*, p. 42; H. Mackowitz, 'Meister Hugo und die romanischen Wandmalereien im Raume Brixen', in H. Fillitz and M. Pippal (eds), *Akten des XXV. Internationalen Kongresses für Kunstgeschichte* (Vienna, 1985), pp. 47–52; S. Gattei et al. (eds), *Trentino Alto Adige* (Venice, 1979), p. 104.

[43] A. M. Birlauf-Bonnet, 'Überlegungen zur Brixener Malerei in den ersten Jahrzehnten des 13. Jahrhunderts', *Wiener Jahrbuch für Kunstgeschichte*, 37 (1984), 23–39, 187–98; and A. Rainer, 'Die Frauenkirche im Brixner Kreuzgang', *Der Schlern*, 62 (1988), 415–28.

[44] P. and D. Diemer, '"Qui pingit florem non pingit floris odorem": Die Illustrationen der Carmina Burana (Clm 4660)', *Jahrbuch des Zentralinstituts für Kunstgeschichte*, 3 (1987), 43–75, on 55–8; Birlauf-Bonnet, 'Überlegungen zur Brixener Malerei', 23–39, on 38; J. A. Rushing, Jr, 'Adventure and Iconography: Ywain Picture Cycles and the Literalization of Vernacular Narrative', *The Arthurian Yearbook*, 1 (1991), 91–106, on 102 n. 7.

[45] M. Curschmann, '*Der aventiure bilde nemen*: The Intellectual and Social Environment of the Iwein Murals at Rodenegg Castle', in M. H. Jones and R. Wisbey (eds), *Chrétien de Troyes and the German Middle Ages: Papers from an International Symposium* (Cambridge, 1993), pp. 219–27, on pp. 220–1.

[46] P. Bassetti Carlini, 'Castel Rodengo in val Pusteria', in S. Spada Pintarelli (ed.), *Affreschi in Alto Adige* (Venice, 1997), pp. 100–9.

[47] Ott, 'Katalog der Tristan-Bildzeugnisse'; V. Schupp, 'Die Ywain-Erzählung von Schloß Rodenegg', in E. Kühebacher (ed.), *Literatur und bildende Kunst im Tiroler Mittelalter: Die Iwein-Fresken von Rodenegg und andere Zeugnisse der Wechselwirkung von Literatur und bildender Kunst* (Innsbruck, 1982); V. Schupp and H. Szklenar (eds), *Ywain aus Schloß Rodenegg: Eine Bildergeschichte nach dem 'Iwein' Hartmanns von Aue* (Sigmaringen, 1996); and A. Deighton, 'Visual Representations of the Tristan Legend and Their Written Sources: A Re-Evaluation', *Tristania*, 20 (2000), 59–92.

[48] V. Schupp, 'Kritische Anmerkungen zur Rezeption des deutschen Artusromans anhand von Hartmanns "Iwein": Theorie–Text–Bildmaterial', *Frühmittelalterliche Studien*, 9 (1975), 405–42; Ott and W. Walliczek, 'Bildprogramm und Textstruktur: Anmerkungen zu den "Iwein"–Zyklen auf Rodeneck und in Schmalkalden', in C. Cormeau (ed.), *Deutsche Literatur im Mittelalter: Kontakte und Perspektiven, Hugo Kuhn zum Gedenken* (Stuttgart, 1979), pp. 473–500; J. A. Rushing, 'Adventure and Iconography', and *Images of Adventure: Ywain in the Visual Arts* (Philadelphia, 1995).

[49] A. M. Birlauf-Bonnet, *Rodenegg und Schmalkalden: Untersuchungen zur Illustration einer ritterlich-höfischen Erzählung und zur Entstehung profaner Epenillustration in den ersten Jahrzehnten des 13. Jahrhunderts* (Munich, 1986).

[50] Ott, 'Geglückte Minne-Aventiure: Zur Szenenauswahl literarischer Bildzeugnisse im Mittelalter. Die Beispiele des Rodenecker *Iwein*, des Runkelsteiner *Tristan*, des Braunschweiger *Gawan*- und des Frankfurter *Wilhelm-von-Orlens*-Teppichs', *Jahrbuch der Oswald von Wolkenstein Gesellschaft*, 2 (1982–3), 1–32.

[51] A. M. Rasmussen, 'Medieval German Romance', in R. L. Krueger (ed.), *The Cambridge Companion to Medieval Romance* (Cambridge, 2000), pp. 183–202, on p. 190.

[52] Rushing, 'Adventure and Iconography', 103 n. 13.

[53] Curschmann, '*Der aventiure bilde nemen*' and *Vom Wandel im bildlichen Umgang mit literarischen Gegenständen* (Freiburg, 1997).

[54] Rushing, 'Adventure and Iconography' and *Images of Adventure*.

[55] Curschmann, '*Der aventiure bilde nemen*'.

[56] Rushing, *Images of Adventure*, pp. 7–9.

[57] Curschmann, '*Der aventiure bilde nemen*', pp. 225–6.

[58] Rasmussen, 'Medieval German Romance', p. 197.

[59] Rushing, *Images of Adventure*, p. 245. For analogous examples of the Nine Worthies, see section on La Manta (this essay, below) and M. Viaggi, 'La pittura profana della Venezia tridentina nel sec. XIV e XV, Parte II, V: Le pitture profane a Castel Roncolo', *Studi Trentini di Scienze Storiche*, 29 (1950), 326–48, on 340–1.

[60] H. Obermair and H. Stampfer, 'Edilizia e cultura abitativa nella Bolzano tardomedievale', in A. Bechtold (ed.), *Castel Roncolo: Il maniero illustrato* (Bolzano, 2000), pp. 397–409; and Dematté and Lucía Megías, 'Immagini di dame e cavalieri: Affresche cavallereschi ed arturiani in Trentino Alto Adige', in Dematté (ed.), *Il mondo cavalleresco tra imagine e testo* (Trent, 2010), pp. 13–43, on p. 23 n. 15.

[61] The Tristan cycle is done in an elegant greyish-green *grisaille* with white highlights and touches of red. This style resembles that of the Master of Ambrass (see the recent *Wiener Musterbuch* facsimile published by Codices Illustres). For similar stylistic examples, datable to the late fourteenth or early fifteenth centuries, see a Louvre drawing reproduced in E. Castelnuovo and F. De Gramatica (eds), *Il Gotico nelle Alpi, 1350–1450* (Trent, 2002), p. 238; and manuscript illuminations in G. Canova Mariani, *La miniatura a Padova dal Medioevo al Settecento* (Savignano sul Panaro [Modena], 1999), pp. 152, 153, 160. Theodore Mommsen hypothesised that a lost fresco cycle of Illustrious Men in the Carrara palace at Padua may have been *grisaille* (Canova Mariani, *La miniatura a Padova*, p. 518.)

[62] Loomis and Loomis, *Arthurian Legends*, p. 49.

[63] Ibid.

[64] The Seelos drawings are reproduced in Walter Haug et al. (eds), *Runkelstein: Die Wandmalereien des Sommerhauses* (Wiesbaden, 1982).

[65] M. Scherer, *About the Round Table*, pp. 10–13, 20–1, 40–1.

[66] Rushing, *Images of Adventure*, pp. 19, 245–56.

[67] G. Gerola, 'Per la datazione degli affreschi di Castel Roncolo (Runkelstein)', *Atti del Reale Istituto Veneto di Scienze, Lettere, ed Arti*, 82 (1922–3), 511–21.

[68] E. Tea, 'Gli affreschi di Castel Roncolo presso Bolzano', *Archivio per l'Alto Adige*, 17 (1922), 67–86.

[69] A. Morassi, *Storia della pittura nella Venezia tridentina: Dalle origini alle fine del Quattrocento* (Rome, 1934), pp. 295–323.

[70] Viaggi, 'La pittura profana'; on the hunting scenes, see 328–9; and on the medallions and allegorical figures, see 337–9; for dates, names and epithets, see 340.

[71] S. Spada Pintarelli, *Affreschi in Alto Adige* (Venice, 1997).

[72] N. Rasmo, *Pitture murali in Alto Adige* (Bolzano, 1973); his figure 35, for example, shows the castle itself portrayed in one of its own frescoes (p. 46).

[73] Rasmo, *Pitture murali*, p. 156.

[74] O. Trapp, *Tiroler Burgenbuch*, 5 vols (Bolzano, 1981), V, pp. 109–76.

[75] A. Grebe et al. (eds), *Burg Runkelstein* (Regensburg, 2005).

[76] Haug et al., *Runkelstein: Die Wandmalereien* (1982) and Curschmann's *Vom Wandel im bildlichen Umgang mit literarischen Gegenständen* (Freiburg, 1997).

[77] A. Bechtold (ed.), *Castel Roncolo: Il maniero illustrato* (Bolzano, 2000), translated as *Schloss Runkelstein: Die Bilderburg* (Bolzano, 2000).

[78] According to the 1407 inventory, the Gonzaga palace contained several rooms which were probably frescoed, including a camera 'Lanzalotti'. See M. Tomasi, 'Pittura murale "arturiana" in Italia (XIII–XIV secolo): produzione e fruizione', in *Modi e forme della fruizione della 'materia arturiana' nell'Italia dei secc. XIII–XV* (Milan, 2006), pp. 33–66, on p. 59.

[79] See photo in A. Cicinelli, 'Nuove indagini e risultati per la Sala del Pisanello a Mantova', in P. Marini (ed.), *Pisanello* (Milan, 1996), pp. 479–85, on p. 480.

[80] G. Paccagnini, 'Il ritrovamento del Pisanello nel Palazzo Ducale di Mantova', *Bollettino d'Arte*, 52 (1967), 17–19; and 'Il Pisanello ritrovato a Mantova', *Commentari: Rivista di critica e storia dell'arte*, 19 (1968), 253–8.

[81] Paccagnini and M. Figlioli, *Pisanello alla corte dei Gonzaga: Mantova, Palazzo Ducale. Catalogo della Mostra* (Milan, 1972), close-up photos (unpaginated pp. 65–71).

[82] B. Degenhart, 'Pisanello in Mantua', *Pantheon*, 31 (1973), 364–411. See Chapters 4 and 12 in this volume.

[83] J. Woods-Marsden, *The Gonzaga of Mantua and Pisanello's Arthurian Frescoes* (Princeton, 1988), pp. 20 and 92–8, respectively.

[84] Woods-Marsden, *Gonzaga of Mantua*, pp. 72–87.

[85] Tomasi, 'Pittura murale', pp. 42–5 (on dates) and p. 47 (on armour).

[86] V. Bertolucci Pizzorusso, 'I cavalieri di Pisanello', *SMV*, 20 (1972), 37–48; Woods-Marsden, *Gonzaga of Mantua* (pp. 15–18); and L. Syson et al. (eds), *Pisanello: Painter to the Renaissance Court* (London, 2001), pp. 52–3.

[87] Paccagnini, *Pisanello alla corte*, p. 61; E. L. Goodman, 'The *Prose Tristan* and the Pisanello Murals', *Tristania*, 3/2 (1978), 22–35; and Whitaker, *Legends*, pp. 133 and 134 n. 35.

[88] Goodman, 'The *Prose Tristan*', 29–30.

[89] G. Giovannoni and G. Pasetti, *Il sangue e la coppa: Itinerari graaliani nella Mantova matildica e gonzaghesca* (Mantua, 1993).

[90] A. Cicinelli, 'Nuove indagini e risultati per la Sala del Pisanello a Mantova', in Marini (ed.), *Pisanello* (Milan, 1996), pp. 479–85, on p. 484.

[91] G. Pasetti, *Il ciclo del Pisanello e la letteratura epica cavalleresca* (Brescia, 1998), p. 12.

[92] Marcello Castrichini published a scientific study of restoration work, including charts showing the phases of Pisanello's work, amounts painted in a single day, close-up photos of fragments and strata of the wall: *Pisanello: restauri e interpretazioni* (Todi, 1996). From a technical standpoint this book is fascinating; however, these skilled art restorers do not seem to grasp chivalric visual and narrative tropes. The captions constantly refer to one cleaned panel as 'Dame sotto il baldacchino e gentiluomini' ('ladies under a baldachin, and gentlemen'; p. 23). The drapery above is not a *baldacchino*, as is evident by comparison with a true *baldacchino* portrayed elsewhere in the same cycle. Indeed, diagram 84 labels the latter correctly as a *baldacchino* and the one above the head of the '*dama*' as a *vessillo* (banner or flag). The '*dama*' is surely a comely young knight with his helmet removed. He wears armour and sits astride a warhorse as do the *gentiluomini* who surround him. For a contemporary point of reference, see the discussion of the 'effeminate' Tristan painted at Saint Floret, later in this chapter (p. 215). The authors also refer to a young black man's head as *testo di paggio* (page's head; p. 21). However, this is clearly an adult male, and the scale of the figure matches the knights who surround him. Why would this figure not represent the 'Saracen' Palamedes in the company of his peers, who also have their helmets removed?

[93] Cicinelli, 'Nuove indagini', p. 482.

[94] Cicinelli, 'Nuove indagini', p. 484.

[95] L. Ventura, 'Pisanello, nuovi risultati e nuovi problemi: Gli esiti delle ricerche del centenario', *Civiltà mantovana*, 31 (1996), 95–107, on 104.

[96] L. Ventura, 'Noterelle pisanelliane: Precisazioni sulla data del ciclo cavalleresco di Mantova', *Civiltà mantovana*, 27 (1992), 19–53, esp. 33–7.

[97] Apparently, a partial cleaning had been undertaken in autumn 1962 under the direction of François Enaud; see P. Deschamps and M. Thibout, *La peinture murale en France au début de l'époque gothique de Philippe-Auguste à la fin du règne de Charles V (1180–1380)* (Paris, 1963), p. 223 n. 8.

[98] Loomis and Loomis, *Arthurian Legends*, p. 59.

[99] F. Cigni (ed. and trans.), *Il romanzo arturiano di Rustichello da Pisa* (Pisa, 1994). 'Frequente nel romanzo il *topos* della bellezza fisica di Tristano', which echoes the prose *Tristan* (p. 15 n. 36).

[100] Deschamps and Thibout, *La peinture murale*, fig. 73.

[101] Personal communication, quoted by Deschamps and Thibout, *La peinture murale*, p. 226.

[102] Whitaker, *Legends*, p. 128.

[103] A. Luyster, 'Time, Space, and Mind: Tristan in Three Dimensions in Fourteenth-Century France', in J. Eming et al. (eds), *Visuality and Materiality in the Story of Tristan and Iseut* (Notre Dame, 2012), pp. 148–77, on pp. 150, 154–6, 166–8.

[104] Deschamps and Thibout, *La peinture murale*, unnumbered plate of Iseut, on p. 182; Whitaker, *Legends*, pp. 128–9; Luyster, 'Time, Space, and Mind', pp. 154, 172.

[105] Loomis and Loomis, *Arthurian Legends*, p. 59.

[106] Whitaker, *Legends*, p. 128.

[107] This usage survives in Andrea da Barberino (d. 1431/3), where an embattled knight has his 'fish' cut off. The earliest Oxford English Dictionary reference to a 'codpiece' dates from 1460.

[108] F. Mazzini, 'Anticipazioni sugli affreschi della Torre di Frugarolo', in L. Tamburini (ed.), *Studi e ricerche di Storia dell'arte in memoria di Luigi Mallé* (Turin, 1981), pp. 91–6.

[109] A. Vitale Brovarone, 'Diffusione dei testi letterari nel Piemonte tra '400 e '500', in *Histoire linguistique de la Vallée d'Aoste du Moyen Age au XVIII siècle* (Aosta, 1985), pp. 132–77, on p. 137; E. Rossetti Brezzi, 'Testimonianze trecentesche nel territorio alessandrino', in G. Romano (ed.), *Pittura e miniatura del Trecento nel Piemonte* (Turin, 1997), pp. 15–35, on pp. 30–4.

[110] M. L. Meneghetti, 'Figure dipinte e prose di romanzi. Prime indagini su soggetto e fonti del ciclo arturiano di Frugarolo', in E. Castelnuovo (ed.), *Le Stanze di Artù. Gli affreschi di Frugarolo e l'immaginario cavalleresco nell'autunno del Medioevo* (Milan, 1999), pp. 75–84.

[111] G. R. Perino, 'Restituzione grafica della sala con gli affreschi del ciclo arturiano', in Castelnuovo (ed.), *Le Stanze di Artù*, pp. 66–72.

[112] E. Cozzi (ed.), *Tristano e Isotta in Palazzo Ricchieri a Pordenone: Gli affreschi gotici di soggetto cavalleresco e allegorico* (Pordenone, 2006), pp. 14, 15.

[113] A. Donadello (ed.), *Il libro di messer Tristano ('Tristano Veneto')* (Venice, 1994).

[114] Cozzi (ed.), *Tristano e Isotta*, pp. 22–4.

[115] Various descriptions of the frescoes are available in English: see Loomis and Loomis, *Arthurian Legends*, p. 39; N. J. Lacy, 'Nine Worthies', in Lacy (ed.), *Arthurian Encyclopedia* (New York, 1986), pp. 407–8; Scherer, *About the Round Table*, pp. 13–15 and 30; and Whitaker, *Legends*, p. 142. Scherer also discusses La Manta from the standpoint of Hector in *The Legends of Troy in Art and Literature* (London, 1963), pp. 63–4.

[116] C. F. Biscarra, 'Studio preparatorio per un elenco degli edifici e monumenti nazionali del Piemonte', *Atti della Società archeologica e belle arti per la provincia di Torino*, 2 (1877), 255–79, on 276.

[117] P. D'Ancona, 'Gli affreschi del Castello di Manta nel Saluzzese', *L'arte*, 8 (1905), 94–106, 183–98.

[118] M. Piccat, 'Le scritte in volgare dei Prodi e delle Eroine della sala affrescata nel castello di La Manta', *Studi piemontesi*, 20 (1991), 141–66, on 161 and 165.

[119] A. M. Finoli, '"Le Donne, e ' cavalier . . .": il *topos* dei nove prodi e delle nove eroine nel *Chevalier Errant* di Tommaso III di Saluzzo', in *Il confronto letterario*, special issue of *Quaderni del Dipartimento di lingue e letterature straniere moderne dell'Università di Pavia*, 7 (1990), 109–22, on 120.

[120] M. L. Meneghetti, 'Il manoscritto fr. 146 della Bibliothèque Nationale di Parigi, Tommaso di Saluzzo e gli affreschi della Manta', *Romania*, 110 (1989), 511–35.

[121] N. Gabrielli, *Arte nell'antico marchesato di Saluzzo* (Turin, 1974), p. 226.

[122] Gabrielli, *Arte nell'antico marchesato*, p. 57. Special care was taken in executing the Hector-Valerano figure; recent restoration revealed that it was done in two days, not one as the others were. See M. L. Meneghetti, '"Sublimis" e "Humilis": Due stili di scrittura e due modi di rappresentazione alla Manta', in C. Ciociola (ed.), *'Visibile parlare': Le scritture esposte nei volgari italiani dal Medioevo al Rinascimento* (Naples, 1997), pp. 397–408, on pp. 401–2.

[123] D. Arasse, 'Portrait, mémoire familiale e liturgie dynastique: Valerano-Hector au château de Manta', in A. Gentili et al. (eds), *Il ritratto e la memoria materiali*, 3 vols (Rome, 1989), I, pp. 93–112, on pp. 93, 95.

[124] In 1942 Gabrielli had proposed Giacomo Jaquerio as the artist and remained convinced of this in her 1974 book *Arte nell'antico marchesato* (p. 57). Meneghetti summarises the various myths and hypotheses in '"Sublimis" e "Humilis"', pp. 398–9.

[125] G. Romano (ed.), *La Sala baronale del castello della Manta* (Milan, 1992), p. 3.

[126] Romano (ed.), *La Sala baronale*, p. 2.

[127] '[U]no stile del vestire destinato a non durare oltre il 1415–20' ('A style of dress destined not to last beyond 1415–20'), in R. Passoni, 'Nuovi studi sul Maestro della Manta', in Romano (ed.), *La Sala baronale*, pp. 37–60, on p. 37.

[128] A particularly nice photograph taken in 1884 shows the ceiling glowing with natural daylight admitted from a window (Romano [ed.], *La Sala baronale*, p. 74); see also comments by Elena Ragusa, 'Il soffitto dipinto della sala baronale', in the same volume, p. 113.

[129] In addition to literary subjects, historical rulers could be portrayed, as at Turin (Castelnuovo and de Gramatica [eds], *Il Gotico nelle Alpi*, pp. 234–7).

[130] Castelnuovo, *Le Stanze di Artù, schede*, p. 179; Cozzi, 'Tavolette da soffitto tardogotiche di soggetto cavalleresco a Pordenone', in G. Fiaccadori and M. Grattoni d'Arcano (eds), *In domo habitationis: L'arredo in Friuli nel tardo Medioevo* (Venice, 1996), pp. 78–83, on p. 82.

[131] Cozzi, 'Tavolette da soffitto', p. 83.

[132] Other beautiful wooden ceilings survive at Palazzo Davanzati in Florence. A custodian there informed me that the red paint used contained arsenic, which protected the wood against insects. For the same reason, red paint was traditionally used on American farm buildings.

[133] Cozzi, 'Tavolette da soffitto', p. 81.

[134] A brief description of all three examples, the architectural history of the Ricchieri palace and photographs may be found online (as of this writing) at: *www.comune.pordenone.it/comune/in-comune/ strutture/museoarte*. The various studies by Cozzi include a photographic sampling of the images.

[135] Cozzi, 'Per la diffusione dei temi cavallereschi e profani nella pittura tardogotica. Breve viaggio nelle Venezie tra scoperte e restauri recenti', in Castelnuovo (ed.), *Le Stanze di Artù*, pp. 116–27, on p. 126.

[136] Cozzi, 'Tavolette da soffitto', p. 83, and 'Per la diffusione', p. 126.

[137] F. Bologna, *Il soffitto della sala magna allo Steri di Palermo e la cultura feudale siciliana nell'autunno del Medioevo* (Palermo, 1975), pp. 16, 31 n. 65.

[138] Whitaker, *Legends*, p. 129.

[139] Bologna, *Il soffitto*, pp. 4–5.

[140] Bologna, *Il soffitto*, pp. 13–14.

[141] Bologna, *Il soffitto*, p. 16.

[142] E. Gabrici and E. Levi, *Lo Steri di Palermo e le sue pitture* (Milan and Rome, 1932; Palermo, 1993).

[143] P. Toesca, *La pittura e la miniatura nella Lombardia dai più antichi monumenti alla metà del Quattrocento* (Milan, 1912; Turin, 1987); H. Bresc, *Livre et société en Sicile (1299–1499)* (Palermo, 1971); Bologna, *Il soffitto*, p. 27.

[144] Bologna, *Il soffitto*, fig. 36.

[145] Gabrici and Levi, *Lo Steri di Palermo*, pp. 97, 99, 101, 104.

[146] Ibid., p. 96.

[147] P. Rajna, 'Intorno a due antiche coperte con figurazioni tratte dalle storie di Tristano', *Romania*, 42 (1913), 517–79.

[148] L. Morelli, 'Un trapunto trecentesco', *Dedalo: Rassegna d'arte*, 2 (1922), 770–83.

[149] A. Santangelo, *A Treasury of Great Italian Textiles*, trans. P. Craig (New York, 1964); and D. Fouquet, *Wort und Bild in der mittelalterlichen Tristantradition* (Berlin, 1971).

[150] A. Colby, *Quilting* (New York, 1971), pp. 13–17, 80, 122–3.

[151] Ott, 'Katalog', '"Tristan" auf Runkelstein', and 'Tristano e Isotta'; Whitaker, *Legends*; and Walworth, 'Tristan in Medieval Art'.

[152] R. Koechlin, *Les ivoires gothiques français*, 2 vols and portfolio of plates (Paris, 1924), I, p. 31.

[153] M. Tomasi, '"Les fais des preudommes ausi com s'il fussent present": gli avori cavallereschi tra romanzi e immagini', in Castelnuovo (ed.), *Le Stanze di Artù*, pp. 128–37, on p. 186.

[154] D. Gaborit-Chopin, *Ivoires du Moyen Age* (Fribourg, 1978); O. Zastrow, *Museo d'arte applicate: gli avori* (Milan, 1978); and E. Merlini, 'La "Bottega degli Embriachi" e i cofanetti eburnei fra Trecento e Quattrocento: una proposta di classificazione', *Arte cristiana*, n.s. 76 (1988), 267–82.

[155] Gaborit-Chopin, *Ivoires du Moyen Age*, p. 131.

[156] R. H. Randall, 'Popular Romances Carved in Ivory', in P. Barnet (ed.), *Images in Ivory: Precious Objects of the Gothic Age* (Detroit and Princeton, 1997), pp. 59, 63, 68, 69, 75.

[157] Zastrow, *Gli avori*, item 195.

[158] Zastrow, *Gli avori*, photos 182–4.

[159] See L. Martini, 'Note storiche e bibliografiche', in *Avori bizantini e medievali nel Museo Nazionale di Ravenna* (1990), pp. 43–57, esp. pp. 44–5, on the problems of doing such research.

[160] Julius von Schlosser found evidence for the presence of German ivory craftsmen in Venice in 1457–1516 ('Die Werkstatt der Embriachi in Venedig', *Jahrbuch der Kunsthistorischen Sammlungen des allerhöchsten Kaiserhauses*, 20 [1899], 220–82, on 258). Randall points out how a northern Italian painted ivory box imitated a Sicilian model, but the French-language motto suggests the court of Savoy (*The Golden Age of Ivory: Gothic Carvings in North American Collections* [New York, 1993], p. 139).

[161] Fiaccadori and Grattoni d'Arcano (eds), *In domo habitationis*, p. 243.

[162] Koechlin, *Les ivoires gothiques*, I, p. 450.

[163] See von Schlosser, 'Die Werkstatt', p. 232 and plates XXXIII–XXXV.

[164] See von Schlosser 'Die Werkstatt', p. 253.

[165] L. Gargan, *Cultura e arte nel Veneto al tempo del Petrarca* (Padua, 1978), pp. 37–8: '*schacum elephanti etc. regis Artusii*'.

[166] Koechlin, *Les ivoires gothiques*, I, pp. 391–2. In *Arthurian Legends*, Loomis and Loomis call this a goblet base (p. 67, fig. 126).

[167] Koechlin, *Les ivoires gothiques*, II, p. 385, item 1058; II, p. 408, item 1137. See also Castelnuovo, *Le Stanze di Artù* (photo p. 188) for an interesting doubling of the motif.

[168] Koechlin, *Les ivoires gothiques*, I, pp. 393, 439, 491–2, 513; II, p. 386, item 1061. For photos, see also Loomis and Loomis, *Arthurian Legends*, pl. 140; L. Martini, 'Note storiche e bibliografiche relative agli oggetti dal sec. XII al XIV', in Martini et al. (eds), *Avori bizantini e medievali nel Museo Nazionale di Ravenna* (Ravenna, 1990), fig. 26; and Castelnuovo, *Le Stanze di Artù*, p. 183.

[169] Koechlin, *Les ivoires gothiques*, I, pp. 490, 492 n. 3; II, p. 455, item 1288. See also Loomis and Loomis, *Arthurian Legends*, pl. 157.

[170] See Koechlin, *Les ivoires gothiques*, II, items 994, 997, 1000, 1005, 1009, 1023, 1024, 1041, 1052, 1054, 1056, 1058, 1061, 1067, 1070, 1082, 1113, 1137, 1188, 1204, 1253, 1279, 1280, 1286, 1323. Of course, modern locations do not necessarily prove medieval ownership.

[171] On this image (item 1296 in Koechlin, *Les ivoires gothiques*), see Martini, 'Note storiche', pp. 87–8, details and photo. Her essay includes photos of courtly scenes preserved in other Italian museums.

[172] For a production map, see T. Wilson, *Ceramic Art of the Italian Renaissance* (Austin, 1987), p. 9.

[173] T. Hausman, *Majolika: spanische und italienische Keramik vom 14. bis zum 18. Jahrhunderts* (Berlin, 1972), p. 111.

[174] C. L. Joost-Gaugier, 'Bartolomeo Colleoni as a Patron of Art and Architecture: The Palazzo Colleoni in Brescia', *Arte lombarda*, 84–5 (1988), 61–72.

[175] For ivories, see von Schlosser, 'Die Werkstatt', p. 263.

[176] Wilson, *Italian Maiolica of the Renaissance* (Milan, 1996), p. 170.

14

ARTHURIAN ART REFERENCES

Gloria Allaire

General Arthurian Art Studies

Boskovits, Miklós. 'Arte lombarda del primo Quattrocento: un riesame', in *Arte in Lombardia tra Gotico e Rinascimento* (Milan, 1988), pp. 9–49.

Canova Mariani, Giordana et al. (eds). *La miniatura a Padova dal Medioevo al Settecento* (Savignano sul Panaro [Modena], 1999).

Castelnuovo, Enrico (ed.). *Le Stanze di Artù: Gli affreschi di Frugarolo e l'immaginario cavalleresco nell'autunno del Medioevo* (Milan, 1999). [Exhibition catalogue; various fresco cycles.]

Castelnuovo, Enrico, and Francesca de Gramatica (eds). *Il Gotico nelle Alpi 1350–1450: Catalogo* (Trent, 2002).

Cozzi, Enrica. 'Aspetti di una cultura allegorica e profana nella pittura murale trecentesca delle Venezie', in Comitato Manifestazioni Tomaso da Modena, *Tomaso da Modena e il suo tempo: Atti del Convegno internazionale di studi per il 6° centenario della morte. Treviso 31 agosto–3 settembre 1979* (Treviso, 1980), pp. 327–36. [Survey of late medieval wall decoration in north-eastern Italy.]

Cozzi, Enrica. 'Il mondo cavalleresco: L'Italia nord-orientale', in Castelnuovo and de Gramatica, *Il Gotico*, pp. 238–51. ['Finding list' of courtly themes; comparative iconography.]

Cozzi, Enrica. 'Temi cavallereschi e profani nella cultura figurativa trevigiana dei secoli XIII e XIV', in Luigi Menegazzi (ed.), *Tomaso da Modena: Catalogo (Treviso, S. Caterina, Capitolo dei Domenicani, 5 luglio–5 novembre 1979)* (Treviso, 1979), pp. 44–59. [General study of courtly art in Treviso area.]

Dematté, Claudia, and José Manuel Lucía Megías. 'Immagini di dame e cavalieri: Affreschi cavallereschi ed arturiani in Trentino Alto Adige', in Claudia Dematté (ed.), *Il mondo cavalleresco tra immagine e testo*, Collana Labirinti, 126 (Trent, 2010), pp. 13–43. ['Finding list' of decorated palaces and castles, new restorations, bibliography.]

Dunlop, Anne. *Painted Palaces. The Rise of Secular Art in Early Renaissance Italy* (University Park, Pennsylvania, 2009).

Eming, Jutta, Ann Marie Rasmussen and Kathryn Starkey (eds). *Visuality and Materiality in the Story of Tristan and Isolde* (Notre Dame, IN, 2012).

Fox-Friedman, Jeanne. 'King Arthur in Art', in Helen Fulton (ed.), *Companion to Arthurian Literature* (Chichester and Malden, MA, 200; rpt 2012), pp. 381–99.

Frugoni, Chiara. 'Le decorazioni murali come testimonianza di uno "status symbol"', in Gabriella Rossetti Pepe (ed.), *Un palazzo, una città: il Palazzo Lanfranchi in Pisa*, Archeologia, storia, progettazione, 1 (Pisa, 1980), pp. 141–58.

Lacy, Norris J. (ed.). *The Arthurian Encyclopedia* (New York, 1986).

Lacy, Norris J. and Geoffrey Ashe, with Debra N. Mancoff (eds). 'Arthur in the Arts', in *The Arthurian Handbook*, 2nd edn (New York, 1997), pp. 197–270.

Loomis, Roger Sherman. *Arthurian Legends in Medieval Art*, Part II in collaboration with Laura Hibbard Loomis (London, 1938).

Lucía Megías, José Manuel. 'Frescos caballerescos y artúricos en el norte de Italia. 1: Tres castillos en los alrededores de Trento', *Letras* 59–60 (2009), 209–30. Online: *http://bibliotecadigital.uca.edu.ar/repositorio/revistas/frescos-caballerescos-arturicos-norte-italia.pdf*. [Brief summary of discoveries; 29 plates.]

Martindale, Andrew. *Painting the Palace: Studies in the History of Medieval Secular Painting* (London, 1995), pp. 136–43. [Fifteenth-century secular decor of Northern Italy.]

Meuwese, Martine. 'The Shape of the Grail in Medieval Art', in N. J. Lacy (ed.), *The Grail, the Quest and the World of Arthur*, Arthurian Studies, 72 (Cambridge, 2008), pp. 13–27. [50 colour plates.]

Morassi, Antonio. *Storia della pittura nella Venezia tridentina: Dalle origini alla fine del Quattrocento* ([Rome], 1934).

Neri Lusanna, Enrica. 'Interni fiorentini e pittura profana tra Duecento e Trecento: Cacce e giostre a Palazzo Cerchi', in Klaus Bergdolt and Giorgio Bonsanti (eds), *Opere giorni: Studi su mille anni di arte europea dedicati a Max Seidel* (Venice, 2011), pp. 123–30.

Ott, Norbert H. 'Katalog der Tristan-Bildzeugnisse: Zusammengestellt', in Hella Frühmorgen-Voss (ed.), *Text und Illustration im Mittelalter: Aufsätze zu den Wechselbeziehungen zwischen Literatur und bildender Kunst*, Münchener Texte und Untersuchungen zur deutschen Literatur des Mittelalters, 50 (Munich, 1975), pp. 140–80. [First attempt to catalogue all Tristan images.]

Ott, Norbert H. 'Tristano e Isotta nell'iconografia medioevale', in Michael Dallapiazza (ed.), *Tristano e Isotta. La fortuna di un mito europeo*, Quaderni di Hesperides, Serie manuali, 1 (Trieste, 2003), pp. 208–24. [Pan-European survey; bibliography. Italy on pp. 215, 218.]

Rasmo, Nicolò. *Pitture murali in Alto Adige* (Bolzano, 1973). [Survey of frescoes, castles.]

Scherer, Margaret R. *About the Round Table: King Arthur in Art and Literature* (New York, 1945; rpt 1974).

Tomasi, Michele. 'L'arredo della casa', in Max Seidel (ed.), *Storia delle arti in Toscana: il Trecento* (Florence, 2004), pp. 251–74. [Florentine interiors, non-Arthurian.]

Tomasi, Michele. 'Pittura murale "arturiana" in Italia (XIII–XIV secolo): produzione e fruizione', in *Modi e forme della fruizione della 'materia arturiana' nell'Italia dei sec. XIII–XV, Milano, 4–5 febbraio 2005*, Incontro di Studio, 41 (Milan, 2006), pp. 33–66.

Van Hoecke, Willy, Gilbert Tournoy and Werner Verbeke (eds). *Arturus Rex: Acta Conventus Lovaniensis 1987*, Mediaevalia Lovaniensia Series I, Studia XVII, 2 vols (Leuven, 1991).

Walworth, Julia. 'Tristan in Medieval Art', in Joan Tasker Grimbert (ed.), *Tristan and Isolde: A Casebook*, Arthurian Characters and Themes, 2 (New York, 1995; rpt 2002), pp. 255–99.

Whitaker, Muriel. 'Early Arthurian Art', in Norris J. Lacy (ed.), *A History of Arthurian Scholarship*, Arthurian Studies, 65 (Cambridge, 2006), pp. 198–219.

Whitaker, Muriel. *The Legends of King Arthur in Art*, Arthurian Studies, 22 (Cambridge, 1990).

Cathedral Decoration

The Modena Archivolt

[Armandi Barbolini, Marina.] *Lanfranco e Wiligelmo: Il Duomo di Modena* (Modena, 1985). [Catalogue of 1984 Exhibition.]

Chiellini Nari, Monica. 'Le favole, i simboli, il "ciclo di Artù": il fronte istoriato nella "Porta della Pescheria"', in Chiara Frugoni, Chiellini Nari and Cristina Acidini Luchinat (eds), *La Porta della Pescheria nel Duomo di Modena* (Modena, 1991), pp. 32–59.

Fox-Friedman, Jeanne. 'King Arthur in Art', in Fulton, *Companion*, pp. 382–3.

Fox-Friedman, Jeanne. 'Messianic Visions: Modena Cathedral and the Crusades', *Res: Anthropology and Aesthetics*, 25 (1994), 77–95.

Gowans, Linda. 'The Modena Archivolt and Lost Arthurian Tradition', in Van Hoecke et al., *Arturus Rex: Acta*, II, pp. 79–86.

Hutchings, Gweneth. '*Isdernus* of the Modena Archivolt', *Medium Aevum*, 1/3 (1931), 204–5.

Lacy, Norris J., et al. *The Arthurian Handbook*, pp. 199, 205–6.

Loomis, Roger Sherman. 'Modena, Bari, and Hades', *Art Bulletin*, 6 (1923–4), 71–4.

Loomis, Roger Sherman. 'The Modena Sculpture and Arthurian Romance', *StM*, n.s. 9 (1926), 1–17.
Loomis, Roger Sherman. 'Some Names in Arthurian Romance', *PMLA*, 45 (1930), 416–43.
Loomis, Roger Sherman and Laura Hibbard Loomis. *Arthurian Legends*, pp. 4, 5, 8–10, 32–5, plates 4–8.
Lorenzoni, Giovanni, and Giovanna Valenzano. *Il duomo di Modena e la basilica di San Zeno* (Verona, 2000). [Excellent photos.]
Mazzadi, Patrizia. 'Il mito di Artù nelle città italiane: esempi iconici e testuali', in Cora Dietl and Claudia Lauer (eds), *Studies in the Role of Cities in Arthurian Literature and in the Value of Arthurian Literature for a Civic Identity: When Arthuriana Meets Civic Spheres* (New York, 2009), pp. 117–34, on pp. 125–30.
Piconi, Sergio. 'Restauri nel Duomo di Modena: la Porta della Pescheria e il bassorilievo di Agostino di Duccio', in Enrico Castelnuovo (ed.), *Wiligelmo e Lanfranco nell'Europa romanica: Atti del Convegno . . . Modena, 24–27 ottobre 1985* (Modena, 1989), pp. 189–96. [Close-up photos of *Artus* and *Winlogee*, p. 192.]
Scherer, Margaret E. *About the Round Table*, p. 5. [Close-up photo.]
Stiennon, Jacques, and Rita Lejeune. 'La légende arthurienne dans la sculpture de la cathédrale de Modène', *Cahiers de civilisation médiévale*, 6 (1963), 281–96.
Stokstad, Marilyn. 'Modena Archivolt', in Lacy, *Arthurian Encyclopedia*, pp. 390–1.
Whitaker, Muriel. *Legends*, pp. 86–8.

The Otranto Mosaic
Alioto, Angela. 'Per una lettura simbolica della storia arturiana del mosaico della cattedrale di Otranto', in Gaetano Lalomia (ed.), *Studi in onore di Bruno Panvini*, special issue of *Siculorum Gymnasium*, 53 (2000), 1–17.
Barba, Giovanni. *L'opera ingenua: una nuova lettura del mosaico pavimentale della cattedrale di Otranto. Romanzo storico illustrato* (Perugia, 2005). [Historical novel.]
Fox-Friedman, Jeanne. 'King Arthur in Art', in Fulton, *Companion*, pp. 383–4.
Gianfreda, Grazio. *Il mosaico di Otranto: Biblioteca medioevale in immagini*, 2nd edn (Frosinone, 1965); 6th rev. edn (Lecce, 1998). [Colour photos.]
Haug, Walter. 'Artussage und Heilsgeschichte: Zum Programm des Fußbodenmosaiks von Otranto', *Deutsche Vierteljahrsschrift für Literaturwissenschaft und Geistesgeschichte*, 49/4 (1975), 577–606.
Haug, Walter. *Das Mosaik von Otranto: Darstellung, Deutung und Bilddokumentation* (Wiesbaden, 1977). [Excellent analysis and photos.]
Lacy, Norris. J. et al. *Arthurian Handbook*, p. 210.
Loomis, Roger Sherman, and Laura Hibbard Loomis. *Arthurian Legends*, pp. 8, 10, 31, 36; figs 9, 9a.
Mazzadi, Patrizia. 'Il mito di Artù nelle città italiane', in Dietl and Lauer, *Studies in the Role of Cities*, pp. 117–34, on p. 131.
Ruggieri, Ruggiero M. 'Avventure di caccia nel regno di Artù', in François Pirot (ed.), *Mélanges offerts à Rita Lejeune, professeur à l'Université de Liège*, 2 vols (Gembloux, 1968), II, pp. 1103–20. [Discusses beasts, links to Otranto creature.]
Saporetti, Claudio. *Mosaico: Una storia inventata per un'interpretazione vera del capolavoro pavimentale di Otranto* (Rome, 2006). [Fictionalization.]
Schulte, Alice. 'Mosaik von Otranto und ein Vergleich mit dem Mosaik von Teurnia', in Gustav A. Küppers-Sonnenberg, Wilhelm Haiden and Schulte (eds), *Flecht- und Knotenornamentik: Mosaiken (Teurnia und Otranto). Beiträge zur Symboldeutung*, Aus Forschung und Kunst, 16 (Bonn, 1972), pp. 155–230.
Settis Frugoni, Chiara. 'Per una lettura del mosaico pavimentale della cattedrale di Otranto', *Bullettino dell'Istituto storico italiano per il Medio Evo e Archivio muratoriano*, 80 (1968), 213–56, esp. 237–41; plates.
Settis Frugoni, Chiara. 'Il mosaico di Otranto: modelli culturali e scelte iconografiche', *Bulletino dell'Istituto storico italiano per il Medio Evo e Archivio muratoriano*, 82 (1970), 243–70, plus six unnumbered plates.

Stiennon, J. and R. Lejeune. 'La légende arthurienne', 281–96, esp. 294; fig. 24.
Stokstad, Marilyn. 'Otranto Mosaic', in Lacy, *Arthurian Encyclopedia*, p. 411.
Whitaker, Muriel. *Legends*, pp. 88–9, 91.
Wierschin, Martin. 'Artus und Alexander im Mosaik der Kathedrale von Otranto', *Colloquia Germanica*, 13 (1980), 1–34. [Historical context and contemporary literary evidence.]
Willemsen, Carl Arnold. *L'enigma di Otranto: Il mosaico pavimentale del presbitero Pantaleone nella Cattedrale*, Italian trans. Raffaele Disanto, Civiltà e Storia, 1 (Galatina, 1980).
Willemsen, Carl Arnold. *Das Rätsel von Otranto: das Fussbodenmosaik in der Kathedrale. Eine Bestandsaufnahme*, German trans. Raymund Kottje (Sigmaringen, 1992). [67 pages of plates, some in colour. In Italian as *L'enigma di Otranto*.]

Castles and Palaces

Castel Rodengo
Ackermann, H. 'Die Iwein-Fresken auf Schloß Rodenegg', *Der Schlern*, 57 (1983), 391–421.
Barbieri, Alvaro, and Rosanna Brusegan. 'Iwein a Castel Rodengo', in Sonia Maria Barillari and Margherita Lecco (eds), *Testo e Immagine: Espressione linguistica e comunicazione iconografia dall'antichità all'età contemporanea*, special issue of *L'Immagine Riflessa: Testi, società, culture*, n.s. 11/1–2 (2002), 189–211.
Bassetti Carlini, Paola. 'Castel Rodengo in Val Pusteria', in Silvia Spada Pintarelli (ed.), *Affreschi in Alto Adige* (Venice, 1997), pp. 100–9. [Summarises dating controversy; plates.]
Birlauf-Bonnet, Anne Marie. 'Überlegungen zur Brixener Malerei in den ersten Jahrzehnten des 13. Jahrhunderts', *Wiener Jahrbuch für Kunstgeschichte*, 37 (1984), 23–39, 187–98 [Revises dating.]
Bonnet, Anne Marie. *Rodenegg und Schmalkalden: Untersuchungen zur Illustration einer ritterlich-höfischen Erzählung und zur Entstehung profaner Epenillustration in den ersten Jahrzehnten des 13. Jahrhunderts*, tuduv-Studien, Reihe Kunstgeschichte, 22 (Munich, 1986). [Fine photos; schematic reconstructions of individual scenes.]
Castelnuovo, Enrico. *Le Stanze*, photos on pp. 77, 117.
Curschmann, Michael. '*Der aventiure bilde nemen*: The Intellectual and Social Environment of the Iwein Murals at Rodenegg Castle', in Martin H. Jones and Roy Wisbey (eds), *Chrétien de Troyes and the German Middle Ages: Papers from an International Symposium*, Arthurian Studies, 26, Institute of Germanic Studies, 53 (Cambridge, 1993), pp. 219–27.
Curschmann, Michael. 'Images of Tristan', in Adrian Stevens and Roy Wisbey (eds), *Gottfried von Strassburg and the Medieval Tristan Legend: Papers from an Anglo-North American Symposium*, Arthurian Studies, XXIII, Publications of the Institute of Germanic Studies, 44 (London, 1990), pp. 1–17, on pp. 5–7.
Curschmann, Michael. *Vom Wandel im bildlichen Umgang mit literarischen Gegenständen*, Wolfgang Stammler Gastprofessur für Germanische Philologie, Vorträge 6 (Freiburg, 1997), plates 1–5.
Deighton, Alan. 'Visual Representations of the Tristan Legend and Their Written Sources: A Re-Evaluation', *Tristania*, 20 (2000), 59–92.
Diemer, Peter, and Dorothea Diemer. '"Qui pingit florem non pingit floris odorem": Die Illustrationen der Carmina Burana (Clm 4660)', *Jahrbuch des Zentralinstituts für Kunstgeschichte*, 3 (1987), 43–75, on 55–8. [Dating controversy of Rodengo murals.]
Garber, Josef. *Die romanischen Wandgemälde Tirols* (Vienna, 1928), pp. 109–10.
Gattei, Sandro, Roberto Mainardi, Sandro Pirovano and Nicolò Rasmo (eds). *Trentino Alto Adige* (Venice, 1979), pp. 167–71, plate 162.
Mackowitz, Heinz. 'Meister Hugo und die romanischen Wandmalereien im Raume Brixen', in Hermann Fillitz and Martina Pippal (eds), *Akten des XXV. Internationalen Kongresses für Kunstgeschichte, Wien, 4.–10. September 1983*, Eröffnungs- und Plenarvorträge, Arbeitsgruppe 'Neue Forschungsergebnisse und Arbeitsvorhaben', 9 (Vienna, 1985), pp. 47–52, illus. 1–4.

Masser, Achim. 'Die "Iwein"-Fresken von Burg Rodenegg in Südtirol und der zeitgenössische Ritterhelm', *Zeitschrift für deutsches Altertum und Philologie*, 112 (1983), 177–98.

Masser, Achim. Review of A. M. Bonnet, *Rodenegg und Schmalkalden*, *Anzeiger für deutsches Altertum*, 100 (1989), 91–7.

Ott, Norbert H. 'Geglückte Minne-Aventiure: Zur Szenenauswahl literarischer Bildzeugnisse im Mittelalter. Die Beispiele des Rodenecker *Iwein*, des Runkelsteiner *Tristan*, des Braunschweiger Gawan- und des Frankfurter *Wilhelm-von-Orlens*-Teppichs', *Jahrbuch der Oswald von Wolkenstein Gesellschaft*, 2 (1982–3), 1–32.

Ott, Norbert H. and Wolfgang Walliczek. 'Bildprogramm und Textstruktur: Anmerkungen zu den "Iwein"-Zyklen auf Rodeneck und in Schmalkalden', in Christoph Cormeau (ed.), *Deutsche Literatur im Mittelalter: Kontakte und Perspektiven, Hugo Kuhn zum Gedenken* (Stuttgart, 1979), pp. 473–500.

Rainer, A. 'Die Frauenkirche im Brixner Kreuzgang', *Der Schlern*, 62 (1988), 415–28.

Rasmo, Nicolò (ed.). *L'età cavalleresca in Val d'Adige* (Milan, 1980), pp. 40–53. [Photos.]

Rasmo, Nicolò. 'Der Iwein-Zyklus auf Schloss Rodeneck', *Burgen und Schlösser im Österreich*, 13 (1977–8), 22–7. [Plates.]

Rasmo, Nicolò. *Pitture murali in Alto Adige*. [Plates, black and white and colour.]

Rasmussen, Ann Marie. 'Medieval German Romance', in Roberta L. Krueger (ed.), *The Cambridge Companion to Medieval Romance* (Cambridge, 2000), pp. 189–90, 197.

Rushing, Jr, James A. 'Adventure and Iconography: Ywain Picture Cycles and the Literarization of Vernacular Narrative', *The Arthurian Yearbook*, 1 (1991), 91–106.

Rushing, Jr, James A. *Images of Adventure: Ywain in the Visual Arts*, Middle Ages Series (Philadelphia, 1995). [Includes survey of criticism.]

Rushing, Jr, James A. 'The Medieval German Pictorial Evidence', in W. H. Jackson and S. A. Ranawake (eds), *The Arthur of the Germans: The Arthurian Legend in Medieval German and Dutch Literature*, Arthurian Literature in the Middle Ages, 3 (Cardiff, 2000), pp. 257–79.

Rushing, Jr, James A. Review of Schupp and Szklenar, *Ywain auf Schloß Rodenegg*, *Speculum*, 73 (1998), 592–3.

Schupp, Volker. 'Kritische Anmerkungen zur Rezeption des deutschen Artusromans anhand von Hartmanns "Iwein": Theorie–Text–Bildmaterial', *Frühmittelalterliche Studien*, 9 (1975), 405–42.

Schupp, Volker. 'Die Ywain-Erzählung von Schloß Rodenegg', in Egon Kühebacher (ed.), *Literatur und bildende Kunst im Tiroler Mittelalter: Die Iwein-Fresken von Rodenegg und andere Zeugnisse der Wechselwirkung von Literatur und bildender Kunst*, Innsbrucker Beiträge zur Kulturwissenschaft, Germanistische Reihe, 15 (Innsbruck, 1982), pp. 1–27. [Pre-restoration photos of entire cycle: views of room and close-ups.]

Schupp, Volker, and Hans Szklenar (eds). *Ywain auf Schloß Rodenegg: Eine Bildergeschichte nach dem 'Iwein' Hartmanns von Aue* (Sigmaringen, 1996).

Szklenar, Hans. 'Iwein-Fresken auf Schloß Rodeneck in Südtirol', *BBIAS*, 27 (1975), 172–80.

Whitaker, Muriel. *Legends*, pp. 124–5, colour plates 13–14.

Castel Roncolo

Arnholt di Danneburg, Riccardo. *Il Castello di Roncolo presso Bolzano ed i suoi affreschi* (Modena, 1924).

Bechtold, André (ed.). *Castel Roncolo: Il maniero illustrato* (Bolzano, 2000). [Collection of essays, photos.]

[Becker, A.] 'Schloß Runkelstein und seine Wandgemälde', *Mittheilungen der k.k. Zentral-Kommssion zur Erforschung und Erhaltung der Kunst- und Historischen Denkmale*, n.s. 4 (1878), xxiii–xxix.

Castelnuovo, Enrico. *Le Stanze*, pp. 80, 113.

Castelnuovo, Enrico and Francesca de Gramatica. *Il Gotico nelle Alpi*, pp. 138, 142, 243–6, 248, 289.

Curschmann, Michael. *Vom Wandel im bildlichen Umgang*, plate 20.

Dörrer. 'Vintler, Hans', in Wolfgang Stammler and Karl Langosch (eds), *Die deutsche Literatur des Mittelalters: Verfasserlexikon*, 14 vols (Berlin, 1933–2008), IV (1953), cols 698–702; V (1955), col. 1112.

Eming, Jutta et al. (eds). *Visuality and Materiality*, pp. 272–3. [Colour plate: Tristan and dragon.]

Gattei, Sandro et al. (eds). *Trentino Alto Adige*, pp. 294, 301–2; plates 292–4.

Gerola, Giuseppe. 'Per la datazione degli affreschi di Castel Roncolo (Runkelstein)', *Atti del Reale Istituto Veneto di Scienze, Lettere ed Arti*, 82 (1922–3), 511–21.

Gottdang, A. '"Tristan" im Sommerhaus der Burg Runkelstein: Der Zyklus, die Texte und der Betrachter', in Eckart Conrad Lutz, Johanna Thali and René Wetzel (eds), *Literatur und Wandmalerei, I: Erscheinungsformen höfischer Kultur und ihre Träger im Mittelalter (Freiburger Colloquium 1998)* (Tübingen, 2002), pp. 435–60.

Grebe, Anja et al. (eds). *Burg Runkelstein*, Burgen, Schlösser und Wehrbauten in Mitteleuropa, 20 (Regensburg, 2005).

Haug, Walter. 'Das Bildprogramm im Sommerhaus von Runkelstein', in Haug et al. (eds), *Runkelstein: Die Wandmalereien*, pp. 15–62.

Haug, Walter, Joachim Heinzle, Dietrich Huschenbett and Norbert H. Ott (eds), *Runkelstein: Die Wandmalereien des Sommerhauses* (Wiesbaden, 1982). [Seelos drawings reproduced.]

Heinzle, Joachim. 'Die Triaden auf Runkelstein und die mittelhochdeutsche Heldendichtung', in Haug et al. (eds), *Runkelstein: Die Wandmalereien*, pp. 63–93.

Lacy, Norris J., et al. *Arthurian Handbook*, p. 211.

Loomis, Roger Sherman and Laura Hibbard Loomis. *Arthurian Legends*, pp. 4, 38, 48–50, 79–84, 104.

Malfér, Viktor. *Die Triaden auf Schloß Runkelstein: Ihre Gestalten in Geschichte und Sage*, 3rd edn (Bolzano, 1980).

Morassi, Antonio. *Storia della pittura*, pp. 295–323.

Ott, Norbert H. 'Geglückte Minne-Aventiure', 1–32.

Ott, Norbert H. '"Tristan" auf Runkelstein und die übrigen zyklischen Darstellungen des Tristanstoffes: Textrezeption oder medieninterne Eigengesetzlichkeit der Bildprogramme?', in Haug et al. (eds.), *Runkelstein: Die Wandmalereien*, pp. 194–239.

Rasmo, Nicolò. *Affreschi medioevali atesini* (Milan and Venice, 1972).

Rasmo, Nicolò. 'Gli affreschi medioevali di Castelroncolo', *Cultura atesina*, 18/1–4 (1964), 1–24; 61 plates.

Rasmo, Nicolò. *Affreschi del Trentino e dell'Alto Adige* (Trent, 1971), pp. 210–11.

Rasmo, Nicolò. *L'età cavalleresca*, pp. 36, 74, 134, 144, 156, 170, *passim.*; plates 135–41. [Excellent photos.]

Rasmo, Nicolò. *Pitture murali in Alto Adige*, pp. 41–8, 75; colour plate XXVI.

Rasmussen, Ann Marie. 'Medieval German Romance', in Krueger, *Cambridge Companion*, pp. 196–7.

Rushing, Jr, James A. *Images of Adventure*, pp. 19, 245–56.

Scherer, Margaret R. *About the Round Table*, pp. 10–13, 20–1, 40–1. [Photos of castle exterior, pre-WW II.]

Schupp, Volker. 'Der Bilderzyklus von Tristan und Isolde auf Schloß Runkelstein bei Bozen und der Roman des Gottfried von Straßburg: Der Mythos von der eigenständigen Fassung', in Martin Ehrenfeuchter and Thomas Ehlen (eds), *'Als das wissend die meister wol': Beiträge zur Darstellung und Vermittlung von Wissen in Fachliteratur und Dichtung des Mittelalters und der frühen Neuzeit. Walter Blank zum 65. Geburtstag* (Frankfurt am Main, 2000), pp. 195–215.

Spada Pintarelli, Silvia. *Affreschi in Alto Adige*, pp. 20–1, 162–74.

Stokstad, Marilyn. 'Runkelstein Murals', in Lacy, *Arthurian Encyclopedia*, p. 465.

Tax, Petrus W. 'Der Pleier' in Lacy, *Arthurian Encyclopedia*, pp. 427–9.

Tea, Eva. 'Gli affreschi di Castel Roncolo presso Bolzano', *Archivio per l'Alto Adige*, 17 (1922), 67–86.

Tomasi, Michele. 'Pittura murale', pp. 36, 46, 47, 50, 52–4, 57–8; figs 4, 8.

Trapp, Oswald. *Tiroler Burgenbuch*, 5 vols (Bolzano, 1981), V, pp. 109–76; various plates.

Viaggi, Marisa. 'La pittura profana della Venezia tridentina nel sec. XIV e XV, Parte II, V: Le pitture profane a Castel Roncolo', *Studi Trentini di Scienze Storiche*, 29 (1950), 326–48.

von Lutterotti, Otto R. *Schloß Runkelstein bei Bozen und seine Wandgemälde*, rev. 2nd edn (Innsbruck, 1964).

von Schlosser, Julius. *L'arte di corte nel secolo decimoquarto*, trans. Gian Lorenzo Mellini (Cremona, 1895; rpt 1965), pp. 43–4.

Whitaker, Muriel. *Legends*, pp. 129–32; plates 15–16.

Weingartner, Josef. *Die Kunstdenkmäler Südtirols*, 3 vols (Innsbruck [1951]), III, plates 29–32.

Weingartner, Josef. 'Die profane Wandmalerei Tirols im Mittelalter', *Münchner Jahrbuch der bildenden Kunst*, n.s. 5 (1928), 1–63.

Bolzano, Casa Schrofenstein

Castelnuovo, Enrico, and Francesca de Gramatica. *Il Gotico nelle Alpi*, p. 246.

Obermair, Hannes, and Helmut Stampfer. 'Edilizia e cultura abitativa nella Bolzano tardomedievale', in Bechtold, *Castel Roncolo*, pp. 397–409. [*In situ* photos of badly damaged chivalric frescoes.]

Mantua, the Sala di Pisanello

Algeri, Giuliana. 'Il ciclo pisanelliano', in Giuliana Algeri (ed.), *Il Palazzo Ducale di Mantova* (Mantua, 2003), pp. 63–85. [Summary of criticism; history and ongoing restoration efforts of entire complex and gardens; photos of restored frescoes, *sinopie* and room.]

Bellosi, Luciano. 'The Chronology of Pisanello's Mantuan Frescoes Reconsidered', *The Burlington Magazine*, 134 (1992), 657–60.

Bertolucci [Pizzorusso], Valeria. 'I cavalieri di Pisanello', *SMV*, 20 (1972), 37–48; rpt in *Morfologie del testo medievale* (Bologna, 1989), pp. 75–86.

Castrichini, Marcello. *Pisanello: restauri e interpretazioni* (Todi, 1996).

Cicinelli, Aldo. 'Nuove indagini e risultati per la Sala del Pisanello a Mantova', in Paola Marini (ed.), *Pisanello* (Milan, 1996), pp. 479–85. [Exhibition catalogue; *schede* pp. 118–23, pp. 128–31 pertain to the *Sala*.]

Degenhart, Bernhard. 'Pisanello in Mantua', *Pantheon*, 31 (1973), 364–411.

Fox-Friedman, Jeanne. 'King Arthur in Art', in Fulton, *Companion*, pp. 390–1.

Giovannoni, Giannino, and Giovanni Pasetti. *Il sangue e la coppa: Itinerari graaliani nella Mantova matildica e gonzaghesca* (Mantua, 1993).

Goodman, E. L. 'The *Prose Tristan* and the Pisanello Murals', *Tristania*, 3/2 (1978), 22–35.

Lacy, Norris J., et al. *Arthurian Handbook*, p. 211.

Paccagnini, Giovanni. *Pisanello*, trans. Jane Carroll (London and New York, 1973). [Trans. of *Pisanello e il ciclo cavalleresco*.]

Paccagnini, Giovanni. *Pisanello e il ciclo cavalleresco di Mantova* (Milan, 1972).

Paccagnini, Giovanni. 'Il Pisanello ritrovato a Mantova', *Commentari: Rivista di critica e storia dell'arte*, 19 (1968), 253–8.

Paccagnini, Giovanni. 'Il ritrovamento del Pisanello nel Palazzo Ducale di Mantova', *Bollettino d'arte*, 52 (1967), 17–19.

Paccagnini, Giovanni, with Maria Figlioli. *Pisanello alla corte dei Gonzaga: Mantova, Palazzo Ducale. Catalogo della Mostra* ([Milan], 1972), esp. pp. 60–93.

Pasetti, Giovanni. *Il ciclo del Pisanello e la letteratura epica cavalleresca*, Galleria e Museo di Palazzo Ducale, Percorsi, 1 (Brescia, 1998).

Puppi, Lionello (ed.). *Pisanello: Una poetica dell'inatteso* (Cinisello Balsamo [Milan], 1996). [Colour plates.]

Syson, Luke, and Dillian Gordon, with Susanna Avery-Quash. *Pisanello: Painter to the Renaissance Court* (London, 2001). [Exhibition catalogue.]

Tomasi, Michele. 'Pittura murale', pp. 38–45, 47, 50–1, 58–9; figs 2, 3, 9, 14.

Ventura, Leandro. 'Noterelle pisanelliane: Precisazioni sulla data del ciclo cavalleresco di Mantova', *Civiltà mantovana*, 27 (1992), 19–53. [Archival evidence for dating.]

Ventura, Leandro. 'Pisanello, Nuovi risultati e nuovi problemi: Gli esiti delle ricerche del centenario', *Civiltà mantovana*, 31 (1996), 95–107. [Summary of criticism, not only for frescoes.]

Whitaker, Muriel. *Legends*, pp. 132–6.

Woods-Marsden, Joanna. *The Gonzaga of Mantua and Pisanello's Arthurian Frescoes* (Princeton, NJ, 1988).

Woods-Marsden, Joanna. 'Pisano, Antonio', in Lacy, *Arthurian Encyclopedia*, p. 427.

Saint Floret (Issoire, in Auvergne, France)

Courtillé, Anne. *Histoire de la peinture murale dans l'Auvergne du Moyen-Age* (n. p., 1983), pp. 139–42. [Survey of region's murals.]

Courtillé, Anne. 'La Peinture murale en Auvergne au temps de Jean de Berry', in Alain Salamagne (ed.), *Le Palais et son décor au temps de Jean de Berry* (Tours, 2010), pp. 195–209.

Curschmann, Michael. 'Images of Tristan', in Stevens and Wisbey (eds), *Gottfried von Strassburg*, pp. 1–17, on p. 9.

Dauvergne, Anatole. 'Note sur le château de Saint-Floret', in France, Comité Impérial des Travaux historiques, *Mémoires lus à La Sorbonne: Archéologie*, vols 1–3 (1861, 1863, 1864). [Photocopy of an annotated typescript.]

Deschamps, Paul, and Marc Thibout. *La peinture murale en France au début de l'époque gothique de Philippe-Auguste à la fin du règne de Charles V (1180–1380)* (Paris, 1963), pp. 182, 222–7, plate CXLII.

Loomis, R. S. and L. H. Loomis. *Arthurian Legends*, pp. 8, 22, 57–61, figs 92a–105.

Luyster, Amanda. 'Time, Space, and Mind: *Tristan* in Three Dimensions in Fourteenth-Century France', in Eming et al., *Visuality and Materiality*, pp. 8–9, 116, 148–77. [Colour plates and schematic plan.]

Ott, Norbert H. 'Katalog', in Frühmorgen-Voss (ed.), *Text und Illustration*, pp. 141–2.

Il romanzo arturiano di Rustichello da Pisa, ed. and Italian trans. Fabrizio Cigni (Pisa, 1994), pp. 11–13. [Plot summary.]

Scherer, Margaret E. *About the Round Table*, pp. 14–16, 44–5.

Whitaker, Muriel. *Legends*, pp. 127–9.

Frugarolo

Castelnuovo, Enrico. *Le Stanze di Artù: Gli affreschi di Frugarolo*.

Lorenzo Gradín, Pilar. '"Quei che *le mura* empion di sogni": Lanzarote y la Dama del Lago en el norte de Italia', *MR*, 29 (2005), 415–32. [Frescoes compared to *Lancelot* illuminations; detailed analysis of scenes.]

Mazzini, Franco. 'Anticipazioni sugli affreschi della Torre di Frugarolo', in Luigi Tamburini (ed.), *Studi e ricerche di Storia dell'arte in memoria di Luigi Mallé* (Turin, 1981), pp. 91–6.

Meneghetti, Maria Luisa. 'Figure dipinte e prose di romanzi. Prime indagini su soggetto e fonti del ciclo arturiano di Frugarolo', in Castelnuovo (ed.), *Le Stanze*, pp. 75–84.

Meneghetti, Maria Luisa. 'Modi della narrazione per figure nell'età della cavalleria', in Marco Praloran, Serena Romano, Gabriele Bucci et al. (eds), *Figura e racconto: narrazione letteraria e narrazione figurative in Italia dall'Antichità al primo Rinascimento ... Atti del Convegno di studi, Losanna, 25–26 novembre 2005*, Etudes lausannoises d'histoire de l'art, 9 (Florence, 2009), pp. 89–109. [Plates.]

Perino, Giorgio Rolando. 'Restituzione grafica della sala con gli affreschi del ciclo arturiano', in Castelnuovo (ed.), *Le Stanze*, pp. 66–72.

Rossetti Brezzi, Elena. Contribution in Castelnuovo and de Gramatica, *Il Gotico nelle Alpi*, pp. 410–13.

Rossetti Brezzi, Elena. 'Testimonianze trecentesche nel territorio alessandrino', in Giovanni Romano (ed.), *Pittura e miniatura del Trecento in Piemonte*, Arte in Piemonte, 11 (Turin, 1997), pp. 15–35, on pp. 30–4.

Tomasi, Michele. 'Pittura murale', pp. 36, 48, 54, 56.

Vitale Brovarone, Alessandro. 'Diffusione dei testi letterari nel Piemonte tra '400 e '500', in *Histoire linguistique de la Vallée d'Aoste du Moyen Age au XVIIIe siècle: Actes du seminaire de St. Pierre (Aosta, 16–17–18 maggio 1983)* (Aosta, 1985), pp. 132–77, on p. 137.

Pordenone, Palazzo Ricchieri

Battaglia Ricci, Lucia. 'Frammenti di storie dipinte', in Gilberto Ganzer (ed.), *Le favolose historie di Palazzo Ricchieri: Testimonianze tardogotiche nei soffitti lignei di Pordenone* (Treviso, 2008), pp. 51–65, 93–115.

Cozzi, Elena (ed.). *Tristano e Isotta in Palazzo Ricchieri a Pordenone: Gli affreschi gotici di soggetto cavalleresco e allegorico* (Pordenone, 2006).

La Manta

Arasse, Daniel. 'Portrait, mémoire familiale et liturgie dynastique: Valerano-Hector au château de Manta', in Augusto Gentili, Philippe Morel and Claudia Cieri Via (eds), *Il ritratto e la memoria: materiali*, 3 vols (Rome, 1989), I, pp. 93–112.

Bernardi, Marziano (ed.) *Tre monumenti pittorici del Piemonte antico* (Turin, 1957), pp. 70–87.

Biscarra, C. F. 'Studio preparatorio per un elenco degli edifici e monumenti nazionali del Piemonte', *Atti della Società di archeologia e belle arti per la provincia di Torino*, 2 (1877), 255–79, on 276.

Castelnuovo, Enrico. *Le Stanze*, p. 113.

Castelnuovo, Enrico, and Francesca de Gramatica. *Il Gotico nelle Alpi*, pp. 18, 19, 232, 237.

D'Ancona, Paolo. 'Gli affreschi del Castello di Manta nel Saluzzese', *L'arte*, 8 (1905), 94–106, 183–98.

Fajen, Robert. *Die Lanze und die Feder: Untersuchungen zum* Livre du Chevalier errant *von Thomas III., Markgraft von Saluzzo*, Imagines Medii Aevi, Interdisziplinäre Beiträge zur Mittelalterforschung, 15 (Wiesbaden, 2003).

Fajen, Robert. 'Malinconia di un lignaggio: Lo *Chevalier Errant* nel castello della Manta', *Romania*, 118 (2000), 105–37.

Finoli, Anna Maria. '"Le Donne, e ' cavalier . . .": il *topos* dei nove prodi e delle nove eroine nel *Chevalier Errant* di Tommaso III di Saluzzo', in *Il confronto letterario*, special issue of *Quaderni del Dipartimento di lingue e letterature straniere moderne dell'Università di Pavia*, 7 (1990), 109–22.

Gabrielli, Noemi. *Arte nell'antico marchesato di Saluzzo* (Turin, 1974).

Lacy, Norris J. 'Nine Worthies', in Lacy, *Arthurian Encyclopedia*, pp. 407–8.

Loomis, R. S. and L. H. Loomis. *Arthurian Legends*, pp. 4, 39; fig. 14.

Meneghetti, Maria Luisa. 'Il manoscritto fr. 146 della Bibliothèque Nationale di Parigi, Tommaso di Saluzzo e gli affreschi della Manta', *Romania*, 110 (1989), 511–35; rpt in Romano, *La Sala baronale*, pp. 61–72.

Meneghetti, Maria Luisa. '"Sublimis" e "Humilis": Due stili di scrittura e due modi di rappresentazione alla Manta', in Claudio Ciociola (ed.), *'Visibile parlare': Le scritture esposte nei volgari italiani dal Medioevo al Rinascimento*, Pubblicazioni dell'Università degli Studi di Cassino, Sezione Atti, Convegni, Miscellanee, 8 (Naples, 1997), pp. 397–408; plates.

Morassi, Antonio. *Storia della pittura, passim*; fig. 208.

Passoni, Riccardo. 'Nuovi studi sul Maestro della Manta', in Romano, *La Sala baronale*, pp. 37–60.

Piccat, Marco. 'Le scritte in volgare dei Prodi e delle Eroine della sala affrescata nel castello di La Manta', *Studi piemontesi*, 20 (1991), 141–66.

Ragusa, Elena. 'Il soffitto dipinto della sala baronale', in Romano, *La Sala baronale*, p. 113.

Romano, Giovanni (ed.). *La Sala baronale del castello della Manta*, Quaderni del restauro, 9 (Milan, 1992). [Archival documentation, technical comments on latest restoration and colour analysis. Photos of manuscripts, frescoes and castle exterior.]

Scherer, Margaret E. *About the Round Table*, pp. 13–15, 30. [Photos of exterior, pre-WW II.]

Scherer, Margaret E. *The Legends of Troy in Art and Literature* (New York and London, 1963), pp. 63–4.

Silva, Romano. *Gli affreschi del Castello della Manta: Allegoria e teatro* (Cinisello Balsamo [Milan], 2011). [Post-restoration colour photos, including room layouts; bibliography.]

Syson, Luke and Dillian Gordon. *Pisanello: Painter to the Renaissance Court*, p. 98.

Toesca, Pietro. 'Antichi affreschi Piemontesi', *Atti della Società piemontese di archeologia e belle arti*, 8 (1910), 52–64, on 61–3.

Tomasi, Michele. 'Pittura murale', pp. 34, 36, 37, 45, 47, 50, 54, 55, 58–60; figs 1, 6, 13.

von Schlosser, Julius. *L'arte di corte*, p. 51; plates 12, 31, 32, 58, 59.

Whitaker, Muriel. *Legends*, p. 142.

Wooden Ceiling Panels

Cantarutti, Novella. 'Tavolette friulane di soggetto cortese-cavalleresco', *Quaderni utinensi*, 1–2 (1983), 17–18.

Cozzi, Enrica. 'Per la diffusione dei temi cavallereschi e profani nella pittura tardogotica. Breve viaggio nelle Venezie tra scoperte e restauri recenti', in Castelnuovo, *Le Stanze*, pp. 116–27.

Cozzi, Enrica. 'La pittura della prima metà del XV secolo nel Friuli occidentale', in *Il Quattrocento nel Friuli occidentale*, II: *Studi urbani. L'avvio di una ricerca. La dimensione artistica*, Itinerari del Quattrocento. Atti del Convegno . . . dicembre 1993, 2 vols (Pordenone, 1996), II, pp. 113–34.

Cozzi, Enrica. 'Tavolette da soffitto tardogotiche di soggetto cavalleresco a Pordenone', in Fiaccadori and Grattoni d'Arcano (eds), *In domo habitationis: L'arredo in Friuli nel tardo Medioevo* (Venice, 1996), pp. 78–83.

Cozzi, Enrica. *Tristano e Isotta in Palazzo Ricchieri a Pordenone*, pp. 65–9.

Dachs, Monika. 'Eine Cremoneser "Tavoletta da soffitto" im Besitz des Oberösterreichischen Landesmuseums in Linz', *Jahrbuch des Oberösterreichischen Musealvereines, Gesellschaft für Landeskunde*, II, Berichte 134/1 (1989), 113–31. [Northern Italian wooden ceiling remnants, non-Arthurian.]

Palermo, Palazzo Chiaramonte 'Lo Steri'

Bologna, Ferdinando. *Il soffitto della Sala Magna allo Steri di Palermo e la cultura feudale siciliana nell'autunno del Medioevo* (Palermo, 1975). [Photos and schematic charts of layout.]

Di Marzo, Gioacchino. *La pittura in Palermo nel Rinascimento: Storia e documenti* (Palermo, 1899).

Gabrici, Ettore, and Ezio Levi. *Lo Steri di Palermo e le sue pitture*, Regia Accademia di Scienze, Lettere ed Arti di Palermo, Supplemento agli Atti, 1 (Milan and Rome, 1933; rpt Palermo, 1993). [Extensive photographic evidence; schematic chart identifies content of images where possible.]

Loomis, R. S. and L. H. Loomis. *Arthurian Legends*, pp. 61–3; figs 106–16.

Scherer, Margaret E. *About the Round Table*, pp. 43, 46.

Whitaker, Muriel. *Legends*, p. 129.

Decorative Objects

Textiles

Colby, Averil. *Quilting* (New York, 1971), pp. 13–17, 80, 122–3.

Fouquet, Doris. *Wort und Bild in der mittelalterlichen Tristantradition: Der älteste Tristanteppich von Kloster Wienhausen und die textile Tristanüberlieferung des Mittelalters*, Philologische Studien und Quellen, 62 (Berlin, 1971), pp. 53–4.

Fox-Friedman, Jeanne. 'King Arthur in Art', in Fulton, *Companion*, pp. 386–7.

Gabrici, Ettore, and Ezio Levi. *Lo Steri di Palermo*, pp. 94–6; plates XCIX, C, CI.

Lacy, Norris J. et al. *Arthurian Handbook*, pp. 213–14.

Loomis, R. S. and L. H. Loomis. *Arthurian Legends*, pp. 8, 63–5, figs 117–19.

Morelli, Lidia. 'Un trapunto trecentesco', *Dedalo: Rassegna d'arte*, 2 (1922), 770–83.

Ott, Norbert H. '"Tristan" auf Runkelstein und die übrigen zyklischen Darstellungen des Tristanstoffes: Textrezeption oder medieninterne Eigengesetzlichkeit der Bildprogramme?', in Haug et al. (eds), *Runkelstein: Die Wandmalereien*, pp. 194–239, on pp. 231–3.

Ott, Norbert H. 'Tristano e Isotta nell'iconografia medioevale', p. 218.

Proto Pisani, Rosanna Caterina, Marco Ciatti et al. (eds). *La 'coperta' Guicciardini: Il restauro delle imprese di Tristano*, Problemi di conservazione e restauro, 27 (Florence, 2010).

Rajna, Pio. 'Intorno a due antiche coperte con figurazioni tratte dalle storie di Tristano', *Romania*, 42 (1913), 517–79; rpt in Guido Lucchini (ed.), *Scritti di filologia e linguistica italiana e romanza*, Pubblicazioni del 'Centro Pio Rajna', Sezione Seconda, Documenti 1, 3 vols (Rome, 1998) III, pp. 1547–1614.

Santangelo, Antonino. *A Treasury of Great Italian Textiles*, trans. Peggy Craig (New York, 1964), p. 41.

Schuette, Marie. 'Eine wiedergefundene Tristanstickerei', in Paul Clemen (ed.), *Karl Koetschau von seinen Freunden und Verehrern zum 60. Geburtstag am 27. März 1928; Beiträge zur Kunst-, Kultur- und Literaturgeschichte* (Düsseldorf, 1928), p. 35.

Schuette, Marie, and Sigrid Müller-Christensen. *The Art of Embroidery*, trans. Donald King (Tübingen, 1963; London, 1964), plate 169.

Stokstad, Marilyn. 'Embroidery', in Lacy, *Arthurian Encyclopedia*, p. 151.

Walworth, Julia. 'Tristan in Medieval Art', in Grimbert (ed.), *Tristan and Isolde*, pp. 274–5; figs 7–8.

Whitaker, Muriel. *Legends*, pp. 106–8.

Ivory Objects

Eming, Jutta et al. (eds). *Visuality and Materiality*, pp. 280, 327. [Turin ivory pieces.]

Gaborit-Chopin, Danielle. *Ivoires du Moyen Age* (Fribourg, 1978).

Gabrici, Ettore and Ezio Levi. *Lo Steri di Palermo*, pp. 100, 101, 130, 140.

Gargan, Luciano. *Cultura e arte nel Veneto al tempo del Petrarca* (Padua, 1978). (1425 inventory; chess game '*regis Artusii*', pp. 37–8.)

Koechlin, Raymond. *Les ivoires gothiques français*, 2 vols and portfolio of plates (Paris, 1924).

Loomis, R. S. and L. H. Loomis. *Arthurian Legends*, pp. 66, 70, 76; figs 125, 157.

Martini, Luciana. 'Note storiche e bibliografiche relative agli oggetti dal sec. XII al XIV', in Martini et al. (eds), *Avori bizantini e medievali nel Museo Nazionale di Ravenna. Catalogo*, (Ravenna, 1990), pp. 43–57, 87–9, 106, 122.

Merlini, Elena. 'La "Bottega degli Embriachi" e i cofanetti eburnei fra Trecento e Quattrocento: Una proposta di classificazione', *Arte cristiana*, n.s. 76/724 (1988), 267–82.

Randall, Richard H., Jr. *The Golden Age of Ivory: Gothic Carvings in North American Collections* (New York, 1993), pp. 139–40, 146.

Randall, Richard H., Jr. 'Popular Romances Carved in Ivory', in Peter Barnet (ed.), *Images in Ivory: Precious Objects of the Gothic Age* (Detroit and Princeton, 1997), pp. 63–79.

Rossi, Attilio. 'Les ivoires gothiques françaises des Musées Sacré et Profane de la Bibliothèque Vaticane', *Gazette des beaux-arts*, 3rd ser. 33–4/575 (1905), 390–402. [Tristan and Iseut mirror cover, 399.]

Tomasi, Michele. '"Les fais des preudommes ausi com s'il fussent present": Gli avori cavallereschi tra romanzi e immagini', in Castelnuovo, *Le Stanze*, pp. 128–37; plates 24–30.

Trexler, Richard C. 'The Magi Enter Florence: The Ubriachi of Florence and Venice', *Studies in Medieval and Renaissance History*, The University of British Columbia, first n.s. 1 (1978), 127–218.

von Schlosser, Julius. *L'arte di corte*, plates 20, 24–7.

von Schlosser, Julius. 'Die Werkstatt der Embriachi in Venedig', *Jahrbuch der Kunsthistorischen Sammlungen des allerhöchsten Kaiserhauses*, 20 (1899), 220–82.

Zastrow, Oleg. *Museo d'arti applicate: Gli avori* (Milan, 1978).

Ceramics

Hausmann, Tjark. *Majolika: spanische und italienische Keramik vom 14. bis zum 18. Jahrhundert*, Kataloge des Kunstgewerbemuseums Berlin, 6 (Berlin, 1972).

Joost-Gaugier, Christiane L. 'Bartolomeo Colleoni as a Patron of Art and Architecture: The Palazzo Colleoni in Brescia', *Arte lombarda*, 84–5 (1988), 61–72.

Wilson, Timothy. *Italian Maiolica of the Renaissance*, Parnassus, 1 (Milan, 1996).

Wilson, Timothy and Patricia Collins. *Ceramic Art of the Italian Renaissance*, in co-operation with British Museum Publications (Austin TX, 1987).

Other Decorative Objects

Haug, Walter, et al. (eds). *Runkelstein: Die Wandmalereien*, p. 224. [Maternity tray, colour plate.]

Loomis, R. S. and L. H. Loomis. *Arthurian Legends*, p. 70, figs 126, 135.

Stokstad, Marilyn. 'Louvre Tray', in Lacy, *Arthurian Encyclopedia*, p. 341.

Tea, Eva. 'Gli affreschi di Castel Roncolo', 81 n. 1. ['Un tavolino intagliato' with Tristan and Iseut, at Milan, Museo del Castello Sforzesco.]

van Marle, Raimond. *Iconographie de l'Art profane au Moyen-Age et à la Renaissance et la Décoration des Demeures* (The Hague, 1932), II, pp. 464ff. and image 483. [Maternity tray made in Verona.]

Whitaker, Muriel. *Legends*, p. 115. [Maternity tray, photo.]

Manuscript Illumination

Arte Lombarda dai Visconti agli Sforza: Palazzo Reale, Milano, Aprile-Giugno 1958, intro. Gian Alberto dell'Acqua (Milan, 1959). [Exhibition catalogue.]

Avril, François, and Marie-Thérèse Gousset, with Claudia Rabel. *Manuscrits enluminés d'origine italienne*, Paris, Bibliothèque Nationale, Département des manuscrits, Centre de Recherche sur les manuscrits enluminés, 2: *XIIIe siècle* (1984); 3: *XIVe siècle, I. Lombardie-Ligurie* (Paris, 2005).

Avril, François and Yolanta Załuska. *Dix siècles d'enluminure italienne (VIe–XVIe siècles)* (Paris, 1984).

Benedetti, Roberto. '"Qua fa' un santo e un cavaliere . . .": Aspetti codicologici e note per il miniatore', in Gianfranco D'Aronco et al. (eds), *La grant Queste del Saint Graal / La grande Ricerca del Santo Graal: Versione inedita della fine del XIII secolo del ms. Udine, Biblioteca Arcivescovile, 177* (Tricesimo [Udine], 1990), pp. 31–47.

Berti Toesca, Elena. 'Un romanzo illustrato del Quattrocento: Il romanzo di Lancillotto, codice palatino 556', *L'Arte*, n.s. 10 (1939), 135–43.

Bertolucci Pizzorusso, Valeria. 'Testi e immagini in codici attribuibili all'area pisano-genovese alla fine del Duecento', in Marco Tangheroni (ed.), *Pisa e il Mediterraneo: Uomini, merci, idee dagli Etruschi ai Medici* (Milan, 2003), pp. 196–201.

Bertoni, Giulio. *Poesie leggende costumanze del medio evo*, 2nd edn (Modena, 1927), pp. 231–68. [Estense MS α T.3.11 (Est. 59).]

Biblioteca Nazionale Centrale, Firenze, *Le grandi biblioteche d'Italia* (Florence, 1989).

Biblioteca Nazionale Centrale, Firenze. MS Palatino 556, *Tavola Ritonda*. [MS images online: *www.bncf. firenze.sbn.it/Bib_digitale/Manoscritti/Pal_556*.]

Cadei, Antonio (ed.). *Il Trionfo sul tempo: Manoscritti illustrati dell'Accademia Nazionale dei Lincei, Palazzo Fontana di Trevi, 27 novembre 2002–26 genn. 2003*, Ministero per i Beni e le Attività Culturali (Modena, 2003). [*Tristano Corsiniano* MS description, plate on pp. 125–6.]

Castronovo, Simonetta, and Ada Quazza. 'La circolazione dei romanzi cavallereschi fra il XIII e l'inizio del XV secolo tra Savoia e area padana', in Castelnuovo, *Le Stanze*, pp. 91–106; *schede* 5, 6, 10, 14.

Cigni. 'Mappa redazionale di *Guiron le Courtois* diffuso in Italia', in *Modi e forme della fruizione della 'materia arturiana' nell'Italia dei sec. XIII–XIV: Milano, 4–5 febbraio 2005*, Incontro di studio, 41 (Milan, 2006), pp. 85–117.

Contini, Gianfranco (ed.). *Mostra di codici romanzi delle biblioteche fiorentine: VIII Congresso Internazionale di Studi Romanzi, 3–8 aprile 1956* (Florence, 1957).

Cziep, Norbert. '*Daz was ein dinc, daz hiez der Gral*', *Imagination*, 2/3 (1987), 27–8. [BNCF, Pal. 556.]

Dachs, Monika. *Der Codex Palatino 556 der Biblioteca Nazionale in Florenz und der illustrierte Ritterroman in Italien* (Vienna, 1987).

Dachs, Monika. 'Der Codex Palatino 556 der Biblioteca Nazionale in Florenz: *La Tavola Ritonda*', *Rivista di storia della miniatura*, 1–2 (1996–7), 115–22.

Dachs, Monika. 'Eine Cremoneser "Tavoletta da soffitto"', plates 11, 12. [BNCF, Pal. 556.]

Dachs, Monika. 'Zur Illustration des höfischen Romans in Italien', *Wiener Jahrbuch für Kunstgeschichte*, 42 (1989), 134–54.

Debae, Marguerite. 'La bibliothèque de Marguerite d'Autriche duchesse de Savoie', in Agostino Paravicini Bagliani (ed.), *Les manuscrits enluminés des comtes et ducs de Savoie* (Turin, 1990), pp. 147–70.

Degenhart, Bernhard. 'Pisanello in Mantua', 406–9.

Degenhart, Bernhard, and Annegrit Schmitt. *Corpus der italienischen Zeichnungen*, 8 vols, Berlin (1980–2010).

Degenhart, Berhhard, and Annegrit Schmitt. 'Frühe angiovinische Buchkunst in Neapel. Die Illustrierung französischer Unterhaltungsprosa in neapolitanischen Scriptorien zwischen 1290 und 1320', in Friedrich Piel and Jörg Traeger (eds), *Festschrift Wolfgang Braunfels* (Tübingen, 1977), pp. 71–92.

Durrieu, Paul. 'Les Manuscrits à peintures de la Bibliothèque incendiée de Turin', *Revue archéologique*, 3, series 4 (1904), 394–406. [Two Arthurian mss. damaged in fire.]

Fabbri, Francesca. 'Romanzi cortesi e prosa didattica a Genova alla fine del Duecento fra interscambi, coesistenze e nuove prospettive', *Studi di Storia dell'Arte*, 23 (2012), 9–32.

Faietti, Marzia. 'La *Tavola Ritonda*, Zuliano degli Anzoli e la bottega dei Bembo', in *PAL 556*, pp. 59–82.

Flores d'Arcais, Francesca. 'Les illustrations des manuscrits français des Gonzague à la Bibliothèque de Saint-Marc', in *Essor et fortune de la chanson de geste dans l'Europe et l'Orient Latin: Actes du IXe Congrès International de la Société Rencesvals pour l'Etude des Epopées Romanes: Padoue-Venise, 29 août–4 septembre 1982*, 2 vols (Modena, 1984), II, pp. 585–616.

Flores d'Arcais, Francesca. 'Letteratura cavalleresca e arti figurative nel Veneto dal XIII al XIV secolo', in Giosuè Lachin and Francesco Zambon (eds), *I Trovatori nel Veneto e a Venezia: Atti del Convegno internazionale, Venezia 28–31 ottobre 2004*, Medioevo e Rinascimento veneto, 3 (Padua, 2008), pp. 39–46.

Gathercole, Patricia M. 'Illuminations on the Manuscripts of Rusticien de Pise', *Italica*, 44/4 (1967), 400–8.

Gengaro, Maria Luisa, and Luisa Cogliati Arano (eds). *Miniature lombarde: Codici miniati dell'VIII al XIV secolo* (Milan, 1970).

Giaccaria, Angelo (ed.). *Biblioteca Nazionale Universitaria di Torino. Manoscritti danneggiati nell'incendio del 1904: Mostra di recuperi e restauri* (Turin [1986]).

Gousset, M.-T. 'Etude de la décoration filigranée et reconsitution des ateliers: le cas de Gênes à la fin du XIIIe siècle', *Arte Medievale*, 2 (1988), 121–52.

Guerrieri, Francesco (ed.). *Disegni nei manoscritti laurenziani (sec. X–XVII): Firenze, ott. 1979–febb. 1980* (Florence, 1979). [Exhibition catalogue.]

Longobardi, Monica. 'Due frammenti del *Guiron le Courtois*', *SMV*, 38 (1992), 101–18. [Photos of two pen designs.]

Loomis, R. S. and L. H. Loomis. *Arthurian Legends*, pp. 20, 22, 58–9, 93 n. 23, 99, 107–8, 114–21; plates 305–39.

Luyster, Selon Amanda. 'Playing with Animals: The Visual Context of an Arthurian Manuscript (Florence, Palatino 556) and the Uses of Ambiguity', *Word and Image*, 20 (2004), 1–21.

Macciotta, Leonida (ed.). *Eroi e miti della* Tavola Rotonda, intro. Antonio Viscardi; Italian trans. of texts Carla Cremonesi and Anna Maria Finoli (Milan, 1960).

Morato, Nicola. *Il ciclo di Guiron le Courtois: strutture e testi nella tradizione manoscritta*, Archivio romanzo, 19 (Florence, 2010).

Perriccioli Saggese, Alessandra. 'Alcune precisazioni sul *Roman du Roy Meliadus*, MS. Add. 12228 del British Museum', in Emanuela Sesti (ed.), *La miniatura italiana tra Gotico e Rinascimento: I: Atti del II Congresso di Storia della Miniatura Italiana, Cortona 24–26 settembre 1982*, Storia della Miniatura, Studi e documenti 6, 2 vols (Florence, 1985), I, pp. 51–64.

[Perriccioli Saggese, Alessandra]. *I romanzi cavallereschi miniati a Napoli*, Miniatura e arti minori in Campania, 14 (Naples, 1979).

Pourquery de Boisserin, Juliette. 'La mise en scène de la parole dans les miniatures de trois manuscrits de *Guiron le Courtois*', in Jean-Pierre Montier (ed.), *À l'oeil. Des interférences textes/images en littérature* (Rennes, 2008), pp. 17–25.

Rasmo, Nicolò . 'Il Codice Palatino 556 e le sue illustrazioni', *Rivista d'arte*, 21 (1939), 245–81.

Rasmo, Nicolò. *L'età cavalleresca*, 23. [BNCF, MS Pal. 556.]

Il romanzo arturiano di Rustichello da Pisa, ed. and Italian trans. Cigni 1994. [Colour facsimile of BnF, MS. fr. 1463.]

Savino, Giancarlo. 'Ignoti frammenti di un *Tristano* dugentesco', *Studi di filologia italiana*, 37 (1979), 5–17. [Pistoian fragments; photo of illumination.]

Scherer, Margaret R. *About the Round Table*, pp. 23, 59, 65–7, 69.

Stones, M. Alison. 'Arthurian Art Since Loomis', in Van Hoecke et al. *Arturus Rex: Acta*, II, pp. 21–54. [General theoretical remarks.]

Stones, M. Alison. 'Aspects of Arthur's Death in Medieval Illumination', in Christopher Baswell and William Sharpe (eds), *The Passing of Arthur: New Essays in Arthurian Tradition* (New York, 1988), pp. 52–102. [List of MSS, some produced in Italy.]

Stones, M. Alison. 'The Illustrations in BN, fr. 95 and Yale 229: Prolegomena to a Comparative Analysis', in Keith Busby (ed.), *Word and Image in Arthurian Literature* (New York, 1996), pp. 203–83; plates. [BNCF, MS Pal. lat. (sic) 556, *Tavola Ritonda*, on pp. 216–19.]

Stones, M. Alison. 'Manuscripts, Arthurian Illuminated', in Lacy, *Arthurian Encyclopedia*, pp. 359–74; see 'Italian Manuscripts' on pp. 367–8.

Stones, M. Alison. 'Manuscripts, Illuminated', in Lacy et al. (eds), *The New Arthurian Encyclopedia* (New York, 1991), pp. 299–308.

Sutton, Kay. 'Milanese Luxury Books: The Patronage of Bernabò Visconti', *Apollo*, 34 (1991), 322–6.

Tagliani, Roberto. 'Una prospettiva veneziana per il *Tristano Corsiniano*', *MR*, 32 (2008), 303–32. [Plates.]

Tavola Ritonda: Manoscritto Palatino 556. Firenze, Biblioteca Nazionale Centrale, ed. Cardini (2009).

Thibault Schaefer, Jacqueline. 'The Discourse of the Figural Narrative in the Illuminated Manuscripts of Tristan (c. 1250–1475)', in Busby, *Word and Image*, pp. 174–93, plates.

Toesca, Pietro. *La pittura e la miniatura nella Lombardia dai più antichi monumenti alla metà del Quattrocento* (Milan, 1912; rev edn Turin, 1987), pp. 78–9, 98–9. [Plates of BnF mss.: fr. 755 *Tristan*; fr. 343 *Lancelot*; nouv. acq. fr. 5243 *Guiron*.]

Tordella, Piera Giovanna. 'Le icone disegnate del Manoscritto Palatino 556. La dimensione esecutiva come veicolo di lettura critica', in *PAL* 556, pp. 103–12.

Walworth, Julia. 'Tristan in Medieval Art', in Grimbert, *Tristan and Isolde*, pp. 292, 294; pl. 17, 18.

Whitaker, Muriel. *Legends*, pp. 53–5, 61–7, 70–5.

BIBLIOGRAPHY: PRIMARY TEXTS

Gloria Allaire

Critical Editions, Facsimiles, Transcriptions

Principal Texts

Allaire, Gloria. 'Un nuovo frammento del *Tristano* in prosa (Biblioteca Nazionale Centrale di Firenze, ms. Nuovi Acquisti 1329, Maculatura 44)', *LI*, 53/2 (2001), 257–77. [Fragmentary prose text transcribed.]

Andreas Capellanus. *De amore*, ed. and trans. Patrick Gerard Walsh, *Andreas Capellanus on Love* (London, 1982).

Ariosto, Ludovico. *Orlando furioso secondo l'edizione del 1532 con le varianti delle edizioni del 1516 e del 1521*, ed. Santorre Debenedetti and Cesare Segre, Collezione di opere inedite o rare, 122 (Bologna, 1960).

Arnaut Daniel. Mario Eusebi (ed. and trans.), *Il sirventese e le canzoni* (Milan, 1984).

Boccaccio, Giovanni. *Amorosa Visione*, ed. Vittore Branca, in *Tutte le opere di Giovanni Boccaccio*, V. Branca (gen. ed.), I Classici Mondadori, 9 vols (Milan, 1974), III.

Boccaccio, Giovanni. *Corbaccio*, ed. Giorgio Padoan, in *Tutte le opere* (1974), vol. V, tome 2.

Boccaccio, Giovanni. *De casibus virorum illustrium*, ed. Pier Giorgio Ricci and Vittorio Zaccaria, in *Tutte le opere* (1983), IX.

Boccaccio, Giovanni. *Elegia di Madonna Fiammetta*, ed. Carlo Delcorno, in *Tutte le opere* (1994), vol. V, tome 2.

Boccaccio, Giovanni. *Esposizioni sopra la Comedia*, ed. Giorgio Padoan, in *Tutte le opere* (1965), VI.

Boiardo, Matteo Maria. *Opere*, 1: *L'inamoramento de Orlando*, ed. Antonia Tissoni Benvenuti and Cristina Montagnani, La letteratura italiana, 18/1 (Milan and Naples, 1999).

Brunetto Latini. *Tresor*, ed. Pietro G. Beltrami et al. (Turin, 2007).

Brunetto Latini. *Il Tesoretto*, ed. Julia Bolton Holloway, at *http://www.florin.ms/Tesorett.html*. [From Florence, Bibl. Medicea Laurenziana, MS Strozziano 146.]

Casanova, Giacomo. *Histoire de ma fuite des prisons de la République de Venise qu'on appelle les Plombs* (Bordeaux, 1884).

Conti di antichi cavalieri, ed. Alberto Del Monte, Testi e studi romanzi, 1 (Milan, 1972).

Conti di antichi cavalieri copiati da un codice della biblioteca di casa Martelli, ed. Pietro Fanfani (Florence, 1852).

Contini, Gianfranco (ed.). *La letteratura italiana delle Origini* (Florence, 1970). [*Tristano Riccardiano* and *Tavola Ritonda* excerpts.]

De Bartholomaeis, Vincenzo. *Tristano: Gli episodi principali della leggenda in versioni francesi, spagnole e italiane* (Bologna, 1922). [Transcribed excerpts.]

El Cuento de Tristán de Leonis, edited from the unique manuscript Vatican 6428, ed. George Tyler Northup, The Modern Philology Monographs of the University of Chicago (Chicago, 1928). ['The Italian-Hispanic Group'.]

Dante Alighieri. *La Commedia secondo l'antica vulgata*, ed. Giorgio Petrocchi, Edizione Nazionale, Società Dantesca Italiana, 4 vols (Milan, 1967; rpt Florence, 1994).

Dante Alighieri. *Convivio, 2: Testo*, ed. Franca Brambilla Ageno, Edizione Nazionale (Florence, 1995).

Dante Alighieri. *De vulgari eloquentia*, ed. Pier Vincenzo Mengaldo, in Mengaldo et al. (eds), *Opere minori*, La letteratura italiana, Storia e testi 5/2, 2 vols in 3 tomes (Milan and Naples, 1979), II.

Dante Alighieri. *Opere*. I: *Rime. Vita nova. De vulgari eloquentia*, ed. Claudio Giunta, Guglielmo Gorni and Mirko Tavoni, I meridiani (Milan, 2011).

Dante Alighieri. *Rime*, in Domenico De Robertis and Gianfranco Contini (eds), *Opere minori*, La letteratura italiana, Storia e testi 1/1, 2 vols in 3 tomes (Milan and Naples, 1995), I.

degli Agostini, Niccolò. *Innamoramento de messer Lancilotto et madonna Ginevra, nel quale si trattano le horribili prodezze e le strane venture di tuti li cavalieri erranti nella Tavola rotunda* (Venice: Zoppino, 1521).

degli Agostini, Niccolò. *Innamoramento de messer Tristano e Madonna Isotta,* Libro I (Venice: Simon de Luere, 1515); Libro II and III (Venice: Benedetto Bindoni, 1520).

degli Agostini, Niccolò. *Il libro e terzo e ultimo del innamoramento di Lancillotto de Zenevra . . . agiuntovi el fine de tuti li libri de Lancilotto del strenuo milite Marco Guazzo* (Venice: Zoppino, 1526).

Di Benedetto, Luigi (ed.). *La leggenda di Tristano*, Scrittori d'Italia, 189 (Bari, 1942). [Excerpts of *Tris. Ricc.* (ed. Parodi), *Tav. Rit.*, *Tristano Corsiniano* and 'La morte di Tristano' (*cantare*).]

Fazio degli Uberti. *Il Dittamondo e Le Rime*, ed. G. Corsi (Bari, 1952).

Fossa, Evangelista. *Libro novo de lo innamoramento di Galvano* (Milan, 1494).

Francesco da Barberino. *Reggimento e costumi di donna*, ed. Giuseppe E. Sansone, 2nd edn (Turin, 1957; rpt Rome, 1995/7).

Il Gatto lupesco *e Il* Mare amoroso, ed. Annamaria Carrega, Gli orsatti (Alessandria, 2000).

Guittone d'Arezzo. *Canzoniere: I sonetti d'amore del Codice Laurenziano*, ed. Lino Leonardi (Turin, 1994).

Guittone d'Arezzo. *Le Rime*, ed. Francesco Egidi, Scrittori d'Italia, 175 (Bari, 1940).

Guittone d'Arezzo. *Lettere*, ed. Claude Margueron, Collezione di opere inedite o rare, 145 (Bologna, 1990).

Henricus of Settimello. *Elegia*, ed. E. Bonaventura, 'Lo libro d'Arrighetto fiorentino disposto di grammatica in volgare', *StM*, 4 (1912–13), 110–92.

Henricus of Settimello. *Elegia*, ed. Clara Fossati, *Arrigo da Settimello: Elegia*, Edizione Nazionale dei testi mediolatini, 11 (Florence, 2011).

Inquisitio in partibus, ed. F. Schneider, 'Die Einsiedler Galgan von Chiusdino und die Anfänge von San Galgano', *Quellen und Forschungen aus italienischen Archiven und Bibliotheken*, 17 (1914–24), 71–7.

L'Intelligenza: poemetto anonimo del secolo XIII, ed. Marco Berisso, Biblioteca di scrittori italiani (Milan and Parma, 2000).

King Artus: A Hebrew Arthurian Romance of 1279, ed. and trans. Curt Leviant (New York, 1969; rpt Syracuse, NY, 2003).

Macrobius. *Commentary on the Dream of Scipio*, trans. W. H. Stahl (New York, 1952).

Leggenda antica di San Francesco, trans. V. Gamboso, in *Fonti francescane: Scritti e biografie di san Francesco d'Assisi* (Padua, 1983).

Matthew of Vendôme. *Ars versificatoria*, ed. Franco Munari, *Mathei Vindocinensis: Opera*, 3 vols, Edizioni di Storia e letteratura, 144, 152, 171 (Rome, 1977–88).

Monte Andrea da Firenze. *Le rime*, ed. Francesco Filippo Minetti, Quaderni degli 'Studi di filologia italiana', 5 (Florence, 1979).

Niccolò de' Rossi. *Il Canzoniere di Niccolò de' Rossi*, I: *Introduzione, testo e glossario*, ed. Furio Brugnolo, 2 vols, Medioevo e Umanesimo, 16 (Padua, 1974). [BAV, MS Barb. Lat. 3953: Isotta's letter to Tristano from *Roman de Tristan*.]

Il Novellino, ed. Alberto Conte, I novellieri italiani, 1 (Rome, 2001).

Paul the Deacon. *History of the Langobards* [sic], trans. W. D. Foulke (Philadelphia, 1907).

Petrarca, Francesco. *Opera omnia* (Basileae: Per Sebastianum Henricpetri [sic], 1581).

Petrarca, Francesco. *Poesie minori del Petrarca: sul testo latino ora corretto*, ed. Domenico Rossetti, 3 vols (Milan, 1829–34).

Petrarca, Francesco. *Les remèdes aux deux Fortunes, 1354–66; De remediis utriusque Fortunae*, ed. Christophe Carraud, 2 vols (Grenoble, 2002).

Petrarca, Francesco. *Trionfi, Rime estravaganti, Codice degli abbozzi*, ed. Vinicio Pacca and Laura Paolino, Opere italiane, I meridiani (Milan, 1996; 2nd edn 2000).

Poeti del Duecento, ed. G. Contini, 2 vols, La letteratura italiana, Storia e testi, 2 (Milan and Naples, 1960).

'Poeti della corte di Federico II', ed. Costanzo Di Girolamo et al., in *Poeti della Scuola Siciliana*, I meridiani, 3 vols (Milan, 2008).

Prose di romanzi: Il romanzo cortese in Italia nei secoli XIII e XIV, ed. Felice Arese, Classici italiani, 3 (Turin, 1962). [Anthology of prose romance excerpts.]

Rime due e trecentesche tratte dall'Archivio di Stato di Bologna, ed. Sandro Orlando, Collezione di opere inedite o rare, 161 (Bologna, 2005).

Dal Roman de Palamedés *ai* Cantari di Febus-el-Forte*: Testi francesi e italiani del Due e Trecento*, ed. Alberto Limentani, Collezione di opere inedite o rare, 124 (Bologna, 1962).

Ruggeri Scudieri, Jole M. 'Due lettere d'amore', *Archivum Romanicum*, 24 (1940), 92–4.

Sacchetti, Franco. *Il Libro delle Rime*, ed. Alberto Chiari, Scrittori d'Italia, 157 (Bari, 1936).

Sacchetti, Franco. *Il Trecentonovelle*, ed. Antonio Lanza, I classici italiani (Florence, 1984).

San Galgano e la spada nella roccia: con testo volgare inedito del XIV sec., ed. Franco Cardini, I Classici cristiani, 254 (Siena, 1982).

Il Tristano Biancorusso, ed. and trans. Emanuela Sgambati, Studia historica et philologica, 15, Sectio Slavoromanica, 4 (Florence, 1983).

Tristán de Leonis (Valladolid, Juan der Burgos, 1501), ed. María Luzdivina Cuesta Torre (Alcalá de Henares, 1999).

Visio sancti Pauli: The History of the Apocalypse in Latin Together With Nine Texts, ed. Theodore Silverstein, Studies and Documents, 4 (London, 1935).

Visione di Tugdalo, ed. Francesco Corazzini (Bologna, 1972; rpt 1968). [Includes fourteenth-century Italian version.]

La visione di Tungdal, ed. Margherita Lecco (Alessandria, 1998).

Zorzi, Bertolomé. *Der Troubadour Bertolome Zorzi*, ed. Emil Levy (Halle, 1883).

Cantari

'Il cantare di Astore e Morgana', ed. Daniela Delcorno Branca, in Luigi Reina (ed.), *Humanitas e Poesia: Studi in onore di Gioacchino Paparelli*, Università degli Studi di Salerno, Istituto di Lingua e Letteratura italiana, 2 vols (Laveglia, 1988), I, pp. 5–20.

I Cantari di Carduino, giuntovi quello di Tristano e Lancielotto quando combattettero al petrone di Merlino: Poemetti cavallereschi, ed. Pio Rajna, Scelta di curiosità letterarie inedite o rare dal secolo XIII al XVII, 135 (Bologna, 1873; rpt Bologna, 1968; rpt Rome, 1998). [MS Ricc. 2873.]

Cantari cavallereschi dei secoli XV e XVI, in Giorgio Barini (ed.), Collezione di opere inedite o rare dei primi tre secoli della lingua, 89 (Bologna, 1905).

Cantari del Trecento, ed. Armando Balduino, Scrittori italiani, Sezione letteraria (Milan, 1970).

Cantari fiabeschi arturiani, ed. Daniela Delcorno Branca, Biblioteca medievale, 76 (Milan and Trent, 1999).

Li chantari di Lancellotto, ed. E. T. Griffiths (Oxford, 1924).

Cantari novellistici dal Tre al Cinquecento, ed. Elisabetta Benucci, Roberta Manetti and Franco Zabagli (Rome, 2002).

Cantari di Tristano, ed. Giulio Bertoni, Istituto di filologia romanza della R. Università di Roma, Testi e manuali, 1 (Modena, 1937); rpt in *CN*, 47 (1987), 5–32.

'Il Cavaliere del Falso Scudo. *Cantari due di anonimo fiorentino del sec. XV*', ed. Carlo Milanesi, in Cesare Riccomanni (ed.), *Raccolta di scritture varie pubblicata nell'occasione delle nozze Riccomanni-Fineschi* (Turin, 1863), pp. 79–84.

Cigni, Fabrizio. 'Un nuovo testimone del cantare *Ultime imprese e morte di Tristano*', *SMV*, 43 (1997), 131–91.

De Robertis, Domenico. 'Cantari antichi', *Studi di filologia italiana*, 38 (1970), 67–175. [On 134–8, excerpts from *Cantare di Tristano* in BNCF, MS Magliab. VIII, 1272 and Milan, Bibl. Ambrosiana, MS N. 95 Sup.]

Delcorno Branca. 'I cantari di Tristano', *LI*, 23/3 (1971), 289–305. [Text transcribed from MS Tempi 2.]

'*Morte del Tristano*', in Giulio Bertoni, *Poesie leggende costumanze del medio evo*, 2nd edn (Modena, 1927), pp. 315–16. [Transcription of MS Ambrosiano, N. 95 Sup., fol. 253v.]

Ponzela Gaia: cantare dialettale inedito del sec. XV, ed. Giorgio Varanini, Scelta di curiosità letterarie inedite o rare dal secolo XIII al XIX, 252 (Bologna, 1957).

Ponzela Gaia: Galvano e la donna serpente, ed. Beatrice Barbiellini Amidei, Biblioteca medievale, 80 (Milan and Trent, 2000).

Pucci, Antonio. *Gismirante. Madonna Leonessa*, ed. Maria Bendinelli Predelli. English translations by Joyce Myerson, Amanda Glover and Andrea Saunderson. British Rencesvals Publications, 6 (Edinburgh, 2013).

'*La Struzione della Tavola Rotonda*', ed. Maria Bendinelli Predelli, *Letteratura italiana antica*, 13 (2012), 17–111.

'*Ultime imprese e morte di Tristano*', ed. Armando Balduino, *Cantari del Trecento*, pp. 105–27.

'*Vendetta della morte di Tristano*', ed. Giulio Bertoni, in *Cantari di Tristano*, pp. 68–93.

French and Occitan Romances

Chrétien de Troyes. *Le Chevalier au Lion*, ed. and trans. David Hult, Lettres Gothiques, 4539 (Paris, 1994).

Chrétien de Troyes. *Cligés*, ed. Stewart Gregory and Claude Luttrell, Arthurian Studies, 28 (Cambridge, 1993).

Chrétien de Troyes. *Erec und Enide: Textausgabe mit Varientenauswahl, Einleitung und erklärenden Anmerkungen*, ed. Wendelin Foerster, Romanische Bibliothek, 13 (1890; rpt Halle/Saale, 1934).

La Folie Lancelot: A hitherto unidentified portion of the Suite du Merlin contained in MSS B.N. 112 and 12599, ed. Fanni Bogdanow (Tübingen, 1965).

Guiron le Courtois: Étude de la tradition manuscrite et analyse critique, ed. Roger Lathuillère, Publications romanes et françaises, 86 (Geneva, 1966).

Jaufre, ed. and trans. Charmaine Lee, Biblioteca medievale, 105 (Rome, 2006).

Le Livre de Alixandre, empereur de Constentinoble et de Cligés son filz: roman en prose du XVe siècle, ed. Maria Colombo Timelli, Textes littéraires français, 567 (Geneva, 2004).

La Mort le roi Artu, ed. Jean Frappier (Geneva, 1956; rpt 1964).

Richart d'Irlande. *Les Prophecies de Merlin*, ed. Lucie A. Paton, 2 vols (New York and London, 1926–7). [From MS 593 in the Bibliothèque municipale of Rennes.]

Le Roman d'Eneas, ed. J. J. Salverda de Grave, Biblioteca normannica, 4 (Halle, 1891).

Le Roman de Tristan en prose, ed. Renée L. Curtis, 3 vols (Munich, 1963; Leiden, 1976; Cambridge, 1985).

Le Roman de Tristan en prose, Philippe Ménard (gen. ed.), Textes littéraires français, 9 vols (Geneva, 1987–97).

Le Roman de Tristan en prose: Les deux captivités de Tristan, ed. Joël Blanchard, Bibliothèque française et romane, Série B: Éditions critiques de texte, 15 (Paris, 1976).

Le Roman de Tristan en prose (version du manuscrit fr. 757 de la Bibliothèque nationale de Paris), Philippe Ménard (gen. ed.), Les classiques français du Moyen Âge, 123, 133, 135, 144, 153, 5 vols (Paris, 1997–2007).

Thomas. *Le Roman de Tristan*, ed. Joseph Bédier, Société des anciens textes français, 2 vols (Paris, 1902–5).

Le Livre du Chevalier Errant

Tommaso III di Saluzzo. Marco Piccat (ed.), *Il Libro del Cavaliere Errante (BnF ms. fr. 12559)* (Boves, 2008). [Contains *Le Livre du Chevalier Errant*, crit. edn Laura Ramello, pp. 37–575; Italian prose trans. Enrica Martinengo, pp. 577–1049. Name Index, Glossary, coloured plates of MS illuminations.]

Tommaso III. von Saluzzo. *Le Livre du Chevalier Errant, kritische Edition*, ed. Robert Fajen (Wiesbaden, forthcoming).

Ward, Marvin James. 'A Critical Edition of Thomas III, Marquis of Saluzzo's "Le Livre du Chevalier Errant"' (unpublished Ph.D. dissertation, University of North Carolina, Chapel Hill, 1984).

Girone il Cortese / Meliadus / Compilation of Rustichello da Pisa

Alamanni, Luigi. *Girone (Gyrone) il Cortese* (Venice: Comin da Trino di Monferrato, 1549).

Girone il cortese: Romanzo cavalleresco di Rustico o Rusticiano da Pisa, volgarizzamento inedito del buon secolo, ed. Francesco Tassi (Florence, 1855).

Levy, John Fligelman, '*Livre de Meliadus*: An edition of the Arthurian compilation of B.N.F. f. fr. 340 attributed to Rusticien de Pise' (unpublished Ph.D. dissertation, University of California, Berkeley, 2000).

Il romanzo arturiano di Rustichello da Pisa, ed. Fabrizio Cigni (Pisa, 1994). [Facsimile of BnF MS fr. 1463, transcribed with facing modern Italian trans.]

Queste del Saint Graal

'*La grant Queste del Saint Graal*', ed. Aldo Rosellini, in Gianfranco D'Aronco et al. (eds), *La grant Queste del Saint Graal: Versione inedita della fine del XIII secolo del ms. Udine, Biblioteca Arcivescovile, 177* (Tricesimo [Udine], 1990).

La Inchiesta del Sangradale: Volgarizzamento toscano della Queste del Saint Graal, ed. Marco Infurna, Biblioteca della Rivista di Storia e Letteratura Religiosa, Testi e documenti, 14 (Florence, 1993).

Ruggeri Scudieri, Jole M. 'Versioni italiane della *Queste del Saint Graal*', *Archivum Romanicum*, 21 (1937), 471–86. [Transcription of four *Queste* fragments in Veneto dialect, bound in Venice, Biblioteca Marciana, MS. Graec. II, cod. XVII.]

La Version Post-Vulgate de la Queste del Saint Graal *et de la* Mort Artu*: troisième partie du* Roman du Graal, ed. Fanni Bogdanow, 4 vols in 5 tomes, S.A.T.F., Paris, I, II, IV/1 (1991); III (2000); IV/2 (2001).

La Storia di Merlino / Vita di Merlino

Pieri, Paolino. *La Storia di Merlino*, ed. Mauro Cursietti, I topazi, Testi volgari antichi, 4 (Rome, 1997).

La Storia di Merlino di Paolino Pieri, ed. Ireneo Sanesi, Biblioteca storica della letteratura italiana . . . III (Bergamo, 1898).

Messer Zorzi. *Historia di Merlino,* or *Vita di Merlino con le sue profetie* (Venice: Lucas Dominici, 1480).

La Tavola Ritonda

M[arti], M[ario]. 'La *Tavola Ritonda*', in Cesare Segre and Mario Marti (eds), *La prosa del Duecento*, La letteratura italiana, Storia e testi, 3 (Milan, 1959), pp. 663–735. [Excerpt.]

La Tavola Ritonda o l'Istoria di Tristano: Testo di lingua, ed. Filippo-Luigi Polidori, Collezione di opere inedite o rare dei primi tre secoli della lingua, 8–9, 2 vols (Bologna, 1864–6).

La Tavola ritonda, ed. Filippo-Luigi Polidori, rpt with intro. Marie-José Heijkant, Biblioteca medievale, 1 (Milan and Trent, 1997; rpt Trent, 1998).

Tavola Ritonda: Manoscritto Palatino 556, Firenze, Biblioteca Nazionale Centrale, ed. Roberto Cardini, I codici miniati, 2 vols (Rome, 2009). [Facsimile edn with transcription and critical apparatus. High-resolution images of the entire manuscript may be seen on line at *http://www.bncf.firenze.sbn.it/ Bib_digitale/Manoscritti/Pal_556/main.htm.*]

Tavola Ritonda, ed. Emanuele Trevi, Classici Rizzoli (Milan, 1999).

Tristan and the Round Table: A Translation of La Tavola Ritonda, trans. Anne Shaver, assisted by Annette Cash, Medieval and Renaissance Texts and Studies, 28 (Binghamton, 1983).

Il Tristano Corsiniano

Tagliani, Roberto. 'Il *Tristano Corsiniano*, edizione, studio codicologico, iconografico e linguistico' (unpublished Ph.D. dissertation, University of Siena, 2006) *www.unisi.it/ricerca/dottorationweb/filologia. . ./abstract_tagliani.pdf.*

Il Tristano Corsiniano, ed. Michele Galasso (Cassino, 1937).

Il Tristano corsiniano: Edizione critica, ed. Roberto Tagliani, Atti della Accademia Nazionale dei Lincei, Classe di scienze morali, storiche e filologiche, Memorie, ser. IX, vol. 28/1 (Rome, 2011). [With MS facsimile on CD-ROM.]

Il Tristano corsiniano, transcription with English trans. Gloria Allaire, Arthurian Archives, 8, Italian Literature (Cambridge, forthcoming).

Il Tristano Panciatichiano

Banchi, Luciano. *Il castello delle pulzelle, racconto inedito tratto dall'Istoria del Sangradale (Nozze Morelli-Brini)* (Siena, 1884).

Il Tristano panciatichiano, ed. and trans. Gloria Allaire, Arthurian Archives, 8, Italian Literature, 1 (Cambridge, 2002).

Il Tristano Riccardiano, ed. E. G. Parodi (Bologna, 1896). [Includes excerpt of *Panc.*]

Il Tristano Riccardiano

M[arti], M[ario], '*Tristano Riccardiano*', in Cesare Segre and Mario Marti (eds), *La prosa del Duecento*, pp. 555–661. [Excerpt.]

Il romanzo di Tristano, ed. Antonio Scolari, Testi della cultura italiana, 17 (Genoa, 1990). [New edn of *Tristano Riccardiano*.]

Il Tristano Riccardiano, ed. E[rnesto] G[iacomo] Parodi, Collezione di opere inedite o rare di scrittori italiani dal XIII al XVI secolo, R[eale] Commissione pe' testi di lingua nelle provincie dell'Emilia, 74 (Bologna, 1896).

Tristano Riccardiano, rpt of critical edn by Parodi; Marie-José Heijkant (intro.), Biblioteca medievale, 16 (Parma, 1991).

Tristano Riccardiano, rpt of critical edn by Scolari; F. Regina Psaki (trans.), Arthurian Archives, 8, Italian Literature, 2 (Cambridge, 2006).

Il Tristano Veneto

Donadello, Aulo. 'La redazione veneta del *Romanzo di Tristano*' (unpublished Ph.D. dissertation, University of Padua, 1987).

Il libro di messer Tristano ('Tristano Veneto'), ed. Aulo Donadello, Medioevo Veneto (Venice, 1994).

Review (anon.) of Donadello, *Il libro di messer Tristano*, *Medium Aevum*, 65/1 (1996), 183.

Il Vecchio Cavaliere (The Old Knight)

Breillat, Pierre. 'La *Table Ronde* en Orient. Le poème grec du vieux chevalier', *Mélanges d'archéologie et d'histoire*, 55 (1938), 308–40.

Brownlee, Marina Scordilis. 'The Politics of an Arthurian Prequel: Rustichello, Palamades, and Byzantium', in José Manuel Hidalgo (ed.), *La pluma es lengua del alma: Ensayos en Honor de E. Michael Gerli*, Juan de la Cuesta Hispanic Monographs, Homenajes, 39 (Newark, DE, 2012), pp. 53–77. [In appendix, translation of *The Old Knight* in collaboration with Fotini Skordili.]

Goldwyn, Adam J. 'Arthur in the East: Cross-Cultural Translations of Arthurian Romances in Greek and Hebrew, Including a New Translation of Ο Πρέσβυς Ἱππότης / *The Old Knight*', *LATCH: Journal of Literary Artifacts in Theory, Culture, and History*, 5 (2012), 75–105.

'Ο Πρέσβυς Ἱππότης: The Old Knight. A New Edition of the Greek Arthurian Poem of MS Vaticanus graecus 1822*, ed. Thomas H. Crofts, trans. Dimitra Fimi, forthcoming.

Il vecchio cavaliere, ed. and trans. Francesca Rizzo Nervo, Medioevo Romanzo e Orientale / Testi, 6 (Soveria Mannelli, 2000).

Zibaldone da Canal

Merchant Culture in Fourteenth-Century Venice: The Zibaldone da Canal, ed. and trans. John E. Dotson, Medieval and Renaissance Texts and Studies, 98 (Binghamton, 1994). [Prose *Tristan* fragment, pp. 125–7.]

Zibaldone da Canal: Manoscritto mercantile del sec. XIV, ed. Alfredo Stussi, Fonti per la storia di Venezia, Sez. 5: Fondi Vari (Venice, 1967), pp. 73–5. [Prose *Tristan* fragment.]

English Translations

Boccaccio, Giovanni. *Amorosa visione*, ed. and trans. Robert Hollander, Timothy Hampton and Margherita Frankel (Hanover, NH, 1986). [Bilingual edn.]

Boccaccio, Giovanni. *Boccaccio's Expositions on Dante's 'Comedy'*, trans., intro. and notes by Michael Papio (Toronto, 2009).

Boccaccio, Giovanni. *The Corbaccio*, trans. Anthony K. Cassell (Urbana, 1975).

Boccaccio, Giovanni. *The Elegy of Lady Fiammetta*, trans. Mariangela Causa-Steindler and Thomas Mauch (Chicago, 1990).

Boccaccio, Giovanni. *The Fates of Illustrious Men*, trans. Louis Brewer Hall (New York, 1965).

Chrétien de Troyes. *The Knight of the Cart*, in David Staines (trans.), *The Complete Romances of Chrétien de Troyes* (Bloomington, IN, 1990).

Dante Alighieri. *Dante's Il Convivio (The Banquet)*, trans. Richard Lansing, Garland Library of Medieval Literature, 65 (New York, 1990).

Dante Alighieri. *De Vulgari eloquentia*, ed. and trans. Steven Botterill, Cambridge Medieval Classics, 5 (Cambridge, 1996).

Dante Alighieri. *Inferno*, trans. Robert Hollander and Jean Hollander; intro. and notes by Robert Hollander (New York, 2000).

Dante Alighieri. *Paradiso*, trans. Robert Hollander and Jean Hollander; intro. and notes by Robert Hollander (New York, 2007).

Drukker, Tamar S. 'A Thirteenth-Century Arthurian Tale in Hebrew: A Unique Literary Exchange', *Medieval Encounters*, 15 (2009), 114–29. [Translation and analysis of *King Artus*.]

King Artus: A Hebrew Arthurian Romance of 1279, ed. and trans. Curt Leviant, Studia semitica neerlandica, 11 (New York, 1969; rpt Syracuse, NY, 2003). [Biblioteca Apostolica Vaticana, MS Urb. ebr. 48.]

Petrarca, Francesco. *Letters of Old Age: Rerum senilium libri I–XVIII*, trans. Aldo S. Bernardo, Saul Levin and Reta A. Bernardo, 2 vols (Baltimore, 1992).

Petrarca, Francesco. *Petrarch's Remedies for Fortune Fair and Foul: A Modern English Translation of De remediis utriusque fortune, with a Commentary*, trans. Conrad H. Rawski, 5 vols (Bloomington, IN, 1991).

Rossetti, Dante Gabriel. Sally Purcell (ed.), *The Early Italian Poets* (Berkeley, CA, 1981).

Wilhelm, James J. (ed. and trans.), 'Cantare on the Death of Tristan', in Wilhelm (ed.) *The Romance of Arthur: An Anthology of Medieval Texts in Translation*, (New York, 1994), pp. 295–303.

BIBLIOGRAPHY: STUDIES

Gloria Allaire

Ackerman, R. W. 'Arthurian Literature', in Strayer (ed.), *Dictionary*, I, pp. 572–3.

Agamben, Giorgio. 'Comedìa', in *Categorie italiane. Studi di poetica e di letteratura*, Biblioteca Universale Laterza, 634 (Rome, 2010), pp. 3–26.

Albert, Sophie. 'Des mythes pour penser le roi. Lectures de la figure d'Uterpandragon, du *Lancelot* en prose au *Roman de Meliadus*', *Questes*, 13 (2008), 24–37.

Albertini Ottolenghi, Maria Grazia. 'La Biblioteca dei Visconti e degli Sforza: Gli inventari del 1488 e del 1490', *Studi Petrarcheschi*, n.s. 8 (1991), 1–238.

Alfie, Fabian, and Andrea Dini (eds). *'Accessus ad Auctores': Studies in Honor of Christopher Kleinhenz*, Medieval and Renaissance Texts and Studies, 397 (Tempe, 2011).

Alhaique Pettinelli, Rosanna. *Forme e percorsi dei romanzi di cavalleria* (Rome, 2004).

Alhaique Pettinelli, Rosanna. *L'immaginario cavalleresco nel rinascimento ferrarese* (Rome, 1983).

Allaire, Gloria. 'Arthurian Material in Italy', in Kleinhenz (ed.), *Medieval Italy*, I, pp. 68–9.

Allaire, Gloria. 'Cantare', in Kleinhenz (ed.), *Medieval Italy*, I, pp. 180–1.

Allaire, Gloria. 'Literary Evidence for Multilingualism: The *Roman de Tristan* in its Italian Incarnations', in Kleinhenz and Busby (eds), *Medieval Multilingualism*, pp. 145–53.

Allaire, Gloria. 'Un nuovo frammento del *Tristano* in prosa (Biblioteca Nazionale Centrale di Firenze, ms. Nuovi Acquisti 1329, maculatura 44)', *LI*, 53 (2001), 257–77.

Allaire, Gloria. 'An Overlooked Italian Manuscript: The *Tristano Corsiniano*', *Tristania*, 24 (2006), 37–50.

Allaire, Gloria. Review of Delcorno Branca, *Tristano e Lancillotto in Italia*, *Speculum*, 76/2 (2001), 430–3.

Allaire, Gloria. 'Tavola Ritonda', in Kleinhenz (ed.), *Medieval Italy*, II, pp. 1070–1.

Alvar, Carlos. '*Tristanes* italianos y *Tristanes* castellanos', in Fabrizio Cigni and Maria Pia Betti (eds), *Testi, generi e tradizioni nella Romània medievale: Atti del VI Convegno della Società Italiana di Filologia Romanza, Pisa, 28–30 settembre 2000*, special issue of *SMV*, 47 (2001), 57–75.

Alvar, Carlos, and Lucía Megías, José Manuel. 'Hacia el códice del *Tristán de Leonís* (cincuenta y nueve nuevos fragmentos manuscritos en la Biblioteca Nacional de Madrid)', *Revista de Literatura Medieval*, 11 (1999), 9–135.

Ambrosini, Riccardo. 'Spoglio fonetico, morfologico e lessicale del *Tristano Corsiniano*', *L'Italia Dialettale*, 20 (1956), 29–70.

Ambrosini, Riccardo. 'Su alcuni dittonghi aberranti del *Tristano Corsiniano*', *Annali della Scuola Normale Superiore di Pisa*, series II, 24 (1955), 109–14.

Antonelli, Armando. 'Un nuovo frammento bolognese del *Lancelot en prose*: trascrizione e prospettiva di ricerca', *Parola*, 13 (2009), 115–32.

Asín Palaciós, Miguel. *Islam and the* Divine Comedy, trans. Harold Sunderland (New York, 1926; rpt London, 1968).

Aslanov, Cyril. *Evidence of Francophony in Mediaeval Levant: Decipherment and Interpretation (MS Paris BnF copte 43)* (Jerusalem, 2006).

Aslanov, Cyril. *Le français au Levant, jadis et naguère: à la recherche d'une langue perdue*, Lingustique française, 12 (Paris, 2006).

Aslanov, Cyril. 'Languages in Contact in the Latin East: Acre and Cyprus', *Crusades*, 1 (2002), 155–81.

Avalle, D'Arco Silvio (ed.). *Concordanze della lingua poetica italiana delle origini (CLPIO)*, Documenti di filologia, 25 (Milan, 1992).

Avalle, D'Arco Silvio. *Le maschere di Guglielmino. Struttura e motivi etnici nella cultura medievale* (Milan and Naples, 1989).

Avril, François and Marie-Thérèse Gousset. *Manuscrits enluminés d'origine italienne*, 3: *XIVe siècle*, I: *Lombardie-Ligurie* (Paris, 2005).

Bandini, Anton Maria. *Catalogus codicum manuscriptorum Bibliothecae Medicae Laurentianae*, 5 vols (Florence, 1778), V: *Italicos scriptores exhibens*.

Barattelli, Bianca. 'Due proposte per la zoologia fantastica del *Detto del Gatto lupesco*', *Studi Linguistici Italiani*, 13/1 (1987), 222–31.

Barber, Richard. 'The Grail Quest: Where Next?', in Norris J. Lacy (ed.), *The Grail, the Quest and the World of Arthur*, Arthurian Studies, 72 (Cambridge, 2008), pp. 173–84.

Barbiellini Amidei, Beatrice. 'A proposito di dame al bagno e *dames à la cuve*', *ACME. Annali della Facoltà di Lettere e Filosofia dell'Università degli Studi di Milano*, 61 (2008), 95–121. [On *Ponzela Gaia*.]

Barini, Giorgio. 'Tristano in Italia', *Nuova Antologia*, 193 (1904), 658–74.

Bartuschat, Johannes. '"Il mare amaro dell'amore": Autour du *Mare amoroso*', in Claude Cazalé-Bérard et al. (eds), *La mer dans la culture italienne*, Cahiers d'Italies (Paris, 2009), pp. 47–58.

Battaglia Ricci, Lucia. 'Frammenti di storie dipinte', in Gilberto Ganzer (ed.), *Le favolose historie di Palazzo Ricchieri: Testimonianze tardogotiche nei soffitti lignei di Pordenone* (Treviso, 2008), pp. 51–65, 93–115.

Baumgartner, Emmanuèle. 'Compiler/accomplir', in Jean Dufournet and Nelly Andrieux-Reix (eds), *Nouvelles recherches sur le* Tristan en prose *(Etudes réunies par J. Dufournet)* (Paris, 1990), pp. 33–49.

Baumgartner, Emmanuèle. *La harpe et l'épée: Tradition et renouvellement dans le* Tristan en prose, Moyen Age (Paris, 1990).

Baumgartner, Emmanuèle. 'Histoire d'Helain le Blanc: du *Lancelot* au *Tristan* en prose', in Jean-Claude Aubailly (ed.), *'Et c'est la fin pour quoy sommes ensemble'. Hommage à Jean Dufournet*, 3 vols (Paris, 1993), I, pp. 139–48.

Baumgartner, Emmanuèle. 'The Prose *Tristan*', trans. Sarah Singer, in Burgess and Pratt (eds), *Arthur of the French*, pp. 325–92.

Baumgartner, Emmanuèle. *Le* Tristan en prose*: Essai d'interprétation d'un roman médiéval* (Geneva, 1975).

Bec, Christian. *Les livres des Florentins (1413–1608)*, Biblioteca di 'Lettere italiane', 29 (Florence, 1984).

Beer, Marina. *Romanzi di cavalleria: il 'Furioso' e il romanzo italiano del primo Cinquecento* (Rome, 1987).

Beltrami, Piero G., Maria Grazia Capusso et al. (eds). *Studi di Filologia romanza offerti a Valeria Bertolucci Pizzorusso*, 2 vols (Pisa, 2006).

Benedetti, Roberto. 'Appunti su libri francesi di materia bretone in Friuli', in Paola Schulze-Belli and Michael Dallapiazza (eds), *Liebe und Aventiure im Artusroman des Mittelalters* (Göppingen, 1990), pp. 185–92.

Benedetti, Roberto. 'Frammenti arturiani: Percorsi e nuove individuazioni. *L'Estoire del saint Graal*', in Paradisi and Punzi (eds), *Storia, geografia, tradizioni manoscritte*, special issue of *Critica del testo*, 7/1 (2004), 257–93.

Benedetti, Roberto. 'Un frammento del *Roman de Tristan en prose* fra tradizione toscana e tradizione veneta (Udine, Archivio di Stato, fr. 110)', *SMV*, 49 (2003), 47–69.

Benedetti, Roberto. '"Qua fa' un santo e un cavaliere . . .": Aspetti codicologici e note per il miniatore', in Gianfranco D'Aronco et al. (eds), *La grant Queste del Saint Graal: Versione inedita della fine del XIII secolo del ms. Udine, Biblioteca Arcivescovile, 177* (Tricesimo [Udine], 1990), pp. 31–47.

Benedetti, Roberto, and Stefano Zamponi. 'Notizie di manoscritti: Frammenti del *Guiron le Courtois* nell'Archivio Capitolare di Pistoia', *LI*, 47 (1995), 423–35.

Benedetto, Luigi Foscolo. 'Non "Rusticiano" ma "Rustichello"', in *Uomini e tempi: pagine varie di critica e storia* (Milan, 1953), pp. 71–85.

Bénédictins du Bouveret. *Colophons de manuscrits occidentaux des origines au XVIe siècle*, Spicilegii Friburgensis Subsidia, 4, 6 vols (Fribourg, 1973), III.

Benozzo, Francesco. 'Per la storia di un *topos* del ciclo bretone: il combattimento in incognito di Tristano e Lancillotto (i testi del gruppo cornico)', *Francofonia*, 16/31 (1996), 21–46.

Benozzo, Giuseppina Brunetti, et al. (eds). *Culture, livelli di cultura e ambienti nel Medioevo occidentale: Atti del IX Convegno della Società Italiana di Filologia Romanza, Bologna, 5–8 ottobre 2009* (Rome, 2012).

Benvenuti, Anna Papi (ed.). *La spada nella roccia: San Galgano e l'epopea eremitica di Montesiepi* (Florence, 2004).

Bertolini, Lucia. 'Censimento dei manoscritti della *Sfera* del Dati: I manoscritti della Biblioteca Nazionale Centrale e dell'Archivio di Stato di Firenze', *Annali della Scuola Normale Superiore di Pisa*, ser. III, 18/2 (1988), 417–57.

Bertolini, Lucia. 'La lingua del Palatino 556', in *PAL 556*, pp. 19–58.

Bertolucci Pizzorusso, Valeria. 'L'arpa d'Isotta: Variazioni testuali e figurative', in Jean-Claude Faucon et al. (eds), *Miscellanea Mediaevalia: Mélanges offerts à Philippe Ménard*, Nouvelle Bibliothèque du Moyen Âge, 2 vols (Paris, 1998), I, pp. 101–19.

Bertolucci, Valeria. 'I cavalieri di Pisanello', *SMV*, 20 (1972), 37–48; rpt in *Morfologie del testo medievale* (Bologna, 1989), pp. 75–86.

Bertolucci Pizzorusso, Valeria. 'Nuovi studi su Marco Polo e Rustichello da Pisa', in Morini, *La cultura dell'Italia padana*, pp. 95–110.

Bertolucci Pizzorusso, Valeria. 'Pour commencer à raconter le voyage: Le prologue du "Devisement du Monde" de Marco Polo', in Baumgartner and Laurence Harf-Lancner (eds), *Seuils de l'oeuvre dans le texte médiéval* (Paris, 2002), pp. 115–30.

Bertolucci Pizzorusso, Valeria. 'La réception de la littérature courtoise du XIIe au XIVe siècle en Italie: nouvelles propositions', in Barbara K. Altmann and Carleton W. Carroll (eds), *The Court Reconvenes: Courtly Literature across the Disciplines: Selected Papers from the Ninth Triennial Congress of the International Courtly Literature Society, University of British Columbia, 25–31 July 1998* (Cambridge, 2003), pp. 3–13.

Bertolucci Pizzorusso, Valeria. *Scritture di viaggio. Relazioni di viaggiatori e altre testimonianze letterarie e documentarie* (Rome, 2011).

Bertolucci Pizzorusso, Valeria. 'Testi e immagini in codici attribuibili all'area pisano-genovese alla fine del Duecento', in Marco Tangheroni (ed.), *Pisa e il Mediterraneo. Uomini, merci, idee dagli Etruschi ai Medici* (Milan, 2003), pp. 196–201.

Bertoni, Giulio. *La Biblioteca Estense e la coltura ferrarese ai tempi del duca Ercole I, 1471–1505* (Turin, 1903).

Bertoni, Giulio. 'I *lais* del romanzo in prosa di Tristano', *StM*, 2 (1929), 140–51.

Bertoni, Giulio. 'Lettori di romanzi francesi nel Quattrocento alla corte estense', in *Studi su vecchie e nuove poesie e prose d'amore e di romanzi* (Modena, 1921), pp. 253–61.

Bertoni, Giulio. 'Notizie sugli amanuensi degli Estensi nel Quattrocento', *Archivum Romanicum*, 2 (1918), 29–57.

Bertoni, Giulio. *Poesie–leggende–costumanze del medio evo*, 2nd edn (Modena, 1927), pp. 231–68. [Mentions *Tris. Ricc.*, *Tris. Panc.*, *Tav. Rit.*]

Bertoni, Giulio. Review of L. F. Benedetto, edn of *Il Milione*, in *GSLI*, 92 (1928), 285–93.

Bogdanow, Fanni. 'Arthur's War against Meliadus: The Middle of Part I of the Palamède', *Research Studies. Washington State University*, 32 (1964), 176–88.

Bogdanow, Fanni. *La Folie Lancelot: A hitherto unidentified portion of the Suite du Merlin Contained in MSS B.N. 112 and 12599* (Tübingen, 1965).

Bogdanow, Fanni. 'Fragments d'un nouveau manuscrit du *Lancelot* en prose', *Romania*, 89 (1968), 399–416. [29 folios from two exemplars preserved at Modena.]

Bogdanow, Fanni. 'The Fragments of Part I of the "Palamède" preserved in the State Archives of Modena', *Nottingham Mediaeval Studies*, 13 (1969), 27–48.

Bogdanow, Fanni. 'A Hitherto Unidentified Manuscript of the *Palamède*: Venice, St. Mark's Library, MS. Fr. XV', *Medium Aevum*, 30 (1961), 89–92.

Bogdanow, Fanni. 'A Hitherto Unnoticed Manuscript of the Compilation of Rusticien de Pise', *French Studies Bulletin*, 38 (1991), 15–19.

Bogdanow, Fanni. 'The Italian Fragment of the *Queste del Saint Graal* preserved in the Biblioteca Nazionale Centrale, Florence, and its French Source', *Medium Aevum*, 69 (2000), 92–5.

Bogdanow, Fanni. 'A New Fragment of the *Tournament of Sorelois*', *Romance Philology*, 16/3 (1963), 268–81.

Bogdanow, Fanni. 'A New Manuscript of the *Enfances Guiron* and Rusticien de Pise's *Roman du roi Arthur*', *Romania*, 88 (1967), 323–49.

Bogdanow, Fanni. 'Un nouvel examen des rapports entre la *Queste post-vulgate* et la *Queste* incorporée dans la deuxième version du *Tristan en prose*', *Romania*, 118 (2000), 1–32.

Bogdanow, Fanni. 'Part III of the Turin version of *Guiron le Courtois*: A hitherto unknown source of MS B.N. fr. 112', in Frederick Whitehead, A. H. Diverres and Frank-Edmund Sutcliffe (eds), *Medieval Miscellany presented to Eugène Vinaver by Pupils, Colleagues and Friends* (Manchester, 1965), pp. 45–64.

Bogdanow, Fanni. 'Quelques fragments inconnus de la mise en prose du *Merlin* de Robert de Boron', *Romania*, 90 (1969), 371–81.

Bogdanow, Fanni. *The Romance of the Grail: A Study of the Structure and Genesis of a Thirteenth-century Arthurian Prose Romance* (Manchester and New York, 1966).

Bogdanow, Fanni. 'Some Hitherto Unknown Fragments of the *Prophécies de Merlin*', in F. J. Barnett et al. (eds), *History and Structure of French: Essays in Honour of Professor T. B. W. Reid* (Totowa, 1972), pp. 31–59. [Modena MS fragments, in French with Italian traces.]

Bogdanow, Fanni. 'La tradition manuscrite de la *Queste del Saint Graal*: Versions *Vulgate* et *Post-Vulgate* en Italie', in Danielle Buschinger and Wolfgang Spiewok (eds), *Die kulturellen Beziehungen zwischen Italien und den anderen Ländern Europas im Mittelalter: 4ème Congrès annuel de la Société Reineke (Florenz, 28.–31. Mai 1993)*, Jahrbücher der Reineke-Gesellschaft, series 4; Wodan, 28 (Greifswald, 1993), pp. 25–45.

Bogdanow, Fanni, and Richard Trachsler. 'Rewriting Prose Romance: The Post-Vulgate *Roman du Graal* and Related Texts', in Burgess and Pratt, *Arthur of the French*, pp. 342–92.

Bologna, Corrado. 'La letteratura dell'Italia settentrionale nel Trecento', in Alberto Asor Rosa (gen. ed.), *Letteratura Italiana: Storia e geografia, 1: L'età medievale* (Turin, 1987), pp. 511–600.

Bologna, Ferdinando. *Il soffitto della sala magna allo Steri dei Palermo e la cultura feudale siciliana nell'autunno del Medioevo* (Palermo, 1975).

Boni, Marco. 'Note intorno al MS. Marc. Fr. XXIII del "Roman de Tristan" in Prosa', *SMV*, 1 (1953), 51–6.

Boni, Marco, and A[nna] Valeria Borsari. 'Una reminiscenza del *Roman de Tristan* in prosa nell'*Aspremont V⁴-CHA* e negli *Aspramonti* italiani', in *Atti dell'Accademia delle Scienze dell'Istituto di Bologna*, Classe di Scienze morali, Anno 68, *Rendiconti*, 62/2 (1973–4), 36–54. [Bibl. Marciana, MS fr. IV and Chantilly, Musée Condé, MS 470 (703).]

Borsellino, Nino, and Walter Pedullà (eds). 'Il romanzo', in *Storia generale della letteratura italiana*, I: *Il Medioevo: Le origini e il Duecento* (Milan, 1999), pp. 307–10.

Braghirolli, Willelmo, Paul Meyer and Gaston Paris. 'Inventaire des manuscrits en langue française possédés par Francesco Gonzaga I, capitaine de Mantoue, mort en 1407', *Romania*, 9 (1880), 497–514.

Brambilla Ageno, Franca. 'Una fonte della novella di Alatiel', *Studi sul Boccaccio*, 10 (1977–8), 145–8. [Prose *Tristan* apparent source for story of Tristan's ancestors.]

Branca, Vittore. 'Nostalgie tardogotiche e gusto del fiabesco nella tradizione narrativa dei cantari', in *Studi di varia umanità in onore di Francesco Flora* (Milan, 1963), pp. 88–108.

Brand, Peter, and Lino Pertile (eds). *The Cambridge History of Italian Literature*, rev. edn (Cambridge, 1999).

Breillat, Pierre. 'Le manuscrit Florence Palatin 556: La *Tavola Ritonda* et la liturgie du Graal', *Mélanges d'Archéologie et d'Histoire de l'École française de Rome*, 55 (1938), 341–73.

Breillat, Pierre. 'La *Quête du Saint-Graal* en Italie', *Mélanges d'Archéologie et d'Histoire de l'École française de Rome*, 54 (1937), 262–300.

Breillat, Pierre. 'Une traduction italienne de la *Mort le Roi Artu*', *Archivum Romanicum*, 21/4 (1937), 437–69. [BNCF, MS Panc. 33.]

Bresc, Henri. *Livre et société en Sicile (1299–1499)*, Centro di Studi filologici e linguistici siciliani, Bollettino, Supplementi, 3 (Palermo, 1971).

Brownlee, Marina Scordilis. 'The Politics of an Arthurian Prequel: Rustichello, Palamedes, and Byzantium', in José Manuel Hidalgo (ed.), *'La pluma es lengua del alma': Ensayos en Honor de E. Michael Gerli*, Juan de la Cuesta Hispanic Monographs, *Homenajes*, 39 (Newark, DE, 2011), pp. 53–77.

Bruce, J. Douglas. *The Evolution of Arthurian Romance from the Beginnings down to the year 1300*, 2nd edn, 2 vols (Gloucester, MA, 1958).

Brunel-Lobrichon, Geneviève. 'Un nouveau fragment des *Prophéties de Merlin* à Bologne', in Cornagliotti, *Miscellanea di Studi romanzi*, I, pp. 91–8.

Bruscagli, Riccardo. 'Matteo Maria Boiardo', in Enrico Malato (ed.), *Storia della letteratura italiana, Il Quattrocento* (Rome, 1996), III, pp. 635–708.

Bruscagli, Riccardo. *Studi cavallereschi*, Biblioteca di letteratura, 1 (Florence, 2003).

Brusegan, Rosanna. 'Les insertions lyriques dans les *Tristan* italiens. Le lai en Italie au Moyen Âge', in Laurence Harf-Lancner et al. (eds), *Des Tristan en vers au Tristan en prose: Hommage à Emmanuèle Baumgartner*, Colloques, congrès et conférences sur le Moyen Âge, 8 (Paris, 2009), pp. 63–83.

Brusegan, Rosanna. 'L'intertexte français du *Dit du chat-loup: Detto del gatto lupesco*', in Huguette Legros (ed.), *Remembrances et Resveries: Hommage à Jean Batany* (Orléans, 2006), pp. 233–61. [Edn and French trans.]

Bullard, Melissa Meriam. *Filippo Strozzi and the Medici: Favor and Finance in Sixteenth-Century Florence and Rome* (Cambridge, 1980).

Burgess, Glyn S., and Karen Pratt (eds). *The Arthur of the French: The Arthurian Legend in Medieval French and Occitan Literature*, Arthurian Literature in the Middle Ages, IV (Cardiff, 2006).

Burrow, John. *A History of Histories: Epics, Chronicles, Romances and Inquiries from Herodotus and Thucydides to the Twentieth Century* (London, 2007). [Arthurian legend in Giovanni Villani, on p. 279.]

Busby, Keith. 'La bibliothèque de Tommaso di Saluzzo', in Claudio Galderisi and Jean Maurice (eds), *'Qui tant savoit d'engin et d'art': Mélanges de philologie médiévale offerts à Gabriel Bianciotto*, Civilisation Médiévale, 16 (Poitiers, 2006), pp. 31–9.

Busby, Keith. 'Chrétien in Italy', in Alfie and Dini, *'Accessus'*, pp. 25–38. [Wales, MS 444-D prose *Yvain*.]

Busby, Keith. *Codex and Context: Reading Old French Verse Narrative in Manuscript*, Faux-Titre, 221–2, 2 vols (Amsterdam, 2002).

Busby, Keith. 'Livres courtois en mouvement: dans les marges codicologiques de la francophonie médiévale', in Isabelle Arseneau and Francis Gingras (eds), *Cultures courtoises en mouvement* (Montreal, 2011), pp. 227–48.

Busby, Keith (ed.). *Word and Image in Arthurian Literature* (New York and London, 1996).

Busby, Keith, and Catherine M. Jones (eds). *'Por la soie amisté'. Essays in Honor of Norris J. Lacy* (Amsterdam and Atlanta, 2000).

Busby, Keith, and Ad Putter. 'Introduction: Medieval Francophonia', in Kleinhenz and Busby (eds), *Medieval Multilingualism*, pp. 1–13.

Cabani, Maria Cristina. *Le forme del cantare epico-cavalleresco* (Lucca, 1988).

Cadioli, Luca. 'Scoperta di un inedito: il volgarizzamento toscano del *Lancelot en prose*', *MR*, 37 (2013), 177–92. [Fondazione Franceschini, MS 1, Italian prose *Lancelot*.]

Caïti-Russo, Gilda. 'Tristan et l'origine de la littérature romanesque en Italie', *Revue des Langues romanes: Varia*, 110/2 (2006), 457–67.

Caldarini, Ernesta. 'Da Lancillotto al Petrarca', *LI*, 27/4 (1975), 373–80.

Calzone, Sergio. '"Conta la vera storia": le "prose di romanzi" tardo-duecentesche e un contributo alla ricerca delle loro fonti', in *La Macchina meravigliosa: Il romanzo dalle origini al '700*, L'Avventura Letteraria, Teoria e storia dei generi letterari (Turin, 1993), pp. 1–12.

Campbell, Laura Jane. 'The Devil's in the Detail: Translating Merlin's Father from the *Merlin en Prose* in Paulino Pieri's *Storia di Merlino*', *Arthuriana*, 23/2 (2013), 35–51.

Campbell, Laura Jane. 'Translation and Réécriture in the Middle Ages: Rewriting Merlin in the French and Italian Vernacular Traditions' (unpublished Ph.D. dissertation, Durham University). Online: *http://etheses.dur.ac.uk/705/*.

Canova, Andrea, and Paola Vecchi Galli (eds). *Boiardo, Ariosto e i libri di battaglia* (Novara, 2007).

Cappelli, A. 'La Biblioteca estense nella prima metà del secolo XV', *GSLI*, 14 (1889), 1–30.

Capelli, Roberta. 'Caratteri e funzioni dell'elemento cavalleresco-cortese nella lirica italiana del Due e Trecento', in Picone (ed.), *La letteratura cavalleresca*, pp. 91–122.

Capelli, Roberta. 'Presenze arturiane nella lirica italiana delle origini', *Quaderni di lingue e letterature*, 31 (2006), 43–56.

Capelli, Roberta. 'Presenze arturiane nella lirica italiana delle origini (2a parte)', *Quaderni di lingue e letterature*, 32 (2007), 17–27.

Capelli, Roberta. *Sull'Escorialense (lat. e.III.23). Problemi e proposte di edizione*, Medioevi, Studi, 9 (Verona, 2006).

Capusso, Maria Grazia. *La lingua del 'Divisament dou Monde' di Marco Polo*, I: *Morfologia verbale* (Pisa, 1980).

Capusso, Maria Grazia. 'La mescidanza linguistica del *Milione* franco-italiano', in Conte (ed.), *I viaggi del Milione*, pp. 263–83.

Capusso, Maria Grazia. 'La produzione franco-italiana dei secoli XIII e XIV: convergenze letterarie e linguistiche', in Renato Oniga and Sergio Vatteroni (eds), *Plurilinguismo letterario* (Soveria Mannelli, 2007), pp. 159–204.

Cardini. 'L'avventura cavalleresca nell'Italia tardomedievale: modelli letterari e forme concrete', in Centro di studi tardoantichi e medievali di Altomonte (ed.), *Mediterraneo medievale. Scritti in onore di Francesco Giunta*, Biblioteca di storia e cultura medievale, Studi e Testi 2, 3 vols (Soveria Mannelli, 1989), I, pp. 243–88.

Cardini, Franco. *Alle radici della cavalleria medievale*, Pensiero Storico, 76 (Florence, 1981).

Cardini, Franco. 'Concetto di cavalleria e mentalità cavalleresca nei romanzi e nei cantari fiorentini', in Donatella Rugiadini (ed.), Comitato di studi sulla storia dei ceti dirigenti in Toscana. *I ceti dirigenti nella Toscana tardo comunale: Atti del III Convegno, Firenze, 5–7 dicembre 1980* (Florence, 1983), pp. 157–92; rpt in Cardini, *L'acciar de' cavalieri: Studi sulla cavalleria nel mondo toscano e italico (secc. XII–XV)* (Florence, 1997), pp. 73–110.

Cardini, Franco. *San Galgano e la spada nella roccia: San Galgano, la sua leggenda, il suo santuario con un testo inedito volgare del XIV secolo*, I Classici Cristiani, n.s. 2 (Siena, 2000).

Careri, Maria. 'Per la storia di un testimone poco utilizzato del *Brut* di Wace (*membra desiecta*)', in Beltrami, *Studi di Filologia romanza offerti a Valeria Bertolucci Pizzorusso*, I, pp. 419–24.

Carozza, Davy. 'Elements of the *roman courtois* in the Episode of Paolo and Francesca (*Inferno* V)', *Papers on Language and Literature*, 3 (1967), 291–301.

Carrai, Stefano. 'Il lamento di Francesca, il silenzio di Paolo', *Nuova Rivista di letteratura italiana*, 9/1 (2006), 9–26.

Castelnuovo, Enrico (ed.). *Le Stanze di Artù: Gli affreschi di Frugarolo e l'immaginario cavalleresco nell'autunno del Medioevo* (Milan, 1999).

Cavagna, Anna Giulia. '"Il libro desquadernato: la carta rosechata da rati". Due nuovi inventari della
    libreria visconteo-sforzesca', *Bollettino della Società pavese di storia patria*, n.s. 41 (1989), 29–97.

Cavaliere, Alfredo. *La leggenda medievale di Tristano e Isotta* (Rome, 1974).

Ceccarelli Lemut, Maria Luisa. 'I pisani prigionieri a Genova dopo la battaglia della Meloria: la
    tradizione cronistica e le fonti documentarie', in Renzo Mazzanti (ed.), *1284: L'anno della Meloria*
    (Pisa, 1984), pp. 75–88.

Cerrini, Simonetta. 'Libri dei Visconti-Sforza: Schede per una nuova edizione degli inventari', *Studi
    Petrarcheschi*, n.s. 8 (1991), 239–81.

Chandès, Gérard. 'Recherches sur l'imagerie des eaux dans l'oeuvre de Chrétien de Troyes', *Cahiers de
    civilisation médiévale*, 19 (1976), 151–64.

Chênerie, Marie-Luce. 'Étude et édition des fragments du *Tristan en prose* de Toulouse', *BBIAS*, 50
    (1998), 231–64.

Cherchi, Paolo. 'Gli *adynata* dei trovatori', *Modern Philology*, 68/3 (1971), 223–41; rpt in *Andrea, i
    trovatori e altri temi romanzi* (Rome, 1979), pp. 19–51.

Ciàmpoli, Domenico. *I codici francesi della R. Biblioteca nazionale di S. Marco in Venezia* (Venice,
    1897).

Cian, Vittorio. 'Per la fortuna della leggenda di Tristano e d'Isotta nell'Italia del Rinascimento', *GSLI*, 25
    (1929), 391.

Ciccuto, Marcello. *Il restauro de 'L'Intelligenza' e altri studi dugenteschi* (Pisa, 1985).

Cigni, Fabrizio. *Bibliografia degli studi italiani di materia arturiana (1940–1990)*, Biblioteca della
    ricerca, Medio evo di Francia, 2 (Fasano, 1992).

Cigni, Fabrizio. 'Bibliografia degli studi italiani di materia arturiana: Supplemento 1991–2005', in *Modi
    e forme*, pp. 183–226.

Cigni, Fabrizio. 'Copisti prigionieri (Genova, fine sec. XIII)', in Beltrami, *Studi di Filologia romanza*, I,
    pp. 425–39.

Cigni, Fabrizio. '*Guiron, Tristan* e altri testi arturiani. Nuove osservazioni sulla composizione materiale
    del Ms. Parigi, BNF, fr. 12599', *SMV*, 45 (1999), 31–69.

Cigni, Fabrizio. 'Manoscritti di prose cortesi compilati in Italia (secc. XIII–XIV): stato della questione
    e prospettive di ricerca', in Guida and Latella (eds), *La filologia romanza e i codici*, II, pp. 419–41.

Cigni, Fabrizio. 'Manuscrits en français, italien, et latin entre la Toscane et la Ligurie à la fin du XIIIᵉ
    siècle: implications codicologiques, linguistiques, et évolution des genres narratifs', in Kleinhenz and
    Busby (eds), *Medieval Multilingualism*, pp. 187–217.

Cigni, Fabrizio. 'Mappa redazionale di *Guiron le Courtois* diffuso in Italia', in *Modi e forme*, pp. 85–117.

Cigni, Fabrizio. 'Memoria e *mise en écrit* nei romanzi in prosa dei secoli XIII–XIV', *Francofonia*, 45
    (2003), 59–90, esp. 86–90.

Cigni, Fabrizio. 'Per la storia del *Guiron le Courtois* in Italia', in G. Paradisi and A. Punzi (eds), *Storia,
    geografia, tradizioni manoscritte*, special issue of *Critica del testo*, 7/1 (2004), 295–316.

Cigni, Fabrizio. 'Per un riesame della tradizione del *Tristan* in prosa, con nuove osservazioni sul ms.
    Paris, BnF, fr. 756–757', in Benozzo, *Culture, livelli di cultura*, pp. 247–78.

Cigni, Fabrizio. 'Pour l'édition de la *Compilation* de Rustichello da Pisa: la version du Ms Paris, B. N.,
    Fr. 1463', *Neophilologus*, 36 (1992), 519–34.

Cigni, Fabrizio. 'Prima del *Devisement du monde*: Osservazioni sulla lingua della compilazione arturiana
    di Rustichello da Pisa', in Conte (ed.), *I viaggi del* Milione, pp. 219–31.

Cigni, Fabrizio. Review of Heijkant, *La tradizione del 'Tristan' in prosa in Italia*, *SMV*, 36 (1990),
    267–78.

Cigni, Fabrizio. Review of Scolari (ed.), *Il romanzo di Tristano*, and Heijkant (ed.), *Tristano Riccardiano*,
    in *Rivista di Letteratura Italiana*, 11/1–2 (1993), 323–37.

Cigni, Fabrizio. 'La ricezione medievale della letteratura francese nella Toscana nord-occidentale', in
    Edeltraud Werner and Sabine Schwarze (eds), *Fra toscanità e italianità. Lingua e letteratura dagli
    inizi al Novecento*, Kultur und Erkenntnis, 22 (Tübingen and Basel, 2000), pp. 71–108.

Cigni, Fabrizio. '*Roman de Tristan* in prosa e *Compilazione* di Rustichello da Pisa in area veneta. A proposito di una recente edizione', *LI*, 47 (1995), 598–622.

Cigni, Fabrizio. 'Storia e Scrittura nel romanzo arturiano: i chierici e l'origine merliniana del "libro di corte"', in *Mito e storia*, pp. 363–83.

Cigni, Fabrizio. 'I testi della prosa letteraria e i contatti col francese e col latino. Considerazioni sui modelli', in Lucia Battaglia Ricci and Roberta Cella (eds), *Pisa crocevia di uomini, lingue e culture. L'età medievale, Atti del Convegno di Studio (Pisa, 25–27 ottobre 2007)* (Rome, 2009), pp. 157–81.

Cigni, Fabrizio. 'Tristano e Isotta nelle letterature francese e italiana', in Dallapiazza (ed.), *Tristano e Isotta*, pp. 29–129.

Cingolani, Stefano. 'Frammenti di codici in volgare dall'Archivio di Stato di Viterbo, I', *Pluteus*, 4/5 (1986–7), 247–53.

Cingolani, Stefano. Review of edns by Günter Holtus and Peter Wunderli, *Romanistisches Jahrbuch*, 40 (1989), 215–21.

Classen, Albrecht. 'The Tristan-and-Isold Motif in Sixteenth-Century Italian Literature: Straparola's Reception of a Medieval Narrative: A New Source of the *Tristan* Reception History', *Tristania*, 24 (2006), 79–94. [Ordeal of hot metal motif from *Tav. Rit.*]

Clough, Cecil H. 'The Library of the Gonzaga of Mantua', *Librarium. Revue de la Société Suisse des Bibliophiles*, 5 (1972), 50–63.

Comba, Rinaldo and Marco Piccat (eds). *Immagini e miti nello* Chevalier Errant *di Tommaso III di Saluzzo: Atti del Convegno, Torino, Archivio di stato, 27 settembre 2008*, special issue of *Bulletino della Società per gli Studi Storici, Archeologici ed Artistici della Provincia di Cuneo*, 129/2 (2008).

Conte, Alberto. '*Ur-Novellino* e *Novellino*: ipotesi di lavoro', *MR*, 20 (1996), 75–115.

Conte, Silva. *Amanti lussuriosi esemplari: Semantica e morfologia di un vettore tematico*, Testi, studi e manuali, 23 (Rome, 2007).

Conte, Silva (ed.) *I viaggi del* Milione. *Itinerari testuali, vettori di trasmissione e metamorfosi del* Devisement du Monde *di Marco Polo e Rustichello da Pisa nella pluralità delle attestazioni* (Rome, 2008).

Conti, Andrea, and Mario Arturo Iannaccone. *La spada e la roccia: la storia e la leggenda* (Milan, 2007).

Contini, Gianfranco. 'Postilla angiolieresca', in Giancarlo Breschi (ed.), *Frammenti di filologia romanza. Scritti di ecdotica e linguistica, 1932–1989*, Archivio Romanzo, 11, 2 vols (Florence, 2007), I, pp. 495–500.

Corcoran, Patrick. *The Cambridge Introduction to Francophone Literature* (Cambridge, 2007).

Cordié, Carlo. 'Alla ricerca di Demogorgone', in Giuseppina Gerardi Marcuzzo (ed.), *Studi in onore di Angelo Monteverdi*, 2 vols (Modena, 1959), I, pp. 158–84.

Cornagliotti, Anna (ed.). *Miscellanea di Studi romanzi offerta a Giuliano Gasca Queirazza per il suo 65° compleanno*, 2 vols (Alessandria, 1988).

Coronedi, P. H. 'La leggenda del San Graal nel romanzo in prosa di Tristano', *Archivum Romanicum*, 15 (1931), 83–98. [MS evidence for *Queste* in Italy.]

Coronedi, P. H. Review of Gardner, *The Arthurian Legend in Italian Literature*, *Archivum Romanicum*, 16 (1932), 185–7.

Corti, Maria. 'Emiliano e veneto nella tradizione manoscritta del *Fiore di Virtù*', *Studi di filologia italiana*, 18 (1960), 29–68; rpt in Corti, *Storia della lingua e storia dei testi* (Milan and Naples, 1989), pp. 177–216.

Cozzi, Enrica. 'Per la diffusione dei temi cavallereschi e profani nella pittura tardogotica. Breve viaggio nelle Venezie, tra scoperte e restauri recenti', in Castelnuovo (ed.), *Le Stanze di Artù*, pp. 116–27.

Creazzo, Eliana. '*En Sesile est un mons mout grans'*: La Sicilia medievale fra storia e immaginario letterario (XI–XIII sec.)*, Medioevo romanzo e orientale, Studi, 14 (Soveria Mannelli, 2006), pp. 146–68.

Crescini, Vincenzo. 'Il bacio di Ginevra e il bacio di Paolo', *Studi danteschi*, 3 (1921), 5–57.

Cristiani, Emilio. 'I combattenti della battaglia della Meloria e la tradizione cronistica', *Bullettino Storico Livornese*, 1/3 (1931), 165–71; 2/1 (1932), 18–42.

Cristiani, Emilio. 'I dati biografici ed i riferimenti politici dei rimatori pisani del Dugento', *SMV*, 3 (1955), 7–26.

Cuesta Torre, María Luzdivina. *Aventuras amorosas y caballerescas en las novelas de Tristán* (León, 1994).

Cuesta Torre, María Luzdivina. 'La venganza por la muerte de Tristán: la reconstrucción de un episodio del *Tristán* castellano del ms. de Madrid a la luz de sus paralelos con versiones francesas e italianas y con el *Tristán el Joven* de 1534', in Antonio Chas Aguión and Cleofé Tato García et al. (eds), '*Siempre soy quien ser solía': Estudios de literatura española medieval en homenaje a Carmen Parilla* (A Coruña, 2009), pp. 83–105.

Culianu, Ioan P. *Expériences de l'extase: Extase, ascension et récit visionnaire de l'héllenisme au moyen âge* (Paris, 1984).

Curtis, Renée L. 'Les deux versions du *Tristan* en prose: examen de la théorie de Löseth', *Romania*, 84 (1963), 390–8.

Curtis, Renée L. 'A Romance within a Romance: The Place of the Roman du Vallet à la Cote Mautailliée in the Prose *Tristan*', in *Studies in Medieval French Language and Literature Presented to Brian Woledge in Honour of his 80th Birthday* (Geneva, 1988), pp. 17–35.

Dallapiazza, Michael (ed.). *Tristano e Isotta. La fortuna di un mito europeo*, Quaderni di Hesperides, Serie manuali, 1 (Trieste, 2003).

Dardano, Maurizio. 'Il *Tristano Riccardiano* e la *Tavola Ritonda*', in *Lingua e tecnica narrativa nel Duecento*, Biblioteca di Cultura, 3 (Rome, 1969), pp. 222–48.

De Frutos Martínez, María Consuelo. 'La adaptación de los personajes tristanianos en Italia: el *Tristano Riccardiano*', in Pilar Lorenzo Gradín (ed.), *Los caminos del personaje en la narrativa medieval: Actas del Coloquio internacional, Santiago de Compostela, 1–4 diciembre 2004* (Florence, 2006), pp. 165–84. [Focus on Lancelot and Tristan.]

de la Mare, Albinia. 'The Library of Francesco Sassetti (1421–90)', in Cecil H. Clough (ed.), *Cultural Aspects of the Italian Renaissance: Essays in Honour of Paul Oskar Kristeller* (New York, 1976), pp. 160–201.

De Robertis, Domenico. 'Censimento dei manoscritti delle *Rime* di Dante', *Studi Danteschi*, 38 (1961), 167–276.

Del Guerra, Giorgio. *Rustichello da Pisa* (Pisa, 1955).

Del Monte, Alberto. '"Desuz le pin": Postilla tristaniana', in Del Monte (ed.), *Civiltà e poesie romanze*, Biblioteca di filologia romanza, 2 (Bari, 1958), pp. 60–88. [*Tavola Ritonda* and *novella*.]

Delcorno Branca, Daniela. 'Appunti sui romanzi di Merlino in Italia fra Tre e Quattrocento', *Schede umanistiche*, 1 (1993), 5–30.

Delcorno Branca, Daniela. 'L'Ariosto e la tradizione del romanzo medievale', in *Ludovico Ariosto: Convegno internazionale (27 sett.–5 ott. 1974)*, Atti dei Convegni dei Lincei, 6 (Rome, 1975), pp. 93–112.

Delcorno Branca, Daniela. *Boccaccio e le storie di re Artù*, Il Mulino, Ricerca (Bologna, 1991).

Delcorno Branca, Daniela. 'I cantari di Tristano', *LI*, 23 (1971), 289–305.

Delcorno Branca, Daniela. 'Le carte piene di sogni', Introduction to *PAL 556*, pp. 3–18.

Delcorno Branca, Daniela. 'Il cavaliere dalle armi incantate: circolazione di un modello narrativo arturiano', *GSLI*, 159 (1982), 353–82; rpt in Picone and Bendinelli Predelli, *I cantari: Struttura e tradizione*, pp. 103–26.

Delcorno Branca, Daniela. 'Dal romanzo alla novella e viceversa: il caso dei testi arturiani', in Gabriella Albanese, Lucia Battaglia Ricci and Rossella Bessi (eds), *Favole–Parabole–Istorie. Le forme della scrittura novellistica dal Medioevo al Rinascimento, Atti del Convegno di Pisa (26–28 ott. 1998)* (Rome, 2000), pp. 133–50.

Delcorno Branca, Daniela. 'Dante and the *Roman de Lancelot*', in Norris J. Lacy (ed.), *Text and Intertext in Medieval Arthurian Literature* (New York, 1996), pp. 133–45; rev. and trans. into Italian as 'L'alto principe Galeotto' in *TLI*, pp. 225–38.

Delcorno Branca, Daniela. '"*De Arturo Britonum rege*": Boccaccio fra storiografia e romanzo', *Studi sul Boccaccio*, 19 (1990), 151–90.

Delcorno Branca, Daniela. 'Diffusione della materia arturiana in Italia: per un riesame delle "tradizioni sommerse"', in Benozzo et al. (eds), *Culture, livelli di cultura e ambienti*, pp. 321–40.

Delcorno Branca, Daniela. 'Eremiti e cavalieri: tipologia di un rapporto nella tradizione epico-romanzesca italiana', in Beltrami, *Studi di Filologia romanza*, I, pp. 519–41.

Delcorno Branca, Daniela. 'Interpretazioni della fine nella tradizione italiana della *Mort Artu*', in *Mito e storia*, pp. 405–25.

Delcorno Branca, Daniela. 'Lecteurs et interprètes des romans arthuriens en Italie: un examen à partir des études récentes', in Kleinhenz and Busby (eds), *Medieval Multilingualism*, pp. 155–86.

[Delcorno] Branca, Daniela. 'La morte di Tristano e la morte di Arcita', *Studi sul Boccaccio*, 4 (1967), 255–64.

Delcorno Branca, Daniela. *L'Orlando Furioso e il romanzo cavalleresco medievale*, Saggi di 'Lettere italiane', 17 (Florence, 1973).

Delcorno Branca, Daniela. 'Per la storia del *Roman de Tristan* in Italia', *CN*, 40 (1980), 211–29.

Delcorno Branca, Daniela. 'Prospettive per lo studio della *Mort Artu* in Italia', in *Modi e forme*, pp. 67–83.

Delcorno Branca, Daniela. 'Romanzi arturiani', in *Enciclopedia dantesca*, 6 vols (Rome, 1973), IV, pp. 1028–30.

[Delcorno] Branca, Daniela. *I romanzi italiani di Tristano e la Tavola Ritonda*, Pubblicazioni della Facoltà di lettere e filosofia, Università di Padova, 45 (Florence, 1968).

Delcorno Branca, Daniela. *Il romanzo cavalleresco medievale*, Scuola aperta, Lettere italiane, 45 (Florence, 1974).

Delcorno Branca, Daniela. 'Sette anni di studi sulla letteratura arturiana in Italia: Rassegna (1985–92)', *LI*, 44/3 (1992), 465–97.

Delcorno Branca, Daniela. 'Le storie arturiane in Italia', in Piero Boitani, Mario Mancini and Alberto Vàrvaro (eds), *Lo spazio letterario del Medioevo*, II: *Il Medioevo volgare*, III: *La ricezione del testo* (Rome, 2003), pp. 385–403.

Delcorno Branca, Daniela. 'Une *Tavola Ritonda* du XVe siècle: le ms. Palatin 556 de la Bibliothèque Nationale de Florence', *BBIAS*, 49 (1997), 319–20.

Delcorno Branca, Daniela. '*Tavola Ritonda*. La materia arturiana e tristaniana: tradizione e fortuna', in Vittore Branca (ed.), *Dizionario critico della letteratura italiana*, 4 vols (Turin, 1973), III, pp. 471–76; 2nd edn (Turin, 1986), IV, pp. 270–6.

Delcorno Branca, Daniela. 'La tradizione arturiana in Boccaccio', *LI*, 37 (1985), 425–52.

Delcorno Branca, Daniela. 'La tradizione della *Mort Artu* in Italia', *Critica del testo*, 7/1 (2004), 317–39.

Delcorno Branca, Daniela. 'La tradizione italiana dei testi arturiani: Note sul *Lancelot*,' *MR*, 17/2 (1992), 215–50.

Delcorno Branca, Daniela. 'I *Tristani* dei Gonzaga', in Jean-Claude Faucon, Alain Labbé and Danielle Quéreuil (eds), *Miscellanea Mediaevalia: Mélanges offerts à Philippe Ménard*, Nouvelle Bibliothèque du Moyen Âge, 46, 2 vols (Paris and Geneva, 1998), I, pp. 385–93.

Delcorno Branca, Daniela. *Tristano e Lancillotto in Italia: Studi di letteratura arturiana*, Memoria del tempo, 11 (Ravenna, 1998).

Delcorno Branca, Daniela. 'Tristano, Lovato, e Boccaccio', *LI*, 42 (1990), 51–65.

Delcourt, Thierry. 'Un fragment inédit du cycle de la Post-Vulgate', *Romania*, 109 (1988), 247–79.

Desideri, Giovanella. '*Et indefessa vertigo*. Sull' immagine della ruota della Fortuna: Boezio, *Lancelot* e *Commedia*', *Critica del testo*, 8/1 (2005), 389–426.

Desole, Corinna. *Repertorio ragionato dei personaggi citati nei principali cantari cavallereschi italiani*, Pluteus, Testi, 4 (Alessandria, 1995).

Di Domenico, Adriana. 'Un cavaliere sotto l'insegna del leone rampante: Una nuova ipotesi di commit-tenza', in *PAL 556*, pp. 113–22. [Proposes Piero Maria Rossi (1413–82) as commissioner of the book.]

Dinzelbacher, Peter. *Vision und Visionsliteratur im Mittelalter*, Monographien zur Geschichte des Mittelalters, 23 (Stuttgart, 1981).

Dionisotti, Carlo. 'Appunti sui "cinque canti" e sugli studi ariosteschi', in *Studi e problemi di critica testuale: Convegno di studi di filologia italiana nel centenario della Commissione per i testi di lingua, 7–9 aprile, 1960*, Collezione di opere inedite o rare, 123 (Bologna, 1961), pp. 369–82.

Dionisotti, Carlo. *Boiardo e altri studi cavallereschi* (Novara, 2003).

Donà, Carlo. 'Cantari e fiabe: a proposito del problema delle fonti', *Rivista di studi testuali*, 6–7 (2004–5), 105–37.

Donnarumma, Raffaele. *Storia dell' Orlando innamorato: Poetiche e modelli letterari in Boiardo* (Lucca, 1996).

Dronke, Peter. 'Francesca and Heloise', *Comparative Literature*, 26 (1975), 113–35.

Drukker, Tamar S. 'A Thirteenth-Century Arthurian Tale in Hebrew: A Unique Literary Exchange', *Medieval Encounters,* 15 (2009), 114–29.

Duchesne-Guillemin, J. 'L'Iran antico e Zoroastro', in H.-C. Puech (ed.), *Storia delle religioni*, II: *Da Babilonia a Zoroastro*, 7 vols (Rome and Bari, 1977), pp. 309–80.

Dumézil, Georges. *Le livre des héros: légendes sur les Nartes* (Paris, 1965).

Edmunds, Sheila. 'The Medieval Library of Savoy', *Scriptorium*, 24 (1970), 318–27; 25 (1971), 253–84; 26 (1972), 269–43.

Entwistle, William J. *The Arthurian Legend in the Literatures of the Spanish Peninsula* (New York, 1975), pp. 110–20. [Mentions Italian parallels.]

Eusebi, Mario. 'Reliquie del *Tristano* di Thomas nella *Tavola Ritonda*', *CN*, 39 (1979), 39–62; rpt in Eusebi and Eugenio Burgio (eds), *Saggi di filologia romanza* (Florence, 2005), pp. 255–84.

Everson, Jane E. *The Italian Romance Epic in the Age of Humanism: The Matter of Italy and the World of Rome* (Oxford, 2001).

Everson, Jane E. Review of Psaki trans. *Italian Literature*, II: *Tristano Riccardiano*, *Medium Aevum* 76/1 (2007), 170–1.

Fabbri, Francesca. 'Romanzi cortesi e prosa didattica a Genova alla fine del Duecento fra interscambi, coesistenze e nuove prospettive', *Studi di Storia dell'Arte*, 23 (2012), 9–32.

Faietti, Marzia. 'La *Tavola Ritonda,* Zuliano degli Anzoli e la bottega dei Bembo', in *PAL 556*, pp. 59–82.

Fajen, Robert. *Die Lanze und die Feder: Untersuchungen zum* Livre du Chevalier errant *von Thomas III, Markgraf von Saluzzo*, Imagines Medii Aevi, Interdisziplinäre Beiträge zur Mittelalterforschung, 15 (Wiesbaden, 2003).

Falzon, Alex R. *Re Artù in Toscana: Inchiesta sul ciclo arturiano in Toscana dal XII secolo a oggi* (Siena, 1996).

Ferrante, Joan M. *The Conflict of Love and Honor: The Medieval Tristan Legend in France, Germany and Italy*, De Proprietatibus litterarum, Series practica, 78 (The Hague and Paris, 1973).

Finoli, Anna Maria. '"A celle rose clamée . . .": lettere d'amore ne Le Chevalier Errant di Tommaso III di Saluzzo', in Andrea Fassò, Luciano Formisano and Mario Mancini (eds), *Filologia romanza e cultura medievale: Studi in onore di Elio Melli*, 2 vols (Alessandria, 1998), I, pp. 304–17. [Debts to *Tristan en prose* and other French literary sources.]

Finoli, Anna Maria. *Prose di romanzi: Raccolta di studi (1979–2000)* (Milan, 2001). [Several studies on the *Livre du Chevalier Errant.*]

Folda, Jaroslav. *Crusader Art in the Holy Land, from the Third Crusade to the Fall of Acre, 1187–1291* (Cambridge, 2005).

Folena, Gianfranco. 'La cultura volgare e l' "umanesimo cavalleresco" nel Veneto', in V. Branca (ed.), *Umanesimo europeo e umanesimo veneziano*, Civiltà europea e civiltà veneziana, Aspetti e problemi, 2 (Florence, 1963), pp. 141–58; rpt in *Culture e lingue nel Veneto medievale*, Filologia Veneta, Testi e studi (Padua, 1990), pp. 377–94.

Folena, Gianfranco. *Culture e lingue nel Veneto medievale* (Padua, 1990).

Folena, Gianfranco. 'Ernesto Giacomo Parodi', *LI*, 14 (1962), 395–420.

[Folena, Gianfranco]. Review of Ambrosini, 'Spoglio fonetico', *La Rassegna della Letteratura Italiana*, 60 (1956), 540–1.

Fontanella, Lucia and Alessandro Vitale Brovarone. 'Due frammenti francesi all'Accademia delle Scienze di Torino: *L'Estoire du Graal* e il *Tristano* torinese', in Cornagliotti, *Miscellanea di Studi romanzi*, I, pp. 291–314.

Formisano, Luciano, and Charmaine Lee. 'Il "Francese di Napoli"', in Paolo Trovato (ed.), *Lingue e Culture dell'Italia meridionale (1200–1600)* (Rome, 1993), pp. 133–62.

Fotitch, Tatiana. *Les lais du roman de Tristan en prose d'après le manuscrit de Vienne 2545. Edition critique*, Münchener Romanistische Arbeiten, 38 (Munich, 1974).

Foulon, Charles et al. (eds). *Actes du 14ème Congrès International Arthurien: Rennes, 16–21 Août 1984*, 2 vols (Rennes, 1985).

Franceschetti, Antonio. 'Italian Literature: Epic and Chivalric', in Strayer (ed.), *Dictionary of the Middle Ages*, VI, pp. 637–40.

Frappier, Jean. 'Plaidoyer pour l'"architecte", contre une opinion d'Albert Pauphilet sur le *Lancelot en prose*', *Romance Philology*, 8 (1954–5), 27–33.

Galimberti, Paolo M. 'Censimento dei frammenti manoscritti della Biblioteca Queriniana di Brescia', *Aevum*, 76 (2002), 471–551.

Gallais, Pierre. *Perceval et l'initiation. Essais sur le dernier roman de Chrétien de Troyes, ses correspondances 'orientales' et sa signification anthropologique* (Paris, 1972).

Gardner, Edmund Garratt. *The Arthurian Legend in Italian Literature* (London and New York, 1930; rpt 1971).

Gardner, Edmund Garratt. 'The Holy Graal in Italian Literature', *Modern Language Review*, 20 (1925), 443–53.

Gaunt, Simon. 'Galeotto fu il libro e chi lo scrisse: l'amore in tre nella letteratura cortese', in Paolo Oderico and Nicolò Pasero (eds), *Corrispondenza d'amorosi sensi. L'omoerotismo nella letteratura medievali. Atti del I Atelier di Antropologia e Letterature medievali (Genova, 27–28 maggio 2005)* (Alessandria, 2008), pp. 215–33.

Gaunt, Simon, and Ruth Harvey. 'The Arthurian tradition in Occitan Literature', in Burgess and Pratt, *Arthur of the French*, pp. 528–45.

Gerritsen, Willem P., and Anthony G. van Melle (eds). *A Dictionary of Medieval Heroes: Characters in Medieval Narrative Traditions and Their Afterlife in Literature, Theatre and the Visual Arts*, trans. Tanis Guest (Cambridge, 2000), p. 277.

Gherardini, Laura. 'Il testimone fiorentino del *Tristano* di Goffredo di Strasburgo', in E. De Angelis (ed.), *La giovane germanistica italiana, Pisa 25–7 settembre 2006* (Pisa, 2006), pp. 106–17.

Gherardini, Laura. 'Il *Tristano* a Firenze: Un manoscritto della Biblioteca Nazionale Centrale', *Annali della Facoltà di Lettere e Filosofia dell'Università di Siena*, 18 (2007), 29–47. [German-language MS Banco Rari, 226, bound, owned in Italy.]

Giannetti Ruggiero, Laura. 'L'incanto delle parole e la magia del discorso nell'*Orlando Furioso*', *Italica*, 78 (2001), 149–75. [Arthurian precedents for *O. F.*]

Gianni, Alessandra (ed.). *Santità ed eremitismo nella Toscana medievale. Atti delle giornate di studio, 11–12 giugno 1999* (Siena, 2000).

Giannini, Gabriele. 'Il romanzo francese in versi dei secoli XII e XIII in Italia: il *Cligès* riccardiano', in *Modi e forme*, pp. 119–63.

Gimber, Arno. 'La continuación castellana del *Tristán de Leonís* de 1534 y su traducción italiana de 1555', in Javier Gómez and Folke Gernert (eds), *Literatura caballeresca entre España e Italia (del 'Orlando' al 'Quijote')* (Salamanca, 2004), pp. 415–28.

Ginzburg, Carlo. *Ecstasies: Deciphering the Witches' Sabbath*, trans. Raymond Rosenthal (New York, 1991).

Girbea, Catalina. 'Flatteries héraldiques, propagande politique et armoiries symboliques dans quelques romans arthuriens (XIIe–XIIIe siècles)', in Denise Turrel, Martin Aurell et al. (eds), *Signes et couleurs des identités politiques du Moyen Âge à nos jours* (Rennes, 2008), pp. 365–80.

266 GLORIA ALLAIRE

Goldwyn, Adam J. 'Arthur in the East: Cross-Cultural Translations of Arthurian Romances in Greek and Hebrew, Including a New Translation of Ὁ Πρέσβυς Ἱππότης / *The Old Knight*', *LATCH: The Journal of Literary Artifacts in Theory, Culture, and History*, 5 (2012), 75–105.

Goodman, E. L. 'The *Prose Tristan* and the Pisanello Murals', *Tristania*, 3/2 (1978), 22–35.

Gousset, Marie-Thérèse. 'Étude de la décoration filigranée et reconstitution des ateliers: le cas de Gênes à la fin du XIIIe siècle', *Arte Medievale*, 2 (1988), 121–52.

Graf, Arturo. 'Appunti per la storia del ciclo brettone in Italia', *GSLI*, 5 (1885), 80–130.

Graf, Arturo. 'Artù nell'Etna', in Graf, *Miti, leggende, e superstizioni del medioevo* (Florence and Rome, 1892), II, pp. 303–59; rpt Zürich and New York, 1985; rpt Milan, 2002, pp. 375–408.

Gregory, Tullio (ed.). *I sogni nel medioevo. Seminario internazionale, Roma 2–4 ottobre, 1983* (Rome, 1985).

Grendler, Paul F. 'Chivalric Romances in the Italian Renaissance', in J. A. S. Evans and R. W. Unger (eds), *Studies in Medieval and Renaissance History*, o.s. 20 (New York, 1988), X, pp. 59–102.

Grimbert, Joan Tasker. 'Changing the Equation: The Impact of Tristan-Love on Arthur's Court in the Prose *Tristan* and *La Tavola Ritonda*', in Lacy (ed.), *The Fortunes of King Arthur*, Arthurian Studies, 64 (Cambridge, 2005), pp. 104–15.

Grimbert, Joan Tasker. 'The "Matter of Britain" on the Continent and the Legend of Tristan and Iseult in France, Italy, and Spain', in Helen Fulton (ed.), *A Companion to Arthurian Literature*, Blackwell Companions to Literature and Culture, 58 (Chichester, 2009; rpt 2012), pp. 145–59.

Grimbert, Joan Tasker. 'Translating Tristan-Love from the Prose *Tristan* to the *Tavola Ritonda*', *Romance Languages Annual*, 6 (1994), 92–7.

Grimbert, Joan Tasker (ed.). *Tristan and Isolde: A Casebook*, Garland Reference Library of the Humanities, 1514, Arthurian Characters and Themes, 2 (New York, 1995; rpt 2002), pp. xiii–cii.

Guida, Saverio. 'Per il testo della *Tavola Ritonda*. Una redazione umbra', *Siculorum Gymnasium*, n.s. 32 (1979), 637–67.

Guida, Saverio. 'Sulle "fonti" della *Tavola Ritonda*', in *Umanità e Storia. Scritti in onore di Adelchi Attisani*, 2 vols (Messina, 1971), II, pp. 129–55.

Guida, Saverio and Fortunata Latella (eds). *La Filologia romanza e i codici: Atti del I Convegno della Società Italiana di Filologia Romanza, Messina, 19–22 dicembre 1991* (Messina, 1993).

Hasenohr, Geneviève. 'Copistes italiens du *Lancelot*: Le manuscrit fr. 354', in Danielle Buschinger and Michel Zink (eds), *Lancelot-Lanzelet: Hier et aujourdhui. Recueil d'articles . . . pour fêter les 90 ans de Alexandre Micha*, Wodan, 51; Serie 3, Tagungsbände und Sammelschriften; Actes de colloques et ouvrages collectifs, 29 (Greifswald, 1995), pp. 219–26.

Hatcher, Anna G., and Mark Musa. 'The Kiss: *Inferno* V and the Old French Prose *Lancelot*', *Comparative Literature*, 20 (1968), 97–109.

Heijkant, Marie-José. 'L'assedio della città di Gippi nel *Tristano Riccardiano*', in Giovanni Angeli and Luciano Formisano (eds), *L'imaginaire courtois et son double: Actes du VIème Congrès triennal de la Société International de littérature courtoise (ICLS) (Fisciano [Salerno], 24–28 juillet 1989)*, Pubblicazioni dell'Università degli Studi di Salerno, Sezione Atti, convegni, miscellanee, 35 (Naples, 1992), pp. 323–31.

Heijkant, Marie-José. 'La compilation du *Tristano Panciatichiano*', in Bart Besamusca, Willem P. Gerritsen, Corry Hogetoorn and Orlanda S. H. Lie (eds), *Cyclification: The Development of Narrative Cycles in the Chansons de Geste and the Arthurian Romances*, Koninklijke Nederlandse Akademie van Wetenschappen Verhandelingen, Afd. Letterkunde, Nieuwe Reeks, 159 (Amsterdam, 1994), pp. 122–6.

Heijkant, Marie-José. 'The Custom of Boasting in the *Tavola Ritonda*', in Logan E. Whalen and Catherine M. Jones (eds), *'Li premerains vers': Essays in Honor of Keith Busby*, Faux titre, 361 (Amsterdam, 2011), pp. 143–56.

Heijkant, Marie-José. '"E re non è altro a dire che scudo e lancia e elmo": il concetto di regalità nella *Tavola Ritonda*', in Carlo Donà and Francesco Zambon (eds), *La regalità*, Biblioteca medievale, Saggi, 9 (Rome, 2002), pp. 217–29.

Heijkant, Marie-José. "'E' ti saluto con amore": Messaggi amorosi epistolari nella letteratura arturiana in Italia', *MR*, 23 (1999), 277–98.

Heijkant, Marie-José. 'L'emploi des formules d'introduction et de transition stéréotypées dans le *Tristano Riccardiano*', in Keith Busby and Erik Kooper (eds), *Courtly Literature: Culture and Context. Selected papers from the Fifth Triennial Congress of the International Courtly Literature Society, Dalfsen, The Netherlands, 9–16 August, 1986*, Utrecht Publications in General and Comparative Literature, 25 (Amsterdam and Philadelphia, 1990), pp. 271–82.

Heijkant, Marie-José. "'La figura del mondo": Tristan als das Idealbild des Rittertums in der *Tavola Ritonda*', in Matthias Meyer and Hans-Jochen Schieuwer (eds), *Literarische Leben: Rollentwürfe in der Literatur des Hoch- und Spätmittelalter, Festschrift Volker Mertens zum 65. Geburtstag* (Tübingen, 2000), pp. 269–82.

Heijkant, Marie-José. 'Iseut aux Blanches Mains dans le *Tristano Riccardiano*: le motif de l'*homme entre deux femmes* et le motif de la *femme abandonnée*', *Tristania*, 16 (1995), 63–76.

Heijkant, Marie-José. 'La mésaventure érotique de Burletta della Diserta et le motif de la pucelle esforciée dans la *Tavola Ritonda*', *Zeitschrift für romanische Philologie*, 118/2 (2002), 182–94.

Heijkant, Marie-José. Review of Allaire, *Il Tristano panciatichiano* edn, *Romance Philology*, 58 (2006), 136–47.

Heijkant, Marie-José. Review of Ros Domingo, *Arthurische Literatur der Romania*, in *Estudis Romànics*, 26 (2004), 384–9.

Heijkant, Marie-José. 'The Role of the Father of Iseut in the Italian Versions of the Prose *Tristan*', *Tristania*, 20 (2000), 31–40.

Heijkant, Marie-José. 'Die seltsame Gefangenschaft von Tristan und Lancelot bei der Dama del Lago in der *Tavola Ritonda*', in Trude Ehlert (ed.), *Chevaliers errants, demoiselles et l'Autre: höfische und nachhöfische Literatur im europäischen Mittelalter, Festschrift für Xenja von Ertzdorff zum 65. Geburtstag*, Göppinger Arbeiten zur Germanistik, 644 (Göppingen, 1998), pp. 245–56.

Heijkant, Marie-José. *La Tavola Ritonda*, rpt of critical edition by Filippo-Luigi Polidori, Biblioteca medievale, 1 (Milan and Trent, 1997; rpt 1998).

Heijkant, Marie-José. *La tradizione del 'Tristan' in prosa in Italia e proposte di studio sul 'Tristano Riccardiano'* (Nijmegen, 1989).

Heijkant, Marie-José. 'The Transformation of the Figure of Gauvain in Italy', in Raymond H. Thompson and K. Busby (eds), *Gawain: A Casebook*, Arthurian Characters and Themes, 8 (New York, 2006), pp. 239–53.

Heijkant, Marie-José. 'Tristan im Kampf mit dem treulosen Ritter: Abenteuer, Gralssuche und Liebe in dem italienischen *Tristano Palatino*', in Xenja von Ertzdorff and Rudolf Schulz (eds), *Tristan und Isolt im Spätmittelalter: Vorträge eines interdisziplinären Symposiums vom 3. bis 8. Juni 1996 an der Justus-Liebig-Universität Gießen*, Chloe, Beihefte zum Daphnis, 29 (Amsterdam and Atlanta, 1999), pp. 453–72.

Heijkant, Marie-José. 'Tristan "pilosus": La folie de l'héros dans le *Tristano Panciatichiano*', trans. Sabine Raaijmakers Costa, in André Crépin and Wolfgang Spiewok (eds), *Tristan-Tristrant: Mélanges en l'honneur de Danielle Buschinger à l'occasion de son 60ème anniversaire*, Wodan, 66 (Greifswald, 1996), pp. 231–42.

Heijkant, Marie-José. 'Tristano in prospettiva europea: A proposito di un recente volume', *LI*, 57/2 (2005), 272–86.

Heijkant, Marie-José. 'Le *Tristano riccardiano*: une version particulière du *Tristan en prose*', in Foulon, *Actes du 14ème Congrès*, I, pp. 314–23.

Heinrich von Freiberg. *Tristan*, ed. Danielle Buschinger, Göppinger Arbeiten zur Germanistik, 270 (Göppingen, 1982), pp. xiv–xviii. [German Arthurian texts extant in Italian MS libraries.]

Heinz-Mohr, Gerd. *Lexikon der Symbole: Bilder und Zeichen der christlichen Kunst* (Düsseldorf and Cologne, 1971; rpt Freiburg im Breisgau, 1995).

Heller, E. K. 'The Story of the Magic Horn: A Study in the Development of a Mediaeval Folk Tale,' *Speculum*, 9/1 (1934), 38–50.

Hoffmann, Annette. 'Il rapporto testo-immagine: un caso particolare', in *PAL 556*, pp. 83–102.

Hoffman, Donald L. 'The Arthurian Tradition in Italy', in Valerie M. Lagorio and Mildred Leake Day (eds), *King Arthur Through the Ages*, Garland Reference Library of the Humanities, 1269, 2 vols (New York, 1990), I, pp. 170–88.

Hoffman, Donald L. 'Lancelot in Italy', in Carol Dover (ed.), *A Companion to the Lancelot-Grail Cycle*, Arthurian Studies, 54 (Cambridge, 2003), pp. 163–72.

Hoffman, Donald L. 'Merlin in Italian Literature', in Peter H. Goodrich and Raymond H. Thompson (eds), *Merlin: A Casebook*, Arthurian Characters and Themes, 7 (New York and London, 2003), pp. 186–96.

Hoffman, Donald L. 'Radix Amoris: The *Tavola Ritonda* and its Response to Dante's Paolo and Francesca', in Grimbert, *Tristan and Isolde*, pp. 207–22.

Hoffman, Donald L. 'La Tavola Ritonda', in Lacy et al. (eds), *The Arthurian Encyclopedia* (1986), pp. 541–2; rev. edn *The New Arthurian Encyclopedia* (1991), p. 444.

Hoffman, Donald L. 'Tristano panciaticchiano [*sic*]', in Lacy et al. (eds) *The Arthurian Encyclopedia* (1986), pp. 579–80; rev. edn *The New Arthurian Encyclopedia* (1991), p. 473.

Hoffman, Donald L. 'Tristano Riccardiano', in Lacy et al. (eds), *The Arthurian Encyclopedia* (1986), p. 580; rev. edn *The New Arthurian Encyclopedia* (1991), p. 473.

Hoffman, Donald L. 'Was Merlin a Ghibelline? Arthurian Propaganda at the Court of Frederick II', in Martin B. Shichtman and James P. Carley (eds), *Culture and the King: The Social Implications of the Arthurian Legend, Essays in Honor of Valerie M. Lagorio*, SUNY Series in Mediaeval Studies (Albany, 1994), pp. 113–28.

Hollingsworth, Mary. *Patronage in Renaissance Italy from 1400 to the Early Sixteenth Century* (Baltimore, 1994).

Holtus, Günter. 'L'état actuel des recherches sur le franco-italien: corpus de textes et description linguistique', in François Suard (ed.), *La Chanson de Geste: Écriture, Intertextualités, Translations*, Littérales, 14 (Paris, 1994), pp. 147–71.

Holtus, Günter. 'La "matière de Bretagne" en Italie: quelques réflexions sur la transposition du vocabulaire et des structures sociales', in Foulon, *Actes du 14ème Congrès*, I, pp. 324–45.

Infurna, Marco. 'Un ignoto volgarizzamento toscano della *Estoire del Saint Graal*', in Antonio Daniele (ed.), *Omaggio a Gianfranco Folena*, 3 vols (Padua, 1993), I, pp. 295–305.

Infurna, Marco. 'La *Queste del Saint Graal* in Italia e il manoscritto udinese', in D'Aronco et al. (eds), *La grant Queste*, pp. 51–7.

Iragui, Sebastian. 'The Southern Version of the Prose *Tristan*: The Italo-Iberian Translations and their French Source', *Tristania*, 17 (1996), 39–54.

Jauss, Hans Robert. 'The Alterity and Modernity of Medieval Literature', *New Literary History*, 10/2 (1979), 181–229.

Jauss, Hans Robert, and Erich Köhler (eds). *Grundriss der romanischen Literaturen des Mittelalters*, IV/1: *Le Roman jusqu'à la fin du XIIIe siècle* (Heidelberg, 1978).

Joris, André. 'Autour du *Devisement du monde*. Rusticien de Pise et l'empereur Henri VII de Luxembourg (1310–1313)', *Le Moyen Âge*, 100 (1994), 353–68.

Jossa, Stefano. *La fondazione di un genere: il poema eroico tra Ariosto e Tasso* (Rome, 2002).

Kappler, Claude et al. *Apocalypses et voyages dans l'Au-delà*, Études annexes de la Bible de Jérusalem (Paris, 1987).

Kennedy, Elspeth. 'The Placing of Miniatures in Relation to the Pattern of Interlace in Two Manuscripts of the Prose *Lancelot*', in Busby and Jones (eds), *'Por la soie amisté'*, pp. 268–82.

Kennedy, Elspeth. 'The Scribe as Editor', in *Mélanges de langue et de littérature du Moyen Âge et de la Renaissance offerts à Jean Frappier*, Publications romanes et françaises, 112, 2 vols (Geneva, 1970), I, pp. 523–31.

Kent, Dale. 'The Florentine *Reggimento* in the Fifteenth Century', *Renaissance Quarterly*, 28 (1975), 575–638.

Kent, Dale. *The Rise of the Medici Faction in Florence 1426–1434* (Oxford, 1978).

Kerth, Thomas. 'Tristan, Legend of', in Strayer (ed.), *Dictionary of the Middle Ages*, XII, pp. 199–201.

Kleinhenz, Christopher. 'Dante as Reader and Critic of Courtly Literature', in Keith Busby and Erik Kooper (eds), *Courtly Literature: Culture and Context: Selected Papers from the 5th Triennial Congress of the International Courtly Literature Society, Dalfsen, The Netherlands, 9–16 August, 1986* (Amsterdam and Philadelphia, 1990), pp. 379–93.

Kleinhenz, Christopher. 'Italian Arthurian Literature', in Lacy et al. (eds), *The Arthurian Encyclopedia* (1986), pp. 293–9; rev. edn *The New Arthurian Encyclopedia* (1991), pp. 245–8.

Kleinhenz, Christopher. 'Italian Arthurian Literature', in Lacy (ed.), *A History of Arthurian Scholarship*, Arthurian Studies, 65 (Cambridge, 2006), pp. 190–7.

Kleinhenz, Christopher. 'Italy', in Lacy (ed.), *Medieval Arthurian Literature: A Guide to Recent Research*, Garland Reference Library of the Humanities, 1955 (New York, 1996), pp. 323–47.

Kleinhenz, Christopher (ed.). *Medieval Italy: An Encyclopedia*, 2 vols (New York, 2004).

Kleinhenz, Christopher. 'The Quest Motif in Medieval Italian Literature', in Busby and Lacy (eds), *Conjunctures: Medieval Studies in Honor of Douglas Kelly* (Amsterdam, 1994), pp. 235–51.

Kleinhenz, Christopher. 'Tristan in Italy: The Death or Rebirth of a Legend', *Studies in Medieval Culture*, 5 (1975), 145–58.

Kleinhenz , Christopher and Keith Busby (eds). *Medieval Multilingualism: The Francophone World and its Neighbours* (Turnhout, 2010).

Köhler, Erich. *L'Aventure chevaleresque: idéal et réalité dans le roman courtois, études sur la forme des plus anciens poèmes d'Arthur et du Graal*, trans. Éliane Kaufholz (Paris, 1974).

Krauss, Henning. 'Der Artus-Roman in Italien', in Jauss and Köhler (eds), *Grundriss der romanischen Literaturen*, IV/1, pp. 667–75.

Lacerenza, Giancarlo. '*Mēlek Arṭûś*. I temi arturiani ebraizzati nel *Sēfer ha-šēmād*', in Giovanni Carbonaro, Eliana Creazzo and Natalia L. Tornesello (eds), *Medioevo Romanzo e Orientale. Macrotesti fra Oriente e Occidente (Atti del IV Colloquio Internazionale, Vico Equense, 26–29 ottobre 2000)* (Soveria Mannelli, 2003), pp. 101–18.

Lacy, Norris J., 'The Sense of an Ending: *La Mort le roi Artu*', in C. Dover (ed.), *A Companion to the Lancelot-Grail Cycle* (Cambridge, 2003), pp. 115–24.

Lacy, Norris J. et al. (eds). *The New Arthurian Encyclopedia* (New York and London, 1996).

Lacy, Norris J., and Geoffrey Ashe (eds). 'Italian Literature', in *The Arthurian Handbook* (New York, 1997), pp. 125–30.

Lagomarsini. 'Dalla *Suite Guiron* alla *Compilazione guironiana*: questioni preliminari e strategie d'analisi', *SMV*, 57 (2011), 242–6.

Lagomarsini, Claudio. 'Rustichello da Pisa ed il *Tristan en prose*: un esercizio di stemmatica arturiana', *SMV*, 58 (2012), 49–77.

Lagomarsini, Claudio. 'La tradizione compilativa della *Suite Guiron* tra Francia ed Italia: analisi dei duelli singolari', *MR*, 36/1 (2012), 98–127.

Lagomarsini, Claudio. 'Tradizioni a contatto: il "Guiron le Courtois" e la "Compilation arthurienne" di Rustichello da Pisa. Studio e edizione critica della "Compilazione guironiana"' (unpublished Ph.D. dissertation, University of Siena, 2012).

Lahdensuu, Laura. 'Predicting History: Merlin's Prophecies in Italian XIIth–XVth Century Chronicles', in Erik Kooper (ed.), *The Medieval Chronicle III: Proceedings of the 3rd International Conference on the Medieval Chronicle, Doorn/Utrecht 12–17 July 2002* (Amsterdam and New York, 2004), pp. 93–100.

Larner, John. 'Chivalric Culture in the Age of Dante', *Renaissance Studies*, 2/2 (1988), 115–30.

Lathuillère, Roger. 'La Compilation de Rusticien de Pise', in Jauss and Köhler (eds), *Grundriss der romanischen Literaturen*, IV/1: *Le Roman jusqu'à la fin du XIIIe siècle*, pp. 623–5.

Lathuillère, Roger. Guiron le Courtois. *Etude de la tradition manuscrite et analyse critique* (Geneva, 1966).

Lathuillère, Roger. 'Le manuscrit de *Guiron le Courtois* de la Bibliothèque Martin Bodmer à Genève', in *Mélanges de langue et de littérature . . . Jean Frappier*, II, pp. 567–74.

Le Goff, Jacques. *The Birth of Purgatory*, trans. Arthur Goldhammer (Chicago, 1986).

Le Goff. 'L'*exemplum* et la rhétorique de la prédication aux XIIIe et XIVe siècles', in Claudio Leonardi and Enrico Menestò (eds), *Retorica e poetica tra i secoli XII e XIV, Atti del secondo Convegno internazionale di studi dell'Associazione per il Medioevo e l'Umanesimo latini (AMUL) in onore e memoria di Ezio Franceschini, Trento e Rovereto, 3–5 ottobre 1985* (Perugia, 1988), pp. 3–29.

Le Roy Ladurie, Emmanuel. *Montaillou: The Promised Land of Error*, trans. Barbara Bray (New York, 1978).

Lecco, Margherita. '*Bruto di Bertagna* e Andrea Cappellano. Analisi delle fonti e considerazioni comparative su un *Cantare* del XIV secolo', *Forum Italicum*, 38/2 (2004), 545–61.

Lecco, Margherita. 'Letteratura d'autore e fiaba. Livelli letterari e commistioni tipologiche in due *Cantari* del XV secolo', *Testo*, 57 (2009), 19–33.

Lecco, Margherita (ed.). *Materiali arturiani nelle letterature di Provenza, Spagna, Italia*, Studi e Ricerche, 49 (Alessandria, 2006).

Lee, Charmaine. 'Artù dall'Italia alla Spagna', in Roberta Morosini and Cristina Perissinotto (eds), *Mediterranoesis: Voci dal Medioevo e dal Rinascimento mediterraneo* (Rome, 2007), pp. 43–60.

Leonardi, Lino. 'Bella scoperta: Riappare il cavalier Lancillotto', *Il Sole 24 Ore*, 143 (26 May 2013), 41.

Leonardi, Lino. 'Un nuovo frammento del *Roman de Tristan* in prosa', in Domenico De Robertis and Franco Gavazzeni (eds), *Operosa parva per Gianni Antonini* (Verona, 1996), pp. 9–24. [Fragment of a version that circulated in Italy.]

Leonardi, Lino. 'Il torneo della Roche Dure nel *Tristan* in prosa: versioni a confronto (con edizione dal ms. B.N., fr. 757)', *CN*, 57 (1997), 209–51.

Levarie Smarr, Janet. 'Boccaccio, Giovanni', in Lacy et al. (eds), *The Arthurian Encyclopedia* (1986), pp. 51–3; rev. edn *The New Arthurian Encyclopedia* (1991), pp. 42–3.

Levi, Ezio. *I lais brettoni e la leggenda di Tristano* (Perugia, 1918). [Extract from *Studj Romanzi*, 14.]

Levy, John Fligelman. '*Livre de Meliadus*: An edition of the Arthurian compilation of BNF f. fr. 340 attributed to Rusticien de Pise', 2 vols (unpublished Ph.D. dissertation, University of California, Berkeley, 2000).

Lewis, Clive Staples. *The Allegory of Love: A Study in Medieval Tradition* (Oxford, 1936).

Limentani, Alberto. 'Note sullo stile epico-romanzesco di Martino da Canal', in *Atti del 2° Congresso Internazionale della Société Rencesvals, 12–16 settembre 1961*, special issue of *CN*, 21 (1961), 220–8.

Limongi, Donatella. 'Le maculature della Biblioteca Nazionale Centrale di Firenze', *Accademie e Biblioteche*, 59 (1991), 55–7.

Lomagistro, Barbara. 'Tristano e Isotta nelle letterature slave', in Dallapiazza (ed.), *Tristano e Isotta*, pp. 175–88. [Newly discovered Veneto text.]

Longobardi, Monica. 'Altri recuperi d'archivio: le *Prophécies de Merlin*', *SMV*, 35 (1989), 73–139.

Longobardi, Monica. 'Ancora nove frammenti della *Vulgata*: l'*Estoire du Graal*, il *Lancelot*, la *Queste*', *Giornale Italiano di Filologia*, 46 (1994), 197–228. [Transcriptions with four plates showing MS illuminations.]

Longobardi, Monica. 'Censimento dei codici frammentari scritti in antico francese e provenzale, ora conservati nell'Archivio di Stato di Bologna', in Morini, *La cultura dell'Italia padana*, pp. 23–44.

Longobardi, Monica. 'Due frammenti del *Guiron le Courtois*', *SMV*, 38 (1992), 101–18.

Longobardi, Monica. 'Frammenti di codici dall'Emilia-Romagna: un primo bilancio', *CN*, 48 (1988), 143–8.

Longobardi, Monica. 'Frammenti di codici in antico francese dalla Biblioteca Comunale di Imola', in *Miscellanea di studi in onore di Aurelio Roncaglia a cinquant'anni dalla sua laurea*, 4 vols (Modena, 1989), II, pp. 727–59.

Longobardi, Monica. 'Frammenti di codici dall'Emilia-Romagna: secondo bilancio', in Guida and Latella, *La Filologia Romanza e i codici*, pp. 405–18.

Longobardi, Monica. 'Un frammento della *Queste* della Post-Vulgata nell'Archivio di Stato di Bologna', *SMV*, 33 (1987), 5–24.

Longobardi, Monica. '*Guiron le Courtois*: Restauri e nuovi affioramenti', *SMV*, 42 (1996), 129–68.

Longobardi, Monica. 'Nuovi frammenti del *Guiron le Courtois*', *SMV*, 34 (1988), 5–25.

Longobardi, Monica. 'Nuovi frammenti della Post-Vulgata: la *Suite du Merlin*, la Continuazione della *Suite du Merlin*, la *Queste* e *La Mort Artu* (con l'intrusione del *Guiron*)', *SMV*, 38 (1992), 119–55.

Longobardi, Monica. 'Recupero di codici romanzi dall'Archivio di Stato di Bologna', *Romania*, 113 (1992–5), 349–72.

Longobardi, Monica. 'Scartafacci romanzi', in Mauro Perani and Cesarino Ruini (eds), *'Fragmenta ne pereant': Recupero e studio dei manoscritti medievali e rinascimentali riutilizzati in legature*, Le tesserae, 4 (Ravenna, 2002), pp. 213–48.

Longobardi, Monica. 'Una sola moltitudine: pluralità onomastica nel romanzo arturiano', in Pilar Lorenzo Gradín (ed.) *Los caminos del personaje en la narrativa medieval: Actas del Coloquio Internacional (Santiago de Compostela, 1–4 diciembre 2004)* (Florence, 2006), pp. 185–209.

Loomis, Roger Sherman. *Arthurian Legends in Medieval Art*, Part II in collaboration with Laura Hibbard Loomis (London, 1938).

Loomis, Roger Sherman (ed.). *Arthurian Literature in the Middle Ages: A Collaborative History* (Oxford, 1959).

Loomis, Roger Sherman. *Celtic Myth and Arthurian Romance* (New York, 1927).

Loomis, Roger Sherman. *The Development of Arthurian Romance* (London, 1963).

Loomis, Roger Sherman. 'Edward I, Arthurian Enthusiast', *Speculum*, 28 (1953), 114–27.

Lorenzo Gradín, Pilar. '"Quei che *le mura* empion di sogni": Lanzarote y la Dama del Lago en el norte de Italia', *MR*, 29 (2005), 415–32.

Löseth, Eilert. *Le Roman en prose de Tristan, le Roman de Palamède et la Compilation de Rusticien de Pise: Analyse critique d'après les manuscrits de Paris*, Bibliothèque de l'École des Hautes Études (Paris, 1890; rpt New York, 1970).

Löseth, Eilert. *Le Tristan et le Palamède des manuscrits français du British Museum: étude critique*, Videnskapsselkapets Skrifter, ser. II: Historik–Filosofik Klasse, 4 (Kristiania, 1905).

Löseth, Eilert. *Le Tristan et le Palamède des manuscrits de Rome et de Florence*, Videnskapsselkapets Skrifter, ser. II: Historik–Filosofik Klasse, 3 (Kristiania, 1924).

Lot, Ferdinand. *Étude sur le* Lancelot en prose (Paris, 1954).

Lusignan, Serge. *La langue des rois au Moyen Âge: le français en France et en Angleterre* (Paris, 2004).

Luyster, Selon Amanda. 'Playing with Animals: The Visual Context of an Arthurian Manuscript (Florence, Palatino 556) and the Uses of Ambiguity', *Word and Image*, 20 (2004), 1–21.

Luzio, Alessandro and Rodolfo Renier (eds). *La coltura e le relazioni letterarie di Isabella d'Este Gonzaga* (Milan, 2005); rpt of *GSLI*, 33 (1899), 1–62.

Maddox, Donald. 'The Arthurian Intertexts of *Inferno* V', *Dante Studies*, 114 (1996), 113–27.

Malanca, Alessandra. 'Le armi e le lettere: Galasso da Correggio, autore dell'*Historia Anglie*', *Italia medioevale e umanistica*, 48 (2007), 1–57.

Malanca, Alessandra. 'Le fonti della materia di Bretagna nell'opera di Galasso da Correggio', *Giornale italiano di filologia*, 61 (2009), 271–98.

Malavasi, Giuseppe. *La materia poetica del ciclo brettone in Italia: in particolare la leggenda di Tristano e quella di Lancillotto* (Mirandola, 1901; Bologna, 1903).

Maracchi Biagiarelli, Berta. 'L'*Armadiaccio* di Padre Stradino', *La Bibliofilía*, 84 (1982), 51–7.

Martineau, Anne. 'Les géants dans *Guiron le Courtois*', *Études Médiévales*, 9–10 (2008), 178–95.

Matarrese, Tina. 'Il racconto cavalleresco dal cantare ai canti: *L'inamoramento de Orlando* di M. M. Boiardo', in Picone (ed.), *La letteratura cavalleresca*, pp. 225–38.

Mazzadi, Patrizia. 'L'érotisme dans le mariage: exemples dans les roman courtois', in Danielle Buschinger (ed.), *Érotisme et sexualité. Actes du Colloque international des 5, 6 et 7 mars 2009 à Amiens* (Amiens, 2009), pp. 167–75.

Mazzadi, Patrizia. 'Il mito di Artù nelle città italiane: esempi iconici e testuali', in Cora Dietl and Claudia Lauer (eds), *Studies in the Role of Cities in Arthurian Literature and in the Value of Arthurian Literature for a Civic Identity: When Arthuriana Meets Civic Spheres* (New York, 2009), pp. 117–34.

Mazzanti, Renzo (ed.), *1284: L'anno della Meloria* (Pisa, 1984).

Mazzatinti, Giuseppe. 'Inventario dei codici della Biblioteca Visconteo-Sforzesca redatto da Ser Facino da Fabriano nel 1459 e 1469', *GSLI*, 1 (1883), 33–59.

Mazzatinti, Giuseppe, et al. (eds). *Inventari dei manoscritti delle Biblioteche d'Italia*, 116 vols (Forlì, 1898–).

Mazzocato, Mirielle. 'The Dismantling of the Chivalric Code: Literature and Society in the *Tavola Ritonda*' (unpublished doctoral dissertation, Macquarie University, 1997).

Mazzocco, Elizabeth H. D. 'An Italian Reaction to the French Prose Lancelot-Grail Cycle: Matteo Maria Boiardo and the Knight's Quest for Identity', in William W. Kibler (ed.), *The Lancelot-Grail Cycle: Text and Transformations* (Austin, 1994), pp. 191–205.

Mélanges de langue et de littérature du Moyen Age et de la Renaissance offerts à Jean Frappier, professeur à la Sorbonne, par ses collègues, ses élèves et ses amis, Publications romanes et françaises, 112, 2 vols (Geneva, 1970).

Ménard, Philippe. '"Monseigneur Robert de Boron" dans le *Tristan* en prose', in Laurence Harf-Lancner et al. (eds), *Des 'Tristan' en vers au 'Tristan' en prose: Hommage à Emmanuèle Baumgartner* (Paris, 2009), pp. 359–70.

Meneghetti, Maria Luisa, 'Temi cavallereschi e temi cortesi nell'immaginario figurativo dell'Italia medievale', in Picone (ed.), *La letteratura cavalleresca*, pp. 173–90.

Mermier, Guy. 'Tristan, Roman de', in Strayer (ed.), *Dictionary of the Middle Ages*, XII, pp. 202–3.

Meyer, Paul. 'De l'expansion de la langue française en Italie pendant le Moyen-Age', in *Atti del Congresso internazionale di scienze storiche (Roma, 1–9 aprile 1903)*, 4 vols (Rome, 1904), I, pp. 61–104.

Michon, Patricia. 'L'épisode de la folie de Tristan dans le *Tristano Panciatichiano*', *Le Moyen Âge: Revue d'histoire et de Philologie*, 101/3–4 (1995), 461–73.

Michon, Patricia. 'Les premières années de Tristan au royaume de Léonois dans les versions romanes de la légende arthurienne', in Christine Ferlampin-Acher and Denis Hüe (eds), *Enfances arthuriennes*, Medievalia, 57 (Orléans, 2006), pp. 313–21.

Middleton, Roger. 'The Manuscripts', in Burgess and Pratt (eds), *The Arthur of the French: The Arthurian Legend in Medieval French and Occitan Literature* (Cardiff, 2006), pp. 81–2.

Milanesi, Gaetano. *Sulla storia dell'arte toscana: Scritti vari* (Siena, 1878; rpt Soest, 1973).

Minervini, Laura. 'Le français dans l'Orient latin (XIIIe–XIVe siècles). Éléments pour la caractérisation d'une *scripta* du Levant', *Revue de Linguistique Romane*, 74 (2010), 119–98.

Minnis, Alastair J. 'Late-Medieval Discussions of "Compilatio" and the Role of the "Compilator"', *Beiträge zur Geschichte der deutschen Sprache und Literatur*, 101 (1979), 385–421.

Mito e storia nella tradizione cavalleresca: Atti del XLII Convegno storico internazionale, Todi, 9–12 ottobre 2005, Atti dei Convegni del Centro italiano di studi sul basso medioevo, n.s. 19 (Spoleto, 2006).

Moakley, Gertrude. *The Tarot Cards Painted by Bonifacio Bembo for the Visconti-Sforza Family: An Iconographic and Historical Study* (New York, 1966).

Modi e forme della fruizione della 'materia arturiana' nell'Italia dei sec. XIII–XIV: Milano, 4–5 febbraio 2005, Incontro di studio, 41 (Milan, 2006).

Montorsi, Francesco. 'L'autore rinascimentale e i manoscritti medievali: sulle fonti del *Gyrone il cortese* di Luigi Alamanni', *Romania*, 127 (2009), 190–211.

Moore, Edward. *Contributions to the Textual Criticism of the* Divina Commedia, *including the complete collation throughout the* Inferno *of all the mss. at Oxford and Cambridge* (Cambridge, 1889).

Morato, Nicola. *Il ciclo di* Guiron le courtois: *Strutture e testi nella tradizione manoscritta*, Archivio romanzo, 19 (Florence, 2010).

Morato, Nicola. 'Figure della violenza nel romanzo arturiano in prosa', in Praloran et al. (eds), *Figura e racconto*, pp. 163–91.

Morato, Nicola. 'Un nuovo frammento del *Guiron le Courtois*. L'incipit del ms. BnF, fr. 350 e la sua consistenza testuale', *MR*, 31/2 (2007), 241–85.

Moreschi, Beatrice. Review of Malavasi, *La materia poetica del ciclo brettone in Italia*, *GSLI*, 46 (1905), 176–81.

Morini, Luigina (ed.). *La cultura dell'Italia padana e la presenza francese nei secoli XIII–XV (Pavia, 11–14 settembre 1994)*, Letteratura, Università degli studi di Pavia, Dipartimento di scienza della letteratura e dell'arte medievale e moderna, 9 (Alessandria, 2001).

Morosini, Roberta. 'The "In-between Representational Spaces" of Medieval Mediterranean Legends: Arthur, Alexander, Muhammad', in Amity Law and Julian Deahl (eds), *Mapping the Medieval Mediterranean, c. 300–1550: An Encyclopedia of Perspectives in Research* (Leiden, forthcoming).

Morosini, Roberta. '"Prose di romanzi" . . . or novelle? A Note on the Adaptations of "franceschi romanzi." The Case of the *Tristano Riccardiano* and the *Novellino*', *Tristania*, 22 (2003), 23–48.

Morreale, Laura and Susanna Barsella. *French of Italy*, online at *www.fordham.edu/academics/ programs_at_fordham_/medieval_studies/french_of_italy/index.asp*.

[Motta, E.] 'I libri francesi della libreria Sforzesca in Pavia (1470)', *Bollettino storico della Svizzera italiana*, 6 (1884), 217–18.

Moura, Jean-Marc. *Littératures francophones et théorie postcoloniale* (Paris, 1999).

Muir, Lynette R. 'A Reappraisal of the Prose *Yvain* (National Library of Wales MS. 444–D)', *Romania*, 85 (164), 355–65. [Debts to Rustichello.]

Mula, Stefano. 'Dinadan Abroad: Tradition and Innovation for a Counter-Hero', in Keith Busby, Bart Besamusca and Frank Brandsma (eds), *The European Dimension of Arthurian Literature*, Arthurian Literature 24 (Cambridge, 2007), pp. 50–64.

Murgia, Giulia. '*Osservare vogliam la legge di Dio*. La riflessione sul diritto nella letteratura arturiana italiana', *Between*, 2/3 (2012). *http://www.Between-journal.it/*.

Murgia, Giulia. 'La *Tavola Ritonda* tra intrattenimento ed enciclopedismo' (unpublished Ph.D. dissertation, Università degli Studi di Cagliari, 2012).

Murrell, E. S. 'Quelques manuscrits méconnus du *Roman de Tristan* en prose', *Romania*, 56 (1930), 277–81.

Muth, Miriam. 'Calculated Nostalgia: The Creation of Three Arthurian cycles in Late Medieval Europe', in Denis Hüe, Anne Delamaire and Christine Ferlampin-Acher (eds), *Actes du 22ᵉ Congrès de la société internationale arthurienne, actes en ligne* (2008) at: *http://www.sites.univ-rennes2.fr/celam/ ias/actes/pdf/muth.pdf*. [Cites *Tav. Rit.*]

N[eri], F[erdinando] Review of Gardner, *The Arthurian Legend*, *StM*, n.s. 9 (1931), 182.

Neri, Ferdinando. 'La voce *lai* nei testi italiani', *Atti della Reale Accademia delle scienze di Torino, Classe di scienze morali, storiche e filologiche*, 72 (1936–7), 105–19.

Noakes, Susan J. 'The Double Misreading of Paolo and Francesca', *Philological Quarterly*, 62 (1983), 221–39.

Northup, George Tyler. 'The Italian Origin of the Spanish Prose Tristram Versions', *Romanic Review*, 3 (1912), 194–222.

Northup, George Tyler. 'The Spanish Prose Tristram Source Question', *Modern Philology*, 11 (1915), 259–65.

Oldoni, Massimo. '*A fantasia dicitur fantasma* (Gerberto e la sua storia)', *StM*, 18 (1977), 629–704; 21 (1980), 493–622; 24 (1983), 167–245.

O'Sharkey, Eithne M. 'The Influence of the Teachings of Joachim of Fiore on some 13th-century French Grail Romances', *Trivium*, 2 (1967), 47–58.

Otten-Froux, Catherine. 'Les Pisans en Egypte et à Acre dans la seconde moitié du XIIIᵉ siécle: Documents nouveaux', *Bollettino Storico Pisano*, 52 (1983), 163–90.

Padula, Lenore Marie. 'The *Tristan Riccardiano*: A Study of its Composition and its Relations with the French Versions' (unpublished Ph.D. dissertation, Boston College, 1983).

Papio, Michael. 'Lancelot', in Kleinhenz (ed.), *Medieval Italy*, II, p. 599.

Papio, Michael. 'Tristan', in Kleinhenz (ed.), *Medieval Italy*, II, pp. 1096–7.

Paradisi, Gioia, and Arianna Punzi. 'La tradizione del *Tristan en prose* in Italia e una nuova traduzione toscana', in Gerold Hilty (ed.), *Actes du XXème Congrès International de Linguistique et de Philologie Romanes. Université de Zurich (6–11 avril 1992)*, 5 vols (Tübingen and Basel, 1993), V, pp. 323–37.

Paradisi, Gioia, and Arianna Punzi. 'Il *Tristano* dell'Archivio Storico di Todi', *Critica del testo*, 5 (2002), 541–66.

Parkes, M. B. 'The Influence of the Concepts of "Ordinatio" and "Compilatio" on the Development of the Book', in J. J. Alexander and M. T. Gibson (eds), *Medieval Learning and Literature. Essays Presented to R. W. Hunt* (Oxford, 1976), pp. 115–40.

Pastore Stocchi, Manlio. 'Le fortune della letteratura cavalleresca e cortese nella Treviso medievale e una testimonianza di Lovato Lovati,' in Comitato per le celebrazioni, *Tomaso da Modena e il suo tempo: Atti del Convegno Internazionale di Studi per il 6° Centenario della morte* (Treviso, 1980), pp. 201–17.

Pastré, Jean-Marc. 'Les deux chiens de la matière de Tristan', in Danielle Buschinger and Wolfgang Spiewok (eds), *Hommes et animaux au Moyen Age: IVème Congrès au Mont-St-Michel*, Wodan, 72 (Greifswald, 1997), pp. 67–79. [Comparative; includes *Tav. Rit.*]

Patch, Howard Rollin. *The Other World according to Descriptions in Medieval Literature*, Smith College Studies in Modern Languages, n.s. 1 (Cambridge, MA, 1950).

Pellegrin, Elisabeth. *La Bibliothèque des Visconti et des Sforza, ducs de Milan, au XVe siècle*, Publications de l'Institut de Recherche et d'Histoire des Textes, 5 (Paris, 1955).

Pellegrini, Flaminio. Review of *Tristano Riccardiano*, ed. E. G. Parodi, *Rassegna bibliografica della letteratura italiana*, 4 (1896), 212–14.

Petronio, Giuseppe (gen. ed.). *Dizionario enciclopedico della letteratura italiana*, 6 vols (Bari, 1966–70), V, p. 338. ['Tristano'.]

Petrucci, Armando. *Catalogo sommario dei manoscritti del Fondo Rossi: Sezione Corsiniana*, Indici e Sussidi bibliografici della Biblioteca, 10 (Rome, 1977), pp. 19–20 and pl. III. [*Tristano Corsiniano*]

Petrucci, Armando. 'Storia e geografia delle culture scritte (dal secolo XI al secolo XVIII)', in *Letteratura italiana: Storia e geografia, II: Produzione e consumo*, 6 vols (Turin, 1988), II, pp. 1195–1241.

Petrucci, Armando. *Writers and Readers in Medieval Italy: Studies in the History of Written Culture*, ed. and trans. Charles M. Radding (New Haven, 1995).

Petti Balbi, Giovanna. 'Il libro nella società genovese del sec. XIII', *La Bibliofilía*, 80 (1978), 1–46.

Petti Balbi, Giovanna. 'Società e cultura a Genova tra Due e Trecento', in Società Ligure di Storia Patria, *Genova, Pisa e il Mediterraneo tra Due e Trecento: per il VII centenario della Battaglia della Meloria, Genova, 24–27 ottobre 1984, nella sede della Società ligure di storia patria*, Atti della Società ligure di storia patria, n.s. 24/2 (98) (Genoa, 1984), pp. 121–50.

Piccat, Marco. 'Il libro del Cavaliere Errante: l'edizione', *Studi Piemontesi*, 37 (2008), 81–9.

Picone, Michelangelo. 'Dante e la tradizione arturiana', *Romanische Forschungen*, 94 (1982), 1–18.

Picone, Michelangelo. '*Le donne e 'cavalier*: La civiltà cavalleresca nella *Commedia*', *Rassegna europea di letteratura italiana*, 29–30 (2007), 11–32.

Picone, Michelangelo. '"*Ecco quei che le carte empion di sogni*": Petrarca e la civiltà cavalleresca', in Picone (ed.), *La letteratura cavalleresca*, pp. 139–52.

Picone, Michelangelo (ed.). *La letteratura cavalleresca dalle* chansons de geste *alla* Gerusalemme liberata*: Atti del II Convegno Internazionale di Studi, Certaldo Alto, 21–23 giugno 2007, Ricerca* (Ospedaletto [Pisa], 2008).

Picone, Michelangelo. 'La "matière de Bretagne"', in Picone and Bendinelli Predelli, *I cantari: Struttura e tradizione*, pp. 87–102.

Picone, Michelangelo. 'Personaggi cavallereschi nel *Decameron*: il caso di Guglielmo Borsieri (I.8)', in Lorenzo Gradín, *Los caminos del personaje*, pp. 275–91.

Picone, Michelangelo. 'Temi tristaniani nella lirica dei siciliani', in Raffaella Castagnola and Georgia Fioroni (eds), *Le forme del narrare poetico* (Florence, 2007), pp. 21–34.

Picone, Michelangelo. 'Tracce tristaniane nella lirica dei siciliani', in Alfie and Dini, *'Accessus'*, pp. 39–50.

Picone, Michelangelo, and Maria Bendinelli Predelli (eds). *I cantari: Struttura e tradizione. Atti del Convegno Internazionale di Montréal, 19–20 marzo 1981*, Biblioteca dell' 'Archivum Romanicum', Ser. 1, Storia, letteratura, paleografia, 186 (Florence, 1984).

Picone, Michelangelo, and Luisa Rubini Messerli (eds). *Il cantare italiano fra folklore e letteratura: Atti del Convegno internazionale di Zurigo, Landesmuseum, 23–25 giugno 2005* (Florence, 2007).

Pietropoli, Cecilia. 'Le peregrinazioni di un mito: Interpretazioni e riscritture tardomedievali della vicenda di Tristano e Isotta', in Giuseppe Sertoli and Gofreddo Miglietta (eds), *Anglistica e . . . : Metodi e percorsi comparatistici nelle lingue, culture e letterature di origine europea*, I: *Transiti letterari e culturali (Atti del XVIII Convegno AIA, Genova, 30 settembre–2 ottobre 1996)*, 2 vols (Trieste, 1999) I, pp. 129–40. [*Tav. Rit.*]

Pioletti, Antonio. 'Artù, Avallon, l'Etna', *Quaderni Medievali*, 28 (1989), 6–35.

Pioletti, Antonio. *Forme del racconto arturiano: Peredur, Perceval, Bel inconnu, Carduino* (Naples, 1984).

Pirot, François. *Recherches sur les connaissances littéraires des troubadours occitans et catalans des XIIᵉ et XIIIᵉ siècles. Les 'sirventes-ensenhamens' de Guerau de Cabrera, Guiraut de Calanson et Bertrand de Paris*, Memorias de la Real Academia de Buenas Letras de Barcelona, 14 (Barcelona, 1972).

Poggioli, Renato. 'Tragedy or Romance? A Reading of the Paolo and Francesca Episode in Dante's *Inferno*', *PMLA*, 72 (1957), 313–58.

Poli di Spilimbergo, Silvia. 'Un ricordo della Pulzella Gaia in Eubea', *LI*, 25/3 (1973), 356–60.

Polley, Elaine. 'La retransmission de la *Queste* Vulgate par le *Tristan en prose*', *Questes*, 11 (2007), 7–25.

Popolizio, Stephen. 'Literary Reminiscences and the Act of Reading in *Inferno* V', *Dante Studies*, 98 (1980), 19–33.

Pourquery de Boisserin, Juliette. 'L'énergie chevaleresque: Étude de la matière textuelle et iconographique du manuscript BnF fr. 340 (*Compilation* de Rusticien de Pise et *Guiron le Courtois*)' (Ph.D. dissertation, Université de Rennes 2, 2010). Content viewable at *tel.archives-ouvertes.fr/tel-00458206/en/*.

Praloran, Marco. 'La letteratura cavalleresca nell'Europa del Rinascimento. Alcune osservazioni preliminari', in Alberto Roncaccia (ed.), *'Pigliare la golpe e il lione': Studi rinascimentali in onore di Jean Jacques Marchand*, Studi e saggi fuori collana, 11 (Salerno, 2008), pp. 275–92.

Praloran, Marco. *'Maraviglioso artificio': Tecniche narrative e rappresentative nell'Orlando innamorato* (Lucca, 1990).

Praloran, Marco. 'Il racconto per immagini nella tradizione cavalleresca italiana', in Praloran et al. (eds), *Figura e racconto*, pp. 193–232. [Plates.]

Praloran, Marco, and Nicola Morato. 'Nostalgia e fascinazione della letteratura cavalleresca', in Gino Belloni and Riccardo Drusi (vol. eds), *Il Rinascimento italiano e l'Europa*, II: *Umanesimo e educazione*, Treviso-Costabissara (Vicenza, 2007), pp. 487–512.

Praloran, Serena Romano, Gabriele Bucci et al. (eds). *Figura e racconto: narrazione letteraria e narrazione figurativa in Italia dall'Antichità al primo Rinascimento . . . : Atti del Convegno di studi, Losanna, 25–26 novembre 2005*, Etudes lausannoises d'histoire de l'art, 9 (Florence, 2009).

Prestwich, Michael. *Edward I* (London, 1988; 2nd edn 1990).

Proto Pisani, Rosanna Caterina. *La 'coperta' Guicciardini: il restauro delle imprese di Tristano*, Problemi di conservazione e restauro, 27 (Florence, 2010).

Psaki, F. Regina. 'Chivalry and Medieval Italian Romance', in Roberta L. Krueger (ed.), *The Cambridge Companion to Medieval Romance* (Cambridge, 2000), pp. 203–17.

Psaki, F. Regina. '"Le donne antiche e ' cavalieri": Women in the Italian Arthurian Tradition', in Thelma S. Fenster (ed.), *Arthurian Women: A Casebook*, Garland Reference Library of the Humanities, 1499 (New York, 1996), pp. 115–31.

Punzi, Arianna. 'Arturiana italiana: In margine ad un libro recente' [review of Delcorno Branca, *Tristano e Lancillotto*], *Critica del testo*, 2/3 (1999), pp. 985–1007.

Punzi , Arianna. 'Entre ses bras', in Anatole Pierre Fuksas (ed.), *Parole e temi del romanzo medievale*, I libri di Viella, 70 (Rome, 2007), pp. 101–37. [Cites *cantare La morte di Tristano*.]

Punzi, Arianna. 'Per la fortuna dei romanzi cavallereschi nel Cinquecento: il caso della *Tavola Ritonda*', *Anticomoderno*, 3 (1997), 131–54.

Punzi, Arianna. 'Per una nuova edizione della *Tavola Ritonda*', in Giovanni Ruffino (ed.), *Atti del XXI Congresso Internazionale di Linguistica e Filologia Romanza (Palermo 18–24 settembre 1995)*, 6 vols (Tübingen, 1998), VI/7, pp. 727–39.

Punzi, Arianna. 'Tristano e la negazione della cavalleria', in Picone (ed.), *La letteratura cavalleresca*, pp. 37–58.

Punzi, Arianna. *Tristano. Storia di un mito*, Biblioteca medievale, Saggi, 18, Rome.

Radaelli, Anna. 'Il testo del frammento Vb^2 del *Roman de Tristan en prose* (Bibl. Apostolica Vaticana, Vat. lat. 14740)', *SMV*, 50 (2004), 185–223.

Ragni, Eugenio. 'Cantari', in Vittore Branca (ed.), *Dizionario critico della letteratura italiana*, 3 vols (Turin, 1973), I, pp. 480–8.

Rajna, Pio. '*Arturi regis ambages pulcerrime*', *Studi danteschi*, 1 (1920), 91–9.

Rajna, Pio. 'Contributi alla storia dell'epopea e del romanzo medievale, V: Gli eroi brettoni nell'onomastica italiana del sec. XII', *Romania*, 17 (1888), 161–85, 355–65.

Rajna, Pio. 'Dante e i romanzi della Tavola Ritonda', *Nuova Antologia*, 55 (1920), 223–47.

Rajna, Pio. *Le fonti dell'*Orlando Furioso: *ricerche e studi* (Florence, 1876; 2nd edn, 1900; rev. ed. F. Mazzoni, Florence, 1975).

Rajna, Pio. 'Un frammento delle *Enfances Hector* da un codice perduto', *Romania*, 51 (1925), 542–54.

Rajna, Pio. 'Intorno a due antiche coperte con figurazioni tratte dalle storie di Tristano', *Romania*, 42 (1913), 517–79; rpt in Guido Lucchini (ed.), *Scritti di filologia e linguistica italiana e romanza*, Pubblicazioni del 'Centro Pio Rajna', Sezione Seconda, Documenti, 1, 3 vols (Rome, 1998), III, pp. 1547–1614.

Rajna, Pio. 'Ricordi di codici francesi posseduti dagli Estensi nel secolo XV', *Romania*, 2 (1873), 49–58.

Rasmo, Niccolò. 'Il codice Palatino 556 e le sue illustrazioni', *Rivista d'Arte*, 21 (1939), 245–81.

Razzoli, Giulio. *Per le fonti dell'*Orlando Innamorato *di Matteo Maria Boiardo, Parte I: I primi trenta canti del poema* (Milan, 1901).

Renoir, Alain. 'The Terror of the Dark Water: A Note on Virgilian and Beowulfian Techniques', in Larry D. Benson (ed.), *The Learned and the Lewed: Studies in Chaucer and Medieval Literature*, Harvard English Studies, 5 (Cambridge, MA, 1974), pp. 147–60.

Renzi, Lorenzo. *Le conseguenze di un bacio: L'episodio di Francesca nella* Commedia *di Dante* (Bologna, 2007).

Renzi, Lorenzo. 'Da Ginevra a Francesca: per una storia del bacio', in Gianfelice Peron (ed.), *L'ornato parlare. Studi di filologia e letterature romanze per Furio Brugnolo* (Padua, 2007), pp. 431–53.

Renzi, Lorenzo. 'Il francese come lingua letteraria e il franco-lombardo. L'epica carolingia nel Veneto', in Girolamo Arnaldi and Manlio Pastore Stocchi (eds), *Storia della cultura veneta*, I: *Dalle origini al Trecento* (Vicenza, 1976), pp. 563–89.

Riccini, Marco. 'Funzioni narrative negli episodi onirici della *Tavola Ritonda* e nei romanzi italiani di Tristano', in Gabriele Cingolani and Riccini (eds), *Sogno e racconto: Archetipi e funzioni. Atti del Convegno di Macerata (7–9 maggio 2002)* (Florence, 2003), pp. 84–96.

Rizzo Nervo, Francesca. 'Il "mondo dei padri" nella metafora del "Vecchio Cavaliere"', *Studi di Filologia Bizantina*, 3 (1985), 115–28.

Rizzo Nervo, Francesca. 'Nuove linee interpretative per *Il vecchio cavaliere*', in *Byzantina Mediolanensia. Atti del V Convegno di Studi Bizantini* (Milan, 1996), pp. 375–80.

Roncaglia, Aurelio. 'La statua di Isotta', *CN*, 31 (1971), 41–67.

R[oques], M[ario]. Review of Pierre Breillat, *La* Quête du Saint Graal *en Italie*, *Romania*, 67 (1942–3), 139–40.

Ros Domingo, Enrique. *Arthurische Literatur der Romania: Die iberoromanischen Fassungen des Tristanromans und ihre Beziehungen zu den französischen und italienischen Versionen* (Bern, 2001).

Ros [Domingo], Enrique. 'Gallica, Italica, Hispanica: Anmerkungen zu einer umstrittenen Dreiecksbeziehung. Zur Theorie des italienischen Ursprungs der spanischen Fassungen des Tristanromans', in Peter Wunderli, Iwar Werlen and Matthias Grünert (eds), *Italica–Raetica–Gallica. Studia linguarum litterarum artiumque in honorem Ricarda Liver* (Tübingen and Basel, 2001), pp. 655–77.

Rosenberg, Samuel, N. 'Galeotto Before the Fall', in Alfie and Dini (eds), *'Accessus'*, pp. 51–9.

Rossetti, Dante Gabriel. *The Early Italian Poets*, ed. Sally Purcell (Berkeley, 1981).

Rossi, Luciano. '"Bere l'amore": per mare con Enea e Tristano', in Fabrizio Beggiato and Sabina Marinetti (eds), *Vettori e percorsi tematici nel Mediterraneo romanzo: Convegno [Roma (Villa Celimontana), 11–14 ottobre 2000]*, Atti, Medioevo Romanzo e Orientale, Colloqui, 6 (Soveria Mannelli, 2002), pp. 11–32.

Roussineau, Gilles. 'Remarques sur les relations entre la *Suite du Roman de Merlin* et sa continuation et le *Tristan en prose*', in *Miscellanea Mediaevalia: Mélanges offerts à Philippe Ménard*, Nouvelle Bibliothèque du Moyen Âge [46], 2 vols (Paris, 1998), II, pp. 1149–62.

Rovang, Paul R. 'Hebraizing Arthurian Romance: The Originality of *Melech Artus*', *Arthuriana*, 19/2 (2009), 3–9.

Rozsnyói, Zsusanna. *Dopo Ariosto: Tecniche narrative e discorsive nei poemi postariosteschi*, L'interprete, 66 (Ravenna, 2000).

Ruggieri, Ruggiero M. 'Avventure di caccia nel regno di Artù', in François Pirot (ed.), *Mélanges offerts à Rita Lejeune, professeur à l'Université de Liège*, 2 vols (Gembloux, 1968), II, pp. 1103–20.

Ruggieri, Ruggiero M. 'Dante, Petrarch, Boccaccio e il romanzo epico-cavalleresco', *LI*, 8 (1956), 385–402.

Ruggieri, Ruggiero M. 'La Fata Morgana in Italia: un personaggio e un miraggio', *CN*, 31 (1971), 115–24.

Russell, Jeffrey Burton. *A History of Heaven: The Singing Silence* (Princeton, NJ, 1997).

Russo, Luigi. 'La letteratura cavalleresca dal *Tristan* ai *Reali di Francia'*, *Belfagor*, 6 (1951), 40–59.

Saggini, Romilda. '*Lancelot-Graal* (Un nuovo frammento ritrovato a Biestro)', *Letterature*, 11 (1988), 7–41.

Saksa, M. 'Cavalleria e iconografia', in Franco Cardini and Isabella Gagliardi (eds), *La civiltà cavalleresca e l'Europa: ripensare la storia dell cavalleria. Atti del I Convegno internazionale di studi (San Gimignano, 3–4 giugno 2006)*, Storia (Ospedaletto [Pisa], 2007), pp. 139–58.

Salmeri, Filippo. 'Il tema del peccato e della salvazione nella *Tavola Ritonda'*, *Studi in onore di Bruno Panvini*, special issue of *Siculorum gymnasium*, n.s. 53/1–2 (2000), 483–504.

Sandler, Florence. 'A Jewish Encounter with Arthurian Romance', *Arthuriana*, 12/2 (2002), 69–77.

Santoro, Caterina. 'La Biblioteca dei Gonzaga e cinque suoi codici nella Trivulziana di Milano', in Istituto Nazionale di Studi sul Rinascimento, *Arte, Pensiero e Cultura a Mantova nel Primo Rinascimento in rapporto con la Toscana e con il Veneto: Atti del VI Convegno internazionale di studi sul Rinascimento. Firenze–Venezia–Mantova, 27 settembre–1 ottobre 1961* (Florence, 1965), pp. 87–94.

Savino, Giancarlo. 'Ignoti frammenti di un *Tristano* dugentesco', *Studi di Filologia Italiana*, 37 (1979), 5–17.

Sayers, William. 'Sea Changes in Thomas's *Roman de Tristan* and Dante's *Inferno*, Canto 5', *Romance Quarterly*, 51/1 (2004), 67–71.

Scaglione, Aldo. *Knights at Court: Courtliness, Chivalry, and Courtesy. From Ottonian Germany to the Italian Renaissance* (Berkeley, 1991), esp. pp. 169–276.

Scalon, Cesare. *Libri, scuole e cultura nel Friuli medioevale: 'Membra disiecta' dell'Archivio di Stato di Udine*, Medioevo e umanesimo, 65 (Padua, 1987).

Schmolke-Hasselmann, Beate. *Der arthurische Versroman von Chrestien bis Froissart: zur Geschichte einer Gattung* (Tübingen, 1980).

Schmolke-Hasselmann, Beate. *The Evolution of Arthurian Romance: The Verse Tradition from Chrétien to Froissart*, trans. M. Middleton and R. Middleton (Cambridge, 1998).

Scolari, Antonio. 'Sulla lingua del *Tristano Riccardiano*', *MR*, 13 (1988), 75–89.

Scolari, Antonio. 'Volgarizzamenti e intertestualità: il sogno erotico di Pallamides', in Massimo Bonafin (ed.), *Intertestualità: Materiali di lavoro del Centro di ricerche in scienza della letteratura* (Genoa, 1986), pp. 89–100.

Scott, John A. 'Dante's Francesca and the Poet's Attitude towards Courtly Literature', *Reading Medieval Studies*, 5 (1979), 4–20.

Scuderi, Ermanno. 'Valori e precorrimenti d'arte nel *Tristano* e nella *Tavola ritonda*', *Orpheus: Rivista di Umanità Classica e Cristiana*, 15 (1968), 91–7.

Segre, Cesare. 'Appunti su *Le Chevalier Errant* di Tommaso III di Saluzzo', in *Dai metodi ai testi: varianti, personaggi, narrazioni* (Turin, 2008), pp. 279–86.

Segre, Cesare. 'Deconstruction and Reconstruction of a Tale: From *La mort le roi Artu* to the *Novellino*', in *Structures and Time: Narration, Poetry, Models*, trans. John Meddemmen (Chicago, 1979), pp. 58–64.

Segre, Cesare. 'Distruzione e ricostruzione di un racconto: Da *La mort le roi Artu* al *Novellino*', in *Le strutture e il tempo. Narrazione, poesia, modelli* (Turin, 1974), pp. 79–86.

Segre, Cesare. *Fuori del mondo. I modelli nella follia e nelle immagini dell'Aldilà* (Turin, 1990).

Seppilli, Anita. *Sacralità dell'acqua e sacrilegio dei ponti* (Palermo, 1990).

Serra, Giandomenico. 'Le date più antiche della penetrazione in Italia dei nomi di *Artù* e *Tristano*', *Filologia Romanza*, 2 (1955), 225–37.

Sgambati, Manuela. 'Note sul *Tristano Bielorusso*', *Ricerche slavistiche*, 24–6 (1977–9), 33–53.

Sharrer, Harvey L. 'Malory and the Spanish and Italian Tristan Texts: The Search for the Missing Link', *Tristania*, 4/2 (1979), 37–41.

Shaver, Anne. 'The Italian Round Table and the Arthurian Tradition', in Guy R. Mermier (ed.), *Courtly Romance. A Collection of Essays*, Medieval and Renaissance Monograph Series, 6 (Detroit, 1984), pp. 203–22.

Sleiderink, Remco. 'De stem van de meester. De hertogen van Brabant en hun rol in het literaire leven (1106–1430)' (Ph.D. dissertation, Universiteit Leiden, 2003).

Smarr, Janet L. 'Boccaccio, Giovanni,' in N. J. Lacy (ed.), *The New Arthurian Encyclopedia* (1991), pp. 42–3.

Sommer, Elvira. 'Per la leggenda di Tristano in Italia', *Atti del Reale Istituto Veneto di Scienze, Lettere ed Arti*, 67/2 (1907–8), 967–78.

Sommer-Tolomei, Elvira. 'La leggenda di Tristano in Italia. La leggenda di Tristano e Isotta nei poemi stranieri', *Rivista d'Italia*, 13 (1910), 73–127.

Soriano Robles, Lourdes. '"E que le daria ponçoña con quel el muriese": los tres intentos de envenenamiento de Tristán a manos de su madrasta', *CN*, 61 (2001), 319–33.

Soriano Robles, Lourdes. '"E qui vol saver questa ystoria, leçia lo libro de miser Lanciloto": a vueltas con el final original de *Tristan en prosa* castellano', *SMV*, 49 (2003), 203–17.

Spiewok, Wolfgang. 'Tristan en Italie. A propos des relations culturelles entre la cour de Prague et les villes du Nord de l'Italie à la fin du Moyen Age', in Buschinger and Spiewok (eds), *Die kulturellen Beziehungen zwischen Italien und den anderen Ländern Europas im Mittelalter: IV. Jahrestagung der Reineke-Gesellschaft* (Florenz, 28.–31. Mai 1993) (Greifswald, 1993), pp. 179–86.

Spreti, Vittorio. *Enciclopedia storica-nobiliare italiana*, 7 vols (Milan, 1928–35).

Stanesco, Michael. 'Le destin européen de la littérature arthurienne', in *Modi e forme*, pp. 7–32.

Stewart, Pamela D. 'Italian Literature: Prose', in Strayer (ed.), *Dictionary of the Middle Ages*, VI, pp. 658–61.

Stierle, Karlheinz. 'Il mondo cavalleresco nella *Commedia*', in Picone (ed.), *La letteratura cavalleresca*, pp. 123–38.

Stoppino, Eleonora. 'Il destino della storia: genealogie e gerarchie di modelli nel canto XXXIV dell'*Orlando furioso*', *Schifanoia: Rivista dell'Istituto di Studi Rinascimentali di Ferrara*, 26 (2004), 211–22.

Stoppino, Eleonora. '"Lo più disamorato cavaliere del mondo": Dinadano fra *Tristan en prose* e *Tavola Ritonda*', *Italica* 86/2 (2009), 173–88.

Strayer, Joseph R. (gen ed.). *Dictionary of the Middle Ages*, 13 vols (New York, 1982–9).

Sunderland, Luke. *Old French Narrative Cycles: Heroism Between Ethics and Morality*, Gallica, 15 (Cambridge, 2010).

Susi, Eugenio. *L'eremita cortese: San Galgano fra mito e storia nell'agiografia toscana del XII secolo* (Spoleto, 1993).

Tagliani, Roberto. 'La lingua del *Tristano Corsiniano*', *Rendiconti dell'Istituto Lombardo, Accademia di Scienze e Lettere*, 142 (2008), 157–295.

Tagliani, Roberto. 'Il personaggio di Dinadan nella tradizione del *Tristan en prose*', *Critica del testo*, 13/2 (2010), 101–37.

Tagliani, Roberto. 'Una prospettiva veneziana per il *Tristano Corsiniano*', *MR*, 32 (2008), 303–32.

Tavola Ritonda: Manoscritto Palatino 556, Firenze Biblioteca Nazionale Centrale, ed. Roberto Cardini, Intro. Daniela Delcorno Branca, I codici miniati, 2 vols (Rome, 2009). [Facsimile edition with transcription and critical apparatus.]

Thomas, Antoine. 'Les manuscrits français et provençaux des ducs de Milan au château de Pavie', *Romania*, 40 (1911), 571–609.

Tiretta, Gianna. 'La lingua del *Tristano Corsiniano*' (laurea vecchio ordinamento, Università degli Studi di Padova, Area 10: Scienze dell'antichità, filologico-letterarie e storico-artistiche, 1942).

Tissoni Benvenuti, Antonia. 'Il mondo cavalleresco e la corte estense', in Istituto di Studi Rinascimentali di Ferrara, *I libri di Orlando Innamorato: Mostra bibliografica. Ferrara–Reggio–Emilia–Modena*, Saggi (Modena, 1987), pp. 13–33.

Toynbee, Paget. 'Dante and the Lancelot Romance', in *Dante Studies and Researches* (London, 1902), pp. 1–37.

Trachsler, Richard. *Clôtures du cycle arthurien. Etudes et textes*, Publications romanes et françaises, 215 (Geneva, 1996).

Trachsler, Richard. 'Rustichello, Rusticien e Rusta pisa. Chi ha scritto il romanzo arturiano?', in Giuseppina Brunetti and Gabriele Giannini (eds), *'La traduzione è una forma': trasmissione e sopravvivenza dei testi romanzi medievali. Atti del Convegno (Bologna, 1–2 dicembre 2005)*, special issue of *Quaderni di Filologia Romanza*, 19 (2007), 107–23.

Trachsler, Richard. 'Il tema della *Mort le roi Marc* nella letteratura romanza', *MR*, 19 (1994), 253–75.

Traxler, Janina P. 'The Lady or the Horse: Tristan at the Grail Pentecost', *Arthuriana*, 19/1 (2009), 32–46.

Valesio, Paolo. 'Inferno V: The Fierce Dove', *Lectura Dantis*, 14–15 (1994), 3–25.

van der Meulen, Janet Froukje. 'Au coeur de l'Europe. Littérature à la cour de Hainaut-Hollande (1250–1350)' (Ph.D. dissertation, Universiteit Leiden, 2010).

Varanini, Giorgio. 'A proposito della Pulzella Gaia in Eubea', *LI*, 26/2 (1974), 231–3.

Vàrvaro, Alberto. 'L'utilizzazione letteraria di motivi della narrativa popolare nei romanzi di Tristano', in *Mélanges de langue et de littérature . . . Jean Frappier*, II, pp. 1057–75.

Vayra, Pietro. 'Le Lettere e le arti alla Corte di Savoia nel secolo XV: Inventari dei castelli di Ciamberì, di Torino e di Ponte d'Ain 1497–98 pubblicati sugli originali inediti', *Miscellanea di Storia Italiana*, 26 (1884), 6–212.

Verde, Armando F., and Raffaella Maria Zaccaria (eds). *Lo studio fiorentino 1473–1530: Ricerche e Documenti*, Istituto Nazionale di Studi sul Rinascimento, 6 vols (Florence, 1973–2010).

Vidossich, G. 'La lingua del Tristano Veneto', *Studj Romanzi*, 4 (1906), 67–148.

Villoresi, Marco. *La letteratura cavalleresca: Dai cicli medievali all'Ariosto*, Università, 219, Lingua e letteratura italiana (Rome, 2000).

Villoresi, Marco. 'Niccolò degli Agostini, Evangelista Fossa, Francesco Cieco da Ferrara. Il romanzo cavalleresco fra innovazione e conservazione', in Villoresi (ed.), *La fabbrica dei cavalieri: cantari, poemi, romanzi in prosa fra Medioevo e Rinascimento* (Rome, 2005), pp. 345–83.

Vinaver, Eugène. 'The Prose Tristan', in Loomis, *Arthurian Literature in the Middle Ages*, pp. 339–47.

Vinaver, Eugène. *The Rise of Romance* (Oxford, 1971).

Visani, Oriana. 'I testi italiani dell'*Historia di Merlino*: prime osservazioni sulla tradizione', *Schede umanistiche*, n.s. 1 (1994), 17–62.

Viscardi, Antonio. 'Arthurian Influences on Italian Literature from 1200 to 1500', in Loomis, *Arthurian Literature in the Middle Ages*, pp. 419–29; rpt in Viscardi, *Ricerche e interpretazioni mediolatine e romanze* (Milan, 1970), pp. 657–68.

Viscardi, Antonio. 'Introduzione', in *Letteratura franco-italiana* (Modena, 1941), pp. 7–49.

Viscardi, Antonio. 'Motivi brettoni ne *La Spagna* e ne *Li fatti di Spagna*', in *Studi in onore di S. Santangelo*, special issue of *Siculorum Gymnasium*, 8 (1955), 261–74; rpt in Viscardi, *Ricerche e interpretazioni*, pp. 441–54.

Viscardi, Antonio. 'La *Quête du Saint Graal* dans les romans du Moyen Âge italien', trans. G. Peyronnet, in *Lumière du Graal: Études et textes présentées sous la direction de René Nelli* (Paris, 1951), pp. 263–81; rpt in *Ricerche e interpretazioni mediolatine e romanze* (Milan, 1970), pp. 397–414.

Viscardi, Antonio. 'Romanzi cortesi', *Enciclopedia dantesca*, 2nd rev. edn, 6 vols (Rome, 1970–8, rev. 1996), IV, pp. 1030–2.

Viscardi, Antonio. *Storia della letteratura italiana dalle origini al Rinascimento*, Storia delle letterature di tutto il mondo (Milan, 1960).

von Moos, P. 'Sulla retorica dell'*exemplum* nel Medioevo', in Claudio Leonardi and Enrico Menestò (eds), *Retorica e poetica tra i secoli XII e XIV*, Atti del secondo Convegno internazionale di studi dell'Associazione per il Medioevo e l'Umanesimo Latini (AMUL) in onore e memoria di Ezio Franceschini, Trento e Rovereto, 3–5 ottobre 1985 (Perugia, 1988), pp. 53–77.

Walters, Lori J. (ed.). *Lancelot and Guinevere: A Casebook*, Arthurian Characters and Themes, 4 (New York, 1996; rpt 2002), pp. xxxv–xxxviii.

Ward, H. L. D. *Catalogue of Romances in the Department of manuscripts in the British Museum*, 3 vols (London, 1883).

Warnock, Robert G. 'The Arthurian Tradition in Hebrew and Yiddish', *King Arthur Through the Ages*, 1 (1990), 192–200.

Weaver, Elissa. 'Tristan Studies in Italy: A Review of Current Scholarship', *Tristania*, 4/1 (1978), 3–14.

West, G. D. *French Arthurian Prose Romances: An Index of Proper Names* (Toronto, 1978).

Wiesmann-Wiedemann, Frederike. 'From Victim to Villain: King Mark', in Nathaniel Smith and Joseph T. Snow (eds), *The Expansion and Transformation of Courtly Literature* (Athens, GA, 1980), pp. 49–68.

Zambon, Francesco. 'Dinadan en Italie', in Keith Busby and Roger Dalrymple (eds), *Comedy in Arthurian Literature*, Arthurian Literature, 19 (Cambridge, 2003), pp. 153–64.

Zambon, Francesco. Review of Heijkant, *La tradizione del* Tristan *in prosa in Italia*, MR, 16 (1991), 247–53.

Zanni, Raffaella. 'Il Barberiniano latino 3536 e la tradizione del *Tristan en prose*', *Parola*, 12 (2008), 35–67. [Unedited Italian translation/reworking.]

Zingarelli, Nicola. 'Le reminiscenze del *Lancelot*', *Studi danteschi*, 1 (1920), 65–90.

Zink, Michel. 'Moulin mystique. A propos d'un chapiteau de Vézelay: figures allégoriques dans la prédication et dans l'iconographie romanes', *Annales*, 31 (1976), 481–8.

Zumthor, Paul. *Merlin le prophète. Un thème de la littérature polémique de l'historiographie et des romans* (Lausanne, 1943; Geneva, 2000).

BIBLIOGRAPHICAL ADDENDUM

BIBLIOGRAPHY: PRIMARY TEXTS

Les Aventures des Bruns: Compilazione guironiana del secolo XIII attribuibile a Rustichello da Pisa, ed. Claudio Lagomarsini, Archivio Romanzo, 28 (Florence, 2014).

Guiron le Courtois: roman arthurien en prose du XIIIe siècle, ed. Venceslas Bubenicek (Berlin: De Gruyter, 2015).

Lais, épîtres et épigraphes en vers dans le cycle de Guiron le Courtois, ed. Claudio Lagomarsini, Textes littéraires du Moyen Âge, 36 (Paris, 2015).

Lancellotto de Lac. Volgarizzamento toscano del Lancelot en prose, Luca Cadioli (ed.), forthcoming.

La Struzione della Tavola Ritonda. I Cantari di Lancillotto, ed. Maria Bendinelli Predelli (Florence, 2015).

BIBLIOGRAPHY: STUDIES

Albert, S. *'Ensemble ou par pièces': Guiron le Courtois (XIIIe–XVe siècles): la cohérence en question* (Paris, 2010).

Cadioli, Luca and Sophie Lecomte (eds). *Prolégomènes à l'édition du cycle de Guiron le Courtois* (Paris, forthcoming).

Carbonaro, Giovanna. 'Il cronòtopo del "Vecchio Cavaliere" (Ἱππότης ὁ πρεσβύτης)', in Gaetano Lalomia et al. (eds), *Forme del tempo e del cronotopo nelle letterature romanze e orientali, X Convegno Società Italiana di Filologia Romanza, VIII Colloquio Internazionale, Roma, 25–29 settembre 2012* (Soveria Mannelli [Catanzaro], 2014) pp. 363–73.

Garzya, Antonio. '"Matière de Bretagne" a Bisanzio', in Garzya, *Il Mandarino e il quotidiano: Saggi sulla tetteratura tardoantica e bizantina* (Naples, 1983), pp. 263–81.

Gaunt, Simon. *Marco Polo's Le Devisement du Monde: Narrative Voice, Language and Diversity* (Woodbridge, Suffolk, 2013).

'Il romanzo in prosa tra Francia e Italia: stato della questione e nuovi percorsi di lavoro': Tavola Rotonda. Fabrizio Cigni, Roberto Tagliani, Lino Leonardi, Claudio Lagomarsini. SMV, 17 (2011), 227–46.

Infurna, Marco. 'I romanzi del Graal in Italia', in Franco Cardini and Isabella Gagliardi (eds), *La civiltà cavalleresca e l'Europa: ripensare la storia della cavalleria, atti del 1 convegno internazionale di studi, San Gimignano, Sala Tamagni, 3–4 giugno 2006* (Pisa, 2007), pp. 229–42.

Lagomarsini, Claudio. 'Le cas du compilateur compilé: Une œuvre inconnue de Rusticien de Pise et la réception de Guiron le Courtois', *Journal of the International Arthurian Society*, 3/1 (2015), 55–71.

Lagomarsini, Claudio. 'Due giunte inedite (Febusso e Lancillotto) alla corona di sonetti sugli affreschi giotteschi di Castel Nuovo', *Studi Medievali*, 56/1 (2015), 195–223.

Lagomarsini, Claudio (with L. Leonardi, N. Morato, I. Molteni). 'Images d'un témoin disparu. Le manuscrit Rotschild (X) du *Guiron le Courtois*', *Romania*, 132/2 (2014), 283–352.

Lagomarsini, Claudio. 'La tradition manuscrite du Roman de Guiron, deuxième branche du cycle de *Guiron le Courtois*', in *Actes du XXVIIe Congrès international de linguistique et de philologie romanes (Nancy, 15–20 juillet 2013)*, forthcoming.

Leonardi, Lino, et al., 'Immagini di un testimone scomparso. Il manoscritto Rothschild (X) del Guiron le Courtois', in Annalisa Izzo and Ilaria Molteni (eds), *Narrazioni e strategie dell'illustrazione. Codici e romanzi cavallereschi nell'Italia del Nord (secc. XIV–XVI)* (Rome, 2014), pp. 55–104.

Meneghetti, Maria Luisa. *Storie al muro. Temi e personaggi della letteratura profana nell'arte medievale* (Turin, 2015).

Murgia, Giulia. *La Tavola Ritonda tra intrattenimento ed enciclopedismo* (Rome, 2015).

Murgia, Giulia. 'L'allegoria nella letteratura profetica merliniana', in Patrizia Serra (ed.), *In altre parole. Forme dell'allegoria nei testi medioevali* (Milan: 2015), pp. 153–202.

Ruggieri, J. M. 'Versioni italiane della *Queste del Saint Graal*,' *Archivum Romanicum*, 21 (1937), 471–86.

Ruggieri, J. M. *Archivum Romanicum*, 24 (1940), 92–4.

Serre, Antoine. 'Auvergne: le roman de Tristan et Iseut par les fresques du château de Saint-Floret.' *Archeologia*, 86 (1975), 31–41.

Ulrich, J. 'Eine neue Version der *Vita di Merlino*,' *Zeitschrift für romanische Philologie*, 27 (1903), 173–85.

Wahlen, Barbara. *L'Écriture à rebours. Le Roman de Méliadus du XIIIe au XVIIIe siècle* (Geneva, 2010).

Wetzel, René. 'La famille des Vintler et le programme des peintures murales de Castelroncolo (Runkelstein) près Bolzano dans le contexte de la civilisation courtoise', in Stefan Matter (ed.), *Paroles de murs: peinture murale, littérature et histoire au Moyen Âge* (Grenoble, 2007), pp. 75–89.

Zinelli, Fabio. 'I codici francesi di Genova e Pisa. Elementi per la definizione di una scripta'. *Medioevo Romanzo*, 39/1 (2015), 82–127.

The following short list of reviews of The Arthur of the Italians by expert Italianists and Arthurianists offer valuable complements (not only compliments) to this volume. The additions, reservations, nuances, and bibliography in these reviews form part of the larger panorama the volume aimed at compiling, and we thank the reviewers for their expert contributions and corrections.

Bart Besamusca, *Queeste* 22.1 (2015), 113–16.

Kevin Harty, *Parergon* 32.1 (2015), 214–16.

Marco Infurna, *Lettere Italiane*, 57.1 (2015), 192–5.

Antonio Contreras Martin, in *Medievalia* (Institut d'Estudis Medievals, Universitat Autònoma de Barcelona, Spain), 18/1 (2015), 231–7.

Nicola Morato, 'Artù italiano e iberico (sec. XII–XVI): Appunti in margine ai volumi VII e VIII di ALMA', review article, 9344 words.

INDEX OF MANUSCRIPTS

GENERAL INDEX